THE
EUROPEANS
IN AUSTRALIA

For my wife, with love.
Twenty-five years.

THE
EUROPEANS
IN AUSTRALIA
A HISTORY

―

volume two

Democracy

ALAN ATKINSON

OXFORD
UNIVERSITY PRESS

OXFORD
UNIVERSITY PRESS

253 Normanby Road, South Melbourne, Victoria 3205, Australia

Oxford University Press is a department of the University of Oxford.
It furthers the University's objective of excellence in research, scholarship,
and education by publishing worldwide in

Oxford New York

Auckland Bangkok Buenos Aires Cape Town Chennai
Dar es Salaam Delhi Hong Kong Istanbul Karachi Kolkata
Kuala Lumpur Madrid Melbourne Mexico City Mumbai Nairobi
São Paulo Shanghai Taipei Tokyo Toronto

OXFORD is a trade mark of Oxford University Press
in the UK and in certain other countries

National Library of Australia
Cataloguing-in-Publication data:

Atkinson, Alan.
  The Europeans in Australia: a history. Volume two: Democracy.

  Bibliography.
  Includes index.
  ISBN 0 19 553642 8.

  1. Democracy—Australia. I. Title.

994

Typeset by OUPANZS
Printed in China through The Bookmaker International Ltd

Contents

List of Illustrations

Maps

Plates

Abbreviations

AONSW	Archives Office of New South Wales
AOT	Archives Office of Tasmania
CO	Colonial Office records (Public Record Office, London)
HRA	*Historical Records of Australia*
HRV	*Historical Records of Victoria*
ML	Mitchell Library (State Library of New South Wales)
MLSA	Mortlock Library of South Australiana
SLV	State Library of Victoria
SROWA	State Records of Western Australia
SRSA	State Records of South Australia
WAA	Western Australian Archives

Conversions

This book uses units of measurement that applied in the period. To change feet to metres multiply by 0.3. To change miles to kilometres multiply by 1.61. To change acres to hectares multiply by 0.4.

Acknowledgments

Most of the first three chapters of this volume and parts of Chapters 10, 11, and 12 were written in Melbourne during 1998–99. For the first six months of that period (while on Study Leave from the University of New England) I had the benefit of a McGeorge Fellowship at the University of Melbourne, an honour in itself but a fine thing also because it allowed for residence in the McGeorge house, among bellbirds, on the Yarra River at Ivanhoe. The remainder of the time in Melbourne was funded by a Large Grant from the Australian Research Council.

The bulk of the volume, however (like most of Volume 1), was written in Armidale, with short research trips elsewhere. Funding from the University of New England has supported the long-term business of research and writing. In July 2003 I embarked on a five-year research fellowship, thanks once again to the Australian Research Council, and at the beginning of my tenure of that fellowship this work was brought to a close.

So I have to thank three institutions for making this volume possible: mainly my own university (New England) but also the University of Melbourne and the ARC. At both universities I have also drawn heavily on library skills and resources and I am very grateful indeed for the attention of staff at the Dixson and Baillieu libraries respectively. The inter-library loan service at the Dixson Library has been especially important. In Sydney the Mitchell Library (State Library of New South Wales) and the state government Archives Office have been a much-used resource and likewise the La Trobe Library (State Library of Victoria) while I was in Melbourne. Other state libraries and archival repositories have also been unfailingly helpful. The Archives Office of Tasmania is one of the most perfectly pleasant places of its kind.

The manuscript of this volume has been read by a number of people and I have been enlightened by their comments and corrections. Parts have been seen by Anne Coote and Meg Vivers. Parts have been read at seminars at the University of New England, the University of Melbourne, and the Australian National University. In each case discussion has pushed the work forward. The volume as a whole has been read piece by piece over the last few years by Marian Quartly, Miriam Dixson, and Nicolas Rothwell. Their kindness in doing this work for me and the care they have taken with it, especially under pressure as the deadline approached, have been really central to the whole exercise. In October 2003, when all was nearly done, Stuart Macintyre agreed to do the same job almost all at once.

I have done my grateful best with the frequently meticulous comments all four have made.

For research assistance I am grateful to Dan Byrnes, Patricia Curthoys, Caroline Evans, Andrew Messner, and Trin Truscett. It has been particularly useful to have a scholar as dedicated as Dr Curthoys to look at material for me in Sydney. The following have helped me with points of information and with publications that might otherwise have been difficult to find: Anne Coote in Sydney, Hamish Maxwell-Stewart in Tasmania, Grant Ramsey of the Church of Christ in Armidale, Tom Stannage in Perth, Marion Diamond in Brisbane, Rob Linn and Susan Magarey in Adelaide, Marjorie Tipping in Melbourne, and Meg Vivers in Armidale. I am also extremely grateful to the publisher's editor, Helen Yeates, for her patience with last-minute changes. Michael Roach drew the maps.

The Department of History at the University of New England, now part of the School of Classics, History and Religion, has been an unfailing source of support and encouragement. It continues to be one of the best places of its kind in Australia for work in colonial history. Usefully from my point of view, Studies in Religion now flourish here too. Majella Franzmann, Norma Townsend, John Atchison, Frank Bongiorno, John Ferry, and more recently David Roberts have all cast light in one way or another on the subject matter of this volume. My undergraduate and research students have made an impact on the development of ideas. Class discussions in History 155 ('Colonial Australian History') and 271/371 ('Power and Protest') echo in the writing throughout, and the historiography of violence was broached among a captive audience in History 379 ('Violence, Law and Order in Australian History'). The research students who have worked with me on the period covered by this volume cannot all be listed here, but Ann Bartlett, Anne Coote, Patricia Curthoys, Elaine Dunn, Erin Ihde, Helena Farland, Phillip Gregory, Peter Hammond, Rob Leach, Kerry Maher, Marie McInnes, Rob Meppem, Andrew Messner, Patricia Miles, Margaret Slack-Smith, Eric Turner, and Beverly Zimmerman have made a particular impression.

Finally, I am grateful to my family. In thinking now through the direction this volume has taken it is hard to avoid finding my wife, Catherine Pound, somehow or other at the end of every important line of enquiry. That alone would justify the dedication. Tom has reinvigorated the literary side of things and Catherine and Elizabeth have each made a certain solid, subtle difference too.

Foreword

I

This is Volume 2 of *The Europeans in Australia*. The three volumes altogether are meant as a history of common imagination in Australia and in
this one I do not wander much from that leading theme. As with the first
volume, common imagination is presented here partly, but only partly, as
it showed itself in the minds of powerful individuals. In Volume 1 those
were mostly governors – Arthur Phillip, John Hunter, Philip Gidley King,
William Bligh, Lachlan Macquarie. Such men very obviously touched the
thoughts of the mass. Like everyone else they were created by their circumstances but, more than everyone else, they were also creators – more
indeed than anyone who has ruled in Australia since. The small numbers
of the colonial population in that period and the limited spaces they lived
in meant that the way in which a few leading figures – nearly all men –
thought and spoke deeply affected everyone else.

The same is much less true for the period to be covered this time, from
about 1820 to the early 1870s. Now the most significant individuals for
my purpose are more miscellaneous. Some were powerful, some not. Some,
such as Saxe Bannister, attorney-general of New South Wales (to be mentioned often below), thought in startling ways, and yet it is hard to know
exactly what mark they made on the world around them. In any period,
how is it possible to measure the impact of ideas that are never translated
into action but which disturb conversation so much in their passing?

But the greatest challenge in the pages below lies in coming to grips
with the imagination of large numbers of people considered altogether.
This was an intriguing task in Volume 1. Now there are new complications.
From the 1820s the Europeans in Australia were much more numerous and
varied. It is therefore harder to comprehend the range of thought and
harder to decipher difference and disagreement. Attachment to place is just
as problematic. There were now many more places in Australia where
Europeans lived. With Volume 1 there were only a few small settlements –
the Sydney area (including the mouth of the Hunter), Norfolk Island and,
in Tasmania, the Derwent and Port Dalrymple. Now Europeans were
widely scattered and moving quickly further out. By the end of the 1820s
settlement in New South Wales was already extending in all directions

beyond a hundred miles from Sydney. Provincial capitals were set up in the north, south, and west – at Maitland, Goulburn, and Bathurst. At the same time in Tasmania (still Van Diemen's Land) the two original towns, Hobart and Launceston, were linked by new settlement and the island looked at last like a single community. A new colony began on the continent's west coast, at Swan River (Western Australia), and another in 1836 on the Gulf of St Vincent (South Australia), together with settlements at Port Phillip and nearby harbours (later Victoria).

The invasion of Australia became so much more rapid from the 1820s mainly because of pastoral enterprise. Cattle and sheep needed larger acreage than crops. Subsequent riches supported many more people. The pace of immigration from Europe grew far beyond anything that could have been predicted in earlier years, with people continuously vanishing into new corners of the continent. Unpredictability, in fact, is an unstated theme in much of what follows – best epitomised by the goldrush of the 1850s. Planning and idealism were compromised over and over again by unforeseen change. Hopes for justice between Aborigines and Europeans, for instance, were several times overturned, not only by outright opposition but also by the speed of events.

Governments remained a perpetual backstop, and there were always strong hints of the 'dictatorial benevolence' outlined in Volume 1. And yet governments often failed to manage. Speed of movement, of course, depends on space and Geoffrey Blainey pointed out many years ago the importance of distance in Australian history.[1] The impact of rapid change was compounded by the vast spaces within which it happened.

For a moment in the 1830s there were precise hopes, at least in London, that the European population might be kept within limited boundaries, but it was a task beyond current skills. By the 1850s Europeans were already living in large numbers in the northern half of the continent, in what was to be (from 1859) Queensland. By the early 1870s there was a peppering of settlement on the Gulf of Carpentaria, in the Northern Territory (at Port Darwin), and along the De Grey and Fortescue Rivers in the north of Western Australia. The completion in 1872 of the Overland Telegraph, which not only crossed the continent north to south – 1700 miles – but also linked Australia with the rest of the world, was certainly a magnificent triumph. But otherwise governments often fell short in the management of such distances.

Somewhere in these vast spaces, and within a year or two of the building of the telegraph, my own great-grandfather sat in the dark on successive nights listening to a concertina. He belonged to one of the first droving trips from northern Queensland to Adelaide. It took eleven months. The musician's efforts charmed the cattle, as such noises do, and a particular bullock, so W.B. Perry told his children, used to come from the mob and stand with its head down, also listening. This small story points to the fact that *The Europeans in Australia* is caught up with the flesh and memory it describes.

It involves its author in a type of self-reflection. It is also based on hopes of embracing the continent in imagination as Perry must have done. The writing is not really detached and 'objective', a point revisited below.

In this period among the Europeans in Australia there was more variety of age than hitherto. Relatively and absolutely, there were more old people. Some had spent all their lives here. There were also more children, especially from the 1830s, when thousands of young labouring families arrived in New South Wales and South Australia. The dramatic constitutional and economic changes that happened in all the colonies during the 1850s and '60s were partly generational. They were linked to the ambitions of youth – to the way in which the ideals of the old and middle-aged gave way to the ideals of the bustling, crowded young.

The first volume was called *The Beginning*. The second is called *Democracy*. This is not to say that the fifteen chapters that follow are full of accounts of political manoeuvring. They include only a little about political ideas in any narrow sense. Today the word 'democracy' often represents a large bundle of ethical principles, a way of life, and even in the mid-nineteenth century it implied more than just a method of electing representatives – more than the abolition of the property franchise and the right to vote by mere manhood. It represented a great shift in common imagination and common ties. In this volume, then, democratic ideas are interwoven with dealings between men and women, among races and between God and humanity (God being still a speaking, listening figure of power for most). Democracy was most obviously a phenomenon of the 1850s but by my understanding it had gradually taken root in Australian minds (even including minds for whom the word 'democracy' was anthema) during several decades beforehand. The period around the 1830s was really more interesting – hopes were more generous, exploratory, and open-ended – even than the years of fruition. It blossomed with possibilities afterwards lost. That earlier moment occupies many pages below.

These great changes depended on methods of communication, on ways of getting and staying in touch. This volume, even more than Volume 1, is concerned with a revolution in communications, a little like the one that transformed the world during the last years of the twentieth century. And as in the twentieth-century case, this revolution had a global dimension. By the 1840s attitudes that might be called global had started to emerge as a result of newly massive quantities of books (fact and fiction), pamphlets, and newspapers, and as a result of the unprecedented speed with which these, plus letters of all kinds, now moved around the world. So far democracy gave the vote to men alone. Female suffrage was to be the work of another generation. But both men and women began to understand themselves in new ways, to find flattering images of themselves in a fast-moving, far-flung literate culture. Democracy itself was a deliberate import and belonged to the same phenomenon. It was part of the way in which Australia adjusted to the wider world.

In the 1820s and '30s well-read men and women were also delighted with the process of talking to and gathering stories from the poor. They opened their ears in new ways. In a society made up of rank and title, imagination delighted as never before in the speech and decision-making power of the lowly. These issues became the raw material of public debate, of detailed schemes and common fancy. Many of the stories thus collected were put into print and laid before innumerable readers. Numerous voices of the poor therefore began to appear in public during these years. The result gratified the rich, but the reading masses, including many of the poor themselves, were affected too. In short, people of all kinds now saw their own reflection, or something like it, on paper. It was an experience bound to overwhelm, whether suddenly or slowly, old ideas of who they were.

The American literary critic, Harold Bloom, has explained the impact of 'self-overhearing' in the evolution of imaginative writing. Much of William Shakespeare's importance, according to Bloom, lies in his wonderful ability to produce characters who reflected upon themselves, who thought of themselves as actors and of the world as a stage – as actors shifting with peculiar uncertainty from part to part. Shakespeare drew out sudden facets of personality, a series of convolution, inversion, and contradiction, a multiplicity within a single voice. Hamlet, says Bloom, is still 'the leading self-overhearer in all literature', his mind suspended by the playwright above its own wavering image.[2] Historical circumstances are crucial for invention like this. Shakespeare's skill fed on new mental habits of his time. Volume 2 of *The Europeans in Australia* is about a similar process, and one of vast historical importance. In the nineteenth century the ubiquity of print and manuscript led to something very like 'self-overhearing', but as a social and collective experience, among Europeans in Australia and Europeans everywhere.

As with Volume 1, then, a great deal of what follows is about the power of writing. Already during the 1820s many of the well read had begun to see how the written word, carefully used, might turn the world upside down. This understanding, this obsession sometimes, was even more widespread now. It became habitual among many working men and women. Altogether, democracy had its roots partly in the imagination of the rich, but year by year the dance of ideas was first mimicked and then subverted by 'the poorer sort'.

II

Dwelling on the history of imagination makes a difference to the shape of Australian history. It seems as a result that behaviour can have its inspiration in imagery more than in logic, in single words and sentences – in snatches of language – more than in any train of reasoning. Routine patterns of thought appear below more often than sequential cause and effect.

Much is said, for instance (especially towards the end), about images of interconnectedness. By mid-century imagined webs and networks of movement, as in a factory, were overwhelmingly common. Human experience the world over, according to William Godwin, was 'one common sensorium', an all-inclusive jigsaw of feeling and thought. So, apparently, was creation itself, a great engine working by action and interaction. Such ideas shaped the essays of Thomas Carlyle, the planning of railways, the theories of Alexander von Humboldt, and the language of everyone, including the semi-literate, who wanted to sound in step.

This was also therefore an age of *system*. The very word 'system' was a favourite. The power to discover, to invent, and to manage systems was now the high road to intellectual respectability, at least among men. The expansion of knowledge and virtue, of cultural and spiritual well-being, seemed to depend on recognising the way in which one great system, or some tributary system or systems, fitted together. The rules of free enterprise used the same logic. The continents and seas ideally composed one market – a single system of intelligence, energy, and profit. The new racism (a subject for the final chapter) was convincing in just the same way.

The Europeans in Australia had their own reasons for being in love with systematic thought or with thought about system. They were extremely remote from people like them in Europe and North America. System, expansively understood, closed the gap. System made sense of geography, which in those days was a type of theoretical knowledge new to most people. System showed how a particular place sat within a universal scheme. Democracy was systematic in the same way, making colonists part of something bigger. When men of all kinds voted on election day, each in his own place, the engine of paper set in motion was one applicable in theory all over the world. More immediately, democratic voters took advantage an intricate system of protocols and lists, of classification and measurement – all of it a piece of power.

Men were thought to understand system better than women. Women were meant to be in awe of it. But women often suspected that the power they knew best, intrinsic to family and household, was really more profound. Introducing her famous story of *Mary Barton* (1848), about the life of the poor in Manchester, the Englishwoman Elizabeth Gaskell wrote, 'I know nothing of Political Economy, or the theories of trade. I have tried to write truthfully; and if my accounts clash with any system, the agreement or disagreement is unintentional'. All she aimed to do, she said, was describe a 'state of feeling'.[3] She meant a state encompassing the effects of life and death, issues more massive, in fact, than any system.

Over two hundred years women have often told deliberately alternative stories like Mrs Gaskell's, stories about feeling. The twentieth-century novelist Virginia Woolf wrote about the possibility that tales traditionally told by women have done more to keep intact 'the thin veil of civilisation' than high intellect and system. Men have suggested the same too sometimes. In

The Old Curiosity Shop Charles Dickens told of an elderly villager who was something of a scholar but who also upheld the faith of his more humble neighbours. He took local legends seriously. Poring over local records in paper and stone and guiding visitors around local graves he avoided, said Dickens, the methods of 'that stern and obdurate class', the exact and systematic historians. '[H]e trod with a light step and bore with a light hand upon the dust of centuries, unwilling to demolish any of the airy shrines that had been raised above it, if any good feeling or affection of the human heart were hiding thereabouts.'[4]

The mysteries of feeling, the contingent, close-knit and particular, in other words, were this man's index of truth. Was he right, was he wrong – or both? Elizabeth Gaskell was clearly on the same side, but it is easy to find evidence to the contrary. Dickens himself was not sure. The numerous stories set out in the chapters below focus a good deal on people like Dickens, who struggled to reconcile the values of systematic thought and the values of feeling, the global and the intimate – in increasingly global circumstances. Saxe Bannister was one. So was George Fletcher Moore, in Western Australia. So was the wandering philanthropist, Caroline Chisholm.

So was Barron Field, judge of the New South Wales Supreme Court. In 1819 the government printer in Sydney published Field's *First Fruits of Australian Poetry*, the earliest book of its kind written in Australia. It contained only two pieces of verse and in both of them Field worried over the task of finding poetry at Botany Bay. He delighted in the life of the country, its animals, flowers, and insects:

> beetles of enamelled wings,
> Or rather, coats of armour, boss'd,
> And studded till the ground-work's lost.

He was aware of the systematic knowledge of Australia, but he balanced it with something sweeter and more sacred:

> Tho' thousands of thy vegetable works
> Have, by the hand of Science (as 'tis call'd)
> Been gather'd and dissected, press'd and dried,
> Till all their blood and beauty are extinct;
> And nam'd in barb'rous Latin, men's surnames,
> With terminations of the Roman tongue;
> Yet tens of thousands have escap'd the search,
> The decimation, the alive-impaling,
> Nick-naming of GOD's creatures – 'scap'd it all.[5]

'[T]ens of thousands' indicates unlimited mystery. Many of the invaders felt the same appeal and this feeling – mysterious in itself – is, as I say, one of the main issues below.

III

This book is written by one of the heirs of the Europeans in Australia, as the reference to W.B. Perry shows. It is also written from within a community of scholarship. It depends on the active help of the individuals and institutions named in the Acknowledgments. But it also draws on the writing and talking of many more men and women who are now, or who have been once, active in the skilful deciphering of the past.

The following chapters make use of various Australian methods of history writing. Echoes of what was once called 'the new social history', a phenomenon of the 1970s and '80s, will be obvious. The scholarly journal, the *Push* (1978–92), and the bicentennial volume *Australians 1838* were exemplars of this approach in Australia.[6] Here it is adapted to some of the concerns of the 1990s and since – ethnicity, mobility, language. Issues of 'identity', on the other hand, equally new but a blunt instrument for historians, I barely mention. There is also little here of the radical nationalist tradition, highly influential for a generation or more since the 1950s, and still with its echoes in much good and mediocre writing.[7] And there is nothing to comfort what might be called the *Quadrant* school of historians, a mushroom growth from around 2000–03.[8] Radical nationalist history was splendidly productive, especially as a means of exploring the political aspects of working life in Australia, but it never worked well as an open-ended means of exploring imagination in history (or conscience: see below) and it is now past its usefulness. *Quadrant* writing, for all its boldness, undermines the main purposes of humane scholarship.[9]

The immediate aim of the *Quadrant* writers has been to show that the injury done to Aboriginal people by the European invasion is much less than we once thought. Even more important, that injury, they say, is irrelevant to the shared emotion of living Australians. The *Quadrant* school strips from the history of settlement its very real aspect of tragedy. And yet even the settlers themselves – the best of them – could see the high moral complexity of what they did. Historical sensibility of the kind condemned by *Quadrant* writing has in fact enriched Australia since 1788.

The main achievement of the *Quadrant* campaign lies in the way in which it forces Australian historians to take a long-term view of their trade. History writing is both art, in the broadest sense, and empirical science. *Quadrant* shows that the science can poison the art. Done well, history is literature. Its purpose lies in enlarging ideas of shared humanity. The *Quadrant* school has two main boasts. It is dispassionate, not compassionate, and its text is well tied to its footnotes.[10] Accurate footnotes matter. But good scholarship, in the widest sense, ought to recall the remark of Edward Gibbon, one of the great pioneers of modern history writing: 'The bloody actor is less detestable than the cool unfeeling historian.'[11] The soldier or murderer might destroy life. The 'unfeeling historian' instead of enlarging empties out the human dignity of the dead. In the end the humanities, including history, are underpinned by compassion.

The Europeans in Australia is the result of more than thirty years spent piecing together a method of writing useful for my purposes. Some resulting premises and methods have been set out in my book *The Commonwealth of Speech* (Australian Scholarly Publishing 2002).[12] This volume is written, then, with fairly clear guidelines. It is not the duty of historians to be objective, in the strictest meaning of that word, because the material they work with is not object but human – a distinction of crucial importance for the period of this volume. It is not their duty to be dispassionate at every stage because in their research and writing they handle and memorialise passions like their own. It is the duty of historians to be, wherever they can, accurate, precise, humane, imaginative (using moral imagination above all), and even-handed.

In this volume the first chapter deals mainly with the 'native-born', the earliest generation of European men and women born in Australia. This initial detail underlines the difference between a local and particular civilisation and a global one. The native-born were typically rural and their knowledge of the world was narrow. Their character seemed interesting in their own time (at least during the 1820s) and historians have considered it often since, including Russel Ward, Ken Macnab, Portia Robinson, and John Molony.[13] In the sketch offered here I concentrate on the moral attitude of the native-born – fierce self-respect and family loyalty on the one hand and, as I see it, a suspicion of difference on the other.

Throughout the volume this theme of inward-looking simplicity runs beside evidence of the eagerness with which the Europeans in Australia looked to Britain and, later, the United States. The importing of outside ideas to Australia is an old topic in Australian history, explored by some of the best scholars, from Michael Roe, in *Quest for Authority in Eastern Australia* (1965), to John Gascoigne, in *The Enlightenment and the Origins of European Australia* (2002).[14] The 1820s saw a sudden opening out, a rapid increase in traffic, investment, and immigration, bringing the colonies into closer touch with the outside world. Chapter 2 begins my examination of this process. New ideas came mainly through written works and well-read immigrants. It was sheer quantity that made the difference – the number and variety of new publications, the frequency of letter writing, and the man-hours now spent on the bureaucratic management of the empire. This all added up to a critical mass that turned the direction of civilisation in Australia. Writing affected ideas about information (Chapter 2), storytelling (Chapter 3), power (Chapter 4), distance (Chapter 5), and civility (Chapter 6). All these things have been said before but here they are drawn together within a single line of thought.

The well-known Sydney politician William Charles Wentworth figures in several early chapters. My image of Wentworth is linked to my image of the native-born, since he was one of them, but I see him too as a lawyer, not only arguing about political rights but also using the law as a weapon. My characterisation of Wentworth opens up an argument about the relationship of law, order, and conscience, an argument that runs above and below the surface throughout the volume. Wentworth's feud with the Macarthurs, a great landed family, is an old story, told many times. In pursuing the broad themes of this volume I have turned that story inside out. As Manning Clark and others have suggested, Wentworth's ideas about nation and government echoed like thunder among his own generation.[15] They seemed to matter in the same way during most of the twentieth century. However, the Macarthurs represent a deeper and richer pattern of thought and one that ought to mean more today than Wentworth's.

But it is Saxe Bannister who does most to fuel this part of the work. Bannister was the product of a village in Sussex and he spent less than three years in Australia. He represents the great story of Australia's long, anxious, ambivalent relationship with the wider world and with the kind of ideals that come from trained and abstract thought. Bannister was an intellectual and his extraordinary faith in literacy as the basis of universal order and as a means of empowering the mass, both Black and White, anchors the early parts of the volume. It makes up a story of ethical purpose and painstaking intelligence combined. No one has written much about Bannister (though Judith Wright once hoped to do so). It has been impossible even to find a portrait of him to reproduce here.[16]

Chapter 4 shows how the convicts in the two original penal colonies, New South Wales and Van Diemen's Land, understood the link between writing and power. With more space my account of the convicts might have ranged much further, making more, for instance, of the brilliant new work now being done with the convict records in Sydney and Hobart. At the University of New England, even as this volume went to press, Peter Hammond produced an important thesis on everyday convict violence that proves the limitations of any account like mine, which dwells mainly on the way order worked.[17] The detail here builds on my own earlier writing and on that of John Hirst, with a little of Joy Damousi, Kay Daniels, Kirsty Reid, and Hamish Maxwell-Stewart. The balance that Maxwell-Stewart strikes between violence and enterprise in convict life is particularly inspiring.[18]

There are similar limits to my story of the colonisation of Western Australia and South Australia (Chapter 5). Much is crowded out in order to make room for arguments about common imagination, especially, in this case, sense of geography and distance. The miscellaneous movement of peoples figures more largely here than the actions of government. The character of Sydney was a leading point in Volume 1. Sydney matters again in Volume 2. My account of the founding of South Australia makes it more contingent on Sydney than with most previous historians. The link is Bass Strait. The early European uses of the strait have engaged several scholars – Lyndall Ryan, Brian Plomley, Kristen Anne Henley, Iain Stuart, Rebe Taylor. Their work makes it easy to imagine how this stretch of water, extended in the west to Kangaroo Island, affected early nineteenth-century ideas about Australia as a whole – about the continent as a pattern of traffic and space.[19] This spatial approach appears throughout the volume. It is part of the type of imagining I attribute to W.B. Perry, and to anyone who tried to make their way more or less unaided over large parts of the country.

Australian historians have seldom gone out of their way to compare fundamental habits of authority from colony to colony. Lionel Frost is an exception, but his main interest is the later nineteenth century.[20] Others have written about notions of order within each, from Douglas Pike (South Australia) to Stuart Macintyre (Victoria).[21] This volume uses such work in taking difference as a given. There is some relevant detail especially in Chapters 5 and 11. And yet, such difference can certainly be overstated. For instance, as I say in Chapter 5, the ideals that set up South Australia overlapped with those transforming New South Wales at the same time – the 1830s.

My chapter on 'Men and Women' (7) takes advantage of a small part of the great mass of writing on gender history since the late 1960s. I pursue especially the open-endedness and moral ambiguity of dealings between men and women, inspired mainly by the work of Miriam Dixson, Marilyn Lake, and Marian Quartly. A new book about Elizabeth Fry by the Dutch scholars Annemieke van Drenth and Francisca de Haan has solved a central problem in the chapter by explaining something of the cooperative power of women among women during the 1820s and '30s – an argument easily translated to stories of men among men. A recent article by Iris Marion Young on 'masculinist protection', with its neat distinction between good and bad manhood, also overlaps here.[22] Both publications nourish ideas about the relationship between gender and conscience (and for conscience, see again below).

As for race, in Chapter 8 and throughout I depend on the parameters laid down at the beginning of the 1980s by Henry Reynolds and Lyndall Ryan.[23] Their early work extended all at once the imaginative boundaries of Australian history. As a result Aborigines became a subject of detailed scholarship and Australian historians began to qualify themselves for work as intricate as any we have taken on. From the beginning this new body of writing was a remarkable exercise in moral imagination and it has been gradually more refined. Keith Windschuttle's new multi-volume project questions its achievement. Windschuttle has so far managed to set a figure for the number of Aboriginal deaths at the hands of Europeans in colonial Tasmania. He cites that figure as if it was a maximum, but his own evidence proves that it is really a minimum.[24] Even from the point of view of factual detail Windschuttle's work so far has barely affected the tradition followed here.

The last part of this volume, Chapters 10 to 15, moves from the 1840s to a little past 1870. The goldrush of the 1850s is a topic that has been pored over by generations of scholars, with Geoffrey Serle and Weston Bate pre-eminent.[25] I deal with the frenzy of the goldrush years partly for what it says about publicity and communications, following to some extent in the footsteps of F.G. Clarke, in *The Land of Contrarieties* (1977). Like Clarke I think that for all the goldrush excitement little in Australia was absolutely new in 1851–55. Another scholar with an argument weighted like this is Anne Coote, whose brilliant doctoral work sees the light in 2004.[26] I have worked, too, with Serle's story of Melbourne as a cultural phenomenon, during the height of the goldrush and afterwards. Like Sydney earlier on, by this time Melbourne was central to the imagining of Australia, its spatial character, its past, its future. I have had no space to do Melbourne justice.

In the way it describes the beginning of constitutional democracy during the 1850s, this volume is part of a tentative movement to revive interest in a subject long neglected – even in Australian schools. Some work of the highest standard was done in the 1970s and '80s (by Allan Martin, for instance), when there was a better sense than there is today of the creative importance of mid-nineteenth-century Australia.[27] Interest in the history of republicanism has helped again lately, but still too little, to reopen a field crucial to our understanding of the roots of present liberty and public order.[28]

In Australia and overseas an unexpected result of widespread, eager literacy was a new attitude to individual sensibility – the cult of feeling. It was obvious in published fiction (especially novels written for women) and in forms of worship (women worked their way forward here too). What I say about feeling in Chapter 14 depends largely on the argument of the American scholar Ann Douglas, in *The Feminization of American Culture* (1996). *The Fall of Public Man* (1977) by another American, Richard Sennett, has been useful here too, because of its penetrating description of private feeling and public life. Detail on the sudden outbreak of bushranging in New South Wales during the 1860s – an upsurge of the native-born – casts into stronger light the cult of feeling, or so I say here. Some of the ideas at this point were greatly helped by an excellent new doctoral thesis on bushranging by Susan West (University of Newcastle), which reshapes an old topic.[29]

I make Bass Strait an important field of action in earlier chapters. From the 1850s new interest in the north of Australia transformed the imagined shape of the continent. Henry Reynolds' book, *North of Capricorn* (2003), makes this point beautifully.[30] Northern waters, including Torres Strait and the Gulf of Carpentaria, now seemed likely to match the old importance of the south. This shift enormously complicated the moral dimensions of settlement. The last chapter in this volume (15) glances at the relations of Black and White on the Queensland pastoral frontier (up to about 1870), and the notorious Native Police. Here the writing of Ray Evans has been my main support.[31]

The work of the Native Police raised, and raises, large questions about civilisation, violence, and the rule of conscience in Australian history. Already in Chapter 6 there are arguments about conscience and violence among the Europeans themselves. Chapter 9 sketches the relationship between conscience and religious faith in the 1830s and 1840s. The material on feeling and religion in Chapter 14 carries the argument into the 1860s. Against this background Chapter 15 looks at conscience and race.

In this volume imagination and conscience are set side by side. Overseas, something like this was attempted, for instance, in 1985 by Thomas Haskell in his study of the origins of European humanitarianism.[32] Among Australian historians a little was done, but much more implicitly, between the two world wars. In the age of fascism several men and women used Australian history to explore links between private principle and public authority. Take Keith Hancock's *Australia* (1930). 'The ideal of "mateship"', Hancock said, ' ... appeals very strongly to the ordinary good-hearted Australian', and he immediately went on to explain the moral basis of government. 'Good-heartedness' became in his pages an historical phenomenon and a public fact, worth weighing in the scales of scholarship.[33] For a long time after Hancock wrote this, the radical nationalist approach crowded out such inquiry. Ideology came before conscience. But it has been taken up again lately. Note the way in which Henry Reynolds makes use of Richard Windeyer's reference in 1844 to a 'whispering in the bottom of our hearts' – a passing regret at the dispossession of the Aborigines. Such sensibility has figured largely in Reynolds' later work.[34]

Finally, this volume says something about changing perceptions of the land. It is commonly thought that the Europeans in Australia began to be moved by their natural surroundings only during the last years of the nineteenth century, the years of Henry Lawson, 'Banjo' Paterson, and the Heidelberg School – a sensibility neatly in step with the birth of national feeling. The Heidelberg painter, Tom Roberts, aimed, he said, to 'make others feel what beauty there is in [the bush]'. But historians have been too ready to agree with Roberts that no one had done the same before.[35] In fact, many similar efforts had been made fifty years earlier. Men and women like Roberts rebelled against the blindness of their parents' generation, the generation that features in the final chapters below. Their grandparents, my main heroes, they forgot. The history of imagination in Australia was already more complicated than they knew.

Most clearly, Volume 2 of *The Europeans in Australia* follows in the tracks of Volume 1, making as much use as possible of the reviews and other comments that volume met with.[36] Like most books, this one belongs to the talk and writing within which it was born.

PART 1

Still They Kept Coming

Naturae Amator, 'The Natural History of the Colony. – No. 10', 23 March 1841.[1]

On the 6th of March last, after a heavy shower of rain had refreshed the thirsty ground, I first observed a few winged forms flitting by, which were soon followed by thousands; all along the road between North and South Adelaide these swarms kept rather increasing than diminishing for several hours, till the whole atmosphere was full of them, alighting everywhere in hundreds.

The wind was strong during this time, and they all flew in the same direction, as if borne along by it. The dampness of the air caused numbers to fall to the ground, while myriads of others succeeded and passed over them. Those that fell into the various pools that continually appeared were soon drifted to the opposite sides, and their wings acting as sails, they were borne forwards as quickly as their flying companions; few, however, reached the haven in safety, most of them losing their wings or legs, or having their fragile bodies glued to the clammy earth. The numberless insects thus sailing in the still pools looked like an immense fleet in miniature. Still they kept coming till the close of day, when the darkness hid them from sight.

They must have been originally upborne in some cloud or mist, as they evidently were all descending, and they much resembled at a distance a shower of sleet. The immense multitudes that everywhere filled the air might easily be seen by looking at some dark background, as the body of a tree. They were, apparently, very feeble, few being able to rise again after once descending to the ground.

I captured several, but was obliged to be very careful, as the wings easily came off, and on confining them they were soon in an apterous condition, the insects themselves dying soon afterwards. Poultry eat them with avidity.

Chapter 1

Bound by Birth

I

Among the ancient inhabitants of Australia are its ants. Their millions of cities cover the continent, so that, go where you like, they are underfoot. Ants attach themselves to certain spots, and they move about their landscape with each moment shaped – so it seems to the human eye – by small decisions. They act as if convinced of their right to the earth.

John Hunter, who came on the First Fleet in 1788 and was second Governor of New South Wales, found the antipodean ants to be of various sizes and colours, mainly black, white, and reddish brown, all agile and shiny as they hunted in and out among debris and yellowed leaves. The high-stepping red bulldog ant *(Myrmecia gulosa)*, sometimes an inch long, impressed him most. '[I]f you tread near the nest, (which is generally underground, with various little passages or outlets) and have disturbed them', he wrote, 'they will sally forth in vast numbers, attack their disturbers with astonishing courage, and even pursue them to a considerable distance'. They bite hard. The pain, which Hunter called 'most acute', lingers like a bee-sting.[1]

It may be this species that features in one of the most ghastly episodes of colonial fiction. In James Tucker's *Ralph Rashleigh* (written in 1845) bushrangers left a constable naked, stunned but alive, pinned to an antbed. Within hours only fragments of flesh remained. 'Them's the little boys', the leading man remarked, 'for polishing a bone.'[2]

Other ants lived among foliage, bark, and blossom, falling in showers on the skin of blundering Europeans, especially in summer. Hunter found some in nests built against trees, as big as a large beehive. '[A]nother kind', he said, 'raises little mounts on the ground, of clay, to the height of four feet'. Ants are enterprising. Louisa Meredith, a housewife in Tucker's time, wrote of small black ants (probably *Iridomyrmex*), which got into every kind of sweet stuff, whatever the barrier. They had fixed lines of communication and day and night, she said, their 'runs' were a moving stream.

> One day I observed a bright yellow circle on the ground, and on stooping to see what it might be, discovered a quantity of the golden-coloured petals of a small kind of cistus which grew near, neatly cut up into little bits (about the sixteenth of an inch wide), heaped all around an ant-hole, and crowds of my tiny household foes or their relatives busy in various ways. … I watched the indefatigable little creatures for some time, until I became quite cramped from my crouching position, and still the same routine of business went on with unabated activity.

She had also seen them at the bottom of her garden, dispatching grains of sugar.[3] They were among the keenest exploiters of European settlement.

This volume is designed to watch, like Mrs Meredith, the activities of an eager, mobile species. Had she been able she would have stepped through the circle of yellow cistus and, lit by the blue aperture through which she had come, inspected the palace of the ants. The intention here is much the same.

My subject matter, the Europeans in Australia, set upon the country, ant-like, in a ceaseless stream, increasing with the years. As Louisa Meredith said of the ants, 'their industry was unwearied … [and] their plans of business … on a most extensive scale'.[4] Between January 1788, the time of the First Fleet, and December 1815, according to the best record, a total of 15,057 convicts (11,627 men and 3430 women) travelled from Great Britain and Ireland, together with nearly 3000 free people. Many went back again, many died early, but many additions were born here. The European population of Australia at the end of 1815 was said to be a little over 15,000, scattered in interesting patterns over the landscape. Of these, 2000 lived in Van Diemen's Land (now Tasmania). The rest were on the mainland, nearly all within a day's journey from Sydney. At that point among the adult population some four in every ten were still convicts, but of those four at least one had a ticket of leave or, by some other means, was practically free.[5] In short, less than a third of the adults were under penal discipline, and even those might seem to have ambitions of their own.

In 1815 about a quarter were children. Between three and four hundred were born each year. Australia – its floor of dry sticks and leaves, its walls of endless eucalypt, copper-coloured, grey-blue, dim pink, the ceaseless sound and movement of its birds and insects, the unblinking sky – was their only home. It was a vast theatre, displaying episodes of anthill savagery. However, the remoteness of this country from Europe, its scanty population and cultural poverty, compounded the simplicity of childhood. Children born elsewhere arrived with immigrant parents, and even for them the memory of that elsewhere soon dwindled within the sealed horizon. Minds were closed by more than isolation. Many of the poorer

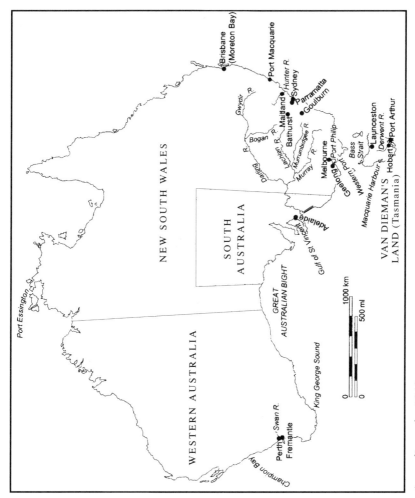

Australia to the 1840s

Europeans who came to Australia in the first years – the first White swarm – were the kind of people who, wherever they might live, took their circumstances as they found them, their thoughts shaped by immediate need and their imaginations depending on their own experience. And like the ants, as we see, they might bite hard.

There were numerous children on the two ships, *Ocean* and *Calcutta*, which anchored in October 1803 at Port Phillip, on the south coast of New South Wales. The parents were among nearly five hundred men and women who anticipated living in that wilderness – at Sullivan Bay, just inside the harbour's mouth – for the rest of their lives. George Harris, who came with them as deputy surveyor-general, sent home to his mother his first impressions of the wildlife. He was much troubled by ants, mosquitoes, and sandflies. The country also teemed with black swans, 'in flocks of hundreds', and with pelicans, ducks, pigeons, and smaller birds – 'some ... extremely beautiful'.[6] On 17 November 1803 the authority of the lieutenant-governor, David Collins, was proclaimed by the public reading of his commission. A week later Ann Thorne, a soldier's wife, gave birth to a boy who was christened 'William James Port Phillip'. In February, the site being found unsuitable (there was no fresh water), the party moved to the mouth of the Derwent River, on the south-west coast of Van Diemen's Land, where a settlement had been formed from Sydney, the first on the island, some months before. The boundary across which they sailed, Bass Strait, was later to be a vital highway for the Europeans in Australia. Catherine Potaski was born as they rode at anchor in Risdon Cove, in the interval before her mother was carried ashore. She grew up around the campsite – eventually a town – that was named after Lord Hobart, Secretary of State for the Colonies. Her father was John Potaski, a convict, probably a native of Poland, who had brought to the Antipodes his wife and their infant, English-born son.[7]

By July 1804 there were nineteen children under ten years old at the Derwent. By September 1807 there were forty-seven. Their horizons were dense and narrow and they were not open-minded humanitarians. Variety of life among animals must have meant more to them than variety among their own species. Catherine Potaski, exploring the smaller aspects of her universe, might have learnt about ant architecture, ant commerce, and ant anger. Ants were one of a number of species easily recognisable even to the most unlearned new arrivals. (Did this little girl know, as anyone from Cornwall might have told her, that ants bore the souls of babies who died without baptism?) It was likewise comforting to find at the Antipodes 'our old friend' the crow, looking the same though sounding different. 'He sings the "quaw, quaw" as in Britain,' said one newcomer, 'but the last quaw is lengthened into a horrible scream and seems to end in a pitiful groan'. Scholars thought that crows talked among themselves and with this idea an early writer about bush life in Van Diemen's Land listened to three in a tree above his head.[8] No doubt children did the same. Given the smallness of settlement, it was difficult to walk far without coming to some wilderness of feathered discussion, particularly along creeks and rivers where birds were legion. Anyone splashing in the rivers, on island or mainland, set off the 'feathered savages' living along the banks. '[S]uch a yelling, screaming, shouting, laughing ... it is at first difficult to believe', said one traveller, 'that such sounds do not proceed from human throats'.[9]

Kangaroos (foresters, wallabies, and kangaroo rats) were more strange and, like crows, innumerable on the Derwent. Their peculiar habits were part of the theatre of camp life and they provoked laughter in children. 'They are the most innocent animals that I know of', said a ship's captain. Newly captured, he said, they would eat flowers and berries from your hand. Easily killed, they were delicately flavoured, and kangaroo meat was sometimes cooked in what came to be called a 'sticker up', with slender pieces threaded on a stick and hung across an open fire. They also yielded the 'handsomest leather for boots and shoes that can be found'. Such footwear was easily made up on marches through the bush.[10]

This was bushmanship, as learnt by the first Australian-born generation. So was knowledge as to what native fruits were edible and how to find your way home. A story was told at the Derwent of one of their girls who went to London, where she was separated from her friend in the heart of the city. Finding herself 'bushed' (a later colloquialism), 'she gave breath to a shrill and prolonged "Cooie" ... to the no small amazement of the passers-by'.[11]

Children probably learnt such skills, and the associated language, before they knew much about the European mysteries of reading and writing. Among their teachers were the Aborigines. In 1810 it was proposed in the *Sydney Gazette* that Aboriginal and European children should, as far as possible, grow up together. The Black children would then become like their playmates, but at the same time they should be taught 'to honour their [own] parents, [and] to esteem their relatives', and the little Europeans should learn their language.[12] In fact, a type of intimacy already existed, but it was deeply ambivalent. At times it was fond and familiar, and some said that the 'unusual levity and wildness' of White children was learnt from the Blacks. But it was also terrifying. In 1834 Lancelot Threlkeld, a missionary in New South Wales, constructed a list of nearly two dozen Aboriginal words commonly used among Europeans, probably taken from dialects around Sydney. They included *cudgel* (tobacco) and *wicky* (bread), both items valued by the Blacks. But they also included *woomerrer*, *boomering*, *mogu* (axe), *gummy* (spear), *gibber* (stone), *hillimung* (shield), and *jerrund* (fear). (The spelling was Threlkeld's.)[13] Such a list suggests that when White and Black talked together it was often about fighting.

Certainly there was violence for European children to see and remember and they had reason to fear the Blacks. The very fact that Aborigines lived among them made brutality, when it happened, more terrifying. It might add to the callousness of daily life. On the Hawkesbury, near Sydney, in 1797 two Aboriginal boys, known as Jemmy and little George, aged about fifteen and eleven, were murdered by Europeans – tied up, shot and chopped about with a cutlass – in revenge for the killing of two neighbours.[14] The Blacks, too, seemed to turn without warning from the sharing of meals to the shedding of blood. They rarely killed White children, but they moved in a way that sometimes must have given the settlers, young and old, a sense of being under the eye of hatred. In May 1805, for instance, on separate occasions the huts of two Hawkesbury families were surrounded and attacked. The Aborigines seem to have waited until the father was gone, but both times they let the mother and children escape. Sarah Stubbs was told by her enemies that they would not hurt her, but they carried all her things away. Elizabeth Lamb and her three small children could see the Blacks close by for 'some considerable time'. They seemed harmless. But then they climbed a stony outcrop, lit fires among the rocks, and picking up the flames suddenly descended on the house.[15]

On the Derwent during the first two years of settlement the small farmers (free immigrants) were usually on friendly terms with the Aborigines, who worked for them and traded crayfish for bread and potatoes. But there was also scattered violence and a number of deaths on both sides. During the following decade Aboriginal babies were often stolen and by 1820 large numbers lived and worked in farming families. More than thirty had been baptised. They lived as a lesser breed among Europeans of their own age, going about their work, as Mrs Meredith might have said, as 'household foes'.[16]

The children of the invaders, embedded in such circumstances, were not likely to take an expansive view of the world. On the other hand, they were not uneducated. The first full inquiry into their aptitude and schooling took place in 1819–21, as part of a survey of life in the Antipodes commissioned by the government in London. The commissioner in charge, John Thomas Bigge, was accompanied by an assistant, or secretary, Thomas Hobbes Scott, and it was Scott who paid attention to the White children. He found them a singular race; the boys and young men brave, articulate, and well-informed about their own world, and also manageable, he said, 'when treated with mildness'.[17] Being manageable, they were also teachable. Rich ex-convicts were supposed to have 'a great contempt for wisdom acquired through the medium of books', but it did not follow that they wanted their children illiterate. The Reverend Richard Cartwright, chaplain on the Hawkesbury, testified that parents were eager to have their offspring educated, 'whatever may be the irregularity of their own lives'. They came to school for unpredictable periods between about four and twelve years old.[18]

It was common for children in and around Sydney to turn up with more or less regularity, but less so in Van Diemen's Land, where the schools themselves were few and teachers inferior. In New South Wales by the 1820s about four in every five young native-born men and three in every five women knew (at least) how to sign their own names, which was a marked improvement on their parents. In Van Diemen's Land the girls especially lagged behind and only two in five could sign.[19] Everywhere girls usually spent less time at school than boys and many could read without being able to write.

With such knowledge, in whatever degree, and with family stories, came an awareness of the mother country. Young crows were thought to learn from their elders about old nesting places they had never seen.[20] The same was true of the Europeans in Australia.

Hobbes Scott, Bigge's assistant, found here a dominion of adolescents, and he was charmed with the effect. 'They are conscious of their freedom,' he said, 'and tho' having daily the most horrid examples before their eyes [that is, the behaviour of the convicts] are rarely if ever infected by them'. Bigge called the young people 'quick and irascible, but not vindictive'.[21] The girls were said to be 'excessively rude and boisterous' and according to Bigge those in the Female Orphan School at Parramatta, near Sydney, were particularly wild – 'their tempers and dispositions are not very easily controlled'.[22] Other observers were more kind. The faults of the native-born girls, so a gentleman said, were part of their 'simplicity of character' for, 'like all children of nature, [they are] credulous, and easily led into error'.[23]

From 1810 to 1821 the Governor of New South Wales (still including Van Diemen's Land) was Major-General Lachlan Macquarie. His successor (1821–25) was Sir Thomas Brisbane. From about the end of Macquarie's time the character of the native-born, male and female, was one of the leading topics of educated conversation, especially on the mainland. It was their 'simplicity of character', their image and their self-image as 'children of nature', which made them seem especially interesting. They were a new variety of humanity, as curious as the wildlife in this remote corner of the world. Educated Britons of a previous generation had looked to alien communities, especially 'noble savages' at the edges of the empire (including Aborigines), with the hope of finding the essence of human nature. Now there was a growing interest in the poor and primitive at one's own doorstep, people who could be thought of as simple versions of oneself. Fellow Britons, from Britain to the Antipodes, were intriguing now for their own sake.

At Home the most telling samples of simple humanity lived in remote villages and uplands. In her novels Maria Edgeworth told of rural Ireland. William Wordsworth wrote of the English north-west and Elizabeth Gaskell (rather later) of the Yorkshire dales. 'Such dare-devil people,' said Mrs Gaskell, ' – men especially, – & women so stony & cruel in some of their feelings & so passionately fond in others'.[24] But most interesting were the Highlanders of Scotland. Scottish manners were displayed to the world in the poetry of Robert Burns in the 1780s and '90s, and more brilliantly still by Sir Walter Scott. In Scott's novels, beginning with *Waverley* (1815), polished English was mixed up with broad Scots dialect gathered from beyond the border of literacy. Picking up snatches of outlandish conversation and weaving them through his stories, Scott startled and amused. He thereby preserved in print the old life and soul of Scotland. In such a place society was like leather and iron. Loyalty was the sweetest love, habit the highest principle. The brutal and the good were strangely mixed. Virtue was linked to violence. Scott's novels were extremely popular and their appeal lay in making readers wonder at the ancient inwardness of the world around them.

In Australia educated men and women looked to their own 'children of nature', the native-born. The first person, as far as we know, to put into writing the sounds of Australian English, was Major West, an Irishman who was surgeon at Windsor on the Hawkesbury. ('Major' was his Christian name.) In October 1823 the *Sydney Gazette* published two pieces that West had sent as letters to the editor over the signatures 'Mary Merino' and 'Betsey Bandicoot'. Both were provoked by an earlier correspondent, 'Fanny Flirt'. Fanny had had some hard things to say about advertisements in the *Gazette*, about the lack of reading for women and about the native-born – an unpolished breed, she called them. Mary Merino answered this insult on behalf of the native-born ladies. Betsey Bandicoot wrote for the commoner sort.[25]

It is Betsey Bandicoot's letter, then, which best presents the accents of the native-born. West had spent five years as medical superintendent at the Female Orphan School and there he must have listened well to the chatter of corridor and playground:

> What a *murree*-fuss Miss Fanny Flirt has made about your Paper [so Betsey declared]; for my part I'm never so pleased as when reading your *adver-tyzements*, and thinks them *prefarable* to the *polly-tics* about *peepall* we don't care a farthing for; only as I am *purdigusly* fond of poetry, I should like to see them all jingling in rhyme.

And again:

> Miss Fan Flirt is very much mistaken if she thinks because she has seen the *lions* in *Lunnon Tower* [the Tower of London was a forerunner of London Zoo], that we don't know *what's what* for all that ... I supposes she conceits there's never not one like her at the *pye-anney-foart* [piano-playing was a standard skill for ladies], but its all gammon a'ter all – *boojeree* me if its any thing else.

'Murree' was an Aboriginal word for 'many', 'very', or 'big'. 'Boojeree' (less common among Whites) meant 'good', though Betsey used, or invented, another meaning. West made these terms dance with words of cockney origin ('gammon', 'what's what'), just as he mixed up Sydney news with London lions.[26]

II

Places are important for children, especially intimate places, where feelings, sounds, and smells enfold your body. Places can hold you safe. They enwrap your bones. Sir Walter Scott's earliest memory was of lying in the hide of a newly killed sheep, an old Scottish cure for infant weakness. A little girl who came to the Derwent with Governor Collins was to remember the first nights on shore, sleeping in a tent made of a blanket and sticks, and later in a hollow tree. Her memory was also imprinted with the sharp taste of seaweed gathered and cooked when food was short. William Macarthur, born at Parramatta, remembered the bed he shared with one of his two older sisters. One night a few months before his fifth birthday the other sister, arriving in the dark from England with their father, got in with him. He woke in the night surprised by the bigness of his bed-mate and when she hugged him said, 'oh! Mary, how kind you have grown'. Both William and the little girl at the Derwent also looked back to the touch and sound of Aborigines, 'with whom', according to the girl, 'the children were often left'. So, like Betsey Bandicoot, they picked up snatches of the language. In William's case, Tjedboro (son of the warrior Pemulwuy), who lived in the house with them, 'restrained me in some of my boyish pranks'.[27] Margaret Ready was a sawyer's child deserted early by her mother. What infant impressions lingered with her? Her father spent long periods in the bush, leaving her as a baby in convict huts nearby, or else wrapped in a blanket among leaves and lizards, within earshot of his axe.[28]

Toys were scarce. William Macarthur remembered only a small wheelbarrow. One day, wreathed with clematis, it broke – 'my grief was intense'. Charles Tompson, who grew up on the Hawkesbury, recalled the noises of childhood, including the 'merry clanking and a roaring sound' of one enchanting spot, the blacksmith's forge at Castlereagh.[29] William Charles Wentworth, son of a convict woman (the surgeon D'Arcy Wentworth was his reputed father), thought back to climbing on the rocks above the heavy shining waters of Sydney Harbour, attempting 'with eager haste ... / To catch a glimmer of the distant skiff'. Jane Maria Brooke also played at the edge of the harbour. She was to remember the beach at Woolloomooloo, small enough to be encompassed by a child's eye and a child's feet, the sand 'quite White and Sparkling' with 'shoals of Blueback Crabs running on it'.[30]

Birds and animals, native and imported creatures mixed up together, were always the main source of wonder for immigrants. A koala impressed its first discoverers with the 'graveness' of its face, suggesting 'a more than ordinary portion of animal sagacity'. A parrot had 'pretty sly eyes'. A pos-

Forester Kangaroo, by Louisa Anne Meredith. No animal, she said, 'can have a sweeter expression'.

Source: Louisa Anne Meredith, *Tasmanian Friends and Foes: Feathered, Furred and Finned* (Hobart 1880), p. 15, reproduction courtesy of Mitchell Library, State Library of New South Wales

sum displayed 'a very mild and pleasing expression', emus 'a very gentle look'. Such characters seemed to have stories of their own. You could imagine malice, retribution, the feuding of species, frequent murder. Obed West recalled dingoes, yellow in the undergrowth, coming to the back door of his father's house at Rushcutters Bay and snatching hens. Goannas could be forced with sticks to poke out their long blue tongues, and the colour was said to show that they were poisonous.[31] Little black fleas, being both immigrant and indigenous, were an older enemy. Everybody in Australia swarmed with fleas, according to a surgeon, 'and those persons who are habitually unclean are a moving mass'. At first light in the morning, according to another grown-up (he might have been talking to a child), on his getting out of bed and walking about, the fleas 'spring upon my legs'. These 'little tigers' then 'begin to phlebotomize me with their diminutive but sharp proboscis. This is the way they give me pepper, in return for which I let fly my battering ram upon them [his fist?]'. Or else, 'I roll their little legs and arms together and crush them to death with my thumb nail'.[32]

Domestic dogs, used mainly for hunting kangaroos, were everywhere, which partly explains the fleas. In Launceston there were dogs tied up at every door, who 'conceive themselves justified in attacking not only those who approach their posts, but every one who walks quietly by'. Some dogs' names – Lion, Neptune, Smut, Rapp – appear in Hobart government records.

Wrapped up in bed children might lie listening to the noise of dogs. A bark would come from some far-off spot, and then an answering chorus from every direction:

> the barkings and their echoes mingling in strangest mimicry; so that even the animals themselves would suddenly pause, and seem to listen and wonder to hear their deep-mouthed clamours thus answered; and then they would utter again one sharp single bark, and listen.[33]

Birds were even more articulate. Talkative and many-coloured native birds were offered in Sydney streets for a guinea each, and wonderful stories were told of their conversational skills. William Addy, a Hawkesbury settler, owned one which, he said, could address each of his family by name. It was eventually killed by a hawk, exclaiming in its death throes, 'Oh the Hawk! Zounds the Hawk!' The Sydney Gazette published an account of a man with several parrots that he was teaching to speak, but they got away by eating through the wooden bars of their cage. A month later, out riding, he was struck by a brightly tinted bird flying about him, 'and when he had half persuaded himself this could be no other than his little talkative favorite, every doubt was removed by an invitation to "be quick, be quick"'. But (said the Gazette) the escapee was teasing and the man not quick enough.[34] Peopled with such creatures – their sayings invented or echoed by rumour – Australia was a vivid mixture of the familiar and the weird.

Where literacy is imperfect, as among the early Europeans, people may have a better ear and imagination for voices, for living speech. The kind of awareness that lives mainly in speaking and listening is different from that which lives mainly in writing and reading – so that here I cut into the hidden sinews of colonial society. In any circumstances speaking exists simultaneously in speaker's breath and listener's ear. It echoes on the instant from soul to soul. Among people ruled by speech, as most of the first settlers were, human voices, heavenly, homely, sweet, or brutal, were easily mingled with the voices of animals. Animal voices had a human power, hard now to appreciate. Their hissings conveyed hatred as real as any. They whimpered with genuine love. In such worlds of speech notions of frog and prince, sphinx and pharaoh, serpent and Ancestor, are interchangeable. The sirens whose lethal songs descended on Ulysses looked like birds. So does the Holy Ghost. During the nineteenth century insects, birds, and animals were ubiquitous – no room, no bed was without them – and they were everywhere in conversation. Pigs, especially under the knife, seemed to copy human passion. Such similarities occur to us now much less readily. Only the bush today has clear echoes, for instance, of the villain in Ralph Rashleigh, when he spoke of ants: 'Them's the little boys for polishing a bone.' All this means that during the first generations of settlement numbers of Europeans in Australia, men, women, and children – all used to watching and listening to beasts – found a powerful immanence in the new land. It had many impulses and expressions like their own.

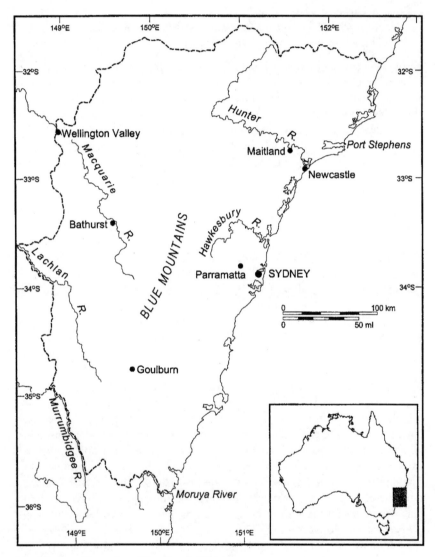

The Limits of Location, New South Wales

Charles Harpur was born on the Hawkesbury in 1813. Largely self-educated, he became a skilled poet. His finest piece, 'A Midsummer Noon in the Australian Forest', carried imagination to a site enveloped within the 'mighty stillness' of the bush. Its scenery is intimate, idle, thick with grasshoppers, ants, cicadas, and beetles. The mind's eye reaches down to the colours of the dragonfly, 'Each rich spot nor square nor round, / But rudely heart-shaped', and the stanzas end with the poet alone among insects:

> O 'tis easeful here to lie
> Hidden from Noon's scorching eye,
> In this grassy cool recess
> Musing thus of Quietness.[35]

Charles Tompson, also a native-born poet, wrote at eighteen his 'Retrospect; or, A Review of my Scholastic Days'. He described the rectory at Castlereagh on the banks of the Nepean (upstream from the Hawkesbury), which had been his home. Under the Reverend Henry Fulton the house had been a boarding school for prosperous farmers' sons – 'Fair Castlereagh! I trace thy landscape round, / Each well known spot to me is sacred ground.' He remembered the river, where he had swum with his friends, a clump of 'rich acacias waving o'er the rill' and a lofty view of tree-tops, a 'green redundancy' shifting beneath him like the ocean.[36]

The introspection of Harpur and Tompson can be found among many of the native-born, including the less educated. They shared a lazy pleasure in homes and land. Betsey Bandicoot boasted of the male of her species, 'Bill Kangaroo'. Bill was a quiet young man – 'whistling and smoking is Bill's delight'. He had his herds of cattle and he was heir to one of the Hawkesbury's small-holders. He had no reason to hurry. He was a typical currency lad, stretched maybe, like Harpur, among the dragonflies. In some such place, said Betsey, he 'lounges like any *swell*, with a nice short pipe, and smoaks and whiffs, and whiffs, and whiffs and smoaks, all the afternoon'.[37]

Commissioner Bigge called the native-born 'slender in their limbs'. The men were a byword for height – thirty-six of them were found on the Hawkesbury over 6 feet tall. Such stature, far beyond the average in England, was partly the result of abundant food, because better nutrition in childhood adds inches to average height in any community. (In Massachusetts in those days, says Edith Wharton, 'the "natives" were easily singled out by their lank longitude'.)[38] But abundance was a mixed blessing. The quantity of sugar used among the Europeans in Australia, for instance, was enormous. Figures for the mainland in 1828 show that each individual ate on average two pounds of it (about a kilogram) a week, and since most of the convicts must have had less than that, the rest of the population, including children, had more. Girls were said to begin losing their teeth even before they were grown up.[39] Also, vast quantities of peaches and other fruit (which, as Bigge remarked, were 'in England ... only in use amongst the opulent classes') were consumed by both pigs and native youth. 'O, it would make you shine your buttons, as the saying is,' declared Betsey, 'to see how Bill will swig off a pot of peach-cyder'.[40]

Abundance meant waste. The first farmers measured their well-being by quantity rather than refinement. Bigge found them improvident and un-skilled, working with hoes rather than ploughs, unfamiliar with manuring and prepared to crop their soil as long as it gave anything back. A descrip-tion of the home of a small settler in Van Diemen's Land brings to the mind's eye a cottage of logs or mud, thatched with straw, a pigsty and cat-tle-yard nearby and a backdrop of 'wool, bones, sheep-skins, wasted manure, ... confused heaps of ploughs, harrows, carts, fire-wood, and water-casks', plus 'a few quarters of mutton or kangaroo' hanging from a tree, a host of wandering hens, and 'a numerous tribe of dogs and idlers; the former barking, the latter lounging about'. Barns were also built of logs, timber being an infinite resource.[41] In a few places the land was so excessive in its produce that the people almost gave up work. On Norfolk Plains, in northern Van Diemen's Land, the wheat was sometimes self-sown and went on for years without interference. The first settlers there also lived on the sheep of their larger neighbours, using an intricate system of theft, which involved them and their children learning the habits of the flocks and moving in the secret recesses of the bush.[42]

Bill Kangaroo, as Betsey remarked, was a cavalier. '[W]hen mounted on his horse, [he] looks quite the thing, with his bran-new fustian *coatee*, and *brass-hammer-handled* whip, cutting and slashing away through the bush, and all round the farm.' The cavalry saddles then used in Australia, though awkward for bush work, must have added to Bill's military air. And what sound could beat 'the loud *coo-hee* of a currency lad riding over the blue mountains'? These were the glories of local manhood. On horseback Betsey herself was a notable sight, 'galloping without a saddle, a'ter Bill, when he has a mind for a bit of a frisk'. But she did not mimic his dignity. On horse or on foot she had no need even for shoes: 'I never thinks of putting them on, only when I goes shopping to Sydney.' There was little feminine delicacy among the native-born women. Their shoeless habits were said to give them feet bigger than the men's and, presumably, soles horny and black. According to one observer, their faces were not pretty – 'there is a cast of countenance peculiar and repelling'. Others spoke of the indecent freedom with which they mingled with their men, 'either at work, at their merry-makings, or bathing in the rivers', where they 'swim and dive like water-hens' and, like water-hens, unclothed. They were indeed 'a *half* dressed or *over* dressed gen-eration who seem born for no other purpose but to gossip with their male acquaintance'.[43] And yet the women were said to be better workers than the men. In a story from the 1820s a housewife on the Hawkesbury disappointed her husband by bearing only daughters. At the birth of the third she demanded, 'Gerrah, why, what are you boddering about? [The voice is Irish.] If I don't make my *darters* better *min* than one half the crathers I see crawling about the counthry-side, I'll ate 'em every one'.[44]

It was female impertinence to talk of the young men 'crawling'. 'Crawler', said a traveller, was 'one of the most opprobrious [terms] in the colonial vocabulary'. Sheep and ruined horses were crawlers. So were convict shepherds, men who lived behind their flocks.[45] A crawler moved feebly through life, blind to the shining spaces of the land. Ants, intent and busy, were not crawlers, nor was any man who could ride and use his fists. The contemporary ballad about Jack Donahoe, the bushranger, sketches the crawler's brilliant antitype: 'We'll wander over valleys, we'll gallop over plains / And we'll scorn to live in slavery, bound down with iron chains.'

During the 1820s horses became a noble addition to the equipment of native-born men. The abundance of horses, steadily increasing from the earliest years, like the abundance of dogs, was one of the great facts of the period. It was notorious that sheep did well here. So did horses. The distance from Europe made it hard to import them in large numbers because they were easily hurt by pitching at sea, but the climate suited them. In 1806 there had been only 285 horses on the mainland, one for every eleven or twelve White men, but by 1828 there were 12,479, nearly one for every two.[46] In Van Diemen's Land horses were also on the increase, but they were not yet so common. In 1819 there was still only one for every nine or ten men. Nor were they so widely distributed. On the Derwent a quarter of all the horses belonged to two great landowners and as late as 1832 the beasts of burden used by local farmers were mainly oxen, 'horses being scarce'.[47]

Such signs of rank – horses for the rich, oxen for the poor – were clear-cut in Van Diemen's Land. But on the mainland children grew up among horses. How many, of nearly all ranks, felt the comfort of horses in the bush, 'their sagacity', as the surgeon Peter Cunningham called it, 'in recognising places where they have once been, and in finding their way home'? How sweet, then, the feel of that hard barrel body, for if you lose yourself riding, as Cunningham said, 'the best way is to lay the bridle loose upon the mane, when your trusty guide will be sure to carry you home by the most direct route'.[48] Horses, when headed homeward, hurried along half-visible tracks with the confidence of ants. Experience with horses shaped the Europeans' understanding, rich and poor, of their own circumstances. In such ways they peopled the country with knowing beasts.

III

In May 1819 there appeared in London a book by William Charles Wentworth, entitled *Statistical, Historical, and Political Description of The Colony of New South Wales, and Its Dependent Settlements in Van*

Diemen's Land. The title page carried two boasts. The author called himself 'A Native', meaning a native of New South Wales, and his work, he said, contained a list of 'the Advantages which these Colonies Offer for Emigration, and their Superiority in Many Respects over those Possessed by the United States of America'. The preface, however, promised only 'a hasty production, which originated in the casual suggestions of an acquaintance'. Wentworth had left New South Wales for England in March 1816, intending to train for the law. On arrival he had announced to the Wentworth family patron, Lord Fitzwilliam, a leading member of the parliamentary opposition, that he had chosen that profession with the hope of benefiting his native land. He aimed, he said, to understand 'the excellence of the British Constitution' so that one day he might help to win for 'my country ... a participation in its advantages'. Never a crawler, young William was sometimes distracted by other ambitions. In April 1817 he wrote to the Colonial Office in London with an offer to explore Australia, 'even from its Eastern Extremity to its Western'.[49] But he always came back to issues of liberty.

Wentworth's best friends in England, to begin with, were the Macarthurs. John Macarthur had left his wife and daughters in the colony in 1809, following the deposition of Governor Bligh, hoping to use that event as a trigger for far-reaching reform. Instead the coup had been discredited and the Colonial Office had prevented him from coming home again. (See Volume 1.) His two elder sons were already in England and his

William Charles Wentworth as a young man, a drawing (detail) by an unknown artist showing something of the pugnacious lines of his face.

Reproduction courtesy of Mitchell Library, State Library of New South Wales two younger ones went with him. The Wentworths were likewise involved against Bligh, and Macarthur offered William all the help he could. 'I really do not know,' the young man wrote home to Sydney, 'what I should have done, on one or two emergencies, without him'. In talking of New South Wales they agreed about the flaws in government and the need for something more 'permanent and respectable'. Briefly Wentworth idolised Macarthur. He was hunting for father-figures and their passions matched – both angry, egotistical, and visionary. When Macarthur sailed home in April 1817 he left Wentworth with the hope that he might marry his eldest daughter, Elizabeth.[50]

Wentworth was already close to Macarthur's son, John, also a law student and native-born. It was John junior who suggested he write his book. Both young men were keen observers of public life and both disliked the authoritarianism of the British government in the postwar years. Wentworth believed that the Tories were tightening their grip on British liberties and young Macarthur thought much the same. But when the book was half written not only did they quarrel about money but also Wentworth heard of Elizabeth's decision against him. He seriously thought of marrying someone else, for the gratification, he admitted, 'of a splenetic revenge', but much of his book was a joint production all the same.[51] It sprang from his early talks with the Macarthurs, father and son.

Wentworth's book was the first attempt by a native Australian to tell the story of his country. The history of nations and empires, according to current orthodoxy, was a cyclical process, in which success, however gilded and dazzling, always carried the seeds of failure. The story had been modified, but not superseded, by the greatest historian of the day, J.C.L. Simonde de Sismondi, whose recent *Histoire des Républiques Italiennes du Moyen Age* had been immediately translated into English. Imperial Rome, its majesty and its humiliation, was the blueprint. Hardy and determined people, as the Romans had once been, began on the path to glory by conquering their neighbours. Their power made them rich. Then their wealth made them soft, unmanly, and tyrannical. Their vices made them weak, and in the end their authority fell apart, in war or revolution. With the defeat of Napoleon Bonaparte in 1815 Britain seemed to be at the height of its power. But Rome's example, neat and obvious, suggested an early decline.

New South Wales, on the other hand – 'my oppressed country', as Wentworth called it – was a place where liberty was still unborn and the cycle not begun. He argued hard about the relationship of colonial and metropolitan power, of an infant nation and its parent state. In his birthplace there was neither trial by jury nor any elected legislature, such as Englishmen possessed everywhere else, and the people were hedged in with restrictive tariffs. One day, he knew, they would enjoy their destiny. But Britain's rulers seemed 'yet to learn that the reign of injustice and tyranny involves in its very constitution the germ of its duration and punishment'.[52]

This was the argument of a young man who wanted to cut a figure. The Whig opposition certainly liked what he wrote but the Tory journal, the *Quarterly Review*, scoffed at the 'dictatorial and menacing tone' of this 'stripling Australian', this 'beardless Solon'. A complimentary copy left at the Colonial Office met with politeness – 'return Mr Wentworth my best thanks for this interesting publication' – but no more.[53]

Wentworth read new novels and poetry as well as history. Like most educated men and women he kept up with the works of Sir Walter Scott. He may have seen Scott's first novel, *Waverley*, before he left Sydney. During the northern winter, 1817–18, just as he began to write on New South Wales, there appeared another piece of Scott's fiction, *Rob Roy*.[54] As with Lord Byron, the other bestseller of the day, Scott's writing held up mirrors for educated young men. It offered new images of manhood for a new generation. The popular interest in manliness went back to the age of the brotherhood of man, the age of revolutions. But since the end of the French war ideas had taken a different turn. The end of a period in which men have died for mighty causes leads to a reshaping of idealism. Peace needs different virtues. The new man described by Scott and Byron combined high spirits and sensibility, boldness and gentleness, virility and polish, but sometimes as well an icy discrimination, a passion *without* action. The new man was a lofty spirit who made his mark by travelling, by writing and reading, by conversation, oratory, and thought.

Parts of Wentworth's book were almost copied from *Rob Roy*. Four years earlier, with Gregory Blaxland and William Lawson, he had found a way across the Blue Mountains (Chapter 2). Their expedition had opened a road between Sydney and its outer hinterland and by 1817 the great western plains were already settled by Europeans. The journey up and across the mountains had left a deep impression on Wentworth. In *Rob Roy* the hero, Frank Osbaldistone, also a young man, described his own journey from Glasgow into the Scottish Highlands. He gazed at the scenery through which he walked – 'High hills, rocks, and banks, waving with natural forests ... [which] as their leaves rustled in the wind and twinkled in the sun, gave to the depth of solitude a sort of life and vivacity.' It was a place, said Osbaldistone, 'where all the ordinary features of nature were raised and exalted', and within which a man, as he laboured upwards, might feel himself both insignificant and serene. Writing at the same time, in the second canto of *Childe Harold's Pilgrimage*, Byron declared, that 'to me, / High mountains are a feeling'.[55] Both authors, read by Wentworth as they appeared, must have distilled his own memories for him, word by word, signposting the landscape of his heart.

Within the Scottish Highlands, among the higher reaches of a difficult country, Osbaldistone found a rebel people, whose lawlessness was partly a result of poverty. Wentworth gave a matching account of New South Wales, of a people reduced to 'privation and misery' through the authoritarian policies of the British government. Here, he said, the poor naturally resort to 'making inroads on the possessions of their richer neighbours'.[56] Scott's Highlanders concealed themselves among their mountains, where the narrow passes made movement dangerous for government troops. Their skill was in the ambuscade, or ambush. In New South Wales, should the British government continue its foolish tyranny, said Wentworth, the people might speedily withdraw to the Blue Mountains, within a natural fortress of narrow ridges and of 'chasms inaccessible to the most agile animal of the forest'. 'Of what avail', he demanded, 'would whole armies prove in these terrible defiles, which only five or six men could approach abreast? What would be the effect of artillery on advancing columns crowded into so narrow a compass?'[57] The story of *Rob Roy*, fresh in the minds of most of his readers, gave the answer.

Among a literate public great novels can make a pervasive impact and Scott created a market unique so far in the history of fiction. His mountains and forests were symbols of the people who lived in them. Among readers in New South Wales a similar aura surrounded the native-born, especially the young men – children of the forest and 'sons of the soil'. Edward Smith Hall, a Sydney newspaper editor, wrote of these youths in rousing terms. '[T]here exists ... in the Territory', he told the Governor in 1827, 'a race of Men already arrived at an adult state, who, scattered in the distant and silent woods of their country, unknown, unfelt and unheard of as a political body, are yet destined to be the Fathers of the succeeding generation and the inheritors of our Lands'. From these men, as Wentworth said in verse, 'each glorious feat, each deathless grace, / Must yet proceed'.[58] Within thirty years of first settlement there was already a European soul within the land, a jewel for the future.

The narrow passes that Walter Scott admired, their green shadow beneath 'twinkling' leaves, were places where forest and mountain dwellers could swarm in secret. (In *Ivanhoe*, published in 1819, Scott likewise drew his reader into the forest paths of the English midlands, the haunts of Robin Hood.) There was feeling, both tightly pitched and strong. The native-born Australians were a proud people. Harpur the poet wrote as one of them. He was, he said, 'a man of the woods and mountains'. He was 'stern and self-reliant, and thence plain, and even fierce', and he owed his character to '*natal* nearness ... to the *incunabula mundi*' – the swaddling bands of the earth.[59] He had been cradled at the edge of settlement, among the opal and bronzed eucalyptus, within a fabric of bush tracks intricate as an ant-bed, where he might have learnt his manners from that shining red beast, *Myrmecia gulosa*.

Harpur's less literate contemporaries displayed a similar self-consciousness but without a bookish shine. They lived within a crevice of faith, among questions yet unborn. But whatever their rank and education, the native-born men were typically, so Hall remarked, 'high-minded even to arrogancy'. Hobbes Scott called them manageable, 'when treated with mildness'. Others found them 'most punctual and observant of religious duties'. They were rarely drunk, and statistical evidence proves that they were remarkably law abiding. They were also proud of being British. And yet, when offended, they took the law into their own hands. They 'revenge their own quarrels', said Hall.[60] Bigge was right. They were 'quick and irascible'. But he was wrong to say that they were 'not vindictive'. Through their sunny sense of their own significance there ran a childlike bigotry, a brazen thread little noticed because it was usually indulged. They had raw notions of right and wrong, rooted in loyalty, and their wrath could be terrible. It was such hidden hardness, perhaps, which could make the girls' faces strangely repelling.

The Kables were farmers on the Hawkesbury. They had several sons who were 'a terror to the peaceable inhabitants', but also devoted to land and family. Freeborn, they thought they were 'subject to no control or legal obligation' and they bullied the local police. Charles Kable, for instance, once set upon Constable Wood, 'putting his hands under Wood's Ears and lifting him up, saying that's the way all Bu[gga]rs like you ought to be hanged'.[61] Likewise, at the Derwent, the Potaskis did well, accumulating land across the estuary from Hobart, with a home at Kangaroo Point. It was said of the parents that John Potaski, though a skilled farmer, was an 'incorrigibly bad' man and his wife a 'low-bred, dirty, idle Connaught woman'.[62] The two children, Joseph and Catherine, had been brought up in 'filth, ignorance, and idleness' and the boy was apparently a rich mix of pride and brutality. His father argued with a neighbouring gentleman, Alfred Thrupp, agent for the late commandant at Hobart, Major Geils, over payment for a property that the Potaskis leased from Geils and Thrupp took away wheat instead of rent. On 21 September 1820, at dead of night, Joseph went with four other men to Thrupp's home at Risdon. They intended robbery, but young Potaski went further. The master was absent but Mrs Thrupp had given birth nine days before and was still in bed. Joseph repaid his father's injury by raping her. The robbery alone was a capital offence and all were hanged.[63]

William Puckeridge was the same. His family, including his twice-widowed mother, lived by fishing in Sydney Harbour and by taking in laundry. The mother, Ann Puckeridge, or Sneyd ('old woman Sneyd'), was given to drink. On the evening of 19 February 1827 Puckeridge was told by a friend named Holmes that his mother was lying in Donovan's yard with a man, or men, about to take liberties with her. The two ran to Donovan's. There were no likely men about and having seen to Mrs Sneyd they stood waiting. After a polite altercation with a boy they heard Donovan's lodger arrive and Puckeridge called in the dark, 'who are you[?]'. The man, faltering, said, 'I am Paddy McCooey'. Somehow this was enough and the ambush was sprung. 'Paddy McCooey are you[?]', said Puckeridge, 'arra then Bye Jesus Paddy McCooey' – and he hurled words about his mother. Holmes told him to hit 'the Irish Bugger'. Puckeridge knocked McCooey down, kicked him and, egged on by Holmes and a party of girls ('stamp his guts out[!]'), jumped with his knees on his victim's stomach. The girls included Jane Lindsay (sixteen), Phoebe Hanks (fifteen), and Louisa Sly (eleven), all native-born. One of them yelled, in those accents so interesting to Major West, that it served McCooey right.[64]

McCooey died that night of a ruptured liver and on 16 March Puckeridge and Holmes were convicted of murder. But a petition was immediately circulated asking for mercy. The signatories included 'several Gentlemen of rank' and 'a number of Ladies' who were moved, presumably, by the fact that Puckeridge the fisherman was a sample of human nature proud and faithful, a man whose simple anger might have been invented by Sir Walter Scott. Here were two sons of the soil rushed into violence by filial devotion. The executive council, meeting to consider the case, was persuaded that in spite of everything heard at the trial the two might have been provoked and changed their sentence from death to seven years servitude at Moreton Bay.[65] Had they not been native-born, and had their victim been a lady, like Potaski's, they would certainly have been hanged.

There was much worse to come. Such loyalty – the iron momentum of soul and muscle – drove a wedge between the White natives of Australia and the Black. In June 1838 John Fleming, born on the Hawkesbury in 1816, led a party of convicts and ex-convicts to the murder, in a single winter's evening, of at least twenty-eight old men, women, and children of the Kamilaroi people, at Myall Creek, near the Gwydir River (Chapter 8). Fleming belonged to a network of Hawkesbury families whose reasons for hating the Blacks went back to his childhood and beyond. They lay among the *incunabula mundi*, the swaddling bands of antipodean earth. The immediate cause of his savagery at Myall Creek was apparently a recent attack by Aborigines far to the south, in which the stockmen of a neighbouring Hawkesbury family were killed.[66] His own victims were found after a long hunt on horseback, caught as they huddled in a bark hut, roped elaborately together and led to a place chosen for the purpose. There they were shot, hacked about, and decapitated with swords. Their bodies were burnt. The pattern of slaughter – the hard faith, the strange mixture of daring and cowardice, the deliberate, roundabout method of retaliation – was all of a piece with the work of Potaski and Puckeridge. There was a faint echo too of the 'splenetic revenge' planned by young Wentworth. This was the blunt, blind piety, *in extremis*, of the first native-born.

Chapter 2

The Well Read

I

When James VI, King of the Scots, became King of England in 1603 – creating the twin dominions that were to be known as Great Britain – he gave up Edinburgh for London, and he ruled Scotland afterwards from a distance. 'This I must say for Scotland', so he boasted and marvelled, ' ... here I sit and govern it with my pen; I write and it is done; and by a Clerk of the Council I govern Scotland now, which others could not do by the sword'.[1]

Power can depend on skill. As with King James, official power among the first Europeans in Australia came not only from force but also from writing, from postage, and from the publication of works in print. Those who can reach like this over many miles must triumph over those who live within a concealed and narrow universe (as in Chapter 1). The creation of Great Britain was only the beginning. In the early nineteenth century the British Empire extended further than any empire had done before, thanks not only to the sword but also to the pen and publicity. Echoing King James, John Stuart Mill said in 1852, 'the whole Government of India is carried on in writing' – and he meant, once again, from London.[2] And the process of writing, plus the habits of thought produced by writing and reading, created in turn a type of regime different from those whose main machinery was living speech. Writing conveyed its own sense of history and purpose, of distance and place.

The efficient use of writing, especially polished literacy, depends on long training. It involves a measured flight from the world of talk. In the early years of the nineteenth century about two-thirds of the population of Britain and half the population of Ireland could read. Fewer could write, especially women, and ease in writing and reading was even more limited. Many subjects of the empire resembled the man described by Harriet Beecher Stowe, who was 'in the habit of reading in a sort of recitative half-aloud, by way of calling in his ears to verify the deductions of his eyes'.[3] Individuals of superior education, who trusted their eyes, who were well acquainted with books and who dealt daily with pens, paper, and postage, made best use of the empire. They might see about them as if from an elevated point, and in doing so they might also see themselves within a wider horizon. Writing is a peculiar mirror. As I write this book I go back from time to time to its earlier passages and they almost seem to be the work of some other man. With literacy, one gets used to many images even of oneself. The centre of imperial bureaucracy, the knot of streets around Whitehall in London's West End, was an increasingly sophisticated place, full of 'reflecting' individuals – capable of thinking, that is, in reflective ways. Those who found favour there, whether they lived in Europe or at the outskirts of empire, were likewise fluent in their writing and reading.

Most of the high idealism of the late eighteenth and entire nineteenth centuries was tied to an understanding and misunderstanding of writing's promise. As a medium effective among the majority of the people literacy was something new and reformers were giddied with hopes of penetrating, all at once, the depths of society at home and abroad, of colouring millions of minds they never met – and at the same time recreating themselves. Their success was both more and less than they thought it would be. Such overshooting the mark and such falling short are, in fact, main points for this volume.

Much depended on the readiness of the people to submit to literate order. Among a population of traditional habits, commands and suggestions in writing seem feeble compared with speech. In order to rule effectively by this means it was important to replicate as far as possible the old familiar power of voices, especially the voices of men. The empire's greatest achievement was the bending of large numbers, scattered across continents and oceans, to a new type of directive. Illiterate men and women were taught that a piece of writing, properly framed (headed, for instance, with royal insignia) had to be obeyed. Within the first British settlements in Australia it was obvious to everyone that the original skeleton of common life was made of paper. The First Fleet, which arrived in 1788, brought enough food to feed a thousand people for about two years, and its collection, storage, transportation, and weekly distribution was a triumph of administrative skill. So was the management of supplies sent by sea thereafter. In the same way, long-term self-sufficiency depended on fixed property rights, another administrative issue. Governor Macquarie had been a military administrator in India and Egypt and he knew how lives depended not only on large-voiced orders but also on desk work. During his time there was a stronger feeling of ownership of the soil and its resources, owing partly to the passage of the years, but also to the Governor's efforts to settle men and women securely under the law. He was, besides, a man of great physical presence. Broad-shouldered and ebullient, his voice was impressive. The distinctive mix of writing and speech explains his successes.

To begin with, Macquarie tried to copy in Australia aspects of Scotland, his birthplace, and of India, where he had spent many years of his manhood. Scotland – six generations after King James moved south – or at least its most civilised parts, featured literacy, well-ordered towns, and good roads. In British India some of the same virtues were strengthened by military government. Mainly a soldier, Macquarie found a special sweetness in the packed order of garrison life, and during his first years in Australia the towns, especially Sydney and Hobart, supported his ideals most of all. But from about 1814 his priorities began to shift. His wife, Elizabeth Henrietta, had a more resilient mind than he did and her imagination took over in his middle years. During spring 1814 Mrs Macquarie's interest in the Aborigines led her husband to found a school at Parramatta to which Black parents might send their children. He also granted land to individual Blacks and he set aside reserves of several thousand acres where they might become farmers.[4] In 1816 husband and wife presided at the first of a series of annual feasts, or 'congresses', for the remnant of nearby peoples, bringing White authority face to face with Black.[5]

This was part of a large program by which the Aborigines were brought within the pale of British government. It fitted not only Mrs Macquarie's idealism but also the Governor's belief that his own power was in fact absolute and imperial throughout the eastern half of the continent. Printed up, he scattered it abroad in multiple copies. In May 1816, for instance, the Governor instructed Aborigines to stop fighting each other, 'not only at and near the British Settlements but also in their own wild and remote Places of Resort'.[6] Whatever its whimsical ambition, this was part of a noble effort to rebuild the moral foundation of European power.

At the same time the Governor also settled his method of dealing with the richer settlers on the mainland. The social division between ex-convicts and free immigrants had always been observed more or less. Macquarie had ignored it at first, believing only that ex-convicts who behaved well should be given chances to succeed. Once again Mrs Macquarie's ideas were more wholesale. As a woman she could afford to be careless about office forms and precedents. And for a lady she was unconventional. Unlike other governors' wives she never used her drawing room as a centre of power, manipulating the elite and sorting out female quarrels. Instead, she dealt directly with men, including ex-convicts and others of middling rank. The Governor made a virtue of her preferences.[7] He wanted to know his people in detail and he looked to men who worked among the mass. Capable ex-convicts thus became pillars of his government.

Among the mass of the people, convict and ex-convict, the charm of the Governor's presence and the power of his voice left a deep impression. 'The very sentiments and phrases of General and Mrs Macquarie', so a newspaper editor recalled in later years, 'were diluted and ramified for popular use, and their very manners and gestures copied and served up in private Society'.[8] But the well read were less enchanted. In Britain and in most British colonies the lynchpins of daily government were the justices of the peace, or magistrates. They were usually gentlemen, who in their own minds represented the best standards of British civilisation and who gave their unpaid time to local affairs. The impartiality of the courts depended on their self-respect. Whether in Britain or the Antipodes these were not the sort to mimic a governor as the poor and ignorant might do.

Simeon Lord was one of two ex-convicts appointed to the bench by Macquarie in his early years (the other died) and by 1814 resentment hardened against him. Lord had made himself rich in New South Wales and he was a leader among the people of middling rank. But as Ellis Bent, the judge-advocate (the colony's only judge until 1814), told the Secretary of State in London, a criminal background must colour anyone's authority as a magistrate. Lord had besides sprung from 'the lower and uneducated order of society'. Under Macquarie, said Bent, the magistrates had become mere 'agents to the Governor'.[9] Nor could men of education and independence make themselves useful in other ways because Macquarie kept a close eye on any activities rivalling his own. He even stopped the formation of an agricultural society, which might have focused the minds of wealthy men on the improvement of the soil. 'I am disgusted with every thing here', wrote Robert Townson, a distinguished botanist and mineralogist, a Doctor of Laws and a large landowner. 'I can neither benefit myself nor be of any benefit to the Colony.'[10]

In Macquarie's middle period relations between Blacks and Whites had also come undone. In 1814, after eight years of peace, Aborigines from the remote bush began to organise themselves. '[W]hen the Moon shall become as large as the Sun', so they were said to have threatened, they would 'commence a work of desolation, and kill all the whites before them'.[11] Several groups, especially the Gandangara, joined forces on the southern frontier. They were probably inspired by the leadership of Cannabayagal, a giant among his fellows and a man held in awe among both Black and White.[12] In March 1816 matters reached a crisis. At one farm the head of the mistress was cut off, a man killed, the house plundered and pigs speared. Macquarie had accused the settlers themselves of 'unprovoked cruelty'. Now he sent detachments of the 46th Regiment out against the Blacks. They scoured the country from the Hawkesbury to the Illawarra and in a night-time attack 40 miles south of Sydney, the Appin massacre, killed Cannabayagal and thirteen others. Supreme in his own imagination, Macquarie outlawed ten more Aborigines. He called them 'banditti', as if they were fugitives from the power of the Crown.[13]

There was peace, but this military expedition set an awful precedent. Many settlers were now growing rich and they had enough men and horses to take the same kind of action themselves, so that by the 1820s killing parties, official and unofficial (precursors to the massacre at Myall Creek), were common. In June 1824, for instance, young William Lawson, heir to a local fortune, spoke of taking up arms against his Wiradjuri neighbours and of the slaughter of 'a hoard [sic] of their women', and soon afterwards three Black women were indeed found murdered in his neighbourhood. The Wiradjuri, for their part, were said to have been scalping men alive. It is impossible to say how many 'hoards' were thus dealt with, but from this time there was something like warfare along the mainland frontier and, perhaps, frequent glee like Lawson's.[14]

The Governor also had to deal with multiplying problems of convict discipline. Between 1804 and 1813 the men and women arriving each year on transports from Britain and Ireland had never numbered more than six hundred. Afterwards the total was never less than a thousand. In 1820 it was nearly four thousand.[15] The end of the Napoleonic Wars in 1814–15 meant the massive demobilisation of troops in southern England and a sudden unemployment of capital. The same had been true of every great military effort in Britain since the late seventeenth century, but this time the impact of the Industrial Revolution and the rapid growth of British population (it had doubled since 1750) made the social problems permanent. The long-term incidence of crime passed beyond any precedent in Britain.

The number of men and women now dealt with by the criminal courts and the number transported made changes in management impossible to avoid. Besides, new ideas about penal discipline called for the rigorous control of individual prisoners through a highly trained prison bureaucracy and finely articulated buildings. Government in both Sydney and Hobart was transformed as a result. Macquarie built a massive edifice, the Hyde Park Barracks, to house the convict men now employed on government works in Sydney, and he began a government farm at Emu Plains on the Nepean River, 36 miles away, for 300 more, plus a penal settlement at Port Macquarie, north of Sydney, for secondary offenders.[16] He also built a new Female Factory (a prison for women convicts) at Parramatta. Van Diemen's Land became for the first time a place of regular transportation from Britain. To begin with only 294 convict men had been sent to the Derwent from England, and 199 more in 1812 to keep up the labour supply, with others forwarded occasionally from Sydney. In 1815, when the European population of the island was nearly 2000, barely a fifth were convicts.[17] There was little regular discipline and to begin with there were separate governments, at Hobart and Launceston. David Collins, the first lieutenant-governor at Hobart, was authoritarian, but in the old style of Governor Phillip. After his death, in 1810, a succession of officers of the garrison took charge until the arrival of a new ruler (for the whole island), Major Thomas Davey, in 1813. But Davey, like Collins, was a man of the First Fleet. He was never interested in penal theory and Launceston, in particular, was left to its own devices.

Lieutenant-Governor William Sorrell, who took charge of Van Diemen's Land in April 1817, was more in step with the times. Sorrell's understanding of the new penal theory meant he was well prepared when the first of a long series of convict ships arrived in the Derwent at the end of 1818. Some of Sorrell's ideas on convict management were to be realised only in later years, but he tightened up surveillance throughout the island.[18] He cut a path for George Arthur, his zealous successor.

In Europe and North America ideas about public authority were changing so quickly that it was hard for remote officials to keep up. The end of the war with France seemed to promise a new Enlightenment, an age for young enthusiasts, men and women who valued private morality, individual ambition, piety, and free enterprise. Lachlan Macquarie, now in his last years as Governor, was behind the times. For instance, he was always anxious to nurture well-ordered households. But he was not interested in stamping out vice among unmarried women, including convicts, as the new thinking required. He had no vision of the state ministering to fallen virtue. Here the Governor found himself eclipsed by his senior chaplain on the mainland, the Reverend Samuel Marsden, who believed, like many of the new generation in Britain, that good men must organise against the unregenerate mass who were predators on women. For a moment Samuel Marsden mattered at Whitehall. In 1817 William Wilberforce, the great anti-slavery campaigner, received from one of the chaplain's local allies a long story of vicious convict management in New South Wales. Wilberforce (once Macquarie's friend) sent it to the Colonial Office, where it joined a thick file on the same subject. 'I fear', he said, 'he has not been at all attentive to the morality of the Colony which ought to have been the grand object'.[19] In fact, morality had been the Governor's great concern, but morality of a different caste.

Macquarie's thoughts on economics were also obsolete. New South Wales, said the *Edinburgh Review*, 'appears to have suffered a good deal from ... the ignorance of its Governors'. They knew nothing of 'the principles of Adam Smith' and of the bright promise of free enterprise. Major Robert Torrens, a famous writer on political economy, told Lord Bathurst, the Secretary of State, that New South Wales was like 'an overgrown pauper ... an enormous and wholesale Workhouse'. It must be drawn within the management revolution that was transforming Britain itself. By skilled exposition of 'the science of wealth', he said, 'the convicts might ... be made not only to produce for themselves whatever they require to consume, but ... to create a surplus which would speedily replace to Government the expenses of transporting them'. Bathurst was usually cool with enthusiasts.[20] But the sheer weight of opinion, the appeals to reason and to new doctrine, made their mark.

By this time the Governor was also breaking the law. Much of the power used by rulers in the Antipodes conflicted with the British constitution.

Strictly speaking, they had no authority except in emergencies over free men and women. They had no right to take their money in duties and taxes and no right to punish them under local law. Even the power of governors over transported convicts was technically debatable. So far it had been possible to bypass fine points of law because settlement was small, fragile, and remote from the rest of the world. Also, there were hardly any gentlemen (except officials) and it could be said to follow that there was no civil community, because among the British gentlemen were a fundamental source of civility and order. But by 1815 much of this had changed. Ellis Bent asked Lord Bathurst to tell him how judges like himself were supposed to act when they knew that the local laws were so defective. Macquarie himself accidentally underlined the point when he ordered the flogging without trial of a free immigrant and two former convicts for trespass on the government domain. The flogging of free men was rare enough. Their punishment by executive order was probably unprecedented, except at small outposts such as the Derwent. A petition describing this piece of tyranny was immediately drawn up by some of the Governor's critics in Sydney, numerously signed and sent to London.[21] Such protests, compounded by doubts about expenditure and the future of transportation, and by new management theory, led the Secretary of State to appoint a commission of inquiry.[22]

This was the inquiry mentioned in Chapter 1. John Bigge, lately chief justice of Trinidad, was named commissioner in September 1818. He was thirty-eight years old and familiar with postwar priorities. He arrived in New South Wales a year later with Hobbes Scott, his secretary, and with orders to examine all the settlements, their society, commerce, administration, judiciary, and schools, and to make suggestions for improvement. Never before had so much of antipodean life been ordered into writing, the commissioner and his secretary, assiduous as ants, gathering and storing a vast quantity of detail for carriage back to Whitehall. They returned home in 1821 and their findings, in three volumes, were presented to the Secretary of State during 1822–23. The spirit of improvement evident all through them was to touch every European on the continent in coming years.

II

'There is, in the climate of Australia, an Ionian elegance.' One glimpses here, in the air and sky, the brilliance of Greece. So an unnamed writer said in 1826. As we watch the birth of this new civilisation we must hope, the same man went on, that a similar elegance will one day permeate 'its national manners'. Climate and manners were closely attuned in contemporary thinking. It seemed self-evident that a country washed with light, such as ours was, must be sure of enlightenment in heart and mind. 'We are here marching into the forest,' this writer continued, 'displacing its silent gloom with cheerful voices, bidding the wilderness to smile, and conferring names on its solitary streams, glens, and mountains'. It was our duty to do so, for, he asked – jaunty in an age of triumphant peace – 'What are we without polished affections, the attractions of science and literature, the influence of imagination and hope, the lustre of futurity?' In forcing our way among Australian trees, letting in light and thought, we 'uphold and extend the magical dominion of the human mind'.[23]

Some of the White native-born, denizens of the forest themselves, resented that dominion. In poetry published the same year (1826) Charles Tompson damned the destruction of the landscape of his youth. He wrote of 'rude invasions ... the spoiling axe':

> Thus Art extends her civilizing reign,
> Bows the tall wood and casts it on the plain,
> Drives Nature's beauties from their seat away,
> And plants a train less lovely far than they.

In Hobart another of the first generation, Sarah Ann Cartwright, made a tangible statement of priority by planting natives along her garden front, recreating a little of the bush in town.[24] But William Charles Wentworth, also a native, would have none of this. The postwar conquest, the spirit of improvement so well represented by Commissioner Bigge (though Wentworth quarrelled with Bigge), was a work of glory:

> Be theirs the task to lay with lusty blow
> The ancient giants of the forest low,
> With frequent fires the cumber'd plain to clear,
> To tame the steed, and yolk the stubborn steer,
> With cautious plough to rip the virgin earth,
> And watch her first-born harvest from its birth.

The forests that Tompson spoke of were pleasant to look at, Wentworth agreed. They consisted mainly of the native apple, 'which is very beautiful, and bears in its foliage and shape a striking resemblance to the [English] oak'. But it was useless, except as firewood.[25] And why, indeed, should anything be sacred just because it lives in someone's childhood memory? At the same time in England the poet John Clare bemoaned the fact that 'an old wood stile [had been] taken away from a favourite spot it had occupied all my life'. '[I]t hurt me', he said, 'to see it was gone for my affection claims a friendship with such things'.[26] Clare, like Tompson, was a poet of romantic inclination. Against the spirit of improvement he appealed to the high court of his own feelings and to the precedent of his early years. These, for men like Wentworth, were an extremely feeble jurisdiction.

A more robust taste was to be satisfied by levelling hills and raising valleys, by buying, catching, or killing things so far beyond control, by bringing mysteries under 'the magical dominion of the human mind'. James
Ross, one of the best thinkers in Van Diemen's Land, wrote about the joy
of laying things low – 'The idea of destruction, I am sorry to say, gives a
zest to many of the pleasures of man.' He included even the making of loud
human noises. In 1823 Ross and some friends visited Lake Echo, at the
centre of the island. There, at sunset, they stood enraptured before a scene
of lengthening shadows, two exquisite islets and in the foreground black
swans embosomed on the still water. Aroused by a sudden sense of mastery, Ross took a shot at a swan. Blood and feathers apart, by his own
account the result was even more beautiful than the scene he had
destroyed. 'The echo that succeeded the report continued to reverberate in
a circle as it were round the shores in three distinct and successive parts.
The effect was sublime, and we exulted in a sort of rhapsody.'[27]

Mastery of this kind was thrilling when managed alone. But better still
was mastery in concert, with others of like mind as audience or associates.
Best of all was making a mark on the world to the acclamation of one's
sex and species. In this spirit the grazier Gregory Blaxland began, in
Macquarie's first years, to think of ways of crossing the Blue Mountains,
the massive high country that had so far formed the western boundary of
settlement at Sydney. Blaxland was moved partly by practical difficulties
shared by most owners of livestock – a scarcity of feed, and of forest pasture in particular, caused by drought, over-stocking, and successive plagues
of larvae called army worm. Some Europeans had been well acquainted
with the mountains since the 1790s and several good bushmen had found
their way far into their interstices and across their rugged backs. John
Wilson, once a convict on the First Fleet and a man who lived with pleasure in the bush, had boasted in Sydney in 1798 of having looked down on
miles of open country to the west. He and others like him had also ventured to the south-west, across easier ridges. In May 1813 Blaxland and
William Lawson (father of the Lawson mentioned earlier), together with
young Wentworth – three propertied men, plus four subordinates – set off
westward, more or less in Wilson's tracks. They pushed through successive
thickets until, as Wentworth put it (Wilson had not boasted in verse), 'as a
meteor shoots athwart the night, / The boundless champaign burst upon
our sight'. They had the Governor's support in principle, but at first
Macquarie was not inclined to make much of their success. Late in 1813,
however, he sent a party headed by the government surveyor, George
Evans, and it was Evans who made the first European descent onto the
western plains.[28]

The crossing of the Blue Mountains shows how speech and writing
worked among the invaders. The most effective forms of enterprise were,
once again, coloured by literacy. They belonged to the polished community

of the written word. Men like Wilson learnt bush skills early, from each other and from the Blacks, and tales of their journeys beyond the frontier circulated as bush wisdom, by word of mouth. In that way a shared sense of geography was laid down. (Fact was mixed with fable. Stories brought on the First Fleet told of a quite different settlement within walking distance of Sydney, a place where life was easy, and as late as 1816 the *Gazette* warned against 'the ridiculous expectation' of finding such a place.)[29] But it was not until Blaxland, Lawson, and Wentworth took advantage of customary knowledge that the discovery of land across the mountains became a science. It became the subject of cartographic skill, announced in the press and in reports to Whitehall. Evans the surveyor went even further. With such gentlemanly information he began the conquest of the plains. In New South Wales public order – literacy, legality, military power – were vital to every large event. Nothing of this kind could have been done on the say-so of people like Wilson.

Macquarie tried to focus such energy in his own name. Blaxland, Lawson, and Wentworth received no public praise until the Governor himself could lay before the world, through the *Gazette,* an account of Evans' discoveries. There followed an even more detailed public narrative of his own trip across the mountains, in 1815.[30] All this was symptomatic of the way in which the Governor resented the initiative and advice of leading settlers. He was also determined not to allow organised debate and consultation among the well read, such as the Blaxlands and the Lawsons. With curious perversity he resisted the spirit of the age.

Since the early seventeenth century most British colonies had had legislatures made up of leading men – a nominated board called a legislative council and often a second, elected chamber, modelled on the House of Commons. In New South Wales Macquarie gloried in the absence of both.[31] He had no thought of duplicating among the Europeans his annual meetings with the Blacks. He differed here from some of his predecessors and from many at Whitehall. Governor Hunter (1796–1800) had tried to make his officers organise themselves for the public good and when this effort failed Hunter's friend, the surgeon William Balmain, had told the British government that it must send out gentlemen settlers who could form an elite.[32] Advice such as this had led to a grant of 5000 acres for John Macarthur, 2500 for Walter Davidson, 2000 each for Robert Townson and his brother, and 12,000 altogether for Gregory and John Blaxland, all in 1805–06.

Such men were meant as the superstructure of a civil society. Their numbers multiplied in Macquarie's time, especially after the war, as immigrants, including senior officials, arrived with enough money to justify large grants. Also, older families began to prosper. The new flood of convicts meant more labour and a better market for meat and grain. By the beginning of the 1820s there were nearly a hundred freeholders on the mainland and nearly twenty in Van Diemen's Land with at least a thousand acres each.[33] Overseas trade also quickened, adding to the wealth of towns-people in Sydney and Hobart. Among the rich the intended spirit of public order – Governor Hunter's dream – began at last to show itself. Macquarie saw it as 'intrigue'. He retaliated, all the same, by making use of it himself, backing up his friends in town against the rural gentry. In June 1816 he called a five-day meeting of his magistrates, a deliberate show of strength that led to the founding of the first significant institution outside govern-ment, the Bank of New South Wales. He also increased the muscle of the Sydney-based Benevolent Society and in 1819 he approved two meetings in town to petition Whitehall for trial by jury and the lifting of restrictions on trade.[34] The minds of leading men, both for and against him, were further focused by the presence of Commissioner Bigge, and by the understanding that Bigge's report might mean radical change. When Macquarie gave up the government, in December 1821, many such men had made a habit of meeting for public ends.

Good meetings depend on habits of ritual and civility. The meetings that began in Macquarie's last years established a useful routine. Geog-raphy was also important because daily movements shaped the way people talked together. In New South Wales there were two main centres of pop-ulation, Sydney and Parramatta, 15 miles apart and as places of business (each had a Government House) their purposes were complementary. Sydney was a port and Parramatta an agricultural town, the home, for instance, of the Macarthurs and Blaxlands and of many small farmers sus-picious of Sydney traders. In Van Diemen's Land matters were less neat. There, too, there were two main towns, Hobart on the Derwent and Launceston on the north coast, but they were about a hundred miles apart and not interdependent, pulling, indeed, against each other. Even with the whole island ruled from Hobart (from 1812) two busy ports remained, with two rich hinterlands. And in both places the biggest landowners were also traders, a type of mixed enterprise that had been given up on the main-land long before. All this meant for Van Diemen's Land a failure of cen-tralised collective effort. In both Hobart and Launceston the typical landowner-wholesaler bought up wheat from neighbouring farmers for the Sydney market and if the Sydney price was high, then it was he who made the profit. He had nothing in common with his suppliers. As one of them complained, they had 'long since made over to him the whole of their pro-duce, at perhaps a dollar a bushel, for what is called "property" [goods from his shop], charged at an enormous rate'.[35]

The prominent men on the island made a good deal of money. But it did not translate into useful, settled authority because they were divided north and south, and because (like the officers of the New South Wales Corps in earlier days) they had no moral standing. There was no one among them who combined energy and a far-sighted intellectual power. Nor did rank bind society, as it sometimes did in the settlements around Sydney.

On both mainland and island there were, as yet, no big manufacturers or landlords and no fixed communities of labourers or tenant farmers. The people on the large estates were nearly all male convicts, assigned by government. For instance, the properties of John Blaxland (12,000 acres at Parramatta and Liverpool) were worked by sixty-four men, fifty-eight of them assigned convicts, and four women.[36] It was impossible for such people to put down deep roots. There were few or no families among them and the best workers were usually allowed to make their own way with tickets of leave after a few years' servitude. Some big employers were determined to create something permanent. But most, on both mainland and island, thought of their people as a resource to be used, and often used up, from season to season.

With Macquarie gone such men were free to organise, to give fresh thought to the future. The Philosophical Society of Australia and the Sydney Institution sprung to life on the mainland, both the work of the judge of the Supreme Court, Barron Field. The first met to hear learned papers on topics from local astronomy to Aboriginal life. It was small, exclusive, and died early. The second was a reading club that built up its own library.[37] More important were two agricultural societies, at Parramatta and at Hobart. Such societies were already common in Britain. They were designed to encourage skilled enterprise among farmers and intellectual leadership by the rural gentry. Like any organisation dedicated to large-scale enlightenment, they relied on that easily ignored model of official ingenuity, the postal service. During the 1790s British workingmen of literate habits had formed 'corresponding societies' that spread a revolutionary message nationwide through the post. The agricultural societies were the corresponding societies of the elite. The very word 'correspondence', in the sense of letter-writing, was part of the fashionable talk of the day and the agricultural societies were ideal institutions for the convict colonies in 1822. They were private bodies but they could work well with government, and the enterprise they wanted to encourage was vital to the life of the country.[38]

Both societies helped to focus graziers' attention on the breeding of fine wool for the British market. The gentlemen at Parramatta succeeded in forming a network of correspondents, a worldwide web (in 1825 a special committee was formed to manage mail), and they introduced new livestock, crops, and pasture. They also condemned some importations. Timor ponies, for instance, they described as 'diminutive, useless ... [and] expensive'.[39] Politically, the Parramatta society was a counterpoise to the Bank of New South Wales, to which many small farmers were said to be bound by debt. It was part of a movement that gave the farming interest on the mainland its own leaders and spokesmen. Articulate landowners also made use of the *Sydney Gazette* and, with his members at his back, the society's president, Sir John Jamison (12,000 acres), sent long letters to the Governor on customs and currency reform. The *Gazette* might remark that it was 'no small matter to attack an army of shopkeepers or merchants', but this the rural gentlemen around Parramatta might now do.[40] Nothing similar happened in Van Diemen's Land. There the Agricultural Society belonged to the south of the island and it was managed by landowners who were also Hobart wholesalers. Its president, Edward Lord (35,000 acres), had acquired £70,000 credit from local small farmers. Some in the Hobart society were keen improvers, but to start with it was mainly a combination against cattle thieves and fractious labourers.[41]

Members of the Hobart society also threw themselves into a campaign for the independence of Van Diemen's Land from Sydney. At the end of Macquarie's time the lieutenant-governor, though he was now responsible for the whole island, still answered to the Governor of New South Wales. Nor did the islanders have a Supreme Court of their own, sailing instead to Sydney or waiting for judges to come south on circuit. This was inefficient. Edward Lord and others complained, for instance, about the difficulty of suing their debtors.[42] More important, Sydney and Hobart were now competitors for British capital and emigration and it seemed wrong for one to depend on the other. The independence of Van Diemen's Land would mean the single-minded promotion of the island and the local spending of local income. When Whitehall at last gave New South Wales a very small, nominated legislative council, in 1823, it was yet another backward step for Van Diemen's Land because all the members were mainland men with mainland interests.[43]

Hobart received its own Supreme Court in May 1824. In the same month Sorrell's successor, Colonel George Arthur, arrived. Arthur himself wanted independence, and he offered his arguments in an early letter Home. To an observer in England, he said, Sydney and Hobart might look like neighbours, but the traffic between them was scarce and slow. The islanders, especially the convicts, needed a ruler who could give orders without constant reference abroad. Also, the problems caused here by so many free immigrants were beyond a Sydney governor. Arthur sensed, too, the local resentment of Sydney, sometimes 'carried to a very blameable and unnecessary extent' but often justified. He and Governor Brisbane should be allowed to represent the interests of their own communities on an equal footing.[44] He put his case well and from June 1825 Van Diemen's Land was free.

Macquarie had been the first to make official use of the name 'Australia'. He meant Van Diemen's Land as well. But in Hobart, as early as 1822, 'Australia' meant the mainland alone, and some educated islanders, looking back to the discovery of their south-east coast by the Dutchman, Abel Janszoon Tasman, in 1642, began to call themselves 'Tasmanians'. Both names were soon in use but neither was well understood. For instance, about this time the master of a ship just arrived at the Derwent from Port Jackson was asked if he had any Australians on board. Staring, he shouted back, 'Australians! what are they?'[45]

III

Two of the best minds among the Europeans in Australia during the 1820s belonged to two senior members of the Sydney government. There was 'Ionian elegance' in both. Thomas Hobbes Scott, Bigge's former secretary, was now archdeacon of New South Wales. Saxe Bannister, who figures largely in this volume, was attorney-general. Scott was the son of a clergyman but in his youth he had attached himself, almost as a son, to the eminent English radical, John Horne Tooke. His picture hung in Tooke's parlour at Wimbledon, near London, and he ate often at Tooke's table. Tooke's notoriety (he was charged with high treason in 1794), his scholarship, and conversation made the house a centre of political and intellectual debate and Scott imbibed his master's enthusiasm. He thought like Tooke that the tyranny of present times was the result of corruption at the top and helplessness among the mass. The law and the constitution were good in theory. But in practice – this is Scott, echoing Tooke – 'no-one who had not wealth, power and powerful friends had any chance of justice'.[46]

Horne Tooke was a democrat, but he was not a democrat like his famous contemporary, Tom Paine. Paine's attacks on the old constitution were ignorant and wicked, so Tooke thought, because it was public order alone, ancient precedent, which could guarantee the rights of Englishmen. Government itself might be guilty, as it was at present, of suppressing rights. But in that case government must be denounced by men of learning and judgement.[47] Tooke was a penetrating lawyer and also a philologist, whose great work, *The Diversions of Purley*, transformed the study of language in England. He thought of language as a political tool, available in the cause of liberty but currently abused. He was one of the pioneers of a new age of communications, for this – the late eighteenth and early nineteenth centuries – was a moment of revolution in communication skills, in communication method, and in communication theory. The way we speak and write, including grammatical structure, was fundamental, Tooke said, 'to the rights and happiness of mankind in their dearest concerns', especially in the courts of justice, where life, liberty, and property can hang on words. Language is a glorious art, 'an art springing from necessity, and originally invented by artless men' (plain men, of the kind who peopled *Waverley* and *Rob Roy*). Words, properly understood, take their substance from action and from the material world, things immediate to all humanity, and to work well they must be transparent. The current system of knowledge, so Tooke believed, the system manifest in the universities and courts of law, confused meaning with empty abstractions.[48] It was a system marshalled against the poor.

By 1812 Hobbes Scott had served his political apprenticeship at Tooke's dinner table. In the same year his partnership in the City of London (a firm of wine, hop, and brandy merchants) was bankrupt. He had entered Oxford with the idea of following his father into the Church, had served as Bigge's assistant, was ordained and came back to the Antipodes as archdeacon in 1824. He was never devout. His caste of mind was rational, secular, and utilitarian, like those other admirers of Tooke, the philosophical radicals. James Mill, friend of Jeremy Bentham and father of John Stuart Mill, was a well-known example.[49] Besides, he was easily carried away by personality. Even a friendly observer thought him too 'defective in temper, in civil courage, and in *state*' for a church dignitary. But he was determined to make his mark here. The Church of England was responsible for the education of the people and Scott planned a network of elementary parish schools, plus a grammar school and an institution teaching technical skills and farming. The whole structure, including scholarships for the sons of the poor, was to be funded from land grants managed by trustees, and Scott also wanted a special grant for the endowment, 'probably at a remote period', of a university.[50] His great purpose was to make writing, and the authority writing might entail, equally available to all the people. In this way he aimed to shift the balance of power in society. The essential flaw of traditional schooling, so Scott believed, harking back not only to Tooke but also to Jean-Jacques Rousseau, was that 'instead of teaching *things*, it has taught only *words*'. Also, instead of judgement it taught only memory.[51] This was education for slaves.

Without reform, said Scott, 'neither N.S.W. or Eng[lan]d will have real justice'. Children must be taught, in common language, 'the nature and elements of Government' and its significance for their own lives. Justice must be their daily bread and literacy its guarantee. All depended on strong action by government itself. The people must be compelled to open their minds. Indeed, only by compulsory attendance – a distant prospect – could all children be persuaded to take their diet of redemption. '[Dam]n 'em', said Scott, with only a touch of humour (Tooke also swore, to his friends' regret), '*they sh[oul]d have it willy nilly!*'[52]

Bannister, a younger man, arrived like Scott in 1824. He, too, had links with the philosophical radicals and he agreed that communication, including schooling, was fundamental to common justice. But he was also influenced by his own grammar-school teacher, the Reverend Vicesimus Knox. Knox was famous as a compiler of school texts crammed with English prose and poetry. A man of dramatic ambition, he aimed to broadcast – to pelt the people – with literary jewels. He also loved whimsy. Knox was less materialist than Tooke and he questioned the teachings of Rousseau. From him Saxe Bannister inherited a belief that words had their own splendid magic, a power apart from the world of 'things'. Knox liked fairy stories, 'those little books, which are sold by itinerant peddlers to children and servants, and which are thought too despicable to deserve the attention of the learned'. In their unpretentious way, he said, they opened infant minds to the riches of humanity. Latin and Greek likewise, though shadow-languages from the past, were a worthy feast for children in secondary schools.[53]

Knox also valued memory. Little children took possession of language, he believed, through their wonderful power of recollection.[54] This notion led the philosophical radicals to gather in support of the experimental infant schools founded in and around London from 1819, and Bannister himself brought literature about such schools to New South Wales. He started one in the crypt of St James' church, Sydney, which within two years housed eighty children between eighteen months and six years of age. The joining of so many infant voices in song and recitation was a new experiment and the school had many visitors. The singing was peculiar to current sensibility, as fresh as Creation itself.[55]

It was a truth newly realised that good laws and good administration could change the character of a people. The education of the masses was a cause which suddenly caught fire in Britain, and also in New South Wales and Van Diemen's Land. The Wesleyan Methodists and evangelical Anglicans had established Sunday schools in Sydney and Hobart from 1815, and in 1820 Governor Macquarie opened the Georgian Public School, for five hundred 'children of the poor'. But these were partial efforts. The hopes of Scott and Bannister went much further. And yet their efforts were compromised from the start. Scott's Church of England included only two-thirds of the local population, other religious leaders were beginning to move and Anglicans themselves differed on the teaching of the poor. Some thought mainly of discipline and it was possible, too, to argue, with Vicesimus Knox, that language was sometimes *meant* to be mysterious. As well as being taught to reason, children must sometimes sit wondering (even frightened, like Aboriginal children at the feet of *their* teachers), tongue-tied by miracles.

Saxe Bannister liked to drop in on his school at St James' church. He was childlike himself, easy with the young but awkward with adults. His few home visitors he received with 'reserve and hauteur', standing, for instance, in conversation instead of handing them a chair. In court he blundered through common civilities, though his speeches, once begun, were not only long but also 'amusing – original – expansive'. He carried everywhere a moral enthusiasm, a wandering, jabbing eagerness, which seemed to some a little mad. He could look like both hero and fool. He and Scott were both bachelors and their unusual temper limited their close friendships to the Macarthurs at Elizabeth Farm. At this time the Macarthur homestead, on a low hill overlooking the Parramatta River, was something like a villa of the High Enlightenment, a glasshouse for modern virtues. It included a fine garden with olive trees (the first in this country), oaks and oranges, 'magnificent mulberry trees of thirty-five years' growth, umbrageous and green', and roses 'in great variety ... [filling] the air with fragrance'. John Macarthur had given his children an interest in educational and political theory, and he and two sons had lived briefly at Vevey, Rousseau's favourite place, where the light danced on Lake Geneva. They had called on Sismondi the historian nearby. Scott took a cottage on Elizabeth Farm.[56] Bannister was the more difficult talker but the family found him worth the effort – 'clever, unaffected, and just odd enough to make a pleasing companion'.[57] The archdeacon spent five years in New South Wales and the attorney-general two-and-a-half. These were periods long enough to make the Macarthur household pivotal for the rethinking of life in Australia.

In strict logic the principles I have described gave government a duty to emancipate, through literacy, not only the children of the poor but also young Aborigines. Bannister came easily to this conclusion and Scott followed. Governor Macquarie had tried to give the Aborigines a secure place under government, to assimilate their rights with the rights of Europeans. But apart from the hanging of one convict, in December 1820, for the murder of an Aboriginal man, little happened in his time to prove to the Blacks that they might be safe under White government.[58] Before coming to New South Wales Bannister had published a paper that proved two large points. First, the fate of a colonised people depended on timing. In North America, he believed, vital chances had been lost in the mid-seventeenth century, during the first and second generations of settlement. Also, like Horne Tooke (both were lawyers), Bannister was intrigued with common wrongs. He was angered not so much by the British invasion of the new world as by all the small savageries that followed. He had 'shuddered', he said, 'with indignation and sorrow upon hearing accounts ... of the barbarous personal tyranny' suffered by the American Indians. In New South Wales he found 'frequent and gross injustice' in official and unofficial dealings with the Blacks. '[C]ommon right, in matters of life and death, ... [were] constantly outraged, by our neglecting the plainest principles of equity.' Commercial law was Bannister's specialty and he always focused on property rights, which he thought the state must guarantee for both moral and prudential reasons. He railed especially against the practice of taking land, with no thought of compensation, from British subjects who happened to be indigenous. The empire ought to represent universal justice. That could only happen, he said, if we were 'just at every step'. We must think of the Aborigines as citizens in the fullest sense, as 'rational beings'.[59]

To be rational was to be capable of managing property. Also, to be rational was to be teachable. To be teachable was to be drawn by curiosity. Bannister believed that humanity naturally made its way towards the light of higher civilisation. He saw intellectual energy all about him, as an entomologist sees insects. It was 'a cruel sophism', he said, to suggest, as many did, that peoples like the American Indians and the Australian Aborigines were incapable of mental effort.[60] Official justice and native curiosity must be linked, and that depended on literacy. Reading must nurture curiosity and at the same time secure the daily rights and enterprise of all citizens. Impressed by such logic, put to him, perhaps, in the drawing room at

Elizabeth Farm, Hobbes Scott not only added infant schools to his blueprint for the Europeans (places using, as he put it, 'gentleness rather than coercion, and … the plainest methods of ocular demonstration'), but he also prepared the ground for the wholesale teaching of Aboriginal children. He began a new school at Blacktown, he sent out a questionnaire to well-read men acquainted with the Blacks, and he appointed an agent to discuss with all the native peoples within reach the subject of their children's education.[61]

Saxe Bannister's ambitions for what he called 'clear-sighted, vigorous philanthropy' went further again. Tooke had argued for the ameliorating power of common English words, rightly used. Bannister believed, with parallel logic, that Aboriginal words must be the fabric binding the native people to their new government. White men in authority must learn to speak with Aborigines in their own languages. Aboriginal grammar must be analysed and, most important, expressed in print – some new Horne Tooke must come forward for the Blacks – so that the message of common citizenship might be universally received.[62] The natives must see their own image, rendered in their own tongue, absolute, precise, and fixed – fixed in ink. Powers of reflection, the knowledge of self-in-the-world, would quickly follow.

In spring 1824 Bannister introduced Lancelot Edward Threlkeld, lately a missionary in Tahiti, to Governor Brisbane. Threlkeld was about to undertake a mission to the Aborigines and, with government support, he settled among the Awabakal at Lake Macquarie, north of Sydney. His aims coincided with Bannister's and they kept in touch. Threlkeld made it his business to report abuses to the attorney-general and in July 1826 he sent him the story of Jackey Jackey, suspected of murdering a stock-keeper. The soldiers, said Threlkeld, had kept this man one night in gaol at Wallis Plains:

> The next morning he was brought out, tied to two saplings and the Officer [Lieutenant Nathaniel Lowe] commanded the Soldiers to shoot him – One fired at him, the ball hit him on the back of the neck, the black turned round his head and looked at him, the next fired, and the bullet cut along the jaw, and broke the bone; the black turned his head round again[,] another soldier stepped up and blew his head to pieces.

'Such a lawless proceeding', Threlkeld wrote, 'committed in such a brutal manner fills me with feelings too strong for utterance'.[63] Bannister attended to such reports as best he could (Chapters 3 and 8). But more hopeful, to his mind, was Threlkeld's commitment to understanding the speech and moral idiom of the Blacks. By such vehicles both hoped to make events like this impossible, ensuring that British law was equally efficient among Black and White. With it they aimed to make acceptable the beauties of English civility, sadly remote as they might seem at present, English commerce, and Christian faith.[64]

McGill, or Biraban, of the
Awabakal people, a portrait by
Alfred Agate, 1839.

Source: Charles Wilkes, *Narrative of the
U.S. Exploring Expedition, During the
Years 1838, 1839, 1840, 1841, 1842*
(London 1845), p. 89. Reproduction
courtesy of Mitchell Library, State
Library of New South Wales.

Opening page of Luke's Gospel, which McGill and Lancelot Threlkeld translated
from English into Awabakal. Decorated by Annie Layard.

Reproduction courtesy of Auckland Public Library, New Zealand

All turned on the written word, that engine whose levers ought to be universally accessible. Aborigines, currently living in a world of voices, were to be given the power that followed from reading and writing in one's mother tongue. Threlkeld was a zealous Protestant and he must have been struck with the way in which his project partly resembled the emancipation of English itself from Latin in the age of Chaucer and Wycliffe. 'Christianity', he said, 'does not make its votaries mere machines, but teaches them how to give an answer to every one that asketh a reason of their hope'.[65] Threlkeld's 'votaries' were Bannister's 'rational beings'. Conscience and curiosity would be drawn together by the incoming light. Bannister, even more than Threlkeld, was in love with print. Print guaranteed the independent life of the mind and the free comparison of ideas. '[T]here is nothing', he thought, 'like a universal printing'. He advised Threlkeld to be cautious in applying established philological rules to 'the expressions of a simple people', but he urged him, all the same, to get an Aboriginal grammar published as soon as possible. Mistakes might be ironed out later by discussion among the well informed.[66] Threlkeld responded with two songs (untranslated) in the *Sydney Gazette*, and, in 1827, with his first attempt at a grammar – *Specimens of a Dialect, of the Aborigines of New South Wales*. A translation of Luke's gospel, *An Australian Grammar* and *An Australian Spelling Book* followed within the next ten years. The gospel, which according to Threlkeld was mainly the work of his assistant, the Awabakal man McGill, was never published.[67]

For some years Bannister continued to hope that even 'the laws of the Aborigines' might be codified, printed, and applied as far as possible by colonial courts.[68] But among his supporters in Sydney the most radical hopes were long dead. In his work for European children, Hobbes Scott increased the number of parish schools on the mainland from fifteen to thirty-six, including five infant schools, and he had reason to believe that Governor Arthur would take up his work in Van Diemen's Land. But with Bannister gone (in October 1826; see Chapter 3) and with a better knowledge of race relations, the archdeacon gave up his blueprint for the Blacks. Likely costs exploded and inquiry proved that with the quickening pace of invasion, livestock already being 100 miles from Sydney, the moment for thorough justice had passed. Too much now depended on graziers and stockmen, often men like the younger Lawson.

The scheme's intellectual premises were also adrift. As Governor Brisbane's successor, Ralph Darling, pointed out, there was no single Aboriginal language on which reconciliation might rest. Threlkeld might make headway among the Awabakal, but the empire here confronted a great jigsaw of tongues. Also, as it soon turned out, even with the shared knowledge of each others' language – Black and White – on both sides deep tracts of mind and soul lay beyond reach.[69] Clear-felling can leave persistent undergrowth, and the neatness of grammar hides a tangle of idiom and myth. Words had none of the clean convertibility imagined by Tooke's disciples and Bannister, for one, had overlooked the difference between his own world and the world he aimed to win in Australia. As late as 1982 the Aboriginal playwright Jack Davis, a worker in English, said: 'There will always be differences. I don't care what it is: there will always be differences between black and white.' He meant differences especially in words, in the deeply patterned colours of speech.[70]

The attorney-general left his mark all the same among a few of the well read in New South Wales, men and women of active conscience. His eagerness was felt among them at a moment of peculiar creativity. Scott and the Macarthurs at Elizabeth Farm both carried forward his ideas on schools. In England Bannister had written not only his book on the Indians and another on conveyancing but also one called *Essays on the Proper Use and Reform of Free Grammar Schools* (1819).[71] John Macarthur was the leading figure in the foundation of the Sydney Public Free Grammar School, in October 1825, and he must have worked with Bannister's advice. The Sydney school, a project so far unique in Australia, was meant for reconciliation among the Europeans themselves. It was designed to turn out a new elite, drawn from among the people. At a time when differences between Protestants and Catholics were fundamental to community life, there was to be 'no exclusion on the ground of religious tenets'. Nor was religious dogma to be imposed within. And at a time of uneasiness between free immigrants and ex-convicts the school was to be a hallmark of cooperation. The trustees included not only several Macarthurs and both judges of the Supreme Court but also five leading ex-convicts (four men and one woman), some of them school parents. The Macarthurs soon withdrew and for a while the effort foundered, but Sydney College (now Sydney Grammar School) was the result.[72]

Bannister also focused public talk about race, and his ideas were to resurface elsewhere in the continent during the 1830s and '40s (Chapters 8 and 10). John Macarthur himself thought anew about the 'reclaiming' of the Aborigines, a question that had always interested him.[73] Macarthur's children, however, belonged to a new generation of educated men and women and in their own time they were to discover the intractability of relations between Black and White. Here was a rock on which were to be broken any number of bright intentions. It was indeed hard to recreate 'Ionian elegance' in the Antipodes. There was no simple equation, as there seemed to be in the Greek isles, between cobalt sky and silver earth. Australia had its own questions. By now there were more fruitful hints in Rousseau and Sismondi – in the more unpredictable blues of Lake Geneva – than there could be in anything ancient and fixed.

Chapter 3

Making a Name

I

Henry Savery arrived a convict in Van Diemen's Land in December 1825, on board the transport *Medway*. In terms of social background and education he was a cut above most of his fellow passengers. He was the son of a substantial banker in Bristol and proud of his descent from several landed families in the West Country. He had been at various times a sugar refiner, a marine insurance agent, and editor of the *Bristol Observer*. He had lately (it was said) accumulated between £30,000 and £40,000 by negotiating bills with fictitious names and addresses, and in December 1824 he had been charged with fraud. He was arrested near Portsmouth, at the last moment, trying to escape to America under the name 'Servington'. (His lineage included the old knightly family of de Servington.)[1]

Fanciful names were Savery's stock in trade. English readers had lately delighted in a series of satirical sketches written by an individual calling himself 'The Hermit in London' and Savery, when he got to know Hobart, boldly used the title 'The Hermit in Van Diemen's Land' for a similar series in the *Colonial Times*. He there presented leading local men and women thinly concealed as 'Mr Sitfall', 'Mr Scribewell', 'Mrs Doubtmuch', 'Mr Cockatrice', and so on. He was 'Simon Stukeley', the Stukeleys being another piece of old gentility.[2] In 1830–31 he followed this effort with a three-volume novel published in Hobart, in which he told an embroidered story of his own life, now using the name 'Quintus Servinton' (with no 'g'). Over more than a thousand pages he coolly observed the unravelling of his own respectability. Both characters, Stukeley and Servinton, were self-portraits set among people Savery knew, but they were very different types – proof of his imaginative range.[3] Stukeley was a judge of others, Servinton a convict.

Australia, for Europeans, was a place for self-enamelling, for living out a newer story, and writing was the way to do it. Men like Scott and Bannister, true heirs of the Enlightenment, might think differently. For them, and for masters of bureaucracy like Governor Arthur (Savery's contemporary in Van Diemen's Land), the written word served a different purpose. For them, as literacy theorists might say, writing was 'message-focussed'. Used as they used it, it was meant to make identity absolutely certain. It carried knowledge abroad. It seemed to pin down rights and obligations and it offered a rational order, accessible from above and below, to government and people. It promised to trim common dealings of prejudice and doubt. It would help to straighten ways of thinking. 'So Architects do square and hew, / Green Trees that in the Forest grow.'[4] But writing also has a life of its own. Of course, it defines the individual and the world. It tells a man who he is. But, like a sudden wind in the branches, it can change things utterly. The very idea of being at Europe's Antipodes still, after a generation of settlement, dazzled faith and undermined identity. That process was amplified by writing and reading. Works such as Savery's were like some spherical mirror, some great green bubble let loose above the Australian landscape. The immigrant people saw themselves anew.

On the mainland one of them, Alexander Harris, who seems to have arrived about a year after Savery reached Van Diemen's Land, also lived with disguises. He was the son of a dissenting minister and apparently known to literary men in London. He was young and physically strong and he tried his hand as a drover, sawyer, and rough carpenter. He changed at least his Christian name and he may have been the John Harris who figures as a cedar-cutter on the Illawarra, south of Sydney. But unlike most labourers Harris carried a pocket book to record his feelings.[5]

Harris lacked Savery's skill in depicting character, but his accounts of colonial labour were unbeaten. The hewing of green trees was itself a mystery, and Harris's sawing days produced some vivid detail. 'A cedar-sawyer's cuts', he said, 'are very deep, and a deep cut makes the saw move very stiff'. He noted too, 'when first cut[,] ... the splendid crimson of some of the planks', and when burnt 'the pink lambent flame' that proved the greenness of the timber. And of an evening's rest:

> The success of the day, the prospect of a good cutting or an advantageously shaped log on the morrow, the pleasant perfume of the pipe, the cheering pot of tea again and again repeated, with each new yarn, or joke, or laugh, the busy and pompous excursions and barkings of the dog, the pattering shower, the clouds of fireflies that dance along in their countless angular courses where the cold stream tumbles among great stones in the bed of the creek – such are the objects which occupy [the tired sawyer's] ... senses and his thoughts.[6]

Rather, such were the feelings of the gentleman-sawyer, comparing perfume with tobacco, the pattern of human voices with a dog's barking, easy sensibility with sore muscles. To begin with Harris seems to have kept such images to his pocket book, publishing much later in London. Henry Savery was less hesitant and *Quintus Servinton* was to be Australia's first novel produced wholly on the spot.

Printing and publishing, putting on a show in multiple copies, became part of the life of Sydney and Hobart early in the 1820s. Savery's writing was the fruit of a decade of colonial self-display, although newspapers themselves went back even further. The *Sydney Gazette* had existed since 1803, and in Hobart the *Derwent Star* (1810–12) had been followed by the *Van Diemen's Land Gazette* (1814) and by the *Hobart Town Gazette* (from 1816). The *Sydney Gazette* was the most substantial. But while Lachlan Macquarie was Governor at Sydney, and during Sorrell's first years as lieutenant-governor at Hobart, the two *Gazettes* were monopolised by official notices.

Macquarie's departure gave more room to both. The *Sydney Gazette* was the first to open up its pages to free discussion, to begin with mainly on customs duties and the currency. Some letters to the editor, always using pen names, were so long that they had to be issued as supplements and soon a box was attached to the door of the press office for the use of correspondents.[7] Then, during winter 1823 the *Sydney Gazette* began to publish verse, reviving a practice of its earliest years. Two poets shone, Charles Tompson ('Australasianus'), only sixteen years old, and the elderly ex-convict schoolmaster, Laurence Hynes Halloran ('Lorenzo'). The same happened in Hobart from April 1824, with the expansion of the *Hobart Town Gazette* from two pages to four. There the earliest verse came mainly from Evan Henry Thomas, a Protestant Irishman of various occupations.[8] But in Hobart, except for Savery, writers did not usually play with names and characters as they did in Sydney. Verse was signed with initials. Nor did they show the same interest in landscape and the native-born. There was less depth of imagination here, and less variety of talent.

This was partly a matter of size and age. Hobart had been founded in 1803 and Macquarie had laid out its streets in 1811, but the engine of town life took time to hum. An immigrant exploring on the morning of his arrival in 1817, when it was still called 'the camp', saw only, as he put it, 'the beginning of a town'. The seeds of civilisation were 'interspersed with the poles and scaffolding of houses being built, ... as if a lot of people had come only the night before, and had begun to set up a city to dwell in'. By 1820 the free adult population was about 500, when the figure for Sydney was already 4000.[9] During the next decade Hobart's numbers grew ten times while Sydney's only doubled, but differences remained. Hobart's sudden success made it a town of transplanted Englishness. There were few adult native-born in Van Diemen's Land in 1820 – it was too early – and by 1830 they were lost among the flood of newcomers.[10] In Sydney in 1820, on the other hand, a quarter of the free adults were natives. In 1828 the *Sydney Gazette* announced the death of the colony's first great-grandmother, with

Launceston, a pen and ink sketch made in 1830 by William Lyttleton. By this time the town had a newspaper, the *Advertiser*, and had become something more than a remote village-port.

100 descendants.[11] The romantic appeal of the new generation, their youth, their passion, their bigotry, gave a colour to Sydney that Hobart lacked. In Sydney, too, rich ex-convicts were more obvious and no citizens remodelled themselves more keenly.

In both places, all the same, crowds gave a larger dimension to town life. Both became theatres within themselves, vividly coloured and full of sound. The newspapers, especially, gave a sparkle to daily events and to daily speech and encouraged a thirst for stories. More than that, they imposed a new mental order on all who joined in the stories as writers and readers. They encouraged precision – if not accuracy – as to who people were and when things happened. In settlements without newspapers public statements (lost-and-found, for instance) were limited to town criers and to notice-sheets stuck in central places, which placed a premium on gossip and individual memory. Note an episode in Launceston in 1824, which we know about from court records, there being no newspaper. Bridget Humphreys ('wife of Serjt Humphreys') told of paying four pints of rum for some French lace belonging to Mary Hewitt ('Jack the Casker's wife'). She wanted the lace stitched to a child's cap and she gave the job to Katherine Simpson, who lost both articles. 'I had the Cap cried', said Mrs Simpson, 'but heard nothing of it or the Lace'. Ann Mayall, a washer-woman, said she heard it cried, 'and a reward of five Guineas offered for it'. It all happened 'about a fortnight after the last men were executed at

Launceston', said Mrs Humphreys, 'I think about two months ago'.[12] This is the way events made their mark in places like Launceston. Knowledge was shaped by an all-enveloping familiarity and everything depended on speaking and listening.

The press changed all this in obvious and exciting ways. 'Fanny Flirt' (Chapter 1), sensing the possibilities, wanted it to cater to her own tastes and she cannot have been alone. To this purpose raw scraps of information, such as those from Launceston, might be cut and stitched (as I have done with these) so as to create a small comedy of manners. Fanny Flirt might have been delighted to witness this little drama, well presented in print. In their pages editors lifted up certain men and women before the mass of their fellows, changing them into typed characters – 'Lorenzo', 'Mrs Doubtmuch' – but still set against a familiar backdrop, the brick and slab, the promontories and waterways that made up each town. Size matters, including the size of community, and the new methods of publicity matched the size of Sydney and Hobart. The gap that might now exist between well-known names and the people who heard about them, the hint of mystery that now divided players and audience, the crystallisation of script and stage, the unpredictability of local colour and local cadence – all this was possible because the towns were thick with faces and because any face might be sketched on paper.

Public characters are always shaped by stereotypes of gender. During the nineteenth century, and ever since, there have been various models of manhood and womanhood, of gendered high ideals. Among early nineteenth-century Europeans there was a powerful consensus, with minor variations, about the best types of manhood (Chapter 1). The works of Byron and Scott were full of them. But for the moment there was not much to guide, and less to excite, the imagination of women and girls, as they sought models for themselves in what seemed to be a new age. So far, good women were only the chaste and private beings on whom good men depended. However, makers of serial literature in Europe and North America were already exploring women's imagination as a field of profit.[13] Fanny Flirt's demand was symptomatic of the same need here.

The *Sydney Gazette's* new prosperity led in October 1824 to the establishment of the *Australian*, followed in May 1826 by the *Monitor*. The *Australian* was a man's paper. It featured contests in the law courts, constitutional reform, fisticuffs, and horse racing. Here was the range of interests and attitudes that the verse of Byron, in his many-faceted manhood, had covered all at once: 'A little breath, love, wine, ambition, fame, / Fighting, devotion, dust, – perhaps a name.'[14] The first proprietors and editors of the *Australian*, Robert Wardell and William Charles Wentworth, were both young, unmarried, trained at the English bar, eager for notoriety, and angry with the restraints of life in New South Wales. The *Australian* also amused male readers with occasional reports of criminal cases at the

Sydney Police Office, written up as dramas ridiculing women. In one, the main characters were:

> Mistress Elizabeth Jackson, otherwise Montague, a comely dame, fat, fair, and forty – landlady of a certain rendezvous for weary travellers ... situated on the Rocks; ... her daughter, *Miss* Montague, a blushing *demoiselle* – Mistress Sally St Leger, otherwise 'Swallow' [a washerwoman] ... and lastly, Mistress Walton, vender and retailer in general, of tea, tobacco, soap, and the like groceries.

The more strongly women made their feelings known the sillier they seemed. Especially laughable for readers of the *Australian* was news of their wrestling in the street, pulling at each other's hair and flesh.[15]

Newspapers also opened the way for men to skylark in print, pretending to be women. At a picnic near Sydney in 1824 the 'fickle mind' of one of the girls upset an admirer, who wrote to the *Australian* complaining of female behaviour. 'Kitty Currency' replied in a jaunty letter that the *Australian's* editors refused to use because it also mentioned the 'big wigs and ugly black gowns' that they wore as barristers in court. Kitty sent it instead to the *Gazette* and provoked an answer in that paper signed 'Crocus'. The original Crocus, 1500 years before (according to Edward Gibbon's *Decline and Fall of the Roman Empire*), was a native chieftain who fought for Constantine. This new Crocus was also a homespun warrior. He was sure, he said, that Kitty was male, a low character aiming 'to amuse some of Sydney's bon vivants, while grinning between the glass and the newspaper'. 'Un Ami', a young native, was also outraged by Kitty's 'indecent and insulting letter' and condemned all correspondence appearing over female names. '[T]hough they bear the semblance of advocating the cause of my countrywomen,' he said, '[they] are intended to depress and hold them up to ridicule'.[16]

On the other hand women, as writers themselves, could dress their feelings for decent exhibition. In both Sydney and Hobart women published poetry. 'Sidneia' sent two poems to the *Sydney Gazette* about 'vanish'd joy' and Ann Stanhope Gore, native-born and only fifteen, wrote one for the *Australian* called 'Eathlina's Lament', in which an Irishwoman mourned her nation in English and Gaelic. Readers in Hobart were offered lines by Mary Leman Grimstone, a writer of powerful imagination and an advocate of women's rights who, in England, had contributed to *La Belle Assemblée*, a monthly 'addressed particularly to the ladies'. The work of yet another female poet was turned down by the editor of the *Hobart Town Gazette* because it was too full of 'mysterious grandeurs'. She was only ten.[17]

Some women were fascinated by the contrast between privacy, especially their own (ladylike privacy, inward-looking and fragile) and the brazen permanence of print. At Denham Court, near Sydney, the lady of the house, Christiana Brooks, kept a journal of public news, written up as if in a newspaper and coloured by her own opinions (especially on finance), shaped by her reading of the local press. She affected to be tired sometimes of the Sydney papers. Weeklies she might look forward to 'with great avidity', but twice-weeklies, so she said, were too much. She read them all the same.[18]

Another reader reminded the *Monitor's* editor, Edward Smith Hall, that as 'news-mongers' ladies were good for circulation.[19] In fact, from the beginning Hall had appealed to women readers. He made no effort to flatter the men, arguing against boxing and betting at the races, and he dwelt on the needs of women shoppers. He complimented Mrs Wemyss and Mrs Cowper for their management of the Sydney sewing school and Mrs Richard Jones for her patronage of the painter Richard Reid. In 1827 he published a letter arguing that 'the Australian fair' ought to cultivate 'the *higher* faculties of the mind'.[20] He tried to get original poetry from women and in 1826–27 he ran three prose pieces signed 'Corinna', which, taken together, constitute the first effort by a woman to publish her attachment to Australia, including the 'sacred character' of its 'white majestic Gum trees'. He followed this with a serialised letter supposed to be from a girl in Sydney to her sister in the country. The writer enjoyed, as she put it, 'nice lodgings in George Street'. But she had trouble with the chest of drawers in her room. '[W]hen you push one side in,' she said, 'the other comes out, like a widow's fat, under the influence of Mrs. Dillon's Patent Stays, (to be had at 74, George-street.)'. 'I went a shopping there,' she rattled on, 'such dresses Susan as made my very eyes water! why your best bombasine, when compared with what I saw, is only like a bark-hut to Government-house!' (Perhaps the author was Mrs Dillon herself.) Her young man, who used hot irons to curl his whiskers, had bought her a blue glass monkey with emerald eyes.[21]

Hall's paper greatly enriched public debate in colonial Australia. He shared with Saxe Bannister, whom he much admired, a passion for equity. The minds and experiences of women he saw as proper parts of a good moral landscape. Editorialising about a poor housewife fined for giving lodging to a convict against the regulations, he was forced, he said, to give it up: '[W]e really cannot argue on the subject – we are absolutely choked with grief and indignation to see such goings-on.' Struck by the sight of washerwomen sweating in summer at the public tanks (the source of the Tank Stream), he urged the government to build shades for them to work under.[22]

Hall thought that details from the law courts were unsuitable for family consumption. But he would not spare his female readers from the more brutal subject of relations between Black and White. He wrote in 1826 of an 'extirpating war' beyond the Blue Mountains, and of the colony 'stained with blood' and he once carried a letter that described in ghastly terms an

Aborigine on Sydney's north shore. This man was a victim of syphilis, said the letter-writer, his head 'food for myriads of vermin', his body beset by 'a host of tantalizing flies'. Here was 'the image of the Creator' consumed – eaten up – by our invasion. Hall set the piece in italics.[23] So he shouted from his pages about types of misery that for other editors were only passing colour on the local stage.

II

The name 'Corinna', used by the *Monitor's* author, might have carried some readers back two centuries to a poem by Robert Herrick, called *Corinna's going a Maying* – 'Come, let us goe, while we are in our prime; / And take the harmlesse follie of the time.' This antipodean Corinna put pen to paper, 'ready', she announced, 'to act in the theatre of fancy, and discourse in language beyond the *platitude* of ordinary life'.

During the 1820s, in both New South Wales and Van Diemen's Land, there was an eagerness for 'harmlesse follie' and a longing for 'the theatre of fancy'. Something similar – a real theatre – had existed in earlier years. During the 1790s small groups of convicts and soldiers had acted in plays and in Sydney a playhouse had been purpose-built and patronised by the Governor and officers.[24] But all had long since passed away. Plays had not been encouraged by Governor Macquarie. Now the idea re-emerged. Late in 1824 a plan for a theatre in Sydney was broached in a letter to the *Australian* from the young Jewish merchant, Barnett Levey. Shares were to be offered for a building to house a company of local amateurs. '[O]ur curency lasses' he said (he was a bad speller), 'would be very much joyed at such an establishment'. There was already a theatre at the convict establishment at Emu Plains, 36 miles away on the Nepean River. Among the convicts there was no need to put up an expensive building, although their audience did include distinguished local families.[25] In Sydney, on the other hand, the cost of evincing 'the theatre of fancy' in some solid and respectable fabric was more than Levey and his friends could manage. It was also soon clear that Governor Darling would not license an institution in the heart of town open to all comers and dedicated, in effect, to the careless mingling of virtue and vice.[26]

But, as I have said, the common life of Sydney and Hobart already had its theatrical aspects. Even the town Aborigines – in some eyes the lowest of the low – might be the stuff of imagination. In 1825 Barron Field, late judge of the Supreme Court, published his impression of the Blacks he had seen in Sydney streets, degraded as they were by abuse, drink, idleness, and charity. They were, he said, 'the Will Wimbles of the colony'. (Will Wimble was a character familiar to readers of Sir Roger de Coverley.) They were 'the carriers of news and fish; the gossips of the town; the loungers on the quay. They know everybody; and understand the nature of everybody's business, although they have none of their own'. They were a backdrop to the traffic of town life; indeed a moral backdrop, a point Field conceded in a flash of art. 'They bear themselves erect,' he told his readers, 'and address you with confidence, always with good-humour, and often with grace'. And, he said, in spite of their fallen state they were not beggars. '[T]hey accept of our carnal things in return for the fish and oysters, which are almost all we have left them for their support.'[27] Here was theatre Darling could not ban.

Levey had more success with concerts, which were more morally straightforward than plays. A series of five was presented during winter 1826 by the Sydney Amateur Concert Society, and the same thing was tried in Hobart. On the first night in Sydney the audience numbered 120, mainly men. But good reports drew women and families and on the third night, six weeks later, the audience totalled about four hundred. There were no women on stage to start with, a point lamented by Hall of the *Monitor*. 'There is ... a charm', he said, 'in the sweet and plaintive tones of the *Female* voice, which finds its way in a peculiar manner to the soul'. Two women joined in due course, and yet on such occasions men always had a better chance of setting up as public characters. Levey himself took to the stage, and his comic songs and mimicry were enormously popular. John Edwards, leader of the group, was also an actor. 'The countenance of this gentleman,' remarked Hall, 'his attitude, the *soul* which he infuses into every thing he undertakes, reminds us of one of the ancient bards, so beautifully portrayed in Ossian, and [in] the works of Scott'.[28]

Men in both capitals were keen to set themselves in the public eye and thanks to the newspapers notoriety spread far beyond the radius of daily conversation. Editors themselves were public figures, struggling to attract all eyes from one issue to the next. They played parts. James Ross, of the *Hobart Town Courier*, called himself 'quite a literary and scientific character':

> I write my articles, engrave my vignettes, set the types, adjust the press, correct the proofs, fold up and direct my papers, make out accounts, receive and pay money, sell my books and papers, answer queries and advertisements, &c., all with my own hand. With me the words are not infrequently printed before the ink of the manuscript is dry.[29]

For such men the editorial page (page two of each issue) was a platform to act upon. E.S. Hall's account of himself breaking down – 'we really cannot argue on the subject – we are absolutely choked with grief and indignation' – mixed real feeling with a touch of drama.

But the law courts worked best. Judges and magistrates were obviously actors, always venturing their dignity before the crowd. Henry Savery, as 'The Hermit', showed how the pomp of petty sessions in Hobart could be translated into comedy:

> Those of my readers who have ever seen a duck waddling and sidling through a farm-yard, first looking on one side and then another, casting up its eyes, all the time making a discordant noise, as if to testify its importance, can picture to themselves the gait, attitudes, and expression of one of these Gentlemen [the justices], as he made his way through the assembled multitude, to take his seat, on the bench.[30]

'Can picture to themselves … .' From 1824 both New South Wales and Van Diemen's Land possessed Supreme Courts, complete with chief justices, puisne judges, attorneys- and solicitors-general, masters, registrars, prothonotaries, clerks, and criers, plus power, cunning, and injured innocence, altogether a fine tapestry of European life. Here was rich material for characters, rich material for picturing as one liked.

In Sydney the two stars in the new legal system were the young barristers (and owners of the *Australian*), Wardell and Wentworth. Wardell was the senior man but Wentworth the more dazzling. It was also Wentworth who made their paper shine. While he wrote for it, as a rival editor admitted, the leading articles showed 'a brilliancy of imagination – a depth of thought – and a commanding peculiarity of style' rare in the Antipodes. In court the two were larger than life. Anxious, as Wentworth said, not to be 'degraded … to a level with the old practitioners', and aware of the value of mimicking Westminster Hall, they were among the few to wear wigs and gowns.[31] They shared offices in Macquarie Place. They also shared cases and the combined luminescence of 'the brothers in law' could create a *cause célebre*. In May 1827 they appeared for Lieutenant Nathaniel Lowe of the mounted police, charged with the murder of Jackey Jackey, 'alias *Commandant*, alias *Jerry*, an aboriginal native', the man whose killing Lancelot Threlkeld had reported the year before (Chapter 2).

In this case, even before the accused could enter his plea, his counsel gave a daring display of the questions they were prepared to ask about the rule of law in the Antipodes. They argued against the jurisdiction of the court, citing Bacon, Grotius, and Puffendorf to prove that the killing of Aborigines was not actionable. These people, they said, had no understanding of legal process. They therefore had no legal significance, alive or dead. They were quite different from the 'rational beings' of Bannister's imagination. They were therefore beyond the law. Or rather they – and we in dealing with them – were subject only to 'the laws of nature'. Thus 'nothing could be fairer', Wardell told the court, than to do as Lowe was alleged to have done – 'to punish them in the very way in which they themselves would punish others falling into their hands'. Besides, they were cannibals ('anthropophagi', eaters of human flesh), which made them liable to extermination. '[D]estroying one of them', he went on, 'would be no more than destroying that which was offensive to heaven'. The chief justice dismissed these arguments and the trial began, but Lowe was acquitted all the same. Bannister himself had lately resigned, after months of argument with the Governor, and the efforts of the acting attorney-general were feeble and confused. More important, the defence lawyers managed to find several individuals happy to testify that the key prosecution witness, a convict, was a man of lies.[32]

The rooms from which Wardell and Wentworth conducted their business were a new centre of power in New South Wales. The two had a new way of talking about civility and order. Or rather, they gave dignity to old and hitherto undignified ways. Wigs and gowns, parchment and pink ribbon, Grotius and Puffendorf, all the weighty ornaments of learning that they handled so easily, were brought to bear *against* the government. Best was Wentworth's anger, which gave a new dimension to the endless quarrelling of public life. His love of hitting back, his coarse swearing, his red face, all became facts of public significance. The courts, bars, and streets he frequented were full of anecdotes. On a Friday evening in February 1825 he was walking with two other gentlemen down to the quay. As they passed the government domain they were stopped by a sentry. Wentworth shouted against this invasion of his liberty (the firelock in his face) and was taken to the guardhouse. He was released minutes later by order of the major of brigade, but he wrote next day to Governor Brisbane demanding the names of the men responsible. He intended, he said, to punish them at law, for the sake of 'my own character and the rights of my fellow citizens'. The names were given. But Wentworth's anger was sometimes spent in the heat of the moment and he did nothing else until he heard that the Governor himself had held an inquiry. That was equally insulting and he wrote again. An inquiry without the complainant present was 'a solemn mockery of justice ... a military insult [added] to ... military outrage'. Besides, 'I never called upon His Excellency to avenge my Wrongs. I knew and know how to avenge them myself'.[33]

These remarks were copied into the office letter-book by Wentworth's clerk and the letter of which they formed part was delivered to Government House by his messenger. Such men (nameless now) were Wentworth's shadows, the vehicles of his passion. He was soon widely adored and his name bandied about, as the *Gazette* remarked, 'unceremoniously ... by the rabble'.[34] He was one of themselves in sentiment and language and yet, in dress, in wealth, in learning, in boldness, in rhetorical power, inexorably above them. In short, he was a hero.

Wentworth was a giant among the early Europeans in Australia. The dramas that shape a nation's common life, its field of shared imagination – certain stock characters, certain moral themes, certain favourite endings – must be the work of many authors. But some authors, thanks to their intellect and imagination, do more than others. Among our national dramas the trial of Nathaniel Lowe was a typical early episode. Wentworth's was a world of men, acquisitive, literate, English-speaking, White. Even educated women might see more commotion than delight in his 'depth of thought', which may be why Elizabeth Macarthur chose not to marry him. Wentworth was not interested in the criminal poor and he was not usually interested in the Aborigines, except as enemies. His commonwealth of men was secular and commercial, a fabric of relations managed by experts like himself. Most of his clients were shopkeepers and merchants and he dispatched for them (at 11s. 6d. each) a continuous flow of letters of demand to debtors and unwanted tenants. Judges might have the final word in most cases, but Wentworth found the colonists eager to settle out of court, so that often events were interpreted just as he liked.[35]

This was a world grounded in the law of nature, in straightforward language, brotherhood, and anger. As Wentworth said, he knew about revenge. It was a type of action that left no room for other people's pain. The legal ceremony in which he specialised (including letters of demand) was like duelling. It was a finely wrought medium of passion. It was not, as Horne Tooke and Hobbes Scott thought, a lynchpin for civility. Defending savages at law, such as Bannister wanted to do, seemed no more sensible than appealing to their honour with swords and pistols.

Wentworth had returned to New South Wales full of the idea of antipodean society remodelled. 'Soon', he declared (in the famous poem he wrote about his native land, published in 1823), 'may a freeman's soul, a freeman's blade, / Nerve ev'ry arm, and gleam thro' every glade'. All necessary order in the Antipodes would repose in such freemen's souls. Freemen, bound to each other by brotherhood, were to quarrel and prosper as they liked and, as they liked, to trample the unfree underfoot. Wentworth's ideas were shaped by a kind of Byronic republicanism, an important point of difference with the enemies he made here. These included Hobbes Scott. Though himself a radical, Scott assumed a moral pivot, a fixed point beyond society on which enlightenment might turn and, never a republican, he looked to God's vicegerent, the King in England. He stressed his own tenure of the King's commission and 'His Majesty's gracious intentions for providing for his Church and Schools'.[36] The royal conscience was for him the spirit of the improving state, sacred, irresistible, ever-busy remodelling life. It was this difference in moral perspective that divided Wentworth from Scott and his friends.

In reality, it was the carefully created image of the royal conscience that mattered most, a painted sun fixed above the public stage. As a piece of theatre Scott's idealising of monarchy, common also at Whitehall, appealed with significant power to the imagination of the people. It engrafted a soul within the imperial engine of pen and paper and it gave many of the subjects of empire a vivid sense of what the philosopher-statesman Edmund Burke called *'a power out of themselves'*, an absolute standard of virtue.[37] The inked image of St Edward's crown, the focal point of the royal insignia, its looped gold, its little cross, left a mark on thousands of subject minds. The invention of this empire-wide faith in monarchy was a work of genius, and one with power to last. For Wentworth, ever Byron's disciple, it was nonsense. Far from glorifying public office, he looked for flesh, blood, and frailty behind all titles.

And yet both Wentworth and Wardell were themselves poseurs. More, they were tricksters. They knew how to cut corners for their clients and their clients were grateful for it. Aiming to shift guilt from himself to an innocent man, one John Sprawls, for instance, called at the office in Macquarie Place and emerged confident that 'Mr Wentworth ... will stand his friend at the Criminal Court'.[38] The partners understood their business. They sprang to the high wire, as in Lowe's case, and they ducked through loopholes in the law. They defied authority. What Scott called their 'craftiness and subtlety of *technicalities*' made them wonderful to watch. And all the time they conjured up an image of an opposing villainy, as if they were scripting some melodrama. The wickedness of others gave their own skill a kind of storyline. Their chosen enemies were the rural magistrates, especially at Parramatta. More narrowly, they took aim at the Macarthurs at Elizabeth Farm, plus Scott and Bannister, a party they called 'the Merinos' or 'the Faction'.[39]

In theory the Europeans in Australia had always been governed, and had governed themselves, by vague notions of the common good. In theory conscience prevailed and that meant the conscience of the King at Home and of his Governor. As one old settler recalled, in earlier days the governors had been all-important:

> every shingle that was split, and nail that was driven came under their notice some way or other. If the Governor was observed to stop at a poor fellow's cottage, and give him a nod of approbation, it was remarked that he worked hard for a month after, and became rather select in the choice of his company.[40]

The influence of His Excellency was now, in the 1820s, more implicit, but he still mattered within the moral framework of community. The viceregal conscience, whatever its flaws in fact, was still a mirror for the consciences of lesser men and women.

From this point of view Wardell and Wentworth were, as a letter-writer said in the *Gazette*, '*evil Counsellors*'. They were men of corrupt learning who led their clients to do things 'which the *inward Monitor* [the conscience] condemns'. They pressed their advantage against rules made for the efficiency of government and for the protection of the weak, for Aborigines, convicts, and orphans.[41] Another story of their exploits was immediately famous. Scott was unhappy with the management of the Female Orphan School at Parramatta and he called to account William Walker, the master, and his wife, the matron. The pair consulted instead at Macquarie Place and Wentworth told them to fight. Scott's authority depended on his being King's Visitor of all the government schools but a little inquiry showed that Whitehall had neglected to issue the necessary warrant. On this vital point Scott was beaten in court.[42]

The Walkers resigned all the same, upset by Scott's 'arbitrary' reforms, and they took with them two servants, the Broadbears, husband and wife. This led to an even greater victory. The school was suddenly without women to look after 120 girls, and in his anger the archdeacon charged the Broadbears with leaving without notice. Among the magistrates who heard the case at Parramatta were three of Scott's friends, who had turned up deliberately, provoked (according to John Macarthur) by 'the scandalous state the children were left in'. The Broadbears were sentenced to three months in gaol, but Wentworth once more came to the rescue. He persuaded the Supreme Court to overturn the decision and he had husband and wife sue for damages, on a charge of malicious conviction.[43]

On the day of this trial the Supreme Court was packed. 'It was a case of much importance,' said Judge John Stephen, in his summing up, '… in which persons of high rank were concerned, in which the Magistracy were concerned, and in which the liberty of the subject was concerned'. Liberty won and the Broadbears were awarded £290. At Elizabeth Farm the result of these 'imprudent but otherwise perfectly pure transactions', as James Macarthur called them, was mortifying.[44] As for the archdeacon, he might see himself, in his life's work, fighting for 'real justice'. But he had lost his way in thickets where only the agile survived.

The ambushing of Hobbes Scott was followed by a last blow at Bannister. On the attorney-general's resignation in October 1826 Wardell wrote a parting attack in the *Australian*. He called Bannister incompetent. He was nothing but an intellectual, he said, a 'veritable Dominie Sampson' (the lumbering tutor in Walter Scott's novel *Guy Mannering*). His mind was cluttered with paper, his 'schemes … all Utopian – all chimerical'. 'He would preach to the Blacks, while the Blacks are destroying our property – he would reason with them, while their spears are uplifted.' Bannister hit back, like Hobbes Scott, and equally unwisely. He sued for libel, the case came on just after the Broadbears' victory, and he too lost. 'Oh! what a disappointment!', sneered Wardell in his next issue, 'The plaintiff takes a *non suit*. … Pooh!!! … Sax[e] & Co. – try it again?'[45]

III

During the 1820s there was drama even in the changing physical state of Sydney and Hobart. The very scarcity of fresh water – the creeks running through both towns were now very dirty and much too small – proved how many more people were crowded together. So did the stink of thickened humanity. Hobart saw a sudden gathering of new buildings in stone and

The harbour end of George Street, Sydney, a drawing (detail) made in 1828–29.
The street is full of both animals and people, including Aborigines begging from
passers-by.

Source: John Carmichael, *Select Views of Sydney, New South Wales, 1829* (Sydney 1829),
reproduction courtesy of Mitchell Library, State Library of New South Wales

brick, some of them two-storied and beetling over the old wooden hovels.
In Sydney good brick cottages had been built over a number of years, typically 'one or two stories high', according to Peter Cunningham, 'with
verandas in front, and enclosed by a neat wooden paling; lined occasionally with trim-pruned geranium hedges'. Geraniums thus added their silky,
spiked fragrance to the residue of long settlement. Front doors were often
of local cedar, scented in its own way and painted white or blue.[46]

New pace and sophistication provoked stories among the old inhabitants. 'You may hear people even now,' said Cunningham, speaking of
Sydney, 'in gossipping over old adventures, relate their tales of shooting
parrots, to make pies of, in the middle of our main street – then a crowded
wood'. Another Sydney newcomer delighted in talking with one of the
'fathers of the Colony':

> I find in him a living chronicle of the bye-gone years; – he can give a cor-
> rect history of every old house in the town, and of its occupants; – recol-
> lects when it was a common thing for people to lose themselves in the bush
> at Woolloomooloo ... At that time ... the houses resembled those Robinson
> Crusoe mentions, which are only now to be met with in the obscurest lanes
> of this Antipodean Metropolis.[47]

In Sydney, some said, 'there was never so great unanimity' as in those hard
early days. In Van Diemen's Land there was likewise talk of 'the good old

times'. One Tasmanian spoke with irony: 'You were no sooner landed from England then, and fairly in the streets of Hobart town, than a knowing one would pick you up, and never leave you till he had plucked you like a green goose. Now you may wander about and nobody will notice you.'[48]

Europeans everywhere were becoming interested in history. As the philosopher John Stuart Mill remarked, 'comparing one's own age with former ages, or with our notion of those which are yet to come' had become an everyday habit.[49] Here there were several efforts to record local memories and to make sense of the local past. In 1821 the *Hobart Town Gazette* announced a forthcoming history of Van Diemen's Land, 'from its first establishment to the present period'. In 1822 *A Popular and Statistic History of Van Diemen's Land* (apparently a separate effort) was said to be nearly finished. In Sydney it was suggested that all government orders from the beginning ought to be collected for publication, since even those now obsolete were 'precious as historical relics'. The Sydney press also promised a narrative *History of New South Wales* by Thomas Parmeter, a government surgeon, and nearly three hundred copies were ordered by public subscription (more than the current circulation of the *Australian*), at two Spanish dollars each. These were the first attempts to set out chronicles that told the full story of the first generation. Everyone who had lately written about the colonies, including Wentworth, had published in England for the emigrant market, and emigrants did not want to know about the local past. Local readers did. Parmeter appealed through the press to the recollections of old inhabitants (as did one of the Hobart historians) and he hunted out written records. But not one of these books saw the light.[50]

This interest in their own history says something important about the people themselves. They already had settled ideas about the history of Europe. In 1826, for instance, E.S. Hall was sued for libel by Hannibal Macarthur (a cousin of the Elizabeth Farm family) and his supporters established a fund to pay his costs. In putting down their names the subscribers showed how much they thought in terms of a classic political battle. They used numerous rousing pseudonyms: 'An English Spirit', 'A British Spark', 'John Bull', 'A True Born Scotsman', 'An honest Hibernian', together with some crude samples of Irish Gaelic. They obviously saw themselves as actors in a European story. Some recalled ancient battles: 'The Cause of Russell', 'The Cause for which Hampden bled in the field and Sydney died on the scaffold', 'Wilks [sic] and Liberty!', 'Junius', 'A Descendant of William Tell'.[51] The list gives some idea, so far, of their sense of history. It was tied to the far side of the world. In Australian terms it was unfocused and irrelevant.

The names of John Hampden, William Russell, Algernon Sidney, and John Wilkes epitomised the English sense of self. Here only the image of Lachlan Macquarie – 'the Grand Napoleon of these Austral Realms' – had an equal aura. When news of Macquarie's death in London reached Sydney, in October 1824, the editors of the *Australian* described him as a legislator who in ancient times might have received 'divine honours'. Tompson, the poet, did indeed offer prayers:

> Then stoop, kind Father, from that bright abode,
> Teach Rulers virtue — bid them dare be good.
> Obey the promptures of a gen'rous mind,
> And trace th' example thou hast left behind!

In Van Diemen's Land the *Hobart Town Gazette* remembered the dead ruler as 'a Guardian Angel', 'a Supreme Legislator of the human heart'.[52] Other famous men lived in Macquarie's shadow, his predecessor, William Bligh, his enemy, John Bigge, and his southern deputy, Sorrell.[53]

But such an attitude, focusing on a governor so lately gone, obscured large questions about the history of the colonies. Also, in these settlements there was something both all-embracing and inscrutable about government. It was hard to imagine its inner springs and broader purpose. Altogether it was impossible, as yet, to see the story from outside.[54] A grub beneath the bark might as well try to measure the shape of its tree. Besides, the violent dispossession of the first owners of the land was still underway. The trial of Nathaniel Lowe, and even more his acquittal, gave broad hints of uncontrolled brutality at the edge of settlement. Any 'extirpating war', to use Hall's words, must give an unpalatable edge to the national story.

And yet stories of a limited kind were now being sketched out in both colonies, in conversation, in rhetoric, in fragmentary images taken up and reaffirmed from day to day. While nothing yet was published, the mid-1820s were the turning point. From this period we begin to find a pattern of local historical belief that was to spread and flourish through several generations. Popular history depends on myth – on powerful lies, easily remembered and easily handed down, which colour every other detail known about the past. The political implications can be enormous. In the mid-1820s two national myths took root with remarkable speed in the minds of the people, one in Van Diemen's Land and one in New South Wales. Both omitted the Aborigines. The first, which was the work of Governor Arthur, appears below (Chapter 4). The second, the mainland myth, was largely Wentworth's.

Among the subscribers to Hall's fund, besides the names already mentioned, there were hints, too, of a newer sensibility. There was one 'old hand', one 'Son of Convicts', five enemies of 'the Faction' or 'the Merinos', and one 'Curer of rotten Sheep'. Here we see the early impact of Wentworth's rhetoric, including his book, first published in London in 1819 (see Chapter 1) and now a type of gospel in both colonies. Wentworth offered no connected story. But his writing showed how the grub under the bark might take a better vantage point. Wentworth's rising celebrity meant that some of his angry passages and the large sense of destiny he seemed to offer – disconnected flashes of past, present, and future – became beacons of common faith. Among any people sense of the past shapes sense of the future. Wentworth's enemies might see the defeat of Scott and Bannister as the end of hope in New South Wales. James Macarthur, only twenty-eight years old, spoke now of 'the dread abyss which seems to open before me when I think of futurity'.[55] But one man's abyss was another's green pasture.

Wentworth offered to Europeans in Australia an understanding of the passage of time that was both modish and passionate. In his writing and speeches over thirty years he fixed these settlements within the larger pattern of the British Empire.[56] He made them duplicates of those once-British communities on the western shore of the Atlantic, the United States. And his up-to-date reading took him further. Sismondi's famous *Histoire des Républiques Italiennes du Moyen Age* was newly available in English, as I say in Chapter 1. It told a story of enterprising peoples, the inhabitants of the Italian city-states, men in love with 'liberty and virtue', shaking free of feudalism and growing rich. Wentworth featured this formula – 'liberty and virtue' – in his book but, unlike the Elizabeth Farm circle who favoured virtue, it was liberty he stressed. He copied Sismondi's faith in a republican elite, well organised, well read, and far-sighted.[57] In New South Wales his law clients included the leading ex-convicts in Sydney, but his most important allies were moneyed immigrants, such as Sir John Jamison and Gregory Blaxland. These were men interested as he was in free enterprise and free speech, in using their combined weight in the government of their country.

Politicians like these, in Sydney and Hobart, were preoccupied with two reforms in the late 1820s. They wanted a proper system of trial by jury and an elected legislature. Juries of twelve operated in both colonies, but it was still possible for the accused in criminal cases to opt for a jury of officers. This Wentworth saw as a relic of military autocracy. Juries of twelve were usually made up of men of middling rank (tradesmen and farmers), and here the arguments for reform were complicated by the question as to who might qualify. In European Australia most men of middling rank had been convicts. Many had been pardoned, but some had served their whole term without any evidence of reform. Should all be entitled, as jurymen, to decide on moral issues? It was an important question at a time when law courts were the focus of community life. The right to sit on juries was a mark of authority and citizenship such as any respectable man might hope for. But who was respectable?

Making laws was an even more lofty business. Throughout the empire the work of legislative councils and legislative assemblies called for a degree of education, a breadth of vision, a knowledge of public forms and public speaking, and a quantity of free time (there was no salary) such as only gentlemen could manage. In each of the two Australian colonies there was by now a small council, the members chosen from Whitehall and entitled to discuss (in secret) laws proposed by their governor. In his book Wentworth demanded an elective system, such as most other British colonies had always had. Population alone might justify it and there were already many more potential voters in the Antipodes than there were in some of the island colonies of the West Indies, 'where', as he pointed out, 'houses of assembly have been long established'.[58]

In Van Diemen's Land, even more than in New South Wales, it was professional men and gentlemen-merchants who took the lead in movements such as these. There was a stricter sense of rank in the south and an even clearer belief that forms of liberty were much the same as good manners and respect for property. In March 1827 a public meeting was held at the court house in Hobart to petition the King and parliament for reform. The leaders included Joseph Tice Gellibrand, lately attorney-general, Edward Lord, president of the Agricultural Society, and Anthony Fenn Kemp, once an officer in the New South Wales Corps. All thought that Governor Arthur, with his aggressive intellect and autocratic habits, was unable to behave as a gentleman among gentlemen.[59] It was usual for petitions to the King to go through the Governor, and a deputation from the meeting arranged to see Arthur several days later. They meant to put him in his place and (as Arthur said, but they denied it) instead of waiting for him to name the time they did it themselves: two o'clock. The Governor forgave this 'total absence of etiquette', but he asked that the petition be sent in beforehand. It came when he was busy with someone else. He was still busy at two, and he moved the appointment to three, the visitors being informed as they approached His Excellency's front door. They felt insulted. 'Though points of etiquette, may be waived', they said, 'in individual intercourse, yet Bodies of Men, especially when representing others, cannot dispense with those forms of Courtesy, which Society has established'. They refused to come again and sent their petition to Whitehall over the Governor's head.[60]

The Hobart public meeting was called simply to approve the gentlemen's petition. In Sydney larger issues were already at stake. For Wentworth public meetings were vehicles of education, like newspapers. They *created* public opinion. 'Public meetings', said the *Australian*, 'open the eyes of the people – shew them their strength – moral as well as physical, and convey to their reasoning faculties truths, to which, but for them, they might remain strangers'. Wentworth's public meetings, happening once a year at least, were always dominated by his own voice. But at the same time they offered a magnificent alternative, not only to the little legislative council but also to those private gatherings (at Elizabeth Farm, for instance) 'whose acts', as Wentworth put it, 'had hitherto been palmed off on the people of England as the acts of the Colonists at large'.[61] Wentworth's meetings made public oratory and acclamation the test of truth.

Faith in public meetings was underlined by another part of Wentworth's message. This was the national myth he planted at the heart of common imagination. Sismondi, in his history of the Italian republics, had told of an invading race, corrupt and selfish, at odds with a native people. Sir Walter Scott used the same idea in his writing, especially in *Ivanhoe* (1820) where the story depends on hereditary hatred – 'a line of separation betwixt the descendants of the victor Normans and the vanquished Saxons'.[62] Here was a perfect formula for New South Wales. Stories of evil deeply entrenched, of a poison working down the ages, gripped current fancy. Revenge was a central theme. It was a formula that might easily engender national history, as it did in *Ivanhoe*. Blind to the most obvious and bloody feud in Australia, between Black and White, Wentworth worked on a story of enmity among his own. An aristocratic caste, the Macarthurs and their supposed allies ('the Faction'), were to be the permanent enemies of the population at large. There was a network of kin running the country who hated ex-convicts and who aimed, said Wentworth, to ensure that the taint of criminal conviction would become ingrained, as 'an hereditary deformity'. 'They would hand it down', he said, 'from father to son, and raise an eternal barrier of separation between their offspring, and the offspring of the unfortunate convict'. When John Macarthur read these words in his own copy of Wentworth's book he scribbled beside them, 'false [and the] young man knows it to be so'.[63]

Wentworth did know it. But history needs the poetry of myth, and rhetoric needs example. And on paper hatred, like love, must be idealised. As specimens of oligarchy the Macarthurs were near enough. Besides, as John Macarthur himself understood, elsewhere among 'the respectable people' of New South Wales there were certainly many who did believe that penal bondage left a deep stain. Many must have hesitated to have their sons mix with the offspring of convicts at Macarthur's Public Free Grammar School, an institution deliberately designed to break down caste. There were also ex-convicts, as one of them said himself, who had no wish 'to dine and drink tea with the Emigrants' in order to meet some fictional test of citizenship.[64]

These feelings, as feelings, made little political difference. But the resentment of aristocracy was part of a sense of history and a sense of destiny now emerging among the Europeans in Australia, and especially in New South Wales. It helped to inspire faith in popular power. In bringing it to birth Wentworth was no more bound to tell the truth than was Scott in *Ivanhoe*.

Chapter 4

Convict Opinion

I

Conspicuous in the theatre of colonial life – as both actors and audience – were the convicts, men, women, and teenage children, who came here in their tens of thousands. They lived within a fabric of rules, which were in some respects much older than the settlement itself, going back not only to the prison communities of Britain and Ireland but also through many generations of convict transportation. The first convict ships left Britain for Australia in May 1786 and the last was to sail, for Fremantle on the west coast, in October 1867. But individuals had been carried in bondage from the British Isles to North America and the West Indies since the reign of James I and VI (mentioned in Chapter 2). Indeed, questions as to whether the state might send its subjects abroad by force, whoever they were, had figured in the seventeenth-century arguments about the rights of Englishmen. Regular transportation across the Atlantic began with the Transportation Act of 1718 and between that time and the outbreak of the American Revolution at least 36,000 convicts had been taken to Virginia and Maryland. Nineteenth-century ideas about convict life across the seas were shaped by events in those early years.[1]

During transportation to North America, and for many years after the First Fleet reached Australia, there was no real penal system. There was a system of transportation, the forced exile of convicted men and women. But for an entire generation in this country, as in Virginia and Maryland, there was no integrated scheme of labour and discipline. Officials in Whitehall were yet interested in the experience of convicts outside Britain and they lacked the power to reach so far into the lives of such people, whether in Annapolis or Toongabbie. Only after 1815, with a new generation of politicians and officials in London, was there something like a pervasive apparatus of power for the management of convict life. Only then, presumably, did some convicts begin to look and sound, even smell, distinctive, because of the manner of their existence. Charles Dickens wrote of 'that curious flavour of bread-poultice, baize, rope-yarn, and hearth-stone, which attends the convict presence' (his experience was at the English end).[2] But even then the impress of confinement and bureaucracy was never absolute in Australia. Systematic notions were often a ruler laid on flesh and blood.

It is hard for any administrative system to emerge at all without the neat growth of paperwork. By about 1815 administrators were used to keeping close watch on the way convicts were embarked in Britain, managed in transit, and landed in Australia. But additional skills – the codification of discipline in office and prison, the positioning of officials, each with his own expertise, a proper use of architecture and geography – all these were needed to make an impact afterwards.

To begin with, officials on the spot often failed to understand why they should take such trouble. Theories of criminal punishment worked out in the last decades of the eighteenth century emphasised reform and the care-ful measurement of penalties. Such things were cherished among the avant-garde in Europe but for many years in Australia it was not even clear what a convict was. In New South Wales recently transported men and women often behaved (by administrative default) as if they were free. And on the other hand wives and children of convict men were often listed as convicts. The main point of discipline in the early period was not punishment but keeping people alive and productive. Until the time of Governor King (1800–06) no attempt was made to keep track of how many convicted men and women there were in the Antipodes. King made some comprehensive lists, he sketched out a system of assignment, by which he handed over named convicts to named employers, and he invented tickets of leave, which in theory showed which convicts were allowed to look after them-selves. But it was not until Governor Macquarie's time that a penal bureau-cracy began to take shape. Finally, in spring 1821, a colony-wide muster at last defined and measured the convict population on the mainland, thirty-three years after first settlement.[3]

System was especially slow to take hold in Van Diemen's Land. The old-fashioned tone used there was manifest in Lieutenant-Governor Thomas Davey's revival of the term 'servants of the Crown', invented for convicts by Governor Phillip. Servants were not quite the same thing as prisoners.[4] Women convicts were particularly hard to classify. The new penal theories were not worked out with women in mind and the principles of discipline to be applied to them were still unclear. Only now, in England itself, Elizabeth Fry was beginning the reform of women's prisons (Chapter 7). Echoes of her enthusiasm were to be found occasionally in the Antipodes, in the work, for instance, of the Reverend Samuel Marsden. But trans-ported women were free to marry in the colonies and their condition as wives often subsumed their condition as convicts. Even as assigned servants women in both colonies behaved as if they were free, leaving their places as they liked to take up offers of marriage or, as Lieutenant-Governor Sorrell said, of 'more advantageous employment'.[5] The men might be just as self-sufficient. In December 1816 Macquarie issued an order about the wages to be given to convict labourers and in March 1818 Sorrell adapted it for his own people, in an effort to stop disputes and to keep wages down (the men in Van Diemen's Land had made themselves remarkably expensive).[6] But rules or no rules, labour always had a price.

One test of penal status was the right to deal in property. In Britain convicted felons were supposed to give up all their property to the state. No such rule had been applied to transported men and women in North America (or at least in Virginia) and some convicts in those parts, qualified by their property, had even voted in elections. In Australia to begin with convicts could hold land. As late as May 1824 in Van Diemen's Land, among the convicts in government service, there were married men with families, 'having Houses or Shares of Houses', as the lieutenant-governor himself remarked. Such a man might build 'what is called a skilling or lean-to, which composes the rear of his future house'. He thus became, in principle, a householder, 'and as his means improve he erects a front'.[7] On the mainland by this time there was less latitude. Convicts might accumulate property but they could not defend it in the courts.[8] They continued to arrive with possessions. A surgeon on a transport in 1822 had to make stringent rules to prevent his charges from robbing each other, owing to the rich variety of their chests and packages.[9] Only in 1826 did Governor Darling, in New South Wales, arrange that everything should be given up on arrival, cash going into a savings bank. In Van Diemen's Land a bank was formed especially for this purpose (Chapter 11).[10]

Meanwhile individual convicts made what they could of these loose ends. Even confinement in Macquarie's great new barracks, at Hyde Park in Sydney, might be far from rigorous. Sent there under orders 'to be deprived of all indulgences', James Lawrence (as he later put it) 'had plenty [of] money [and] dress'd to the Nines'. And without confinement anything was possible. James McGreavy arrived in bondage from Ireland in 1817 and his wife Margaret came, also as a convict, a year later. She brought their baby daughter. Within two years they had set up together in Sydney as 'Mr and Mrs McGreavy' and Margaret devised a plan to sell haberdashery in a big way. She began to gather stock in spring 1820 and within two months had a considerable quantity (twenty yards of lace and seven of cotton quilting, shawls, gloves, straw bonnets, stockings), all surreptitiously removed to her house from a dealer's store in Castlereagh Street with the help of the dealer's servant. It was a robbery, said the *Sydney Gazette*, unparalleled in the history of the colony. James McGreavy was more cautious, but both were keen to make money quickly. Neither was inhibited by the fact that they were convicts. They were tried, found guilty, and sent to the penal settlement at Port Macquarie but there they went on getting rich, more steadily and surely, and by the 1840s they had a string of houses for rent in Newcastle.[11] For such men and women, used to handling property and plausibly respectable, this was a land of opportunity, whatever their convict status.

Until the mid-1820s employers in both New South Wales and Van Diemen's Land thought of the assignment system as an employment exchange (like the parish vestries in England), or in other words as an adjunct to a labour market that was otherwise free. Labour in both colonies seemed superabundant, although in fact a more assiduous use of the soil might have used up all the muscle-power available. To a progressive mind, many employers seemed to do too little for the improvement of the country. They also failed to understand that they were agents of the state in the management of their men and women, who were properly a type of human resource. Both points were central to the program of free enterprise and penal rigour outlined by Commissioner Bigge.

This lack of system, penal and economic, meant that from 1788 to the mid-1820s the settled parts of Australia, though a single dominion in law, were not a single dominion in any practical sense. Quite apart from the difference between island and mainland, the varied resources of the country were the basis of numerous regimes, little kingdoms of habit and custom connected only loosely with each other and with the empire as a whole. In the Hawkesbury Valley, 40 miles from Sydney, a community of reprobates gathered in the 1790s who said that 'they did not care for the Governor or the Orders of the colony – they were free men, and wou'd do as they pleased'.[12] All the same, they enjoyed freehold title under law and they looked to the military for protection against the Blacks. Such compromises worked in many ways, as men and women learnt to mix bush life with the certainties of a more conventional order. By Macquarie's time convict stockmen, sent to the frontier by their employers, were beginning to form there the rudiments of a new existence, relying on rations sent from headquarters but also on what they could kill about them. Their horses gave them control of the country and control of themselves. In his wanderings in Van Diemen's Land, James Ross came across a party of Edward Lord's men, including ten or twelve stockmen, all convicts, with a cook and bullock-driver. 'They had constructed a sort of shed or skreen of the boughs of the trees,' he said, and they were in the process of building stockyards, of logs laid zig-zag, six or seven high:

> The men go out in bodies of 4 or 5, and cracking their whips and riding full gallop they hurry the herds without giving them time to escape from their remote recesses, through wilds, wood, and plains, up and down steep hills and along the most dangerous passes, until they enclose them in the yard.

After several days, when they judged they had all the cattle they could col-lect, they roped them one by one and branded them.[13] Such activity – so different from anything they could have known in Britain or Ireland – made men masters of their work, masters of their time, masters of the land they travelled. They could be as self-sufficient as they liked and if they managed well they need have nothing to do with penal discipline.

Dominion was, once again, especially slippery in Van Diemen's Land. Parts of the country were inhabited by old Norfolk Island settlers, trans-ferred to Van Diemen's Land in 1806–08, long used to looking after them-selves. At Launceston, once a separate government, the commandant wrongly styled himself 'His Honour the Lieutenant-Governor' and dis-obeyed orders from Hobart.[14] On the islands of Bass Strait (Chapter 5) there were little settlements of sealers and escaped convicts who had no such rulers at all. These communities made up a jumble of traffic and trade, a patchwork of pieces under no single order. Its most vivid threads were the bushranging gangs. On the mainland Governor Macquarie had an absolute ascendancy in the minds of his people. But in Van Diemen's Land there was a kind of rainbow order, with the bushrangers at its centre. The bushrangers lived by trade. Besides shooting kangaroos for their skins they robbed wholesale, replicating many times over the McGreavys' achieve-ment in Sydney. In March 1815, for instance, they looted the house of Arnold Fisk at Pitt Water, near Hobart, carrying away not only great parcels of clothes, but also tablecloths, bed curtains, and books (Nelson's *Memoirs*, Stern's *Sermons*, Turnbull's *Voyages*, *Tom Jones*, a Bible).[15] At another time the same party spent three days boiling down forty or fifty head of cattle for tallow, 'disposing of the proceeds amongst certain friends of theirs', which meant tying themselves, by clandestine means, to the Hobart market. They named the site of this labour 'the Tallow Chandler's Shop'.[16] In Van Diemen's Land such names stuck to the landscape, proof of the place of bushrangers in common imagination.

In dealing with bushrangers the government was not just putting down outlaws. It was trying to prove that it was in fact the government. During 1814–18, when Davey was lieutenant-governor, this large question focused on the brilliant figure of Michael Howe. Howe's career sums up the wide-open opportunities of convict life before the 1820s. He was a Yorkshireman transported for highway robbery. He arrived at the Derwent in November 1812, took to the bush within a year and soon shared the command of a sizeable gang. He was then in his late twenties, 'a rough sailor-looking fel-low' with deep-set eyes. He was strong and straight and laughed at the lieu-tenant-governor's paunch. Poorly educated, he had all the same 'a taste for ceremony' and a type of refined curiosity. He once borrowed a dictionary from a farmhouse, politely promising to bring it back. He was also intro-spective. He looked to his own nightly dreams for signs of the unfolding of Providence, and he kept an account of them in a notebook bound in kangaroo skin. He modelled himself on the celebrated highwayman, Dick Turpin, aiming 'to rob from the rich to give to the Poor'. Like pirates his gang boasted that 'they were Bushrangers and Free Booters, but no thieves'. In other words, they thought of robbery as a legitimate means of trade. Diabolical threats were part of Howe's theatrical style, but he allowed no violence except in self-defence. He and two of his leading men had been soldiers and their military skill explains both their success and their restraint. '[W]here we As Much Inclined to take Life As you Are', they told Davey, '... We Could Destroy All the partyes you can send out'.[17] Howe also had his intelligence network so that, as he boasted, 'nothing passed in Hobart Town, but what he and his party had immediate information of'.[18] Howe scripted himself a hero.

The sense of right and wrong trumpeted by Michael Howe was more than a match for anything issuing from Thomas Davey. In August 1814 the Hobart magistrates warned Davey that most of the convicts might shortly transfer their obedience to Howe. Even three years later, after several setbacks, the Turpin of the Derwent had the look of success. 'We have fully Satisfied the Eyes of the Publick', he told Davey, 'In All our Actions'. He was confident for the future, relying on the Almighty and sure, as he put it, that 'He who Preserved Us from Your Plots in Publick will Likewise Preserve Us from them In Secret'. And he styled himself 'Lieutenant-Governor of the Woods'.[19]

Howe was a utopian, a dreamer after perfection. He compared his time as a bushranger with 'the life of the damned'. Fond of flowers, he kept a list of those he liked to think of planting when, at last, he could stop running – a wistful weakness that made him, as a later Tasmanian said, like 'one of Byron's ruffian heroes'.[20] He led his gang until April 1817 and by that time they had killed only two settlers, who had forced them to fight, and he then gave himself up to the new lieutenant-governor, Sorrell. In spite of being treated with considerable respect he took to the bush again, was caught, killed his two captors and in October 1818 was finally killed himself.

The Hobart government took advantage of Howe's death with a remarkable piece of propaganda. It immediately issued for general sale a small book written by one of Sorrell's clerks and entitled *Michael Howe, the Last and Worst of the Bushrangers of Van Diemen's Land*. Howe would surely be the last of his kind, so readers were persuaded, because he was a freak born of peculiar and passing circumstances. They were told of the 'wantonly cruel disposition' and of the sins (multiplied in print) of 'this great murderer'. Indeed (as if readers might be tempted to doubt this detail), the 'strong marks of a Murderer' might be seen in his face. And they were assured of the 'inconceivable degree of satisfaction' that 'the people' felt at his death. In England there was a thriving trade in pamphlet biographies of notorious men and this one found a similar market in Hobart. But its main point was less to entertain than to argue for the misery of the bushranger's existence. It sought to prove how much 'the wholesome and mild Laws of civilized society' were to be preferred to 'a licentious life of unrestraint'.[21]

This publication marked an important step forward in the conquest of the island. But it was also typical of the old method of managing convicts. Sorrell addressed his people, not as subjects of a system but as a community. They were invited, as it were, to read the book or to hear it read, and then to make a choice between the government of the town and the government of the woods. This was ruling by persuasion, by stories, always the most effective means of power. But different rulers tell different kinds of stories. This particular story assumed a kind of imagination, among teller and audience, more free and lively than a penal system could produce.

II

By such means the colonial governments hoped to wind their way into the conversation of the people. Though books like this might circulate among them, the convicts were very much a talking rather than a reading community. Their minds were swayed mainly by what they heard, and some could not read at all. Three-fifths of convict women in New South Wales told officials when they arrived that they could read, but since literacy was proof of respectability many may have been stretching the truth. Nor could all the genuine readers read well. Even by their own admission, of those women who said they could read two-thirds could not write. The men seem to have been more skilled. Half said they could both read and write. But among male and female together, whatever the exact truth, at least three in every ten were totally illiterate.[22] Such people could no more convert voices into writing than we can set down magpie song.

I have said that where literacy is imperfect people can have a particularly good ear and memory for voices. In reporting conversations they re-enact them. Among the highly literate, on the other hand, summary methods of reporting – keeping detail clear and orderly – are highly prized. In official writing, in particular, as one governor put it, 'conciseness and compression of thought' are essential.[23] This means using indirect grammatical forms in relaying what other people say. Well-read men and women distance themselves from the living voice, as in: 'It was agreed at our meeting that … .' The more ancient skill survives among many indigenous Australians, for whom it can be sacred. But common samples appear in any corner store or shopping mall, sometimes among perfectly literate people who keep up old habits: 'She said, Sandra, she said, … , and I said, … , and so she said, … .' And again: 'She's like, "How do you know?", and I'm like, "Because I was there".'[24] Such roundabout recollection is like the re-enacting of plays. Convicts lived within an oral world of this kind and so did many of the humbler class of their employers, the latter spending a good deal of time in what a newspaper called 'eternal repetitions of idle and insolent answers made by convicts'.[25] Paper-driven habits of thought might be nourished among leading officials but elsewhere power depended on talk – on intonation, on idiom, on argument, and on the exact recollection of who said what to whom.

Many convict men made their masters into their enemies by nothing more than 'a natural stupidity and abruptness', or in other words by the way they spoke. A good deal depended, as one man said himself, on his remembering 'to keep a still tongue in his head'.[26] In the colonial courts highly mobile tongues passed frequently over old ground as both parties recalled verbal hits backwards and forwards. Thomas Fleming, an overseer for the Van Diemen's Land Company, mislaid his knife. He asked William Plummer, the convict cook, about it. This was Fleming's evidence before the bench, taken down verbatim by the clerk:

> he said he had taken it and should stick to it. I told him he would repent his insolence some day, he said it was a d[amne]d lye, he would not repent. I asked him if he called me a liar, he said yes, you are a liar, a b[lood]y liar, he said something afterwards, I asked him what it was, he said in reply Bollocks, I then called him a d[amne]d Convict, and again told him it was improper language to use to me.

The conversation ended in fisticuffs, and the trial in twelve lashes for Plummer.[27]

Convicts were brought before the magistrates charged with refusing to give answers, with speaking in a sulky tone and with stressing certain words. 'Oh! I know very well how to behave to *a gentleman*', remarked James Burgess, in an exchange – carefully reported – with a landowner, young Edward Archer. For Archer, this sarcastic emphasis and a failure to call him 'Sir' justified taking Burgess to court.[28] Convicts played the same game. 'Last Wednesday evening', Sarah Bellian told the bench at Norfolk Plains, Van Diemen's Land, 'my master's daughter called me a "Government w[hor]e" and "nothing but a good-for-nothing strumpet"'. William Laters told his master, during a heated conversation (as the master reported): 'Oh very well, now give me a pass to go to Mr Sutherland to complain that you threatened to send me to Macquarie Harbour.'[29] William Hurlock said of another convict: '[He] grossly abused me calling me a daylight Robber, an ill looking Bugger and other approbrious names.' Mary Fleming complained of her fellow servants, two men. They 'called me a strumpet, a Bitch', she said, 'and made a disagreeable contemptuous noise with their mouths at me'. In this last case, for the language alone, the court ordered a total of thirty-seven lashes.[30]

In both colonies ideas about right and wrong were embedded in speaking and listening but, it seems, especially in Van Diemen's Land. The island people apparently moved in a more wholly oral world than those on the mainland. Certainly, island children were half as likely to go to school as mainland ones, thanks to the negligence of parents and of government, there being few schools to go to.[31]

Free men and women of a certain rank were happy to join in verbal battles – 'jarrings' and 'bickerings', as the Governor in Hobart called them – with their assigned convicts.[32] But the well read, settling in increasing numbers in the 1820s, drew themselves apart, remarking on the ignorance they saw and heard about them. The line between these two extremes of understanding (as I say in Chapter 2) was stark. And how did convicts themselves feel as they watched their speech taken down by the clerks of court – as if invisible machinery linked bone and tongue with pen and ink? Some could read. Some could write. And on the other hand some might have fine memories for conversation – in the Female Factory at Hobart women acted out plays to pass the time, using memory for script. But few could converse well with their pens, organising ideas on paper. When a convict maidservant called Kitty told a friend, in Hobart in 1830, 'that her mistress was writing a sight of books' (it was one book), she showed her reverence for an alien order.[33]

Among the Europeans in Australia convict women, taken altogether, were the least touched by literate civilisation. Groups of such women might make up a regime of their own. Their lives might be bound by women's voices, women's innuendo, women's irony. The only way for male authorities to deal successfully with the kingdoms of women was by reaching across the imaginative gap as Sorrell had tried to do with the admirers of Michael Howe. This was often difficult.

The Female Factory, Parramatta, in about 1826, a watercolour by Augustus Earle. It was less remote and romantically placed than this picture suggests.

Reproduction courtesy of National Library of Australia

Convict women, in principle, might live in one of three conditions. They might cohabit with individual men as wives and housekeepers, in which case the government usually took no further notice of them. They might be assigned to private employment like convict men, the government interfering only when something went wrong. Or else they might be in one or other of the women's prisons (called 'female factories' though not all were places of forced labour) on the mainland at Parramatta, Newcastle, Moreton Bay, Port Macquarie, and Bathurst, and in Van Diemen's Land at Hobart, George Town, and Launceston.[34] These institutions were jokingly called 'nunneries' and indeed, except for convents, such large, fixed masses of women had rarely existed before among English-speaking people.

Women learnt from other women, in prisons and transport ships, how best to make their way through the rocks and shallows of convict life. Whatever language and ideas they might have had before imprisonment were afterwards shaken down to a common stock. Visitors to women's prisons, in both Europe and Australia, were appalled by the painful din that issued from the inmates, as if from a tree full of raucous birds. In the Female Factory at Hobart all was drowned by 'the utmost confusion of tongues ... in every yard & every room', according to Lady Franklin, the Governor's wife.[35] While on board ship from Europe predictions of the life to come flew from mouth to mouth. For instance, in the words (and spelling) of Mary Hughs, 'I was informed that the mareed weman got their liberty for to do the best they could for themselves and the single weman was kept in confinement'. This was a tangling of the truth. More accurately, in Hobart, according to Mary Haigh, women learnt at the factory 'what houses they can obtain liquor on the sly and those houses at which shelter is to be obtained when they abscond'.[36]

At a time when women of the middle and upper classes were themselves beginning to speak differently – in tones more refined than their mothers might have used – the speech of convict women seemed very raw, 'sometimes so horrible,' remarked a matron, 'that I am obliged to run away with disgust'.[37] Like all people who lived in an oral world the knowledge of these women was handed, or sometimes hurled about, in chunks from one to another. They dealt in proverbs and epithets, in absolutes of vice and virtue. 'Oral cultures', says the great scholar of language, Walter Ong, '... think by means of memorable thoughts, thoughts processed for retrieval in various ways, or, in other words, fixed, formulaic, stereotyped'.[38] Abuse, when practised by women of this kind, was called scolding. On a Saturday night in 1835, in Newcastle, north of Sydney, a constable heard Margaret Smith, a convict, abusing him and his wife outside their door. The wife she called a 'Flamming whore', and the husband an 'infernal vagabond'. '[S]he wished me nor my wife or children', the constable said, 'may never have a days luck as long as we live'.[39] Margaret Smith was almost struggling to cast spells – 'flaming' and 'infernal' being words in which a little of the sacred lingered still. A count of the charges laid against convict women in the police courts of Van Diemen's Land between 1820 and 1839 shows that they were most commonly charged with being away from their work. But improper speech – insolence and arguing, threats and slander – came second.[40]

The tongues of convict women were their leading weapons. They sounded especially bad because they had been toughened through being together, by talking together, by all the collective experience of English and Irish gaols, ships, and factories. It was the sinewy speech they shared that made them especially hard to mould and discipline from above. The 'tricks, manoeuvres and misconduct' of the female convicts, so a Hobart newspaper said, 'have baffled the exertions of every person appointed to control and correct them'. One method succeeded. On the way out both men and women who caused trouble might be made to stand for hours in an upright narrow box on the ship's deck. It worked straightaway with the men, but the women hit back with their voices. A cistern of water was placed on top of the box. 'This was turned over upon those who persisted in using their tongues ... [and] was always and quickly efficacious in quieting them.'[41]

Highly literate people, as I say, were trained in efficient reporting of events and speech. The convict colonies were more and more managed by such people, making faith in writing the basis of government. Between 1815 and 1830 the quantity of paper dealt with by the Colonial Office in London doubled. At the same time the reporting of detail became more complex and specialised. The main period of change was 1822–25, when the number of clerks in the office grew from nine to eighteen. The two leading reformers were Robert Wilmot Horton, under-secretary of state from 1821 to 1827, and James Stephen, who was the office's salaried legal counsel from 1825, but they were symptomatic of something much bigger.[42] Throughout Britain educated public opinion was beginning to apply new pressure to government, to demand a new degree of activity, efficiency, and literate idealism. The philosophical radicals, or utilitarians – acquaintances of Saxe Bannister before he left for New South Wales (Chapter 2) – were the most effective of all.

Reforms must be set out first on paper, as summary 'plans'. Also, such reforms must embody a 'system'. Besides having a clear moral purpose they must make sense in black and white. And they must be carried through with focused expertise, including precise methods of data retrieval – annotation, codification, classification, filing, a careful delegation of duties, and strict accountability from desk to desk. New South Wales and Van Diemen's Land were dramatically affected from 1825, when new governors, Ralph Darling and George Arthur, were appointed to each. Their task, as a malcontent put it, was to create 'a kind of bureauocracy [sic]', a word which then implied uncompromising power. Or, as James Stephen told Arthur, it was to erect 'a christian, virtuous and enlightened state'. And how was this to be done?

'Schools, missionaries, Bibles, prayer books, are the things you want and the weapons you must use.' They were to hit hard with the written word. And not too much talk. Stephen hated what he called 'mere talk for talk's sake'. He sought instead to instil 'the duty of silence'.[43]

Both governors were taciturn. The sharp eyes and compressed lips of George Arthur were his most obvious features.[44] Both were also masters of reporting and they set new standards of efficiency among their subordinates. The number of dispatches passing between Sydney and London was already increasing. The number in 1822 had nearly doubled by 1824 but it had multiplied more than six times by 1827. Arthur managed less than Darling, his population being half the size, but his letters were longer so that, on the whole, just as much paper passed in and out. While in Hobart he also wrote two pamphlets, *Observations Upon Secondary Punishment* (1833) and *A Defence of Transportation* (1835), and his office hours were frequently from eight or nine in the morning until ten or eleven at night.[45] Arthur was a man of eloquence and imagination whereas Darling (so Arthur was informed by Stephen), possessed 'little reach of thought or variety of knowledge'. Certainly Darling failed to make complete sense of Hobbes Scott, his archdeacon, and Saxe Bannister, his attorney-general. Arthur, on the other hand, saw them both as men of his kind. He corresponded with Scott (*'I wish you were nearer'*, wrote the archdeacon) and when Bannister failed in Sydney, Arthur suggested that he come as a judge to Hobart.[46]

Arthur's writing included few statistical returns. He wanted to control his people, not as measured lumps but as individuals. Like Scott and Bannister, his 'reach of thought' led him to embrace others, however humble, as rational beings. He aimed to give his convicts choices. He believed in severe and rigorous punishment and he was merciless in his use of the death penalty.[47] But he also insisted on fairness. He worked hard for a finely articulated administrative system, one which would be perfectly just and in which everything, including every decision at every level, led back to himself. He was like Governor Macquarie in his wish to be all-pervasive, to forge links with everyone under him. But Macquarie had depended not only on his pen but also on the power of his physical presence. Arthur ruled from his office.

Arthur's hope of making an impression on individuals was behind his first significant reform, the creation of a mounted police force made up of 'the best conducted prisoners', originally to deal with bushrangers. The idea of giving horses and firearms to a body of convicts frightened some of his advisers. Ten years earlier, after all, they might easily have deserted to Michael Howe. But as Arthur afterwards explained, those who joined up were looking for favours. Such men weighed the points for and against and went over to government. '[J]ealousy and disunion, as I anticipated, followed amongst the whole class of Convicts, and no longer confiding in each other they ceased to be formidable, and have since been gradually brought into a state of subordination consistent with their condition.'[48] In 1827–28 he went on to divide Van Diemen's Land into nine districts for police purposes. Each was given a full-time police magistrate, who was to be, like the Governor himself, not only a ruler but also a bureaucrat. The honorary magistrates who had so far been responsible for rural law and order, all of them landed gentlemen, now took second place.[49] As a result, the island elite also 'ceased to be formidable' and a genuine autocracy took shape.

The precise management of convicts within each district depended on paperwork (muster lists, registers, passes, and so on) and each police magistrate had to send a continuous series of reports, explanations, and recommendations to Hobart, as well as being in 'constant communication' with other districts. Some came to resent such authoritarianism, including the overbearing comments scribbled on their written work, a practice, so one of them said, which gentlemen 'should not put up with'. Such a regime affected the way they dispensed justice, just as Macquarie's had done in New South Wales. 'One felt when trying a man that the whole thoughts were necessarily directed to know what Colonel Arthur, or the chief police magistrate [Arthur's nephew] would think of it; not to what was the just sentence.'[50]

Arthur's imagination gave him a sense of his own power as something weighty in both space and time. Scott, envisaging an island nation, told him, 'You are rocking the cradle of Hercules', and Arthur probably believed it. As a ruler, his efficiency depended on good communications throughout the island and by the end of his time there were more than 2000 men working on the roads. He even dreamt of extending his government across Bass Strait.[51] He also liked to think of the way his regime might fit within the ongoing order of things. It was Arthur's fond belief that Van Diemen's Land had been a prison, in principle, from its settlement in 1803–04. '[T]he reformation and punishment of numerous Convicts transported from England was the main design', he said, 'in the original establishment of the Colony'.[52] This was certainly a useful belief to work with. It gave him an all-embracing original 'plan' within which his system might sit. It followed that everything done in Van Diemen's Land, and everyone who had come from the beginning, must trim or be trimmed to fit that plan. Even the common rights of Englishmen, sacred in England itself, might be curtailed within an island-gaol.

In fact Whitehall had sent convicts systematically to Hobart only since 1818 and the Sydney government had sent second offenders even more recently (and Hobart sent theirs in the other direction). Until the arrival of Arthur himself convicts had seemed almost incidental to island life.[53] New South Wales had always been more thoroughgoing in its discipline. As recently as 1824 a book published in London made the point very clearly: 'In Port Jackson they seem to bear in mind that the colony is a place of punishment, a circumstance wholly forgotten in Van Diemen's Land.'[54] But under Arthur penal restraint became the beginning and the end of everything. His intellectual authority and the weakness of opposition meant that his understanding of the island's history – the story implicit in all he said and did – was immediately commonplace. Everyone who mattered believed that Van Diemen's Land had always been in theory a prison, Arthur having brought the theory to polished fact. The very first expedition was supposed to have come from New South Wales in 1803, 'with a view', so an author of Arthur's time remarked, 'of forming a penal settlement for persons convicted in that Colony'. Whatever the country might become in due course, said another, 'it was at first a jail, and nothing but a jail on a large scale'.[55] Arthur's methods were entwined, in short, with the very existence of the place.

The commonly understood history of New South Wales had been constructed by Wentworth from popular ideas about authority (Chapter 3), and it was then embroidered and perpetuated by the Sydney press. The agreed history of Van Diemen's Land began as a piece of skilled reporting from Arthur's office. Both stories were to continue as undoubted truth long into the twentieth century. If, in Van Diemen's Land, there were memories of a different truth stretching back beyond Arthur – among admirers of Michael Howe, among family men and women at New Norfolk, among inmates of the female factories – they lived and died in local talk.

III

Educated men and women were sometimes puzzled as to why the convicts did not rise up in mass rebellion. 'How have the many bold and hardened perpetrators of crime … been so tamed and humbled – so led and governed, apparently by a mere thread?', asked Henry Savery, a convict himself. The explorer Charles Sturt thought it might be the air. The delicious climate, he said, made horses and cattle pliable, 'and I cannot but think it has in some degree the same happy effect upon some of the hardened human beings who are sent hither from the old world'. Others pointed to the way in which convicts could do well if they behaved themselves. Commissioner Bigge remarked on the 'considerable profit and indulgence [available] to those who possess either industry or skill'.[56] Clever men were the normal leaders of rebellion, but here they did better by prudence. E.S. Hall, of the Sydney Monitor, took this point a little further. Convicts were docile because they believed that, whatever their suffering, justice existed at the heart of the system. This belief was due originally, he said, to the moral authority of government. Now it depended on the press and public opinion.[57]

Both Bigge and Hall were right, but the reasons were more complicated than they knew. Convicts were now thinking subjects of bureaucracy. As bondage became tighter they learnt with more or less success to manage it.

In various ways Australia had always offered an imaginative challenge for both rich and poor and transportation involved an education in the workings of the nineteenth-century state. A pattern of understanding informed by living speech, the normal thing among the convicts, was reshaped to answer the demands of a literate universe. Governor Macquarie, though a pale prefiguring of Arthur and Darling in this respect, had begun the process. By the end of his time convicts had looked to government rather than to their employers as the main source of power in their lives. John Macarthur, absent from New South Wales between 1809 and 1817, found on his return that convict men had changed in the way they dealt with their masters. They now had a strong faith in what government would do for them, a sense of entitlement. They were 'less respectful', he said, 'and now claim many of those indulgences, as a Matter of right, which they used to receive thankfully as the reward of Merit'.[58]

Pervasive government also meant pervasive corruption. Many convicts were 'extremely Idle and Insolent', remarked another New South Wales employer, because they knew they could pull strings within the police and penal system.[59] These strings ran in intricate ways through the multiplying offices of government. By the 1820s the same was true of Van Diemen's Land. James Ross, writing as editor of the *Hobart Town Courier*, described how convicts might negotiate with the forces of law and order. He had missed one of his men at the printing office:

> Where is Jonathan? Asked I, Oh, Sir, says Tom, Jonathan has got into trouble ... He was buying something this morning, and the dollar that he had paid for it was not a good one, so the constable has got alongside of him and he is trying to make it all right with him. ... The constable, I think, continued Tom, will make it up for ten shillings.

As Ross explained, 'getting into trouble' meant getting caught. 'Making it all right' or 'making it up' meant bribing someone who had the power of punishment.[60] In Macquarie's last years Commissioner Bigge had found evidence of such petty dishonesty wherever he looked. But instead of proving the failure of Macquarie's reforming efforts, as Bigge believed, it really proved their success. Now, at last, there was an administrative system and a police worth corrupting. Now there was a regime that could shape even the language of the people. The ten shillings that Ross mentioned may have been a standard price for service. Also, knowledge of the regime, its strengths and weaknesses, gave the most able convicts power over their daily lives and power over the lives of their weaker fellows. As Bigge understood, these were just the men and women who might otherwise have organised revolt. Through petty corruption the system became, in a sense, their own.

Also, while many could barely read, the clerical skills of a few convicts gave them entry to sites of authority. Some worked as clerks tending 'the springs of Government'. For a price they could falsify records, reducing, for instance, terms of transportation. The lawyers now arriving in large numbers also depended on convict literacy. According to the Presbyterian minister, John Dunmore Lang, convict clerks in lawyer's offices often persuaded trial witnesses to give false evidence. Others worked as teachers and general scribes. The Catholic priest, William Ullathorne, sketched such a man, assigned to a publican:

> tall, grizzly-headed ... with a sharp sinister countenance, his body enveloped in a long, seedy coat, once black ... . This man is considered by the neighbours 'a gentleman' and 'a scholar'. ... he can read, and write, and talk. He keeps the accounts, teaches the children, writes prisoners petitions, and entertains guests.

This might be a man of influence among such neighbours. Convicts and ex-convicts were especially obvious in newspaper offices, not only as press-man and compositors (and these controlled their workplace), but also as reporters and editors.[61] Thus a convict perspective began to shape news and opinion, especially in New South Wales.

Reading and writing were the clue to the penal system, a point obvious even to the illiterate. It was a means of escape, at least in imagination. Writing, or having someone else write as your amanuensis, could breach walls and traverse the imprisoning oceans. The letters that convicts wrote home where their only means of keeping in touch with their earlier selves and with the world that meant most to them. And through writing they dramatised themselves. They made their suffering, which might be painful enough, into a *type* of suffering, an *idea* of pain – a point of reflection. The illicit trade in and out of the Hobart Female Factory included pens, ink, and paper (the latter bought from the factory nurse for sixpence a sheet). With these the women wrote letters which others going out took with them, hidden, for instance, in their stays. At the Launceston factory, by some such means, Maria Turner communicated with her man, Steven Bumstead, a hairdresser, asking him for tobacco and rum: '[M]y dear you had better direct the parcell to the factory and do not let the person that brings them to [the] gate mention my name at all.' And she ended with verse: 'Their is no flower half so sweet / As absent lovers when they me[e]t.'[62]

Also, just as literacy let Whitehall and its agents impose their will at a distance, so it was literacy that let convicts reshape the rules from within. Arthur knew that convict letters to and from England were an engine of communication at odds with his own and he especially regretted that the convicts tended to make light of their sufferings in their letters Home.[63] But it was the newspapers that annoyed both governors most of all. The ideas contained in the newspapers, like those in official orders, made their way everywhere. During 1825–35 the management of the press was a major political issue, with convict influence being the main point in Sydney. According to Lang, who ran a Sydney paper, the colonial press had an impact on the poor much greater than the press did in Britain. Free people of all ranks, he said, bought papers 'to a much greater extent', and as for the convicts, 'they get them from the master after he has done with them in many cases, and in others they are to be had at the public houses'. Illiteracy was no obstacle, since papers were frequently read aloud. Newspapers were also central to the wider market. Sydney's ex-convict dealers preferred to advertise in print, rather than posting notices, and editors, in consequence, treated them well.[64] This only compromised further the government view.

Some newspaper writers were interested in convict rights without having been transported themselves. In Van Diemen's Land between 1829 and 1831 the *Launceston Advertiser* was owned and edited by John Pascoe Fawkner, a convict's son. '[W]e daily see or hear of persons cruelly treating their assigned servants', Fawkner told his readers, 'and no voice raises itself on their behalf ... their very cries and groans, although caused by torture the most intense, are often made a subject of merriment'. He did not hesitate to raise his own voice. In Sydney, E.S. Hall invited any victims of oppression to make their cases known in the pages of the *Monitor*, and he boasted of 'those appeals to a generous public in behalf of Convicts, which we have often made in our journal'.[65] Such publicity strengthened the hand of convict writers. William Angus Watt was transported in 1828. During the next five years he worked as a clerk at the convict settlements at Wellington Valley and Emu Plains and in the offices of the colonial secretary, the sheriff, and Archdeacon

Two labouring men, probably assigned convicts, near a bush homestead in Van Diemen's Land, 1825, one of them reading a newspaper; detail from a watercolour by Augustus Earle.

Reproduction courtesy of National Library of Australia

Broughton. Then, with a ticket of leave, he moved to the *Sydney Gazette*, where most of the printing staff were convicts and where the editor was the ex-convict poet, Edward O'Shaughnessy. Within a year he was virtual editor himself. He was a keen politician, arguing against the cruelty of the convict system and the tyranny of the country magistrates. He published a pamphlet on those subjects in 1835.[66]

By these and other means convicts might learn to control, or at least to understand, their own corner of the system. They might see themselves anew, as part of a system, one item in a many faceted machine. In September 1832 Thomas Chatfield, an assigned man in Van Diemen's Land, wrote to his wife in Sussex. Among other things, he told her about tickets of leave. '[M]en as is transported for 7 years', he said, 'they have to serve four years to their masters where they be signed and then they have a ticket to work for themselves ... men as is for 14 they have to serve 6 years with their master and men as is for life they have to serve 8 before thay have their ticket'. These large administrative facts were common knowledge. Finer details were open to question, and the questions asked were unending. Here again the newspapers served a crucial purpose. In 1834, for instance, a convict employer thought it necessary to write to the *Sydney Gazette* to contradict a statement in another paper: 'That if a master call his convict servant a scoundrel, he [the servant] may turn around and legally box his master's ears.' This 'mischievous propagation', the letter-writer said, must lead both parties into trouble.[67]

Convicts were expected to apply for tickets of leave themselves when they thought they were due. In June 1827 the *Monitor* published a letter from Parramatta signed 'A poor Convict hoping for a Ticket'. The writer complained that a large bundle of applications for tickets, including his own, had been sitting for months on a table in the local courthouse instead of being sent to Sydney. He was quickly answered in the same paper. Any delay in issuing tickets, the second letter-writer said, should not be blamed on the authorities at Parramatta. Under the current rules 'a large printed form, containing every requisite particular of every applicant is periodically transmitted to Head Quarters'. At Parramatta the original forms had rightly stayed where they were.[68]

Most convicts hated authority. 'The feeling of vengeance', said Ullathorne, 'is general indeed, and much more than would be supposed, because it does not always express itself'. With some men and women hatred destroyed any faith or interest in the rules.[69] But taken as a whole, the labouring world of the convicts was sustained by knowledge such as I have described. Employers, too, acquiesced in conditions that were, in truth, imposed partly by government and partly by the convict body, the convicts working well enough as long as the rules were followed. The most immediate issues were hours of work, food, clothing, and living conditions. 'Do you see that', said Benjamin Ray, an assigned man at Port Macquarie, pointing to the sun, 'after that's down I'll work for no man' – and indeed sunset was the official end of the working day. At Merton, in the Hunter Valley, the Ogilvie family argued with their convicts, there being no wheat to include in their rations, the men having refused to take rye instead. 'I went out', Frederick Ogilvie told the Muswellbrook bench, 'and saw the prisoners who said that they wanted their wheat. I told them either to go to their work or to the lock up but they ... walked off to their huts'. When Ogilvie had finished giving his evidence the men in turn offered the bench their varied excuses. One saw the issue with perfect clarity. '[H]e did not take the rye', he said, 'because it is not in the regulations'. The rest fumbled with other reasons. The rye had weevils in it. It was putrid. It could not be well ground or cooked.[70] Each in his own way showed a sense of entitlement such as systems give birth to.

It was this constant pressure on masters and government that ensured that by the late 1830s the agreed convict ration on the mainland included wheat or wheaten flour, instead of maize. Maize was cheaper and it was the staple diet of poor farming families. But a little familiarity with the way things worked made maize bread too coarse for convict tastes. Gradual attrition – frequent jarrings and bickerings, in Arthur's terms – established the convict right to wheat.[71]

At the same time convicts in both New South Wales and Van Diemen's Land were also managed with violence. Soft white bread and the bloodied lash represent two extremes of a finely balanced scheme of forbearance and force. Every convict man knew that, with bad behaviour or bad luck, he was liable to be flogged. 'I always knows how to manage my servants,' so a small farmer said, in a conversation drawn from life by Henry Savery, 'for if they don't please me, or if they be saucy to my wife when she's got a drop or so, I have only to take 'em to the office, and it don't seem nothing to give them a couple of dozen or so'.[72] Before the arrival of Darling and Arthur flogging was almost the only punishment used for male convicts guilty of ordinary infringements of discipline. Both governors, wary of brutalising all concerned, thought it a punishment that should be limited as far as possible. They aimed for a greater range of penalties, hoping to reach the minds of sufferers in more subtle and complex ways. Convict men were now sentenced to chain gangs that worked on the roads, each man being hobbled with shackles linked with a chain to his belt. Both men and women were sentenced to treadwheels, and they were supposed to learn habits of industry from the fact that their muscle-power drove machinery for grinding grain. The most ambitious experiment was solitary confinement, which was meant to isolate individuals for days on end. True efficiency depended on purpose-built cells, but local experience made the cost seem hardly worthwhile. Arthur preferred the treadwheel, which he called 'solitary confinement with hard labour'.[73]

Solitary confinement was a neat and total form of punishment that was strongly supported by penal theorists in Europe. It was a direct hit at the talk-based power of convict life. The chain gangs had some of the same advantage. As Arthur explained on his return to England, he had tried to ensure that the men could not talk as they worked. But he hesitated, he said, to ban speech for its own sake. In managing the convicts his aim was not to destroy common social relations but to present men and women with palpable choices and to make them think. 'I do not know that any advantage is derived from total silence', he said, 'I think the contrary'.[74]

Flogging, though less important, remained vital. The fear of pain was always a part of the penal system. But even with flogging, new principles of accountability meant that magistrates had to add up all cases from year to year for the Governor's inspection (numbers of punishments and numbers of strokes). Thus it appears that by the beginning of the 1830s the number of convicts flogged each year varied between about one in four and one in ten and that the average sentence numbered fifty strokes in New South Wales and thirty-three in Van Diemen's Land. By the time Arthur left, in September 1836, recorded numbers were falling in Van Diemen's Land, but in New South Wales the downward trend had been reversed. In 1832 Richard Bourke had assumed the government in Sydney and he moved to trim the power of magistrates to order floggings. However, in his time gentlemen were more likely than hitherto to find a way around restraint.[75]

Though many convict men were never flogged themselves, nearly all must have seen or heard it done. James Tucker, the convict author of *Ralph Rashleigh*, left the kind of vivid image that must have been familiar among them. '[T]he pain', he said, 'was most harrowingly intense ... it could only be likened to the sensation of having furrows torn in your flesh with jagged wire, and ere they closed filled up with burning molten lead running in streams of fire down your back'. After four dozen the whole body, he said, was 'entirely numbed' and the strokes of the whip felt like 'heavy blows from some huge club'.[76] The shock of being flogged for the first time must have been truly stunning. It happened to Ralph Entwhistle in early summer 1829, when he had been in New South Wales two years. He was twenty-five years old and had been swimming with other men in the Macquarie River when the Governor passed on his way to Bathurst. So far well-behaved, such savage treatment – for simple nakedness – made him, as a gentleman recalled, 'an altered man ... boiling with hatred and revenge'.[77]

It was an article of faith among masters that the convicts were cowards.[78] All the same, convicts with no faith in the system, or whose faith was exhausted, often turned to violence themselves, with vicious cunning, with boldness, or with both. Near Berrima, south of Sydney, in 1836, two convict bushrangers announced their intention 'to go round and flog all the Gentlemen so that they might know what punishment was'. They caught one, at least, and gave him thirty lashes.[79] On two estates, Claggan in northern Van Diemen's Land, and Castle Forbes in the Hunter Valley, there were wholesale mutinies and elsewhere masters were murdered.[80] But it remained true that angry convicts found it hard to collect large numbers behind them in rebellion. Ralph Entwhistle was an exception. He made no obvious move for ten months after his flogging, but then, in October 1830, he left his work and began to move from station to station in the bush near Bathurst gathering men. The news soon reached Sydney and Governor Darling took precautions against a general uprising in those parts. Entwhistle himself aimed, as he said, to 'take the settlement', meaning Bathurst, and he used a war-cry common among Irish rebels, 'Death or liberty!' He had grown up among Irish immigrants in Lancashire, in England's north-west, and six of his leading supporters were Irish. Like an Irish 'Ribbon Boy' – a member of a rural gang – he wore strips of white cloth in his hat. Sure of his own ability to command in battle, he proved it by twice beating the military sent against him. Defeated at last, he and nine others were hanged.[81]

At one point Entwhistle had over 130 men with him, but most of them broke away as they travelled through the bush and hurried back to safety.[82] They may well have joined him in the first place because they were angry about their rations and there was afterwards a government inquiry on the subject. The troubles would prove to masters, said one of the Sydney papers, 'the value and necessity of feeding prisoner servants well, and clothing them comfortably, if they are to be well worked'.[83] To some extent this bloody event was another statement of claims, not against the convict regime but within it. It was about the rules and their fulfilment. By making trouble, not too much but not too little, convicts managed their circumstances. Only the shouts of 'Death or Liberty!' suggest among a few of them much larger dreams.

Chapter 5

'A Most Extensive Scale'

I

The expedition from Sydney westward across the Blue Mountains in autumn 1813, led by Blaxland, Wentworth, and Lawson, with its well-publicised results, led to a new idea of the size of the country. Nearly as important for the European imagination were the two expeditions by the surveyor-general of New South Wales, John Oxley, south-west down the Lachlan River in 1817 and north-west down the Macquarie in the following year. Oxley's journals, published in 1820, presented a picture of Australia quite different from any hitherto. Here was a world truly dazzling. On the Lachlan Oxley found stretches of territory where little seemed explicable, where everything, as he said, 'seems to run counter to the ordinary course of nature in other countries'. Day after day he had gazed on a desert so extraordinary and so depressing as to make him sure that no European would ever come that way again. The Macquarie had been more inviting. There, instead of the dead-level horizon and the fragile red earth of the Lachlan, he found a varied landscape with brilliant water and pasture – 'imagination cannot fancy anything more beautifully picturesque'. Even this time, however, he made his way home through quagmires and thickets, the worst a mass of small iron-bark trees lately burnt, a tangle of blue foliage and black stems set in grey sand, a mass of scrub that poked the horses' eyes and bloodied the shins and knees of the men.[1]

Some Europeans were inclined to imagine that such country was beyond the British Empire in every practical sense. It also seemed to be the domain of a wholly alien people. Even Oxley's successor as surveyor-general, Thomas Livingstone Mitchell, thought like this, though New South Wales technically included all of the eastern two-thirds of the continent (and from 1831 the remainder was defined as Western Australia). Mitchell spoke of 'the colony' as identical with its surveyed territory. He left it, for instance, in 1831, when he crossed the Liverpool Range, at the head of the Hunter Valley. Exploring westward in 1835 it was necessary then, he said, to conciliate the indigenous people 'by every possible means', since he and his companions had become, as he put it, 'rather unceremonious invaders of their country'.[2]

Others took a more sweeping view, and not only of Australia. During these years, among many Europeans there was an expanding sense of the world's geography and an eagerness to occupy vast tracts so far untouched by men and women like themselves. New notions of control over distance were encouraged by the fact that in Europe itself roads were much improved and horse-drawn vehicles were becoming faster, more frequent, and more reliable. Equally important were the rapid improvements in steam-powered travel. From 1819 some trans-Atlantic sailing ships had steam engines attached and within twenty years a few were powered by steam alone. Partly as a result, the shape of the United States was to be transformed by immigration from Europe and then by mass movement inland. Steam trains were likewise running within Britain from 1825. The same willingness to tackle space and distance – the same 'locomotive disposition', as an Englishman called it – had its impact on Australia, although here the steam-powered link with Europe was still to come.[3]

Such boldness was also due to a more common acquaintance with maps. Before the 1830s those few children who learnt geography at school did so not with maps but with lists of places. Cartography, the 'science of princes', had always been associated with government surveillance and military campaigns. It was privileged knowledge. Maps were expensive to print, they were not published widely, and, because they were so unfamiliar, reading them called for specialist skill.[4] One had to be trained to understand a mass of spatial detail in summary, to take a bird's-eye view (just as one might be trained, like the new officials, in the succinct reporting of events). In other words, information basic nowadays to everyone's sense of nationhood – the shape of one's country – was very rare. The more ancient approach affected understanding of distance. The explorer Charles Sturt once met two Irishmen on the lonely western reaches of the Macquarie, both convicts who had escaped from the penal settlement at Wellington Valley. They had provisions for a fortnight and two dogs and they were heading, they said, for Timor.[5] They were probably typical of unlettered men and women in having a fair sense of direction but no idea of the spaces that imprisoned them.

On the other hand, simple experience was a good teacher about some aspects of geography. Some convicts learnt to think about the remote bush as a place of liberty. From Bathurst, for instance, as a rural magistrate explained, runaways 'almost invariably follow the Abercrombie and the Lachlan [Rivers], to the Murrumbidgee', and so to the frontier of European knowledge. And convict stockmen sent by their masters from the better ordered districts to work in those parts spoke of coming from 'inside', as if from prison.[6] Changes in the height of the land also made easy sense. Patrick Byrne, a convict (and an old explorer), spoke to Commissioner Bigge in 1820 about horse traffic which, he said, went 'up' and 'down' between Bathurst and the coastal plain. Three horses that he knew well – Old Ball ('the best draught horse in the Country'), Young Ball, and Turkey – worked, he said, 'drawing *up* provisions from the Nepean'. They 'carried *down* loads of Wool in return'.[7]

Ignorance of maps meant ignorance about the way territories were arranged on the globe. 'Australia is a great big island', so one piece of emigration propaganda told English yeomen in 1835, 'situated in the South Sea, or Indian Ocean: they used to call it, *New Holland*'. Readers were then, in a few words, led around the borders of the 'island', first north, then east, south, and west. It remained very hard to think of yourself positioned on a map. As late as 1857 a woman setting sail from London told a fellow-traveller that there was nothing tangible at the Cape of Good Hope but that on the other hand they might set foot on the equator – 'there is land at the line we shall cross it'.[8] What could she know of the shape and dimensions of this continent?

She, and many thousands like her, came here all the same. During the 1820s and '30s numerous new settlements were made throughout Australia, and the remaining parts of this volume must stretch to embrace them. These were enterprises much less isolated than the tiny bases first formed, during 1788–1803, at Port Jackson, Norfolk Island and Van Diemen's Land. The government in Sydney established outposts for convicts in the extreme western inland, at Wellington Valley, in 1823, to the north at Moreton Bay (Brisbane) in 1824, to the far east on Norfolk Island in 1825 (abandoned since 1814) and on the remote south coast, at King George Sound (Albany) in 1826. In the far north-west a series of military stations existed from 1824 to 1829 at Port Essington, Melville Island, and Raffles Bay, for the protection of British trade in the East Indies. The government in Hobart tried its hand in a similar way, with a penal settlement at Macquarie Harbour on the west coast of Van Diemen's Land in 1822.[9]

There were also settlements made directly from Britain. They included one on the Swan River (Western Australia) and another on the Gulf of St Vincent (South Australia), both of which are detailed below. 'What a proud sight', Wentworth had written in 1819, 'for the Briton to view his country pouring forth her teeming millions to people new hives, to see her forming in the most remote parts of the earth new establishments which may hereafter rival her old'. Twenty years later another writer asked of Australia:

> Say, will the hand that hath in wisdom crowded
> > A water drop with life,
> Leave this vast shore, unpeopled still, and shrouded
> > From human joys and strife.[10]

The question – even in terms of Europeans, let alone indigenous people – was already answered. Between 1815 and 1840 the size of Australia's immigrant population increased fourteen times, from about 15,000 to nearly 210,000. Among this mass of souls nine-tenths still lived in the two original colonies, New South Wales and Van Diemen's Land, but even within these limits people were scattered much further afield than they had originally been.

Everybody in Australia – and especially the unwashed – swarmed with fleas (Chapter 1). But the carcass of the country itself had its teeming creases, where the immigrant people seemed to gather, sometimes in great numbers, sometimes with nothing more than striking energy. Water traffic was still usually much cheaper and quicker than land traffic and waterways were especially attractive for men and women with limited capital and a willingness to brave fortune. In New South Wales, Port Jackson and the Parramatta and Hawkesbury Rivers were thick with traffic and likewise the Derwent in Van Diemen's Land. The seas also nourished enterprise. Coastal New Zealand – the Bay of Islands, Cook's Strait, and the western shore of the South Island – was unofficially settled in the 1820s and '30s by missionaries, small tradesmen, sealers, whalers, and escaped convicts. Similarly, the coastal waters of eastern Australia, north to Moreton Bay and west to Kangaroo Island (in what was to be South Australia) had over-lapping economies of their own, faintly reminiscent of other, more famous waterways, such as the Mediterranean and the intricate passages of the East and West Indies. Such traffic, including pirate trade, worked especially well among archipelagoes. Here it was focused in the region from Kangaroo Island to the eastern end of Bass Strait, the only official settlement of any size being Launceston. These waters, lying between the two original colonies and largely free of both, bounded by two fertile coasts and scattered with landfalls, were an independent source of life.

Ships from Sydney and Hobart came to these parts to gather seal and kangaroo skins, and (at Kangaroo Island) the fine salt that crystallised in the lagoons. King George Sound was sometimes part of such ventures. Seamen were left behind and convicts came from Van Diemen's Land so that there were small camps at various sites, especially at Western Port (on the northern coast), Cape Barren Island, King Island, and the Furneaux Group. Some men raided the mainland on both sides for Aboriginal wives, and as many as a hundred women lived there (including Kangaroo Island) by 1830, some men having several wives.[11] At Kangaroo Island there were perhaps a dozen men, some with families, a type of pirate gang according to one ship's master. They sometimes seemed to have left civilisation far behind, 'living entirely on kangaroos, emus, and small porcupines, and getting spirits and tobacco in barter for the skins which they lay up during the sealing season'. This visitor, who bought 4500 skins, found that the men stank like foxes. With or without families, they tended to live in pairs,

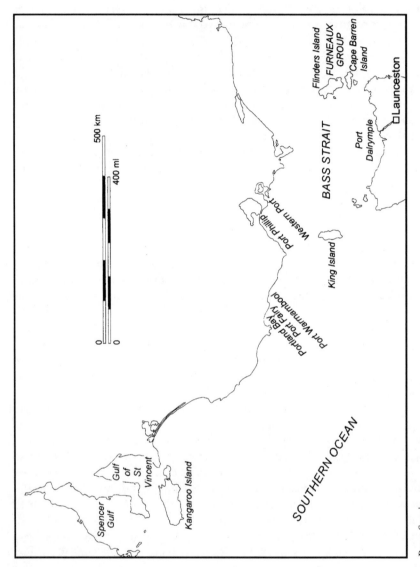

Bass Strait

probably sharing income according to the cooperative system of 'lays' used on sealing and whaling vessels. But a few lived alone with their women, including a man on a small island in Spencer Gulf – extraordinary to exist wholly within a sphere of varied blue – who once sold to a single buyer 7000 wallaby skins, 'very small, fine-furred, and beautifully mottled', at a cost of thirty shillings per hundred, paid in goods. The soapy-yellow, red marbled undersides were cured, presumably, with Kangaroo Island salt.[12]

As the home of a maritime people, fluid and beyond control, this waterway contradicted some of the orthodoxies of colonised Australia. On Preservation Island, at the eastern end of the strait, James Monro managed a settlement of Aboriginal women (four of them his wives) and White men, growing wheat and potatoes and selling mutton-bird feathers to Launceston. The Hobart government named him a constable in 1825. On Kangaroo Island Henry Wallen, with three wives, ran poultry and pigs. Wallen called himself 'Governor', just as, in Van Diemen's Land, Michael Howe had been 'Lieutenant-Governor of the Woods'. '[A]nd to his rule', by one report, 'the others yielded such obedience as was necessary in so primitive a state of society'.[13] However, by this time (the mid-1830s) men with larger ambitions and better education began to take similar advantage of the southern waterways. The Hentys – parents, seven sons, and a daughter – had been farmers in Kent. Like the Straitsmen they had a settled system of enterprise among themselves. Arriving first in Western Australia in 1829, where they took up land at Swan River and King George Sound, by 1833 they had moved their headquarters to Launceston. From there they reached across the Strait to Portland Bay, a site hitherto used as a camp for whalers. At Portland, in November 1834, Edward Henty formed a whaling base himself, with sheep stations nearby. Some of his brothers followed, as did other men from Van Diemen's Land, forming settlements in various inlets – Western Port, Port Phillip, Warrnambool, and Port Fairy.

The Hentys were among the first large capitalists to take advantage of Bass Strait. John Batman, a grazier, and John Pascoe Fawkner, late of the *Launceston Advertiser*, followed, setting themselves up at Port Phillip in 1835. Batman was the leading figure of the Port Phillip Association, with members in Launceston and Hobart. And just as the expedition by Blaxland, Wentworth, and Lawson in 1813 had drawn government after it – where poor men had gone years before – so the arrival of money and education in these waters meant more certain law and order. As we see later, a police magistrate was sent to Port Phillip in 1836 and in 1837 towns were surveyed on its shores.

Water was useful in other ways. Movement inland depended on the fresh water of the rivers and creeks. These were arteries which, in European eyes, fed the body of the country. Men and livestock clung to watercourses or tracked from one to the other as they spread over the land. Graziers pushing outward (or 'inward') from Sydney took various routes.

All came to know Australia by the pattern of its watercourses. In 1818–19 Charles Throsby, a landowner-explorer and the first educated European to be much acquainted with the country south-west of Sutton Forest (the future site of Goulburn), heard in local conversation of 'a considerable river of salt water ... called by the natives, Mur: rum: bid: gie ... [and] described by them, to communicate with the sea, at a great distance, pointing southerly'. He discovered the river himself in 1821.[14] Found in fact to be fresh, it was to be pivotal to future movement. In the north explorers were likewise drawn by stories of the 'Kindur', a vast watercourse said to exist beyond the current frontier of knowledge. Some believed that this river would show the way to a great sea at the heart of the continent. Never properly identified, it was perhaps the Gwydir, which was in fact called by stockmen the 'Big River' and which Thomas Mitchell, in 1831–32, linked up with other northern rivers, proving that all flowed to the Darling.[15] Mitchell's findings, together with stockmen's knowledge, also showed graziers how they might settle, with fair hope of survival, along the meagre lacework of northern watercourses.

The government in Sydney struggled meanwhile to form a well-knit, properly bounded community of Britons, with something like a British sense of place, of closeness, of community, and good order. In the 1820s the surveyor-general's office had drawn a semicircle on its maps, of about 120 miles diameter (three or four days ride), reaching south to the Murrumbidgee and north to the Manning. At first this was meant only to show where freehold title was available. Hence its name, the 'Limits of Location' ('to locate' meaning to take possession). But Mitchell, as surveyor-general, soon filled in the space with the cartographic symptoms of civilisation – counties, parishes, roads, and towns. So the line became 'the limits of the Colony'. Nineteen (later twenty) counties were drawn up, a few around Sydney and the others loosely grouped in three provinces. To the south-west the main highway was to be the Great South Road, extending first to Goulburn, the southern provincial centre, and later to Yass. The Great Western Road led over the Blue Mountains to Bathurst, on the Macquarie. In the north, Maitland was laid out as the capital of the Hunter River valley, but the Great North Road, meant as its lifeline, was precipitous and difficult. Most northern travellers went instead by sea to the Hunter's mouth or by other circuitous tracks to the headwaters. These three main towns, Goulburn, Bathurst, and Maitland, and the network of surveyed roads, overlaying as they did the mapped rivers and creeks, were meant as focal points for rural life.[16]

Surveys were urgent because the immigrants of this period brought with them considerable capital. The investment of wealth, including the forming of large estates, depended on elaborate efforts by government. It also depended on rapidly broadcast and more-or-less reliable information about the uses of the land. In Britain and Ireland educated men and women were urged to sail southward by a number of new books, all published in London. Wentworth promised on his title page to show that New South Wales and Van Diemen's Land could do more for emigrants than the United States and his book sold so well that two bigger editions immediately followed. Partly as a result, the Hunter Valley, barely touched by settlement in 1820, soon supported nearly two hundred landholders, half of them with estates of at least a thousand acres, granted in freehold by the Crown. Similar works appeared on Van Diemen's Land, and more land was granted on the island in 1823 alone – three or four times more – than in the previous ten years combined.[17]

Most of the new immigrants aimed to grow fine wool for sale in London. Thanks to the efforts of pioneer breeders such as John Macarthur and Samuel Marsden, it was now clear that sheep did especially well in Australia, a happy discovery at a time when Britain's main European suppliers were becoming expensive and uncertain. According to Wentworth, writing with heroic optimism, money invested in sheep would 'in the *course of three years, rather more than double itself*'.[18] Wool now became Australia's main export to Europe. In 1821 175,000 pounds were sent Home. By 1830 the figure had increased more than ten times. By 1850 it was 39 million.

The commercial and legal implications were vast. The new fabric of freehold, flung suddenly across the country, was woven and embroidered not only by surveyors but also by lawyers and moneylenders. In Britain itself investment in the industrial and agrarian revolutions had begun to affect even tradesmen and small farmers. Capitalists of all kinds were becoming more familiar with bookkeeping and it was obvious that efficient paperwork, in the colonial capitals and in London, was crucial to the control of such great spaces as these. There was little room for whimsy. Poetry itself struggled to survive in this country (so the writer Louisa Meredith complained) under 'the leaden influence of its ledger and day-book kind of atmosphere'.[19] And more than landed title was at stake. Because of their numbers, the sheep let loose in Australia, and also the cattle – beef for the new population – had to be managed with pen, ink, and agile calculations. Edward Curr, in his *Account of the Colony of Van Diemen's Land* (1824), advised every immigrant proprietor to update stock records at least once a month. The master, his overseer or shepherd, should take care to show 'in separate columns, the numbers of each description of stock, the increase of each kind since the last return, the decrease by death or accident, and the numbers slaughtered for subsistence, with any remarks that may appear necessary'. Such improvements in technique must change an owner's relationship with his animals. One remarked on the difference between the 'sort of domestic or family interest' that he had always felt in his 'old pets' and his new attitude to his sheep – the purpose of his coming out – whose faceless numbers, as he said, were 'a mere matter of profit'.[20]

But old pets were useful too. The same man had a black milking cow that died. He dined that evening, as he put it, 'sumptuously on one of poor dear Cowsy's marrow-bones!' and smiled at the notion of a mourning suit made from her skin.[21]

II

Sites used for homesteads and towns were often chosen for their natural beauty. A charming mix of water and woodland, light and shade, was central to ideas of the picturesque. And yet, in very process of using such a spot much of the beauty was immediately wrecked. The trees must go first, and 'nothing,' so James Macarthur (John Macarthur's native-born son) observed, 'can be more desolating than this operation'. But the pain, he thought, was worth it:

> Fresh attractions, of a more pleasing and permanent character, succeed to those which have been destroyed. Order, utility, comfort, enjoyment, luxury, follow each other step by step, and the charms of culture and civilization, deriving increased beauty and power from their being of our own creation, replace the wilder aspects of nature.

Each new settler was thus, supposedly, attached in his own mind to the land. With the clearing of the trees about his chosen home, so Macarthur believed, whatever the immediate ugliness, 'his prospect embraces a more extensive and cheering horizon'.[22]

Such progress went side by side, all the same, with Bass Strait disorder. Individuals comparable with the Straitsmen were known in New South Wales until the mid-1830s as 'squatters'. This word was soon to change its meaning dramatically, but so far it meant poor men and women, mostly landless ex-convicts, who squatted on Crown land. They lived mainly by running cattle and selling grog. 'In every part of the country', a newspaper editor said in 1835, 'squatters ... have formed stations', and worse, '[t]hey have reared families'. There had thus sprung into existence a breed 'initiated in all the craft and villiany [sic] of their sires'.[23] These squatters lived off their richer neighbours, as one gentleman explained:

> [They] are almost invariably the instigators and promoters of crime, receivers of stolen property, illegal venders of spirits, and harbourers of runaways, bushrangers, and vagrants. ... They keep up a constant intercourse with our assigned servants, and knowing the weak points of each establishment, seize their opportunity and commit depredations, particularly upon cattle, with impunity.[24]

With cunning enough, they might make good money from their livestock, 'which', he said, 'they usually herd in concealed recesses, and dispose of to butchers at a low rate'.[25]

In fact, even freehold farms and estates in the Antipodes might be something like little islands, or 'concealed recesses'. Australia yielded independence in many ways. According to John West, the historian of Van Diemen's Land who lived through much of it: 'Whatever his rank, [the immigrant] … dreams of the day when he shall dwell in a mansion planned by himself; survey a wide and verdant landscape called after his name; and sit beneath the vineyard his own hands planted.'[26] This ambition largely explained the flood of capitalists in the 1820s.

It was not even necessary to leave Europe in order to enjoy, in a vicarious fashion, such dominion and profit. Capitalists working in the City of London and going home to houses in its suburbs joined forces in taking up untamed parts of the continent. Distance meant that they had to be particularly careful with their employees. During the 1820s joint-stock companies were planned to promote investment in several parts of Australia: sites considered almost as new colonies. Two succeeded. The Australian Agricultural Company was formed in 1824, with a promise from Whitehall of a million acres, and the Van Diemen's Land Company with half a million. Long ago similar companies had set up the colonies of Virginia, Pennsylvania, Massachusetts, and Georgia. In every case, besides land, shareholders had wanted men bound somehow to labour on the spot, to remain with their capital. Stable enterprise required a stable workforce, but finding individuals happy to contract themselves at a fixed wage and for a fixed term of years was difficult.

The directors of the two companies recruited their people in Europe with strict regard to skills and moral character. They were to be committed to their workplace by law, like convicts, but in theory they were to be free of convict vices. During its first four years the A.A. Company brought out seventy-four labouring men, thirty-four of them with wives, plus a total of seventy-seven children. Several had changed their minds before they got here, either in England or, in one case, at Rio de Janeiro (where the British consul had to intervene), and more refused to travel the last leg, from Sydney to the company's estate at Port Stephens.[27] As for the servants of the V.D.L. Company, before leaving England they persuaded themselves (so their managers said) 'that Van Diemen's Land is the true Eldorado'. They were disappointed. In 1832 the former attorney-general, Joseph Gellibrand, acted in court for twenty who had escaped from their employers in the far northwest of the island. He successfully argued that the dating of their contracts was invalid, from which it followed that they and all their fellow servants could work wherever they liked.[28]

For a while the British government was happy to give thousands of Australian acres not only to chartered companies but also to rich Englishmen with no intention of leaving home. But by the late 1820s ideas had changed, because officials were now awake to the risk of wasting land and holding up closer settlement.[29] One gentleman who asked too late was Thomas Peel, first cousin to Robert Peel, Home Secretary and later Prime Minister.

Disappointed in New South Wales, Peel turned his attention to the vast, unsettled western part of the continent, still known as New Holland.[30]

Thomas Peel must have understood that British ministers were already interested in this part of the world, hitherto, in European eyes, a place both desolate and extraordinarily remote. They were anxious mainly to pre-empt the French, who were once again exploring the Australian coastline. To begin with the idea in Whitehall was that the whole continent might be ruled from Sydney and in December 1826, as I say, two new penal settlements were formed on the south coast, at Western Port, in Bass Strait, and far away at King George Sound. Darling pointed out that the latter was beyond his boundary, as set out in his commission, and his complaints about having to manage places at such a distance persuaded his superiors that Australia was bigger than they had thought. It was suggested that the East India Company govern the west from Calcutta, but that came to nothing.[31]

There were then some rapid changes of government at Whitehall, and equally quick changes in policy. In January 1828 Darling was told that even the settlement at King George Sound would probably be abandoned. But in January 1829, with the Tories in power, the opposite message arrived. A new colony altogether was to be formed at Swan River, but the Governor, Captain James Stirling, was to be independent of Sydney, taking orders from London and sustenance, should it be needed, from the Cape of Good Hope.[32]

Stirling was a naval officer whose wife's family were East India merchants. He had been in Australia in 1826–27 and was inspired by the possibility of making Swan River part of an Indian Ocean trading network. He and the government botanist from Sydney had spent a fortnight in March 1827 looking over the area. He had decided that it possessed 'the greatest natural attractions', and during 1828–29, in England, he managed to infect with this opinion a powerful circle of supporters. The London press spoke of 'Swan River mania'. Stirling's own family ties were Tory and these, backed up by the Peel network, won him access to the government of the Duke of Wellington.[33] As a result, the type of society first imagined for Swan River was not after all a trading one, tied to the City of London like the companies in the east, but shaped instead by rural hierarchy.

This new settlement was to be made up of an assortment of adventurers, men and women who hoped to make their money from the soil and with no ongoing fund of liquid capital. They also made their plans as farmers rather than graziers, most of them spending much more on equipment and seed than on livestock. Ignorant, apparently, of the money being made from grazing sheep in the older colonies and careless of ocean commerce, many seem to have looked forward to buying and selling among themselves, adrift from the imperial market.[34]

The idea of founding a colony with a parcel of gentry was something new in the Australian experience. It involved a belief that all the refinements of nineteenth-century life might be easily shifted abroad – as if recent improvements in traffic and communications had somehow cancelled distance. Here, indeed, was an invigorating idea. We see its impact, for instance, on ladies eager to escape seclusion. When Elizabeth Fenton arrived by herself in Van Diemen's Land in 1830 she was complimented for her 'astonishing courage'. 'I was much amused', she said, but the world – so she explained to her Hobart friends – had changed. Now, 'every one but very young girls, or very simple old ones, might travel where they list'.[35] In fact, she exaggerated. For most practical purposes the Australian settlements were still cut off from Europe by long and difficult voyages, an obstacle seriously hindering traffic, investment, and news. But Swan River depended on such sweet assurance.

So did the entire constitution of the empire during the 1820s and '30s. The same imagined order and unity can be seen in the way in which Darling and Arthur set up their regimes (Chapter 4). An all-embracing knowledge, sent to Whitehall by efficient governors, was to create a type of administrative machinery that would be perfectly efficient and perfectly just. Since the beginning of Creation distance had caused misunderstanding. Far from home, allegiances might be forgotten and promises fail. Now this was apparently no longer true. Trust and perfect knowledge seemed transportable from one end of the world to the other. Certainly, as far as Swan River was concerned, promises made in Europe were meant to hold in this country. And yet, many, especially among the poor, had no way of grasping precisely what the adventure would really entail. To begin with, trust and *imagined* knowledge was an antidote to fear. It was not to last.

A good deal turned on contractual agreement between the British government and moneyed settlers. Each such settler was promised 40 acres of Crown land for every £3 invested in livestock and farming equipment taken with him, plus 200 acres for every male or female labourer. But full title was to be allowed only when he had improved every acre to the value of one shilling and sixpence.[36] And just as the capitalists were bound by promises to the government, so they bound the rest of the population to themselves. Their prosperity depended on their having a labour force tied to their estates and most used a system of indenture, as the two great companies had done. Their labourers signed up for a predetermined period in return for certain wages and conditions. Terms varied. The Hentys, later settlers in Bass Strait, brought with them by the *Caroline* £6330 worth of stock and equipment together with six married couples (five with children) and six single men. Nearly all the men were old employees and they had promised to serve for five years at Swan River in return for £20 a year, fuel, and board. One man, Charles Gee, wrote a ballad on the way out:

> Come all you English lads that have a mind to go
> Into some foring Contery I would have you for to know
> Come join along with Henty and all his joyful crew
> For a Set of better fellows in this world you never knew.

Living conditions at Swan River in 1830, the first summer of settlement, a drawing by Mary Ann Friend.

This was one of the biggest establishments. Assets worth between £100 and £400 were more usual, plus two or three servants, adding up to an entitlement of between one and four thousand acres.[37]

Stirling soon found that too many of his settlers were 'helpless and inefficient' and, in spite of his original confidence, there was too little useful land. There was no prospect of large, uniformly fertile estates. He struggled to meet the government's promise to settlers by breaking up entitlements into small pieces and by including large areas of bad land with the good. Settlers had begun to arrive in June 1829 and by the end of 1831 more than a million acres had been allocated. But only 200 acres were under cultivation.[38] During the 1830s the European population never reached much more than 2000. The settlers had looked forward to being surrounded by a type of European abundance, an idea implicit in their dealings with government. They certainly found abundance, but of an ancient, indigenous variety. Ants, for instance, busied themselves everywhere, as they did in the east. 'The ground seems alive with white ants,' wrote the lawyer-settler George Fletcher Moore, 'and the trees swarm with them inside and out; every thing here teems with life'. The noises, too, were strange. There was 'an immense quantity' of frogs – this was Moore too – 'some of which make a hard *co-ax, co-ax*, sort of noise, and others a most mournful and horrible bellowing'.[39]

There was a little cause for cheerfulness anywhere. Certainly the settlers were well provided with skilled labour. A list made in 1832 shows a population of 1416 with forty-seven carpenters and sawyers, eight coopers, wheelwrights, and boat-builders, seven brickmakers, two bricklayers, two stonemasons, a thatcher, and a glazier; and, for more common daily needs, six blacksmiths, two butchers, and seven bakers. And life had its pleasures. At about this time a grand piano arrived for the elderly Mrs Leake. Two Aborigines danced to its music. '[T]ank you mem', they said, 'very pretty'.[40]

And yet progress was so slow that even skilled men found themselves short of work. George Stokes, a carpenter, his wife Rachael, and six children arrived by the *Britannia* in 1830, indentured for five years to Lieutenant-Colonel Peter Lautour. Lautour already had money in Van Diemen's Land and his investment in Swan River was second only to Peel's. He had been allowed over 100,000 acres and had sent out an agent to manage his affairs, but when nothing prospered his establishment was broken up and his servants left to themselves. Charles Gee had predicted 'plenty of provishons boys and plenty for to do', and a carpenter should have found ready work in a new settlement, building houses. But according to Stokes, he 'was thrown on the community and on the Government for assistance and support, which occasioned much illness to himself and family, and eventually the death of one of his children'. Stokes could not write (these words were written for him in a letter to Governor Stirling), but like the convicts in New South Wales and Van Diemen's Land he set himself to understand the system by which he had been bound. He only partly succeeded. Having learnt that Lautour had not been able to take up his land he told the Governor that some of his former master's entitlement ought to devolve on him, his wife and his two elder sons, Moses and Carey. This would mean 200 acres each. Having come as part of his master's capital Stokes tried to make himself into someone who could deal with government direct.[41]

His logic was flawed, but his ambitions were typical. Like the servants of the two great companies, indentured labourers at Swan River had arrived with high hopes of future prosperity. And like the convicts, they thought carefully about their rights. Large numbers had come from parts of England which, in 1829–30, were about to erupt in rural revolt because of unemployment and low wages. 'Now England is got very bad,' said Gee, 'of that you well doth know / Provishons they are got very dear, and little for to do.' All must have expected a kind of security and comfort no longer possible at home. They had been promised much and they had imagined more, even the certainty, as George Fletcher Moore remarked, of 'meat and beer three times a day'. None was forthcoming. Instead employers referred back to the indentures and demanded discipline even harder than in England. 'The indentured men', said one magistrate, 'have an opinion that they are slaves and this is so strong in their minds, that it is loss of time to endeavour to remove the impression'. At Swan River periods in gaol were normal for servants who refused to work as they had agreed.[42]

In January 1831 the *Sydney Gazette* reported on the progress of the set-tlement in the west, relying on news lately arrived. 'The people were not actually *starving*', it said, 'but the gloom of despondency was spread over every mind, even the few who had luckily hit upon the more favoured patches of land, having quite enough to damp their spirits in the poverty and wretchedness which they saw around them'. By now the lack of money for further investment had become critical. Stirling had established two towns, Fremantle, on the mouth of the Swan, and Perth, the seat of gov-ernment, 9 miles upriver, and by 1832 – in spite of the rural character intended for the colony – about half the immigrant people were in one or the other. And yet trade was minimal. The towns housed so many because it was hard to survive anywhere else. Only isolation and lack of means pre-vented a mass exodus and, even so, in 1832 more people left Swan River than arrived.[43] Meanwhile the eastern parts of the continent were entering a period of extraordinary prosperity, thanks mainly to the export of fine wool. Wool could be carried over long distances without deterioration, which was part of the reason for its being so important for Australian pros-perity. Its export did not need steam power. A different kind of squatter, rich and respectable, began running stock, both sheep and cattle, over land still ungranted by the Crown.

Awake at last to the same opportunities, leading settlers at Swan River turned their attention to breeding sheep, encouraged especially by the dis-covery of good country inland, in the Avon Valley. There two towns, York and Northam, were laid out.[44]

To begin with, this only meant that problems of distance from Home were compounded with problems of distance within the colony itself. The settlement that remained at King George Sound was now ruled from Perth, more than 200 miles away, and there the awkwardness of being the remote outpost of a remote outpost caused 'the most bitter animosity and dissatis-faction'. At Swan River itself shipping remained scarce, traffic from the Avon was expensive, and there was little money to be spent in making a difference to either. Large numbers of sheep had been eaten before settlers had noticed the value of their wool, leaving barely 2000 head. But by the late 1830s mat-ters began to improve. Inland farmers took charge themselves of the road to the coast, subscribing funds and setting a toll.[45] By 1846 sheep numbers had topped 100,000 (there were seven million in New South Wales) and the European population, at 4290, was growing likewise. Numbers – the press of population round about – softened the impact of being far from home.

III

The settlement schemes of the 1820s and early 1830s were piecemeal com-pared with what was to follow. Just as Britain and its Antipodes began to be bound much more tightly by the continuous mass of fine-woolled fleeces moving in one direction, so they were bound by the continuous mass of people moving in the other. During the ten years 1836–45 about 78,000 men, women, and children, mostly labouring families, reached the Antipodes from Europe, driven by hunger and poverty, with their passages paid under schemes of assisted immigration. The married couples were generally young, with children yet unborn. More than two-thirds of the assisted immigrants landed at Sydney and the European population of New South Wales grew by 143 per cent (reaching 190,000) within those ten years.[46] Here was a demographic change with lasting results (Chapter 14). Also, in 1836 the province of South Australia was established, with a population, ten years later, of 22,000.

More than 26,000 other Europeans paid their own way to the various parts of Australia. These were people who had the means to insist on shaping the world about them. The first capitalists at Swan River had brought with them a certain pride in being far from Sydney, with its authoritarianism and its convicts. So did some new arrivals elsewhere. Many new squatters (the more respectable sort) in marginal parts of New South Wales, such as New England to the north and Port Phillip to the south, had come straight from Europe and they, too, wanted dominions of their own. Some were well organised, well connected, and rich. They were to be most successful at Port Phillip, which was to be separated, at last, in 1851 as the colony of Victoria.

For men and women like these, immigrant labourers were tangible assets. Anyone who bought land in South Australia should realise, said the editor of the *South Australian Gazette,* that he 'does not merely buy clods of earth – he buys labour'.[47] And yet the doctrine of free enterprise also stressed that labourers, like capitalists, were decision makers. They made their way forward by selling their labour to advantage. Gentlemen interested in the settlement of South Australia were especially well read in the requisite theory. They were 'men of book-learning and science'. They belonged, it was said, to 'the new school of political Economists called "Theorists"'.[48] They were men for whom 'plans' and 'systems' were vital to any way forward. In this respect they were different from the founders of Swan River. Not for them the undigested planning, the unthinking and unreading Toryism that had apparently run that project into the sand. Like Thomas Hobbes Scott, Saxe Bannister, and George Arthur, they were students of human motivation, deeply interested in the springs of action operating at all levels of society. But while Scott, Bannister, and Arthur laboured with the vagaries of conscience, for the 'systematic colonisers' human will-power was like a steam engine. In a piece of theory sent to the Colonial Office in 1829 *(Sketch of a Proposal for Colonizing Australasia),* the chief among them, Edward Gibbon Wakefield, bracketed in a particularly neat way the twin turbines that, he said, might drive colonial prosperity – the desire to minimise tax and the reproductive power of young couples.[49]

Suggestions for the planned settlement of Australia's south coast were first made in Britain in 1829. They can probably be traced back to Francis Dixon, a ship's captain who lived by the sale of colonial wool, whale-oil, and skins, and who had spent a good deal of time in southern waters, including Bass Strait. A 'very intelligent man', Dixon had moved in influential circles in Sydney and had married the sister of the surveyor-general, John Oxley. He seems to have met Wakefield and Wakefield's friend, Robert Gouger, in England during the first half of 1829 and echoes of their conversations might be imagined in Wakefield's *Letter from Sydney*, written, in fact, in London and published that autumn in the London *Morning Chronicle*. Wakefield dwelt on sea traffic just as Dixon might have done. '[S]hips, and water to float them on' were the main means of transport in countries like these, he said. It followed that 'New South Wales and Van Diemen's Land are connected, not separated by Bass's Strait', for such traffic 'enables fellow-countrymen and brothers, living on either shore of Bass's Strait, to maintain an intimate connection'.[50]

In fact, such statements were not as true now as they had been a little earlier. While ships still mattered, inland exploration and inland traffic were becoming more and more important to long-distance movement in the Antipodes. Early in 1830, for instance, an expedition led by Charles Sturt travelled down the Murrumbidgee to the Murray (a new discovery), to the Murray's junction with the Darling (whose upper waters Sturt had found in 1828) and so to Lake Alexandrina and the Southern Ocean. The river mouth was barely navigable, but news of this find – of 'a magnificent river falling into the sea at Gulf St Vincent' – nourished English plans for settlement on Australia's south coast.[51] Wakefield had declared in his *Letter* that the southern half of the Australian continent, below 25 degrees south, was 'capable of supporting a dense population'.[52] The area he described was already settled on its eastern and western edges, but the south coast was nearly wholly vacant. The addition of the lower Murray to expert knowledge showed where such population might go.

Wakefield had a strong sense of the maritime empire, interconnected by sea. The settlements in Australia were really, he said, 'one and the same colony'. At some point they would be 'districts of one and the same country', an important fact for British trade.[53] Among the plans of George Fife Angas, the leading British investor in South Australia, was a line of steam-ships running between the new colony, Van Diemen's Land, and New South Wales by way of Bass Strait. And like Wakefield, Angas could see that the Australian colonies had a common interest, which led him to wonder why Whitehall did not work out 'some general and uniform plan' for them, apparently meaning a single government. Early publicity for the new colony predicted that its capital town would become 'the commercial emporium, the London of Australia'.[54]

And yet, as with the Swan River settlers, the founders of South Australia also wanted to be perfect among themselves and they quarantined themselves from other enterprises. Their publicity stressed that this was not a penal colony like its neighbours – 'There will never be a single *convict* sent thither.'[55] And, more important, Wakefield thought that population scattered over large spaces, including such a continent as Australia, was a cause of barbarism. The need for dense settlement – for 'concentration' – was crucial to his thinking. With a population as compact as the populations of Europe, he said, you might expect 'wealth, knowledge, skill, taste, and whatever belongs to civilization'. Without it you must have ignorance, prejudice, and mean-spirited egalitarianism, in short 'a people … rotten before they are ripe'. Experience in the Antipodes had already proved as much.[56] The Straitsmen and the original squatters were extremes of the typical Australian.

There were strong habits of moral and intellectual independence about many of the founders of South Australia, a sense of superiority to old ways and to officialdom. Wakefield himself spoke of the need to circumvent 'the red tape school of politics'. One of his supporters called the Colonial Office a citadel of the 'ancien regime'.[57] They struggled to do things in their own way, but also, because they could not help it, with official underpinning. Three bodies were formed to push their project forward. The South Australian Association (December 1833) was designed to work out and disseminate the principles of systematic colonisation. On the one hand it promoted freedom of opinion, and especially religious equality, in the new land. The whole project was well supported by Dissenters, or in other words by members of those churches that had been formed in dissent from the Established Church of England. On the other hand, free investment was carefully curtailed. Crown land was to be sold not according to the law of supply and demand but at a uniform price, a point pivotal to the machinery of settlement.

It was the association that persuaded the Secretary of State for the Colonies to support the passage of the South Australian Act (August 1834). The South Australian Colonisation Commission (May 1835), a body also made up of systematic colonisers, was then set up to manage the emigration of labourers and the disposal of land. It had to make sure that population numbers matched the area under cultivation and pasture, and one of its members was to be stationed in the colony for that purpose. The commissioners decided that, on average, the use of every 200 acres would need four male agricultural labourers and one other working man, skilled or unskilled. Concentrated settlement was their answer to the risk of a wandering workforce, but so, too, was the equality of the sexes. The number of women sent out was to equal the number of men. And, to complete the circle of calculation, the cost of emigration was to be met by land sales, every four acres to be priced so as to pay for ten adults.

The third body, the South Australian Company (January 1836), was a joint-stock company, like the A.A. Company and the V.D.L. Company, formed to take up land that had not found buyers in the commission's original distribution. All three – the association, the commission, and the company – were all in full operation, spinning off local institutions (the *South Australian Gazette*, a literary association, a lending library) before anyone had left England. Also, land was paid for and a town sketched out. Unlike Swan River, South Australia's patrons were not rural gentry but urban intellectuals. The loving attention they paid to the future capital and to the reading habits of the people is proof of that.

The company's first two vessels reached Kangaroo Island, its headquarters, in July 1836. The government surveying party, including the surveyor-general, William Light, arrived in August–September and the Governor, John Hindmarsh, and resident commissioner came by the *Buffalo* in December. They and other officers of government were sworn in and the settlement proclaimed on the 28th. At the same time the surveyors hurried ahead with the business of dividing up the soil, on which all else depended.

The mass arrival of new immigrants in New South Wales likewise happened during the second half of the 1830s. Here, too, money from the sale of Crown land was set aside to pay for their passage. But here most of the details were worked out on the spot. From 1835 employers who could manage to find their own labourers in Britain might claim part of the cost of bringing them out, as long as they met certain criteria of gender, age, and skill. This was the bounty system and there was also a wholly government system, the people being chosen by agents of Whitehall. Many employers were keen to use these schemes to build up a working population better ordered and more moral than the convicts could ever be. Besides, the convicts were now too few.

There were differences but also similarities with South Australia. In both cases a number of leading men and women were driven by the intellectual challenge of giving a new cast to society. An anchoring to place was to be married somehow to the conquering of distance. Like the systematic colonisers, they were taken with the idea of the empire as a single entity, bound by the continuous passage, from end to end, of trade, information, and people.

Among the innovators in New South Wales was James Macarthur, now beginning his political career, a man whose ideas echoed with the influence of Hobbes Scott and Saxe Bannister. He and his brothers made full use of the bounty system, bringing in 176 men, women, and children to live on their estates.[58] Macarthur was not much given to plans and systems, but in 1837 he published in London his ideas on immigration to New South Wales. Well managed, he said, it would involve 'substituting a virtuous population, for the guilty outcasts who now compose so large a portion of the labouring class of the colony'. The convicts and their children, he said, were not all bad, but it was time to build again on a new foundation. This was Wakefield's emphasis too, but Macarthur added his own perspective. More delicately than Wakefield, he dealt with labouring people as thinking beings. Labour, he said, was not a 'commodity'. The poor in Britain deserved to know that the colonies were partly for their benefit. Wakefield

Bethany, a village for German settlers in South Australia, about 1845, a lithograph by George French Angas. Germans, too, came as assisted immigrants.

Reproduction courtesy of State Library of South Australia

only wanted to persuade labour to move where it were needed. Macarthur wrote of a 'bridge of communication' between Britain and Australia, 'as accessible to the poor as to the rich'. The head of each labouring household in the mother country – a 'rational being', in Bannister's terms – must have good and certain knowledge of the chances abroad. He was entitled to information about the help available to get there, with his family and his small property. The 'resources of the State', Macarthur said, must be placed within his reach, so that he might be, 'in this respect, ... upon an equal footing with his wealthier neighbour'.[59]

Macarthur had grown up among convicts. He knew how the more astute convict men and women found out about the intricacies of the regime that bound them. He knew how individuals with no authority themselves could learn to use the authority of others. He agreed with Scott and Bannister that moral and material progress depended on the careful use of intellect and power by individuals like himself. His ideas about equity (going back to Horne Tooke) laid a peculiar duty on the rich and well read.

He failed to grasp, all the same, the way in which letters and postage shaped a regime like this. The secretary of the South Australian Colonisation Commission was Rowland Hill, who in 1839 was to make his name by the fundamental reform of the British postal system. Hill wanted postage to be frequent, much cheaper (a penny a letter), and pre-paid (with adhesive stamps). Currently letters were paid for on delivery, and the cost was high and often unpredictable. Cheapness and simplicity, Hill said, would encourage letter-writing and, in the end, increase the revenue of government. More important, such small efficiencies, many times over, would transform society. 'There is oftentimes', he said, 'a desire to communicate at short intervals, as one or twice per day, some single fact'. For instance, in cases of serious illness it ought to be possible, for both rich and poor, to send news to friends through the day. Also, a London tradesman ought to be able to tell his wife in the afternoon if he was going to be late home. In more general terms, cheap postage would 'powerfully stimulate the productive power of the country' by allowing every kind of enterprise to communicate on the instant. In the same spirit Wakefield argued that assisted emigrants should be allowed postage free of charge for 'some years' after they reached their destinations. They would then send home frequent news of their prosperity and their friends and relations would follow them out.[60]

The same fascination with the possibilities of postal traffic appears in the way South Australia was advertised in Britain during the 1830s. And not only South Australia. One of George Fife Angas's admirers wrote to him suggesting for Britain itself a 'Central Benevolent Society', which would collect and distribute by post 'every good Plan for aiding the Poor Man to help himself'. Angas and Hill, as the commission's secretary, made full use of the post to persuade the poor to move in thousands to the Antipodes. As Angas's assistant, Samuel Stephens, remarked, 'the only way of getting on is to advertise and publish *extensively*', and never before had any new colony been promoted through such wholesale distribution of the written word. (At the same time there were parallel hopes of publicising more efficiently among 'the criminal population' the idea that Australia was not a pleasant place at all.)[61] Hill suggested that all vital detail about the colony be reduced to a single sheet, 'for ready transmission by the post', and the *South Australian Gazette* was founded especially 'to enable those interested [in the colony] to transmit, free of postage, to all quarters of the kingdom, a full and authentic account of its advantages and prospects'. (Newspapers were posted free of charge.) During its first year and a half the commission spent £900 on books, stationery, printing, and advertising, and £137 on postage, the last sum kept to a minimum by Rowland Hill.[62]

'There is a great difference', Wakefield said in his *Letter from Sydney*, ' ... between looking *to* a place and looking *from* it'. There was a difference between seeing a point on the map, reading about it, and really being there.[63] There was also a difference between writing books and pamphlets about a place, as South Australia's English friends did, and writing letters Home after getting there. New arrivals in both Western Australia and South Australia, as in New South Wales and Van Diemen's Land, were struck with the difference between ideal and reality. Many miles now existed between the two, and between themselves and all they knew best. This was distance hard for imagination to conquer. The remedy in theory was quick and easy postage. Indeed, in South Australia Rowland Hill's hopes were manifest in a flat rate of a penny each for all letters to and from England.[64] But distance remained. Among Europeans in this country immediate links might happen, literally, only in dreams. Poor men and women had some faith in supernatural forms of contact. On the way out in 1822 James Gardner, a convict, dreamt of a member of the family whose birth in England he only heard of twenty years later. In his dream he asked, 'how did you come here[?]', and the child's mother said, with dream-like irrelevance, 'very well'. He made a mental note of the date, sure that the dream meant something. 'I suspect', he said, 'it was the very night he was born'.[65]

Postage, unlike dreams, involved deliberate effort. Unhappily, long periods in a remote place without news, plus the knowledge that your own letters would be months old when they reached home, could be almost paralysing. Poor men and women, unused to linking lives across the globe, were most affected. George Fletcher Moore, at Swan River, noticed that his servants, at least to begin with, would not write at all. 'It arises partly', he said, 'from our not knowing of the sailing of the ships until it is too late', but also, '(I am sorry to say) from their being too fond of playing cards, carousing, and singing, which makes them inattentive to any of their duties. I often ask them to write, yet they forget to do so'. Strangely, however, he felt the same. 'I sat down several times to write, but could not arrange my ideas; I wanted to say something particular to each of you', he said, 'I still wish it; but how to do justice to my own feelings and your affections!' And again, when mail did come, 'I open every letter with fear and trembling at this distance of time and space'.[66] Louisa Clifton found the same, also in Western Australia, ten years later. '[T]he sense of distance', she explained, 'imposes a barrier to communication not as far as feelings are concerned, only in the verbal expression of them. My heart is just as warm as ever, but my pen is frigid and powerless'.[67]

In Europe itself many, including the poor, struggled to duplicate the great river of knowledge, which now flowed, by way of governors' dispatches, into Whitehall. '[W]hen the other men sends home', Mary Arlett told her convict son-in-law, 'they fills up their paper But you did not half fill yours they Lett us know all about the particular of the Country but you said nothing'. Hearing from his sister in Worcestershire, Richard Corbett sat down in the bush near Western Port to answer her questions. She had asked, he said, 'wether we had the same langwig as you'. Did she imagine that his very speech had changed in transit? '[O]ur langwig', he assured her, 'is the same and complections'.[68] In a world supposedly so much smaller she might not have been happy with such a curt reply.

Chapter 6

Conscience

I

Refining the world – brightening the sensibility of men and women and drawing them together in kindly exchange – meant doing something about violence. Hear the story of John Blackman, who in 1837 ran away from school, the King's School at Parramatta. He was twelve or thirteen, the son of free immigrants, and he boarded. 'The cause of my "bolting"', so he later recalled (using school-boy slang), 'was in consequence of my being coated by Mr Forrest [the headmaster] with a long, thin ebony ruler on the hands one Sunday night, for not being able to repeat a whole Watts' Hymn'. He had been badly beaten once before ('I nearly fainted'), and this time he escaped home to Sydney. He was persuaded by his father to go back, but only after the Head guaranteed that it would not happen again.[1]

The King's School was designed to civilise. Robert Forrest, its first head, was an intelligent man and a good teacher. Two years later, on his resignation, the boys thanked him for his gentleness. And yet he easily took to violence. In fact he hit Blackman once more, with a quince stick. But this time, as his victim stumbled under him, Forrest seems to have remembered his promise. He checked himself, 'ordered me to sit on an old tea chest, at the foot of his rostrum', and there were no more beatings.[2]

Europeans, in Australia and Europe, were often checking themselves just as Forrest did. There were now dramatic efforts to make the habits of society less brutal. The reduced frequency of flogging for convicts (Chapter 4) was one result. The origins of such sensibility lie with eighteenth-century humanitarianism but the change was now very quick, as well-read individuals became suddenly aware of the violence that was part of their daily lives. The first children's book published in Australia, *A Mother's Offering to Her Children* (1841), by Charlotte Barton, was mainly about violence. Mrs Barton had her leading character, a mother (modelled on herself), tell her children long stories about shipwrecks, including the sufferings of those on board who fell into the hands of Pacific islanders. The detail was gruesome. 'Such wanton barbarities', little Clara interjects, 'fill one with horror and indignation; and a wish to exterminate the perpetrators'. But the author's main aim was to draw a line between savagery and humanity. Islanders and Aborigines are more prone than we are, so the mother says, to 'unrestrained passions'. 'We should never destroy any thing wantonly', she tells her small listeners. As children we must be kind to animals. 'Some people', she says, 'have a sad cruel habit of throwing insects into the fire!'[3]

Even grown men, as they dealt with animals, now felt the same sudden tug of conscience – of conscience new-modelled. A year after Blackman's adventure Thomas Livingstone Mitchell remarked on his own feelings while exploring along the River Bogan. His dogs had brought down a female kangaroo for the evening meal and, he said, he found himself complicit in their savagery:

> There is something so affecting in the silent and deadly struggle between the harmless kangaroo and its pursuers, that I have sometimes found it difficult to reconcile the sympathy such a death excites, with our possession of canine teeth, or our necessities, however urgent they might be.

Besides, there was a baby, 'warm from the pouch of its mother', which escaped into the long grass. 'The nights were cold', said Mitchell, 'and I confess that thoughts of the young kangaroo did obtrude at dinner, and were mingled with my kangaroo-steak'.[4] Similar self-conscious joking echoed also in a remark made on the far edge of the continent by George Fletcher Moore. Newly arrived at Swan River, Moore was sorry to see so much sand and so few stones, 'not even a pebble to be flung at a bird; a benevolent action, in which from old habit, I frequently feel a desire to indulge'.[5]

Of course, animals themselves lived by violence. Mrs Barton wrestled with this fact. Her young readers were told of a purple beetle 'sadly tormented by ... little black ants' and of two swallows whose career was cut short by a cat and a magpie. For we must remember, she said, 'that a wise and good God, has destined one thing as food for another'. And yet we must feel for the victims too. The swallows in her story were the best of married couples, existing for each other and for 'their tender little ones'. They lived – briefly – within a world of duty and affection that was a model for humankind. The nest they built (a 'mighty task') was a little paradise, a place woven from self-sacrifice. For women like Charlotte Barton all virtue was explained by family life. The good community was the good home writ large. We too had our 'remorseless cat' and our 'greedy magpie' – our frontier savages – but we must behave well, all the same, among ourselves.[6] Behaving well among ourselves is the main point of this chapter.

Animals made a powerful imaginative impact (Chapter 1). In Britain the first law against their mistreatment was passed in 1822 and the Society for the Prevention of Cruelty to Animals was formed in 1824. Feeling for animals was supposed to echo feeling for humankind, but not always in the interests of gentleness. The coincidence of feeling could sharpen as well as soften cruelty. English farm labourers maimed livestock in revenge against employers and in Ireland the hocking of cattle (cutting their hamstrings) was an old form of protest. According to twentieth-century scholarship, living creatures, including human beings, often attack other members of their own species by using the 'illusion of violence', with substitute targets for instance. Animals are a substitute easily available to those of us who cannot bring ourselves to make a direct hit at our kind. Escaped convicts who besieged Major MacLeod's house at Claggan, in northern Van Diemen's Land, tied up a favourite horse and shot at it. Thomas Holden, a convict shepherd near Yass, in New South Wales, hurt his mistress by slashing at one her rams. '[H]e would take good care', he said, 'that she should not have many [lambs] from his flock the coming season'.[7] Animal symptoms of fear and pain, so much like human voices, drove triumph home.

Violence was an old prerogative of men and boys. It might be justified by the need for security or the need for food, but it might also be a means of retribution or sheer pleasure. Much depended on the ease with which one might lay one's hand on a stick, a stone, a gun, or a knife. A weapon can shape and even authorise the harm it causes. Forrest's quince stick, held tight, had its own logic. 'Our strong arms be our conscience', says Shakespeare's Richard III, 'swords our law'.[8] Providentially, stones were scattered for use against other parts of God's creation. And yet, so both men and women increasingly argued, such behaviour was sadly like the 'unrestrained passion' of the savage.

The new difficulties with violence arose partly from revulsion with its results. John Blackman, in order to impress his father, 'held out both my battered hands'. The sight of bruises and blood, though still intriguing – as it always is – seemed more ugly than it once had been, jarring apparently with a new sense of right. There was a new balance of wonder and disgust. English farmers were shocked to find their horses' tongues torn out by angry labourers. Parliament, by a law of 1832, brought to an end the dissection, in public, of criminals' bodies after execution. Consider, too, the cutting off of heads. Throughout the British Empire no one had been sent to the block since the Jacobite rebellion of 1745, but until lately there had been no objection to the public decapitation of bodies already dead. On ordering a punitive expedition against Aborigines in 1790 Governor Phillip required heads to prove the numbers killed.[9] Also, when men were outlawed a price might be offered for their heads, as the best means of identification. In Van Diemen's Land in the time of Michael Howe the heads of bushrangers were carried to Hobart while their other remains were left in the scrub. In July 1833 the head of Yagan, an Aboriginal warrior and a declared outlaw, was likewise cut off following his death near Fremantle. But as a sign of the times, perhaps, it was not handed in to government, remaining instead a private trophy before being sent for anatomical study to England.[10] Only science now seemed to justify the dissection of human flesh.

Among gentlemen duelling had always been thought a necessary evil, wrong in law but justified when honour was at stake. Now duellists, including Europeans in Australia, hoped to prove their courage without killing. For cynics it was all bombast or, as a Sydney versifier put it, 'guns and swords, / And great big words', and in fact (as far as we know) only three Australian duels were fatal. In one case, at Fremantle in 1832, William Nairne Clark killed George French Johnson, but he was so clearly shaken by Johnson's death that the criminal court acquitted him even of manslaughter. A year later, when another duel was threatened, the president of the civil court moved quickly to stop 'this evil'.[11] Duels were most common at Port Phillip, where there were numerous young gentlemen whom the magistrates found hard to keep under. At least fifteen duels were fought there between 1839 and 1845. But they were a kind of play-acting. All concerned were usually happy 'to turn the affair into a joke'.[12]

These shifts of attitude were pivotal to the history of civility and conscience in Australia. Referring to the new methods of punishing convicts, the Quaker missionary James Backhouse (who was here in the 1830s) spoke of changes taking place among those men 'who have gained some degree of victory over themselves'. Others, who still liked to use violence

Flogging in Van Diemen's Land, 1837, a newspaper sketch. The convict is tied, as usual, to a triangle. The gentleman on the hill calls it 'butchery', but the gentleman on the spot threatens hanging as well.

Source: *Cornwall Chronicle*, 9 September 1837

to enforce obedience, remained 'in bondage', he said, 'to their own evil passions'. They must do more harm than good, for an overbearing master 'is often the exciting cause of the insolence in the prisoner, which occasions him to be brought before a magistrate and to receive flagellation'. In short, violence used by men who ought to know better kept up a cycle of violence. Contrariwise, their self-restraint would surely be mimicked among the rest. The poor must also be better educated. According to the Church of England Bishop of Australia, good schooling 'diminishes the ferocity of men'.[13] It was supposed to give one a stronger sense of one's own place within Creation, of moral responsibility and of cause and consequence. It linked one to a greater, more abstract universe. A 'reflecting' being, thus created, was a creature of conscience.

Perhaps, on the contrary, it was the rich, not the poor, who needed civilising most. Perhaps conscience depended on something simpler than literacy. Some radicals believed that gentlemen typically governed by terror. Alexander Harris took this view. 'There is among working men', he said, 'a strong and ineradicable and very correct sense of what is fair'. It was up to masters to treat them with corresponding moderation. One of the old settlers on Kangaroo Island, being pursued by the sub-inspector of police, Alexander Tolmer, came to give himself up and found Tolmer asleep. He roused him: 'There Mr Tolmer, don't say I am not a Man or I could have shot you with your own Gun.' He knew without being taught that it was a cool head that made him a civilised being. And yet, most influential voices agreed that the poor and illiterate were most impetuous. In the high Yorkshire dales Mrs Gaskell (Chapter 1) had found the people not only 'passionately fond' but also 'dare-devil', 'stony & cruel'. Even the English political philosopher John Stuart Mill, a radical himself, was appalled by what he called the 'selfishness & brutality' of the 'uncultivated herd'.[14]

Certainly, to some extent, conscience depended on upbringing and circumstance, on fashion, time, and place. The weight of principle was to fall at a different angle, for instance, among the next generation, who people this volume's last chapters.

And yet, among all ranks and in a timeless way violent ambitions existed side by side with moral disgust. Sometimes blood lust was only fantasy. Convicts on Norfolk Island might happily think of killing their commandant, as they did in 1834, cutting him in four and sticking the quarters up around the island.[15] Whether they could have done it is another matter. John Brackfield, a settler at South Creek, near Sydney, was indeed murdered by his convict servants, four men and a woman. One man strangled him with a black silk handkerchief and another finished him off with a hammer. The men had made their plans together, but the woman, Eliza Campbell, insisted on being involved. She, too, wanted Brackfield dead. He was urging her to sleep with him, she said, otherwise 'he would take me to Atwood's, the constable, and send me to the factory for the two figs of tobacco he found in my box'. The men's only purpose was robbery and it is not clear why they made themselves murderers. But they were in awe of Eliza Campbell. They were stupid, according to the newspaper reporter who saw the trial, but she was 'a woman of more than ordinary understanding'. She asked them after the deed to wound her too, to make her look innocent, and she must have already been concocting the vivid and plausible tale she was to tell afterwards. But 'they had not the heart'. Nor was she altogether callous. When the undertaker asked her to help him with the body (when no one yet suspected her) it was only under orders that she 'tremblingly complied'. And yet, in the end she insisted she was guilty and the men tried to exonerate her.[16] Such dappled shifts of motivation – such simultaneous loathing and embracing of violence – appeared everywhere throughout the colonies.

Between 1830 and 1849, not counting charges against Aborigines, there were two murder trials in Western Australia and twelve in South Australia, compared with 294 in New South Wales. The newer colonies had much smaller populations, but this difference still suggests that there was less risk of fatal violence there. It was the convict presence that made all the difference in New South Wales, and as convict numbers began to dwindle in the 1840s murders also grew fewer.[17]

It was commonly argued that a population of free immigrants must be more moral and humane than one made up of convicts. For similar reasons those in charge of assisted immigration made sure that the number of women equalled, as far as possible, the number of men. It seemed obvious that violence in the convict colonies was due not only to ingrained wickedness but also to the imbalance of the sexes. The proportion of men to women who had come as convicts was six to one. As a result the men did not typically live in families. For companionship they relied on each other, and masculine, almost animal solidarity often seemed at odds with the rule of conscience. Convict men, so E.S. Hall said (with a little exaggeration), were like wild bulls who had been 'separated by the master bulls from the general herd'. They spent their time 'fighting and tearing each other to pieces'.[18] Their weapons were usually workplace tools. William Johnson killed Morris Morgan at Moreton Bay with an axe. John Hammill killed George Williamson at Grose Farm, near Sydney, with a spade. ('I am guilty of striking him, my Lord, but he struck me first.') Edward Tufts killed John Jones near Cassilis, in the upper Hunter Valley, by stabbing him in the groin with sheep shears.[19] Convicts laid their hands more easily on such instruments than on firearms, which they were allowed to carry only on the remote frontier. Once again, the pattern was different in South Australia. Of the fourteen White men tried for murder or attempted murder in Adelaide during the first five years of settlement twelve used firearms – muskets, pistols, or fowling-pieces.[20]

South Australia was meant to be a concentrated settlement, gathered tightly about its capital town. For a while, certainly, Adelaide absorbed not only a good deal of investment but also most of the arriving immigrants. Early experience suggested that good land was scarce and that most of it was near the capital, and besides the many women who had come with children gravitated towards town, or never left it. A census in 1840 found three men in South Australia for every two women, with half the men and nearly two thirds of the women and children living in Adelaide.[21] And yet there were also many who liked to work at a distance from the heart of things. German immigrants – Lutherans from Prussia whose passage had been paid by George Fife Angas – settled as market gardeners in tight communities at Klemzig, 4 miles down river from Adelaide, and at Hahndorf, 14 miles to the south-west. By 1842 some were already in the Barossa valley, 30 miles away. Squatters used land on the lower Murray, close to the Port Phillip district of New South Wales. And the rougher parts of the Adelaide Hills were inhabited by escaped and former convicts from the penal colonies. In January 1840 the *South Australian Register* said that of the twenty-five prisoners currently awaiting trial in the Supreme Court all but five were transportees.[22] Such men called the hills 'the Tiers', a name used for high country in Van Diemen's Land. This coastal country, in spite of the dreams of the systematic colonisers, was still an extension of Bass Strait. By the same token firearms were not only brought to Adelaide by sea. They also came overland, with parties from the east armed against Aboriginal attack. South Australia was not the moral citadel its founders had hoped for.

On the other hand South Australians could not always blame outsiders for the breakdown of peace and high principle. The large number of family men and women now arriving in both New South Wales and South Australia was meant to make violence irrelevant to social life. But families nourished their own kind of brutality. Between 1836 and 1841, throughout the mainland colonies, nine women were charged with killing their newborn babies, six in New South Wales and three in South Australia. All were unmarried. Infanticide was a crime little known within the mainland penal system.[23] Among convict women childbirth, with or without marriage, had always been common and there was no punishment beyond being sent to one of the female factories, where mother and child, though parted early, were looked after by government. Only one of the six mothers charged in New South Wales was a convict and in her case the baby's death was clearly an accident. Among immigrant women, on the other hand, motherhood without marriage was often a deep source of shame. One of the women charged in South Australia belonged to the German community at Klemzig, a people tightly knit, devout, and severe – as virtuous as Charlotte Barton's swallows. Another was a settler's daughter, nineteen years old, who with her two younger sisters had cut her baby's throat.[24]

Not only marriage, but also a woman's livelihood depended on her reputation. Mary Ann Atkin, a free servant in Melbourne, looked pregnant, but she denied it until a neighbour's dog, exploring an empty posthole, found the body of a new-born baby girl. It had been beaten about the head with something like a piece of wood. Onlookers heard Mary Ann say as she stood among them, desperate to avoid suspicion, that 'whoever had done the deed ought to be hanged'. But eyes turned to her, she was medically examined, and finally confessed.[25]

She was obviously guilty but the case was dismissed. There was no useful evidence, according to the chief justice, because confession had been given under duress and everything else was circumstantial. Throughout the colonies most infanticide trials ended thus, the courts refusing to inflict the extreme punishment allowed. Judges might think, as one of them said himself, that killing one's own offspring was 'a crime the most horrible and revolting in its nature'.[26] But it was hard not to be sympathetic when the crime had been caused by the dictates of conscience. It was also hard to escape the fact (though it might hide in silence at the back of one's mind) that most of the aims of civilised, reflecting society – food, comfort, safety – were underpinned by violence.

II

W.H. Leigh, a ship's surgeon visiting South Australia in the late 1830s, woke up one winter morning to a fatal drama. '[O]n turning my eyes on the floor as I lay in bed,' so he later told his diary, 'I saw an enormous tarantula [a spider] marching majestically along'. His first thought was to destroy it, but then:

> I saw a scorpion in full chace of him. Watching them still, I beheld, to my great amusement, the scorpion overtake the gentleman who was so cavalierly walking the course, and jostle up against him to provoke the caitiff to combat. No sooner was that done than a deadly battle ensued … The tarantula worked his mandibles in fine style, and the scorpion slewed around his tail with wonderful agility. I could see that he whipped the sting into him so deep, it was almost beyond his strength to extract it; in the mean time, writhing with agony, but with uncommon strength, the tarantula tumbled him over and over savagely. I began to wonder which would gain the battle – when lo! Another black scorpion issued from a crack in the floor, and came up 'nine knots an hour' to the field. I now saw the poor tarantula stood little chance.

The sting of the second scorpion ended it all. The two victors 'were walking off together', said Leigh, 'when I entered the field, and gently embracing the dear creatures, put them carefully, with the dead chief, into my *bottle* of *preserves*'.[27]

Leigh made a joke of his story, but his feelings were engaged all the same. The struggle, he said, 'must have been dreadful for the combatants'.

For a similar but different type of narrative go to Louisa Meredith, as she tells of walking in the bush during a journey across the Blue Mountains from Sydney. She found no fighting.

> Strange birds [she said] were fluttering and whistling in the trees; thousands of grasshoppers, large and small, leaped up wherever I went, tumbling down again in their helpless way, with all their legs abroad, and taking a few seconds to gather themselves into place again for a fresh jump; myriads of ants, of various sizes and species, were as busy as ants always are, running hither and thither, up and down the smooth-barked gum trees, in long lines reaching from the ground far beyond my sight into the tall branches.[28]

Mrs Meredith found among the insects a benign peace. Leigh's creatures killed for the joy of it. Hers, and she felt for them too, led a life in which each individual went about its work, bumbling, gentle, and busy. She trod among them in a similar spirit whereas Leigh, in the end, gathered up for his own purposes the living and the dead.

The planning of settlement in Australia, from colony to colony and here and there within each, engaged many minds. Anyone who reflected on the best ways of ordering society here, or anywhere else, had to use their imagination very much as these two did. The problems were more complex. But still creatures were to be envisaged caught up in a pattern of moral

Louisa Anne Meredith,
a photograph probably
taken in the early 1860s by
Bishop Francis Nixon.

Reproduction courtesy of Allport Library
and Museum of Fine Arts, Hobart

imperatives, dealing with each other for a variety of ends within a visionary fabric of good and evil. Leigh saw in his three characters a little cameo
of aggression and loyalty. Louisa Meredith dreamt of quiet industry, as if
within some well-run household. The contrast was one between impulse
and principle, and in thinking about principle Mrs Meredith, like many
others in her day, was interlinking habits of work. Good labour was reliable labour, labour shaped by obedience, foresight, and self-respect. Her
ants apparently had habits of reflection. The two great companies and the
projects at Swan River and in South Australia all depended on an adequate
and predictable workforce, men and women 'as busy as ants always are'.
It was important that the supply of labour should match the demand, that
immigrants should focus their ambitions on the spot, marry and put down
roots. Too many men would lower wages, plunging all into poverty. Too
few would send wages up and halt investment. The Swan River settlers and
the two companies had tried to solve the problem with long-term indentures, but in South Australia the answer seemed to lie with better planning.

South Australian employers took conventional precautions all the same
(Chapter 5). The third law passed, within a week of settlement being proclaimed, was designed to enforce workplace agreements, and masters made
good use of it. To begin with labour was too scarce. Capital poured into
the building of Adelaide and workmen were in high demand. They were
keen to sell their labour to the highest bidder, by so that by spring 1837
broken work agreements were a 'daily occurrence', and magistrates struggled to cope with the number of men sent in for trial.[29]

Also, men and women were sometimes sick. In New South Wales and
Van Diemen's Land hospitals had been an obvious aspect of government
and anyone might be admitted, whether they could pay for it or not. Even
in Western Australia the hospital, though makeshift, was managed on this
principle. Among human beings self-reliance was to be hedged about with
fatherly providence, and good fathers are people of conscience. Patients in
Perth were asked to pay (in weekly instalments) only after they had been
released, and some never paid at all. Other cases of hardship were dealt
with on their merits. Sarah Day, for instance, had three children, an absent
husband, apparently a sailor, and an injury of some kind that stopped her
working. Her man had left her with only a shilling a week but government
added a little to help her through.[30] In South Australia Captain Hindmarsh, the Governor, wanted to use the same principles of government welfare, arguing for instance that the colonial surgeon, Thomas Young Cotter,
should care for the poor whether they could pay or not. But Cotter himself
thought like the systematic colonisers. The poor must learn to support
themselves, he said, even in emergency. It was their own consciences that
mattered, not those of their superiors. This was part of their training in
civility. Under the same rubric public institutions should depend as much
as possible on the voluntary efforts of the people.[31] In Adelaide a hospital,

a mud hut, was built by government very early but no money was put aside for it. A report in 1838 found that its operation depended on 'casual charity even for the daily support of those patients who have been from time to time admitted'.[32]

For Hindmarsh the conventional power of governors was the lynchpin of society. Working men and women might well agree. Having been brought to this part of the world with high hopes, they believed they had a right to look to him in their disappointment. But Young thought that men should make their own way forward independent of their superiors. Those who failed fell outside his vision, because only the deserving poor were members of his good community. In June 1838, for instance, he published in the *Southern Australian* an address 'To the Working Classes of South Australia'. His readers, he told them, belonged to a 'splendid scheme of Colonization', and it was up to them to rise to the opportunities placed before them. They must no longer 'live from hand to mouth, spending your earnings in reckless extravagance'. They must plan their lives, 'adopting habits of economy and forethought' and scorning the charity of the state. He suggested a 'Medical Club' funded by themselves, a type of benefit society on which they could depend in times of ill health.[33]

Cotter's was the way of the future everywhere. The third Governor of South Australia, George Grey, struggled with serious unemployment during 1841–42, during an economic crisis of unprecedented severity that affected all the colonies. He provided labour for unemployed men but, unlike Hindmarsh, he insisted that their claims to payment must depend entirely on the work they did.[34] In New South Wales Sir George Gipps, Governor from 1838, reformed the system by which all Aborigines in contact with settlement were given a blanket each year, a tacit acknowledgement of the great fact of dispossession. Just as assisted immigrants felt a sense of entitlement, the Blacks thought that they had a right to blankets. The Governor wanted them to learn that only work gave them rights.[35]

Talking itself depends on the mix of impulse and conscience, of patterning and surprise. Everywhere among the Europeans in Australia the right to speak one's mind and the power to talk well made up the best expression of liberty – liberty at least as understood by men. Charles Brown, a convict, argued with his mistress, asking her, so she said, 'if I wished to lock his lips'. Despite his bondage, he believed that he had a right to speak 'where and when he thought proper'. 'I have freedom of speech', declared Richard Roberts, a young man, native-born, during a heated conversation in Sydney. You do, said his friends, but there was no need to shout. 'I have a peculiar kind of voice,' he replied, 'and sometimes it echoes'.[36] By this time William Charles Wentworth had made his name in Sydney as an unrivalled public speaker. His voice echoed too, but to better effect than Roberts'. Wentworth now had an established following, especially among former convicts who had made a little money. Men who were still in bondage looked to Hall of the *Monitor* to defend them. But among those who had done their time – who could defy authority – the sound of Wentworth was sheer delight.

Wentworth spoke for men who were in a position to pay taxes, and who wanted a voice as to how much they paid. He had no interest in convict grievances. In fact, he wanted convict rights cut back, with heavier penalties for runaways and for men who would not inform on each other.[37] He was not always a man of delicate conscience. The rights of free men, men with control over their lives, were another matter. During the 1830s the campaign continued in New South Wales for an elected legislature and a great meeting was held in Sydney in January 1833 to demand an assembly. The cause now enjoyed wide support. As the *Sydney Herald* pointed out, there were 'not two men in the Colony who do not perceive the advantages that might be derived from a House of Assembly'. But how many of these supporters might have been called 'reflecting'? For how many was this a matter of conscience and of moral standing? There were questions, for instance, as to whether a criminal past should limit a man's right to vote or to be elected. The principal reformers ignored such fine points, leaving the campaign perfectly uncomplicated by moral issues.[38]

The wished-for assembly would be a forum in which the leaders of public opinion might contend with government, and such leaders were now, it seemed, numerous, respectable, ready, willing, and able. Many who supported reform hoped to cut back the cost of government, which by now was borne on local taxes. Many again were provoked by the policies of Governor Bourke, who seemed too gentle in managing the penal system. An elected assembly might insist on rigorous discipline.[39] In fact officials at Whitehall blocked reform precisely because they refused to hand over convict management to local politicians. They did not trust to local conscience and no elective system was to come, in fact, until transportation ended.

The meeting also interested James Macarthur, who aimed to use it in more subtle ways. Two petitions had been drawn up beforehand, for submission to the King and to the House of Commons. Sir John Jamison, former president of the Agricultural Society, proposed the first, but when he was on the point of moving its adoption Macarthur rose from his seat. He asked his listeners to think more carefully about the obstacles and advantages of the business. He had in his pocket a plan for a 'General Committee', a body of varied views and with time and skill to deliberate on the best way to achieve what he called 'a more efficient and popular Legislature'. It was to be a kind of institutionalised collective conscience. He wanted local leaders to take the burden of policy on themselves and at the same time to hunt for the kind of middle way that might have some chance of succeeding at Whitehall.[40] Wentworth's aims were antagonistic. Macarthur's aims were cooperative. He thought of the colony itself as a moral enterprise in which various interests might be gathered to a common end. From a local point of view Macarthur, like Horne Tooke and Hobbes Scott, believed that the well read and conscientious ought to provide the basis on which the people at large might build. Wentworth was happy to castigate British ministers, but he would have left the work to them.

Here was a drama that summed up, for any observant historian – then or now – some of the great issues of the day. But a mass of noise, fumbling and elegant, coarse and ephemeral, made its impact too. Macarthur's voice was thin, his manner courtly, and this audience had come for stronger stuff. He sat down to hisses and shouts of 'Question!', Jamison began again and was again cut short. The sheriff now suggested from the chair that it was not prudent to accuse the Secretary of State of telling lies, and Wentworth leapt to his feet – entering the field like the second scorpion. Amid 'tremendous cheering' he turned on the sheriff: 'We ... do not come here to solicit your advice. You are the mere shadow of this meeting, and have exceeded your duty.' The next speech was his own. He filled it with jokes about their British masters ('The Secretary of State has become too habituated to fingering our money'); about local officials (they vote annually 'a large sum of money out of our pockets into their own') and about the Church ('Gentlemen, do any of you know the use of an Archdeacon?'). Whitehall had appointed a commercial representative at the Bay of Islands, whose salary was paid from Sydney. 'This gentleman may be sent to New Zealand', declared Wentworth to the wide-eyed crowd, 'to strut about in his uniform and be stared at by the savages – they may make a roast of him for all I care – *(loud laughter)* – but why should £500 a year of our money be voted into his pockets without our consent?' After all this – a continuous rush of oratorical power met with waves of laughter and cheers – the master sat down, as the reporters put it, 'much fatigued'.[41]

For months the petitions were carried around for signature and were at last sent off with more than six thousand names. The member of parliament who took charge of the petition to the House of Commons suggested a permanent pressure group and the Australian Patriotic Association was formed in May 1835. Though unelected and expensive to join (at £1 per annum), the association looked like a little parliament, with members debating whatever they liked and with forms of etiquette like Westminster itself. To the optimistic eye it was 'our now firmly established COLONIAL HOUSE OF ASSEMBLY'. During its career it included a rainbow of opinion – not only liberal reformers like Wentworth but also sometime admirers of Governor Darling and radicals new from Britain. In December 1835 it sent Home two alternative constitutions for the colony. But nothing came of either and by 1838 the association had collapsed.[42]

Ideas of combining like this, of summing up in political form the variety of colonial life and of doing something truly historic, were also obvious in Van Diemen's Land. The Political Association was formed in Hobart, similarly designed to push for a new constitution, to 'represent the Colonists to the Local Government' and to debate the future.[43] As in Sydney, its members included not only old leaders but also newly arrived radicals. The men and women coming in such large numbers to all four colonies included many inspired by new ideas about public order and ready to ask fundamental questions, including questions of conscience, for this part of the world. The secretary of the Political Association and its guiding light was Thomas Horne, said to be a relative of Horne Tooke. It was probably thanks to Horne that membership of the association was open to all and free of charge. And on the other hand it was probably lack of funds that caused it to die early.[44]

The people in Adelaide also made much of their public meetings and here, too, gatherings drew together a variety of types in great conflicts of principle and in tangled patterns of speech and gesture. Governor Grey's attempts to solve South Australia's economic problems were much debated and a stormy meeting was held in the theatre at Adelaide in February 1842. A labouring man named Worthy Nicholls, amid 'great uproar, cheers, hisses, cries of "order", &c.', demanded the Governor's resignation. Grey was inexperienced and badly informed, he said, while he (Nicholls) knew what he was talking about – 'He had worked through a cotton factory, and afterwards in a sweep's cellar; but he had since learnt to disprove the principles of the rich and educated.' A few books of the right kind, such as Thomas Paine's *Rights of Man*, had given him insight superior, he thought, to that of men who had been reading all their lives. He received some encouragement from one man of his own kind, but the meeting was managed by the well read. Nicholls obviously resented not only their authority but also their style – the ease with which they put their message across and the way they forced on him the conventions of debate. 'He was no speaker [himself]', joked Nathaniel Hailes, in moving the third resolution, 'and, in fact, had he been, Mr Nicholls would have taken the *shine* out of him'. Nicholls stood up again at the end with angry words about the local press, which ought to have done more, he said, to explain and promote 'the universal rights of man'. They had been seduced from their duty by 'large land[ed] possessions and many other interests they have in the colony'. Printed truth and the power of conscience had been enfeebled, he thought, by greed.[45]

Freedom of speech was all very well. As Nicholls accidentally proved, it could do little without being organised. A small number of associations made up of men with opinions more or less like his – men, that is, who thought they knew better than the well read – appeared from time to time in this part of the world. In every case the idea was to raise up some fundamental principle against the selfishness and violence of those in power. Impermeable and obvious on the printed page, these ideas were to be fixed – so their proponents hoped – in the daily round, spreading a golden influence abroad. There were meetings, for instance, in humble rooms in Clarence Street, Sydney, of the 'Colonial Society for the advancement of the

Social System, as propounded by Robert Owen'. Owen, an Englishman, taught that self-reliance had its roots in community life, in common kindness and the better sharing of wealth. Here, indeed, was a regime of conscience. Among other things, the founder had worked out plans for 'Villages of Unity and Mutual Cooperation' and he set up one himself, called 'New Harmony', in the United States. A Sydney Owenite, or Socialist, boasted of having been in 'constant attendance' on the great man for three years in England – 'I took great pleasure in calling him father, for he was more than *father* to many of us'. The Clarence Street group tried hard to spread the word, but with limited success.[46]

And yet such views, or something like them, might be found among 'the rich and educated' too (though providing differently for the uses of power). The concern for rebuilding on firm and certain principles was everywhere, from Adelaide, the dream city of the systematic colonisers, to Port Stephens, where the Australian Agricultural Company still hoped to combine virtue and profit. The imaginings of Charlotte Barton – her tableau of mother and father swallow and 'their tender little ones' – was the same thing writ small.

III

When men and women in Europe made up their minds in the first place to come to Australia they took a step that might be a means of improving and even saving their lives. But the risks were high. During the long voyage out they were very much in the hand of God. They knew about shipwrecks. They might also have known how easy it was for disease to sweep through a vessel, carrying off the children in particular. Fragile lives were more fragile at sea. When Clarinda Parkes stepped on board the *Strathfieldsaye* at Gravesend in March 1839 with her husband Henry, an ivory turner, she was heavily pregnant.[47] They had given up first Birmingham and then London as places where he might find work. London impressed them only with its noise and filth. She had never been to sea before, she had already lost two babies and the chances of safe childbirth on board must have seemed small. She took that step in order to save what she had. 'I am very glad we are going', she said, 'for I believe if we were to stay in London it would kill Henry outright in a short time'.[48]

On decisions of this kind were built the European communities in Australia. Breaking with the convict past, gathering instead such a mass of people as would change the character of the place – this revolution depended on the decisions of the poor, on the way in which they pieced together ideas of an improved existence. They had to weigh advantage and disadvantage, risk and probability, chances in the short term and chances in the long term, their attachment to kin, both here and there. In thinking matters through

Henry Parkes himself was careful not to talk to 'private individuals' who had been in the country. He had an obsessive reverence for the written word and he put his faith entirely in official, printed information. Others worked differently. Briefly in England, James Macarthur spoke to a party of assisted emigrants embarking at Bristol. '[T]hey were well satisfied', he said, 'that it was a good country to go to', and they told him they had come to this conclusion by reading letters sent home by convicts.[49]

Many well-read men and women were intrigued to think that the choices of the poor might be fundamental to society. Indeed, such choices had always mattered in Australia. The convicts certainly had had no choice in coming and, once here, they might fumble from bad to worse, as the murderers of John Brackfield did. But there were many whose instincts, obvious in their speech and expressions, matched the schemes of men and women in power. The Macarthurs themselves had in their employment one of the largest bodies of convict men to be found anywhere. Their system of management had been carefully worked out over many years – 'where a man behaves well [we] make him forget, if possible, that he is a convict'.[50] This was prudent from the employers' point of view because it made men more productive. But it also improved the way they made up their minds.

The decisions of women mattered too, a fact recognised most clearly in New South Wales, where women had always been central to the purposes of the state.[51] It was a point reinforced by some governors' wives. During 1800–06 Anna King had gathered ladies about her, especially in managing the Female Orphan School. Elizabeth Macquarie's power had been even more obvious. Less interested than Mrs King in the affairs of women, she had managed all the same to add to the womanly tone of government. In the early 1820s Ann Cowper, wife of the Sydney chaplain, and Jane Wemyss, wife of the deputy commissary-general, ran a sewing school for the daughters of the poor. With such skills they hoped that girls could make their own way and take their choice of husbands. Mrs Wemyss, said to be the cleverest of Sydney's ladies, was also interested in the work of Lancelot Threlkeld among the Aborigines. Since she managed much of her husband's life it may also have been thanks to her that William Wemyss found places in the commissariat for young native-born men.[52] Individuals like Jane Wemyss thought that the reasoning and consciences of women mattered in the world and that their ambitions might justifiably shape those of everyone else.

In Sydney the ladies' heyday came with Governor Darling's wife, Eliza. Mrs Darling worked with the Female Orphan School, the Female Factory at Parramatta (a ladies' committee and sewing classes), and the Benevolent Society (caring for women in childbirth). She began a Female Friendly Society (a kind of savings bank for poor women, including convicts) and on her advice the Governor founded the Sydney Dispensary, which gave medical advice to the poor.[53] But the Female School of Industry, which trained and educated the daughters of the poor, was Mrs Darling's main interest.

'[S]orely against my good will [she] has appointed me Treasurer & Secretary', remarked Fanny Macleay, daughter of the colonial secretary (the Governor's leading official), 'I am very angry, Papa well pleased'.[54] The school was run by ladies and depended wholly on voluntary donations, nearly half of them from women. Government surgeons and clergy (and some clergy wives) had always worked this way in Sydney, cooperating with governors' wives in schemes of public welfare. The Sydney Dispensary and the lying-in arrangements at the Benevolent Society both depended on medical expertise. And all charities were kept alive by the pastoral work of the clergy, who had a duty to bring the poor to the attention of the rich.[55]

In Van Diemen's Land there was little of this feminised form of government. Ladies there had long been scarce. Mrs Davey and Mrs Arthur, the first two wives at Government House, both kept to their drawing rooms. As for clergy, the mainland had Samuel Marsden, William Cowper, and other evangelical Anglicans, all building bridges between government and private life, as well as Thomas Hobbes Scott. But in Van Diemen's Land the Reverend Robert Knopwood had no large ideas and William Bedford, senior chaplain during the 1820s, was ineffectual. In both colonies there were newspapers managed by devout and philanthropic men. But Hobart and Launceston had nothing like E.S. Hall's *Monitor*, a paper which made much of the good works of women (Chapter 3). Public power in Van Diemen's Land had a military, masculinist simplicity, and officials tended to disregard 'the weaker sex'. With all his ambition, George Arthur made no effort to duplicate the female authority to be found to the north.

The Arthurs were succeeded in 1836 by Sir John and Lady Franklin. Jane Franklin was an avid reader and traveller and she made Hobart a bright focus of intellectual life. The Natural History Society (afterwards the Royal Society of Tasmania) and Christ's College were her work. But, thanks partly to old island habits, success like Mrs Darling's was beyond her. Her attempts to improve the lives of women convicts were a complete failure. She needed more tact, but she also needed, as she said herself, 'such a power as must silence objections, and bear down opposition, and override prejudice'. The newspapers in Hobart set her up as proof of the evils of female authority, while her husband's officials offered politeness – 'the outward semblance', as she called it, 'of readiness and civility' – but no more.[56] Most important, she failed to change the habits of the Van Diemen's Land gentry who, unlike those in New South Wales, rarely joined forces for the good of the poor.[57]

Besides, Lady Franklin came too late. During the 1830s, even before her time in Van Diemen's Land, the empire underwent great changes in the style and purpose of public life. The suggestion that ladies might be part of good government was suddenly less convincing. The principles of free enterprise also made rapid headway so that more was now left to the unaided individual, whether rich or poor. Poor men in particular were less eager to lean on the power of gentlemen and they looked even less to gen-tlewomen. More was heard of Worthy Nicholls' resentment of 'the rich and educated' and more, too, of his idea that labourers must train themselves to outwit the rich. At the same time the great surge of paper that had begun in the early 1820s, the bureaucratic tide on which Darling and Arthur had been lifted to power, had begun to fall away. In the early 1830s the num-ber of letters passing between Whitehall and Sydney – where there was a new Governor (Richard Bourke) – dropped again by a quarter. The same happened among officials within the colony. In the ten years from 1836 the European population in New South Wales was to double, and yet the number of reports and requests posted to government headquarters hardly changed at all.[58]

There was a new understanding of the way individuals ought to work and live together, a new scheme for social life, new methods of reflection. Power, including the power of conscience, was to be more dispersed. Government was to be less self-sufficient and less centralised. Whitehall had been briefly seen as a steam engine turning wheels worldwide. But even in Australia, where the penal system continued to demand some such effi-ciency, this vision seems to have failed. By the end of his time (1831) Darling's system had clogged at its heart, making him, in the words of William Macarthur, 'a weak and most ineffective ruler'.[59] Throughout the empire there were already new ideas about the way in which methods of communication ought to shape society. It was no longer all-important that great quantities of detail should flow in a settled pattern among officials, moving especially towards the executive. Instead, the most telling traffic was of a more intricate and glittering kind. The gathering of information continued (Chapter 10), but it was now hunted up in a multiplicity of ways, drawn even from the mouths of the lowest of the low. The visit by the Quakers James Backhouse and George Washington Walker to all the colonies in 1832–38 was typical. Men of a new age and unaccountable to government, their methods were very different from those of Com-missioner Bigge. As George Arthur said, they 'took means of acquiring information, which persons usually resorting to the colony had never thought of before'. They went everywhere on foot and they talked to every-one, gathering from the convicts, in particular, 'a great fund' of detail.[60]

From now on society was to be considered not as a hierarchy, either feu-dal or bureaucratic, but as a network of points – points, as it were, on a horizontal plain, on a map, points whose main dimension was geography. Its lifeblood was to be private travel, newspapers, and letters, altogether a kind of social electricity moving, as Rowland Hill desired, quickly, easily, and with a wonderful life of its own.

Efficiency depended not just on speed but once again on style. Facility was everything. Wisdom must be succinct. Hill himself wrote beautifully and Wakefield's liquid wit was part of the reason for his sudden success.

Charles Dickens' first book, *The Pickwick Papers* (1836) – full of brilliant talking – was an immediate bestseller. The new methods of literary expression were shaped by journalism. Words must sell quickly. Among Europeans everywhere the uses of print were expanding beyond imagination. 'At no former era has Literature, the printed communication of Thought, been of such importance as it is now', said Thomas Carlyle. This meant that moral truth no longer resided in ancient authority. 'The true Church of England', Carlyle said, 'at this moment, lies in the Editors of its [England's] Newspapers'. Between 1801 and 1851 the number of newspapers purchased per head in Britain more than tripled. Already in 1827 every ship reaching Hobart from Europe was said to carry 3000 of them. As a Sydney editor remarked, it was impossible to keep up with readers' demand for 'correct information on *trifling* occurrences of the day'.[61]

There were more adventurous ways of gathering news and of writing it up. '[B]lended anecdote, narration and instruction' was the recipe for success among public speakers, as one of them said, and likewise in print. All kinds of information must be made saleable, breaking through the surface of events and laying souls open – going to the marrow of common life, so that readers might see their own personalities, or something like them, reflected in print. Press reporters must use a racier style than their predecessors, 'manlier and more philosophical', so they boasted, a style of 'warmth and substance', picturing human beings of all kinds, 'endowed with passions and struggling with ills'.[62]

How much was to be trusted to a small number of the very best brains? Even in South Australia, a community born of intellectual principle ('systematic colonisation') there were worries on this point. George Stevenson of the *South Australian Gazette* spoke with scorn of those who went on about 'the Principles of the Colony'. They 'delude themselves and their silly followers by extravagant dreamings of some republican Utopia – "the freest of the free" – which has never existed but in their own distempered imaginations'. He wanted something more well-worn, rich, and kind. In New South Wales, James Macarthur spoke fiercely of those who tried to make human beings fit some intellectual pattern, and he was thinking of the systematic colonisers. Even 'the conqueror in his career of bloodshed' was moved by a nobler impulse, Macarthur said, than mere ideologists, who 'contemplate with indifference and even with satisfaction the ruin of thousands, rather than give up one jot or title of a hypothetical theory'.[63] Such disenchantment was typical of the middle decades of the nineteenth century. The outlook of ladies (hesitantly expressed) and the new journalism (carrying all before it) offered two alternatives. The latter especially was shot through with streetwise irony. Both felt for the complexity of daily life, its colour and feeling.

Established law, the conventions governing meetings, habits, and speech, and, overlapping with all of these, the power of conscience, were fundamental to most common ambition. Everyone, in fact, wanted predictability such as Mrs Meredith found among the interlinking lives of the bush. There might be disagreements as to what the right principles were and how they should shape actions and voices. But the disagreements themselves were part of the shaping.

Consider the adventure of Mary Maloney and Sarah McGregor. Both arrived in New South Wales as convicts in 1831. Mary was eighteen and born in County Clare, Ireland. Sarah was sixteen and born in Liverpool. Mary had a stormy temper and was tattooed on her left arm. Sarah, a children's nurse, looked more docile but she was also easily angered. Both were good-looking – 'extremely pretty', by one account – with ruddy complexions and brown hair, and neither was much more than 5 feet tall. These were details that were to add to their celebrity.[64] They were assigned as servants in the same household, near Illawarra's brilliant blue coast, south of Sydney, and they became close friends. Their duties included washing the verandah each morning and, with the approval of their mistress, Jemima Waldron, they took it in turns.

Mrs Waldron was herself newly arrived, but her life was different. Sarah and Mary had nothing but their friendship, and that depended on the exigencies of the convict system. Mrs Waldron had the settled affection of her family, good property, and high connections. Captain Waldron, a gentleman-settler, was (so she said herself) 'the best of husbands, fathers, and masters'. They had twelve children and they were building up a freehold estate.[65] And yet, as Louisa Meredith might have put it, Mrs Waldron had her 'household foes'. Something about her husband made him hated by their convicts, men and women.

On a summer morning in 1834 Jemima Waldron emerged from her dressing room into the hard early sunlight, a little weak from her latest childbirth. She found the captain smoking on the verandah and he 'rejoiced', as she later put it, 'at seeing me rejoin the family breakfast table'. Mistress once again, she remarked that the verandah had not been washed. Sarah said she had done it and Mary, suddenly passionate, backed her up. But 'my husband', Mrs Waldron said, 'overhearing what passed, called out, Jemima, don't let them persuade you it has been done, as I will take my oath water has not been on it'. There was a violent argument – the two girls had had rum before breakfast – and Captain Waldron followed them back to the kitchen. There, as he leant against the doorpost, his pipe in his hand, he told Mary that her language was so bad that she must go off for punishment. Sarah shouted, 'if Mary goes I will go too; we came together, and we will go together'. To make sure of this result she ran at the captain and hit him on the neck.[66]

Waldron, 'a very thin spare man', was taken by surprise. He fell hard on the paving outside and the girls set upon him with their fists, like the black ants around Mrs Barton's purple beetle. Mrs Waldron called for help, amid 'the cries of my children who flocked around me', and in her weakness made what she called 'a feeble effort to go towards him'. None of the convict men moved and the captain was rescued at last by his twelve-year-old son. Meanwhile Sarah (once again in Mrs Waldron's words) 'made her way to my daughter's bedroom window, in which she broke three panes of glass; my daughter jumped from her bed, and begged for her life'. Given to apoplexy, the master had a stroke and was dead in a fortnight.[67]

The two were tried for murder. The case caused enormous interest and the courtroom was packed with onlookers drawn partly by the youth and beauty of the accused and partly by the sad figure of Jemima Waldron, who gave her evidence dressed in black and carrying her baby. The judge, William Westbrooke Burton, told the jury that a verdict of murder depended on whether the victim's death was due mainly to his being beaten or mainly to his stroke. The jury decided on the first, the judge told them to reconsider, the jury stood fast and Burton at last reached for his black cap. Mary, both before and after the trial, according to the reporter of the *Gazette*, displayed 'the most disgusting levity', but Sarah was stunned. On hearing the sentence of death she collapsed in tears. She suddenly said she was pregnant and could not hang. A 'jury of matrons' (married women with knowledge of childbirth) was quickly put together and after spending half an hour with her in the jury room they emerged to say that she was indeed pregnant, but not 'with *quick* child'. The judge said this was nonsense. They retired again. Now they said she was not with child at all.[68]

The audience was divided between Mrs Waldron and the girls. Which side should the rules favour? Sarah's 'mildness of countenance' made it hard to think of her as a murderer and the 'matrons' obviously hoped to save her. When they decided against it one of them was violently accosted by a woman in the crowd. Besides, Waldron himself was said to have been 'a passionate man, and easily excited'. The girls '*must* have received some provocation', so the editor of the *Australian* (a lawyer) put it, 'which, although it could never justify them in striking their master, brings them within that merciful regulation of our laws which allows for the frailty of human nature'. 'Severe punishment these women richly deserve', said his colleague at the *Gazette*, 'but whatever feelings of indignation their atrocious conduct may excite, justice is due even to them'.[69]

In the end the sentence was reduced to three years hard labour in the Female Factory. There Mary and Sarah found that the other women, who might have pitied them had they hanged, resented the fact that they had escaped. They were deeply hurt, they said, by being taunted all the time as 'murderers'. Their experience had taught them some of the fine points of the law and of the way it was interwoven with the dictates of conscience. They had never meant to kill anyone, they said. It was hard being 'hunted like wild beasts' for a crime they never committed.[70]

PART 2

Their Method of Utterance

Naturae Amator, 'The Natural History of the Colony. – No. 3', 30 November 1840.[1]

I remarked in my last on the noise occasionally made by some of the Coleoptera [sic; in fact Hemiptera]. … I have discovered four sorts of this insect [cicadas]. The largest one is a native of some other warm countries; but the name by which naturalists distinguish it I do not remember. The three most alike in form and color live in trees, only varying in their sizes, which are nevertheless accurately defined. The fourth does not aspire above the lowly flower, and might lately have been seen in great numbers on the North Adelaide hills, keeping up without cessation its shrill cherruping noise.

With regard to the tree species, on a fine day our park lands are all alive with them – the trees themselves seem to sing and answer one-another in the fabled language of the Arabian tales, when the true cause lies concealed. When I first heard this extraordinary fly, I mistook the sound it produces for the notes of a bird. The largest-sized insect is about two inches in length, sometimes rather more. The smallest species is not quite an inch, and the remaining one is nearly between the two in size.

The first may be heard beginning with a monotonous two-syllabled note, which is repeated from six to ten or twelve times, and the only thing I think it can be compared to is the vile notes of some London hurdy-gurdy in miniature, though in truth much more musical. This challenge, as it were, is then answered by some neighbouring aspirant to vocal powers – like two game-cocks trying to out-crow each other – and at the conclusion of each strain the three species in all the adjacent trees join in with their running accompaniment or clock-work note, which in the smallest species amounts from its shrillness to an absolute hiss. These curious sounds may be heard to a great distance.

... The whirring noise which they all make in common seems to proceed from between the thorax and abdomen of these insects but though I have held in my hand at different times several of all the sorts while in the act of showing their prowess, I cannot, after the minutest scrutiny, understand their method of utterance.

Chapter 7

Men and Women

I

No one made better sketches of family life among small settlers than James Tucker, the convict author. In such imagery we glimpse the dealings of husband and wife. The hero of Tucker's story *Ralph Rashleigh* spent several nights in a loft next to a slab-and-bark farmhouse on the Hawkesbury, near Sydney, in about 1827. The house had obviously expanded over the years, to keep pace with increases in property and children, and Rashleigh found the original dirt-floored, two-roomed hut (kitchen and bedroom) ringed by lean-to additions. Parents, children, and visitors gathered, at least in winter, around a fireplace of slabs lined with clay that extended across most of one side of the kitchen. Seats were set about the hearth, 'a few rough stools, mostly fixed on stumps sunk in the floor', and there were besides, for sitting on, two or three moveable blocks of wood. A big table stood in the middle of the room and a smaller one against the wall. But the chimney drew badly and sometimes in summer, to escape the smoke, the family – as on small farms in England in earlier days – had their meals in the open air.[1]

Rashleigh looked to see what the sleeping arrangements were. He could find nothing that could be called bed linen, though there were blankets and in the parents' room a patchwork quilt, badly worn and dirty. There were no feather mattresses. '[E]ach ... slept on beds of chaff contained in rough ticks [bags], many of which, being the worse for wear, suffered their contents to escape through their numberless orifices.' Chaff littered the dirt floor and was piled in corners, making nests for fleas. The beds were made of slabs and sheets of bark, fixed to the wall like berths on a ship, and 'only the one belonging to the father and mother ... [was] furnished with any attempt at curtains, which for economy's sake were confined to the foot of the bed and one side. The berth being fixed in a corner, all was thus enclosed'. The curtains around this, the marital bed and the most elaborate piece of furniture in the house, were of blue striped 'shirting' and were tied back with ribbons, easily loosed to make a tent of privacy.[2]

About this time the magistrates at Launceston had occasion to note, from the mouth of Mary Rogers, the contents of the house nearby at Emu Plains that she shared with Thomas Grady. Living alone, with no lodgers, servants or children – and therefore no need for bed curtains – like Rashleigh's couple she and Grady possessed blankets (four) and a quilt. But they also owned a pair of sheets, and for clothes she probably did better than Rashleigh's housewife, putting on, if she liked, a different dress, stockings, cap, and apron every day of the week (and she had three irons – one 'Italian' – to smooth them with). Grady, apparently, had three pairs of trousers and four shirts. This was very desirable comfort. Another writer told of a one-roomed hut on the mainland that was the home of a Scottish couple, together with their two small children and an old convict shepherd. There was a single bunk for the family and the man slept on the floor. It was a tiny place, so the woman complained, 'mair fit for a box for a penny show at a fair, than for Christian folk to leeve in, and it was'na dacent their being so near auld Bob, wha' could'na but ken every thing that was going on'.[3]

Even in wealthy families small babies might sleep with their parents. Sophia Dumaresq and her husband Henry, Eliza Darling's brother, shared their bed with their infant son. From her home in Sydney Mrs Dumaresq wrote to an English friend about Henry's midnight kindness:

> Whenever his boy wakes during the night which he usually does 2 or 3 times for me to nurse him, Col[onel] Dumaresq takes him and holds him out [above the chamber pot], wh[ich] the young man quite understands and immediately performs what is required of him. Where would you find another Papa to do as much[?][4]

And on the other hand, some married women chose to sleep quite alone. Annie Baxter, a gentleman-squatter's wife, thought it a type of prostitution to share her bed with her husband, who had proved himself a brute by lying with Aboriginal women. She advised a friend who had similarly suffered to do as she did, or in other words to reject her husband's embraces. 'I *could* not consent to place myself', she said, 'in the most intoxicating, rapturous position, with a wretch who had so far ill-treated, [and] abused me!'[5]

What of marriages where couples had no choice but to spend both days and nights, even over many years, at a distance? 'Catherine my dear you are my own / my heart lies in your heart' – so Edward Kennedy, a Scottish ploughman, said of his wife at the moment of his being transported. It was a message to himself rather than to her, since it was tattooed on his right arm. 'Constant and true I will prove', the tattoo went on, 'for now and for ever more'.[6] Kennedy may have promised too much because with the best will in the world exile for years or for ever to such a remote place could bring even the best love to an end. Many said it amounted to divorce. In other words, marriages made at Home must cease in law when husband or wife was sent to the Antipodes. After all, marriage meant living together. It meant sharing bed and board – 'my heart lies in your heart' must have some palpable reality. When intimacy was forever destroyed then surely marriage no longer existed? But this understanding was at odds both with Church doctrine and with the great nineteenth-century scheme of empire. The dominions ruled from Whitehall were now understood to be a single community worldwide and it was therefore necessary to identify, with crystal clarity, all the subjects of the Crown wherever they might be. Identity, especially for women, included marital condition. Men and women who were British subjects were no longer to be allowed to make and remake their names and their civil commitments beyond the gaze of government. Dealings between men and women might be hidden, say, behind unloosed blue-striped curtains. But they must also be exposed by the red-tape of ubiquitous empire.

The strengthening of administrative ties from one hemisphere to the other during the time of Governor Darling, Governor Arthur, and the settlement at Swan River – the 1820s – also made it possible, at least in theory, to bind labourers here by promises made in England (Chapter 5). In the same way officials could now insist that marriages were made for life, though the partners might live at opposite ends of the earth. (As yet there were no laws for divorce.) All convicts, male and female, were asked about their marital state when their ships weighed anchor in Port Jackson or the Derwent, and their replies – written down on the spot as part of the 'convict indent' – were held against them should they apply as convicts to marry here. If, according to the indent, they were already bound by law in Britain or Ireland then they must produce a letter or some other piece of paper to show that their first spouse was now dead.[7]

This exacting approach might have strange results. Robert Simpson and Ann Durrant were both convicted at Aberdeen, in Scotland, and both sentenced to fourteen years transportation. Simpson called himself, among other things, a 'lapidary', or cutter of gemstones. He was also known as 'Robert Smart' and 'John Duncan' and he had been convicted twice before. According to the indent, he was brown-haired, brown-eyed, and ruddy (facts more certain than his name). Ann Durrant had been born in the East Indies and was possibly a soldier's daughter. She had dark brown hair, hazel eyes, and pale skin. Her face was scarred with small-pox and her left arm was tattooed with 'ADIDHD' (possibly her parents' initials with her own). She had been married to a sailor named Brown, long since drowned, and had three children. For a time she and Simpson had lived together in Aberdeen. They had been sentenced together for receiving stolen goods and, although they came in different ships, they soon found each other again in New South Wales.[8]

They had some early trouble. Simpson was sentenced to a road gang and his ticket of leave was put back four years. But ten years after leaving

Scotland he managed a boat on the Parramatta River and they had a house nearby. Transportation for such couples was only a phase in the interweaving of intimacy and distance that shapes every lifetime love affair. With age both had changed. Ann's hair was grey and Robert now went to church and worried about living in sin. According to the Presbyterian minister who sent in their application for leave to marry (both were still convicts), 'his demeanour has been so christianlike that I would have admitted him to our communion had he not made known this preventive circumstance'. The application was debated in the colonial secretary's office with some relish for its logical complexities. According to the indent, both the man and the woman had said when they got here that they were already married, but they had clearly not been married to each other. Her name was given as 'Ann Durrant, or Brown', and she said she had three children while he said he had none. We may guess in fact that, like many such convict couples, these two had said they were married because they felt married. All they wanted now was that this old, settled affection should receive the blessing of the Church. However, the final decision in Sydney forbade it, on the grounds that one or both must be married already to somebody else. [9]

For some couples movement to the Antipodes and life thereafter was a shared adventure. George and Margaret Stevenson arrived with the first Governor of South Australia, John Hindmarsh, in 1836. George was Hindmarsh's secretary, clerk of council, and editor of the *South Australian Gazette*. Margaret had produced books with her late husband, the assistant editor of the London *Globe*, a paper on which George had also worked. They were newly married and on the way out they kept a joint diary, clearly believing, like many avante-garde couples, that marriage was the pairing of equal minds. Sometimes Margaret wrote about George – his conclusion, for instance, within a month of landing, that in South Australia 'all the trees ... incline to the north east' because of the prevailing winds. With such knowledge (learnt, she said, from American Indians) no one should get lost. Sometimes George wrote about Margaret. She had been upset by the proclamation he composed for Hindmarsh on the subject of the Aborigines – 'My Wife, whose interest in the Aborigines is great, thinks it profanation to put such serious language into the mouth of a swearing & totally irreligious person like the Governor.'[10]

In January 1836, a month after their arrival, the Stevensons visited the South Australian Company's headquarters on Kangaroo Island. The local manager was Samuel Stephens, who in England had been assistant to George Fife Angas. Highly regarded by Angas, Stephens was out of his depth giving orders in a new settlement. Worse, he had lately married Charlotte Beare, widowed mother of his superintendent of buildings and a woman obviously beneath him in rank and education. The Governor asked George Stevenson to investigate, but it was Margaret who entered their conclusions in the diary. Having worked already within two productive marriages, she had an eye for intimacy:

Mrs Stephens [she said] is a tall raw boned person of at least 15 or 16 years older than her husband, & illiterate to a painful degree; still in this short visit I ... who perhaps saw more of her than the gentlemen, can say that I saw something to admire in the manner in which she managed the wayward, fidgetty temper of Mr Stephens, without seeming in the least discomposed. Notwithstanding the circumstances connected with the marriage, she is liked & respected and it is very probable after all, that the temporary welfare of the Company during Stephens' administration may be safer in her hands than in his, can she but manage to preserve or rather to increase her influence over him by this, to him, imperceptible means.[11]

Stephens kept his position for the time being, but he was replaced in the following year. Meanwhile George Stevenson made his reputation as editor of the *Gazette*. Some of his public writing must have been his wife's.

Margaret Stevenson understood that, given the old ideas of the world, a woman must seem subordinate to her husband. The influence of wives must be 'imperceptible'. Charlotte Stephens' tact, which Mrs Stevenson so much admired, was not shared by every woman who came married to Australia or who found a husband here. Men were held, and held themselves, responsible for the material welfare of their families. They were supposed to know more about the wide world than women, to make the difficult decisions and to guarantee to doubtful wives that all would be well. Their self-importance was invested in the outcome. Many husbands, at sea or after arrival, must have shared the experience of Thomas Atkinson, an assisted immigrant (and my great-grandfather's brother), who came with his wife and three small children. His shipboard diary includes the entry, for instance, when well out to sea: 'Another bitter lecture for not finding time to buy more cheese and some onions before we started.'[12]

To comfort themselves in such circumstances men liked to think that only they could really feel the high adventure involved in emigration. Men were easily lifted, as Atkinson said of himself, 'above the bustle of every day life'. '[A] man', he told his diary, 'should be alone on the boundless deep fully to appreciate the scene – Clouds – Sunshine, and unbounded view – The voiceless rolling deep'.[13] He especially liked to be on deck during the early watches of the morning, when his family was asleep. Samuel Stephens might have felt the same. However incompetent he was on the spot, his refined abilities had been proved, after all, as one of the systematic colonisers, men well above 'the bustle of every day life'.

Movement from hemisphere to hemisphere should have underpinned the authority of men, since so much depended on them. With luck and common courage any husband might become a hero of empire.[14] In fact, poor men, whether they came with families or not, frequently found themselves at the mercy of the elements while in transit and – for long after they arrived – at the mercy of men, or even women, of higher rank. At sea especially they had to fit within a tight bureaucratic system that proved, every moment of the day, that they were by no means in control. Resentment was not to be cooled

A married couple with a friend contemplating an immigrant vessel at Port Adelaide, South Australia, 1840s, a watercolour (detail) by Samuel Thomas Gill. The clothes suggest middling rank, with poverty perhaps behind them.

Reproduction courtesy of National Library of Australia

in every case by dreaming on deck. This was most true of male convicts, and experience of the penal system, with its often bloody humiliation, made some men brutal. Those who lived on the islands of Bass Strait included sailors and escaped convicts. The women they had with them were Aborigines brought from the mainland, sometimes as children. Abducted and raped, they were kept under in ways that sailors and convicts themselves had suffered. 'What do they flog them for?', the missionary, George Augustus Robinson, asked some Aboriginal men who had been to the islands.

> 'If they take biscuit or sugar [he was told] they flog them; plenty women steal biscuit'. 'What do they steal biscuit for? Don't the white men give them plenty?' 'No, little bit, sometimes very little bit'. 'How do the women live?' 'On what they can catch; on limpets, mussels, crawfish and mutton birds. The white men flog the black women for nothing and flog the women belonging to other white men ... .'

Even the method of flogging was the same – 'the white men tie the black women to trees and stretch out their arms ... and then they flog them very much, plenty much blood, plenty cry'.[15]

The very failure to prosper, the whole point of emigration, might bring out a man's worst parts. The immigrant community at Swan River hovered for a time on the brink of collapse and there was much drinking, violence, and demoralisation, a sense of hopelessness among the settlers, as Governor Stirling said, 'either with the state of things here, or with their own want of power to surmount the difficulties pressing about them'. Assaults on women soon became 'very prevalent'.[16] Not many cases were brought to trial, but the court records suggest all the same that women and girls lived in frequent risk of attack. Thomas and Elizabeth Dent arrived by the *Marquis of Anglesea* in August 1829. They were both in their late 30s, they had three children already and twin girls were born here. They had been farmers in Kent, but at Swan River they opened a public house, normally a good way of making money quickly. Public house management depended on home-making skills and womanly attention to detail, and wives often took charge. This may explain why the Dents' marriage now began to come apart. Thomas Dent, used to command, found in his wife's behaviour 'many petty vexations'. From her point of view, her husband seemed 'cruel and tyrannical'. 'He treats me more like a slave than as mistress of our house.' At last she complained of his beatings and the magistrates gaoled him. When he came home, she said, 'on my offering my hand to him he knocked me down on a chest with such violence that the lid of the chest was broken'. She complained again and this time the members of the bench were careful to make sure that her own behaviour was correct. They looked at a letter she had sent him in gaol. It was not respectful, lacking, at the beginning and the end, 'those endearing epithets, which might be expected, from an affectionate wife, addressing a beloved husband'. But in the circumstances that seemed excusable. Nor, apparently, had she ever answered him back. On his return, she said, she had 'taken the greatest pains to calm his mind knowing that he was greatly irritated at having been sent to Jail'. He said she called him 'bugger'. She denied it. 'But I acknowledge', she said, 'that when he has been pinching my arm till I could bear it no longer, and has throttled me till I was nearly suffocated, I have called him "beast and brute" '.[17]

The magistrates could see the marks on Mrs Dent's neck and they were willing to believe that 'delicacy ... prevented her from exposing others'. Even the marital bed, no doubt, was no longer the sweet spot it might once have been. Dent was sentenced to three months' hard labour. Two years later the eldest of their girls, Ann (aged eleven), was assaulted – nearly raped – by another man. Thomas Dent eventually gave up any hope of doing well in the new land, took to drink, and applied to government for help. 'He complains of great debility', the government surgeon reported, 'but as it is not occasioned by illness, it is possibly for want of sufficient food'. A little flour was allowed each week to his wife and from that, presumably, Thomas Dent, in no sense a hero of empire, had his share.[18]

II

Knowledge of all kinds seemed to depend at this time on drawing contrasts and listing differences – on classification. Animal and plant life was classified, into orders, genera, and species. Human beings were classified, by gender, phrenological characteristics, complexion, and much else. 'System', too, was vital, classification being the application of system. The idea of system had been popular among European intellectuals for nearly two hundred years. The body itself was a system and so were collective bodies of humanity.[19] System was to be understood by dissection, and the mind must consume and digest each dissected part on its own so as to classify and comprehend the whole. Systematic colonisation depended on the subdivision and careful description of emigrants. A good penal system listed and separated moral types. The pattern thus imagined was dynamic, not static. Indeed, it almost seemed that systems had wills of their own, or moral characters. James Ross, the Van Diemen's Land writer, said of the minute classification of convicts: 'It is the beauty indeed of the system that it is incessantly improving and purifying itself.'[20] Systems like this could be trusted. Good systems were like beehives, thick with energy. What every bee looked like was important. But what mattered most was what each one did within the hive, and the aggregate life of them all.

In Britain, the world's biggest beehive, work was now strictly defined as male and female. At harvest time, for instance, women no longer walked through the crop with their sickles, as they had once done, side by side with men.[21] In Australia, among the convicts, careful management made separation of the sexes pivotal as a means of reinforcing the nature and duties of each. In the early years a few of the transport ships to Sydney had carried men and women together. Ships' surgeons might argue that their requirements differed (with special attention necessary for women in childbirth), but little was done. After 1815 there were no more shared vessels, steps were taken to stop female convicts from sleeping with the seamen in transit and, in the penal colonies themselves, institutions were built for large numbers, exclusively male and female. In 1830 at Norfolk Plains, in Van Diemen's Land, Mark Woodrooffe was sentenced to twenty-five lashes for talking to a female servant. 'No man', he said, as he left the court, 'can keep me from a Woman unless he puts me in Gaol'. Now this was easily done, and for thousands all at once.[22]

Convict men so much outnumbered convict women that, even out of prison, there were great hordes of them alone, men among men, in many cases for life, 'deprived', as one newspaper put it, 'of the natural rights of their sex and nature'.[23] In prison this vast sameness produced a peculiar kind of solidarity. Women, although they moved often in and out of the factories, also depended on each other more than they had done in previous years. They, too, thought more about what they might do as women, en masse. By the late 1820s the factories were places where anger itself had become contagious.[24] At Parramatta the first mass outbreak happened in October 1827. The women's breakfast ration included an ounce of sugar, for their maize-meal porridge, but they had been given salt instead. This caused some rioting and the matron ordered, as punishment, that they be docked bread as well as sugar. Irate and hungry, early on a Saturday morning, 27 October, the women seized axes, pickaxes, and crowbars and broke down the main gate. They numbered at this time between three and four hundred and, as the *Sydney Gazette* put it, they 'quickly poured forth, thick as bees from a hive, over Parramatta and the adjoining neighbourhood'. Village women in England frequently rioted when they thought the price of bread too high and, as in England, these women made straight for the bakers' shops. But in England bread, once snatched from the counter, was usually paid for (at a 'fair' price). At Parramatta the frightened bakers 'threw into the street whatever loaves the women required'. There was no talk of payment and, shouting 'Starvation!', the women went also for the butchers. Most of them were caught and returned to the factory, but they took with them, gathered in their aprons, large quantities of food.[25]

The leaders were ordered to the punishment cells, 'but so determined were the rioters,' said the *Gazette*, 'that, though opposed by a military force, they succeeded in rescuing their companions, declaring, that if one suffered, all should suffer'. The Parramatta women were now in such a state that some said a complete regiment of troops was necessary '*to keep them in awe*'. But sometimes soldiers were part of the problem. At Hobart members of the garrison threw food in over the factory wall. The women's male overseer confiscated it and, as he later complained, 'between 30 & 40 of the Women followed me clapping their hands and hooting me out of the Yard'. Female ambition blossomed. During an uproar at Parramatta in 1831, when an outbreak seemed likely, one 'Amazon' declared her aim of going down to the capital, to the office of the Sydney *Monitor*. The editor, E.S. Hall, had often argued that good women were needed in New South Wales and, just as often, that convict women were not the kind he meant. 'She proposed', so she said (or so she was reported), 'to demolish the press, and scatter the types, and thus be revenged of their political enemy, the editor, who was always holding them up as the worst and vilest of their sex'.[26]

In Van Diemen's Land Lady Franklin thought that it was 'much more difficult to deal with the women than the men'. A settler on the mainland said the same: '[T]he female convicts are *now* [in 1834] in a more insubordinate state, if possible, than the males.' Each female factory had become a gathering point for enormous numbers, a focus of sentiment that made the inmates feel their strength as women. They learnt, at least, that if they stuck together they would be hard to bend and sometimes there were hints among them of almost military order. Women assigned to households in inland New South Wales, according to the same settler, 'are continually boasting of the pleasures they enjoy in the Factory'. Inspired by a sense of shared fate, one of his own women told him, 'if all the *prisoners* in the

Colony were of her mind, they would turn out, and cut one half of the [profanity] settlers' throats'.[27]

At the same time a more subtle and, in the end, a more powerful challenge to old understanding was to be found among women in general. The different characteristics (or presumed characteristics) of manhood and womanhood were now, as I say, increasingly interesting. They were explored in writing of all kinds – religious and moral treatises, works of political economy, verse and prose, fact and fiction. Once read, they could be applied to one's self, one's wife, one's husband, one's sons, one's daughters, to male and female humanity real and fictional, near and far. New ideas about similarity – the similarity of all men, the similarity of all women – took shape, lifted beyond the local and the palpable, beyond the small circles with whom an individual might speak from day to day. Thoughts about manhood and thoughts about womanhood became abstract, multi-layered, and extraordinarily powerful, worth inscribing on men and women worldwide.

Ladies began to take an intense interest in the poor of their own sex, including convicts. In 1816, in England, Elizabeth Fry, moved by what she had seen during visits to the female cells at Newgate, decided to give her life to alleviating the helplessness of poor women, especially those in gaol. Mrs Fry's work was in some ways in step with the ideas of men like Scott and Bannister, George Arthur and James Macarthur. Like them she was eager to feel the decision-making power of the poor. Also, she was a devout Quaker and Quakers took seriously the equal value of every soul, of whatever sex or rank. But most of all Mrs Fry was moved by new ideas about womanhood.

Elizabeth Fry's methods of convict management depended largely on conversation, on dealing with women one by one. Face to face, she implemented current thought. 'Much good', she said, 'may be effected by instructing the female criminals *individually*'. Their knowledge of religion was most important, but useful conversation must also do something for their intellectual and moral character, and they must be encouraged to manage better from a material point of view.[28] According to John Ruskin, the English writer, 'woman's power is for rule, not for battle ... her intellect is ... for sweet ordering, arrangement, and decision'. In order to use this power, so Mrs Fry believed, women must be free from the overbearing power of men. Without protection by women like herself, female prisoners not only suffered physical cruelty, including rape, they were also morally and spiritually degraded. Even high-minded men could not properly manage the deeper needs of women. When she visited Newgate and other prisons she spoke to the inmates as one of them – of 'us' rather than 'you'. She believed in what she called the 'common bond of sisterhood' and she was sure that all women, well dealt with, could feel it.[29]

Elizabeth Fry deliberately inspired other educated women in the same work. One of them, Charlotte Anley (a cousin of Henry Dumaresq), came to Sydney in 1836. Experience in Newgate had shown Miss Anley what might be done 'where woman will plead with woman, upon the broad ground of christian charity'. A Quaker too, she was known in England as the author of *Influence: A Moral Tale for Young People* and *Miriam: or, The Power of Truth* (which went through ten editions in twenty years). During a visit to the Female Factory at Parramatta she was, as she put it, 'literally *hemmed* in by … women' and there she met Mary Maloney and Sarah McGregor, convicted in 1834 of murdering Captain Waldron. Mrs Fry advised ladies not to talk to criminals about their past misdeeds – 'it frequently leads them to add sin to sin, by uttering the grossest falsehoods' – but this was often hard to avoid. They longed to tell their stories. Miss Anley had a detailed conversation with Mary Maloney, who argued hard that they were not really murderers. '[W]e couldn't help it that he died', she said, 'and we were sorry for it, although he deserved it'. Charlotte Anley set down their conversation in her next book, *The Prisoners of Australia*:

> I replied that I could readily believe the *act* of murder [in their case] to be one of awful passion, and not of premeditated crime. Here she interrupted me, looking up with an expression of deep emotion, such as I can never forget, and exclaiming, 'Then you *do* believe *that*.' – 'Yes', I replied, 'I could scarcely think otherwise of a *woman*.'

There was a pause and Mary, touched with this unexpected hint of sisterhood, said, 'May God bless you for that!' Miss Anley was pleased to report that this was the first time Mary Maloney had been seen to cry.[30]

As for convict men, their places of mass confinement were all at a distance from Sydney and Hobart. Any committing new crimes while in bondage were sent to Newcastle, on the mouth of the Hunter River, between 1804 and 1824, and to Port Macquarie, further up the mainland coast, from 1821. Northward again a prison settlement was formed at Moreton Bay in 1824, and to the remote east on Norfolk Island in 1825. In Van Diemen's Land there were bases at Macquarie Harbour (Sarah Island) from 1821, on Maria Island, off the north-east coast, from 1825, and on the Tasman Peninsula, at the entrance to Storm Bay (the outer mouth of the Derwent), from 1832. To begin with some of these institutions included women. As late as 1838, one third of the prisoners at Moreton Bay were female.[31] However, by then the main penal settlements, one for each colony, were on Norfolk Island and the Tasman Peninsula, and here the imprisoned population was wholly male. The peninsula held not only men, at Port Arthur and the Coal Mines, where they worked in extreme hardship underground, but also boys at Point Puer.

The new penal discipline fell more heavily on men than it did on women. The men themselves knew it, if only from their experience of flogging, which women did not share. '[H]e cried out *loudly* at every lash', says a record of various episodes of corporal punishment, 'he screamed *dreadfully*'; 'he bellowed at every lash, and writhed with agony'.[32] The flogging of women having ceased in 1817, female voices were never raised in quite this way. Also, government interest in convict women was haphazard and it usually ceased when they found husbands. Both men and women posed an intellectual challenge for male officials, but in the case of the women, as Jane Franklin remarked, the challenge was too much. As a result, she said, 'the subject, as perplexing subjects are apt to be, has been put aside'. Charlotte Anley found it astonishing that issues which seemed to her so urgent should be ignored by leading men in Sydney. Vast numbers of women, needed for the womanly work of making homes, were gathered instead in the factories where they could only make trouble. 'I am no politician', she said (by 'politician' she meant a theorist of government), 'but common sense tells me the reasoning is bad even as a question of policy'.[33]

The technique taught by Elizabeth Fry depended upon the idea that women's souls were different from men's. It followed all the same that an approach like hers might be taken by men with their own sex. Male convicts might be managed as individuals, so as to give them a finer sense of what a man should be. Colin Arrott Browning, who came to Australia six times as a surgeon on male convict ships, during 1831–49, made the attempt (Chapter 9). So did Alexander Maconochie on Norfolk Island in the 1840s (Chapter 10). A tender reverence for women was one of the most important attributes of good men. Lacking women on Norfolk, Maconochie nevertheless gave his men a powerful impression of the young Victoria, still a maiden queen, whose birthday they marked with a dinner and a play. For a moment, as one prisoner said, 'Her Majesty reigned in their hearts'. Impressed with a feeling almost romantic, many of the men briefly showed a sense of duty rare in that place.[34]

At its peak the number of men on Norfolk was 1200. The commandants during the 1830s, Maconochie's predecessors, were conscientious, but they used military methods to impose their will. And this in spite of the fact that the hierarchy they managed was in no sense military. Corruption and petty tyranny met with frequent rebellion, including murder. A full-scale insurrection in January 1834 led to the trial of fifty-five men and the hanging of thirteen. On the Tasman Peninsula there were larger numbers (nearly 2000 by January 1842) but discipline was better.[35] The commandant from 1833 to 1844 was Charles O'Hara Booth, a captain in the 21st Fusiliers. Booth imposed his own distinctive regime, one that depended not on military protocol, as at Norfolk, but on the lively power of his own presence. The only hint of rebellion in his time, soon after his arrival, Booth dealt with instantaneously:

> put on my annihilating countenance [so he noted in his diary] – went down [to] them 375 in number raised my Stentorian voice and made them quake ... heard something like a disposition to insult – but casting my eye pretty sharply round to the spot from whence it came – with by no means a good natured look – prevented a recurrence.

This was Booth's idea of useful conversation. He saw command as a continuous adventure:

> Everything goes on quiet [he reported to Hobart in autumn 1833] nor do I hear of any treason in contemplation – until the dark Nights set in – a nocturnal visit to the Commissariat Store is the intended Plot – we are all ready to receive them, whenever the lads fancy they can effect it with impunity.

He was especially intrigued with the challenge of stopping escapes and he made his territory extraordinarily secure. On his verandah he lined up as trophies the little boats that hopeful but hopeless runaways used in his time.[36]

Booth was also a man of system. To outwit 'the lads' he built twenty-two signal stations linking Port Arthur with the narrow neck, which was the only means of dry-land escape, and he devised a signal system with 11,300 notations. This was his 'great hobby', as Lady Franklin put it, and the main semaphore stood up behind his own house like a ship's mast. The absence of any prisoner, day or night, was immediately noticed, the news ran from semaphore to semaphore and so 'the entire body of constables and watchmen all along the lines is on the alert, until he is discovered or apprehended'. A similar watch was kept on daily misbehaviour. On Norfolk Island corruption was endemic and justice unpredictable. On the peninsula all was clockwork. 'I have adopted the plan', Booth said, 'of not allowing the slightest offence to pass without punishment'.[37]

Convict ingenuity, for good or ill, was Booth's delight. The true man 'is eminently the doer, the creator, the discoverer, the defender', said John Ruskin, and in nourishing ingenuity Booth differed, once again, from Elizabeth Fry. Booth's system was never interrupted by the kind of compassion Mrs Fry spoke of. Instead he aimed for an intricate, interlinked workforce. And once again, he made Port Arthur unlike Norfolk Island. On Norfolk, to make life more arduous, the mass of orange trees planted since the 1790s were cut down and ploughs were banned. The men used hoes instead.[38] Booth, in contrast, searched for varied ways to employ his prisoners. The soil was no good for crops, but an enormous granary and flour-mill were erected and grain was brought from elsewhere. He began shipbuilding. He designed a railway linking the Coal Mines with Port Arthur and Eagle Hawk Neck, the trolleys being pushed by the men. Visitors occasionally rode in them. He was keenly interested in the education of the boys at Point Puer and a few learnt useful trades from convict men. Shoemaking was a major industry and intricate stonework on the church and other buildings showed the skill of the masons.[39]

Governor Arthur was satisfied that the hard labour, the unremitting surveillance and punishment, the 'absolute weariness' of life at Port Arthur, made it a place of terror. His colonial secretary called it 'worse than death'. The unbearable cries mentioned above were common. And yet Booth's system allowed rewards for usefulness. In Hobart it was sometimes said that at Port Arthur present good behaviour allowed officials to forget too easily an evil past.[40] A few men must have watched with interest the experiments of their commandant. Linked to him by an elaborate code, the signalmen must have taken pleasure in the way they gave the network life. Even the railwaymen, certainly beasts of burden, might have felt some thrill in the extraordinary downhill speed of the railway car, which little but galloping horses could match. Pushing no longer they jumped onto its running-board, where they could watch the nervousness of visitors inside. As a visitor said, 'No power on earth could stop you. You come to a curve, and lest the car should fly off, the two men on the one side, keeping only one foot on the car, lean out as far as possible to "carry her round" '.[41]

Uphill was different. The men were 'terribly jaded, running down with sweat, and I saw one of them continually trying to shift his irons from a galled spot on his ankle'.[42]

III

In the story of *Ralph Rashleigh* the hero once ate with an Irish settler family who had poultry in the rafters and, in the same room, two or three pigs, a sick calf, a mare, and newborn foal. The foal came to the table to be fed and 'the younger fry ... enjoyed his tricks in an uproarious manner'. We might imagine the grunts, clucks, and footfall of livestock, the shouts of children and the rougher Irish-turned voices of men and women, primed with rum, including, from the matriarch: 'There wor no *shpuds* (potatoes) to be got in this thieving cullony, bekase they wouldn't grow in id.' Dancing followed, and a fight. 'The children roared, the dogs growled and bayed fiercely, ... the pigs squeaked and the fowls lent their shrill cackling to augment the uproar.'[43]

Such highly charged closeness, steeped in sound (whether richly patterned or chaotic), shapes people's sense of who they are. However, the world was increasingly understood at this time not only by hearing but also by reading – a much quieter affair. Books and newspapers, as I say, opened intellectual gateways for rapidly growing numbers of people, here as in Europe. Reading about men and women made it more natural to think about each, as it were, including oneself, from the outside. More intricate codes of behaviour emerged and were broadcast in print. In this way, with extraordinary speed, manhood and womanhood each became, as it were, keys to public and private order. The idealisation of each was used as a kind of index – or competing indices – of the way societies might be managed, overlapping with other ideologies. It was possible to experiment in this way with prisons, as Mrs Fry and Captain Booth did. But even more intriguing was the possibility that society itself might be run as if it were made up entirely of ideal men or, as a quite different vision, of ideal women.

In Launceston John Pascoe Fawkner, the young editor of the *Launceston Advertiser*, had clear ideas about such things and it was men he looked to. He enlightened his readers with a local story of a woman who had run up a debt of £64.16s.6d. for clothes, bought on her husband's credit and without his knowledge. Having first hidden the clothes – 'expensive, extravagant, and useless articles' – among friends she then gathered them up and left home. The husband refused to pay the bills and it was to be hoped, Fawkner said, that his attitude would make shopkeepers more careful about trusting married women. Otherwise 'any wife may ruin her husband'.[44] Complementary to such rights at home were men's duties abroad, as citizens. In 1830 Fawkner made an effort to get all the men of Launceston to meet and form a 'town guard', for the sake of public order and protection from bushrangers. They were to elect their officers and a committee of management, which meant setting up a structure of power to rival that of the local commandant. 'Tasmania expects that every man will thus perform his share of public duty!!!' Launceston had a self-regarding energy of its own, with its old resentment of Hobart and its oversight of Bass Strait, an almost republican spirit with which Fawkner seems to have been inspired.[45]

The town-guard scheme came to nothing, but five years later, at about the time he moved across the water to Port Phillip, Fawkner went further, sketching on paper a visionary constitution for a town-republic on the northern shore. Here, truly, was a place to be governed by its men – all of them. Launceston people believed that this corner of the mainland was beyond the Sydney government because it was so far outside the Limits of Location. It was therefore open to any kind of settlement, including one created fresh from European recipes. Well read in radicalism, Fawkner himself thought that communities were not formed for the good of their rulers but by the people for themselves. New settlements, like the one he now proposed, ought to prove the 'Natural Liberty of Man' – and he meant, the liberty of men – because such liberty involved 'each individual acting as to him may seem just and conducive to his interest, Comfort or Whim'.[46]

Fawkner planned, on paper, a single town surrounded by land under crops and cattle, with small estates nearby and larger ones at a distance. Mere manhood would confer the right to vote. There was to be a council of three and a president, and any male householder of 'Good Moral conduct and a fair share of talent' might propose himself. In his newspaper Fawkner had argued that female intelligence should be taken seriously. It was not as contemptible, he said, 'as our vanity would lead us to believe'. However, men must rule. Women figured in his Port Phillip scheme only as possible landowners and likely drunkards.[47]

Good manhood meant order, civility, honesty, rational self-control, and respectful regard for other men. It was a parcel of virtues existing from man to man and Fawkner called it 'Independent Feeling'.[48] As a kind of reverse image of his community at Port Phillip consider the penal settlement on Norfolk Island before Maconochie. There the 'peculiar language' of the place, its upside-down moral logic, meant that among the convicts 'a good man' was one of those lost to duty. On Norfolk Fawkner's ideal type was 'bad'. The convict author, Thomas Cook, arrived a prisoner on the island in 1836. He came ashore just as Fawkner planned to do at Port Phillip, setting foot on the beach as a man entering a new existence. But Fawkner wanted manhood perfected. On Norfolk Island, like the thud of the lash, Cook felt the opposite. As they stood together on the sand he and the other men with him were told to take off their clothes so that they could be searched, presumably for tobacco. The memory of this initial indignity, plus the proddings perhaps, summed up Cook's experience on Norfolk. From now on he was, he said, 'Shut out from the World for ever to herd with beings in human form, but whose every action excluded their claim to the appellation of "Man"'. In the female factories women were often punished by having their hair cut off, which they felt as a horrible thinning of their womanhood. Among men, very likely, it was forced nakedness that carried this kind of pain. [49]

John Fawkner's scheme had some echoes on the ground in early Port Phillip. This was in fact a place created by men for their own exclusive purposes, with women often invisible – even around Melbourne they were outnumbered two to one.[50] And nowhere else in Australia was it so readily assumed that the pioneers would take charge and make what they could of the place. '[A]ll are engaged in one object', according to a visitor, and that object was 'gain'. They were 'sharpers', he added, 'who wanted everything for less than cost price'.[51] And yet, selfish or not, they also worked together. Formal combinations – the Port Phillip Association, the Clyde Company – were pivotal to first settlement, and Fawkner did indeed implement his visionary republic to the extent of assembling a 'council' of three in Melbourne in May 1836. He hoped, as he put it, that 'every male inhabitant' might vote for future members. The 'council' succeeded in settling an argument between Fawkner himself and Henry Batman. Then it died.[52]

A police magistrate arrived from Sydney in September 1836 and a deputy governor, or 'superintendent', in 1839. The Governor himself, Richard Bourke, came in March 1837 and named Melbourne and Williamstown in honour of the prime minister and the King. In outward form then, this was no republic. And yet, the making of the place still depended on the voluntary efforts of local men. There was no simple duplication of early Sydney. The public meetings starting about the same time became habitual, and while they did not always achieve much they kept up manly cooperation.[53] The Port Phillip Association was succeeded by a pastoral and agricultural society and by numerous bodies, often short-lived, designed to bring labouring people from abroad.[54] The men who settled along this coast were keen to choose their fellow citizens. An especially ambitious scheme, the Port Phillip Colonization Company, was formed in 1846 with the aim of raising £250,000 to bring family men to the region, especially from Scotland. Its main mover was the Presbyterian minister, John Dunmore Lang, another republican keen to build bodies of men of 'Independent Feeling'. Shares in the company were to cost £20 each, and immigrant men were to be shareholders, purchasing not only a passage but also a chance to buy land and a voice in meetings.[55]

Skill was important for the dignity of manhood. For poor men skill with reading and writing promised most of all. The pen of Thomas Cook, mentioned above, underpinned his life. A clerk sent to Norfolk for forgery, Cook kept his self-respect, so he said, because he possessed 'a heart filled with early affection' and 'a mind capable of powerful reasoning'. His writing was meant to prove both. With such qualities a man might hope to save himself, even at Norfolk, 'from falling into the lowest depth of infamy, never more to rise to the rank of man'.[56] In the autobiography he wrote towards the end of his time on the island Cook created images of the pain and tyranny all about him, images, as he thought, spun from intelligent manhood. He knew that 'system' was one of the key words of rational debate, a word that could connect him to the thoughts of men much greater than himself, and in his 'treatise' he wrote of Norfolk's 'plotting and conspiring System', its 'torturous System', its 'System of rigorous coercion'. Men were absorbed within these systems. There was a 'purloining System', by which overseers stole convict rations, and a 'System of ... Running', by which the strongest men worked on each end of hoeing gangs. The others kept up or were flogged. In due course all this, said Cook, was replaced by the 'admirable System' devised by Maconochie.[57]

Cook wrote, he hoped, a hard-edged argument, a combination of humanity and logic typical of a good man. As for women, they might embellish their sense of self by making parallel efforts towards high culture. The individuals who came to Australia with assisted passages in the 1830s included thousands of women who were drawn by an enlarged sense of what a woman might be. In New South Wales employers assumed that such women would do outdoor work, like their husbands. But they overlooked the new idealism, plus the fact that in New South Wales it was obviously easy to make money and, with money, to be respectable. After 'a short time in the country', one employer said, the women become 'too proud to be industrious'. '[Many] forget they left starvation to come here', said another, a woman herself. 'Oh they are a saucy race. ... The women ... are far worse to manage than the men.'[58] Some immigrants might do nothing but imagine their own improvement, but in New South Wales a quarter were said to have freed themselves from the labour market within four years. They invested mainly in cattle, just as former convicts had done.[59] For those few, at least, pride was justified.

Newcomers were moved, too, by a contrary belief, that by leaving Europe, the source of civilisation, they risked a kind of moral failure.

Children were quickly hardened, just as they had been earlier in New South Wales (Chapter 1). Even gentlemen's sons might have nothing but basic schooling, said a Port Phillip mother, 'with the addition of being taught to swear, smoke and ride'. And as a gentleman himself put it, 'the children become at an early age, adepts with their hands, while their hearts are unimproved and their minds uncultured ... morally, they are little removed from the swarthy aborigines'.[60] James Drummond, a Fellow of the Linnaean Society, came to Perth to manage the botanical gardens. His sons grew into fine bushmen, living and fighting among their tribal neighbours. Two of them stole Aboriginal women and one was killed in consequence. Meanwhile Euphemia, their sister, engaged herself to a former shepherd newly rich. The young men reacted to this last degradation by burning her dress on her wedding morning – and yet the gentility they imagined in themselves must have already tasted ashen.[61]

Where schools were available immigrants' children were pushed hard, not only to read and write but also to read and write in certain ways. Respectability meant not only gathering money and literacy but also taking on the stereotyped manhood or womanhood to be found everywhere on the printed page. Girls promised the most straightforward results. It was easy to understand what a lady was. Besides, good literacy led directly to letter-writing and for girls and women it was letters that most clearly carried female virtue to the wide world. '[T]he private letter', said Eliza Brown, writing privately herself from the remote frontier of Western Australia, is 'woman's weapon'. With it she might cut quietly but hard. The Benedictine nuns, at their 'Educational Establishment for Young Ladies' at Parramatta, promised parents that their girls would learn Christian Doctrine, English, French, Italian, arithmetic, drawing, dancing, music, and needlework, a bundle of skills equalling refinement. And to these they added 'Penmanship' and 'Epistolary Correspondence'. Through letter-writing their alumnae would demonstrate their skills – and muster at least a little power – before the world at large.[62]

Mary Anne Kettle was born in Sydney in 1831. Her mother, the daughter of convicts, was apparently illiterate, and it was her father, a free immigrant, who drove the family forward. Cabinetmaker, then house-builder, then publican, he bought up town properties. Mary Anne was sent first to Mrs Love's school at Concord. Her eyes being weak, she was often at home but, as she later emphasised, she 'never assisted in the public house'. Later she spent a year at Mrs Perrier's boarding school. Then 'my education was finished, excepting music', and for that she went by day to Mrs McMahon. She might now call herself a lady. She was courted by a young physician and she was visited by Captain Roskell, of the merchant ship, *Asia*. At a party at her father's house, she said, 'we were engaged in the "cushion dance" when the Captain kissed me ... [he] kissed other ladies,' she explained, eager to prove that she was not a common female. 'Other gentlemen did the same.'[63]

A party like this was the end product of considerable enterprise. It cost money to build companies of ladies and gentlemen. Not all parents could manage it. Not every girl could learn the cushion dance, nor possess the 'neat desk and small appurtenances of epistle-craft' that novels allowed to young heroines.[64] But a little of such polish might be won even in the elementary schools, which, in every colony, were used from village to village by the mass of the population. In New South Wales and Van Diemen's Land the government-subsidised schools were mainly run by the Church of England and the teachers were men, including convicts. But by the 1840s there were many small independent establishments, in which women, too, struggled to teach the refinements of the literate world.[65] Mothers wanted teachers like Lucy Didsburry, who was one of the rare women to manage a Church of England parish school in New South Wales (in Sydney). Miss Didsbury's class included fifty-six boys and eighty-five girls, but when she was replaced by two men, in rapid succession, the girls fell away by 25 per cent.[66] In Western Australia the Catholic Church established new schools in Perth and Fremantle in 1846–47. The school for boys in Perth drew about thirty pupils immediately, but there were twice as many girls (mostly Protestant) with the Sisters of Mercy at the convent school. 'We would not admit a naughty child', said Sister Ursula, 'and this is, I believe one of the chief recommendations of the school'. Good music and singing were perfect proof of respectability and the nuns knew the special power of womanly voices. Sister Mary Francis sang solo at mass in Perth on Christmas Day 1848. 'The people were all astonished and delighted', said Ursula, '[and] crowds of Protestants came to hear her. I have every hope it will be the means of making many converts amongst the poorer classes'.[67]

Everywhere among the Europeans in Australia girls who reached school age in the 1840s were, on average, much better readers and writers than their predecessors.[68] From now on girls were just as familiar with writing as boys of the same age, an equality hitherto unknown among English-speaking people (except in Scotland). As writers and readers they could handle many aspects of gentility. They read novels. Worldwide, there was now a flood of cheap works of fiction, whose authors asked no more of their readers then an interest in courtship, marriage, and womanly sacrifice. Such books, 'eagerly sought after by milliner's apprentices and lady's maids', were trash, said John Dunmore Lang. Catherine Helen Spence, in her fictional story of South Australia in the 1840s, told of a maidservant who read them in bed 'half the night'. 'There is nothing spoils a servant so much as a taste for reading', said the story's Miss Withering, 'it makes them dislike working'. Besides, 'they fancy when they have read a few books, that they know as much as their mistresses'.[69] This was one reason why they did it.

In such ways women learned new things about womanhood. Reading novels was done silently and alone, but in imagination it drew women together.[70] Similarly, among the multiplying mass of postage during the

Imagined romance, in a picture drawn by an unknown artist for a locally written story. The heroine, a former convict but unstained, first meets her future husband.

Source: 'Lucy Cooper', by John Lang, *Illustrated Sydney News*, 23 December 1854

1840s numerous letters – 'Epistolary Correspondence' – passed among young women, many, no doubt, meditating the subject matter of novels, and many also between young women and young men. They included cards on St Valentine's Day. '[V]alentines were much improved', as one lady said, 'since I was myself a girl'. They were also more of them. In February 1846 Hobart's leading stationer was said to have sold 8000, equalling (if true) eight for every teenage girl in the city.[71]

A style of writing like that of valentines was also used in messages sent through the newspapers. Backwards and forwards, day by day, lovers took up pretended names and declared themselves in the classified columns. Thus, in the *Sydney Morning Herald*:

> [From 'Camelia' to her man:] 'Pride and ingratitude, can I evermore visit thee? No, I cannot.'
> [His reply, next day:] 'Cruel Camelia, reconsider your decision; also those unjust epithets, "Pride and Ingratitude".'
> [From 'Camelia', two days later:] 'If I have been guilty of cruelty, may retribution overtake me, but I have not – my decision I am willing to alter if thou wilt only be amiable and affectionate. Then let us both in friendship meet, with love from our hearts each other greet.'[72]

How thrilling to see yourself masked like this in print! Even life at the wrong end of the world could be like a novel.

Meanwhile men and women went on writing about each other in older ways. In 1849 news arrived of gold discoveries in California and many men left with hopes of finding wealth. John Jamison, a Sydney butcher, wrote back to his wife Elspith of his hardships – 'but my dear, you know what sort of man I am, ... I never meet sorrow half way' – and of how much he missed her. 'My dear wife, some of my friends wonder that I did not bring you with me', and indeed, 'women can make more money in one week than a man can make in two; but that would not satisfy me to see you standing over a wash tub or in service in a cold tent'. He had been a madman to come, he said, but he would persevere. She too must show her usual patience, 'for which I have so often applauded you'.[73] Elspith Jamison sent this letter to the *Herald*, ostensibly to publish conditions on the goldfields. But it may be that she was also pleased, and wanted to show her pleasure, at being addressed as such a woman by such a man.

Chapter 8

Black and White

I

'Are you a black man [?]', John Velvick asked Somed Ali. Velvick was an English labourer. He had been at Swan River for nearly three years, since February 1830, and he had a friend with him. Somed Ali was walking with two other men, Habib and Cassim, and all were lascars, or sailors from an Indian Ocean vessel. This was not a question about the right definition of 'Black' and since Velvick asked it in broad daylight, in a Perth street, he knew the answer before he opened his mouth. Ali said, 'Yes'. Velvick said, 'Will you give me a glass of grog [?]' Ali said he had no grog. Velvick called him a 'black bugger'. Ali now spoke up – 'Oh you are a very nice man, why do you talk so to me?' – which was what Velvick wanted. 'Oh you black bugger', he shouted, 'if you do not give me a glass of Grog I will kick your arse; go along you black bugger'. A number of other White men had gathered meanwhile. They now closed in on the lascars. It may be that Habib and Cassim escaped, but Ali was hit about the head and back with a stick and they tore his shirt.[1]

The lascars got back to their hut but the Europeans increased their numbers and made a larger attack, on the principle that 'they would never let a black man strike a white man'. The lascars were outnumbered four to one and were beaten. Among the onlookers was the merchant James Purkis. He thought the attack was 'one of the most cowardly transactions in which I ever saw white men engaged'. David Patterson, a tradesman, called it 'as barbarous a thing as I ever saw'. On the contrary, according to one of Velvick's friends, it was gorgeous to feel 'some of the black bugger's blood then trickling down his neck'.[2]

The indigenous inhabitants of the British Isles saw people whom they could call 'Black' wherever they went throughout the empire. This included not only Indians and Africans, often scattered far abroad, but also the people who had lived in Australia from the beginning. Their response varied. Relative numbers mattered, because numbers can mean power. In the case of Velvick and Somed Ali the White men made sure of their numbers before their second attack. With the Aboriginal people this was not always easy. In Van Diemen's Land, where the territory was small and the Aborigines probably numbered no more than 4000, it was clear by the late 1820s that invasion might go on until the place was full and the first inhabitants overwhelmed.[3] But on the mainland, though the Aborigines were thinly scattered, given the space they commanded their numbers seemed limitless.

Fearful resentment came most easily to Europeans with a shaky sense of their own importance, the 'unreflecting' poor. Other individuals, like Purkis and Patterson, were more free to glimpse the divinity of human nature behind strange bearing, strange diction, strange complexion. And yet Europeans who were poor and at risk might make the same imaginative leap. Andrew Eaton was an illiterate nailer from Killarney, in Ireland, with dark eyes and a lopsided mouth. In 1835 he was sentenced to fourteen years transportation for a firearms offence. He was about twenty-three and left behind a wife and baby daughter. Since his birthplace was one of the most out-of-the-way corners of Europe, it may be that Eaton had never before seen anyone he could call 'Black', but by spring 1837 he was working as a hutkeeper at Byron Plains, on the extreme north-western frontier of New South Wales. There (two years distant from the mountains of Killarney) he was immediately friends with the people around him. They went with him to visit the neighbouring station at Myall Creek and one of their children, killed by stockmen, he buried, so he said, 'with the assistance of King Sandy [an elder] and twelve or thirteen of the blacks'. 'I was most of the time quite alone', he said. 'They never attacked me at all.'[4]

In any period, strangers who want to take part in unfamiliar talk and ceremony have to watch carefully, keeping their thoughts in step. Eaton clearly did so. Among the Aborigines, equal delicacy appears in an old man, his name unrecorded, whom Charles Sturt met near the River Darling in 1844: 'It was his wont to visit my tent every day at noon, and to sleep during the heat; but he invariably asked permission to do this before he composed himself for rest, and generally laid down at my feet. ... he never asked for anything, and although present during our meals kept away from the table.' And then, 'If offered anything he received it with becoming dignity'. Such things might be said of a good dog, but Sturt mentioned too the 'freedom and grace' of the old man's manners, and the 'intellect and feeling' evident in everything he did.[5]

Intonations of the voice and movements of the body and gaze all matter at such times. The native-born Elizabeth Macarthur (James Macarthur's sister) thought that the Blacks possessed 'more native politeness than is found amongst any people'. Thomas Mitchell, surveyor-general of New South Wales, saw in them a 'natural attentiveness, if I may so call it'. They

were 'very shrewd', said Mitchell, 'easily distinguishing our grades of society, and reading the very mind of a white man in his look'. The Benedictine
brother, Rosendo Salvado, said the same: 'They are aware of even hidden
thoughts.' Sometimes both Black and White could feel, on coming face to
face, both attraction and revulsion. During his expedition to the Darling in
1828, Sturt's party, including Hamilton Hume, met a man who had never
before seen human beings on horseback. 'He had evidently taken both man
and horse for one animal', said Sturt, 'and as long as Mr. Hume kept his
seat, the native remained upon his guard; but when he saw him dismount,
after the first astonishment had subsided, he stuck his spear into the
ground, and walked fearlessly up to him'.[6] As for 'natural attentiveness',
Mitchell told of an Aboriginal man who had been caught in a skirmish
with his expedition on the Bogan in 1835. Wounded with buckshot, he was
brought in to be bandaged. 'He had asked for a bit of fire to be placed
beside him, (the constant habit of the naked aborigines,) and, on seeing a
few sparks of burning grass running towards my feet', said Mitchell, 'he
called out to me "*we, we*", (i.e. *fire, fire!*) that I might avoid having my
clothes burnt'. Mitchell thought this extraordinary in someone who had
never seen Europeans before, who was terrified and at the same time 'suffering from so many new and raw wounds'.[7]

Sometimes, on the other hand, Aborigines seemed to the invaders to
show less delicacy than beasts. In a different mood, Mitchell said that his
bullocks, pricking up their ears at the wild gestures of the Blacks, showed
a dignity far beyond theirs. And after a difficult conference, he said, 'I have
found comfort in contemplating the honest faces of the horses and sheep'.
Encouraged by fear, the idea that Aborigines were no better than beasts, or
were even diabolical, quickly found its place among the mass of Europeans.
Likewise, some Blacks had a name for the invaders which meant 'white
spirit' or 'devil'.[8]

The flood of immigrants during the 1820s made such issues crucial. The
newcomers' understanding of the Aborigines affected their imaginative
grasp of the country itself. It shaped ideas about controlling the land. The
Aborigines were not just Blacks, as lascars might be. Theirs was a more
brightly barbed significance and as a result the relationship of Black and
White within Australia began to be understood, on both sides, within
wider intellectual dimensions. Imagination was reshaped. Saxe Bannister
had addressed these questions as attorney-general of New South Wales in
1824–26, taking them further than anyone else so far. Bannister was not
only an humanitarian and a commercial lawyer but also a scholar interested in the economic history of nations. Since the Aborigines were, in his
view, 'rational beings' they must also be actors within an historical universe. They must therefore be brought to understand, as soon as possible,
their place within that universe and the power they now lived under.
Bannister took seriously Aboriginal claims to the land itself and he hoped
to find ways in which that, and everything else they valued, might be

anchored in law, by which he meant their own law subsumed somehow – girded above and below – by the law of the invaders.

In August 1824, soon after Bannister's arrival and following serious violence around Bathurst, Governor Brisbane declared martial law. The magistrates, working with the military, were thus given summary powers of life and death. Using swift and precise action they were to put an end to lawless, formless violence. This was done on Bannister's advice. No previous governor had thought to use martial law in such crises because it had been understood that although the Aborigines were British subjects force might be used against them, at least on the frontier, without legal difficulty. They could be killed by anyone who considered himself in danger. Bannister thought differently. He believed that the Crown, as the embodiment of British honour, must 'take the lead ... both in the coercion and in the improvement of the aborigines'. He wanted the finely grained mingling of Black and White. He wanted the two parties to mix in their daily lives. But uncontrolled contact, including violence, must be disastrous from any point of view. Where it happened on a large scale government must respond, he said, by 'putting forth an overwhelming force'. Long-term justice was to be born somehow of short-term bloodshed.[9]

Brisbane's successor, Ralph Darling, failed to follow this argument. Martial law was not necessary, he said, 'to put down a few naked

An attack by Aborigines on a farmhouse at Great Swanport, east coast of Van Diemen's Land, in 1828, a drawing by an unknown artist. On one side the Blacks have come through the bush, on the other they halt behind the zig-zag fencing characteristic of such places (see Chapter 10).

Savages'.[10] But in Van Diemen's Land Governor Arthur seems to have admired the broad vision and hard moral logic that Bannister applied to the relationship of Aborigines and government. There the immigration of large numbers of Europeans had been particularly sudden. The killing of several Aborigines at Cape Grim, by employees of the Van Diemen's Land Company, might have been taken as particular proof of the European determination to prevail. 'I was shewed a point of rock', said a traveller in those parts, 'where an old man ... was shot through the head by one of the murderers – who mentioned these circumstances as deeds of heroism'.[11] This and many other examples of casual brutality provoked new resistance from the Blacks, a 'determined spirit of hostility and revenge', and in November that year Arthur, too, declared martial law. Brisbane, in his proclamation, had stressed the need to stop 'mutual Bloodshed'. Arthur also wanted to save lives on both sides, but here the situation differed. The Aborigines in Van Diemen's Land had begun to think of themselves as one people and, faced with a single invading force, they had apparently combined in 'a complete declaration of hostilities against the settlers generally'. They aimed, so the government believed, 'systematically to kill and destroy the white inhabitants' whenever they could. They had also become inventive in the way they armed and organised, and more merciless, especially in the midlands and around Oyster Bay. Between 1824 and 1831 White deaths at the hands of the Blacks averaged one a week.[12]

For these reasons, and because, from an intellectual point of view, he did not follow Bannister all the way, Arthur's proclamation of martial law spoke of 'His Majesty's Subjects' being under attack from 'the Black or Aboriginal Natives of this Island'. And yet, in principle all were the King's subjects. As Bannister knew, this was the very reason for declaring martial law among civilians. The magistrates, arbiters of equal justice, were to use force with an even hand. In the Sydney proclamation 'Black Women and Children and unoffending White Men' were all described as victims of violence and it followed that the culprits too were both Black and White. In Hobart, however, Arthur gathered his power '*against* the ... Black or Aboriginal Natives', as if he were making war on a separate people.[13]

Brisbane's proclamation extended from the Blue Mountains westward, with no outer limit. Arthur, once again with a very different purpose, drew an outer rather than an inner boundary, cutting off the Tasman Peninsula (not yet a penal settlement), the island's north-east corner and its far south and west. These he meant as districts where the Aborigines could escape his new rigour. Even in dealing with Europeans alone Arthur was eager to divide space from space, drawing lines across the island and giving each its own internal order. Unlike Bannister, he was not interested in the mingling of the races. Also (and in spite of the terms of his proclamation), he stretched the power of martial-law discretion far beyond his magistrates. Rewards were offered for the capture of Aborigines and killing was forgiven, so that in effect everyone who was White was given power of life and death. Never before on the island had Europeans, en masse, been so drawn within a single, dramatic act of government – except for the original invasion. Arthur's intellectual authority determined the local sense of history (Chapter 4). In the same way his use of martial law must have sharpened the popular understanding of territory, of a land possessed by European effort and one that Europeans might shoot and kill for.

The situation only worsened and Arthur, still hopeful of disentangling Black and White, drew up a more ambitious plan. In spring 1830 settlers and troops (totalling 2200 men) were formed in a line that was to sweep through the southern midlands, mustering the Aborigines step by step towards the Tasman Peninsula, where they were to be confined. This, the 'Black Line', proved more than anything else the vivid cast of Arthur's imagination. His people were to perform in the drama he thus sketched out, to take up places in the line as it moved, puppet-like, through the landscape. Both soldiers and civilians, they were to be part of a vast and intricate formation of tactics and logistics, their movements on the ground precisely matched with directions on the map, their weapons, their rations, their clothes, all accounted for by a single extraordinary administrative effort. The exercise caused great excitement and it seems likely that most of those involved saw it as a final solution. But while the passing of the line left 'vast destruction' among trees and undergrowth, its prisoners numbered only two.[14]

The sharper geographical sense drawn from these events can be found in a shift of language. Note the more common use, for instance, of the words 'exterminate' and 'extirpate'. 'Exterminate', especially, seems to have become more familiar in local mouths as settlers talked over their Aboriginal problem. Here was a word like 'system' (Chapter 6). Both were dense with Graeco-Latin obscurity and high seriousness. They were spells, incantations, words of policy, appropriate for men who knew something of the wide world. In fact, the exact meaning of 'exterminate' was less clear at that time that it was to be in the following century, after years of use, in Europe itself, for insects, beasts, and human beings. It then meant 'drive out' (its original sense) as well as 'destroy'.[15] In England about this time John Ruskin complained of the 'masked words' he heard all about him, whose implications few thoroughly understood but which everybody used. It was their mixture of vagueness and apparent power that made such words into idols. They were part of a new kind of popular politics, where literacy and part-literacy were intermixed and through which the well read aimed to flatter and seduce the ignorant. Such words, in any age, 'untie the winds' – here the phrase belongs to Shakespeare's Macbeth. It was one Macbeth used as he went from murder to murder. On both island and mainland 'exterminate' became a favourite word. In Sydney in 1827 W.C. Wentworth and Robert Wardell, as counsel for Nathaniel Lowe, called for 'an exterminating war' against the Blacks. With such an imprimatur it was soon a matter of faith that, as another Sydney man said in 1838, they '[are] a set of monkies, and the earlier they are exterminated from the face of the earth the better'.[16]

Graziers and stockmen made organised efforts to destroy all the Black people living about them. They had their methods of communication too, so that the lessons of invasion and ideas about revenge easily extended not only along the frontier but also from one side of the continent to the other. At Swan River eighteen months after Arthur's Black Line, George Fletcher Moore told the story of a labouring man lately arrived from Van Diemen's Land. He was walking with a cart near Perth when he saw what Moore called 'some unoffending natives'. ' "D—n the rascals," said he, "I'll show you how we treat them in Van Diemen's Land," and immediately fired on them.'[17]

What of the combinations made by Aborigines, with the hope of driving out or destroying the invaders? Sometimes settlers imagined tribal alliances that did not exist. At Swan River, for instance, among wild fears of a sudden attack from all sides, Governor Stirling tried to shift the intertribal balance of power, as he understood it, by courting Weeiup, of the Upper Swan people.[18] But in New South Wales the troubles around Bathurst in 1824 certainly involved an alliance of tribes. During the 1830s most of the pastoral frontier was embraced by two enormous groupings, the Wiradjuri (south past the Murrumbidgee) and the Kamilaroi (north to the Macintyre). These were areas of easy movement, languages were widespread and trade and ceremony drew the people together, so that alliances were common. For similar reasons the invaders themselves spread quickly across this country, with settlement sweeping southward from Sydney and Bathurst and north and north-west to the Namoi and Gwydir. Stockmen, cattle, and sheep passed frequently across the land. Faced with growing numbers of Europeans, several Wiradjuri clans took the offensive along the Murrumbidgee late in 1838, in 'a regular guerrilla warfare', as a traveller put it, and with temporary success.[19]

On the lower Gwydir some of the Kamilaroi did the same. In response, and driven perhaps by an exterminating spirit, stockmen organised themselves during winter 1838. On 10 June at least twenty-eight Aborigines were killed at Myall Creek, one of the tributaries of the Gwydir (Chapter 1).[20] The leading man was John Fleming, native-born, and the others were convicts and former convicts. Their homes were scattered along the river for 40 miles and among seven cattle stations, but they organised a meeting at a central point, Bengari, near Gravesend. Fleming himself was absent – out, as he later said, 'after the blacks in another direction' – but he caught up with the main party before they reached Myall Creek. After killing the Aborigines there they crossed the ridge to Byron Plains, where the boy was shot whom Andrew Eaton buried, but where Eaton managed to get most of the people away.

By chance, the deaths at Myall Creek were reported and followed up by a police magistrate from the Hunter Valley and, whatever these and other

Europeans might have done elsewhere, it became the best documented case of its kind. We therefore know that the Aborigines on this station – at least a third of them children and the remainder women and old men – tried to escape by crowding into the main hut. The stockmen tied their wrists, 'with the palms to each other', roped them in a line and led them some distance away, where they were killed, mainly with knives, and hacked to pieces. Their remains were then dragged together and burnt.[21]

These Aborigines had lived around the Myall Creek huts for several weeks. Like Eaton at Byron Plains, one stockman, Charles Kilmeister, had made them especially welcome. According to the superintendent, each evening when he came home Kilmeister danced and sung with them – 'it was altogether through him that the blacks were permitted to be on the station at all'. And yet, when the Aborigines were led away Kilmeister was persuaded to go too, among the murderers. It was he who was sent afterwards to see that every trace of his friends was destroyed.[22]

II

During this very period along the south coast of the mainland, and in particular at Port Phillip and Adelaide, there were attempts to make a new start with the relationship of Black and White. When John Batman reached Port Phillip from Launceston as representative of the Port Phillip Association, in late May 1835, he planned to deal with the Aborigines there as the current proprietors of the soil. He immediately looked for men who had the appearance of local leaders and having found eight – so he later claimed – on 6 June he persuaded them to set their marks to a document that conveyed to the association 600,000 acres to the north and west of the harbour. They were to receive in return forty pairs of blankets, 130 knives, sixty-two pairs of scissors, forty-two tomahawks, forty mirrors, 250 handkerchiefs and equally precise quantities of clothes and flour, plus more of the same each year as 'tribute or rent'.[23]

Settlers in Van Diemen's Land believed to begin with that the power of mainland governors, in Sydney and Perth, went no further than their own areas of settlement (Chapter 7). As late as March 1836 Arthur himself asked for clarification on this point from Sir Richard Bourke, Governor of New South Wales, and the belief that Port Phillip was ruled by no one was at the root of John Fawkner's plan for a town-republic.[24] The same logic meant that settlers might make their own arrangements with the people they found there. Most members of the Port Phillip Association wanted, above all, to be rich, which depended on their getting land as easily as possible. But some were both well read and highly principled in their attitude to race relations. They included the sheriff of Van Diemen's Land, Thomas Bannister, younger brother of Saxe Bannister. On such issues Saxe was an enthusiast, but Tom was obsessive. He seems to have relied especially on his brother's book, published in London in 1830 and entitled *Humane Policy; or, Justice to the Aborigines of New Settlements Essential to a Due Expenditure of British Money, and to the Best Interests of the Settlers.*

Saxe's failure in New South Wales and the recent violence in Van Diemen's Land proved to the younger Bannister that the government in London was not interested in using moral authority in questions of race. To all appearances it acknowledged, he said, 'no power but the bayonet'. '[I]t is *new* to English history', he argued (using phrases from *Humane Policy*), 'to seize distant countries, as has been done in Australia, without at least pretending to compensate the natives'. 'Our object', so he told a highly placed patron in England, hoping that the point would reach Whitehall, ' ... is not possession and expulsion, or what is worse extermination, but possession and civilization'. Having little money to invest in the enterprise himself, he was less concerned with acreage than with the high moral ground. Their proposal, he believed, was 'the only chance for the natives'. It would 'substitute real benefits for them, in the place of the *verbal* benevolence heretofore bestowed'. Joseph Tice Gellibrand, another member, likewise spoke of the Port Phillip opportunity as providential. With the imprimatur of the British government, he said, 'we may expect ... that its effects will extend over the continent of New Holland'.[25]

Batman's agreement with the Port Phillip people was, in fact, a fraud. The marks on the deed were not Aboriginal ones and no Aborigine in such circumstances could have understood the transaction as Batman said they did.[26] And yet an important building was planned on this flawed foundation. The local people were to be converted, very gradually, into informed and free members of a new kind of community. Some in the association believed that in making up their minds about the invaders the Aborigines would be persuaded by positive evidence of the benefits available. They were, after all, 'rational beings'. Choices were to be offered them, and the most promising were in the areas of justice and medicine. In both cases European advantage was surely palpable. In February 1836 the association was able to drive home the virtues of British justice when, after months of harmony, an Aboriginal woman was raped by a shepherd on the Maribyrnong River. The offender was sent back to Launceston for trial and the victim's people were assured of his punishment.[27]

As for medicine, in *Humane Policy* Saxe Bannister had explained the usefulness of qualified surgeons on the frontier. They could not only improve the people's health. They might also seek to understand indigenous cures, discover 'native drugs and minerals' and set up laboratories for teaching the natives. At Port Phillip part of the Bellarine Peninsula was set aside as a formal meeting place for Black and White, with Alexander Thomson, a medical man, in charge. Thomson was to be not only storekeeper, dispensing the blankets, clothes, and food that were to be part of the association's regular 'tribute', but also catechist and surgeon. This was apparently the idea of John Helder Wedge, another member of the association and a former government surveyor. Wedge was particularly interested in traditional skills and it was he who gave most thought to the way in which Aboriginal ingenuity might be turned in new directions. The key, he believed, was a regular system of barter, and he tried it himself at Port Phillip with some success. The point, as Saxe Bannister had said, was to give the Aborigines a place of their own, as self-reliant individuals, within the wider economy. Schooling was crucial. 'The children may be led by degrees', he said, 'to assist in producing their own provisions'.[28] Nothing could make a better impression than the European power to save lives and ease bodily suffering, but much else was to follow.

In August 1835 Governor Bourke declared that Port Phillip was indeed part of New South Wales and in September 1836 he received permission from Whitehall to establish there the normal structures of law and order. All landed title within the colony was derived from the Crown and as a result the association's purchase was disallowed, but members were given £7000 compensation and Bourke also took over their moral obligations to the Aboriginal people.[29] Thomas Bannister asked to be given the management of the settlement and Wedge continued to consider the recreation of the Blacks as free individuals. '[O]n no account', he said, must we 'coerce them to permanent labor'. They must begin as producers themselves, possibly selling fish or baskets.[30] But Bourke had already consulted with Mr Justice Burton. Together they planned for the district a system of 'Black villages', where the people could be taught, as Burton later put it, 'the purposes, duties, and Arts of life'. They were to enjoy the rights of British subjects, plus that security and comfort owed to them as 'the original proprietors of the soil'.[31]

Burton wanted to work, as Wedge and the Bannisters did, by persuasion. His conduct of the trial of the Myall Creek murderers (see later) was to prove that he was deeply concerned about the legal status of the Blacks. But his ideas about freedom were limited and he was more interested in their spiritual than their economic future. He paid no attention to indigenous tongues. There was no point, he said, 'in forming vocabularies and gaining an imperfect knowledge of a necessarily imperfect language'. Nothing in his scheme was to be compulsory, and yet he imagined the Aborigines being brought to a point where their decisions were preordained. The children, for instance, were to be fed and clothed so as to force on their minds an unmistakable contrast with life in the bush. As quickly as possible they were to possess, he said, 'not only a dislike … but an incapacity even to live in it'.[32]

The difference between these two approaches echoed arguments that might be heard now all over the British Empire. Bannister's was the older view, anchored in a secular frame of mind and a utilitarian understanding of the duties of government. In promoting human happiness, all authority must shape itself to the rational inclinations of the people. The ancient cultures of India, especially, had long interested British scholars. British philology had taken large leaps forward through the comparison of Sanskrit and European tongues and British administrators had attempted forms of government that might, in limited ways, make use of Indian ideas about public order. But by the 1820s the British were becoming more absolute in their dealings with the rest of the world and less interested in the mental universe of those they governed. In 1835 the Board of Control for India received from Thomas Babington Macaulay his authoritative 'Minute on Education', which famously argued that 'a single shelf of a good European library was worth the whole native literature of India and Arabia.' The board, said Macaulay, must give the people of India justice and civilisation, but that could only be done with English language and English ideas. It was pointless to spend any time on indigenous learning – on 'medical doctrines', as he put it, 'which would disgrace an English farrier, [and on] astronomy which would move laughter in girls at an English boarding school'. These were people who could not be truly educated with words of their own.[33]

In Australia Threlkeld might argue for the high complexity of Aboriginal language – for its 'extensive dual numbers', its 'conjoint dual cases', its 'various conjugations of verbs'. At Swan River, Robert Menli Lyon (who, like Threlkeld, put together an Aboriginal vocabulary) might find the people strangely similar to ancient Scots, Greeks, and Hebrews. Lyon, too, might argue for the impossibility, the 'utter folly', of trying to govern any people without learning their language. This approach now belonged to the past. Humanitarians everywhere might still argue for Aboriginal claims to the soil and, in fact, such arguments were strengthened in 1835, with the appointment of Lord Glenelg, a keen humanitarian, as Secretary of State for the Colonies. But such logic depended on movements of European conscience, not on any sense of the richness of life in the Antipodes. The opinion of Alexander Maconochie, who interested himself in the welfare of Aborigines as well as the welfare of convicts, was now typical. 'The object is to raise the native', Maconochie said, 'not to descend to his level ... by imperfect, and ... ludicrous efforts to use his jargon'.[34]

Late in 1836 the Governor appointed a missionary, George Langhorne, who was instructed to establish a village or villages at Port Phillip, with the hope of drawing the Aborigines away from their 'wandering habits' and 'proving to them experimentally the superior gratification to be obtained in civilized life'. Land was to be allowed them in small quantities as long as they showed an interest in cultivating it and Langhorne was to make up his own mind whether they should work it as individuals or as groups. Threlkeld's rule was that all Aboriginal labour in such settlements should be 'for common good'. Bourke went further in suggesting that Robert Owen's scheme of shared property, including land, might be useful at Port

Phillip, so that 'cultivation should be for common benefit'. Langhorne agreed. '[B]eing simple in its principle', he said, 'it would be more readily understood by these people who may be said already to practise the system of a community of goods'.[35] A site was chosen across the Yarra River from the newly formed town of Melbourne, and Langhorne made a start. However, Burton's hopes, founded on ignorance, soon evaporated. After two years, he said in disappointment, some boys had learned to read. But the adults had 'in no respect broken off their Native usages'.[36]

South Australia was governed from the beginning in the spirit of Macaulay. The South Australian Act, passed in 1834, declared that all land within the territory was 'waste and unoccupied' and therefore available for purchase from the Crown. However, Lord Glenelg came to office soon afterwards and when letters patent were issued bringing the colony into existence they included a proviso that the government had no intention of impinging on 'the rights of any Aboriginal natives ... to the actual occupation or enjoyment ... of any Lands [they] now actually occupied or enjoyed'.[37] Glenelg also forced the South Australian Commission to agree that any land it planned to sell which was found to be occupied by Aborigines would be bought from them at a fair price. But the commissioners made this agreement with the belief, apparently concealed from Glenelg, that there was in fact no such land. The Aborigines were not 'occupiers' as they understood the word.[38]

White efforts to take and hold the land might be wholly due to greed, as they were with the South Australian Commission. But among Europeans already living here they also came from a sharpened sense of territory, a belief that years of labour, together with the hardship and daily fears associated with frontier life, gave a moral claim to the soil. Talk of 'extermination' depended on that feeling, but a few managed to affirm, on their own terms, a kind of shared possession with the indigenous people. Every land grant at this time included, in theory, an obligation for the proprietor to pay a nominal 'quit rent' to the Crown. With this in mind, perhaps, an unnamed gentleman wrote to the *Sydney Gazette* in 1823. Describing his feeling for 'the people whose land I have taken', he committed himself to an annual payment of a farthing an acre for their benefit – a peppercorn rental. The Port Phillip Association's purchase included annual payments to the Aborigines and at Camden Park, near Sydney, the Macarthur family set aside a paddock and gave regular rations to the local people, as their 'inheritance'. Such arrangements, more or less informal, were made in many places throughout Australia.[39] Some also argued that Aboriginal place names ought to be preserved as far as possible. 'Dutigalla', 'Nearamnew', 'Bareberys', and 'Bearpurt' were all used by the Port Phillip Association for their settlement. Here was acknowledgment more permanent than annual tribute and, happily, even cheaper. James Ross, in Hobart, said that such names gave a distinctive 'nationality' to the land. John Dunmore

Lang, in Sydney, liked them for their independent vigour, so different, he said, from the names of British statesmen with which the soil was otherwise adorned.[40]

Europeans who were interested in Aboriginal language were not always interested in their rights to land. Even Threlkeld thought of them mainly as a labouring people. The possibility of employing Aborigines for private profit had existed from the beginning. In the 1790s some of the officers of the New South Wales Corps had spoken of them as possible slaves and at Swan River problems with immigrant labourers led many settlers to think in the same way. '[O]n them', said George Fletcher Moore, 'we must eventually depend for labour, as we can never afford to pay English servants the high wages they expect, besides feeding them as well. The black fellows receive little more than rice – their simple diet'.[41] In more prosperous places employers occasionally made a point of paying wages. A few Aboriginal families earned both money and rations for work as shepherds, and the Macarthurs employed Yellow Johnny, a horse-breaker at a regular wage of five shillings a week. 'For stockmen', said Threlkeld, 'the blacks are invaluable, they being exceedingly fond of riding on horseback'.[42]

The land rights of the Aborigines, once dismissed, were easily forgotten. It was more difficult to decide, as a matter of day-to-day policy, what rights they might have as a conquered people and as individual British subjects. This point became especially urgent when they lived within areas of settlement, working, or at least living, side by side with Europeans.[43] But while most senior administrators supported equal citizenship in theory very few could decide what it meant in practice. Aborigines had been spoken of as British subjects since the time of Governor Macquarie but the resulting benefits were meagre and inconsistent. In 1820 a convict man, John Kirby, was hanged for the murder, near Newcastle, of 'King' Burrigan. In Van Diemen's Land another received twenty-five lashes for behaviour of 'indescribable brutality' towards Aboriginal women.[44] But though murders multiplied in the 1820s, and several Aborigines were themselves tried and hanged, the only White men thus condemned to death, in Sydney in 1826, were four convict stockmen who murdered a boy called Tommy, at Port Stephens, and all four were reprieved.[45]

The settlements at Swan River and in South Australia both began with announcements that the Aboriginal people had the full protection of the law. Any colonist committing a crime against them, said Governor Stirling, 'will be liable to be prosecuted and tried for the offence, as if the same had been committed against any other of His Majesty's subjects'. Governor Hindmarsh said the same, in his first formal act of government, using the proclamation that his secretary George Stevenson had drawn up for him at sea (mentioned in Chapter 7).[46] But once again the principle was not put into practice. At Swan River a European boy and an Aboriginal man were separately killed early in 1830 and by spring that year there was organised violence on both sides. The law, dressed in motley, then stepped in. In February 1832 three Aborigines were tried and hanged for murder and in July 1835 a carpenter, John McKail, was charged with the manslaughter of Gogalee, an Aboriginal man whom he killed because he wrongly thought he had raided his hut. Several of Gogalee's friends were invited to watch McKail's trial. But they could not give evidence because they could not swear the Christian oath and so he was discharged. He was persuaded to offer compensation in flour and blankets to Gogalee's people and to transport himself to King George Sound.[47]

In 1833 a powerful leadership had emerged among the Aborigines at Swan River, including Yagan and his father, Midgegooroo, of the Beeloo people. Yagan, Midgegooroo, and another man were proclaimed outlaws, which, as the *Perth Gazette* explained, meant that they might be killed on sight. In May Midgegooroo was captured by soldiers. Disarmed and closely watched, had he been White he would have been brought in and tried for his 'crimes'. Indeed, there was a moment of doubt as to the next right move. George Fletcher Moore remarked in his diary, 'the idea of shooting him with the cool formalities of execution, is revolting'. But it was only revolting if the mind were allowed to dwell on Midgegooroo as a creature with all the high trappings of human dignity, or at least as a British subject. Two days later Moore noted, without comment, that he had in fact been shot, 'at the gaol-door, by a party of the military'.[48]

III

It was common, at the beginning of each European settlement along the Australian coast, for the Aborigines to decide that the newcomers were their own dead returned to life. There were exceptions. In the extreme north of the continent the people knew about aliens because they were used to visitors from the East Indies, and this may explain why the military base at Fort Dundas, on Melville Island, was immediately resented by the Tiwi as a citadel of invaders. It lasted for this and other reasons only four years, 1824–28. But in most cases the Aborigines were inclined to think that Europeans were part of their own universe and could be brought more or less easily within the old, familiar scheme of things. Drained of colour as corpses were, it was only hard to understand why they blundered so much in the daily habits of life renewed.[49]

This faith survived longest in the case of William Buckley, a convict who was left behind at Port Phillip when the expedition under David Collins sailed for the Derwent early in 1804 (Chapter 1). Buckley lived among the Aborigines until the men of the Port Phillip Association arrived, and since he had learnt the local language he proved a precious asset to Batman in his negotiations. Without him no agreement could have been made and his help was also crucial afterwards. Many years later again, after Buckley's death, the story of his first meeting with the Blacks was told by the woman who was supposed to have been his Aboriginal wife, Purranmurnin Tallarwurnin. Her words, obviously well polished by her European interviewer, were written down. It seems that Buckley was found lying, Gulliver-like, on the sand, 'sunning himself after a bath in the sea' – presumably a glistening pink. The man who first saw him, the woman said, collected as many others as possible and they crept in on him.

> When they came near he took little or no notice of them, and did not even alter his position for some time. They were very much alarmed. At length one of the party finding courage addressed him as muurnong guurk (meaning that they supposed him to be one who had been killed and come to life again), and asked his name, 'You Kondak Baarwon?' Buckley replied by a prolonged grunt and an inclination of the head, signifying yes.

Further questions and similar answers made them sure, 'and he and they soon became friends. They made a wuurn of leafy branches for him, and lit a fire in front of it, around which they all assembled'. From that time Buckley was one of their own.[50]

In Western Australia a belief that invasion somehow equalled reincarnation was already fading by 1836, at least among young Aboriginal men and women.[51] The disenchantment of the Europeans themselves with the old inhabitants was a parallel process. Like the Aborigines, confronted with something so strange settlers had to cast about for something familiar in order to decide how to act. To begin with they, too, occasionally found in these new faces, both ghastly and attractive, some hint of themselves in earlier form. Figures like Yagan – brave, dignified, and clever – caught the European imagination, as reflections, for instance, of the kind of primitive chief to be found in the writing of Sir Walter Scott. A few well-read settlers were prepared to think that such leaders were antique gentlemen, cruel, impulsive but honourable. Europeans were newly aware of the romantic power of the past, Scott being their teacher, and these richly unpredictable savages were easily seen as its inhabitants. Threlkeld spoke of watching an Aboriginal couple, McGill and his wife Patty, 'in all the playfulness of pure affection, like Abraham sporting with Sarah in the even-tide'. Contrariwise, he referred to the British ruler Boudicca (Boadicea) as 'queen of an Aboriginal tribe'. Robert Lyon, himself apparently a Scot, described Yagan as 'the Wallace of the age'.[52]

The killing of Yagan in July 1833, by two white men (brothers) who had asked him to eat with them, looked like an act of romantic treachery.[53] It echoed the murder of King Duncan by Macbeth, for English-speaking people the most famous betrayal of a noble guest. Aborigines, in short, might do strange things to the European imagination. The pursuit of such mystery meant listening well to their voices and to the inward complexity that those voices seemed to convey. It was infinitely hard. 'What for you so stupid', said McGill, who was Threlkeld's friend and teacher, when he blundered with the language, 'you very stupid fellow'. The world of the women might be especially intriguing. At King George Sound the government surgeon, Isaac Scott Nind, found that the women 'frequently sing while by themselves, and their songs are not always decent'. Their evasiveness summed up all the difficulties of European understanding. '[T]hey are also said by the men to be very fluent in abuse', said Nind, 'and their oratory, as interpreted to us, was sufficiently *piquante*. At their camps there was always a great noise, but it instantly ceased on the approach of a stranger, till it was ascertained who he was'.[54]

Such noises and such silences made up a pattern very hard to unpick. Considered in the mass, Aborigines were a world apart. And yet the newer understanding made them, individual by individual, no more or less than British subjects. They were to be honestly dealt with, not as fixed communities, not as ancient Scots or Hebrews, but one by one, as modern Britons. Everything was meant to depend on the methods of administrators, taking no account of origins, skin colour, or old forms of leadership. Here were no Wallaces or Boudiccas. The Aborigines must come to terms with the nineteenth-century state, a power that governed through the written word, which depended on system, which peeled mystery from old kings, and which transcribed as simple public fact the life of every individual.

Threlkeld and Saxe Bannister had themselves worked for the literacy of the Aborigines. They, too, had aimed to reform Aboriginal relationship with government by rendering all in print, for the equal comprehension of both sides. This effort survived into the 1830s, and especially in Western Australia, the only colony where Aboriginal language can be said to have made a mark, however slight, on leading men. There, during the first years (as I say above), the settlers were forced to depend on the Aborigines.[55] In South Australia settlers who thought carefully about the Aborigines did so on principle, whereas in the west they did so because they needed them, and this need encouraged more even-handed conversation. 'Unlike some of our neighbours', said the editor of the *Perth Gazette*, 'we are disposed to place a certain degree of reliance upon the word of a native'.[56] Such trust meant a more penetrating kind of curiosity. In autumn 1833, at Swan River, Robert Lyon published a vocabulary in the *Gazette*, as part of a series of articles about the Aborigines. This was followed by Captain George Grey's *Vocabulary of the Dialects of South-Western Australia*, also published locally, in 1839. The government's 'Native Interpreter', Francis Armstrong, was a continuous source of useful knowledge and in 1842 his 'Native Grammar' appeared in the *Western Australian Almanack*. At the same time George Fletcher Moore published, in London, the knowledge accumulated so far (including that of the current Governor, John Hutt) in a book he called *Descriptive Vocabulary of the Language in Common Use amongst the Aborigines in Western Australia*.[57] And again, in 1845, the Catholic missionary, John Brady, published a *Descriptive Vocabulary* in

Rome. In South Australia there were only two such books, by the Lutheran missionaries Christian Teichelmann and Clamor Schürmann in 1840, and by Matthew Moorhouse in 1846.[58]

Thus, in the west, Aboriginal tongues were well attended in print. Some of the people themselves, the Nyungar, were acquainted with writing, sensing its power as a means of knowledge, if only because they were often asked to carry written messages. They had their own rapid methods of spreading news, and as letter carriers the Europeans found them 'invaluable', as the Reverend John Wollaston said, 'never failing in what they undertake in this way'.[59] The man who carried a note from shepherds in the York district to their master – 'The devil may take the sheep and you to for weve neither flowr shuger nor meat' – must have seen how voices entered the paper at one end and made their impact at the other. Another Catholic missionary arriving in Perth in the 1840s spoke of 'the kind of veneration which the natives have for books or any papers with writing'. 'Talking papers', as they called them, clearly had an inwardness, a concealed authority, like that of their own most sacred objects. 'They credit them', the same man said, 'with an almost magical power of revealing hidden things, so that, when they want to justify themselves in the face of some accusation, they tell us: "Look at the book or the talking paper, and then you will know who is right!"'[60]

Meanwhile in all colonies continuing efforts were made to impress on the Blacks the majestic truth of British justice. As Saxe Bannister had always argued, it was the duty of the British, as agents of empire, to be 'just at every step' and that depended on the scrupulous administration of the law. The daily demonstration of high principle within instruments of government was, in the end, the only means of proving to the old inhabitants that they might benefit from invasion. This was an argument especially dear to Lord Glenelg, and he impressed it on all colonial governors during his period as Secretary of State, 1835–39. Inspired by these instructions, as soon as he heard of the massacre at Myall Creek, in June 1838, Governor Gipps ordered an inquiry. In a similar spirit, the magistrate whom he sent to investigate, Edward Denny Day, after a fortnight's ride inland, compiled a body of paperwork more weighty and meticulous than any so far yielded by the remote Australian bush.

In November the Myall Creek murderers, all except their leader John Fleming, who had escaped, were brought to Sydney. There were two trials, with eleven accused in the first and seven in the second. The problem with both trials lay in proving the death of a particular, identifiable human being, not only a British subject but also someone recognisable within the ceremonies of British law. This was not the problem that Wentworth and Wardell had suggested in Lowe's case, in 1827. They had never doubted the identity of Lowe's victim – Jackey Jackey, 'alias *Commandant*, alias *Jerry*' – nor that he was dead. Instead they had argued that all Aborigines were beyond the law. In the Myall Creek case it was identities that were

Stockmen on horseback drag away their Aboriginal victims at Myall Creek; the scene as it was imagined by an unknown English artist in 1841.

Source: C. Pelham, *The Chronicle of Crime; or, The Newgate Calendar*, 1 (London 1841)

uncertain. Large numbers had been killed but there were problems with linking, beyond reasonable doubt, the names of culprits to the names of victims. Had Wentworth and Wardell been available for the defence it is likely that these problems would have been insuperable. But Wentworth had retired from the bar and Wardell had been killed by convicts. The dominant figures in both trials, and especially the second, were not counsel but the judges.

The chief justice, James Dowling, heard the first. The charges of murder were couched in various ways, with the hope that one might stick. Some formulas mentioned the victim as 'an aboriginal male black', name unknown. Others tried to pinpoint an individual by referring to 'Daddy' and the attorney-general, John Hubert Plunkett, set out to prove that Daddy, a known person who had been at Myall Creek, had in fact been killed. He relied mainly on the evidence of William Hobbs, who had been in charge at the station and who had reported the killings in the first place.

> I saw some of the bodies [Hobbs told him from the witness box]; they were
> very much disfigured; ... I did know Daddy, he was an old man; he was the
> largest man I ever saw, either white or black; I saw a large body there ... I
> could not swear that it was Daddy's body; ... it was laying on its back;
> there was no head and the fire had destroyed nearly the whole of the flesh;
> I believe it to be the body of a man – the body of Daddy.

But under cross-examination Hobbs had to admit, 'I could not swear that it was a male', and worse, 'I could not swear that the black called Daddy is not now in existence'. In his address to the jury the chief justice agreed that without the body of the victim as described in the charges the prosecution must fail. Armed with this advice, the jury quickly returned with 'Not Guilty'.[61]

Plunkett ordered a new trial. This time the victim was described in some counts as a boy named Charley and in others as 'an aboriginal black child', name unknown. Like Daddy, Charley was easily remembered. Hobbs called him 'very familiar and a forward boy for his age'. This time legal argument stretched the trial over four days, and all three judges sat together in the end. The vaguer charges overlapped with the equally vague ones used previously and this made it look as if the men were being tried twice for the same offence, which the law forbade. On the other hand, the attorney-general now produced several charred bones, picked up during Day's search of the massacre site, including the rib bones of a child six or seven years old. It was only circumstantial evidence, but here at least were physical remains. Once again the defence argued that there was no certainty of the death of anyone the court might name – 'the alleged murdered person was a savage roving amongst his native hills and dales, and who might not be seen by any human being except his own tribe for years'. Once again the jury agreed. But persuaded apparently by the bones, this time they found the seven stockmen guilty of the murder of an unnamed child and on 18 December all were hanged.[62]

As proof of the energy of British justice the second trial was a triumph. It was one of the most significant events of the period for this country. But it also showed that the best hopes for Black and White were now over. The Aborigines were British subjects. That was certain. They were not beings beyond the law. But as individuals – creatures of voice, reason, conscience, and will – large numbers of them had no official existence because it was impossible to name them in the courts. In New South Wales, the project that was to have defined them as 'rational beings', recognised and recognising as such, among their fellow citizens – not just passive, but active heirs of justice – had failed. We must have trials like this, said Plunkett's junior counsel, if we want to protect the Aborigines, 'as we have no way of naming them'. Others were shocked at such a straining of legal principle. Wentworth, now a rich grazier himself, called the hangings 'legal murder'. Richard Windeyer, one of the defence lawyers, admitted that the crime had been 'most horrible' and that the punishment was well deserved. But

Burton had secured it by outmanoeuvring the defence, a 'trick', said Windeyer, beneath the dignity of a British judge.[63]

The logic of the Myall Creek trials was taken a step further in South Australia in 1840. The *Maria*, a passenger vessel travelling from Adelaide to Hobart, was wrecked on a reef off Lacepede Bay, in the colony's south-east, in July. About twenty-five survivors reached the shore and began walking back to Adelaide, more than 100 miles away. They were apparently looked after by the local people until some of the crew took liberties with Aboriginal women and the entire party was then killed. When he heard of the massacre Governor Gawler sent a body of men under the command of the police commissioner, Thomas O'Halloran, to identify the offenders and to enforce some kind of summary justice. The clan in question, the Milmenrura, were persuaded to hand over two men, Mongarawata and Pilgarie, and they were hanged at the site of the murders, with their people watching.[64]

The Governor had proceeded, as he put it, 'on the principles of martial law', though he had made no proclamation. Besides, martial law punished individuals only as a means of restoring order. Gawler's aim was to punish in a situation where the lack of Christian witnesses (qualified to swear an oath) made it impossible, as with Myall Creek, to link named killers with named dead. Elaborate and angry argument followed. Gawler's supporters declared that the Milmenrura were not really British subjects – some said they had forfeited their rights and some that they had never had any. The chief justice himself, Charles Cooper, believed that people like the Milmenrura were beyond British jurisdiction. '[S]uch only of the native population', he said, 'as have in some degree acquiesced in our dominion can be considered subject to our laws'. Acquiescence made men and women knowable, and being knowable they could be held to account. It all depended on their own consent, because 'there must be some submission or acquiescence on their part, or at least, some intercourse between us and them'.[65] In this way the question of Aboriginal rights was tied back to that of the free-willed human being – that lively piece of Creation whose attributes (to use *Macbeth* again) stand 'trumpet-tongu'd' before the listening world.

In a similar spirit James Macarthur, speaking in Sydney in 1842, asked his listeners to imagine the 'intolerable tyranny' involved, from an Aboriginal point of view, in being forced to choose between two types of obedience, two bodies of law, equally insistent, Black and White. A man might be known, and might know himself, as one of his own people or he might have his name enrolled among the newcomers, and this must, or should, be a matter of his own painful choice. During a trial in Perth, Johnston Drummond, one of the government botanist's sons, told of just such a man, Boo-goon-gwert, who had stolen grapes, melons, and potatoes from his father's garden. 'I accused the prisoner of having stolen them, and he said he would submit to be speared in the thigh (the punishment usually inflicted amongst themselves for any transgressions)'. But Boo-goon-gwert had added, with all the fierceness of free will, that if soldiers tried to force on him the justice of the invaders he would hit back hard.[66]

In fact it was too late to make room for the deliberations of individual Blacks. Stockmen, apparently anxious to escape the fate of the Myall Creek murderers, began to use more clandestine methods, distributing flour, for instance, laced with strychnine or arsenic. '[W]hen these men ... get alarmed', said a northern squatter, 'they frequently shoot at a blackfellow, or quietly give him a dose of poison'.[67] These were now acts impossible to adjudicate. At the same time (Chapter 15) almost instinctive notions of racial difference began to be embroidered with new ideas sent abroad in print. As with manhood and womanhood, reading gave a loftier self-consciousness to the individual's sense of race. We began to think in cleverer and more conceited ways – about the shape of our bodies, the timbre of our voices, and the tincture of our skins.

Imagination was driven, too, by a more complex sense of past, present, and future. In England during the 1840s there was a burst of writing about 'Caucasians', 'Teutons', 'Saxons', and 'Anglo-Saxons'. A love of liberty, a high sense of personal duty, and an overwhelming energy were now supposed to be Anglo-Saxon virtues, virtues nourished in the blood from generation to generation down the ages. Their ancestry made the English capable of governing lesser races. Ability gave them a right to rule and, if necessary, a right to exterminate and displace. It was to be some years yet before such ideas – binding common bigotry to complex thought – became a kind of household wisdom, especially in the remote inland. But they were beginning to make their mark. The much-read essayist, Thomas Carlyle, was an early exponent. In a savage moment Carlyle suggested that the whole Black population of the West Indies might not equal – 'in quantity of intellect, faculty, docility, energy, and available human valour and value' – a single street in the heart of London.[68] Macaulay had weighed the books of Europe against the books of India and Arabia. Carlyle weighed people, Black and White.

At the same time the rapid growth of Sydney proved for James Tucker 'the wonted energy of the Anglo-Saxon race'. South Australia's splendour suggested to another writer that 'the energies of the Saxon race are as active in the warmer regions as in their native cooler ones'.[69] The word 'race' was taken up in this way, in our part of the world, with precision and pride. It even seemed that commitment to race might eclipse all other duties. In one of his novels (1847), Benjamin Disraeli, the future prime minister, had a gentleman explain the vast power of England itself in the same way – 'All is race; there is no other truth.'[70] Among many of the Europeans in Australia, surrounded by other 'races' – faces legible by colour, and voices and bearing to match – this formula made immediate sense.

Chapter 9

God and Humanity

I

Europeans long lived in hope of a teeming and glittering mass of water in the middle of Australia, an inland sea. Finding that sea became a great desideratum, for surely, with its heart uncovered, the land would at last make sense. The evidence of Aborigines on both sides of the continent seemed to affirm that a sea did exist. '[I]ts waves are mountains', the story went, 'and in its waters is a creature which devours black men'.[1] In August 1835 an expedition of five men left Bathurst, in western New South Wales, under the leadership of a young settler, Hopkins Sibthorpe, with the intention of following inland the rivers so far known and putting the matter at rest. Moving with unprecedented speed, within three or four weeks the explorers covered 1400 miles. There was of course no sea, but at the end of their journey they made a more surprising discovery – an English-speaking community calling itself 'Southland'. [2]

This was certainly a different kind of heart, a more distinctly human soul. A little inquiry proved that Southland was a loose federation of eleven states whose inhabitants numbered three or four million, partly Aboriginal and partly the descendents of invaders from Europe three centuries before. The laws were liberal and humane. Racial origin made no difference to civil rights. Also, only wild animals were slaughtered for meat, on the grounds that: 'A tame animal is a sort of friend, a member of the family.' In fact, principles of live-and-let-live were stretched as far as possible. Numerous forms of worship existed side by side, differing on many points but acknowledging a 'friendly agreement on essentials'. A leading citizen explained how such variety worked. 'Ours … are "Christian states" ', he said, 'in the sense that the *individual citizens* of them are Christians, but not in the sense of our *laws enforcing* the profession of Christianity, or of any particular religious persuasion'. Anyone could hold public office, whatever their sect. In theory even Christian faith was not required. And yet the discipline of faith was taken seriously and its ministers were supported by government. There was a common understanding that the teachings of Christ were in some sense infallible, and they were the basis of daily life.[3]

The story of Southland was no more true than the supposed Aboriginal tales of the inland sea. Published in London in 1837, it was the work of Lady Mary Fox, daughter of King William IV and Dorothea Jordan. Lady Mary never saw Australia and she seems to have fed her imagination mainly with the exploration journals of Charles Sturt.[4] Another book about religion and this country, *The Convict Ship*, just as remarkable but more accurate, appeared in London seven years later. Colin Arrott Browning, its author, was a naval surgeon who had travelled six times with convicts to New South Wales and Van Diemen's Land. He was much admired by Governor Arthur.[5] In an earlier publication Browning had explained the system he used for the moral and spiritual enlightenment of convict men on their way out. He shared the curiosity of Lancelot Threlkeld, plus the belief of Elizabeth Fry that souls might be won by the to-and-fro of conversation, and he worked out a complicated system of schooling on board ship, encouraging the prisoners to take responsibility for each other's progress. Pivotal to everything was the faith of each man in Browning himself. That was secured by showing them that he wanted to hear the tales of their lives. Browning believed that souls were storied things – that the inner self dances through narrative – and he offered himself as audience.

Mrs Fry was a strong-minded sceptic, but Browning seems to have received what he heard as transparent truth. He persuaded some of the men to write down their stories and a few, well edited, he published in *The Convict Ship*. The poor had always entertained each other with life stories. They had ancient ways of making sense of their lives and the patterns they used in dramatising themselves belonged to the distinctive formalities of an oral culture. One women convict, for instance, telling her own story in Hobart in 1842, spoke of how on the passage from England, 'Singing, dancing and telling the Histories of their past lives beguiled the time away'. Men about to be publicly hanged, as they stood with the rope around their necks, were also allowed to tell their stories. The pattern of the narrative was often the same, with wickedness and redemption the leading themes. The tales told by Browning's men were like that too, but he gave them a gloss of his own, which appears in the way he wrote them up.[6] Given his influence, perhaps they had begun to take the shape he approved of even as they left the lips of each teller.

Browning seems to have been successful with his men to a degree that may have surprised even himself. In his book he told of the voyage on the transport *Earl Grey*, which left Plymouth in October 1842. He began straightaway to impress on the convict passengers their immediate relationship with God – a person to be known face to face, whose speech might gild the air at least as much as any mortal speech. But his message was driven home in an unexpectedly powerful way when, at night in mid-Atlantic, the ship was hit by a thunderstorm. Browning, as he says in the book, jumped from his bunk and ran on deck:

> No language can possibly describe the scene in the midst of which I then stood, and by which I saw and felt myself encompassed. All creation seemed on fire. The thunder, the loudest that ever fell on my ear, prevailed in every quarter; – peal upon peal followed in rapid succession; – the distant roar contrasted with that in which I felt myself enwrapped, and the one or the other never ceased … The thick and Egyptian darkness which intervened was but for a moment, but even that moment gave to the senses and the mind no repose, – it was darkness that was terrific in itself, and gave to the winged thunderbolts and the electric coruscations that covered the face of the heavens, a more piercing glare – a more overpowering vividness.

It was hard for any man or woman of faith to believe that this was anything but the voice and appearance of the Almighty. 'The hour – the very hour of death was felt at hand – the moment of the soul's unclothing.' A thunderbolt hit the fore-royal-mast, split it to pieces and ran around and about through the fabric of the ship. '[F]or a while she seemed on fire', and it appeared she must immediately go down. The convicts had already been affected by Browning's conversation and sermons. This extraordinary experience, far beyond anything they could have known on land, seemed to prove everything he had told them about their own helplessness and the vast and unpredictable power of God. Calm returned, but next morning as he went among them he sensed 'an air of deep seriousness'. The night-time crisis was everywhere, he said, 'the subject of solemn conversation'. Its impact lasted among many of the men for the rest of the voyage and when they were about to disembark at Hobart some put together a written statement to be sent to the Governor, in which each promised to save £10 for transmission to the Chancellor of the Exchequer at Whitehall, 'as a practical expression', they said, 'of our sorrow for the injury we have inflicted on our country and on our society'. This document received 132 signatures, half the number of men on board.[7]

Here are two kinds of piety, and Australia was the site of both. Mary Fox wrote of a place where all lived side by side in rational charity and where the enjoyment of religion was underwritten by good government. Browning spoke of the way in which the finger of God might be laid with shocking impact on individual hearts. During the 1830s and '40s glorious possibilities of both kinds began to be felt in the Antipodes. This was partly a result of a belief that the world as a whole was passing through a period of extraordinary change. The Industrial Revolution had made a profound difference to the circumstances of both rich and poor and those of the poor who tried to make sense of the change turned to their Bibles. Often barely literate, many had a deep reverence for the written word, as a medium of the Word of God and as a final source of truth.

Some thought that the material universe itself was drawing to a close, as predicted in Revelation. In August 1830 John Claborne, a cooper in Bristol, wrote to his daughter, Mary Griffiths, who had lately come as a convict to New South Wales:

> Dear Mary you have often heard me tell of the Changes that must take place in all the world prior to the Kingdom of Christ to be established on earth and now wonderfull things is takeing place both at home and abroad for never was troubles in England as is now the poor is starving in the streets for want of Employment and hundreds is going to America to get labour … and Others is gone to Swan River to sell themselves for a time until they pay for passage over by servitude and the inhabitants is over pressed with taxes and Opp[r]ession so that they know not what to do or where to go: and the King of france [Charles X] is obliged to fly from france and is Come to England for refuge and is arrived in London and we know not what may happen here for [letter torn] oppression is verry great, but I believe and I am sure the time is Verry near that the Kingdoms of all the earth will fall, and the Kingdom of christ will be Established on the Ruins.

He assured her, in bondage far from home, that 'then the lord will gather his children from the four Quarters of the world and release his Captives be where ever they may'. Meanwhile she must read her Bible and, he said, 'put your dependence in him and in due time your deliverance will come'.[8]

An eager religious sensibility was obvious throughout the European world. In some ways these changes dated back to the mid-eighteenth century. John Wesley's Methodism had begun in the 1730s as a revivalist movement within the Church of England. It was now independent and had given birth to smaller and more radical sects. In Australia, as a vigorous and popular body of Protestant faith, Methodism had no equal. In New South Wales and Van Diemen's Land the official number of Methodists was still small, but their multiplying baptisms and marriages (at least among the Wesleyans, or 'Original Connection') proved their energy. In South Australia Maria Gawler, the Governor's wife, described them as 'by far the most numerous body', and they were certainly the most active there in building churches and broadcasting the Word to remote corners of settlement.[9]

The Bible was easily seen as a means of meeting with God. Used to reading out loud (either as readers themselves or as listeners) the poor did not think of print as a silent medium. Read devoutly, the Word of God might fill the sky like Browning's thunder. 'I cannot find one ray or beam of the son of Righteousness', said Isaac Dole, a Sydney locksmith, 'but in the scriptures'.[10] Dole was a former convict, but many other men and women – members of radical fundamentalist sects, mostly labourers or small tradesmen as he was – came to Australia as free immigrants. They hoped to find not only material prosperity but also spiritual freedom. Here they might forget the ubiquitous voice of an Established Church and feel more fully the voice of the Lord. David Doust, a Primitive Methodist from Sussex, received this advice from his father before he sailed for Sydney:

> The way to git on is to git the Bible open before you and read a verse and pray over it, and read it again and pray and let 6 verses last a hour in that way till you feel it is yours and heaven comed down on earth and you are filled with a power that will carry you above and through all.

The experience of 'heaven comed down to earth' might empower a man or woman all alone, but it might also empower Christians gathered among others of like mind. By 1844 two Primitive Methodist ministers had formed a congregation of about two hundred, with a school, in Sydney, calling themselves 'Australian Methodists'.[11] Numerous sects of the same kind gathered in South Australia, famous from the beginning as a place of free worship. By the mid-1840s Adelaide possessed congregations of Bible Christians, Primitive Methodists, and New Connection Methodists, all seeking God by the close reading of scripture.[12] The Lutherans in their rural villages, Klemzig, Hahndorf, Bethany, were also people of the Book.

Others used not only the Bible but also messages received direct from on High. Emanuel Swedenborg had established his Church of the New Jerusalem in England in 1757, with the belief that the Last Judgement, 'the Lord's second advent', had already happened. He was privy, he said, to the inner sense of scripture and he had also been allowed to visit the hereafter. Jacob Pitman, a Swedenborgian, came to South Australia in 1838, equipped with books, periodicals, and tracts, and by 1845 had a congregation of twenty. He wrote his sermons in the celebrated shorthand invented by his brother Isaac, 'and read them slowly and deliberately so that all might understand them'.[13] Meanwhile, in the United States, Joseph Smith had built the Church of Jesus Christ of Latter-day Saints on the authority of *The Book of Mormon* (1830), a volume transcribed from golden tablets to which he had been led by angels. The Mormon gospel spread likewise, by way of Britain, to Australia. The first Mormon missionary, William Barratt, came to Adelaide in 1840, and another, Andrew Anderson, reached Sydney in 1841. Barrett managed very little but Anderson gathered a congregation near Wellington, in western New South Wales. More systematic Mormon preaching began in the 1850s, when eight shiploads of Saints, mainly from regions north of Sydney, crossed the ocean to California, aiming to witness the Second Coming itself at Salt Lake City, the Church's Zion.[14]

This blossoming of religious life made a difference most of all to women. The voices of women themselves (as with the Sisters of Mercy in Perth) became sacred in new ways. In the early years of the century a domestic servant living in Devon, Joanna Southcott, the 'Woman Clothed with the Sun', had prophesied at length – her inspired words filling more than sixty volumes – and had drawn a following of more than a hundred thousand, nearly two-thirds of them women. 'Is it a new thing', she asked, 'for a woman to deliver her people?', and she cited Esther and Judith.[15] She died in 1814 but the hopes she had built up were carried forward by others, both women and men. They included John Wroe, who taught his followers, including many in Australia, of the high place of women in the new dispensation. Wroe, like Joanna, used convoluted sexual metaphor. The gospel was the good seed, and women, he said, in their material existence, received the seed of men. They therefore had authority in the matter of seed, both real and metaphorical, and they must 'separate the tares from the wheat', or in other words the seed of Satan from the seed of Christ. Wroe's idea of 'heaven comed down to earth' was apocalyptic, universal, and woman-centred. 'And Jerusalem, will descend', he prophesied, 'and rest on the woman, and she will bring man from the state of mortal to that of immortality'.[16]

Here was an important change in the way women might think about their spiritual authority. It had long been Christian doctrine that the female part of Creation was subordinate to the male because of Eve's disobedience in the Garden of Eden. Now both men and women might believe that the changes all about them prefigured the Last Days, when Christ would come in majesty to judge the world. The long punishment of womankind was at an end. No longer the ally of Satan, she was to be a source of new truth. No longer the culprit in the Garden, she was herself, as Wroe put it, 'a tree of knowledge of good and evil to the man'.[17] This new sense of womanly authority was felt in various ways, and far beyond the radical sects (Chapter 14).

Many immigrants to New South Wales and South Australia in the late 1830s had come from parts of England affected by millennial hopes and fears. Some of Wroe's people, the Christian Israelites, were to be found in New South Wales when the prophet himself arrived in 1843 and by the 1850s there were several congregations throughout the eastern mainland. On his original visit Wroe spent his time in and around Sydney. His followers met him first at the house of John Beaumont, a coachbuilder and Wroe's old acquaintance, and there, speaking 'in the Spirit', he described to them the coming end of the world. Like Mary Griffiths' father, he explained that remoteness from Europe was no problem:

> as a man's body is convulsed by fits, so this planet will be convulsed in the same way, till all the islands of the sea become one, and Jerusalem be in the centre of it; so that the planet will be a fixed body, then it will be all one season as it will be with the natural immortal body; the planet shall then no more turn upon its own axis, nor the moon withdraw its shining, nor the sun set any more.

The improving spirit of the times would help the poor: '[T]here will be neither hire for man nor beast, but all labour will be done by machinery, with the pressure of the air, so that labouring man will only have to watch it.' On the other hand all wages, he said, would be halved.[18]

Wroe's Australian disciples were apparently farmers and tradesmen rather than labourers. 'Seek not to be employed', he told them, 'but to be employers'. Their worldly competence meant that he could ask of them a certain fraction of their weekly income for the support of the preachers and they received in return a vote in Church affairs. George Frost, a Penrith man, asked, 'how a farmer is to know the amount of his weekly income'. Wroe told him to work out a half-yearly sum and calculate backwards. Trustees were appointed to manage Church funds, a woman for the women's tithes and a man for the men's, and the two were accountable to each other. A man and a woman were also given joint authority 'over the preachers'. The woman in this case was Elizabeth Weavers, native-born, the grand-daughter and wife of convicts.[19]

The Frosts' farm near Penrith, on the Nepean River, was a centre of Israelite fellowship. There, on 8 October, Wroe told his people about the importance of pure marriages. (These and all his sayings were immediately taken down and printed for publication, as inspired truth.) With his 'planet'-centred ideas, the prophet's views of wedlock resembled those of Whitehall. Marriages were lifelong, even when husband and wife lived a hemisphere apart. He now told everyone to step forward who were married here as well as in Europe and three men and one woman obeyed. The woman was Harriet Hoe, once a convict, married in England to Richard Marsh and in New South Wales to Barnabas Hoe. (Barnabas was soon afterwards to be found in the government lunatic asylum.)[20] She was an ardent believer and from the time of Wroe's arrival, she said, 'her body was affected, as if convulsed'. Soon after the meeting, perhaps provoked by being called out, she retired to the bush where she pulled off everything except her shoes and stockings and, picking her way among the fences and farm buildings, the grey slabs hung with blackened hides, she ran into the house. There she danced. According to the written record: 'Her sinews were quite contracted, and her skin wrinkled up.'

Wroe pronounced an exorcism ('Come out of her, Satan ... Come out of her, thou evil spirit, and enter no more') and her body took its usual shape. But, offended by the idea that she was possessed by the devil – that her ecstasy was not divine – she now claimed independence. 'I am the first Eve', she said, ' ... Thou fight for thy kingdom, I'll fight for mine'. After a little doctrinal altercation, she asked Mrs Frost to give her a linen shift and announced to her eager hearers that 'she should wander, with the Bible as her guide'.[21]

II

Ideas about belonging, to God and to one another, were the essence of religious feeling. And for many, for the time being, belonging was most pungent when embodied in speech. The illiterate and semi-literate waited first and foremost on God's Word read out among them. But among the better educated the great weight of intellectual curiosity was shifting in these days from an interest in the voice of Almighty, so enigmatic in its terrible power, to an interest in the voices of other human beings – that vast and pressing babble, which, thanks to population growth, was more numerous and more varied by the moment. Among this generation there was a concern especially with candour in speech, with the openness of souls. How else was the world to be saved from the impact of so many unfamiliar faces? In 1831 the great English novelist and philosopher William Godwin, by now an old man, published an essay 'On Frankness and Reserve'. If speech could always be honest, he said, it would soon 'put down all misrepresentation and calumny, bring all that is good and meritorious into honour, and, so to speak, set every man in his true and rightful position'.[22] This idea of frankness, as something peculiarly precious, figured in many new novels. It made a difference too to forms of piety.

At the same time (I repeat), the printed page was also forcing itself more and more on the attention of the world. Writing was especially valued as the lucid passage of thought, as with speech, from one individual to another. The Bible, for instance, appeared a little less as a sacred article, gilded and dead, and a little more as the living story of God's dealings with humanity. As a result Christ came to the fore more often as man and teacher. It was candid and vivid writing, in scripture and elsewhere – writing that might be scattered to the edge of the reading world – that mattered now. Publicity was all. Catholics stressed the secrecy of the confessional. But for Protestants often the whole point of stories about sinful deeds lay in their repeated retelling. In the same way worshipping together meant speaking frankly with one's fellows. 'We are all members of the great congregation of mankind', said William Godwin (once a Dissenting minister), and 'we should have one common sensorium, vibrating throughout, upon every material accident that occurs'.[23] (Strictly speaking, 'sensorium' meant the senses of the human body, working altogether.) Through honest publication we know and feel as one, and in the same way we spread the Word of God. The peculiar appeal of Methodist ministers lay partly in the fact that they were not only vigorous preachers but also writers in the periodical press. The Reverend Ralph Mansfield, for instance, founded the *Australian Magazine, or Quarterly Register* (1821–22) and afterwards edited both the *Sydney Gazette* and the *Herald*. The preaching and writing of men like him carried a spacious sense of community to colonial readers.

'Speech', said Godwin, 'should be to man in the nature of a fair complexion, the transparent medium through which the workings of the mind should be made legible'.[24] Among Europeans 'fair' was a word of telling ambiguity. It meant both blonde and just. Was truth compatible with black skin? The invaders made many attempts to engage the consciences of

Aborigines – in lasting agreements, for instance, between governors and Black leaders. These agreements involved the sharing of ceremony, as a splendid way of creating 'one common sensorium'. In December 1824, with the end of martial law in New South Wales, some of the Wiradjuri people, including the great warrior Windradyne, hitherto a public enemy for the Europeans, came to the annual conference between Governor Brisbane and the Aboriginal people, at Parramatta.[25] At Swan River in October 1834 relations between the government and the Murray River people, under Calyute, led Sir James Stirling to launch a punitive expedition against them. The battle of Pinjarra involved the deaths of at least fifteen Aborigines, and maybe many more. But from Stirling's point of view it opened the way for an exchange of promises. Ceremony was used here too. There was a corroboree, bread was handed out, and on 2 June 1835 the Aborigines joined in the annual feast at Perth to mark the colony's foundation.[26]

In South Australia the Queen's Birthday in 1840 was likewise marked together by White and Black. In a speech that day Governor Hindmarsh stressed their shared interest and their need to trust one another. All were one under God, he said, 'who made the sun, and the earth, white men, black men, and everything'. Aborigines must realise that God (the god the White men brought with them) knew their transgressions. 'He sees you every where – he is always with you – he is able to save you from every thing bad and to give you every thing good.' If they worked the land like White men and if they did what the missionaries told them, then 'white men and black men will be brothers together'.[27]

Richard Windeyer, defence counsel at the Myall Creek trials, repeated the theme of brotherhood in a speech in Sydney in 1844. He told of being accused by his own conscience about the wholesale murder of the Blacks. 'What wouldest thou?', he replied to these inner promptings, 'Am I my brother's keeper? – Ay, art thou [conscience answered] – and more than thy Brother's blood, his immortal spirit shall be required at thy hands'.[28] Sisterhood was spoken of too, though White women did not usually blame themselves for Aboriginal suffering. Annie Baxter, a landholder's wife, was affronted by the way in which White men hurt women they lived with, whether White or Black. 'For White, or Black', she said, ' – in Sickness or in health – we are Sisters in God!' Eliza Hamilton Dunlop, in a poem published in the *Australian*, drew sympathy even tighter. She imagined herself as an Aboriginal woman who had lost her husband at Myall Creek, escaping with her baby:

> Oh hush thee, dear – for weary
> And faint I bear thee on –
> His name is on thy gentle lips,
> My child, my child, *he's gone*!
> Gone o'er the golden fields that lie

Beyond the rolling cloud,
To bring thy people's murder cry
Before the Christian's God.[29]

This again was a God to whom all was laid open, to whom brothers and sisters of all kinds might appeal together in unity of heart.

All depended, however, on the invaders deciding whether the consciences of Aborigines were in fact like their own. Could there be a single 'sensorium', Black and White? This was a point debated at the highest levels of government from the late 1830s. Since the seventeenth century English courts of law had normally required witnesses to promise, with a Christian oath, that they would tell the truth. More recently other forms of oath had been allowed, mainly to admit the evidence of Muslims and Jews. It was now only necessary that a witness prove religious faith, which meant belief 'in a God, in a future state of rewards and punishments and in the moral obligation of the oath he is about to take'.[30] In fact, this rule assumed a plurality of gods. Every witness might invoke a different one and all depended on the way in which conscience related to the divine. Even so, it excluded Aborigines – they apparently had no sense of an omnipotent being and of rewards and punishments after death. Saxe Bannister had suggested in 1824 that Aborigines ought to be admitted as witnesses on their own terms, but it was not until the humanitarians, including Lord Glenelg, reached positions of power at Whitehall in the mid-1830s that anything was done. Even then, it was hard to find a way around the current rule. Colonial governments might legislate, and thanks to Plunkett, the attorney-general, this happened in New South Wales in 1839. But colonial laws had to match those of England and Plunkett's Act was disallowed.[31]

In 1841 a similar law was passed in Perth and now the Secretary of State responded with an Act of Parliament that abolished the problem. The governments in South Australia and New South Wales moved immediately. In South Australia all legislation was the work of a small council whose members were chosen by the government itself. Its Aboriginal Evidence Act passed without difficulty. But in New South Wales the old nominated council had just been replaced by one in which two-thirds of the members were elected. For the first time public opinion could make its way to the heart of government and as a result the bill in this case was defeated. In both colonies it was widely agreed that the Aborigines were 'notorious' liars. 'The whole study of their lives', Sir Thomas Mitchell said in council in Sydney, 'was, how they should best conceal the working of their minds from the eye of the observer'. William Charles Wentworth backed him up: 'Conscience had been very expressively defined as a bundle of habits, and the whole life and habits of these blacks were the practice of falsehood.'[32]

No orthodox Christian would talk of conscience as 'a bundle of habits'.[33] Conscience was the medium by which God addressed the individual soul. But then, there were Europeans who believed that the Aborigines had no souls.[34] And for their part the Aborigines thought that the invaders were habitual liars too. 'They complain greatly', remarked a Presbyterian minister, 'that the white men do not keep their promises'. One of the reasons why they did not take paid work, he said, was 'that they are cheated of their hire'.[35]

Living and talking among themselves, both Black and White believed in their own transparent candour. Honesty belonged to conversations, from place to place, like with like. The Europeans dealt with their own all-seeing, all-hearing Almighty. The unchanging attitude of the Aborigines was nicely summed up by a man of the Aranda people, a hundred years later: 'We are upright ... we children of the tjibulkara (brightness). When we gaze upon the tjilpa (totemic ancestor) on his own ground, then this is altogether virtuous.'[36] This 'own ground' was the earth continuously turned over, as it were, with native tongues.

With failure of trust on such a scale it was only possible for those who wanted perfect communion between Black and White to try it in small and isolated places, and especially on Christian missions. For missionaries who understood their work this meant relying on a truth that was particular and relative, something inherent in face-to-face exchange. Truth published abroad – absolute and universal truth, printed truth – was in practice less important. What mattered most was that human beings should know each other well and know their God.

In Van Diemen's Land, with the failure of the Black Line (Chapter 8), Governor Arthur had turned to yet another final solution. George Augustus Robinson, a former house-builder who managed a small Aboriginal settlement on Bruny Island, to the south of Hobart, was asked to see whether he could persuade all the remaining Blacks to accept peace. Robinson had already spent a good deal of time in the bush refining his methods of dealing with the Aboriginal people, and between October 1830 and December 1831, by moving carefully through the territory, he was able to make contact with them all, or very close to it. They now numbered less than a hundred. He relied on go-betweens, especially the women Trugernanna and Dray, with whom he had formed a mutual trust. Among the Aborigines of Van Diemen's Land women had an authority as negotiators, which they did not usually possess on the mainland and, as Trugernanna herself was to say much later, Robinson's seemed the only way of saving the remnant of their people.[37]

Underlying these negotiations was an understanding among the Aborigines that they would be given a place to live where they would be safe with Europeans they knew. There was, once again, no treaty. But by the same token, 'we were not taken prisoners', as another of them put it, 'but freely gave up our country ... after defending ourselves', and they did so, the same man said, on the basis of 'an agreement' with the Governor. Under this agreement they were taken to Flinders Island, one of the larger islands of Bass Strait, where they were to be a free community under government, with Robinson himself as their guarantor and guardian.[38] Christian teaching was not part of the agreement, but it was to be part of their reward.

There were also missions on the Australian mainland. Besides Threlkeld's at Lake Macquarie, the Wesleyan Methodists operated at Wellington Valley, in the western inland of New South Wales. At Moreton Bay there was a Presbyterian mission (but with Lutheran ministers) and another run by the Passionist fathers. All of these were abandoned by the mid-1840s. More lasting was the Benedictine monastery at New Norcia, 70 miles north of Perth, begun in 1846. In the very first days Dom Rosendo Salvado, head of the mission, was assaulted by a crowd of white cockatoos, thickening about his head as he ran from tree to tree, and the words of the first Easter mass in those parts, at the edge of a waterhole, had to be shouted above the 'ear-splitting din' of birds come down to drink.[39] The missionaries soon felt, all the same, that their message was received with joy, filling an empty, silent place in the souls of the people.

The missionaries all aimed to give the Aborigines an understanding of Christianity that would qualify them for eternal salvation. What of baptism, the ceremony that makes all one in Christ? 'Often times', said John Bede Polding, Australia's first Catholic bishop, 'we have the happiness of seeing [Aboriginal] fathers bring to us, at Sydney, their children that they may receive a name – it is thus they signify baptism'. This was done, he said, as long as there was a priest on hand in the tribal area who might keep an eye on 'the regenerated infant'.[40] But most other Catholics and all Protestants insisted that baptism must be the reward of faith already perfect and they found extraordinary difficulties in reaching such perfection. Aboriginal language, said Father Luigi Pesciaroli, of the Passionist mission at Moreton Bay, had 'that poverty, that laconism, and all that absence of connection' typical of savage tongues, and it could not be used to convey important truths. Also, while the people seemed docile, 'they are of a treacherous nature even to those who do them good'. There were no Protestant baptisms at all.[41]

The question of truth and lies, so vexing to legislators, took on especially subtle dimensions for the missionaries. Aborigines who were asked about their faith rarely answered as a conscientious European would do. 'Their shrewdness is such', said Salvado, 'that they always shape their replies to what their questioner wants to hear'.[42] Polding told a story of the people he met at Moreton Bay. When he had spoken to them about the meaning of the word 'soul', about the Creator and the afterlife, 'one of the most intelligent amongst them said with *great apparent sincerity*, "We know nothing of these things, but by and by, when you learn our language, you will teach us, and we will believe you", and they all joined in this'.[43] Even Polding, who trusted wherever he could, wondered in this case.

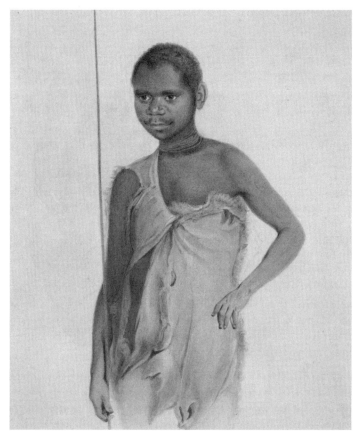

Jemmy, from the Hampshire Hills in north-west Van Diemen's Land, in about 1832, a watercolour by Thomas Bock. Whatever sense of the divine there might have been among the Aborigines it was a largely a mystery even to the most painstaking Europeans.

It was also hard to make the Aborigines understand that Christianity was a matter of faith. Saxe Bannister, who was not keenly religious himself, had thought of them as 'rational beings', but few of the missionaries valued reason in this way. Pesciaroli's colleague, Father Vaccari, said how hard it was to remove 'the prejudices rooted in their minds'. '[A]s far as I can understand', he said, 'they look for practical and material arguments, which alone can convince them'.[44] Such arguments most missionaries refused to offer, thinking it beneath them. Salvado, however, appealed as a matter of course to the reasoning power of the Blacks, their 'shrewdness', as he called it. He displayed his skill in healing wounds and diseases, but he also demonstrated the power of God through miracles. He made a great leap forward, for instance, when he managed to turn back a bushfire by propping up, in its immediate path, a picture of the Virgin Mary.[45]

At most places, and certainly at Flinders Island, the first stage of instruction involved giving the people some idea of the Almighty, especially as their Creator. 'Spoke to the natives about God', Robinson told his journal. 'Asked several of them who made them. They said their father.' He asked another group. 'Some laughed, some repeated the question after me.' One said, 'the Devil'. On another occasion a woman answered, 'Eve', at which a boy retorted, 'what did you say "Eve", ... God is a spirit, is not a woman; God is a white man'. Some asked questions themselves, trying to make this new character live as a traveller in the bush paths of their own imagination – 'whether [God] ... was a big man, whether he eat kangaroo, ... whether he walked about as they did'.[46] As in most Protestant missions, the teaching was often set question-and-answer, but some Aborigines learnt to preach and argue. In time not only God but also Christ and the devil figured in their speculations. The soul played a part too. All these beings belonged to the spirit world and all were to be feared. 'They do not like their breasts to be touched', said James Backhouse, after visiting the island, 'because they say the devil lives there'. Robinson's main task was to make them all – God, Christ, the devil, and the soul – a *dramatis personae*, to make them items of drama, and he partly succeeded.[47] The man Noemy told some enthusiastic listeners in September 1837:

> God *noracoopa* he *coethee* us, you *coethee* God – *coethee* plenty a big one you *taplaldy weethicallee* God send Jesus Christ to save us to *parraway* the Devil, *potheae* you *coethe* the Devil *parraway*, *coethe* God *coethe* Jesus Christ the son of God – you *taplady luthra* you *coethe* you *norocoopa* God make you good man you go top *weekthiekatha*.

'Noracoopa' meant 'very good'; 'coethee' seems to have meant 'hurry to'; 'parraway' meant 'throw away'; and 'taplaldy' meant 'walk'.[48] For the English poor there were similar lessons in *The Pilgrim's Progress*.

As Noemy demonstrated, stories of God were stories about power, and in the end the Aborigines needed to understand, as the basis of their being, the way they belonged within that power. Robinson shared with Salvado a belief in the innate goodness of the Blacks. They were not liars, he said, but 'a remarkably honest people' and as long as they were compliant their chances of salvation were good. '[W]here there is no law there is no transgression, and ... they will be judged only according to the measure of light they have received.' Instruction and the ritual of baptism mattered less, so he believed, than the internal workings of the Holy Spirit.[49] But once again this goodness – this truth – was passing and particular. It lived and died in their talking together and in the way they opened their souls to trusting White men. Robinson's faith in the 'genuine sincerity' of his people was mainly a mirror-image of their faith in him, and this was the highway to everything else.[50] 'If you believed in me', he told them, 'if you confided in me, if you trusted in me, if you like me who am but a man, how much more ought you to abide in Christ'. He was a kind of Prospero. When they set foot on his island he gave many of them new names, as a kind of shadow-baptism. He sometimes added titles. His two 'kings', George and William, were his magistrates, endowed by himself with authority over the rest. 'I have created kings, queens, nobles, counts etc', he said, exulting in his almost God-like influence, 'in a short time I have found names for the whole aboriginal population'.[51] His eye, indeed, like God's, was everywhere.

III

As among the Aborigines, for many Europeans in Australia God was to be approached as a source of bounty. But, as Governor Hindmarsh implied, he was a person to be used with ceremony and skill, like anyone in power. And just as the Aborigines sometimes confused God with the devil, both being spirits, some Europeans thought that any prayer, good or evil, might reach the divine ear.[52] During their trial one of the murderers of John Brackfield (Chapter 6) swore out loud at two crucial prosecution witnesses. When he was hanged, he said, 'he would haunt them as long as God Almighty would give him liberty'. Elizabeth Chittenden, who received the goods stolen from Brackfield's house, cursed them too. She wrote to her husband: 'Give my love to Sprawls and likewise to Antony & Eliza [the murderers] for I am sure that both you and me ought to pray for them night and day.'[53]

The rules of here-and-hereafter were like those of the penal system. They had to be learned and used. A convict named Trennam killed another man at Macquarie Harbour because he was tired of life and wanted to be hanged. He was asked why he did not simply kill himself, but he had weighed his chances of salvation, and he knew that suicide was as much a sin as murder. 'If I kill myself', he replied, as if he were talking about something like tickets of leave, 'I shall immediately descend to the bottomless pit, but if I kill another I would be sent to Hobart Town and tried for my life; if found guilty, the parson would attend me, and I would be sure of going to heaven.'[54]

Imminent death focused European (and sometimes Aboriginal) minds on the relationship between God and humanity, and for many poor men and women a proper funeral was the best insurance for the life to come. Those who lived in remote parts of the Australian bush had no such comfort, and there, according to a Church report, 'the apprehension of being deprived of Christian burial is found to prevail to a painful extent'.[55] This was traditional religion at its simplest. Being Christian for many of the poor was a question of birth, language (English, that is), and skin-colour, but those points settled, it was the rituals of baptism, marriage, and burial that fastened one's fate to the Almighty. Animals – also God's creatures – might often behave and speak a little like human beings, they might live intimately among us, they might even apparently feel love and guilt. But they were not Christian. For many Europeans, Aborigines occupied a doubtful middle ground. They, too, seemed to do everything that White men and women did, and sometimes just as well, and yet in the minds of many they fell at the final hurdle.

Sometimes ideas about belonging to God were very particular indeed. Among the Independents, or Congregationalists, in Hobart, members were forbidden to marry outside the sect. Three women were suspended in one day, in November 1836, for failing to marry 'only in the Lord'. Others (men) were suspended for 'immoral conduct' or 'dishonourable transactions in business'. And others again departed of their own free will, securing God, as they thought, to themselves. Francis and Harriet Edgar resigned after being 'repeatedly grieved' by other members' ideas about religious truth. '[W]hat is advanced by too many at our Church meetings', they said, 'is quite unscriptural, and consequently unprofitable'.[56]

In 1832 the Quakers James Backhouse and George Washington Walker arrived in Hobart, with plans to visit all the British settlements in Australia. They not only gathered information in an entirely new way, as Governor Arthur said (Chapter 6). In doing so, they carried to this country spiritual sensibility of a new kind, an eagerness for speech wherever it might occur – across whatever boundaries – and for careful listening, as the finest manifestation of Christian love. This was, once again, a kind of curiosity shared by many educated men and women arriving in Australia at this time. All were part of what I call (in Chapter 2) a communications revolution. Backhouse explained the way in which he and Walker dealt with convict men, of whatever faith, whom they found at work. They always got them to sit down and rest themselves, he said, 'and if exposed to the sun, we request them to keep on their hats or caps. These little considerations for their personal comfort, often prepare the way for the reception of our counsel'. Their own civility matched what they understood to be the goodness of God. In Hobart they visited a free woman who had been brought up in the Church of England and who shared the old view of religion as a matter of ritual. With her, so Backhouse recalled, 'we had much conversation on the simplicity and the spirituality of the Gospel'. The impact was immediate. 'She said, she perceived that religion was a very different thing from what she had been taught to think it; and that it did not consist in forms and ceremonies, but in an exercise of a soul before God.'[57]

This emphasis on 'little considerations', including the way individuals sat down together, could easily smudge divisions among sects. The generosity of Christ himself was held up as the sublime model for common dealings on earth. As E.S. Hall of the *Monitor* put it, this was 'GENUINE NEW

TESTAMENT Christianity; not the Christianity of *the world*'. Hall and others also used the term 'Bible Christianity' (which was different from the faith of Bible Christians, mentioned above). When the senior Church of England chaplain in Hobart refused to let the Congregationalist minister work among convict women, though unable to do it himself, the Governor, Sir Eardley Wilmot, was shocked. 'Is not the Bible *the Bible*?', he demanded, 'Is not Christianity *Christianity*? Are not the women to be instructed in *Bible Christianity*?'[58] Colin Arrott Browning agreed. Reform among convict men did not depend on sectarian doctrine. In Browning's experience it corresponded exactly 'with the degree of diligence and zeal with which the gospel, in its *divine simplicity*, was brought to bear, from the hour of embarkation, upon their understandings, consciences, and hearts'.[59] And so did convicts themselves. Christian teaching made a difference, even on Norfolk Island, said the twice-convicted Laurence Frayne (admitting he was not a 'religionist' himself), whether the minister was Protestant or Catholic; 'for there is a certain Something in a truely pious man let his religion if a christian be what it may'.[60] That 'certain Something' showed up in the 'little considerations' of Backhouse and Walker. The method of communication mattered as much as the substance. Or rather method and substance were the same thing.

In New South Wales between a quarter and a third of the Europeans were Catholic. Elsewhere the numbers were about one in ten. Convicts had been transported directly from Catholic Ireland to Sydney since 1791, but none had come from Ireland to Hobart and most of the labouring people arriving in the other two colonies were recruited in English parishes. Even in New South Wales, however, for many years the Catholic population had been largely unattended by priests. The first to make much impact was Father John Joseph Therry, who arrived in Sydney in 1820, together with Father Philip Conolly, who went on to Van Diemen's Land. Governor Macquarie had insisted on what he called 'Uniformity in Matters of Religion', and he barely tolerated clergy who did not belong to the Established Church of England.[61] However, by the 1820s officials throughout the empire were beginning to follow British public opinion in their attempts to provide equal freedom for the consciences of Protestant and Catholic. This was a result not only of more liberal feeling among Protestants but also of a renaissance within the Church of Rome itself. Catholics still insisted on the unique authority of their own Church, but they, too, were interested in the simplicity of faith. The Emancipation Act, passed by parliament in 1829, was an important mark of reconciliation. Since the seventeenth century Catholics had suffered many civil disabilities in Britain and Ireland. Now they shared most of the rights enjoyed by Anglicans. Whitehall even began to subsidise Maynooth College, near Dublin, in its training of Catholic priests, and in England as well Catholic education flourished.

In Australia Catholics felt in fits and starts the renewed energy of the Church. As late as 1840 a French Catholic sent as a convict from Quebec to New South Wales was scandalised by the way mass was conducted here. The people 'come to church', he said, ' … with small children who are still infants and who do nothing but cry in the mass. Women are not ashamed to suckle their babies in church during the course of the mass. Lovers hold hands in church as if they were in a private house'.[62] Bishop Polding, arriving in 1835, was startled to see how easily Catholics knelt in prayer side by side with those beyond the faith.[63] They were not yet fully aware that their religion gave them a special place in the sight of God. Marriage to Protestants was now frowned on, and yet in New South Wales Catholic women, who ought to have been most pliable, married Protestant men, making up their own minds afterwards as to their own and their children's faith.[64]

Change had begun with Therry who as an Irishman had marshalled the loyalty of other Irish. He was 'indefatigable in his endeavours to preserve his influence amongst his countrymen,' said Governor Darling, 'and is constantly going from place to place with this view'.[65] In due course other priests had arrived and in 1832 a vicar-general, William Ullathorne, was appointed to Sydney. Ullathorne was English, an intellectual devoted to the revival of Catholicism in England, and eventually became Bishop of Birmingham. He understood the methods of moral influence that underpinned the renewal of the Church throughout the world. Like Backhouse and Walker, he found on reaching Sydney that the feelings of each convict were 'petrified' – 'He never feels the touch of kindness.'[66] Ullathorne was widely read, but he was also vividly attuned to the power of speech. A complex man, he was seemingly struck with the sound of his own voice. This was apparently also true of Saxe Bannister, but whereas Bannister was driven in on himself by shyness, and by anger at the apparent deafness of everyone else, Ullathorne used his priestly office to make speech easier. As a young man, he said, he talked as 'a sort of reflex of whatever was going on in my mind'. The result was scanty and enigmatic. His voice wove a prison around him and to escape it he thought of taking vows of silence, as a Trappist monk. Only later did he learn what he called 'readier habits of converse and lighter modes of speech'.[67] It may have been this self-awareness that opened his ears to the way others spoke – to the silky ease with which they seemed to manage – and to the power of speech as social fabric.

His priestly calling also made Ullathorne value what he saw as the unthinking simplicity of the great mass of humankind, those men and women whom he called 'children of obedience'. On leaving school he spent four years at sea, and the talking of sailors left a permanent impression. They were licentious men, he said. Yet many had 'child-like, kindly and generous hearts'. Each sailor, speaking among his kind, was 'open and unreserved' in a remarkable way – 'His manifestation of himself is like a continuous public confession.'[68]

It was a telling comparison. The confessional for Ullathorne was the measure against which all speech was to be valued. The golden honesty supposedly inherent in the confessional, as many earlier Catholic writers had understood, made it a sublime engine for the discipline of faith. Telling stories in secret to their priests, men and women began to see their own souls mirrored in ancient doctrine and worldwide community. For convicts Ullathorne prescribed 'both general lectures and much individual converse, grounded on the especial frame of mind, disposition of character, and tone of feeling, of each individual person'.[69] Self was to be enamelled in this way with teaching.

Governor Darling, like many Protestants, believed that Catholic priests controlled their people by 'the subjugation of mind'. In fact, the Catholic method of subjugation easily overlapped with that now used everywhere – by Mrs Fry in her dealings with convict women, by Browning in his talks with convict men, by George Augustus Robinson on Flinders Island. All held up the same kind of enlarging, complicating mirror. '[T]he communication of moral impulses to the human mind is a science yet in its infancy', said Alexander Maconochie, 'but from which too much scarcely can be augured'.[70] In 1834 Ullathorne travelled to Norfolk Island in company with an Anglican clergyman, Henry Stiles ('an amiable man with very low doctrines and a limited experience of human nature'). On the way Catholic explained to Protestant the power of the confessional. Stiles was impressed and insisted on Norfolk that anyone wanting holy communion must talk to him first about their sins. During a session with Mary Anderson, wife of the commandant, he suggested that she was guilty of affectation. Mrs Anderson was startled. A Protestant married woman was to be told her sins by no one but her husband. 'Mr Stiles, there is some mistake', she said, 'I am not Mrs Stiles'.[71]

In his own mind, Ullathorne came as a missionary to Protestant and Catholic, Black and White. He thought of himself as a new St Augustine and he spoke of the Catholic Church as 'the Church of Australia'. He not only had to bring men and women back to their old faith and give them a new sense of what that faith was. He also had to convert non-believers. When the boat put in at Norfolk, 'I was determined within myself', he said, 'to be the first to take possession, so I was the first to spring ashore'. He and Stiles had come to attend to the men condemned to death for their part in the mutiny of 1834, and Ullathorne got to the cells first. Of the thirteen who were to hang only three were Catholics, 'but four of the others asked me to take charge of them'. That left four for Stiles. It was a typical percentage. In Sydney, by Ullathorne's account, among men 'of other opinions' condemned to death, about half 'embraced the faith' before they died. And many more, he said, with no immediate fear of dying came to him asking for conversion. A fellow priest counted 250 'dissenters' won in Sydney in a single year.[72]

Anglicans spoke of an unseemly fight for souls, '*a Religious Scramble*', but Catholics exulted in their success.[73] Ullathorne's achievement led to Polding's appointment in 1835 as bishop (later Archbishop of Sydney) and vicar-apostolic. More priests arrived and so did five Sisters of Charity, members of an order newly formed in Ireland. The nuns settled at Parramatta, where they worked with the women of the Female Factory, sitting mainly in chairs out of doors with the women crowded on the ground around them. Their impact in that place of rebellion was like Charlotte Anley's, but much greater. They arrived towards the end of 1838 and in the few weeks before Lent 1839 they had persuaded two-fifths the Catholic inmates to prepare for mass. They could not hear confession themselves, but details of sin and temptation were pressed on them all the same. '[T]hey would as soon speak to a nun', the convicts said, 'as to a priest'. This outpouring of stories made its mark on the whole community. And again, according to Polding, many Protestant women asked the nuns for instruction, 'so that every week some persons were led to the faith and to a holy life'.[74]

'Society without Religion', said John Pascoe Fawkner, 'would soon degenerate into a frightful den of Savages'. Similarly dens of savages might, through religion, be drawn to order. Even violent lunatics were found to fall into a state of 'astonishing' calm on entering a church. In the republic that Fawkner planned for Port Phillip forms of worship were to be strictly observed. He too subscribed to the simplicity of what he called 'Pure Religion', which he equated with the rule of conscience – 'Our duty to Our Creator and also to our Neighbour.' In his scheme a suitable building was to be erected as soon as possible, there was to be worship twice every Sunday and all householders were to take turns in conducting the service, each according to his own faith. A minister was to be appointed as soon as funds allowed, but even then Fawkner assumed that all would continue to meet as one.[75] In fact, the meeting of several sects under one roof was common among the Europeans in Australia. It happened easily among small populations in remote places and at Port Phillip, in due course, there was indeed a church built by general subscription and meant for worship of all kinds. Protestant, that is – the Catholics looked after themselves.[76]

The great challenge for government in Australia was to draw these forms of religious life within a single administrative framework. This was indeed an issue for Europeans worldwide. In England there was talk of making the Church of England a more truly 'national' Church by doctrinal reform, which might bring dissenting sects within the fold. In Germany there were parallel efforts to make Catholics and Protestants equally members of a German nation. In New South Wales profoundly new principles for linking Church, state, and community were laid down in Governor Bourke's Church Act, 1836. The leading Christian churches were all offered government funding, depending only on their numbers and on how much money they could raise among themselves. The Governor also promised to support Catholic and Presbyterian elementary schools on precisely the same terms with those of the old Established Church.

The 'New South Wales system' or 'Australian plan' was soon taken up throughout the British Empire. In South Australia, Lutheran settlements benefited with the rest, and this meant that the government in Adelaide also nourished the teaching of German as a language of daily life.[77] Such a parcel of reform represented an extraordinary shift in ideas about religious truth. The punishment of Eve, as I say, was now apparently ended. But in other ways, too, divine order had changed. God had become many-faced and many-voiced. And yet this refashioning left in limbo the religious character of government itself, which throughout the empire had long been exclusively Anglican. In Germany the philosopher Hegel argued that the priorities of a nation at large need not be Christian at all. The first duty of government, he said, was its people's survival and strength, which might be at odds with anything biblical. It followed for Hegel that the god of the state was neither good nor bad – let alone Catholic or Protestant. Rulers were to be judged for their material success. Some in Australia agreed with him, at least in practice. But many gloried in the possibility that government might be even more clearly a medium of conscience when it was set above sectarian difference. It would be 'Bible Christian'. At last public life, said James Macarthur, including the funding of religion, could be shaped by such rules as, 'Do as you would be done by' – as Christ himself had taught in the Sermon on the Mount.[78]

But how could men in power endorse several truths all at once? In 1836 the Anglicans throughout Australia had also secured a bishop, their former archdeacon William Grant Broughton. Broughton fought hard for the continued supremacy of his own Church. He admitted that 'the State is not a responsible body in the same way that individuals are responsible' (he did not say what state responsibility was). And yet he thought that individuals close to the state, such as himself, must be guided in their work by their own faith. They must have that faith taught in the government-funded schools, interwoven with literacy. Richard Windeyer, an Anglican himself, told the bishop that he had a Catholic servant. He was teaching him, he said, to read and write, but avoiding issues of faith. Did his Lordship approve? If religion could not be taught too, said Broughton, the man should be left ignorant.[79]

Mary Fox, in her story of Southland, had her own solution for such difficulties. Among the Southlanders there was little room for the individual who said that his was the only truth. He might indeed commune with the Almighty, but under Southland law he was to be imprisoned all the same. If he was an 'impious imposter' (so their guide told Hopkins Sibthorpe and his friends) the punishment was just. If, on the other hand, he really was 'a divine messenger' God would free him. The taunters at the Crucifixion, all those years before, had said the same. '[D]escend now from the cross', they demanded of Our Lord, 'that we may see and believe'. But as inhabitants of the nineteenth century the Southlanders felt sure that God would sanction their approach to faith.[80]

Some of Lady Mary's readers might have trembled all the same at such a story. In Southland, and indeed everywhere under the 'Australian plan', it was the responsibility of government to emulate, not King Jesus, but King Herod.

PART 3

The Masses
Unpacked

Naturae Amator, 'Notes on the Natural History of South Australia. – No. III', January 1842.[1]

The insects in consideration are our largest and also most brilliant species of bees (Apidae). These fine insects are in length little less than one inch, and between the expanded wings not quite an inch and a half, with the body very bulky, limbs thick, and the posterior tibiae covered with down. ...

... On the 27th of last July, four-and-twenty of these insects were brought to me, all found in a rotten or decayed log of wood – and this being our midwinter month – in a perfectly torpid state, though the day was mild. They were discovered altogether, and, as it were, packed as closely as possible, apparently to facilitate warmth: they formed two lines of bees in two separate grooves running along the centre of the log, with a small ridge between them; but the most singular circumstance was the way in which these insects had arranged themselves; first came two bees side by side, then one lay across or lengthways, touching with its head and tail (apex of abdomen) those on each side of it; then followed two more in the usual way, and another single one crossways, and so to the end of the groove. ...

... They were all females! and as I before remarked, quite torpid and inert at first, and unable to move their limbs. ... I put them altogether, thinking that, as they were quiet enough before, they would now at least not disagree, but being once disturbed, and also perhaps from feeling the warmth of the outer air, they were not inclined again to settle. After moving their legs they began to set their wings in motion, and the buzzing of one soon excited others to follow its example, the noise and agitation every minute increased, till the whole of this Amazonian band presented nothing but confusion and apparent angry discord. They did not, however, appear at any time to use their wings in flight, for which they seem to require the direct influence of the sun, and the casting away of superfluous moisture.

It was remarkable that during this time they exhaled a strong smell of honey, which continued in this scene of their disputes long after I had removed them, from a store no doubt secreted by them, if not to be actually fed upon, at any rate to preserve their existence during their 'dreamy days'.

Chapter 10

Feeding on Stories

I

A body of people can be made to work smartly enough on a diet of lies. Seasoned correctly, lies can meet a range of needs, though they always taste local. Indeed, however high-minded the hearers, the truth itself may be hard to take raw.

Laurence Frayne was a convict on Norfolk Island. He was an educated man who thought carefully and wrote well. He knew Alexander Maconochie when Maconochie came as commandant to the island in 1840 and he saw in the new ruler the keenness of a revolutionary. According to Frayne, Maconochie understood 'the Science of Gov[ernmen]t'. This term, 'the Science of Government', was a piece of new jargon that Frayne had picked up from reading 'An Essay on Prison Discipline', by James Ross of Hobart. Ross himself read widely in the literature of his day and I am combining nineteenth-century and twentieth-century language when I say that this 'science', as they both called it (Maconochie's methods on Norfolk), depended on a certain 'information order'.[1] In short, the science of government on the island depended on the mass of sayings – all the stories, true and false – which circulated among the convicts and which were harvested as a continuous crop, by Maconochie and other men in power.

Government on Norfolk had controlled the information order for some time. Before Maconochie a passion for storytelling, such as exists in any close-knit body of men, women, or children, had fuelled what Laurence Frayne called 'a System of Espionage'. The ears of the commandants and other officers were always open. They feasted, he said, on 'false informations' so as to justify their cruelty.[2] Thomas Cook, also a convict (Chapter 7), said the same. Such was this 'rage for informations', Cook said, that the convicts chosen by the authorities to spy on the rest had to make themselves into agents provocateurs, 'to hatch plots and form conspiracies, into which the unwary were ensnared', simply, he said, 'to keep pace with their employers wishes'. The regime of lies spread favours among the wicked and destroyed the honest. Those caught in the spies' net endured merciless floggings and long periods in solitary confinement. Frayne was imprisoned for two months, a time 'indeed dreary doleful & truely miserably spent', alone in silent darkness.[3]

All this changed with Maconochie. The information order was now supposed to depend on honest conversation. Convicts opened their hearts to the commandant's 'Godlike System', so that the ruler appeared to them like the shadow of God himself. Frayne had already found comfort in Psalm 12, where the Word of the Almighty is set beside common speech. In this wicked world, says the psalmist:

> Every one utters lies to his neighbour;
> with flattering lips and a double heart they speak.
> May the Lord cut off all flattering lips,
> the tongue that makes great boasts,
> those who say, 'With our tongue we will prevail,
> our lips are with us; who is our master?'[4]

Now the question 'who is our master?' was easily answered. It was Maconochie. According to James Porter, also on Norfolk, the new regime gave men like himself 'a sense of our duty, never to lose the only thing an exile doth possess, his word'. Thanks to Maconochie's science of government, as Frayne put it: 'We considered ourselves as elevated to the Standard of Men once more.'[5]

The authorities in Sydney and London, said Frayne, had never understood that Norfolk Island was at odds with 'the whole reformatory System' they believed in. All would be set right, he thought, when everyone knew the truth, and that, indeed, was another of Maconochie's ambitions.[6] Since government began in Europe men in power had managed by secrecy and intrigue. Now, Frayne wrote, 'under more magnanimous & enlightened circumstances' it was possible for them at last to be frank. Norfolk Island would be in step with the rest of the world. This had also been the hope of Saxe Bannister in his own area of interest and, like Frayne, Bannister made it a question of efficiency as much as goodness. Truth was to be married with power. Government, said Bannister, 'would form sounder conclusions, and act more energetically, when the facts now secret, were sure to be generally known'.[7]

And yet there was still a place for silence. Every man, woman, and child might manage a private information order, a parcel of fact to be taken off to a corner and thought through alone. The agony of his own solitary confinement was something Frayne swore never to forget. But it was so degrading, so much part of his own flesh and soul, that it 'ought', he said, 'never to be known to mankind'.[8]

During the 1840s there were large changes in the science of government, in the information order of the Australian colonies. And not just in
the way facts were gathered. Stories and opinions were now understood,
sorted and catalogued, with a clearer sense of system. They also mattered
more completely for their moral bearing. The law courts were no longer
the only institutions in which obscure, discordant voices were drawn from
all quarters and weighed by the authorities for their moral significance.
Officials and public representatives also collected and sifted opinion. As
newspapers multiplied, especially in the capital towns, they too broadcast
everywhere the judgments of editors and reporters.

Truth itself was thus constituted in new ways.

In 1841, for instance, Sir John Franklin appointed a committee to investigate discipline among women convicts in Van Diemen's Land. Four convicts were called in and they were the first such women ever heard for such
purposes in either colony. They were questioned at length about their experiences since conviction, including general behaviour and attitudes,
assignment, homosexual dealings, and the illegal traffic of goods in prison,
and their answers were taken down verbatim.[9] A parallel effort was made
about the same time by George Grey, Governor of South Australia, to discover the truth about his north-eastern frontier. Numerous stockmen were
now arriving with sheep and cattle from New South Wales, and they were
often ambushed on the way by Blacks. Matthew Moorhouse, the protector
of Aborigines, made detailed reports in June and July 1841 and in August
he was sent with a party of police to look after an expedition currently en
route. On the Rufus River, a tributary of the Murray, they met a party of
the Maraura people and, afraid of immediate attack, the police opened fire.
It was more or less agreed that about thirty Aborigines were killed, though
Moorhouse said twenty-one. There were immediately more reports, and
Grey organised a magisterial inquiry. Among the witnesses was Moorhouse's native interpreter and a captive Maraura man, Pul Kanta. Pul
Kanta was in theory a British subject. His ideas therefore mattered and
they, too, were recorded verbatim, but they yielded little. Drawn from the
very edge of European power and surrounded now by his enemies, he
protested that he had never fought White men. He was asked whether he
thought his tribesmen were 'justly shot', the great moral issue underlying
the inquiry. Here Pul Kanta made a stand. His mouth was shut.[10]

The four colonies all had their legislative councils, which were supposed
to keep government in touch with local understanding. In Van Diemen's
Land, Western Australia, and South Australia members of council were all
appointed by the Crown, but in New South Wales from 1843 two-thirds
(twenty-four in thirty-six) were elected. These elected members set up committees of inquiry on a great range of matters, using them to talk with anyone they cared to invite, and every word was set down in the council's
Votes and Proceedings. By 1850 they had held 713 interviews, besides

sending out large number of questionnaires to gentlemen at a distance from Sydney. Parliamentarians in Britain were already working like this.[11] It was part of a new and deeply penetrating bureaucratic and political impulse now felt throughout the empire, part of the science of government. Most of the witnesses in Sydney were gentlemen and tradesmen but officials of the lowest rank (turnkeys, for instance) and labouring men were asked about their work. Four women appeared (Caroline Chisholm three times), one Aborigine (Mahroot, or Boatswain), and one native of Kisar, a small island near Timor. In choosing their witnesses, in questioning them at length, in pursuing them down the byways of memory and opinion, in drawing such information to a point, and in storing it all up in leather-bound volumes, councillors made their mark on the information order.

This was also the great age of state inquiries, of censuses, and statistics. The civil registration of births, marriages, and deaths created with each certificate a thumbprint story of the subject. Great quantities of official time and money were spent on gathering sketches of the people, on measuring in detail what a statistician in Britain called 'the social progress of this vast and growing empire'. Power seemed to depend so much on information that the very word – 'information' – became a favourite government tool. John Ruskin wrote of seeing everywhere about him 'the spread of a shallow, blotching, blundering, infectious "information", or rather deformation'.[12] New ways of labelling, filing and indexing meant the storage of millions of lives – as if compacted within a single unity, a great polished box, minutely patterned, opaque and seamless. Charles Dickens, unlike Ruskin, was fascinated with the result. Dickens once described with wonder the office of the registrar-general of the United Kingdom, including the tedious work of the 'examiners' who checked the detail of each birth, marriage, and death (1,200,000 that year) as they were copied from the original records to the central registers. One examiner was deaf and two were deaf and dumb, and a useful thing too, because the absence of normal sense helped concentration.[13]

The new bureaucracy was dehumanising. And yet, such labour might be sublime. Among any people, in any degree of civilisation, there is glory in material well wrought. The bureaucratic systems evolving in the mid-nineteenth century set up monuments to everyone they touched. The magic involved in that godlike skill, writing, is remarkable anywhere. It was now extraordinary. Writing gathered millions of lives within a new creation, the ubiquitous state. It caused a 'revolution in social administration', as one historian has put it, a transformation in the way people were tied to their rulers.[14] It also recast the minds of the people themselves.

It changed people's minds because under the new dispensation one's own writing (or whatever one said that was converted to writing) mattered too. Nothing was now more sacred in Europe and among the Europeans in Australia than trade in the written word, the movement and exchange of paper. The reforms of Rowland Hill, offering cheap, frequent, and reliable postage to the entire population (Chapter 5), testify to this enthusiasm. So does the new vividness to be found in novels and newspaper reporting (Chapter 6), where men and women in their millions were scripted in black and white – and yet 'endowed with passions and struggling with ills'. Charles Dickens also visited London's general post office. Each day, he said, more than 200,000 letters arrived and for every item left in the bottom of the sheepskin bags the bag-opener was fined half a crown. In Sydney the penalty was a day's pay.[15] Within this painstaking regime the letters of convicts might draw special attention. Since they were not supposed to manage their own money, in New South Wales transported men and women sent and received letters free of charge. One came for Thomas Cook from his family in England when he had just been moved to a road gang near Port Macquarie, north of Sydney. As he said (in a tale otherwise full of his sufferings), he was immediately given time to walk the 20 miles to get it.[16]

Dennis Kennedy was an Irishman, an inhabitant of Ballangarry, county Limerick. In November 1843, in the evening, as he later reported, he and Ellen Fitzgerald 'went to the priest's house, and got married'. Two girlfriends went with them as witnesses and the priest presumably noted the event in his marriage register. (Had they been married in England the event might have been subject to civil registration as well.) Two days later, at Cork, husband and wife embarked as government-assisted emigrants on the *William Metcalfe* for New South Wales, their names, ages, and occupations ('farm labourer' and 'farm servant') being listed as part of the record of the voyage. They were family number 22. A son, James, was born in April 1845 and baptised by the priest at Campbelltown, south of Sydney, that event being similarly recorded, with the parents' names and father's occupation and address. Kennedy had found good employment on his arrival and a 'Memorandum of Agreement' with his master was lodged with government. He was still there in February 1846 when he spoke with Caroline Chisholm, as she made her way around the settled parts interviewing small settlers. They gave her what she called 'voluntary information'. Besides a wage of £16 a year, Kennedy told her, 'I get 12lb. flour, 10lb. meat, 2lb. sugar, and ¼lb. tea a week, with a house to live in; have two good cows, and above 20l. in money; my wife washes a little'. This statement, one of several hundred, Mrs Chisholm published next year in London, in *Douglas Jerrold's Weekly Newspaper*.[17]

Because it was unspectacular, Kennedy's life was a matter of public interest. And Mrs Chisholm was a figure of power. Like many of the people she spoke with, Kennedy was illiterate and she must have written down his words as they talked. On such occasions she sometimes picked up peculiar fragments of thought. The published transcript of an interview with a Scotswoman in New South Wales ended with: 'Mention this, my Lady, and, if you please, mem, read it over that I may see it's correct – That's very nice, very nice, mem – that will do. How astonished they will be when they hear I am married!' Another Irishman ended his story, as recorded, with advice on format:

> We live pretty well here. Now put it down in three rows, – it will look better when it is printed, – we have –
>> For Breakfast ... Bread, Meat, Tea;
>> – Dinner .... Bread, Meat, Tea;
>> – Supper .... Bread, Meat, Tea;
> with milk, butter, and eggs; in truth, we live well.[18]

Caroline Chisholm was careful with such detail because she shared the new eagerness for writing out lives. She liked to enter into the existence of other people. She caught at every word that, as she thought, proved the decision-making soul behind the sunburnt face. But also, she thought of such stories, laid end to end before the reading world, as a foundation for the great engine of policy now taking shape. They represented the kind of understanding on which government should turn.

The listing of the Europeans in Australia, name by name, had been tried many times since 1788. It had seemed especially important with the convicts. Surnames were the neatest labels by which a government might know its people. Women, more than men, changed their last names, but the weight of government made an impact here too, so that even after marriage convict women might be known by the surnames written down when they arrived. By the 1840s, in the Female Factory at Hobart, even the convicts themselves sometimes referred to each other by surnames alone, as their keepers did, forgetting their older instincts. 'One morning', said Elizabeth Studham, 'Eliza Churchill and I went to draw water'. Then she dropped the 'Eliza'. 'Churchill', she went on, 'called Mrs Littler to the window ...'.[19] And yet for a woman, to be known only by surname – no first name and no 'Mrs' or 'Miss' – was a loss of dignity like the shaving of your head. (Mrs Littler was not a convict.)

There were no family names among the Aborigines. The names they did have were more changeable even than those of European women, but they, too, were packed into lists. At Flinders Island, George Augustus Robinson not only gave out fixed and final names; he also made a comprehensive record, in 1832 and again in 1836.[20] In New South Wales from about the same time rural magistrates also tried to list all the Aborigines living in their districts. If there were to be any hope of knowing them as individuals, of giving them justice, their names, however slippery, must be arranged and digested by government.

Not only their names but also what they said about themselves. True justice depended on the people being more than names. Between 1835 and 1837 a select committee of the House of Commons met to consider the treatment and prospects of indigenous peoples throughout the empire. Its members were moved by the enormous challenge of securing justice where languages, cultures, and patterns of law seemed infinite. The first task was the accumulation of names and related detail, but much had to be done beyond that. The committee twice interviewed Saxe Bannister, and it was he who offered the most complete solution. There must be consistency throughout the empire, he said, but at the same time there must be a nourishing of difference – not difference for its own sake but difference as a key to individual need. From place to place, native languages should be taught in the schools and courts of law should take account of native 'laws and usages'. There should be an agent of the Crown in London to whom the natives might write on all matters. And there should be a great weekly gazette of news and opinion, including statements from indigenous people. Names, married to voices, were to be broadcast in print.

This last was vital. Bannister believed in the published word, in the 'common sensorium' of facts and opinion. The gazette would draw, he said, on many sources. It would be remarked on by all concerned and through such to-and-fro it 'would be made to tell the truth'.[21] From diverse stories would be built a new information order, empire-wide, and from that would come new standards of justice.

At the outer edges of the system, said Bannister, 'protectors' must be appointed as moral agents and gatherers of information. Matthew Moorhouse had just been sent to South Australia, but Bannister wanted an all-embracing network. Natives should themselves be appointed protectors, so that the structure might become their own. James Macarthur said that the poor in Britain should be taught, as decision-makers, how to take advantage of the empire (Chapter 5). Bannister wanted the same for its many peoples.

The committee liked the idea of protectors. So did the Colonial Office. Charles Symmons was appointed for Western Australia and there were to be five protectors in the new district of Port Phillip, with Robinson as chief protector in Melbourne and the others stationed in different quarters. At Port Phillip there was to be some hint of that independent network which Bannister wanted, and some slight hope, to start with, that reform would make a real difference, not only in the assembling of detail but also to the welfare of the people. At Port Phillip, too, large areas were set aside so that the Blacks might go on maintaining themselves. But it was soon clear that the energy, skill and official support that Bannister dreamed of were non-existent.

The first task was a census of the Aboriginal population and an account of tribal groups and boundaries. That was easy. A few schools were also built and there was talk of the children being instructed in their own tongues. A squatter, Charles Griffiths, made suggestions of his own about adapting British law to the needs of the Blacks. But the Europeans spread, as usual, with overwhelming speed and the protectors were a feeble shield between invaders and invaded. There was no agent in London, and no regular way of making government listen to Aboriginal voices. Instead of an imperial gazette, trumpeting stories Black and White, there was only a sceptical local press. By 1849 the protectorate at Port Phillip was given up, an almost total failure.[22]

II

It was by telling stories about the country, and about themselves within it, that Europeans began to know Australia. Whole lives, or significant parts of them, unfolded in the mind's eye – innumerable minds' eyes – within an antipodean landscape and the surrounding ocean. In these days, the settler population was beginning to work with the idea of an existence deeply dyed – gilded and stained – by the new world, including its most distinctive parts, its bush, its villages, its ports, its penal outposts. So much salted blue, so much dried brown. Local writers of fiction made this kind of effort. Alexander Harris's novel *The Emigrant Family* was published in London in 1849, the result of sixteen years in New South Wales. His story moved between the lower Hawkesbury Valley and the southern highlands of New South Wales (between his hero's native home and his place of work). Among other achievements, Harris described the link between these two places with a peculiarly Australian blindness to distance. The long miles, equalling London-to-Liverpool, seem on his pages to be nothing but a passage through the scrub.[23] Since then (to our own day) six or seven generations have moved through such extended banquets of sun and dust. In his own time Harris's sensibility was new.

Putting stories together was a matter of skill. It was also a process embedded in other skills. With skill the new people made and kept themselves. With skill they told stories about the making and the keeping. In that sense the Europeans in Australia clothed themselves in a many-coloured coat of aptitude, a cleverness of their own. Even the legislative councillors who took evidence in committee used a kind of tact appropriate, in a way, to colonial conversation.

Something else was happening at the same time, in Australia and elsewhere. Europeans were beginning to think more carefully about skill itself. One of the results of the Industrial Revolution was that skill seemed newly significant, especially the skill of men (Chapter 7). The most common male dexterity might now seem scientific, because such dexterity seemed to shine with new knowledge, a hint of the future. Australians learnt skills peculiar to the country by a perfectly informal process, skills well expressed and nicely shaped to its hardness, its softness, its beauty, its flaws, and they remarked on such skills accordingly. In the convict colonies even horse and cattle-stealing was 'a sort of science', according to one writer.[24] Who knows how it worked?

Skill was used in managing and describing the landscape. The work of painters such as Conrad Martens in New South Wales and John Glover in Van Diemen's Land showed a penetrating sense of beauty, a visual control of the natural environment. The invaders also experimented with apportioning the body of the land, with measuring and sharing it. Each household of settlers was allotted, as if at a feast, its own piece of sustenance. Distinctions here, indeed, matched ideas about culinary refinement. Cooking and eating habits are a good test of rank. They show different degrees of refinement among rich and poor, heroes and beasts. Shakespeare said so. 'Let's carve him as a dish fit for the gods', says Brutus about the murder of Julius Caesar, 'Not hew him as a carcase fit for hounds'.[25] The most godly attempts to divide up Australia were those of the surveyors-general, Thomas Mitchell, who worked from Sydney, and John Septimus Roe in Perth, each of them with a vast dominion and both tracing lines over the carcase as a whole before they started their meticulous skinning. Both were explorers, mapping as they went. Roe made fifteen major expeditions throughout the great triangle of the south-west, from King George Sound in the south to Champion Bay in the north, an area about the size of Britain. Mitchell covered twice that space again, from the lower Murrumbidgee to the upper Barcoo.

Some of the most urgent skills involved the tackling of Australian distance. The good bushman, as the explorer Ludwig Leichhardt remarked, was a man at ease mentally and physically with the dimensions of the country, who 'can walk for long distances or ride hundreds of miles in one stage'. Thomas Mitchell had his own way of meeting this test. 'I have frequently found', he said, 'that the most dreary road ceases to appear monotonous or long, after we have acquired a knowledge of the adjacent country. The ideas of locality are no longer limited like our view, by the trees on each side'. In other words, every small twist in the road was to be considered symptomatic of a larger feature, of the barely hidden bones of the land. Once surveyed, every such feature had its place on the map, 'which thus determines our position', as we move across it.[26] Mitchell's readiness in remembering maps meant that as he walked or rode he could think of himself travelling ant-like over the back of the country. This skill governed his visual impressions of Australia. It let him balance the immediate with the circumstantial – the narrow track ahead, to be understood step by step, with the limitless, lasting country roundabout.

Assessment of the land was coloured by faith in one's own ability to change parts of it. As surveyor-general Mitchell looked about for the features that could be made to work in the broad progress of settlement. Men and women with less power gave their attention to smaller possibilities. Altogether, applied from day to day in the way each made a living, such skills not only reshaped the land itself. They also coloured the way the invaders thought about the land's surface, and likewise its depth.

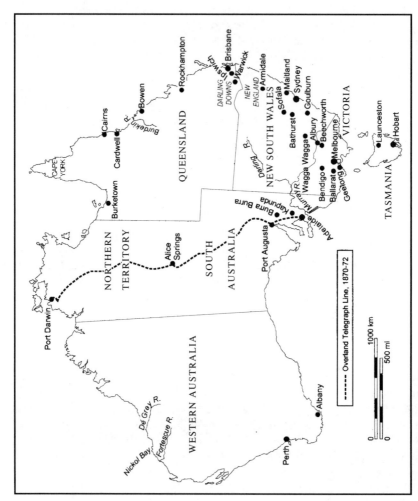

Australia from the 1840s

Settlers hesitated at first to rely on the antipodean soil as a source of life. Life, to invading minds, came from elsewhere. It spilt from the ships and ran over the surface of the land. In other words (whatever government might recommend), most settlers paid less attention to what the earth itself might yield than to the livestock it could carry. Pigs did well from the beginning, goats were also important for a while, and sheep, cattle, and horses were obvious ways of getting rich. Dogs were an extension of yourself, outsmarting other beasts. The early immigrant people saw themselves more often as stockmen and hunters than as farmers. James Gardner, an ex-convict doing well in New South Wales, wrote to his mother in England in 1841 to boast of the marriage he had made. 'My brother in laws', he said, '... have got 800 head of cattle of their own, about 30 breeding mares. As for me, I have got at present 140 breeding cattle, 9 mares and one horse'. And, he went on, 'My father in law says at his death he will divide his stock equally amongst his children, he has got 2 sons and 2 daughters excluding my wife'. Gardner said nothing about the land except that he had too little for his stock.[27] Such men and women set themselves to know, not the wealth to be drawn from the soil, but how sheep, cattle, and horses behaved on it, including the way they bred and multiplied. (Here animal numbers had to match the numbers of sons and daughters.) For many years the man who managed animals was a creature superior to the farmer. He might rely on potatoes and grain, but he had meat too. For Europeans meat was luxury and here, too, by force of habit, heads, tails, feet – all were eaten, and the bones split for marrow. With his dogs the settler fed easily on the fat of the land.[28]

The land was understood in terms of its feed and water and for the way it shaped the movement of livestock. At Swan River to begin with flocks and herds were small enough to allow for bells being attached to each animal to stop them being lost in the scrub.[29] Elsewhere the epitome of rural skill was to be found among the stockmen who gathered wild cattle from the unfenced bush, hurrying them into yards thrown up in the zig-zag American fashion and branding them on the spot. Or it was to be found in the more gradual but still cunning movements of the long-distance drover. Harris wrote of the drover 'wheeling his practised horse' behind his stock, his eye all about him;

> flourishing the eleven-foot thong of his short-handled stock-whip, as one or another of the beasts turned and strove to rush back down the road; bringing it into the herd again with a touch from the hard hide-lash, that sent the pulverized skin and hair ... flying up like smoke.

And again, such a man was to be imagined halting at midday, his quart-pot set on the windward side of an open fire, 'sitting tailor fashion ... watching intently for the full bubble of the water, and directly it showed itself carefully dropping into the pot a capacious handful of tea'.[30] In his storytelling Harris registered these momentary skills and made them picturesque. The men and women who possessed them made assessments of the same kind. In this way the dance of European wrist and finger made its way across the land.

For most farmers the main point about any piece of country was whether it had been cleared, or needed clearing. Clearing was essential for crops, but it made a difference also to the movement of stock. In both New South Wales and Van Diemen's Land the term 'plains' was used for space without trees, whether hilly or not, and a vital distinction was made between 'forest', which was timber with grass, and 'bush' or 'scrub', where grass was scarce. Ideas about fences were especially telling. For many years few fenced even their outer boundaries. The main point of fencing was to keep stock from crops and gardens and many antipodean farmers used only zig-zag fencing, 'the most unsightly of all inclosures', as a visitor said, '... consisting of trunks of trees piled upon each other'.[31] Most farms were also deformed by stumps several feet high, looking like crops of gravestones. As for real crops, their variety was small. Farmers planted just as much as they could manage of the type they understood.[32]

To some English minds such methods were thoughtless and haphazard. Geared to the adventures of animal life, they depended on the unfolding of chance, on stories untold. Colonial farmers tended, as Bishop Broughton remarked, 'to trust to accidents, or as they audaciously call it, to Providence'. 'English notions', as the bishop called them, dictated more careful planning, with the mind of man devoutly matched to the promises of the Creator, as they followed each other season by season. Nevertheless, by the late 1820s a few small farmers, including ex-convicts, were making a new sort of effort, at last digging up old stumps and building good fences.[33] In due course fences were everywhere. Abundance of wood meant that they were normally of split logs, post and rail (mostly taken as triangular segments from the trunk), a method unusual in England. New skills were now imposed on workmen. In 1836, for instance, Thomas Adams, a Van Diemen's Land convict, was given thirty lashes for cutting the rail holes (mortices) near the thin edge of each post rather than the thick.[34]

Where free labour was used pairs of fencers were employed on contract. They first set themselves to collect the timber:

> They ... select the straitest and freest grown trees, fell them with a cross-cut saw, cut them off to proper lengths, and billet them out into as many divisions as the size of the tree will admit; they are then split or run out with wedges into rails or posts; not from heart to bark as is practised in splitting woods in England, but across the silver grain.

Measurements depended on the precise nature of the job in hand:

> Posts are cut five feet six inches, and rails nine feet long. The mortices are cut quite through the posts, about four inches long, and two inches wide; the ends of the rails are sometimes placed one over the other in the mortice,

and sometimes one by the side of the other; which last is much the neatest plan. The ends are trimmed away so as to overlap each other, and project through the mortice on both sides.

Four rails might be used for cultivation paddocks, with the lower three set close to keep out pigs. Otherwise three were enough, or even two where the enclosure was big and timber scarce. As a sample of sophistication still rare, slip-rails might be replaced with swinging gates.[35]

This description of technique appears in James Atkinson's book, *An Account of the State of Agriculture and Grazing in New South Wales*, published in London in 1826. The availability of such advice may explain why the same methods were used very early in Western Australia. George Fletcher Moore announced in his diary in April 1832 that his two labouring men had learnt to use a cross-cut saw, and about this time skilled splitters were beginning to travel the Swan River settlements, the best of them cutting two or three hundred slabs a day. Moore took on a pair, both Irish. He recorded a piece of their conversation that was inspired by one of those long penetrating noises, those painful shouts that the wood itself can make as its fibres – its 'knotty entrails', as Shakespeare says – part beneath the wedge. 'Hah, my joker', said the man with the wedge. 'Are you making him laugh, Paddy?', said the other. 'Laugh is it, ... I'm making him split his sides laughing.'[36]

A farm and farmhouse in South Australia, probably 1849, a brick building surrounded by a garden and post and rail fencing, altogether making up a carefully divided landscape, a lithograph by J.B. Austin.

In South Australia, a place always ready for innovation, such skills were applied very early. Already by 1840 86 per cent of fencing was post-and-rail. With high demand throughout the continent men began to specialise either in splitting or fencing. Such new skills meant a new way of looking at the landscape. The younger generation and more imaginative visitors began to see beauty, because they saw power, both in the cutting of the timber and in the tangible division of the land. 'A real bushman', according to Harris, 'may always be known by the instinctive exactitude with which he hits the true fall of his trees'.[37] Similarly, in the building of stockyards it was siting and layout that mattered. The entrance, for instance, should be set at the end of some natural path through which stock could run without distraction.[38]

In *The Emigrant Family* Harris wrote of his native-born hero walking by night from house to yards: 'The moon was shining with all that brilliancy of light that renders it so remarkable an object as it glides through the lovely skies of the colony, and a plentiful dew was already glistening on the rails, as the young bushman laid his arms upon them, and scrutinized his herd.'[39] The arms, the gaze, the rails themselves, were all of a piece with the new country.

The agricultural societies founded in New South Wales and Van Diemen's Land in 1822 (Chapter 2) had been partly designed to promote a knowledge of the local soil. A similar society existed in Western Australia from 1831, it being well understood, as Moore said, that nothing much could be done without 'a more regular system of agriculture'.[40] Such system must be deliberate. It must be scientific. It must rely on the gathering of information. But it also depended on something instinctive and intimate, on secret – or at least hidden – knowledge, and on changed ways of seeing. Moore himself boasted within two years of arriving that he had 'acquired some knowledge of the indications of soil: mahogany is indicative of sandy land; red gum, of stiff cold clay; wattle, of moisture; and the broom and dwarf grass tree, of what we term *shrubby herbage*'.[41]

This was shared insight. Men and women had to recognise the features of the country on similar terms before they could skin and carve it with skill. Much depended on informal agreement about boundaries because at all stages of settlement, until the last decades of the nineteenth century, it was impossible for the government surveyors to keep up with the demand for their services. Even in Sydney and Hobart, to begin with, householders had done without precise maps. Their right to living space depended partly on the Governor's permission and partly on neighbourly adjustment. Much the same was done in all the colonies later on by owners of sheep and cattle who wanted to use Crown land. These were the squatters. Settling within their boundaries, their skill with the landscape became a type of common sense – a sense held in common and refined with the years. It involved moral obligations. By the late 1830s, for instance, squatters in New South Wales whose boundaries were overstepped by their neighbours appealed to what they called 'old usage'.[42] Old usage depended on old conversation, old stories, and practised ways of seeing.

No European gave a more dramatic exhibition of bushmanship as it was understood by this time than Ludwig Leichhardt. Leichhardt aimed to conquer distance and size – or perhaps to lose himself in it. He was one of a long line of individuals who felt the challenge of Australia's vast dimensions. Matthew Flinders, the original circumnavigator (1802–03), had been followed at sea by Phillip Parker King, who had surveyed the northern coast in four exacting expeditions (1817–22), and, about the same time, by others who wanted glory on dry land. Oxley had hoped to penetrate the heart of the country and Wentworth had once offered to explore it from east to west. But for a while, in the 1820s and '30s, a better understanding of the terrible interior made such ideas seem fanciful. Only with accumulated skill were they revived. In 1840–41 Edward John Eyre set off from Adelaide, hoping to reach the centre and even the north coast. Failing twice, later in 1841 he travelled around the Great Australian Bight from Adelaide to King George Sound. Earlier explorers had used various livestock, including bullocks. Eyre trusted entirely to horses. Well mounted and lightly equipped, he moved quickly through country that would otherwise have killed him.[43] Charles Sturt also made an attempt northwards in 1844–46, being halted by the Simpson Desert. At the same time Leichhardt travelled from Moreton Bay to Port Essington, at the continent's extreme north, arriving in December 1845.

This journey of Leichhardt's was the most remarkable so far. His life's ambition, he said, was 'to investigate the nature of this continent'. He would never leave it 'until I have travelled right across it'. Discovery and mapping were less important to him than the journey itself, and the journey was a steady gathering of skill. Skill, understood as science, gave a man significance in the wider world – 'Just as a dance floor', he said, 'yields under a heavy dancer[,] society yields to the man of moment, no matter how unassumingly he makes his entry'. With skill, painfully gathered, such a man might be as shy as he liked (and Leichhardt was shy).[44] In the bush he learnt to guard against malnutrition and starvation by using indigenous foods that were toxic in their natural state, as Aborigines did, soaking cycad seeds and pandanus fruit, for instance, to release the poison.[45] Experience also added to his control of his animals. In difficult passes man and beast seemed alike. It was 'the spirit', so Leichhardt discovered, some internal fire in both, which mattered in the end.[46] He learnt to rely on the behaviour of birds in searching for water, and he acquired 'a sort of instinctive feeling' when he came across dry creeks as to whether pools might lie up or down stream, 'some', he said, 'being well provided with water immediately at the foot of the range, and others being entirely dry at their upper part, but forming large puddled holes, lower down, in a flat country'.[47] A similar instinct allowed him to find his way in country featureless to the unpractised eye.

Thomas Mitchell thought in terms of the large dimensions of the land and of the points to be entered on maps. Leichhardt was less systematic but more subtle. As with his search for food he copied the Aborigines, conceding that their abilities were far beyond his:

> Trees peculiarly formed or grouped, broken branches, slight elevations of the ground – in fact, a hundred things, which we should remark only when paying great attention to a place – seem to form a kind of Daguerreotype impression on their minds, every part of which is readily recollected.[48]

This willingness to defer, this confidence in trained instinct, was part of Leichhardt's character. The method of 'schooling', as he called it, which he and other bushmen imposed on themselves had been worked out over a generation or more by a cumulative common sense.

III

Stories have a particular point in nations of immigrants. From the beginning, among the Europeans in Australia most people had travelled and tales, true or false, are born of travel. Travel gave kaleidoscopic colour to the travellers' sense of who they were or who they seemed to be. Travelling is like the best kind of reading. We seem different, even to ourselves, as we move through varied parts of the world. By the same token, the business of fetching up detail from someone else's past and present may be one of the most delicate and haphazard aspects of conversation.

In the colonies even those living miles apart might talk in a neighbourly way, brought together by isolation. '[I]t is wonderful', said a woman in the bush west of Melbourne, 'how everything connected with every person, what they say and what they do, flies like wildfire through this place, and when I perchance see any of my neighbours, what wonderful tales we have to hear and relate'. The same eagerness might move a ship's captain – as happened once in the southern Atlantic, en route for Melbourne – to catch a cape pigeon, tie a 'ticket' to its neck giving the details of the ship and its passage and throw it back to sky and sea.[49]

Where people were scarce, in the lonely scrub and unfrequented desert, tales were especially precious. William Wilson Dobie, a squatter, wrote of the quietness of forest country, broken only by '[t]he fall of a branch, the shrill chirp of a cricket, the sudden dart of a snake, the gliding of a lizard through the rustling grass, the hum of insects, and the flight of birds'. It was impossible to read such aural hieroglyphics – so different from the bark of a dog or the clang of a bell. When he came across more familiar signs of life his heart leapt. With a deserted hut: 'Imagination would set eagerly to work, and bring vividly before the mind's eye the shifting scenes of its little story.' Conversations of the dead might be heard about the remains of a fireplace, while animal bones conjured up the jostling of sheep. A life's experience might be drawn, he said, from 'a cracked kettle, the head of a tobacco pipe, and the remains of an old shirt'.[50]

There were many degrees of skill between the stories of Leichhardt and those of William Dobie. And folded in upon such skills were others that were, once again, not so much typical of Australia as typical of the mid-nineteenth century. Storytelling, as Laurence Frayne knew, was a question of power and the purposes of power were changing. In this generation individuals came forward who were peculiarly skilled in reading humanity itself. This knowing attitude towards other people emerged not only in common speech and writing. We also see it in scientific inquiry, in economic theory and in government.

Take the celebrated stories of the American, Edgar Allan Poe. Poe was obsessed with exploring the individual mind. He was just as methodical as Leichhardt and he was also a scientist of sorts. He traced interlinked sensations, watching individuals as they reacted to the world, especially in making their way through a series of small decisions. He was an early writer of detective stories, showing in his famous tale of 'The Murders in the Rue Morgue' (1843) that even the thoughts of someone walking in the street might be analysed if one watched the shifting expressions of the face, the carriage of the head, the hike of the shoulders. For Poe, this proved the power of the masculine mind. 'As the strong man exults in his physical ability', he boasted, '… so glories the analyst in that moral activity which *disentangles*'. It involved, he said, 'a degree of *acumen* which appears to the ordinary apprehension praeternatural'.[51]

It was also a means of influence. Remember William Ullathorne's concern, in the teaching of faith, for 'the especial frame of mind, disposition of character, and tone of feeling, of each individual person'. And it was a method fundamental to penal theory. Alexander Maconochie's favourite science, 'the communication of moral impulses to the human mind', assumed a good knowledge of the receiving party.[52] This work might be done in perfect kindness. But another American, Nathaniel Hawthorne, in his novel *The Scarlet Letter* (1850), showed its sinister side. It might be ghastly as well as sublime. One of Hawthorne's characters (Chillingworth) became a kind of substitute-God as he searched the heart of another (Dimmesdale). 'It is a curious subject of observation and inquiry', said Hawthorne as he meditated the moral of his story, 'whether hatred and love be not the same thing at bottom'. After all, he said, each of them, 'in its utmost development, supposes a high degree of intimacy and heart-knowledge'. Each involved a peculiar penetration in the mastery of souls. Each might be driven by eagerness similar to a miner after gold. This new science was called by some 'ethology'. It underpinned one of the great ambitions of the day, an ambition both oppressive and divine.[53]

New novelists aimed for 'heart-knowledge' themselves, for a hunting-down of humanity. So did many less celebrated writers, including some in

Australia. This was partly the result, once again, of the new masses of human beings to be seen everywhere – great continents of people, increasing by the day and demanding exploration. Dickens' methods grew from the life of nineteenth-century cities, with their endless parade of character, 'busy places,' as he put it, 'where each man has an object of his own, and feels assured that every other man has his'. Anonymous within the crowd, he said, 'his character and purpose are written broadly on his face'.[54] Dickens looked into faces in London streets, while Eugène Sue, in his serial *Les Mystères de Paris* (1842–43), did the same across the Channel. Readers everywhere, including Australia, devoured the results.

But the same might be done in wide open spaces. In April 1835, during Thomas Mitchell's journey along the Bogan River, the botanist Richard Cunningham wandered from the main party with a horse and dog and was never seen again. Mitchell's search for Cunningham occupied a fortnight and he gave a Poe-like account of it (some time before Poe) in his published journal. They found where the poor man lay on 'the first dreary night of his wandering'. They spotted the loss of his horse. They noticed a change in his stride, now 'remarkably long and firm', proving that he had killed and eaten his dog. With new vigour he had clearly headed north trying to find water, 'the direction being preserved even through thick brushes'. They followed him to the river bed, 'and the two steps by which Mr Cunningham first reached water, and in which he must have stood while allaying his burning thirst, were very plain in the mud!' Little more appeared but scraps of clothing. Cunningham had apparently ended his argument with the elements by disappearing into them. (In fact he was killed by Blacks.) Mitchell published a map of Cunningham's last movements, its jagged lines a sketch of pain.[55]

Mitchell proved his anxiety about Cunningham with modish skill. Soon such acumen began to reshape the use of power among the Europeans in Australia. Wherever the well read had room to extend their authority they did it with a similar, scalpel-like testing of lives.

Newspaper journalists, often young men and eagerly fashionable, nourished this skill and by the 1840s few places in the world produced so many newspapers per head as this. Newspapers were useful in places of recent settlement, as a means of keeping up with shifting patterns of trade, and the energy of reporters belonged to town life. Advertisements were 'the principal support', as one authority said, 'of the colonial press', and papers could do well only where there was much to advertise.[56] In Western Australia before 1850 the White population hovered between two and three thousand, and only Perth, Fremantle, and Albany had more than a hundred people each. As a result before 1855 there was never more than one paper in existence there besides the official *Gazette*. South Australia and Port Phillip made better use of the press (Chapter 6). In South Australia between 1838 and 1843, when the population was approaching

10,000, at least eleven papers were begun, most of them weeklies. There was also in London, until 1841, the *South Australian Colonist* – an important source of publicity, as its editor said, in view of 'the increasingly severe competition amongst the colonies in the Australian archipelago'.[57]

A rush of printers to the Port Phillip district led to newspapers not only in Melbourne itself but also in Geelong, Portland, Port Fairy, and Warrnambool, and the wages of reporters, compositors, and pressmen were very high. Proprietors did all they could to train apprentices and import new men.[58] In the older parts of New South Wales it was government that had brought into existence the main points of settlement, but the coastal towns of Port Phillip were the work of commerce, especially from across Bass Strait. It was therefore letters and newspapers rather than government that linked these places to each other and to Launceston, their mother town. It was also the press, carefully orchestrated, that broadcast their virtues in Britain, just as the press had done for South Australia from the start. At Port Phillip the celebrity of reporters meant that they could drink at public bars for nothing.[59]

Here was another way of accumulating facts and deciphering human nature. Even more than listening, reading about other people sharpened one's memory and imagination, and sharpened also the acumen, the disentangling power, which meant so much to Poe. But how was it possible for newspaper readers to make sense of so many lives at once, to draw them together into a single tapestry? How did newspapers contribute to anything like a single information order? So many stories, each urgent in its own way, might be packed into one morning paper – advertisements, notices of shipping, court reports, and other news. Reading laid down quickly, grain on grain, a type of visionary ant-bed within which strangers were like neighbours. Men and women might be unacquainted and yet they might follow each other's fortunes, retelling also what they read. Each reporter, each correspondent, each subscriber, and reader, like a homing insect, carried scraps of detail for the common store.

William Godwin spoke of a 'common sensorium', but George Eliot, one of the newer generation, called the world 'a huge whispering-gallery'.[60] She had a better sense than Godwin of all the loose infinity of human voices. Stories embody moral standpoints. While individual opinions are easily heard in small places, how might they matter among great masses? In the 1830s, travelling in the United States, which he saw as an image of the future for all European peoples, the French writer Alexis de Tocqueville was struck with the way in which the opinions of the many might swamp the opinions of the few. John Stuart Mill wrote not long after of 'the tyranny of society over the individual'.[61] One of the catch-cries of the day was 'Vox populi vox dei' – the voice of the people, united as one, was the voice of God, the two being equally singular and equally potent. Where did this leave the fragmentary story, the individual voice?

Some, more optimistic than de Tocqueville and Mill, believed that within communities the disparate souls were drawn together by daily interaction into a single soul, which was no tyrant but, indeed, a manifestation of the divine. The American essayist Ralph Waldo Emerson spoke of the 'over-soul'. Conversation of any kind, he said, showed the existence of a common nature in the speakers. 'That third party or common nature', he explained, 'is not social; it is impersonal; [it] is God'. This notion of a common nature, in which every individual found his or her own reflection, was taken up by different people in different ways. William Ullathorne used the term '*esprit du corps*' to refer to the living thing that was born of the communal talk on convict ships and at Norfolk Island.[62] German writers spoke of '*Geist*', or spirit of community, including the community of the nation. Such organisms were oneself – one's own identity – in larger form, richer, sweeter, more sensible, more permanent. In the presence of the 'over-soul', said Emerson: 'All are conscious of attaining to a higher self-possession.'[63]

Such sublime agreement created a kind of truth – 'Vox populi vox dei' – and this mattered for politics. Here was a new kind of power for the people as a whole and it led to a new degree of reverence for popular opinion. '[I]t was only by taking the opinions of all classes that the truth in all its majesty could be made known', said James Macarthur.[64] This might be done through general elections, which was Macarthur's point, and in some sense by legislative council inquiries. No method, however, was more weighty than the press.

With similar majesty a flock of birds might move together in the air, as if on a single whim. And indeed, comparisons between animal and human instinct, en masse, were attempted often. South Australian newspapers liked to publish local scientific detail and in 1840–42 a gentleman calling himself 'Naturae Amator', sent in a series of pieces to the *South Australian Register* on 'The Natural History of the Colony'. Among other things he considered the 'social economy' of small creatures. He described a scene during a day of 'general swarming', when the blue air of South Australia was full of ants, male and female, dancing, a three-dimensional curtain of life. Under some rubbish in the corner of a shed, suddenly lifted, he said, a host of 'neuters' were to be seen, running about. 'They all kept within a certain boundary, crossing and recrossing in every direction, and shewing a living mass of countless beings collected together in a small space.'[65] Their one great aim, apparently, was to get the remaining females away. But what made ants behave like this, all to a single end and each in step?

In the study of humanity, attention focused on great cities, places where a 'living mass' likewise lived within 'a certain boundary'. Here, perhaps, the heart of society might be uncovered, its character known and its motives disentangled. For Dickens the air of London, shared over and over, was the filthy breath of a single being. If one could only bring oneself to imagine the moral pestilence that accompanied it, he said, then 'how terrible the revelation!' Every crowded London graveyard, in his view, copied the compact life above, the dead being 'parted from the living by a little earth and a board or two'. And in that place the living might see their own image 'thick and close – corrupting in body as they had in mind – a dense and squalid crowd'.[66]

It had long been conventional wisdom that transported convicts were made worse by being brought in masses together, especially in those 'sinks of iniquity', Sydney and Hobart. The classification of prisoners, solitary confinement, and the lonely labour of shepherding were among the solutions attempted. The layout and management of big towns called for careful planning and well-ordered police, the listing of names and the numbering of houses, so that all – all the dancing ants – might be separately known and separately watched. This was, once again, a matter of system and science. Rulers must probe among the members of society as medical men told over fibres of flesh. To know, and to know in context, made it possible to correct every member and, in due course, the body as a whole. The skills expected of policemen in the streets included a similar discretion – the power to judge, often in an instant, the aims of milling men and women. What Edgar Allan Poe made heroic as detective-work was asked of every convict constable who gave the order to 'move on'.

However, in Australia some thought that it was not only crowds but also isolation, the absence of society, which made men and women wicked. For some, towns were centres of truth. Each, properly organised, might be the heart of a wide-reaching information order. For decades, according to Alexander Harris, convict stockmen, 'scattered among wildernesses', far from 'the sound of holy counsel and spiritual caution ... [had been] left to fester each in his own rankness of soul'. And then, having been corrupted as individuals they often combined. And so they 'ferment into yet more horrible conditions of pollution and iniquity'. The end-result, he said, was the worst evil of all, 'unnatural vice'.[67]

Convict transportation ceased to Sydney in 1840, continuing only to Hobart and from there, in many cases, to the penal settlements at Norfolk Island and Port Arthur. At the same time the inland frontier became even more completely a world of its own. Flocks and herds extended with enormous speed, through the Port Phillip district and northward as far as Moreton Bay and the Darling Downs (later Queensland). In some of these districts there were even small towns. Port Phillip had its coastal settlements from the beginning and in the far north the 1851 census listed not only Brisbane (population 2543), but also Drayton, Maryborough, Ipswich, and Warwick, with more than 200 each. The multiplication of horses (Chapter 1) increased the speed with which the country was overrun. By this time on the New South Wales frontier horses outnumbered men two to one.[68] Horses multiplied problems of law and order, but they were also part of the solution. They added to the independence of stockmen but also to the reach of government, its postal service and police. From 1839 the Governor in Sydney appointed commissioners of Crown lands, one for each of the pastoral districts beyond the Limits of Location, and he backed them up with mounted constables.

The crimes committed in these parts mainly involved violence between Black and White and the stealing of livestock. The 'well-organized bands' that specialised in such theft (the small squatters of earlier times) used the 'science' described above, an exotic skill, which in town made them the subject of many stories, true and false.[69] Rumour fed on the simple disappearance of stock, for whatever reason, on questions of identity, on the possibility of calves taken before branding and of brands forged. All added up to a kind of knowledge peculiar to the bush and at odds with the order in town. The same was true of stories about trouble between stockmen and Blacks. According to the protector in Western Australia such stories, including the testimony of Aborigines themselves, were always 'much exaggerated'. Everywhere news from the edges of settlement was received with scepticism. An Adelaide newspaper remarked how 'correctness ... diminishes in a ratio corresponding to the distance' and in Sydney a letter-writer to the *People's Advocate* contemplated with horror the impact of the bush on 'the intellectual, the reasoning, the thinking faculties' of White men. It was the fate of many there, he said, to 'sink into absolute idiotism'.[70] Almost by definition the inland was a place of untruth.

The power of the newspapers, based in towns, included the power to exalt the rational scepticism of urban life, to define 'correctness'. A few men and women, everywhere, still felt that the barely known parts of the country preserved something of their own – a kind of 'heart-knowledge' intricate and splendid. This had been the point of stories about a great, green-ringed, inland sea. But this was not an attitude fostered by the new generation of journalists. For instance, in winter 1845 a large bone, apparently from some unknown native beast, was found near Lake Colac, west of Geelong. An 'intelligent black' was reported to have said that it belonged to a 'bunyip' and from this point bunyips became a matter of household talk.[71] Amateur scientists did what they could with hearsay evidence and with reputed remains, clothing old bones with the flesh of rural talk.

According to the gentleman-explorer William Hilton Hovell, samples of the species had been seen by White shepherds and Aborigines, 'disporting in clumsy gambols, and inhabiting the waters of the lakes and rivers of the interior'. It was 'a huge animal', Hovell said, and indeed tales of its size were reconciled as if by magic with its quickness in slipping under water. Alexander Macleay, speaker of the New South Wales legislative council, supplied specimens for the Australian Museum and everywhere there were anecdotes. 'He was of a brownish colour', reported another gentleman, who had seen one in the Eumeralla, near Portland, 'with a head something the shape of a kangaroo, an enormous mouth ... [and a] long neck covered

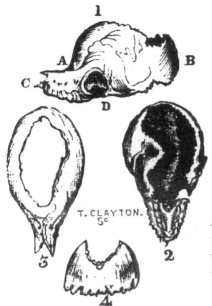

The bones, it was said, of a bunyip, laid before the world in 1847 by W.H. Hovell through the pages of the *Sydney Morning Herald*, drawn by Thomas Clayton.

Source: *Sydney Morning Herald*,
9 February 1847

with a shaggy mane'. There were even reports of a bunyip living in the lake at the botanical gardens in Melbourne. Its 'unearthly howling', said the *Argus*, disturbed the sleep of residents nearby.[72]

But this last was a joke. By now, in town, bunyips were a byword for rural foolishness. The information order under construction left no room for the say-so of 'intelligent blacks' and skilful readers – mainly White men – stood back, uncoupling fact from fiction. They aimed to feel the majesty of truth, 'a higher self-possession', as Emerson put it, in disentangling the tales about them, devising thereby an ordered reality.

Chapter 11

Digging Deep

I

There was much said in these days about self-help and the energy of the individual, especially the individual man. But giving a hand mattered too, and that depended on trust and openness. In their habits of cooperation the Australian settlements varied. The origins and age of each, at least to some extent, made a difference to the way people worked together and so did the relationship of town and country – from Moreton Bay to the Derwent and from inland Western Australia to the anchorages at Port Phillip.

Ideas about working together depended partly on what people thought government could do for them and what they might do by themselves. However brutal and squalid, Sydney and its hinterland had begun as an Enlightenment state, managed (as I say in Volume 1) with dictatorial benevolence. A generation later there was still among the people a pungent 'Botany Bay' style, a startling manner of speech and sense of right that worked strangely with authority – dense with mockery, bold but also clinging. In Van Diemen's Land the manner of power was always more fragile, more busy but not always more effective. In Western Australia survival itself seemed to depend on leading men, including government, working together. In South Australia officials had to deal with methods of brotherhood and a resentment of paternalism that were almost republican. But some officials themselves liked republican ways.

The way in which men and women saved money says a great deal about their sense of self-reliance. The savings banks in Sydney and Hobart were both begun by government, but the Sydney bank was designed for all the poor, bond and free, while Hobart's was meant for convicts alone. The Sydney bank was managed by a board of volunteers, all 'men of standing', and its success depended on the confidence of the poor, whereas in Hobart the convicts had no choice but to hand in their cash. The Sydney bank took deposits of between a shilling and £30 and (at least by 1846) about a fifth of its depositors were women, with domestic servants figuring largely in its books. In Hobart nearly all were men. Men with reliable incomes could commit their funds (including their wives' earnings, which by law they owned) to benefit societies and assurance companies. Women had only the savings bank.[1] In South Australia the savings bank reached out in a similar way, but it was an initiative of the South Australian Company, which was a private concern.[2] Government there did not put out its hand to the poor, and 'men of standing' made the effort alone.

The founders of savings banks in Britain and Australia intended that working men and women should let their money accumulate over the years, to guard against sickness and old age. These institutions were meant to teach the poor to think for years ahead. In fact, at least in Sydney, most depositors saved for the short term. They seem to have thought that savings were meant to be spent at frequent intervals through life. The Sydney bank also worked best for people in town. Elsewhere money might be left with publicans, who needed a name for honesty if they wanted to keep their licences.[3] Such was the network of mutual understanding, the intermeshing of government and individual, which fifty years of settlement had built up.

Cooperation took for granted individual effort. From place to place, in a variety of circumstances, men and women made decisions for their own good. While they might not spend years saving cash they certainly knew that some of the steps they took would matter all their lives. Women, when they married, committed themselves to one man's ability to earn. For men, too, marriage mattered, but much also depended on early decisions about apprenticeship and small investments. The first step, whatever it was, knitted individuals into patterns of trust. This was a great issue of common wisdom. 'A person getting a *start*', said one local authority (and he meant a man), 'and persevering steadily, in whatever occupation it may be, and never letting the *grass grow* under his feet, is sure to do well'. But at this time, he said (he meant the 1840s, when all the colonial economies were uncertain), 'the greatest difficulty ... was, getting something to START upon'.[4]

Some men made their own luck. Benjamin Boyce reached South Australia as a seaman by the *Moffat* and with a mate he jumped ship and made for the hills. There they spent time with the Tiersmen (escaped or freed convicts from Van Diemen's Land), 'but', as Boyce wrote home to his family, 'it was crismas time and thay was all drunk and we culd git nothink to do thear'. (The accent is Lincolnshire.) In due course, he said, 'i ... engaged to go to liv at a dary whear i ad 20 cous to milk every morning'. After three months of milking he noticed Adelaide's need for hay and he went off by himself cutting grass – 'yough mite go and cut a lode of hay in oun day wich it was a selling at four or five pounds a lode'. He worked hard and, he said, 'i out to bean making muny as fast as i culd count it but in stead of that i uest to spend it faster then i earnt it'. Suddenly the market was crowded and, with a companion from his own part of England, Boyce went splitting and fencing. He still spent large sums on drink but he still saved £40 in nine months. He was now ready to marry. '[I] av got all cumpleat', he said, 'but a wife'. Choosing a publican's daughter he had met on board ship, he kept her and their baby son by doing any work that came his way. With another man he shore 14,000 sheep for fifteen shillings a hundred plus rations and there was also harvesting and thrashing wheat. '[I]t his a fine cuntre for a young man to come to thear is plenty of work'. Some new immigrants hardly knew which way to turn, but not him. '[T]hear is no fear of me doing well sum whear for if i cant to wel in oun place then I go to a nother.'[5]

Benjamin Boyce saw himself as a wanderer. He had 'a rovin comichon throo the world'. Men who had served apprenticeships, acquiring a specific skill, might behave differently, staying put, especially as they got older, and trusting to the dignity of their trade. Their training made them what they were. In their search for security they might join forces, so as to shield themselves against sudden disaster, sickness and disability, accidents of trade and weather, and the various vicissitudes of their line of work. They might join trade unions and benefit and assurance societies. Indeed, be-longing in this way was further proof of a man's respectability. In signing up and paying his dues each tested his strength over time and laid down a routine. Among some convict men there had been secret societies where membership depended on the mingling of blood, each man slashing his skin for the purpose. Mingling cash, mingling signatures, eating and drinking together in particular public houses, had much the same effect – learning how to 'voat', as an English baker put it, and how to work on a 'commety'. It gave a man a new look and his voice (with all the forms and frictions of men's conversation) a new weight.[6]

Men at work created space for talking. Note the custom, said to be pecu-liar to Australia, of a 'smoking time', a quarter of an hour each in the morn-ing and afternoon, when '[a]ll the men', according to one authority, 'leave off work and deliberately sit down and smoke'.[7] The way they talked then and on all similar occasions was ruled by custom too. When men argued about wages, for instance, the drift of debate might depend partly on num-bers. This was especially likely, according to Caroline Chisholm, if the men had wives who knew what was going on. '[W]hen they are in large parties', she said, 'a feeling of pride makes a man unwilling to be the first to submit to necessity' (the necessity, that is, of taking less). But 'when in small par-ties, the influence of the women is greater – the wives persuade – [and] the men submit with cheerfulness', so she said, 'to accept lower wages'.[8]

Men of all ranks had rules for meeting. Ludwig Leichhardt, the German, was struck with the methods of discussion used in Australia. They were typically English, he said, and 'whenever Englishmen meet formally to thrash out particular questions, they elect a so-called Chairman or pres-ident, to maintain order'. Meetings might be noisy. Consider the Sydney city council, formed in 1842. 'I have seen four or five speaking at once', said a shorthand reporter, 'the Mayor ... shouts "Order" at the top of his voice, but he is almost inaudible'. And yet even in such debates there was buried a nugget of formality. There was a theory of order, which had justified the meeting in the first place.[9]

Because they were growing fast the leading towns were magnets for men in the building trade and in Australia such men were the first to organise themselves in associations. Carpenters formed benefit societies in Sydney and Perth as early as 1831 and a Builders' Trade Union was formed in Adelaide within two years of first settlement. Hobart had its Carpenters' and Joiners' Society. In these bigger towns men saw each other often at work and they talked easily about wages and conditions. Some unions were also labour exchanges, with books kept to register men looking for jobs.[10]

Some groups, such as the Australian Union Benefit Society in Sydney and the Trades Union Society in Maitland, were apparently meant for all kinds of skilled men.[11] Here, and in Europe and North America, skilled labourers began to see themselves as a single body with a common interest. Typically literate, they read the same books. They absorbed the lessons, for instance, about manhood and violence (Chapter 6). They learnt the difference between 'physical force', which was political activity depending on violence, and 'moral force', where men triumphed because they were self-controlled and well organised. In Britain such elaborate understanding was already nationwide and it was the basis of a new kind of radicalism. Reform by whatever method had two great aims – the abolition of the power of money, which was always erratic and selfish – and the forming of a type of government directly accountable to the organised mass, or in other words to 'the people'. Government must be transparent and the people for their part must be honest and well informed. When that happened, so the radicals said, the distance between government and people would disappear. This was, in fact, another aspect of the communications revolution. To be well informed was to have a clear sense of 'system'. Every man might look about himself as if from a centre of power. He thus attained, once again, 'a higher self-possession'. He thus understood that power was a matter of system and that a flawed system could be changed. In short, men owed it to themselves to convert bad government into good. Managed by moral force, this was democracy. It was underpinned by notions of moral manhood so powerful as to dazzle this generation.

Democrats wanted frequent national elections in which every man would vote and in which all votes would be of equal value. The Chartists – men supremely organised and, in consequence, highly influential – wanted annual voting. They also wanted to be able to send working men to parliament. There were Chartists among the free immigrants to Australia from the late 1830s and Chartist skills made a deep mark on Australian life.[12] In 1843 a meeting of unemployed men in Sydney formed the Mutual

Protection Association in order to pressure government against more immigrant labourers and the revival of transportation, both of which might affect
their wages. They did not say much about democracy but they were organised in a radical fashion, they boasted over 400 members, a newspaper of
their own (the *Guardian*), general meetings once a week, and an active management committee. They aimed to improve the conditions of those whom
they called 'the working classes' (a new term) and they wanted power of a
systematic kind.[13]

Good cooperation depended on men learning about collective management. They had to keep lists, put up posters, and speak in public. They had
to make their demands fit the intricate demands of a man's life, multiplied
by thousands. They had to find and nourish within themselves a common
manhood. In New South Wales and Van Diemen's Land, as working men
became organised they began to think about the convict past, with its ignorance and degradation, as something on which they should turn their backs.
Convictism made men parasites and cowards. Convicts carried on their skin
in red and purple, silvered with sweat, the memory of chaining and the lash.
The mastery of themselves since boyhood made free men, on the other hand,
inhabitants of a purer, brighter world. Their scars – besides the blue-black
of the odd tattoo – were supposedly signs of self-directed labour. With care
they might see beyond gentlemen, however well read. Their own reading,
of radical books, pamphlets, and newspapers, might be slight in quantity
and yet, so they thought, more efficient. In Sydney the socialist disciples of
Robert Owen were small tradesmen (a shoemaker, an upholsterer, a tailor).
But convict discipline proved to them beyond doubt 'the ignorance of our
legislators on that all-important subject, the mental constitution of man'.[14]

The convict regime began to seem alien to the kind of place each colony
must be. Its managers and its victims were all outside the body of trust now
emerging. Many individuals of middling rank took the same view. They
were better men and women, so they thought, than the old elite, who had
made their money from convict suffering.[15] Transportation to New South
Wales having ended in 1840, Van Diemen's Land was now the empire's
only penal colony. Within a few years three in every seven people on the
island was a convict in bondage. Nor were convicts as useful as they had
been. Convict men were no longer assigned to private masters but worked
in 'probation' gangs, though the well-behaved might be hired out (at less
than the free man's wage). No longer dispersed among the free population,
most convicts lived, as it seemed, in great bodies of corruption and vice and
at the same time they competed with the free workforce. '[I]f a free man
went to get work', so one complained, 'the answer generally was, "Oh, I
can get probationers to do it cheaper!"' 'Many a time', he said, 'he had
been deprived of work by the system.'[16]

In 1846 William Gladstone, Secretary of State, decided to suspend transportation to Van Diemen's Land for two years. Whitehall badly needed a

repository for convicts, but Van Diemen's Land's problems were obvious –
so much so that in March 1847 the Governor, Sir William Denison, sent a
questionnaire on the subject to his magistrates. He wanted, he said, 'the
views of the Inhabitants of the Colony' as to whether the colony should continue as a place of transportation and, if so, what reforms were possible. He
asked the magistrates to consult with 'such of the Gentlemen and others in
your neighbourhood who are competent to form opinions on the subject'.
Never before had a Hobart government sought advice in this open-ended
way and while a number of magistrates answered only for themselves a
few took the process even further.[17] Launceston had inspired the democratic
hopes of John Pascoe Fawkner (Chapter 7) and similar independence appears in the way the gentlemen around Launceston now joined to construct
a popular reply. They called a public meeting in town, which in turn set up
a committee to take opinions on the subject. John West, a Congregationalist
minister and editor of the *Launceston Examiner*, used his paper to push the
effort forward, encouraging letter-writers and publishing reports of every
relevant meeting. He composed what he called '39 Articles against the con-
tinuance of Transportation to Van Diemen's Land', and he wrote a pamphlet, *Commonsense*, with a print-run of 3000. Free working men, roused
by the campaign, distributed 1200 copies of his '39 Articles' as a sheet publication at their own expense.[18]

West made himself the moderator of debate in the north. He might pre-
tend sometimes to be impartial but he was confident, he said, that 'at no
distant day the unanimous voice of the community will say, in a tone not
to be disregarded, cease transportation for ever'. This 'unanimous voice'
was to be like Emerson's 'common nature'. It was to be like Ullathorne's
'*esprit du corps*'. It was to be a matter of instinct (moral instinct) en masse.
But that instinct must be called forth with skill – with a type of ingenuity
increasingly prized among public men.[19] Something new was to be found
within the people, a singularity among the noise, and opinion was to shift
all at once, or apparently all at once, because of the way voices were woven
to a single pattern.

Some of the complications of this revolution in method were to be seen
at the second public meeting at Launceston, on 10 May. The proposed chairman, James Cox of Clarendon, was a known enemy of transportation and
some of his opponents, gentlemen who wanted convicts, said that this made
him an unsuitable chairman. The chair must be impartial. Argument around
this procedural point was overwhelmed with shouts of 'Cox, Cox' and 'put
it to the vote'. The 'unanimous voice' prevailed even on such a fundamental
rule – as it had also done in Hobart four days earlier. At Launceston, after
everyone had had their say: 'As one man the meeting rose, and with raised
hands and joyous shouts manifested the opinion of the mass of the community.' And yet, when Denison collated the answers from throughout the
island the numbers for and against more convicts were about equal.[20]

The Launceston leadership already had an agent in London, John Alexander Jackson. Local energy and Jackson's efficiency meant that the Secretary of State now wrestled for the first time with organised popular feeling in the Antipodes. Thanks to Jackson a copy of one official despatch reached Launceston even before its original got to the Governor in Hobart.[21] The idea that representatives of the people might be ahead of Whitehall in this way, equally united, better informed, more efficient, and more moral, was vital to the movement against convicts.

There seemed to be immediate success. Within months of the May meetings Denison announced Whitehall's promise to end transportation. However, within a year the British government decided that convicts who had served a part of their time at Home might be sent with tickets of leave, as 'exiles', to both Van Diemen's Land and New South Wales. This reversal proved to the new enthusiasts that Her Majesty's ministers, hitherto the fountain of honour for Britons abroad, could not be trusted. Where did this leave Laurence Frayne's 'science of government'? It also roused public opinion on the Australian mainland and here, too, 'the working classes' were involved. There was already a new radical body in Sydney called the Constitutional Association with a newspaper, the *People's Advocate*, managed by a Chartist, Edward Hawksley. In both places the leadership was taken by gentlemen. But meetings drew unprecedented numbers because working men believed that the question touched their sense of who they were.[22]

Twenty years before in Hobart Governor Arthur had persuaded his people that the island's existence as a home for Europeans depended on convicts and convict discipline. John West aimed to prove the opposite. 'Van Diemen's Land owes its "existence" to the "presence of convicts"', he said, 'in the same sense that England owes her existence to the presence of barbarians with bodies painted blue'.[23] In 1852 he completed the most exacting piece of scholarship so far managed in Australia, *The History of Tasmania*, and published it from his own press. He retold the island story from the beginning. All, he conceded, had begun with government. But the future depended on the inner strength of the people. They must make a new start. Henceforth, he said, their 'happiness and prosperity' must be drawn with skill from among themselves. This really meant discovering a moral power most hardly knew they had.[24]

By now employers in Western Australia had volunteered to take convicts themselves. As with the South Australians, freedom from transportation had always been a matter of pride in the west. But settlers here had been well aware of the way in which New South Wales and Van Diemen's Land had profited from convict labour and from about 1845 their moral priorities had begun to shift. As livestock began to multiply its owners suffered from the scarcity of hands and convicts seemed to be the answer. They had a newspaper to support them, William Tanner's *Inquirer*, and they could afford to ignore the opinions of the free working men of Perth, a body untouched by Chartism, holding no meetings and possessing no public voice. The pro-convict initiative came from members of the York Agricultural Society and it was backed up by leading merchants in the capital. It led to the arrival both of 'exiles' and of convicts in bondage (all men) from June 1850. The human cargo came with funds for a penal system, a useful bounty in itself.[25]

II

Emerson once told of riding with a woman in the American forest. Among the silence of the trees she said to him 'that the woods always seemed to her *to wait*, as if the genii who inhabit them suspended their deeds until the wayfarer has passed onward'. The silence itself seemed to suggest something living. This feeling of an expectant presence must have been keen in Australia too, although here it was not always silent. Many remarked on noises in the bush that seemed to indicate something wholly mysterious. (This was before there were stories of bunyips.) Robert Dundas Murray, at Port Phillip, was baffled by a voice, as he called it, which came at times 'out of the depths of the forest', apparently calling to intruders in complaint or anger: 'You recognise its tones in the moanings, the uncouth cries and wild shrieks, that at long intervals rise into the air, arrest the ear for an instant, and then cease as suddenly as they broke forth.'[26] He never discovered what it was.

For anyone with ears attuned there was a waiting even more palpable among the rocks beneath. Here, as in America – both countries in which there was much for immigrants to do – it seemed that the very future was living and breathing beneath the surface of the present.

The opening of the Australian scrub was followed by the opening of the earth itself. The territory was gouged and tunnelled first in imagination and then in fact. It was a shared effort and it was a result of the way in which Europeans thought and acted together during the 1830s and '40s. In 1833 Charles Sturt published, as part of an introduction to his account of two expeditions of discovery, the first summary account of the geology of the eastern mainland (leaving out what is now Queensland, so far unexplored). The sandstone of the east coast, he said, gave way along the line of the Great Dividing Range to red granite. That 'primitive rock' was a type of continental skin – blonde, as if European – that stretched as plains to the westward, ribbed here and there with limestone and further on with a variety of schorl (blue, finely grained, and very hard) and mica (rose, pink, and white). To the south-west the sandstone was interrupted by the richer whinstone, and so, once more, by limestone as far as the Yass Plains. There Sturt found quartz, 'in huge white masses', more granite, and, as a type of mottling, sandstone, chlorite, micaceous schist, chalcedony, and red jasper.[27] In South Australia the geologist and linguist Johann Menge made similar surveys, publishing his findings in Adelaide. He was struck with the hornstone of the Barossa Range. 'Veins of opal', he said, ran through it everywhere, including opal agate striped red and blue and opal jasper in red and yellow. Similarities with Iceland suggested hot springs in earlier ages.[28]

In such writing there was a great sense of depth. The country now apparently had bulk and weight. The same appeared in a statement by Leichhardt, which even hinted at something moving within the mass. He had heard, he said, 'men of science' suggest that this continent had once been two large islands, or an archipelago. These had supposedly been 'united by their progressive, and, perhaps, still continued elevation'. Such theories seemed to touch the marrow of the land and new scientific beliefs in Europe, evident in Sir Charles Lyell's famous book, *Principles of Geology* (1830–33), did indeed suggest life underfoot. Over barely comprehensible stretches of time the earth had apparently changed, maturing and aging, shifting and buckling.[29] Like Dundas Murray, Charlotte Barton speculated about sounds heard in the bush, including explosions 'like the loudest cannon', apparently from the rocks beneath. Sir John Herschel, she said, who had studied the subject in Europe, thought that such noises might be caused by 'subterraneous steam … in the process of forming and condensing'.[30] Here was something like a great beast, sighing and settling.

Such insights led to a range of new skills, including more varied methods of mining. The earth's interior might be opened up with more system than hitherto, just as whales were dismembered by crews of seamen for

View of the copper town at the Burra, 1850, a lithograph by Samuel Thomas Gill.

their bones, ambergris, and oil. And just as whalers sometimes stepped into the mouths of their prey we might now contemplate labour of considerable refinement within the ribcage of the earth. We might clothe our bodies with this larger body.

Thanks partly to the way Johann Menge published geological information, deposits of rich minerals were found early in South Australia. In 1841 two labouring men discovered an outcrop of silver and lead within a few miles of Adelaide. Exports from the site continued through the 1840s. Then copper was found to the north at Kapunda. It was exported from 1844 and in the following year copper mining began also at Burra Burra, an even richer field 90 miles from the capital. Many thousands of pounds were immediately invested in the Burra mine and there were soon nearly 2 miles of galleries and chambers underground, lined with green malachite and red oxide and to be traversed, as a visitor put it, candle-lit, with 'divers wendings, prostrations, twistings, turnings, climbings, clamberings, and examinations', and, he added, with frequent exclamations of delight. In 1846 there were 468 people in Burra town, with sawyers, charcoal-burners, and carters around about. It quickly became one of the biggest settlements in Australia.[31]

Europeans also hunted underground for water, with artesian wells. New machinery allowed for a narrow bore reaching down more than 1000 feet and lined with piping to prevent seepage, the water being forced upwards under its own pressure, though not always to the surface. Two attempts were made in South Australia (the first by Menge on Kangaroo Island) and in 1849–50 experts argued in Sydney as to whether this might be the answer to one of the country's most pressing problems, its lack of surface moisture. The Australian Agricultural Company brought out an English engineer, Thomas Paten, to bore at its estate at Port Stephens. Paten's father, an 'eminent well-digger', had long searched under the white chalk of south-east England for a run of pure water to supply London's new millions. His son struggled instead with Australian granite. After many months digging tawny water gushed up in hundreds of gallons, smelling thickly of sulphur. But Paten had to stop at 120 feet. His men had left to dig for gold.[32]

Australian newspapers had already alerted readers to the possibility of local gold. From time to time for many years small nuggets had been found in New South Wales and even in Van Diemen's Land, according to a recent book, the existence of gold was 'beyond mere conjecture'.[33] Now, in March 1851, good quantities were found near Bathurst, on Sturt's red granite plains, and similar discoveries followed elsewhere, including Victoria, which became a separate colony on 1 July. An extraordinarily rich field appeared at Ballarat, north-west of Melbourne, in spring, and others at Buninyong, Mt Alexander, and elsewhere. News of these discoveries soon reached Europe and North America and during the following year 86,000 people arrived in Australia from abroad. There was also hectic movement among the colonies. Launceston was 'almost deserted', at least by its men, and the same was said of most of the villages of South Australia.[34]

Given the feeble response to earlier discoveries, how was this sudden worldwide frenzy to be explained? On the goldfields near Bathurst some said that 'the Almighty blinded the eyes of men until the poor of England had congregated in Australian lands, to enjoy the good He had prepared for them'. A few thought more scientifically. '[A] peculiar process of chemistry has been slowly going on of late years', they argued, which had all of a sudden laid the wealth of the land open.[35] But equally powerful was the chemistry at work among the people themselves. The goldrush was a result of a certain crystallising in daily conversation that profoundly remade the way men thought about 'getting a start'. Only a great shift in communication methods could have convinced so many people so quickly of the chances of being rich and of the possibility of travelling over oceans to do so. As a gentleman remarked, this was not an everyday process. Nothing would have happened without the right encouragement:

> The circumstance of being able to pick up gold like common dirt is, in itself, of so extraordinary a nature, so completely opposed to all our experience, that its first announcement was received with something like a doubting reservation, and had it not been attested by a goodly array of facts, the public were half-disposed to treat it rather as an airy unreality of romance than one of the hard, naked, and practical doings of this material world.[36]

The 'goodly array of facts' was a matter of publicity. The earlier discoveries had not been reported as these ones were because the means of reporting were different. The variety and passage of news from continent to continent meant that information of this kind, 'so completely opposed to all our experience', could not make its mark.

Only in the late 1840s, in Europe, had Australia begun to look like a place where poor men might do well. The United States, on the other hand, had always been a land of opportunity and since 1849 the rush to dig for gold in California had made the world aware of the way riches might be gathered, as if by magic, in remote spots. Now stories of sudden wealth were easily copied for Australia. Besides, local men returning from California knew what to look for. The rushes also depended on that copious ocean traffic that was drawing the world together. '[T]housands now can be transported to scenes and localities', said the same writer, 'where their labour may be made available, and their industry exercised, for their own advantage, and for the creation of an honest and healthy independence'.[37] This had never before been true.

Communication was circular. The flood of people, especially to Victoria, made a difference to the quantity of mail, so that news fed news. The

Arrival of the mail from Geelong in the Main Road, Ballarat, 1855, a lithograph by Samuel Thomas Gill. The flags and numerous notices were typical of goldrush towns. The man in the foreground has on a digger's jumper.

chaos at the main landing place (Hobson's Bay, in Port Phillip) was a telling initiation for new arrivals, but the impact on the postal system was the clearest proof of the immensity of events. By winter 1852 enormous mails, many tons at a time, were beginning to arrive from abroad.[38] Newcomers were always eager to hear from home and always sure that letters addressed to them were on the way. For young married men, especially, the post office was 'the most sacred spot on the diggings'.[39] In Melbourne itself postal administration broke down under the new weight and many letters went astray. By way of experiment a townsman sent one to himself each day for two weeks, except Sundays. Of the twelve only two came back. '[H]e then made his case known publicly in the Newspapers.'[40] The newspapers, indeed, were certain when everything else was in flux.

The government struggled with the administrative techniques already used in Europe to cope with large numbers. In 1853 a new wing was added to the Melbourne post office, with 942 private boxes, all glass-fronted so that owners might check without opening. There was no home delivery and other clients used a complicated system of counter windows backed up with larger boxes, each with 3254 subdivisions arranged alphabetically. '[T]he applicant has only to apply at the window bearing the initial of his name and he is at once readily supplied.'[41] But on the goldfields themselves there was nothing like this. At Bendigo a rail of saplings 100 yards long directed a single queue of waiting men to the office and it might take two hours to move from one end to the other.[42] Here, too, the newspapers helped, publishing long lists of letters whose addressees had so far failed to appear.

Goldrush masses meant new ways of buying and selling. Newspapers had normally been sold by long-term subscription. Now copies were individually priced as a matter of course, making them more easily available to diggers. Also, 'It is a great thing in importing here', a Melbourne dealer wrote home, 'to have every thing in small and convenient packages' – tins of herring, bottles of pickles – because in such a place the market was large and there was no time to weigh goods out for every customer. A bookseller kept on hand 'several thousand volumes' of popular authors, pocket size, and another retailer specialised in diggers' kits – 'all sorts of provisions for taking up [to the diggings]'. Small tins, bottles, and boxes were standard furniture in diggers' tents and used matchboxes especially, of cardboard or timber, were a powerful symbol of goldfields life. They were the 'digger's treasure chest', in which he put his specks of gold.[43]

Diggers learnt to use this regime just as they learnt about digging itself. To begin with many had only the haziest idea about the colony they had chosen, let alone the rest of Australia. One, an American, two weeks after his arrival in Sydney and sitting down at the foot of the Blue Mountains on the way to the western goldfields, informed his diary that 'the Parrot and Parkeet … are about the only birds found in the Island'. Another believed after two months in Victoria that the storekeeper at Forest Creek, with 'thousands of pounds passing through his hands almost daily', was 'the wealthiest man in the Australian Colonies'.[44] Good information was the diggers' first valuable acquisition. There were various ways of getting it and of finding your way about, but even public notices might take an unfamiliar form. At Canvas Town, the permanent camp outside Melbourne where many families were left while their men were at the diggings, slips of paper were pinned to canvas exteriors for advertising purposes – 'Shaving and hair-cutting done here'; 'Clothes are neatly repaired'.[45] On the goldfields themselves the few trees left standing were used as signposts. At Fryers Creek every tree near the main track pointed travellers to nearby shops, at the same time murmuring, as it were, of 'lost Cattle, Servants wanted, Goods for sale'. One tree alone might be 'a complete register and advertising Office'. This was also how friends attempted to find each another. 'In a walk through the diggings you might see a hundred of these notices, beginning with the formula "If this should meet the eye of", &c.' But here, too, newspapers soon stepped in. Their columns of 'Missing Friends' were a leading feature.[46]

In this bottomless flux notices and signs were so important that anyone with artistic skill could make money painting them. Robert Anderson, a young architect, told of making a sign for a shoemaker at Forest Creek. He was given a piece of calico, 10 feet by 6. 'I drew a large boot in the centre

Selling newspapers on the goldfields at Bendigo, 1854, a drawing by an unknown artist.

Source: *Illustrated Sydney News*, 9 December 1854

and on the borders and corners: picks, cradles, spades, scales, snakes and all manner of stuff not forgetting Bead awls and shoemakers tools.' He was paid 30 shillings for four hours' work, and 'my performance', he said, 'earned me roars of applause and laughter'. Some of the more settled places had criers, who were useful for special occasions. Ballarat had 'Bob the Original Bellman' – always drunk but always in demand. At the end of each announcement (for a concert it was 'Roll up! roll up! and enjoy a pleasant evening!') Bob added 'a peculiar burr with his lips'. Another Ballarat crier called himself 'Bill Lungs'.[47]

Men learnt also about mining. Even panning for surface gold, apparently a simple task, called for 'a peculiar knack of so turning the wrist and hand, that every twist sends from the edge of the dish a portion of water, earth, and sand, the whole of the heavier matter [including gold] drawing towards the centre'. It was important, so a digger told his parents in England, to go about the entire business 'sistematically'. It followed in the minds of some men that only those with scientific knowledge could do well. In creek beds near Bathurst Sir Thomas Mitchell, the surveyor-general, noticed educated men working, as he thought, 'more systematically' than others. At deeper levels, in the beds of buried watercourses, such diggers seemed to understand 'the effect of the fluentile currents of past times'.[48] And yet, on the contrary, digging was an equaliser. Experience easily made up for a lack of book-learning – and when diggers bought books they preferred fiction ('little story books') to works of science. On the other hand even experience was sometimes not enough. As you dig down, said another observer, 'the shades of difference distinguishing the good layers from the bad are so subtle that the oldest hands are sometimes taken in by them'. [49]

Experience and a little life together shaped the way in which diggers spoke – just as gravel of weight and size settled with shaking. For instance, they might say that someone 'had just struck the "juggler"', or in other words struck rich. (In killing livestock, as heads were pulled back and throats cut, it was the jugular one aimed for.) The very word 'diggings' was sometimes spelt 'diggins', even by educated men, as if habits of speech had corroded literacy.[50]

Dress, too, was soon a kind of uniform, although it was partly dictated by the way shopkeepers catered for thousands at a time. Rudston Read, one of many who wrote books about the goldrush (such books were another commodity for the mass market), arrived in Sydney in September 1851. Already, he said, only six months after the first discovery of gold, diggers could be recognised by what they wore – 'serge frock, fustians, half boots, cabbage tree hat, and belt round the waist, attached to which was a quart tin pot for boiling tea'.[51] Others wrote about 'jumpers', a new garment to be seen everywhere, belted on the outside. The jumper, by one report, was 'a blue elastic vest, or jersey, like that worn by sailors'. Someone else called it 'an article made like a shirt, but sometimes of fancy patterns'. On the Californian diggings men took their clothes off – there were reports of complete nakedness – but in Australia they dressed up, with, say, 'a gay-coloured handkerchief tied loosely round the neck' and rings of heavy gold. All were thickly bearded, at a time when men were usually clean-shaven (a fashion on the point of changing here and in Europe).[52]

These uniformities were supposedly settled, at least in Victoria, by the end of 1852 – and yet a Melbourne retailer remarked only six months later that 'the blue serge shirts which every one used to wear is now superseded by the black coat and hat'. Men were known and knew each other as diggers by the way they dressed and spoke and at the same time they began to act as a single political body, with certain rights and grievances.[53] Their sheer numbers had already made a difference to the newspaper market. The proprietors of Melbourne's leading paper, the *Argus*, had their own arrangements for reaching the main centres of digger population and within two years they had increased their circulation more than five-fold. The *Argus* was a daily, but the purchase of news every day must have been beyond the routine of most men. At Ballarat Alexander Dick, a digger, bought an *Argus* on Saturdays only and read it through during the week, consuming, as he said, 'every word not even omitting … the notices of impoundings'.[54] The *Gold-Diggers Advocate*, a weekly, began in Melbourne in January 1854, designed especially for the goldfields market. Like

John West in Launceston, the owner and editor, George Black, wanted his paper to be a forum for debate. He wanted his readers to think of it as their own. His letters column was at first headed 'Open Council' and later 'The Diggers Speaking for Themselves'. He was a chairman in print – asking all who wrote in to use only one side of their paper and to leave a margin for editing. They reported various grievances, mainly issues of postage and local justice, and while debate was never energetic the paper sold well. Within five months, Black said, circulation had 'far exceeded our expectation'. But he was soon complaining of a fatal spirit of competition among Victorian papers and in spring the *Advocate* ceased to exist.[55]

III

The lady of Emerson's acquaintance would have sensed no silent presence in the goldrush parts of Australia. Melbourne was 'a perfect Babel'. '[M]en from all nations', wrote an Englishman, newly arrived, 'sit down at the same table and drink from the same Bowl, they each talk and sing in their own tongue ... quarrel, jangle, fight or embrace as their various natures dictate'.[56] On the goldfields the ear was battered with noise, violent, varied, strange, continuous. In daytime there might be a certain calm because the diggers were intent on their work, 'as busy as ants', by one account, 'and as silent as though they belonged to a dumb generation'.[57] But the sound of machinery, the innumerable movements of water, wood, and earth, were obvious – 'like a human beehive', according to another, 'and the rockings of the hundreds of cradles producing an incessant din'.[58] And then:

> At night time when all were in camp [said another man, a poor writer] the noises and scenes were indescribable ... During arrivals home and cooking supper the talking and yelling was incessant. After supper nearly evryone owned a gun or pistol they commenced firing and kept [it up] perhaps a full hour. What with firing of guns and barking of dogs it was deafning.[59]

This happened every evening. It was not only deafening, as another remarked, but also 'a great annoyance to people of weak nerves'. The swearing, 'an almost all prevailing vice', had the same effect ('a man would hardly speak to his *friends* without calling them some sort of unmentionable name').[60] And then as night proceeded and as shooting and barking slackened, musical instruments came out, each player with a tune of his own.

At last human noises gave way to animal ones, the goldfields being surrounded by bush. 'Greatly annoyed by the Croaking of the Frogs at night', so one digger complained, 'they can be heard ½ Mile off'. Kangaroo rats were busy about his tent, and there was, he said, 'a bird which screams ... every now and then suddenly, making a most villianous [sic] row and has often woke me in bed'.[61]

For all the obvious violence the diggings seemed safe, safer than California, according to a writer who had seen both. In California men were unpredictable. There was a callousness, the same writer said, a 'Mephistopheles-mixture of man and fiend' – a '*blazéd*' style of humanity 'sear-hardened' by vice. Here, on the other hand, men seemed bound by 'a higher social discipline'.[62] Emerson wrote of movement wrapped in silence. Here we seem to find the reverse – a kind of peace, or at least a certain routine, a silent assumption of order wrapped in continuous noise. Firearms were everywhere, as one man remarked, but they were unnecessary, 'as everybody is quiet and peaceable'. Certainly, he added, 'if one man tries to plunder another he is generally shot dead, but nothing more'.[63] This peculiar accommodation of violence even affected fights among dogs. At Chok'em Flat, near Fryers Creek, there were 'quite as many dogs as Christians'. Fights were common, but:

> Here again is the good sense of the men … displayed, for if another owner wishes the dogs parted, it is immediately done, but if the dogs have been known previously to quarrel, the owners mutually agree to let them have it out and no one to speak to, or interrupt them.[64]

Fights between diggers themselves were just as well organised, especially if they were meant to decide the possession of a claim.[65]

Some of the noise was for special occasions. A public meeting might become a festival – 'tents and stores decorated with flags of all nations and patterns, guns and pistols … firing in all directions, sky rockets and various fireworks enlivening the scene, Music in the evening'. On Guy Fawkes Day at Forest Creek in 1852, 'never heard such firing salutes nor such bonfires kept up from dusk until 10 pm without ceasing'.[66] Sometimes an individual sound might rise above the mass. One night at Ballarat a peculiar series of noises came from one tent. There were thumps:

> it might have been a bag of flour, [and] a man's voice yelling out You call yourself a wife, you beggarly brute, I'll stop your gallop or [my] names not Tom – then an imitation of a woman's voice. You wretch you wretch you brute do you call yerself a man. Thump went the blows again fell thick and heavy oh! oh! in a wailing woman's voice oh! Tom Tom I'll never do it again.

A few women lived on the diggings and wife-beating was common. A lady visitor, not normally critical of the diggers, found that at Tarrangower 'most of the wives in the camp exhibit in their faces the brutal marks of their husbands' fists!'[67] But this episode was a piece of play-acting – a joke.[68]

The diggers had a strong sense of their own importance and they liked to show off. As a traveller put it, they were 'Strong, healthy, and vigorous, and being the creators of all the enormous wealth that was pouring into the colony [he meant Victoria], they considered their interest the paramount one'. They looked down, he said, 'with a civil sort of contempt upon all other classes'.[69]

Women especially, beaten into submission in some cases, struggled to be heard. For many the wild power of goldrush Australia was summed up in one vice – drunkenness. In October 1853 two petitions were presented to the legislative council in Melbourne asking for a law modelled on one in the American state of Maine that would ban the sale of alcohol on the goldfields. One was a women's petition with 2097 names to it. It argued that drink was everywhere the cause of crime, ruin, madness, and death. 'From our position', they said, 'as "Keepers at Home", we are the greatest sufferers by drunkenness'.[70] The following song issued from the diggings in response, addressed to the two lady organisers:

> Oh! Hester Hornbrook, 'there's a dear',
> Do allow me a glass of beer;
> And Lizzy Singleton, I think,
> You might allow your friends to drink;
> Ah! never mind the law of Maine,
> Our English statute book 'twould stain,
> Because I'm sure, my dear, you know
> That stays and razors kill also.
> Prohibit them, and penknives too,
> Because men cut their windpipes through.

And then think of so many men, razorless and unmarriageable:

> ... our chins, in all their glory,
> Must bow unshaven – unshorn before ye;
> And you must mount the Bloomer dress,
> And never feel our soft caress.[71]

Bloomers were trousers worn in America by emancipated women, who were supposed to have no need of men.

The government did try to prosecute unlicensed publicans, or sly-grog sellers, and to help the effort, so it was said, 'a whole brood of informers instantly sprang up'.[72] In fact, because of the unpredictability of goldfields life, with its rapid movement and its strange mix of individuals, the authorities used spies for various reasons. In Britain, although the 'science of government' demanded openness, state espionage had lately reached new levels of sophistication. In 1848 several states on the European mainland had been racked with revolution and Whitehall feared the infection of men and ideas from across the channel. For British radicals, as a result, spies had become agents of the devil. Here, just as the myriad notices on the goldfields told diggers where to go for what they wanted, spies helped to guide the power of government. Among the diggers, as on Norfolk Island (Chapter 10), spies were the enemies of true men. With artful faces and deceptive tongues, they were candour reversed.

It was said of life on the Californian goldfields that 'there is no general bond of sympathy, but simply that of *manhood*.' This was partly true in Australia. One of the early lessons, especially for newcomers, was the difficulty of making progress alone. Cooperation among men was necessary not only in getting a start but also in order to survive. Partnerships were most easily formed among passengers from the same ship, but compatriots worked together too. Parties of diggers were often distinguished by the way they spoke, from 'the drawling language' of the Americans to the dense lilt of 'the wild Irish', or 'Tips' (presumed to be from county Tipperary).[73] So while there was uniformity and unity among the miners there were also divisions. Differences of nationality raised questions of race. Those who called themselves 'Anglo-Saxons', whether British or Americans, often thought they were better than the rest. 'Certainly', said a goldfields author, 'with few others would an Englishman like to mingle'. And yet even feelings such as these were not entrenched as they were in the United States. In Victoria, when a Black miner (probably an immigrant) was thrown out of 'a place of public amusement' by a White American the latter was fined £50 and the magistrate added that he was sorry he could not make it more. American Indians spoke of their new pleasure in being treated 'as fellow men'.[74]

Status depended mainly on the way men worked, on the way they made a start and on their energy. Initiation was painful and pick-handles might be clammy with blood after the first crop of blisters. Men fell into distinctive types as they put themselves to labour and a little success, or resources brought from home, might lead to some being better off than others. At Ballarat Alexander Dick and his partner joined the ranks of 'bloody furnishers', as others called them, because they could afford to give food and equipment to other diggers in return for a share of their profits.[75] Sometimes superiority was localised, especially on goldfields where more courage and skill were called for. Ballarat was a very rich field but the gold was buried deep and diggers might spend months making their way down, descending 150 feet or more to the subterranean streams, to the 'deep leads' in which their great desideratum was supposed to lie. Teams were needed, some men digging in relays, some carrying away soil as it came to the surface, some cutting slabs to line the shaft and one at least looking after the tent and meals. Without proper reinforcement buried watercourses might break in upon the bottom man and it was fatal to breathe carbon dioxide – the stink of long dead vegetation. Ballarat, said Dick, was 'no place for the weak and the timid'.[76]

Work like this had to be properly funded and some diggers were better than others in finding money to maintain themselves and to cover the chance of failure at the bottom. Local storekeepers and 'furnishers' were the first to invest in the labour of others, but city merchants were soon involved, offering capital as they had done in the grazing boom of the 1830s. Involvement in networks of finance added to the miners' sense of their own importance, and so did the newspapers which, by 1854, existed in Bathurst, Bendigo, Ballarat, and elsewhere. It was the business of local editors to tell the diggers they mattered in the wider scheme of things. At Ballarat, once again, all these things (this is Dick again) 'imparted a degree of arrogance to the speech and bearing of the ... deep miner which was very offensive to those whose lot had been cast in shallower and more easily worked fields'. The Ballarat men called the others 'pipeclay punchers'. Pipeclay, a thick blue, and the red marl that normally lay above it, were both gold bearing. They were deep enough for most – sometimes hidden by nothing but surface soil and a bed of gravel.[77]

Within each colony every digger worked under the same rules. All had to carry a licence, which to start with cost 30 shillings a month. The licences were part of the local information order, linking the authorities by pen and ink to every man on the diggings. The diggers complained that they cost too much and that any system of 'taxation' ought to depend not on their labour but on their earnings. And in Victoria they also complained about the way government used the money – the bad roads and postal service and, most of all, the corrupt police. Grievances came full circle in the way police checked licences, calling miners from the bottom of their shafts, wasting their time and treating all they said as lies. Their own labour surely proved their good citizenship. And yet, in the words of a medical man who worked among them, the police behaved 'so ... as to make the diggers appear like a criminal class, and digging like a crime'.[78]

Public meetings were the usual expression of digger grievances. But in their meetings, as in everything else, they acted as if they were in a play. '[T]hey are like a set of schoolboys', said a goldfields storekeeper, 'they shout and halloo at anything'. They echoed the spirit of duelling at Port Phillip (Chapter 6), full of anger but ending in jokes. 'There would be an animated assemblage', said another man, 'eager participants in semi-rebellious projects, daring speeches and ferocious countenances'. But it quickly passed:

> within an hour every man would be once more at his absorbing business, peaceably rocking his cradle, or examining his trough for far brighter spots in his fortune than were to be found in an upset of the government, a declaration of independence, or any other operation that involved time, combination, and a cessation from gold-digging.[79]

Government was to be laughed at and abused. But it was the still centre of life. It lay at the heart of affairs. There were official rules, for instance, about the size of mining claims and these shaped the dealings of neighbours. In the pastoral districts squatters had arranged their own boundaries but they had taken any intractable arguments to the commissioners of Crown lands. When nothing could be solved with voices or fists, miners went to the goldfields commissioners.[80]

Sometimes such confidence failed. A corrupt and overbearing police force was a continual reminder of the suspicions of government. So were the troops stationed at some goldfield towns and the weekly arguments of local newspapers might deepen the cut of any grievance. It was obvious, for instance, to men of radical mind that the goldfields were governed with no hint of democracy. In New South Wales, Bathurst had its *Free Press* and the diggers were visited by Sydney politicians, including the republican democrat, John Dunmore Lang. In February 1853 there were mass meetings along the Turon River and several hundred armed men marched in formation on the commissioners' headquarters at Sofala. Violence was averted and in due course the government reduced the licence fee. In Bendigo in July a petition was drawn up listing the grievances of Victorian diggers, signed by more than 5000 and taken to the Governor. Here, too, the men organised themselves as a military force.[81] The licence system was reformed, the fee cut back, and the vote offered to men who paid for twelve months at a time.

So diggers organised themselves in order to make their voices carry to the centres of power. On the Victorian fields especially there were many men direct from Europe, including some who knew how to orchestrate popular feeling. Their knowledge showed in Victorian campaigns. Besides its mass petition Bendigo had an Anti-Gold-Licence Association, with a separate committee for each gully. Steps were taken towards setting up a Diggers' Congress, with representatives from all over the colony, and men (and horses and dogs) wore red ribbons to show solidarity with the cause.[82] Ribbons, like the mass petition, was meant to prove the organised weight of numbers which, besides manhood, was the one great, immoveable asset possessed by the people.

A riot at Ballarat in October 1854, inspired by digger resentment, led straightaway to a Reform League, with similar elaborate ambitions. Here, too, the leading men hoped to avoid violence, putting their faith in 'moral force'. At the Turon and Bendigo the troops had responded in a similar spirit and bloodshed was avoided. But a year or more had intervened since these events and the troubles at Ballarat were managed by a new Governor, Sir Charles Hotham, who was determined to show his power. Following the riot Hotham told Ballarat's commissioner, Robert Rede, 'to use force whenever legally called upon to do so, without regard to the consequences that might ensue'. Rede was ready to obey. Neither understood the true priorities of the diggers. Both believed that organised agitation mirrored the European troubles of 1848 and must be put down.[83]

Towards the end of November more troops arrived at the Ballarat diggings. Stones were thrown as they marched in – 'a cowardly affair', said Samuel Lazarus, a digger himself, 'principally carried on by the worst portion of the digging community – old convicts and Tipperary men'. But extreme possibilities now gripped the imagination of miners. There was a mass meeting the next day and everywhere predictions of bloodshed, though few were sure how it would start. 'The diggers were earnestly at work', said Lazarus, 'buying revolvers and ammunition, making long pikes, fixing large knives on sticks, rubbing up old swords, muskets and bayonets and in fact making every preparation for a determined struggle'. On 1 December there was a meeting of 3000 and half of them were armed.[84] At the Eureka lead, where the men were mainly Irish, a large enclosure, or stockade, was built of slabs, patched here and there with wooden vehicles on their sides, and a flag was raised within it, a cross and five stars, white sewn on blue, a design that mimicked the masthead of the *Gold-Diggers Advocate*. Some diggers talked of an attack on the garrison and apparently the stockade was meant as a place of retreat should they fail. But there was still play-acting in the diggers' declarations – a Hamlet-like gap between fantasy and action. 'A wild feeling of poetry', so a later writer recalled, 'as well as of anger fired the breasts of many then'.[85] The poetry was almost an end in itself.

Into this gap, like ancient air at the bottom of a shaft, rushed Her Majesty's forces. 'We will stand no more of this nonsense', said Rede.[86] Just before daylight on Sunday, 3 December, the troops charged down from the camp and overran the stockade. The miners who lay asleep along the fence were hacked about with swords, buildings were set alight and many, trying to escape, were hunted down. The tent of Ann Diamond, a storekeeper, was destroyed. 'I did not know what to do', she said, 'they were just tearing over the people as if they had no feeling at all'. Her own husband was among the dead, and all she had was burnt.[87]

Not since 1804, at Vinegar Hill (Volume 1), had the Europeans in Australia made such havoc among their own kind. Nineteen men were killed on the spot, five of them soldiers, and others died later of their wounds.[88] Several diggers wrote down their memories of the day. Asleep in his tent, Lazarus saw only the aftermath. He struggled to make sense of the story now on everyone's lips. It was hard to believe, he said, 'that Englishmen in Authority [could have] had made such a savage and cowardly use of their power'. He found the same feeling everywhere, the same sense of a world out of order: 'A universal shock has passed through the diggings, a feeling of horror seems to possess almost every mind.' Alexander Dick watched as a new body of troops arrived to confirm the peace two days after the attack. 'I shall never forget', he said, 'the silence and the awe stricken faces as that procession passed slowly along the famous main road'.[89]

The only memoir to be published, a year later, was that of Raffaello Carboni, one of the organisers of the resistance and a native of Urbino, in Italy. Carboni was acquainted with the stage, and in particular with the Teatro Argentina in Rome, where that master of opera, Guiseppe Verdi, had lately cast the history of his own nation in a tumult of music. He could sing snatches of opera and his book, *The Eureka Stockade*, was put together like a piece of Verdi. He, too, recorded a peculiar emptiness after the event. When the wounded were brought together other diggers crowded around them silent and bewildered. 'None', said Carboni, 'would stir a finger'. With a wave of military pistols they were cleared away. As he and other prisoners were marched across the central part of the camp for trial in Melbourne, 'though it was clear daylight, yet did I see only one digger on the whole of the main road'. All were apparently hidden in their tents, as if appalled to find that bullets, so often bruising their night sky, might be part of the noise of morning.[90]

Chapter 12

Ink and Affection

I

This book tells stories from within. The Europeans in Australia were my own people, including at this point my father's grandparents. Ancestors are strange reflections of the present – an early shadow of yourself. John and Eliza Atkinson reached Melbourne in February 1855 with their two small children, Eliza's brother and John's brother and parents, among twenty-seven second-class passengers on board the *Sir Colin Campbell*. John Atkinson's family had been unsettled for a century and frequent movement can create a certain attitude to geography. In their case the mastery of distance involved a mastery of reading and writing. They had been part of a network of printers and booksellers working along the valleys of the Tyne and Tees in northern England, intermarried and publishing through each other's shops. Among their nineteenth-century productions were some printed family trees that show the wandering of their kin: 'went into Worcestershire, and there settled'; 'wounded in W. Indies'; 'd[ied] on cruize in E. Indies'; 'sailed to Valparaiso ... and never since heard of'.[1]

Green Atkinson, John's father, who came with him to Melbourne, had once published books with a younger brother further up the Tees and with their widowed mother further down. One he wrote himself. According to an indulgent friend he was 'a fine classical scholar, an accomplished musician, and ... a perfect master of the English language'. And yet a stranger, maybe with equal truth, spoke of a common dealer who, with his books and stationery, sold roasted corn.[2] In a world that was supposed to be hierarchical it was often hard to decide on the rank and dignity of people like this – writers, printers, publishers. Undistinguished at first sight, they might do surprising things on paper. Labouring with their hands, they might be learned all the same. Print ate into distinctions of status. Charles Dickens began as a reporter and at the height of his fame he was still an editor and publicist. Karl Marx, his contemporary, was both a journalist and a profound scholar. The multiplication of printed works meant that such men and women might have enormous power over the public imagination. 'The printer', boasted a printers' periodical, 'is the Adjutant of Thought' – and that at a time when thought was broadcast in unprecedented ways.[3]

In Victoria the Creswick *Weekly Times* was not exaggerating when it told its readership of diggers:

> Newspapers are amongst the most peculiar characteristics of the present age
> – emanating from the womb of circumstance, and imbued with the vitality
> of current events, they direct the flood of living thought with energetic activ-
> ity; give a tone and hue to society, and, by evoking and directing public
> opinion, act as the alternate curb and spur to both Government and people.[4]

Many overseas papers reached Australia, and the colonies themselves produced growing numbers. The gap between the humble customary status of journalists and printers and their sudden importance in public life was debated here just as it was in Europe. In the Melbourne court of quarter sessions a decade before the goldrush the proprietors of the *Port Phillip Gazette* charged one of the compositors with neglect of duty, under the colonial Masters and Servants Act. The compositor argued in reply that he was not liable because he was not a common labourer. Working with type involved, he said, 'mental ability' of a quite superior kind. George Cavenagh, another owner (of the *Port Phillip Herald*), was called to testify to the contrary. He was certain enough. '[A] man', he told the court, 'might acquire the knowledge of compositing, without being able even to read or understand the sound of a single letter'.[5]

In fact, printing work was fluid, versatile, and demanding. Especially in the smaller offices men moved from one duty to another, reporting, editing, designing, proofreading. Aspiring writers might start as compositors, and compositing rooms often mixed up a range of skills in the making of stories.

The 'companionship' of printers was reinforced by strange hours of labour, elaborate jargon, the squalor and stink of crowded offices, sedentary habits – trousers shiny on the seat – and fingertips raw with handling type. Newspapers especially depended on teamwork. The *Port Phillip Patriot* gave a sketch of a newspaper office about the size of its own – a vivid image probably drawn by a compositor. Imagine, he said, the compositors at their labour:

> That thin stooping figure, with sharp face, high nose, and dark motionless
> eyes, has a genius for setting advertisements. He is the uncontrolled master
> of that department. That fine looking fellow with an oval border of black
> whiskers round his face and corresponding curve of his leg, the wit, orator,
> and gay Lothario of the establishment, has a taste which the Overseer him-
> self does not disdain occasionally to call to counsel. The greasy looking

individual with a bald head, if you keep whiskey from him, and him from whiskey, (no easy task by the by,) will set you a column of close dig without any typographical error. The demure gentleman, with his nose stuck in his composing stick, has a genius for 'scheme work', which technical phrase designates what the vulgar call tables, &c.

In the making of each paper every man at first worked on his own but at a certain stage of the day all gathered to see their combined labour placed on the imposing stone – 'bending over the solid mass of types, touching, examining, scrutinizing, whispering eagerly'. The apprentices stood back – 'they are not allowed to interfere with this part of the ceremony' – but here was one of them newly risen to the rank of journeyman. 'His whole frame thrills as he fingers the CHASE. He feels himself a man.' The work was driven home with mallets and then 'the brawny pressmen' appeared, the presses themselves being normally housed at the back of the building. Carrying 'the ponderous mass' between them, they 'disappear into the press room, whence the dull sound of their process may be heard to issue' – the regular thud of mass production. The printed paper as it emerged was folded by an apprentice and sold on the spot, 'an eager and curious public … crowding the place of publication, to snatch the first damp sheets'.[6]

In the newspaper business profit came from speed (like cutting grain and shearing sheep), and compositors were paid by the line or the letter. Their importance was measured by their quickness, and a competitive spirit, from man to man and paper to paper, helped the sense of fraternity. They might throw names at each other. At Port Phillip it was 'the man Fawkner', 'the stuck-up brat', 'Noodle', 'the Big Drum', 'the Teetotum', 'the Donkey', 'Buggins'. They were a brotherhood all the same, with all the pride of manhood and science combined.[7] Nor were there many of those kindred trades, as in England, which sometimes gave work to women. Rosa Alais, for instance, who hoped to follow her sweetheart, Charles Atkinson, John's brother, to Melbourne, was an etching engraver in Hammersmith. She would have found it hard to make her mark here.

At Port Phillip at the moment of first settlement, newspapers, like fairy godmothers, had told the community about itself and, as with fairy godmothers, their prophesies were self-fulfilling. The district became in their pages 'Australia Felix', a 'province', even a 'colony'. Her 'local press', said the *Gazette*, 'has been the only chronicle of her establishment, her struggles, her prospects, and her success'.[8] In 1848 the press drew attention to the importation of indentured labourers from China. Readers were asked to consider whether such 'foreigners' were part of the social vision that the press itself had sketched out.[9] Agitation against receiving convicts at Melbourne was called an 'Argus movement' by the editor of that paper.[10] And when it was announced, after a decade of demands, that Port Phillip would in fact be a separate colony the newsmen made it their day. A great procession was led by a float carrying a working press, issuing as it passed a summary history of the local industry plus a declaration that: 'The Printers, and all employed in the diffusion of the printed page: all engaged in the all-powerful PRESS, join heart and soul in the People's joy.'[11] In a similar spirit, in 1852–53, when the credit of the colonial government was at its lowest, the *Argus* carried daily in its 'Mercantile' column: 'Wanted, a Colonial Secretary; apply to the Lieutenant-Governor', and 'Wanted a Governor; apply to the People of Victoria'.[12] His Excellency's power, apparently, rested on the people. For that reason it somehow rested on that fabric of daily chatter, the classified ads. It was anchored in what the *Gazette* called 'the market of letters'.[13]

The first newspapers in Sydney and Hobart (Chapter 3) had interpreted local events to local readers. In Victoria, to start with, editors let their minds run more often along their own horizons, linking coastal ports and goldfields and reaching easily to Europe. Here newsmaking was less accountable to immediate truth. It dealt in imagery for strangers because editors made it their duty to tell distant readers about our prospects. The place was thick with print before the goldrush, so that not only the early pastoral boom but also the rush itself was a triumph of public relations. Printing was a trade for families so that emigrant brothers and friends sent stories home to Britain, feeding the papers they had left behind. They modelled themselves on those far-flung commercial enterprises that managed credit, transported goods for sale, and directed the flow of labour around the world. And they were an important adjunct to such business, because the market of letters raised the price of everything else – and everything else raised the price of print. James Backhouse heard a story about this time of a bushman who found a number of hairy caterpillars on a stone, of the kind which moved head-to-tail in a long line. '[H]e directed the head of the first', said Backhouse, 'with a stick, to the tail of the last, and they continued following one another in a circle, for several hours, without seeming to discover the trick that had been played upon them!'[14] In Victoria the printing trade moved like that, circling within its own trajectory, beyond other conversation. But it wove meanwhile a brilliant fabric of image and ideas.

Victorians were said to buy more papers per head than any other population in the world – slightly more than the Americans and six times more than the British. By 1850, of the five daily papers in Australia, one was in Sydney (population 44,000), one was in Geelong (8000), and three were in Melbourne (23,000). The *Argus* (described by a newly arrived compositor as 'a horrid specimen of typography') was the most popular paper in Victoria at the onset of the goldrush. It was extremely cheap and in the tumult of the first years it became Melbourne's great repository for advertising. Of its fifty-six columns arranged over eight broadsheet pages, three-quarters were advertisements. Its pressmen turned out daily as much as 16 miles of paper, including a sea of tiny notices. As in earlier New South

Wales, newspapers in Victoria reached a class of readers that British editors would not have bothered with.[15] Here, too, rank was dissolved. Rich and poor read the same, and much newspaper writing was aimed at the widest possible market.

Some advertisers, it is true, still used the old system of posting notices in public places, but in Melbourne, even with goldrush frenzy at its height, there was only enough such business to employ one man, who offered his services from shop to shop – one brush, one pot of glue. A second billposter began in spring 1853, and as a result each man had time to spare pulling down the work of the other.[16] The main trade was in the columns of the *Argus*.

In Melbourne the goldrush made placelessness a way of life. People in these parts, so a merchant said, 'do not in general feel Australia to be their home'.[17] Attachment to a country depends on being attached to a certain part of it, or at least to the memory of some part. A period of months digging deep in a particular goldfield might make a difference. It certainly anchored political feeling to immediate and practical causes and it seems to have transformed the way in which men made speeches (see below). But otherwise people moved about so much that within any twelve months, in Melbourne, the population of a single street might be wholly changed. Relationships were so easily dissembled and disassembled that much of the certainty of life seemed to be vested not in habits of conversation but in printed publications, in sheets of paper that, having asserted at breakfast that Victoria was a people and a place, might be burned by dark. Even death made sense best on paper. Five of my family were buried in one plot in Melbourne in the 1850s – 'a rich grave', so their survivors put it. But instead of a solid monument fixed in the earth the deaths were marked by announcements in the press and by mourning cards, little masterpieces of typography struck off in multiple copies and broadcast by post.[18]

Among the newspapermen of the goldrush period, some, like George Black of the *Gold-Diggers Advocate*, seem to have been driven by idealism. Others were more entrepreneurial. Hugh McColl was a Scots Presbyterian, good-natured and far-sighted. Arriving in Melbourne in January 1853, he aimed to rise by selling words and in August he started his own paper, the twice-weekly *Banner*. He planned it as a serial suitable for family reading and meant mainly for Melbourne's many Scots. He hoped for a circulation of 3000, relying, as he said, on 'the well-known rule of political economy which teaches that competition will remunerate the speculator without deteriorating the quality of the article in demand'.[19] Within two months the paper's twelve pages were increased to sixteen, containing, the owner boasted, 'more readable matter than any other in the colony', and the business was moved from its original 'little humpey office' to a stone building worth £800 per annum and housing thirty to forty compositors.[20] McColl also produced for separate sale, as the *Banner* announced, a map illustrating the Crimean War, a 'Letter Pocket Book, designed to facilitate correspondence between the colonies and the mother country', and *McColl's Melbourne Monthly Directory*, a regular update of addresses in the city (a perfectly visionary project).[21] For six weeks he printed the *Gold-Diggers Advocate* for Black and from May 1854 the *Shipping Gazette*. According to one of his compositors he held such a brilliant place at the heart of the trade that even the jobbing work he could get if he tried (cards of all kinds, posters, pamphlets, and so on) might bring in £5000 a year. But his accounts were a mess. According to another of his men his method was to 'enter everything in all conceivable little books, or on numerous pages of paper, intending to enter where they should be when you have time, which is practically never'. He also had trouble meeting his costs. In a rough ocean of money-making he ran along the tops of the waves. In March he was said to be planning yet another paper, but the *Banner* itself died in September and McColl was bankrupt.[22]

The *Banner* once carried in its pages a description of a single issue of the *Argus*. Strange to say, this item was not the work of a local writer but was copied from an English periodical called *Leisure Hour*. In other words, *Leisure Hour* made copy from the *Argus* and the *Banner* made copy from *Leisure Hour*. The colonial and other English-speaking presses throughout the world now worked as mirrors on mirrors, shifting words backwards and forwards, for sale and resale, across the seas.[23] *Leisure Hour* here described the colonial newspaper trade from the evidence of one colonial paper. After dwelling on the extraordinary variety of advertisements placed by Victorians the writer turned to the management of the *Argus* office. It seemed a prodigious enterprise, he said, but judging from the ads the proprietors worked on a knife edge. In the apparent height of their prosperity, so said *Leisure Hour* (or so said the *Banner* on the authority of *Leisure Hour*):

> they have actually advertised ... first, for any number of compositors to come forward at once, offering to all payment at the rate of half-a-crown a thousand [this was three times the rate in the 1840s], at which it would be easy to earn thirty shillings a day; secondly, for two strong fellows to turn the machine which prints the paper; thirdly, for a [proof-]reader to read it; fourthly, for £1500 of new nonpareil type, the old being worn out long ago; and fifthly, for any quantity of paper of their requisite size upon which to print it.

It was impossible to imagine in England a good newspaper office wanting all at once, and at the height of production, so many things essential to survival.[24]

The uncertainties of the newspaper world might kill as well as bankrupt. The happy picture of office work published in the *Patriot* was no longer typical in goldrush days. New methods of mass production and mass marketing, evident in thousands of tiny boxes, tins, and jars (Chapter 11), were also used for labour. The big daily papers were set by rows of men crammed into rooms designed for other purposes, hardly leaving their seats for hours on end and night after night. Many must have spent their time piecing together minute advertisements. Their movements were 'confined', as a medical statistician noted, 'to a multitude of small motions of the right hand'. The close air and lack of exercise gave compositors bad lungs. According to the same expert, in England's busiest offices one man in every ten spat blood. Charles Atkinson, Rosa's intended, a compositor at the Melbourne *Herald*, died of phthisis in 1857.[25] On the other hand the wages were so high that compositors might leap the ranks. In January 1855 twenty-six employees of a new Melbourne paper, the *Age*, formed a syndicate and bought the office themselves.[26]

This last move was also proof, once again, of the cooperative habits of Port Phillip (Chapter 5). And yet newcomers to goldrush Melbourne also said how hard it was to make men stick to their word. Gone were the entrenched networks, common especially in rural England – the tight fabric of relations, neighbours, and old friends. Agreements were as transitory as habitations. On his arrival in February 1855 John Atkinson set up with his brother-in-law, who had worked on the London *Times*. Eliza his wife, a determined manager with scant reverence for the skills of men, probably handled the accounts. But the brother-in-law went off to the diggings and John joined in partnership with the bankrupt Hugh McColl and another new arrival, Thomas Stubbs. McColl, who was allowed three years to pay his share, still had his goldfield connections and Stubbs owned three printing presses, a binding press, two tons of type, and other necessaries, all housed in a small iron building in Queen Street. From that address, late in 1855, the firm issued Raffaello Carboni's book, *The Eureka Stockade*.[27]

It did little more of moment. We can only guess at the daily dynamics of the office, but they were not happy. The Atkinsons were orderly and careful. McColl was energetic. But Stubbs was a wanderer who had escaped a wife in England and who, after a brief trial of the partnership, wanted to lose it too. He was advised by William ('Smiler') Shaw, one of the new owners of the *Age*, to try an elaborate ruse. Shaw was to come to the office at night and remove all the equipment and Stubbs was to say in the morning that it had been taken to pay his debts. It was done, and thus set free, for weeks Stubbs bought drinks for his saviour. But then Shaw himself cut loose from the *Age* (it passed to David and Ebenezer Syme), opened a new office with Stubbs' presses, and made them his own.[28]

II

The market of letters was also a market in feelings. Print was bought and sold not only for the facts it conveyed but also because it crystallised emotion. A few standard words, a little rectangle of ink-on-paper in the classified columns (at fixed prices), might be used to convey an infinity of pain. From the Melbourne *Herald*, for instance, in its list of deaths: 'On the 10th instant, of dysentery, Charles James, youngest son of Mr Edward George Atkinson, of Lonsdale street west, aged 11 months, deeply regretted by his parents.' That was a kind of minimum. But even with unlimited space writers had to standardise their language – had to standardise their feelings – so as to make themselves intelligible to a formless mass of strangers. Novels in bound and serial form, now published in vast numbers, drew from men and women emotions that were meant to be the same wherever and whoever the reader might be. Feeling itself, or at least the expression of feeling, was mass produced. This was age of cliché. Intimacy that could cut across oceans was sold wherever the language was spoken. The new passion for candour, or apparent candour, linked to free enterprise, fuelled the old passion for profit.

Consider the experience of an American, Silas Andrews, who came to the Victorian diggings from California. Travelling up the Yarra River from the bay he noticed in the same tawny waters a brig called the *Uncle Tom*, its figurehead, as he said, 'a black man holding a book in one hand the other arm thrown around a beautiful little girl'.[29] It was June 1853, barely a year since Harriet Beecher Stowe's story, *Uncle Tom's Cabin*, had become a sensation in his own country. Mrs Stowe had succeeded in sharing with thousands the agonies involved in black slavery and in making those

The crowd at the General Post Office, Melbourne, on the arrival of mail from England, about 1862, a watercolour by Nicholas Chevalier. Tables are set up on the footpath for the answering of letters.

agonies a public matter – part of 'one common sensorium'. Here before the errant American, on the far side of the world, stood the image of her hero. '[H]ave you seen that work by Mrs Stowe called "*Uncle Tom's Cabin*"[?]', wrote another man in Victoria to his family in England a few weeks later. He knew without thinking that exactly the same package of words would be on offer at the same time, spelling out the same feelings, everywhere.[30]

The same global sense, but free of market pressure, appears in the private letters that men and women sent around the world. Certainly, the goldrush upset efficiency and the burden of physical labour and the hurry to be rich might make it hard to write home. 'I feel now handling the pen', said James Daniel to his brother in England, 'under precisely the same sensation that a cow would handling a new shilling'. But the main problem was sheer distance and, as long as they were carried by sail, the unpredictability of the mails (Chapter 5). In England, even labouring men were used to steam-powered speed and according to *The Times* some hesitated to go for gold because the lack of steamships made this country so remote and postage so uncertain. Daniel longed for steam power, and when the first steamer carrying mail, the *Chusan*, reached Melbourne from Britain in July 1852 he was overjoyed: 'It seems as if our friends at home were brought suddenly quite near to us – for now there seems some degree of certainty in our communications home reaching their destination – all before seemed doubtful or at best tardy.' The combination of steamships and system (the administrative efficiency pioneered by men like Rowland Hill) made all the difference. Daniel's sense of nearness became commonplace. Just as he remarked to his brother, 'I sit down to write just as I was going to have a chat', so a semi-literate woman in New York spoke also of 'chatting' to her digger son – 'a blessed privilege it is that we can convers together althoug so far seperated'.[31]

The Australian colonies themselves seemed closer together. Still under five governments, they began to have the shadowy appearance of one dominion. Towards the end of the eighteenth century, when European settlement began in New South Wales, some in Britain had envisaged a future empire in the South Seas. Enormous territories would here be drawn within the embrace of a single antipodean power. By the 1830s this possibility already had a local charm. A new sense of the Australian past, evident in many casual reminiscences (Chapter 3), meant a keener feeling for the Australian future. William Westbrooke Burton, the Myall Creek judge, had suggested that New South Wales, lying as it did 'between the vast continents of Asia and America, and amongst the "Isles of the Sea"', might well become the seat of 'a Great Empire', its reach extending far beyond its first boundaries.[32] Others dreamt of moral greatness. Government here, said James Macarthur, would be more highly centralised than it was in Britain. We knew all about Asiatic tyrannies. Might not the Australian example, he said, make 'the spirit and the principles of British liberty …

less repulsive in their form and practice, to the habits and manners of the Oriental nations?'[33]

New settlement on the southern coast gave the idea another slant. In South Australia there was a belief from the beginning that faster travel and geographical advantage would make Adelaide the intellectual and political centre of the empire to come. None could know when, but visionaries were happy to wait. And on the other hand, 'we confidently predict', said the *Port Phillip Gazette* in 1841, 'that the commencement of the next century will see the present scattered provinces of Australia … united into a magnificent state, the metropolis of which will be founded on the central plains of Port Phillip'.[34] The British government soon began thinking in the same way, partly because it wanted its worldwide empire more uniform and systematic. The minister at Whitehall, Earl Grey, himself sketched out something like a 'magnificent state' for this continent, with a federal legislature. In 1850, as a first step, he gave the Governor in Sydney the title of Governor-General of all the Australian colonies.[35]

This appointment hinted at new dignity for the Antipodes. Governors-general are princes of a kind. At the same time Grey also gave the colonial governments power to decide on their own tariffs. He hoped that they would set up a free-trade union among themselves, but instead they insisted on customs barriers so that in this case the ideal failed. Buying and selling along the River Murray became an especially vexed issue for New South Wales, Victoria, and South Australia, and customs posts appeared as little citadels of sovereignty along its banks. In the 1820s and '30s the Straitsmen had flourished at the edges of colonial government. Now the river traders did the same, their steamships, with wool, tallow, hides, and so on, posing real problems for inter-colonial cooperation.[36]

There was better luck with postage. A cheap and uniform system was worked out for Australia and New Zealand, with letters prepaid (using adhesive stamps), and antipodean governments cooperated in the hope of a regular and reliable steam link with Home.[37]

It was also possible to agree that most of Australia should be entirely free of British convicts. To enthusiasts the pollution of one colony felt like the pollution of all. In the late 1840s (Chapter 11) Van Diemen's Land was still a penal colony, but it was also the birthplace of inter-colonial efforts to stop transportation. In August 1850 the leadership in Launceston sent their campaign across the strait. There was a 'unity of colonial interests', they said. All were bound 'by blood, language and commerce' and all must agree on an issue like this. Besides, it was easy now for transported men to move about and for that reason alone, as some in Sydney put it, 'transportation to one of these colonies is indirect transportation to them all'. The Australasian League for the Abolition of Transportation was born. It had an executive committee and a 'general conference', provincial councils in Launceston, Hobart, Sydney, Melbourne, and Geelong, and, in due course, committees in South Australia and New Zealand. Its moral purpose was so deeply laid, its sense of community so sweeping, that there were hopes, as the Sydney *Herald* remarked, that that 'this voluntary federation' might take on the even more splendid questions of combined self-government.[38]

Numerous minds seemed to join in the notion of a 'magnificent state'. Federation, surely, might be born at this moment by the will of the people – by a single large sense of right. But the goldrush began, Whitehall decided that it was foolish to send convicts to a place of sudden riches, transportation ended in the east (beginning instead in Western Australia), and the league vanished.

Besides, for all the speeches and editorials about union most of the immigrant people were tightly tied to their own part of the land. Ink could carry a lasting affection only so far. The goldrush drew men to Victoria and it made Melbourne look like a great centre of European settlement. But even on the goldfields it was provincial loyalties that mattered most. Sense of place might be feeble in Victoria itself, but it was powerful everywhere else. Diggers from South Australia were especially patriotic, so the local writer James Bonwick remarked – thinking themselves superior to 'all things Victorian' – and the southern Tasmanians were also 'strongly influenced by party feeling'. In New South Wales diggers from the Hunter Valley stuck together. One Maitland man set up as storekeeper on the Turon and whenever a dray arrived from home he had no trouble finding Hunter men to help unloading it, 'plenty coming voluntarily, and to hear the news'. From the Victorian goldfields, at least, everyone meant to go home (though not everyone did). 'The only settlement I heard abused', said another man, 'was Canterbury, N.Z. ... Van Diemen's Land, and many parts of New South Wales seemed to be far more preferred than Victoria'.[39]

Intimacy might cross oceans – and to considerable effect (Chapter 14). But the conquest of distance worked most obviously in drawing people together within their own corners of Australia and around their capital towns. Newspapers were already making the towns centres of 'correctness'. More quickly now, these centres began to extend their influence – their political ideas, their advertising and trade, their priorities of all kinds. Free enterprise meant the right to buy and sell with perfect liberty and better communications made that liberty more palpable. Hopes of this kind involved the loosening of old restraints, including place-bound hierarchy – and yet, at the same time, it meant the reinforcement of colonial boundaries. Every citizen, especially every man, was to be drawn to his own capital and government. He was to be tributary to his own centre of order and news. Self-reliance was the key. The strength of character and the sense of right to be found among free men were to be the engine of a free state.

In 1851, under new imperial legislation, elected councils like the one already existing for New South Wales met for the first time in Hobart, Adelaide, and Melbourne. (Victoria itself was brought into being by the same law.) All four councils were asked to decide whether they wanted further constitutional reform and more independence, and this question was resolved among them all by 1855–56. Some might say, with George Fife Angas in South Australia, that by focusing on local independence the councils undermined hopes of federal union.[40] So they did. The main issue for each colony was the control of its resources – mainly land and revenue – and such control was soon conceded by Whitehall. They were not likely just yet to complicate this achievement by federating. All four now possessed 'responsible government'. Each was accountable to its own people and four of Australia's original autocrats, the governors in Sydney, Hobart, Adelaide, and Melbourne, handed over most of their power to the elected leaders. The Queen was still the Queen. Her representatives were still important figures, especially in matters touching the imperial link. But otherwise much was changed, with only Western Australia, now a penal colony, untouched.

In each of the new colonial 'nations' there was to be a parliament modelled on Britain's, including something like a House of Lords. Even democrats acknowledged the uses of an upper house (the name in every case was 'legislative council') but they insisted that it be elected because the elective principle was fundamental to the power of the people. In Van Diemen's Land (now officially 'Tasmania'), South Australia, and Victoria the result was an upper house elected by men of property. This, the house of the rich, was designed to stand in the shadow of the people's chamber. In New South Wales the democrats were less successful. Here they had not yet dislodged a deeply rooted class of gentlemen – officials and propertied men, prudent and cunning, who had worked together for many years. The two leading figures, now allies for the most part, were William Charles Wentworth and James Macarthur. Wentworth, no longer a popular idol (he was burnt in effigy on the Turon), drafted the new constitution, and one of his first suggestions was for a colonial peerage. The right to sit in the upper house might descend, he said, from father to son within our better families, as in Britain.

Loosely planned and soon abandoned, this proposal was almost certainly a trick – a decoy for the democrats. It led to compromise, which was probably its real purpose. Under the final arrangement, members were to be neither hereditary nor elected but chosen by government. They were inevitably rich men protecting the interests of the rich. And yet, as Wentworth knew, they must give way in times of crisis, as the House of Lords did, because any government could make new appointments at any time to bolster its votes. Imprisoned by theory, the democrats failed to see that this very undemocratic chamber could be reshaped by anyone – including themselves when their time came to govern. In Hobart, Adelaide, and Melbourne the elected councils were to flout democracy and to hinder ministers for years to come. Sydney's nominees, born of conservative skill, had no choice but to bend with each strong wind.[41]

More urgent was the question of voting for each of the lower houses. Whatever happened with the legislative council, for democrats in all four capitals it was crucial that election to the people's chamber should have nothing to do with wealth. Even a low property franchise – a £10 lease, for instance – was not democracy. Simple citizenship had to be the final source of power. But what was a citizen, and how was the citizen's will to be known?

In South Australia in 1851, within eight weeks of the first meeting of council, one of the members suggested a democratic franchise. He wanted the vote, George Waterhouse said, for 'every man of sound mind and twenty-one years of age, untainted with crime' – or in other words without a convict past. And, he said, he wanted to ensure that every voter was rational and well informed. He wanted him to be literate. Every man registering to vote would be asked, he said, to sign his name as proof of mental ability – a rule that would have disqualified about a quarter of the whole.[42]

The systematic colonisers had aimed to create in South Australia a haven for good men. But they had also hoped to make it a training ground in virtue. Well designed, the colony would make men better the longer they lived in it. Waterhouse himself had mixed feelings about the intelligence of the population at large. 'I believe', he said at another time, 'that the thinking and reflective portion of the community form a small proportion indeed'. But he doubted the rich as much as the poor – 'There are plenty of thinking working men.' His voting rule would encourage literacy, and therefore reflection, among such men because those who could not manage a pen would feel the shame of being shut out from the franchise.[43] The effort failed, but a year later other members were prepared to go even further. Francis Dutton now suggested that everything might rest on manhood alone.[44]

In the minds of members as they debated the question of the franchise, in Adelaide and elsewhere, there lived the image of the deciding citizen, the man with ideas about government. The thinking habits of that man (or rather, that ideal man) – the way in which he set up a debating chamber in his own head – these were to be the basis of any new system. But what were his thinking habits? In Adelaide Robert Torrens, collector of customs, distinguished two ways of voting and the difference between them was fundamental. Men might settle their thoughts by talking and listening. Or they might do it by solitary reading, by reflection. The second way, Torrens thought, was better. Men should have a clear sense of their own intellectual footsteps, as if on a page in front of them – just as Major Mitchell had mapped the movements of Richard Cunningham on the Bogan (Chapter 10). Torrens had no time for what was called 'political atmosphere' – for decision by osmosis. Voters fell too often, for instance, under the sway of 'some pot-house orator of dubious character'. He might have been thinking here of Chartist talk lately evident among the copper miners at Burra. Political decisions, he said, were best formed by reading 'political economy'. Did he mean only scholarly texts? His own father, Major Robert

Torrens, had been a famous writer of this kind, a scathing critic of Governor Macquarie's old-fashioned ideas (Chapter 2), and one of the founders of South Australia. Or did he include well-informed newspapers, available to everyone? It could be argued, certainly, that newspapers led men astray, but they remained indispensable for public debate.[45]

In this new discussion Waterhouse spoke up again for a literacy franchise, but now he suggested a household franchise too. Men might be allowed to vote because they were masters of families. For some in South Australia householders were the best heirs of systematic colonisation. Votes for mere men was a foreign notion here, said Angas. '[I]n the formation of this colony', he said, ' ... provision was made for maintaining the equality of the sexes'. It followed that married men were more complete citizens than single ones. (Only two-thirds of South Australian men were husbands.) South Australia needed, he said, 'the influence of families'.[46] And yet the influence of families – the impact of conversations between husband and wife – was at odds with pure democratic theory. It was inconsistent with the way democrats hoped to shape masculine opinion. It meant a failure of individual self-sufficiency. It meant 'political atmosphere'. It might even mean a kind of indirect voting by women, an unhappy prospect because women seemed to make up their minds in ways irrelevant to democracy. It was hard to explain just what they meant by the perfectly democratic franchise, said another member. He only knew that it did not mean 'that every individual, male or female, should come to hustings and have a vote'. Must it extend to everyone who obeyed the laws? Waterhouse pointed out that that would mean 'foreigners, aborigines, minors, and females'. All taxpayers? Women figured there too.[47] The 'fair sex' was democracy's antitype just as much as the power of money.

It was impossible to insist that voters know their letters. But in South Australia the same point was achieved, perhaps by accident, through coupling manhood suffrage with the ballot. Hitherto in elections throughout the empire the vote had been taken by a show of hands and then, if necessary, by electors stating their preference one by one to the presiding officers. The ballot let them vote alone, just as they were supposed to make up their minds alone. Each recorded his decision on paper and placed the paper in a box, free from the oversight of landlords, employers, and anyone else on whom he might depend in daily life. Alone and uncorrupted he added his brick to the information order, to the edifice of truth manifest in every free election.

The combined reform – manhood suffrage and the ballot – became law in South Australia in March 1856. The idea at first had been that voters should write down on a blank form the candidates they wanted. Instead, it was decided that forms should have all the names listed already, so that voters might cross out those they did not want. Two members of council, with the semi-literate in mind, argued for having the names printed in different colours – but then, names could easily outnumber the colours available. And why make it easy for men who were almost deliberately incompetent? 'He had no desire', said another member, J.B. Neales, 'to take any trouble in legislating for those who could not read and write. A false kind of sympathy was growing up in their favour, as it was for criminals'.[48]

In Tasmania and Victoria the ballot was introduced at about this time too. In neither was it linked at first to manhood suffrage, but in Victoria manhood suffrage soon followed.[49] In Sydney, as in Adelaide, the two came together, in 1858. Citizens must be something like scholars. It was an all-encompassing victory for the market of letters.

III

In the 1850s the staff in the office of Samuel Goode, publisher of the *Melbourne Weekly Despatch* and the *Victorian Weekly Price Current*, included a young apprentice called John McLeish. This boy's antics were to be recalled long afterwards by one of the compositors (using office jargon). Bushrangers were his demigods and he fancied being one:

> With a mask ... made of cardboard, inked over with the roller, and with the customary slits for the eyes, nose, and mouth he would wait in the press-room until the comps. came for the forms to dis., and shouldering the broom, gun style, with the long handle projecting, he would bawl out in a hoarse voice ... 'Bail up! Stand! Hold up yer blooming props!'

Then, 'with a laugh of derision', he bolted into the side lane, 'leaving the comps. considerably startled'.[50]

Publishing itself depended on bringing the thrill of the great world into the office, boiling it down and selling the result. The sharp taste of original events had to be preserved and rendered fit for circulation. All aimed, as the *Port Phillip Gazette* said of itself, at 'that degree of vivacity which can alone gain a hold upon the minds of [an energetic] people'.[51] Creating characters, including masked bushrangers, was an important part of the business. But while it all began by drawing drama into the office, the end result depended on creating a playhouse – or less commonly a debating chamber – within the mind of each reader and listener. Into every imagination there must rush a John McLeish, with something like the same startling impact but also with some chance of making his figure and actions stick.

Raffaello Carboni, of *The Eureka Stockade*, knew all this. Before coming here he had been, as he said, 'an old *Collaborateur* of the European Press', which probably means that he wrote for it. Ink for Carboni was action. It was his belief that British ink, though 'prostituted' sometimes in Victoria, was 'the only ink that dares to register black on white the name, word, and deed of any tyrant through the whole face of the earth'.[52] The ink used by Henry Seekamp, owner and editor of the *Ballarat Times*, for instance, 'now and then ... turns sour', said Carboni, but then 'its vitriol burns stronger'. Printing offices were ruled by their overseers and the *Times* was 'the Overseer of Ballaarat'. Such language mixed up the black patterning of the printed page with the local landscape, its yellow earth and higgledy-piggle of tents. Which was the real world – the world of ink or the world of flesh and blood? Lives were mined for the sense they made in writing. Carboni too, in his book, aimed to 'sharpen my quill and poison my inkstand that I may put to confusion the horrible brood of red-tape that ruled on Ballaarat at the time'.[53]

The Eureka Stockade was timbre and ink. It was born of a passing relationship between men's voices, sounds in the open air of the goldfields, and the newly popular, worldwide universe of print. We hear comparable echoes in Herman Melville's story of *Moby-Dick*, which had been published in the United States four years earlier. Both burned with vivid manhood, with masculine candour and womanless sensuality. Both placed before their readers a circle of men, characters drawn from around the world, and both invited readers (assumed to be men) to read as if they were listening, man to man. Writers, readers, and subjects – all seemed to be wanderers, men on the move, ocean-borne in *Moby-Dick*, chasing gold in *The Eureka Stockade*. And yet so intimate – 'Call me Ishmael', so Melville starts his story. 'Good reader, listen to me', says Carboni, 'fill the pipe, let's have a "blow" together'.[54] And there followed, within the pages of each story, a medley of entertainment such as might be heard among men of varied background living alone together, whether in a ship's hold or on the goldfields at night. Within a single lighted circle were to be heard pieces of theatre and snatches of learning, plus something of the worldly wisdom of the new press.

Robert Torrens might speak of the importance of reading 'political economy'. In the 1850s readers of a new generation, whether male or female, no longer wanted doctrine. They wanted personality and feeling. In Carboni's book voices came from all directions, as they did on the diggings, from men of all languages and complexions, from that 'splendid chest', from this 'thundering mouth', from that 'short, tight-built young chap', from this 'skinny bouncing curl' – his accent affected Californian.[55] The fist-like impact of such talking was like the best speeches on the goldfields and Carboni loved speech-making. Some local orators used styles transplanted from abroad. There was the old-fashioned gentlemanly rhetoric, finely structured, self-effacing, well read. Equally formal in its way was the radical style of the 1830s and '40s, 'chartist slang', as Carboni called it, perfected by speech-making in Britain. Thomas Kennedy, a leader at Eureka, spoke like a Chartist, his oratory, in Carboni's opinion, 'blathered with long phrases and bubbling with cant'.[56]

Colonial rhetoric worked best when it echoed colonial manners. The speeches here had a distinctive tone, and so did the newspaper reporting.

Daniel Deniehy, a watercolour portrait by an unknown artist – a stern idealist but also a master of jokes.

Reproduction courtesy of Mitchell Library, State Library of New South Wales

In colonial papers, according to an English gentleman, 'the meanings are less delicately couched' than at Home. '[T]he witticism, the reproof, the menace, the political disquisitions, are all put forth in course relief.'[57] The same was true viva voce. In New South Wales, Wentworth, as both writer and speech-maker, had helped to lay the groundwork of local style. He was typically witty and blunt. In the 1850s the same thing blossomed in the speeches of the native-born Sydney radical, Daniel Deniehy. Deniehy's first public address, and his most famous, was delivered in the Royal Victoria Theatre in August 1853, a few days short of his 25th birthday, to a meeting called by democrats to condemn Wentworth's scheme for a constitution. The young man boasted of his own abilities. He was scornful about both gentlemanly rhetoric and the newer jargon. He called the latter 'talkee talkee'. (Carboni called it 'yabber yabber'.) '[P]hrases now a-days' Deniehy said, 'seldom [have] … genuine meanings attached to them'. He was a slight man with a thin voice and someone in the pit of the theatre yelled, 'Speak up!' 'He would do his best', he said, 'to respond to that invitation "Speak up", and would, perhaps, balance deficiencies flowing from a small volume of voice by in all cases calling things by their right name'.[58]

Carboni's imagery in *The Eureka Stockade* might burst with noise, but it was writing all the same. Deniehy's words were meant first and last to echo in men's eardrums. Like Wentworth in his early days, in his theatre speech he made his attack on the closed elite, which had always managed New South Wales, a patrician class that now aimed, he thought, to take to itself hereditary titles. He proclaimed instead, as the best guardians of a free land, an aristocracy of freedom – an aristocracy such as existed, he said, '[w]herever human skill and brain are eminent, wherever glorious manhood asserts its elevation'. 'That is God's aristocracy, gentlemen; that is an aristocracy that will bloom and expand under free institutions, and forever bless the clime where it takes root.' Deniehy's mockery was lighter and sharper than any Australian speaker before him. Standing where, each night, plays were acted, he summoned, as he said, to 'the stage of our imagination' a brilliant array of figures – 'these harlequin aristocrats (laughter), these Botany Bay magnificos (laughter), these Australian mandarins (Roars of laughter)' – who dreamt of their own gilded chamber in Macquarie Street. They were a 'bunyip aristocracy', he said, and by that he meant they were no more solid and sensible than the monsters talked of by so-called 'intelligent blacks'. 'Let them walk across the stage in all the pomp and circumstance of hereditary titles.'[59] Let them pass before us as figments of delighted fancy, summed up and dismissed with the laughter of free men.

Laughter. 'How much lies in Laughter', said Thomas Carlyle, 'the cipher-key, wherewith we decipher the whole man!'[60] Deniehy, highly educated but locally born and bred, knew what made Sydney men laugh. He had mastered the joking that had grown out of convict and ex-convict life, the barbed irony that men had learnt to use over long years in their conversations about authority. His wit was quicker than most, but his style was common. About the same time a newcomer arriving by coach at Sofala, the goldfields town near Bathurst, was struck by the same kind of 'colonial chaff' offered to genteel passengers by youths lounging nearby. Someone carrying a leg of mutton had 'bai-bai' shouted after him. Someone with a new pair of knee boots was asked, 'how much he'd take for them, whether he ever *had* paid for them, if he had not stolen them, and how kind it was of his mother to look out for keeping his feet dry'. During the troubles nearby on the Turon a miner was fined £3 for calling out to a party of soldiers in the act of arresting an unlicensed cripple, 'Does your mother know you are out?' and 'Go it Indigo'.[61]

In Victoria laughter was different. Authority was too raw for jokes like this. Here, instead, we find a chaos of men newly met. The music-hall songs, which were offered on stage in Ballarat, Bendigo, and Beechworth, were impudent enough (in an English style) but among themselves the diggers laughed mainly at each other. Take the following story of a meeting at Bendigo to elect men for the local court, an institution won by the crisis at Eureka:

When the Chairman called for a show of hands, it was impossible to tell whether the majority was for or against Mr Knight, and accordingly one party was requested to go to the right and the other to the left. Here a scene of indescribable confusion ensued, which lasted several minutes. The adverse parties kept pushing and struggling past each other, shouting all the time their watchwords – 'No leases on this side!' 'Quartz miners here!' – and actually carrying off recreant friends *vi et armis*. Several who seemed rather bewildered, amongst whom were the German miners, were rushing first on one side and then on the other, to the utmost perplexity, not to be wondered at in the frightful uproar. Let it be understood, however, that not one quarrel arose. The whole affair was conducted with the utmost good nature, and even hilarity. The numbers were so evenly balanced that it was still impossible to tell which side had the majority, and an attempt was made to count each side by marching them down the flat. After a vain attempt, the diggers scampered back to the front of the platform amidst universal cheers and laughter. Another show of hands was then called for, and the Chairman declared the majority to be against Mr Knight.[62]

Similarly, at a meeting called to discuss the Victorian government's Postage Act, in 1854, the result was mightily confused, 'but productive of great merriment'.[63]

Deference and mockery both take hold more firmly with time. Both depend on the yeast of habit. In Victoria there was no settled society, no assumptions based on local custom, as in New South Wales. Men mattered less here for their background and connections. In Victoria, said William Westgarth, meetings were 'a common stage, knowing no monopoly, where individuals of all ranks freely give views on public affairs'. At such meetings the statements of working men, still hesitantly made in Sydney, could affect the way everyone spoke. It was not only a question of what such men said (and according to Westgarth, 'they frequently display more of original and practical thinking than classes of higher training'). It was also how they said it. They were manly and straightforward, but without Deniehy's refinement: 'Now look here mates I just tell ye exactly how it was … .'[64] The writer William Howitt was at one meeting on the goldfields. The crowd had been left restless by a gentlemanly speaker when 'a rough, determined, yet good-countenanced man was lifted up to the front. He evidently did not court the prominence, but … was perfectly self-possessed, his mind was full and his undisciplined tongue "was all there"'. He began with 'Brother diggers!' (A man of another type might have said, 'Gentlemen!', or if a Chartist, 'Brother proletarians!') Howitt recalled:

He bade them be of good heart, but to be united … he advised them to obey the law, but denied the legality of the license-tax … [and he] wound up by 'swearing, while he would die for his Queen', he would shed the last drop of his blood before he would pay another license.

His loyalty and fierceness drew something intangible from the mass. Touched, said Howitt, 'with the glow of feeling around me, I could imagine that I had a cloud for a footstool'.[65]

These were styles created by men for their own purposes. Women, as public speakers, could not hope for such success. As writers they might do as men did but public speaking posed problems of its own. Women were not always impressed with male efforts. One female description of the speeches of Sydney's legislators – 'piebald oratory, magpie prattle, and blatant magniloquence' – almost suggests an alien tongue.[66] But men in turn heard something strange in women's speeches. When the temperance lecturer Susannah Thomas spoke in Melbourne on the evils of alcohol, the *Banner's* reporter was lost between admiration and ridicule. 'The fair speaker', he said, 'expatiated, in a fluent strain of indignant oratory, against the conventional customs of the age, and contrasted the devastations and misery of warfare with the penury and sufferings of intemperance ... She spoke well, and was frequently applauded'.[67] Apparently Mrs Thomas sounded too earnest for manly ears.

Jokes helped men's speeches but they might be crucial for women's. All women with ambition risked ridicule and lady orators must bear with laughter whether they liked it or not. Caroline Chisholm was one who knew how easily, as a public speaker, she might become a figure of fun. She also knew that the best jokes a woman could make in public were the jokes of intimacy, those which drew on the talking of husband and wife – and especially on the teasing, fond or bitter, which fed the life of many marriages. Such teasing ran through the novels of Thackeray and Trollope, which were mainly about life in families. For Matthew Arnold (writing in verse) the beauty of a loving woman included 'the archest chin / Mockery ever ambush'd in'.[68] Women writers gloried less in this kind of fun. As a laughing public speaker Mrs Chisholm made her way alone.

Certainly, she could argue hard about policy. Her abiding interest since 1841 had been the immigration of poor women and families. She wanted, she said, 'a self-creating and co-operating system' for her immigrants. But at the same time her language had the whimsical charm expected of a happy wife. In a pamphlet addressed to the Secretary of State she wrote of the depression of the early 1840s, when 'the Colonial banks rocked like cradles'. Men made bad decisions then, she said, 'throw[ing] away a diamond for a sugar-plum'. In the end, so Caroline Chisholm believed, men were truly men when they were husbands – daily subject to a female voice. The transportation of convicts, so she argued in the same pamphlet, by tearing men from their wives in Britain and Ireland had put asunder those whom God had joined together. It had 'doomed thousands and tens of thousands to the demoralizing state of bachelorism'. The goldrush had done the same. In spring 1854 she made a tour through some of the goldfield towns of Victoria, ostensibly to find out how far those places were suited to farming families. She made speeches wherever she went and crowds of diggers paid her back with laughter and clapping. At Mt Alexander she taunted them with living single. She could hardly pity men, she said, 'who pay so little respect to their own sex as to live without wives when they can so well afford to maintain them (laughter)'.[69] Even her strictures had a joking undertone.

On her return to Melbourne she made another speech, at the Mechanics Institute. She flattered the male part of her audience. 'There is no mistake', she said, 'about digging being hard work. It is hard work. (Laughter.) But men like it. (Renewed laughter.) And I will tell you why they like it. It is because they feel that they can work when they like and rest when they like; that no man is their master. (Loud and prolonged applause.)' And she made fun of herself. She had found diggers afraid of competition and secretive about the chances of doing well. They said, 'I don't mind telling you, Mrs. Chisholm, but we don't like to publish these particulars'. 'Now', she went on, 'I am the worst person in the world, perhaps, to tell a secret to; but I promised them faithfully that what they chose to tell me should be kept a secret until I got to Melbourne'. She dwelt on home life. As long as the living was rough there would be too few wives among the diggers. She talked about the poor lodging houses to be found at the goldfields and on the way there. Most were managed by men, 'and you know very well that men are bad hands at making a pudding. (Great laughter.)'[70]

Daniel Deniehy and Raffaello Carboni dealt with men among men. For Caroline Chisholm everything turned on men and women, on the jigsaw of labour and affection to be found in good households. The perfect marriage for her was one in which the two parties had, as she put it, 'but one mind'.[71] She meant rich and poor – because, just as ideal manhood cancelled rank so did ideal wedlock. In fact for Mrs Chisholm the two perfections went together. Her main interest was always immigrant women. But her success took her among men and by the 1850s she had mastered the global language of democracy. With rare skill she then combined the politics of theory – the theory of equality – with the politics of home life. She was one of the best exponents of the new regime. Tactful and pleasant with gentlemen ('frank, easy, and lady-like', according to one of them), she nevertheless agreed with Deniehy about exclusive elites. During a speech in Sydney in 1860 she called the House of Lords 'dry rot'. Here, she said, the Australian Club, the most select club in Sydney, was 'a sort of House of Lords' – in past years its members had managed the labour market wholly for themselves. This speech she gave during a general election and her chairman made his own joke. 'Mrs Chisholm would make a most excellent representative in the Assembly', he said, 'He would recommend them to put Mrs Chisholm in at the head of the poll'. The lady replied that if they elected her '(laughter)', they ought to know that she might go her own way on some matters. 'She told them now', she said, 'because it was better to tell them now than after she had been in the House. (Renewed applause.)'[72]

There were women in the audience and Mrs Chisholm asked them to come up and sit behind her, remarking on 'the old prejudice' against women 'meddling' in politics. And yet she laughed herself about the election of women and she never said that they should vote. She stood for democracy as it emerged in the 1850s, confident that the population as a whole might happily rely on the votes of men.[73] She gave the men who heard her striking proof of what a woman could do, but she also gave them the respect of a happy, home-bound wife – a respect proven by teasing. Other women were more cynical about manhood suffrage. Surely, they said, it gave even brutal and stupid men new cause for vanity? Surely, as a plain matter of justice it was wrong? Equality itself was just a theory – bad in its premises and bad in its conclusion. Women had never enjoyed rights of office but at least social rank had given power to a few, to the ladies. The democracy of the 1850s offered nothing new and it promised to destroy the little they had long enjoyed. When all were equal, so the theory had it, ladies, like gentlemen, would be irrelevant. 'What!', a feminist asked the *Sydney Morning Herald* in 1857. 'Is it not enough that they should debar us from the franchise, but that they should also seek to deprive us of what little influence we have in the social scale?'[74]

Mrs Chisholm trusted the men. '[D]emocracy in truth', she said, 'is only the popular and pacific voice of the people – their earnest desire for justice'.[75] By the voice of the people she meant the voice of husbands, fraught, she assumed, with the background murmur of wives, with the 'political atmosphere' of home life. It must have been wives who sat on the platform behind her, women who had come with their men. It must have been husbands, typically at least, who laughed with her from the floor as she sketched out their power.

Chapter 13

Railway Dreaming

I

The goldfields were full of noise. And yet, in all the colonies during the 1850s and 1860s, as one generation gave way to another, the multiplicity of voices did not find its way so often into print. We see fewer well-read men and women seeking stories from people unlike themselves. Imagination worked in less strenuous ways. The simplicity of a rich future overshadowed the complexities of the present. Thus was established, piece by piece, what might be called the democratic settlement, a settlement bearing its best fruit, it was to be hoped, in the years to come.

This new dispensation was most ample in the richest colonies, but it was a broad Australian achievement. It was certainly a work of intellectual power. Saxe Bannister had believed that all 'rational beings' were driven by curiosity. It was only necessary to give them opportunities for intellectual improvement and their minds would catch fire, moving inexorably towards the light (Chapter 2). So it proved to be. However, the outcome was more narrowly focused, more morally uncertain than Bannister had imagined. By the 1850s the great mass of the Europeans in Australia were caught up in the progress of Western humanity. It seemed natural now, at least among the young, to be aware of oneself not only as the 'I' of one's own universe – myself, a 'rational being' – but also as a particle. We each of us belonged to a host of similar creatures, all carried forward by the sudden unfolding of Providence.

The democratic settlement was three-sided. In the first place, it was political. All adult males might take part in electing their government. All authority was tied to the ambition and reasoning power of common manhood. Secondly, the democratic settlement had a commercial side. Free enterprise was the orthodoxy of the day and those who prospered proved by their voices and bearing some of the power of the regime. New technology, especially steampower, was part of the same process. Once again, mainly in New South Wales, Victoria, and South Australia, and even before the goldrush, money began to be invested in improved production. Gold added to the business enormously. Vigorous free enterprise meant that the most successful firms swallowed up the others. Throughout New South Wales during 1850–55 the number of soap-makers barely changed but the output of soap nearly doubled. There was also twice as much sugar, although two sugar manufacturers dwindled to one. It was a larger market, but there were fewer tanneries, breweries, and tobacco manufacturers. There were fewer mills grinding grain, but more were steam-driven (rather than depending on water, wind, or horse-power), so that once again smaller numbers meant larger production.[1]

City firms pushed inland. 'The increased facilities of communication', said the *Sydney Morning Herald* at the opening, in 1855, of the Sydney–Parramatta railway (the first in New South Wales), 'are the cords by which the great interests of a country are bound together'.[2] In the 1840s, thanks to better technology, Tooth's brewery had begun to sell to country towns near Sydney, sending local makers out of business. Each such triumph brought another in its train. At Penrith, 40 miles from Sydney, publicans who bought aerated water from a city firm were told by its agent:

> Mr A– or Mr B– , you have ordered two dozen lemonade, two dozen soda water, &c, you had better let me bring you a case of gin, two gallons [of] brandy, rum, or what spirits you may want. I will deliver it to you with the lemonade, &c, it will cost you nothing for the carriage.[3]

Some manufacturers did such things well. Others failed.

Daily or near-daily papers rose and fell in the same way (and again from the years just before the goldrush). In Sydney within twenty years four papers became two – the conservative *Herald* and the liberal *Empire*. In Adelaide, with so many papers to start with, only the *Advertiser* and the *Register* remained. In Melbourne the *Argus*, its presses driven by steam, absorbed five previous titles, competing in the end with the Melbourne *Herald* and the *Age*. The consolidation of business meant a consolidation of stories and a consolidation of policy. Even in disagreement there was a predictability and uniformity of tone. Country papers sprang up everywhere, but they usually mimicked one of the city giants.

Finally, the democratic settlement was obvious in the way government worked. Here was a process directly linked with the first years of settlement – with the dictatorial benevolence described in Volume 1, with the High Enlightenment and the ramifying ambitions of utilitarianism. Here, too, was the science of government. Good communications were especially important, including postage and transport – 'the cords by which the great interests of a country are bound together'. The mass of the people were to be bound together too, rich and poor, men and women, all on equal terms. This had been the great point of utilitarianism, manifest, say, in Rowland

Hill's reform of postage (Chapter 5). The managers were educated men, but everyone was to share in what they did. The girls who flocked in new numbers to school (Chapter 7) could not hope to vote. But they could write and post letters. If it were possible to sort by gender each item now coming into Australian post offices, the handwriting of women and girls would surely be found on a substantial fraction.

Local expertise was too meagre for the great material and administrative machinery needed under the new regime. Reformers appealed to the best authorities at Home, importing thereby a network of both skill and patronage. In South Australia William Hanson, chief commissioner of railways, brought with him some of the prestige of the celebrated railway engineer, George Stephenson, 'an old friend, and my original master'. Frederick Calf, the Adelaide stationmaster, had served under Hanson himself on England's north-eastern line.[4] These networks involved not only technical ability but also scientific knowledge and research. In Britain since the 1840s the state had begun to fund technology and science as the basis of national wealth, and the new recruits carried this understanding to the Antipodes. The best effort was made in Melbourne, where Charles La Trobe, the first goldrush Governor, had married science and the state. There money was abundant – during 1851–70 six times more gold was fetched to the surface in Victoria than in New South Wales.[5] By 1860 five intellectual enterprises reported direct to the Victorian premier – a board of science, a geological survey (with a palaeontologist), a magnetic survey (concentrating on meteorology and astronomy), the zoological and botanical gardens, and the museum of natural history. The 1860 budget allocated £28,139 altogether for these bodies, plus £13,510 for the board of agriculture.[6] Demographic inquiry flourished too. Victoria's system of census-taking and registration of births, deaths, and marriages was 'more comprehensive', it was said, 'in its scope and scientific in detail than any hitherto carried out in any part of the world'. There was also a Royal Society in Melbourne. Senior public servants added much to its debates.[7]

The effort in Victoria was startling, but everywhere democracy, technology, and science seemed interdependent. The native-born poet Charles Harpur, now a middle-aged democrat living in the Hunter Valley, turned his thoughts, as he put it:

> To Freedom in her future prime,
> To Nature's everlasting lore,
> To Science from her tower in time
> Surveying the Eternal's shore.[8]

Here was power over new kinds and degrees of information. Here was acumen. Here was disentangling. Here was the ability to read signs and to see patterns invisible to the untrained and unmanly eye. Such skills embraced both knowledge and judgment. They involved both training by masters and the self-sufficiency of manhood. Hanson, the railway commissioner in South Australia, issued no written instructions to his subordinates. '[Y]ou cannot make a man a machine', he said, 'the best plan is to carefully instruct a man, and then let him carry on his duty in the best way he can'. And even machinery, after all, might behave in ways no orthodoxy could predict. 'There are so many things in running locomotives over which you have no control', said Hanson's subordinate, J.H. Clark. 'A broken spring, or the bursting of a tube, which cannot be foreseen, and may be called the will of God.'[9] A man must understand system, but the charm of the systematic universe lay in the way in which certainty mingled with surprises, almost deliberately testing men's courage.

Men themselves were systems, even machines, and so were women. Those who looked after the insane, as a great reformer of lunatic asylums said, must think of their charges 'at the same time as brothers, and as mere automata'.[10] They must treat them with compassion but also with a firm hand and frequent attention. By the middle decades of the nineteenth century the ambitions of authority, of all kinds, began to take this form. Among one's fellow creatures there might be plentiful evidence, in each case, of an eternal soul but at the same time one confronted the automaton with which the soul was intermingled. The human anatomy was the seat of something eternal. And yet it was also a mechanical maze, a package of 'complicated labyrinths'.[11] Here was the root of that moral uncertainty – at times, indeed, an agonising test of conscience – mentioned above.

The same years saw a boom in the study of gynaecology and of 'the diseases peculiar to women'. In her story *Middlemarch* (1872), George Eliot told with extraordinary subtlety the story of several marriages, and she also explored the authority of Tertius Lydgate, a doctor of the new type. Lydgate, she said, felt 'much tenderness' in managing women, including his own wife, because he understood both their physical vulnerability and 'the delicate poise of their health both in body and mind'.[12] He exercised, in other words, the detachment of the scientific man.

Tenderness of the same strangely objective kind was to be seen in Richard Tracy, the highly successful and popular gynaecologist and obstetrician at the Lying-In Hospital in Melbourne. Women, Tracy thought, were creatures of distinctive complexity, both moral and physical, and easily unbalanced. In themselves they represented a man's universe, both his opposite and his outer edge. '[T]here is something inexpressibly gratifying', he said, 'in the consciousness of having mitigated the sufferings of a being naturally prone to the most generous emotions, but whom agony and anxiety render so querulous and unmanageable'. A patient of his own, according to his casebook, threatened her baby in a post-natal frenzy, shouting that she had given birth to a donkey. At one point there were fifteen women (among 248) confined at the Yarra Bend Lunatic Asylum who were supposed to have been driven mad by childbirth or pregnancy. Tracy's work in saving the lives of women and their babies depended on his surgical skill, which was all at once bold and delicate. But achievements such as his sprang from larger changes in the habits of humanity, from a new understanding of 'the delicate poise of ... body and mind'. The tending of women, he thought, was the best proof of civilisation. They became now 'more and more the object of our care and watchful solicitude'.[13]

Cities, too, were ensouled machines. Like women, to the scientific world they offered comfort and risk combined. Cities also had to be managed with extraordinary discrimination. Melbourne was a chaos of humanity whose redemption seemed to lie in expert tenderness. In the twenty years after the goldrush Sydney grew two and a half times (to 138,000), but Melbourne grew nine times (to 207,000). The other capitals were on a smaller scale altogether, ranging from Adelaide (43,000) to Perth (5000). In Melbourne, during the first year of the goldrush it was said that: 'Every nook ... including the neighbouring suburbs of Richmond and Collingwood, was crowded to suffocation.' The crush became greater with the years and the quantity of rubbish gathered in back lanes and vacant lots was soon enormous.[14] Sewerage problems, bad before the goldrush, multiplied thereafter. There was no underground sewerage system and few proper cesspits, and matter of all kinds made its way in open drains through Melbourne streets. In 1866 a select committee of the legislative assembly heard evidence on the disposal of 'night soil' throughout the city. Privies a generation old had achieved a depth of filth that made the city very unhealthy in summer. Children were especially likely to die of stomach ailments and in some of the most densely populated spots – North Melbourne, Fitzroy, Collingwood – one in ten never reached their fifth birthday, more than twice the figure elsewhere in the city.[15]

The first systematic survey of inner-city life among the Europeans in Australia was made by the *Sydney Morning Herald* in late summer 1851, when a 'special reporter' worked his way through the worst pockets of local squalor, in a city where even some of the locally born were now old men and women. He estimated the tiny quantities of air, per head, in some slum dwellings and he told of an almost tangible stench. Air was, of course, an object of common consumption and the idea of sharing air was a new and intriguing one. Even on shipboard, so Herman Melville ventured in *Moby-Dick* (also 1851), 'the Commodore on the quarter-deck gets his atmosphere at second hand from the sailors on the forecastle'. In Sydney sewage, too, was everywhere, seeping sometimes in a continuous stream through the walls of cellar-homes. We all must learn 'the chemistry of life', said the *Herald* reporter. He meant the impact of dirt. But more broadly, he meant all the hidden links between the human body and its material habitat. Beyond that, indeed, he meant the tight fabric of Creation itself.[16]

Chemistry was now in its early heyday. It was an arena of manly skill that explained all the interconnectedness of the universe. Any fire in a blacksmith's forge, as Thomas Carlyle put it, was 'a little ganglion, or nervous centre in the great vital system of Immensity' – a nicely biological image for a mainly chemical idea. [17] The universe was a great body, or system, and chemistry, by tracing interconnectedness and interaction, proved the power of each item therein. Magnetic impulse and electricity, both apparently aspects of chemistry, seemed to be the great driving forces of the material world. Life itself, leaving divine will out of the question, might be seen as a symptom of magnetism or electricity.

The 'chemistry of life', though universal, was also a science of place. Places, too, were 'vital systems'. Melbourne, which had once seemed placeless (Chapter 12), began to know itself on just these elaborate terms, through its men of science. When, in June 1860, Georg Neumayer, director of Victoria's magnetic survey, made out his first report (dated from the Magnetical, Nautical and Meteorological Observatory on Flagstaff Hill), he provided 262 pages of numerical data, plus several large sheets, about Melbourne's envelope of air – its pressure, humidity, electricity, the relationship between air and ground temperature (the thermometer being laid on the earth's surface and sprinkled with sand), and much else. The Aurora Australis in late summer, seen from Melbourne, was an extraordinary meeting of powers, marked by a bright arch dressed in streamers – 'broad and short', said Neumayer, 'but very distinct, of a pale yellow and greenish yellow color, very bright close to the level bank of cloud on [the] horizon'.[18] God himself might be examined thus, overseeing the city from his patterned throne.

Each human anatomy was touched by the surrounding elements and so was the urban population all at once – and each, in some sense, touched the others. In his report Neumayer quoted his great contemporary and patron, Alexander von Humboldt, on 'the internal connection existing among all natural phenomenon', and on the need to follow such connections wherever they might lead.[19] One urgent issue was the movement of contagious diseases. A belief in bad air, or miasmas, as a prime cause of disease began to be replaced by germ theory in the 1860s, but still much seemed to depend on invisible forces, evident in our physical feelings, our bodily colour and texture. Different places featured different diseases. During summer 1868–69 Melbourne was struck by what seemed like a combination of smallpox and chickenpox. In particular areas, where sufferers had been crowded together, so it was said, '[t]he surrounding atmosphere was ... impregnated with the disease'. Medical men were bewildered. The government's chief medical officer could only suggest that the inflammation was a result of 'some atmospheric or telluric influences', and by 'telluric' he implied a kind of noxious link between people and place.[20]

Melbourne also had problems with its water supply, and here was more evidence of the 'chemistry of life'. From 1857 water was taken from the Plenty River, via the Yan Yean reservoir, using lead pipes lined internally with tin. The interaction of these three elements, water, lead, and tin, meant that the water was almost immediately contaminated with the lead, and within a year there were serious cases of lead poisoning. The house of the governor of Melbourne Gaol was connected to the main with pipes of this kind. The governor himself, wide-girthed George Wintle, remained healthy, but Mrs Wintle, who consumed large quantities of water, suffered badly from stomach-ache and depression. She improved when her doctor gave her rainwater from his own tank, but in his opinion her health was so shattered that there was no hope of full recovery. Another woman died in Melbourne Hospital from the same cause. A post-mortem on her puttied flesh showed not only the deep blue line along the gums which was the clearest sign of lead poisoning, but also grey-blue intestines and extreme constipation.[21]

Victims in such cases might be sceptical about the logic of the experts, which relied so much on unfamiliar mysteries. Dr William Mackie Turnbull told of a patient whose symptoms of lead poisoning were quite obvious to the trained eye. He was a publican and Turnbull visited him at work. 'I am all right,' the man said, 'but I have got a confounded rheumatism'. He had caught it, he thought, on holiday at Christmas at Snapper Point. 'I have nearly lost the use of my arms.' Turnbull watched him pouring grog, lifting his right wrist with his left hand. 'You are suffering from lead poisoning', he said. 'Yet,' the man replied, 'I can lift a weight straight up from the ground, or press it down strongly, but I cannot lift anything with my wrist placed straight out.' He trusted rheumatism. He would not believe Turnbull's talk of lead poisoning.[22]

Larger minds worked in larger ways. A place was to be characterised by both its water and its air. Melbourne water was deeply coloured and Melbourne people found it hard to drink, whatever their knowledge of the 'chemistry of life'. It was 'repulsive', said Dr David Wilkie. The siting of the reservoir meant that it was thick with what Wilkie called 'organic matter'. He meant the droppings of sheep and cattle – 'and there are of course dunghills and privies, and all sorts of impurities, and in heavy floods a great quantity of water must be washed from the gathering grounds into the reservoir'.[23] This was logic resting on the collection of geographical and chemical facts, and also on summary analysis – on the kind of reporting nourished in the previous generation by men like Governor Arthur (Chapter 4).

Still innocent of such logic, the mass of men, women and children lagged far behind. 'Organic matter' notwithstanding, they still lived intimately with beasts. In Collingwood, poverty stricken and tightly packed, for every ten houses there was a cow, a sheep, a pig, or a goat, together with fifty hens or ducks and an unknown number of dogs and cats.[24] The owners were unskilled in reading brackish water and blue-lined gums and ignorant of 'vital systems'. They also ignored scientific laws, taking no action to manage risk. The city's experts all agreed, for instance, on the importance of smallpox vaccination, especially during the mysterious epidemic of 1868–69. There were deaths from the disease and yet many refused vaccination. Peter Edgar, a labouring man, died of it but the men and women who had lived in the same boarding house with him refused to be treated. And yet, said the doctor, 'they knew that he had paid the forfeit of his life to his neglect of this precaution'.[25]

II

In a material sense, Australia was now a richer place. There was more to be bought, for need or pleasure. Many objects on sale came in glass, which was now a first-class symbol of efficiency and abundance. Remember (Chapter 11) the 942 glass-fronted boxes set up in the Melbourne post office – Sydney used the same system from 1855 – and the small bottles used in the sale of items en masse to diggers.[26] Until 1845 the British government had taxed the manufacture of glass and small bottles had cost too much for common use. The tax had not prevented experiments in methods of mass production, partly informed by chemical skill. A population of many millions was being converted into a vast and eager market and the wholesale manufacture of glass was tried on both sides of the Atlantic. In Britain glassmakers moved quickly when the tax was dropped.

In the moulding of bottles wood gave way to metal. This meant among other things that sharply drawn lettering and symbols could be added to the surface, which was useful in showing whether the bottled liquid was alcohol, aerated water, patent medicine, or perfume. New drinks were produced to fill the bottles. Soda water now came in a rainbow of flavours – vanilla, lemon, strawberry, raspberry, blackberry, peach. Sheet glass was also improved. Glass designed for windows came both at lower prices and in bigger pieces (up to 4 feet across), and as clear, smooth and strong as any so far produced. Sheets were also stained for sale – amber, purple, green, yellow, blue, and crimson – thereby, as it were, colouring the air itself.[27]

Coloured windows were meant for churches and for the houses of the rich, but everyone was affected in some way by glass's ubiquity. In Australia the drinking and eating habits of even 'the lower classes', as Louisa Meredith remarked, were manifest in glass. In earlier days bottles had been carefully handled so that they could be used again. Now they were hardly worth keeping. Working people carried beer and soda as they travelled – coming home from town, for instance. 'As each bottle in succession is emptied', wrote Mrs Meredith (her experience was Tasmanian), 'it is shied out at a parrot or a crow, or dashed against a tree; and, consequently, every road is garnished with portions of broken glass'. The flesh inside the hooves of horses (called the frog) and the feet of dogs were cut. 'I am now accustomed to look out for glass bottles as keenly as for snakes; and we often stop, when riding or driving, to dismount and stow some vicious-looking green glass horror safely away in a hollow log.'[28]

Pieces shining in the Tasmanian bush probably came from the Cascade Brewery, near Hobart. But they did not do so originally because Australia's industrial revolution did not reach to glass. As with most breweries, Cascade's porter, ale, and beer was all sold in dark green bottles previously used for British imports. (The colour in this case was due to cheap manufacture and impregnation with iron.)[29] Well packed, bottles traversed the globe and stayed inexpensive to the end. Backstreet cesspits in the capital cities, filled with the rubbish of the poor, in due course contained thousands of samples, dirty, scratched and worn, of this same 'green glass horror'. Separated from the dirt after generations, by archaeologists of a later day, cleaned pieces catch the light still.[30]

The combination of glass and iron (wrought iron and cast iron) produced London's Crystal Palace, a vast glasshouse unlike anything the world had hitherto seen. Glass and iron, together with copious wood, also made up the skeleton and skin of steam-powered passenger trains. In this case iron was the more obvious item and wood formed the casing of carriages. But the quick and pleasant carriage of large numbers at 40 miles per hour would have been hard without glass. Drivers did without windscreens to begin with but first and second-class passengers were always glassed in. The experience of sitting at such windows clarified a point that in earlier times must have been only obscurely understood. When one moves rapidly forward – and railway carriages were several times faster and smoother than any previous means of transport – the view to the front is much clearer than the view sideways. The effect was explained to a parliamentary committee in England by George Stephenson. Indeed, he said, experiment proved that the faster one went the more one's 'power of vision', looking sideways, was enfeebled. Passengers lost themselves in movement.[31] Charles Dickens called this sensation 'railway dreaming', and he wrote a short story with that title in 1856. The story was about himself. He spoke of sitting in 'luxurious confusion', half asleep, stock-still within a rush of energy, and glassed in from the world. 'I take it for granted I am coming from somewhere', he said, 'and going somewhere else. I seek to know no more'. He might as well, he said, be coming from the Moon.[32]

So he imagined. The people of his dreaming he called the Mooninians. In his previous travels he had stood among them, he said, before a building fronted with glass. It was the Mooninian Morgue. Inside the window were Mooninian bodies that had been found dead with no evidence as to who they were and which had been left to be claimed. Living Mooninians moved through, gazing on each face. It was a popular site: 'Cheery married women, basket in hand, strolling in, on their way to or from the buying of the day's dinner; children in arms with little pointing fingers; young girls; prowling boys; comrades in working, soldiering or what not.' What struck the dreamer most was the appearance of the living faces coming out. They were expressionless – as if under glass themselves, with no hint of what they felt.

Two years later the great author published a similar piece, called 'Railway Nightmares'. This time he asked his readers to pick their way through a future disaster, a ruined railway system with a great central station, 'once so full of life, ... now an echoing deserted cavern; its crystal roof is an arch of broken glass'. The sharp fragments seemed to stand for mortality and immortality both at once, for once again glass gave a shine even to death. 'Nothing living is now left', said the storyteller, 'except a wild, half-famished cat, ravenously gnawing a bone as smooth as glass'.[33]

Dickens admired the railways. Trains for him had unhesitating purpose. They moved in nicely judged patterns and with careful timing to their destination. Their efficiency was art and science combined and he was sure that all the ancient abuses of the present day could be swept away by the kind of interactive power that surrounded travellers in trains. Trains represented the precision and transparency of method that was now demanded of authority in all sorts of ways. Here was the 'science of government' manifest in steam, iron, and glass. The Europeans in Australia, as they became self-governing, began to think of trains in the same way. Australian-made glass might be non-existent so far, but Australian iron was ready to hand and the making of Australian railways only needed trained and systematic thought. Nothing could better symbolise the newly independent power of the colonial peoples.

For some, railway dreaming included ideas of federal cooperation. Now that railways were about to come into use here, said Hugh McColl in the Melbourne *Banner*, the various governments ought to cooperate to avoid 'discrepancy of regulations', including a different width of track from one colony to the next. Sir Henry Young, Governor of South Australia, called for an imperial scheme linking Adelaide, Sydney, and Melbourne.[34] But railways were more easily seen as proof of colonial sovereignty. Nowadays, without such 'a system of transit', said the *Sydney Morning Herald*, 'nations cannot exist'.[35] Steadily – each using its own track-width so that the three systems were in fact incompatible – the geographical reach of these three capital cities, Adelaide, Sydney, and Melbourne, their web of connection, was to be wonderfully extended by rail. These were also the three centres most powerfully touched by democracy, and they were to joined soon by Brisbane, capital of the new colony of Queensland. Here we see clearly the science of government laid out across the land.

Australia's first steam-powered train ran the two-and-a-half miles between Melbourne and Hobson's Bay in September 1854. 'The shrill tones of the steam whistle', said the *Argus* on the morning of the first trip, 'will indicate today as significantly as if the cannon were booming in celebration of our independence that a new era has dawned upon us'.[36] In New South Wales a line southward from Sydney had been under preparation since the late 1840s but no trains ran until 1855. In South Australia they began a year later again.

There was thrill and terror in train-travelling. Once one got on board there might be no choice but to go fast. As George Stephenson remarked, every passenger 'must take the speed that is prepared for him'.[37] And the building of tracks and the highly orchestrated passage of the trains meant that the country itself must be ravaged and overrun. Here, too, there seemed no choice. '[T]he scream of to-day', said the *Argus*, still on the theme of the steam-whistle, 'is but the key-note to a thousand others'. There was glory in such havoc. 'The time comes fast', the paper continued, 'when it will sound over plain and hill, for many a mile away from present signs of civilization, scaring the wild animals from their repose, and warning them that their arch-enemy is upon them in earnest at last'. Even livestock will feel a new fear. Cattle on distant plains will 'run roaring to their camps' – for like men, 'it but too often happens, that the most senseless of the group makes the most fuss and roars the loudest'.[38] Indeed, among men challenges like this divided, for all time, the 'senseless' – for whom such power was always frightening – from those who entered with eagerness into railway dreaming.

Once again, gentlemen with appropriate skill and experience were imported from Britain to establish and manage the railways. Less care was taken in the employment of men at a lower level, including engine drivers. Safety, for instance, depended on an understanding of the relationship between speed, gradients, degrees of curvature, and so on, and yet drivers had

The main railway station in Sydney, 1856, a lithograph by Samuel Thomas Gill.

no particular training, except that they began as firemen, stoking the engines. Some were incapable of reading the gradient signs that told the steepness of the track. As a minimum they were only called on to work the engine and to read the signals (red, blue, and green). The men who maintained the lines, gangers, were even less sophisticated. They made full inspections, say twice a day, but many were illiterate and they were not asked to keep written records. They only had to know how to signal with flags to the drivers. Some carried red and green lamps.[39]

There might have been a certain amount of dreaming on board a particular train running from Parramatta to Sydney on a winter morning in 1858. It was travelling at about 40 miles an hour, nearly twice the normal speed on that line. The driver, Robert Boan, had two minutes to make up but he liked anyway to push his engine to the limit. It passed George Carter, driving his bullock team. Carter saw that one of the horseboxes was wobbling badly. It looked unsafe. 'The fireman had his eye on me', Carter recalled, 'and I took my hat off and cooeyed, but it had no effect – he was past me like lightening'. It passed a team of gangers and the leading man, John Fishlock, had the same impression:

> I said, 'It is a case to me if ever that box gets round the curve.' I was on my hands and knees on the down line, and the train was soon out of my sight; but my mate, who was raising the joint, was out at the far end of the lever, and being up higher and out farther could see farther than I could. He said to me, 'That train has gone over.' I said, 'Nonsense.' He said, 'It has, though.' I stopped the men at their work and said, 'Hold on a bit.' I put my ear down on the rails, but I heard nothing, and then I knew something was wrong; so I jumped up and said, 'Come on, men.'

All six passenger carriages had left the line and three had gone over the embankment. The heads of two passengers, George Want, a Sydney lawyer, and Sarah Hackett, an orchardist who kept a fruit stall in the city, were crushed beneath a carriage roof. Another man was saved from the same death only because his wife, with an instinctive movement, had pulled him to her as they fell. When Fishlock arrived he found another woman, Frances de Courcy, trapped under Mrs Hackett and he dragged her out. She and several other passengers were more or less badly injured.[40]

This was Australia's first serious railway accident. There had, however, been a different kind of smash only lately in the life of Mrs de Courcy. Henry, her husband, had collapsed into madness and she had since supported herself and their five children, as well as paying his board in a British asylum. (Only pauper lunatics were supported by the state.) This she managed as a teacher of singing and piano. In 1848 a legislative council committee had declared that steam-powered trains would stimulate 'all the springs of private industry and enterprize, by presenting to them the means of rapid transit'. This had happened for Frances de Courcy. Her first pupils were at Parramatta, where she lived, but the ability to reach Sydney in forty minutes had given her a market there too and she taught six girls in the city, each worth three guineas a quarter. Mrs de Courcy was thirty-three years old, clear-headed, keen, and highly regarded. She had found, she said, how very pleasant it was 'to labor and earn money for one's self'. She might have smiled, in the early part of this trip, as she gazed at the surrounding winds. She had a promise of more pupils, she had just started a dancing class at Parramatta and she was already making £150 a year. The accident, however, left her with a dislocated wrist and a damaged right eye. The trauma alone kept her in bed for three months and even after that she could not teach. 'I could not suffer the noise, as I was deranged, almost, for a time.' Her troubles, indeed, were permanent. Apart from the injury to her eye, the side of her face was paralysed, which hindered her singing, and two of her fingers likewise, which halved her skill on the piano. She might still earn a little. But, as she said, 'I have no hope now; my sight is failing every day, and my whole system is shaken'. Two years later she was dead.[41]

Such mishaps were unfortunate, but they were incidental to the providential power of these machines. There was a rich idealism in railway dreaming. For instance, in Britain the significance of trains for the poor was a matter of lengthy debate. Like better postage, railways seemed to promise for everyone, whatever their rank in life, the cancelling of distance. Many saw the parallel with postage immediately, including Rowland Hill himself. Hill was among those who wanted universal access to the trains. 'I think it very desirable', he said, 'that we should, if possible, give to the poor the same comforts which are enjoyed by the rich, not only as regards travelling, but every other matter'. And, as with postage, economies of scale seemed to promise an easy marriage of equity and economy. '[A] very large addition', Hill said, 'may be made to the traffic with a comparatively small addition to the expense'. The railway, as George Stephenson's son and partner put it, 'is intended for all classes'. In Britain it was especially urgent that the poor should be able to use the trains because rail traffic put other forms of public transport out of business. Third-class carriages attracted large numbers, although many were unroofed and unglazed and some had no seats. Only after some years was it possible for everyone to travel shut in from the weather, to share in the 'luxurious confusion' described by Dickens.[42]

In Australia there was no such debate about the poor, but only because this was a country, as it seemed, where the mass could afford to travel when they liked. The incapable few hardly mattered. Just as newspapers were read here by working men and women far more than they were in Britain, so it must be with train travel. Here, said the surveyor-general in Melbourne, thanks to 'the generally prosperous condition of the people ... the passenger traffic will be greater, in proportion to our numbers, than in any country under the sun'. In Victoria there was no third class at all, as if in declaration that the poor did not exist. In New South Wales, as in England, there were carriages open to the wind but on pleasant days even the rich could have no objection to travelling in them.[43] George Want, killed in the accident of 1858, had earned so much in life that (as the government agreed) only £10,000 could compensate his widow for his death. He had been reading the morning paper in a third-class carriage.[44]

Railways managers aimed to encompass the entire body of each nation, its geographical limits and all its people. Steam trains, said the Sydney *Herald*, will carry 'intellectual dominion ... to the furthest region of this island-continent'. They would be 'the connecting hand between town and town, and village and village'. They would reflect, in other words, the myriad traffic and wonderful interconnectedness of Creation itself. Women passengers were fully catered for. At colonial railway stations there were 'ladies waiting rooms', each with a fireplace and meant as a homely corner within the great web of machinery, and travelling itself, in both Britain and Australia, was as private as possible. Small carriages and compartments were preferred to the many-seated cars used in the United States, with each resembling a tiny drawing room. In Victoria first-class carriages had mahogany panelling, Brussels carpet, and seats of imitation morocco beaded with gilt.[45]

The first railways, in both Britain and Australia, depended on free enterprise. But it was soon clear that wherever railway lines and railway traffic crossed and connected, they needed some single, overseeing power. Besides, only governments had the capital to make such projects secure. From the late 1850s all Australian steam trains were managed by the state. Each railway system was itself a vast engine.[46]

This precision, manifest in the shriek of the whistle, made its mark on life beyond the tracks. It affected the way in which many people thought about time. Before the railways there had been no need for any single, nationwide system of timekeeping. Each small community, in Australia as in Europe, looked to its own clocks, with no supreme point of reference. There was no standard time and travellers reset their watches, if they had any, wherever they stopped. For those within its reach, railway traffic changed all that. Robert Boan's hope of making up two minutes between Sydney and Parramatta was a symptom of the new regime. Trains had to run according to a single timetable and railway station clocks became a crucial point of reference.[47] In remote places, of course, the world might continue at its old pace. Ann Kershaw, who kept a bark hut near Tumut, south of the Murrumbidgee, said of herself, 'I don't know what month it is. I don't know what year this is ... my occupation is only doing the work of my house at home'.[48] And yet a single united territory (one nation) and a single united idea of time were now the main underpinnings of government and from an official perspective, Mrs Kershaw was an anomaly. The stationmasters were even more accountable to each other and to the centre of power than magistrates had been under Governor Arthur (Chapter 4). Most of all they had to watch their clocks. So many 'traffic transactions' depended on the turning hands.

Everyone who joined in the movement of the trains, as George Stephenson said, 'must take the speed that is prepared for him'. Each, echoed his country-man John Ruskin with disgust, thus became 'a living parcel'.[49]

III

Frances de Courcy said her husband was 'deranged'. She used the same word for herself – after the accident she was 'deranged, almost, for a time'. To be deranged was to be derailed. The mind went off its tracks. Insanity was a topic of particular interest now, partly because of the scientific con-cern with human behaviour, the emergence of psychology and sociology. But it also offered – and offers – a brilliant contrast to the symptoms of rea-son and purpose so obvious everywhere, and in train travel most of all.

In England in the 1840s new legislation and the formation of a national inspectorate forced every county to establish an asylum for lunatics, using the latest methods of management. The immediate experience with these asylums matched that of the railways. Just as the trains created their own market by encouraging people to travel, so the new asylum policy 'created' madness. In Britain the numbers sent straightaway for incarceration far outstripped the predictions of the planners.[50]

Drawing the insane apart, into their own institutions, raised a vital question. These repositories of madness defined the boundaries of reason. But were the inmates mainly sane or mainly mad? Might they, or most of them, be cured and returned to the real world, the world of railways, crys-tal palaces, and vanilla soda? Or were they disabled in some fundamental way? At first the more optimistic doctrine prevailed. Asylums were re-named 'hospitals for the insane' and men and women were taken in with a kind of certainty that most would soon be better. Insanity was said to be caused mainly by emotional distress, by some great sadness. Sufferers belonged among us, then, in tender and powerful ways. Often, surely, they might be reasoned into sense.

Rightly heard, lunatic conversation was drenched with feeling, with a strange combination of glassy light and tunnel-like darkness. In February 1854, for instance, Francis Cockburn, an English traveller, visited the asy-lum at New Norfolk, 20 miles from Hobart, in which were held the certi-fied lunatics of Van Diemen's Land:

> One little man, a Frenchman, who had been long in the Asylum, introduced himself to us with a polite bow and a smirk (he had such a mouth!) and begged the official guide to 'show his apartments'; we were accordingly

ushered into a cell (one of eight opening into a passage,) ventilated from above, in which the little man lived. ...

After hunting all through his Bible twice, the little man found and insisted on my reading a verse from, 'Ecclesticks' as he called it. He then favoured us with an oration in almost the following words, "I asked the Doctor for a goose, and he told me it was too big; I then asked him for a fowl, and he told me that it was too big; I then asked him for a pigeon, and he told me that it was too big; I then asked him for a gun that I might go out and shoot some birds to make a pie with, but he would not; gentlemen, *have you some* small change about you?[51]

All this Cockburn published in the story of his travels. In Brisbane, in the new colony of Queensland (see below), when the administration of madness was called into question, the tales of people recently confined were cited at length in parliament. Similarly, in Melbourne there was a coronial inquiry lasting twelve days into the treatment of local lunatics, most of them inmates of the Yarra Bend asylum, and it relied partly on the word of the sufferers themselves. [52] With their often angry grasp on truth, or at least on some truth of their own, the mad in these years seemed hard to ignore.

In Sydney a select committee of the lower house devoted three days to the case of Joseph Wilkes, once a convict on Norfolk Island and now a shepherd in a remote part of the Clarence River valley. Wilkes had made a powerful demand for justice. His wife and two sons had been brutally murdered and, as he told the committee, the magistrate had taken no notice of the obvious suspect. Instead he himself had been arrested and the gentleman had laughed as his wife was dragged away, so he said, for burial. It was a long story, driven by a deep sense of injury but coolly told. Only in time did it dawn on his listeners, sitting in their summer-hot committee room, that Wilkes himself was the likely killer. Had he persuaded himself of his own innocence? They called in Francis Campbell, physician at the Tarban Creek asylum, to hear the man talk about his night-time dreams in prison, in which, he said, he had seen his wife and children:

> Will you give us an account of the conversation? I could almost repeat it word for word. The first sign that I saw of her was my son. My son was standing at my feet, calling out 'Father!'
>
> Where were you then? In the lock-up.
>
> Were you asleep? Between sleep and awake; I was sitting up with the blanket round me so. (*Witness assumes the attitude.*)
>
> Did you at the time, and do you still believe, that you veritably saw her? Yes, I firmly believe that my child was at my feet. He called out 'Father!' I opened my eyes, and stared him full in face.

And, 'He says, "Don't fret, father," says he, "I am happy." I attempted to get up and lay hold of him, but he vanished out of my sight.' Under pressure

Wilkes agreed that these things had not really happened. He stuck to the main part of his story, but it, too, sounded like fantasy to his listeners, though anchored more deeply than his dreams.[53]

By the 1850s each of the colonies had its lunatic asylum, crammed with men and women more or less like these. The keeper at Yarra Bend managed, he said, 'divinities, kings, queens, emperors, prophets, millionaires and speculators', as well as 'several religious enthusiasts or fanatics'.[54] Each was erratic and a world alone. How were theories of interconnectedness, the precise and hopeful theories of the day, to be maintained in such places? There were examples of cheerfulness, as with the New Norfolk Frenchman, but most of the inmates were buried in their own sad past and present. 'I believe many who are insane or infirm of mind', remarked a gentleman who had seen asylums in three colonies, 'have become so from disappointment upon their arrival here – from not being in the position they expected, and depression of mind from any cause, or from excess of drink'.[55] There was a link, in short, between the high hopes of immigrants (Chapters 5 and 7)

A picnic at Heidelberg, near Melbourne, for the inmates of the Yarra Bend Lunatic Asylum, a drawing by Samuel Calvert. Quiet pleasures such as this were designed to nourish peace within troubled minds.

Source: *Illustrated Melbourne Post*, 24 January 1867, reproduction
courtesy of State Library of Victoria

and the crowded asylums. In Victoria the number of men admitted to Yarra Bend grew fivefold during the first two years of the goldrush. Women especially seemed to show their suffering in madness. Of the thirty-five brought to Yarra Bend in 1853, the mind of one had collapsed, it was said, from 'jealousy', another from 'fatigue', two from 'disappointed hopes', and five from 'grief'. God figured especially in the conversations of the women, but the men, too, felt his brutal and arbitrary power.[56]

New principles for the treatment of the insane had been laid down in England by Samuel Tuke, a Quaker, in 1813. Before Tuke experts had said that reason might be restored only by a regime of terror. Physical restraint and beatings had been the usual treatment in the old asylums. Tuke argued for gentleness, and this certainly made sense if madness was caused by grief. The mad must be made to understand that they were not alone. They must be nourished with all possible compassion. Finely worked moral influence, peace and pleasant surroundings held out most hope. Much depended on entirely new buildings, carefully designed and set in spacious grounds.

Some called this the 'soothing system'. For a long time it had seemed to contradict common sense. In the 1830s writers who wanted harsher measures against Aborigines and recalcitrant convicts had called any policy of kindness a 'soothing system', as if savages, criminals, and madmen were all alike. But by the 1840s in Britain, and by the 1850s in Australia, Tuke's principles began to prevail. They were in keeping with the march of civilisation, including new ideas about violence. Their first important advocate in Australia was Robert Willson, Catholic Bishop of Hobart Town, who as a priest in England had helped in the management of his local county asylum and had had several lunatics in his own house. He helped to make the Tasmanian asylum pre-eminent throughout the colonies and he was heard with attention in Sydney and Melbourne. Any of us might be mad one day, said Willson, the dispensation of God being entirely unpredictable. We were surrounded by madness as we were surrounded by death, and that vast fact made it necessary that the management of the insane be utterly changed. There should be new sites, carefully chosen, and large buildings designed on the latest principles, almost regardless of expense. The bishop's first scheme for Tasmania would have cost £65,000, far beyond local resources. In Victoria a government report suggested a building worth $162,313 – more than the sum so far set aside for the new parliament house.[57]

The management of lunacy involved a tangle of moral problems symptomatic of the time. Like free enterprise, like railway dreaming, it called for the reconciliation of impulse and order. Humanity was now defined by the possession of reason. System was the best means of hope. But here were men and women without reason or system. They must be confined and kept in order. But if they were to recover they must also feel free. They must be kept from society and yet they were to be considered social beings. Their behaviour was wild, even violent, but it must be measured and tabulated. Every well settled national population was supposed to contain a fixed proportion of madness and, just as the experts had predicted, the numbers confined in this country grew as the population stabilised and aged – in Victoria in 1869 the proportion per head was found to have doubled in ten years.[58] However, by this time some of the mysteries of the mad had become less intriguing. Tuke's teaching had become common knowledge and untrained amateurs like Willson had given way to men with more professional assurance. The leading figure by the end of the 1860s was Frederick Norton Manning, a physician whom the Sydney government had sent to Europe and North America to investigate the latest methods and who returned with a precise and voluminous report. He was then appointed superintendent at Tarban Creek, which he reformed and renamed 'Gladesville'.[59]

Manning was also an apostle of order among the lunatics of Queensland. In some sense Queensland was itself a kind of hallucination, a mixture of waking and dreaming. Victoria had been separated from the Sydney government in 1851. In the same way, in December 1859, all those parts of New South Wales beyond 29 degrees latitude were cut away, a fifth of the continent with a coastline stretching nearly 1500 miles northward to Cape York. Thus was created the sixth and last of the Australian colonies. It was also the only one to be self-governing from the moment of its birth. Moreton Bay (Brisbane) had been the site of a penal settlement from 1824 to 1839, the Darling Downs had been settled by squatters since 1840, and more recently there had been police establishments not only at Brisbane but also at Port Curtis (Gladstone). But otherwise the paraphernalia of independent power started from nothing. Much depended on the initiative of first Governor, Sir George Bowen, and it was largely because of Bowen that for the time being Queensland did not use manhood suffrage. Squatters were given a monopoly of the nominated upper house and the first premier, R.G.W. Herbert, was the Governor's former secretary.[60] There was little institutional habit or institutional cunning. Unanchored in settled public opinion, in custom or routine, much in Queensland depended for a while on faith almost as drifting as that of Joseph Wilkes.

Just as the older colonies had been a frontier for British capital, Queensland was a hopeful place for speculators living in Sydney, Adelaide, and Melbourne and for squatters short of pasture in the older places of settlement. Possibilities seemed limitless. Sometime beforehand the country at the head of the Gulf of Carpentaria had been visited by the naval explorer John Lort Stokes. It dazzled him just as Queensland as a whole dazzled many. Struck by the sheer vacancy of the air itself – by 'the intensely blue and gloriously bright skies', unsmudged, as it seemed, even by smoke from Aboriginal camps – Stokes had thought it certain that this remote land must be thick one day with 'christian hamlets'. He envisaged 'tapering spires' holding down the blue.[61] Many since agreed that the Gulf would soon draw a busy and copious traffic from India, China, Japan, and the intervening islands. Meanwhile, steam power – ships and trains – would surely solve most of the problems of distance from the south.

The Reverend John Dunmore Lang had suggested that there should be three new colonies in the north-east, which he named Cooksland, Leichartsland, and Flindersland, linked by steamships and with trains running over thousands of miles to converge at Burketown, the Gulf capital and future gateway to eastern Australia. Hopes for Queensland had a blurred and hurtling form and during its first years there was a feeling of intense competition throughout Australia for a stake in those parts. Even as the Brisbane government began to act, a Melbourne writer told the *Argus* that Victoria should make a claim by spinning off a track from its own rail network to the northern coast. There were fortunes to be made there, he said, in cotton and wool. 'We live in fast times certainly', the editor replied. Such wonders would shortly be upon us. But a railway to Burketown, he said, must wait until that place (in the twenty-first century still a small village) became a city.[62]

To begin with settlement was concentrated in the south-east corner, including Moreton Bay, Maryborough, Rockhampton, and the Darling Downs, with a little pocket to the north around Gladstone. In 1861 Europeans numbered 30,000. Ten years later there was four times that number, squatters had extended to the Gulf and only Cape York and the extreme west and south-west were untouched by White ambition. But during that decade there was little of the multifarious skill that was already taken for granted as part of government elsewhere. Railways took a little time to establish, public health was rarely debated, and there was meagre faith, apparently, in the 'chemistry of life'.

The same was true of the management of the insane. For some time the only individual in Queensland who showed an up-to-date interest in lunatic asylums was the government architect, Charles Tiffin, who had visited New Norfolk, Yarra Bend, and Tarban Creek and who made his own proposal for Queensland, stone-built and costing £80,000. The block he meant as offices was in fact built at Woogaroo, on the river between Brisbane and Ipswich, but nothing more was added and it sat in its broad acreage, another promise for the future, sheltering under its inadequate roof about a hundred inmates.[63] A medical man from Brisbane with an interest in madness visited the place in late summer 1869. First he inspected the women, who were gathered on the verandah, their only source of shade. All were 'jumbled up together', with no attempt at classification, the clean among the dirty, the wild among the silent; 'some quiet, modest-looking women' mixed with 'coarse, immodest, raving maniacs – continually giving utterance to the foulest language, at the loudest pitch of their voices'. He looked in on the men. There had been summer rain, mud was several inches deep and several, he said, were 'simply wallowing like pigs in the mire'.[64]

Many Queenslanders might aim to extend their power to Cape York and the Gulf. The people at Woogaroo fixed their thoughts on littler things – though one called himself 'the Omnipotent God' and said his home was heaven. Some heads and faces were bright red because, as proof of independent thought, they refused to keep their hats on. During cold nights the women could not be persuaded to keep their window closed. Henry Challinor, the surgeon superintendent, at first tried to check on the female inmates after they had gone to bed. '[T]hey resented my visit so much that I have not repeated it.'[65] Certainly, the worries of a few were larger. Michael Fahey was deeply miserable because his scapularies (bands worn over the shoulders by Catholic priests) had been taken away, ending, as he thought, his certainty of salvation. John Clancy had to have exactly the same diet each day. Even a touch of milk in his tea he said was poison.[66]

It was easy to lose patience with the mad. In spite of the principles of the 'soothing system' few could be reasoned into health. In due course, here and abroad, insanity began to be attributed to physical causes rather than moral and emotional ones. It was to be cured, if at all, not by forbearance but by medical treatment. There was a dwindling interest in making inmates content and attention turned instead to their physical state. Their voices mattered less and everything was to be deduced from their behaviour and colouring – external abnormalities in life and internal abnormalities in death (if they seemed worth a post-mortem).[67] By this time, at Woogaroo, a series of scandals had forced on government the need to make a radical change. Frederick Norton Manning was called to Brisbane, where he inspected the asylum and spoke before a select committee. A decade earlier there had been no doubt that the care of the insane was a labour of love. Bishop Willson had certainly thought so. But Manning – his language inexorably modern – stressed efficiency for its own sake. '[W]e like to put it on a philanthropic basis', he said, but really we delude ourselves. The main point was 'commercial'. The mad were to be cured, if possible, in order 'to relieve the state of the expense they entail'.[68]

Public opinion might be persuaded still to feel a passing sympathy. The tales of the mad seemed worth hearing, like cries from one's darker self. In each of the colonies newspapers had been happy to carry evidence of mistreatment, and in Queensland the movement for reform had begun only when the papers took it up. 'I am – mad at times', says the Reverend Josiah Crawley, in Anthony Trollope's *Last Chronicle of Barset* (1867). Trollope was a bestselling author, here as in Britain, and his narrative in this case partly turned on Mr Crawley's delusions about past events, including his own actions. What were we to make of such uneven and deeply disconnected ideas of reality? Should we believe, so the parliamentarians in Brisbane asked Manning, the tales of cruelty from Woogaroo? No, was the answer, 'such evidence is not to be relied upon'. The recollections of former lunatics were, for the most part, 'utterly incorrect'. Indeed, 'the persons themselves are often ready to admit it when pressed, although they may think they are speaking the truth at the time the statements are made.'[69]

In fact, to take a larger view of the history of the Europeans in Australia, the same could be said of many never judged to be mad. As time passes and imagination fails, any story, whether sad or exciting, might be emptied of all but a very shadowy and feeble truth. Looking beyond immediate experience, vivid things are to be glimpsed merely on their passing our window. They are to be remembered as Dickens recalled his stay on the Moon.

For a while many were angered by the stories of the insane. Such wild and apparently unnecessary pain was easily shared. The remedy – unlimited kindness and large sums of money – was thought to be at hand. But this was one of those issues, as a Melbourne doctor said at the time, where excited talk, even among the experts, was bound to be exhausted very quickly. Like lunatic rage itself, 'it ends in a frenzy', he said, 'and the passion dissipates'.[70] Our eyes were soon on other things.

Chapter 14

To Feel as One

I

The democratic settlement, as I call it, did not offer uniform and perfect happiness. Votes for all men did not meet many of the deeper needs of the Europeans in Australia. The 'chemistry of life' was not obviously identical with the myriad undercurrents of human affection – though some men and women, who appear in the final chapter, said it was. Reason often contradicted faith. Few of the best things here and now, let alone in the hereafter, were to be nicely embraced by iron and glass.

Europeans in Europe were sometimes just as disenchanted with the tangible aspects of human progress. The poet Matthew Arnold complained,

> ... the world, which seems
> To lie before us like a land of dreams,
> So various, so beautiful, so new,
> Hath really neither joy, nor love, nor light,
> Nor certitude, nor peace, nor help for pain.[1]

He meant, of course, something beyond the pain that bothered individuals like Richard Tracy.

Queensland was a 'land of dreams'. It was a space abundant, so it seemed, with the promises of the day (Chapter 13). In Europe, the same was true of Italy – a place likewise of 'intensely blue and gloriously bright skies' – that for centuries had consisted of a mass of smaller states. In 1861, as the *Sydney Morning Herald* put it, these antique fragments were plunged into a 'revolutionary crucible' and drawn out as one nation, enamelled over with a single idea.[2] The Italians were Catholic, but their new government was designed to be secular, to be managed with a detachment and expertise that had nothing to do with religion. Italy was to be a nation of railways, science, and free enterprise.[3] To begin with, the Pope, Pius IX, remained an independent prince, ruling Rome and a large territory beyond, but in 1870 an Italian army entered the Eternal City and the papal dominions were cut back to a nest of suburbs, the Vatican State.

The battle waged by Pius IX against the new Italy and all it stood for mirrored many battles throughout the European world. The Pope was an enemy of democracy and liberalism. And yet, he was not perfectly reactionary. In order to outflank secular teaching he managed his Church in modern ways and during his time there was new life in Catholic piety. His was a distinctive kind of empire, and it included the Catholic population of Australia.

Indeed, religion of all kinds began to work in a vastly extended fashion. In spite of Matthew Arnold, the new generation – the younger men and women of the 1860s – looked to new methods of certitude, of peace, of help for pain. These methods had a common origin with the methods of the secular state, but they called for a different kind of allegiance. Arnold thought they were rubbish:

> Great qualities are trodden down,
> And littleness united
> Is become invincible.[4]

Millions disagreed. Among the images displaced at this time, to the regret of some like Arnold, was that of God as a figure of inscrutable power – the God of still, small voices, the God of thunder. Inscrutability of any sort seemed to be a thing of the past. It was candour that mattered now.

The efficiency of written communication, its frequency and bulk, its vivid style – like electricity – meant a new kind of spiritual community. It created a new quality of relationship between individuals and among masses. Just as manhood and womanhood were embodied on paper (Chapter 7), so one might imagine, with the aid of writing, a physical link with the rest of humanity. This was a global age.

Technological and administrative invention made the difference. Paper was crammed with living chat (Chapter 12), for which distance seemed immaterial. Photograph portraits, mounted as *cartes de visites* and broadcast to family and friends, might carry the face with the voice. Even the semi-literate wrote with an idea that space between hemispheres was no more than space between pages:

> One moring before brakefast [this is Edward Payne, a labouring man, on an Australian goldfield, telling a story to his family in England] I was standing at the fire and I seen a man coming swing a long and he came up to me and says doue you no a man by the name ted payne I tuch my nos and said heare he stands doant you com from Aylesbury and I say yes and he says dont you no me and lafed I said Jack is that you and he said it is.[5]

That touching of the nose, that laughter, repeated in the letter, echoing again among readers in Aylesbury, Buckinghamshire, summed up all the liveliness of steam-powered script.

The mass market for newspapers and for books added to the community of feeling. Herman Melville seemed to think that his readers might see his lips, or rather the lips of Ishmael, his hero, moving as he told his story of *Moby-Dick* (Chapter 12). Anne Brontë was interested in the dimensions and power of the soul and in *The Tenant of Wildfell Hall* she had something to say about the new possibilities of spiritual life. Even if we never meet again, say her two lovers, we will write. Love's spiritual perfection is possible – even exquisitely refined – in the ready exchange of letters, for thus 'kindred spirits meet, and mingle in communion, whatever be the fate and circumstances of their earthly tenements'.[6] The idea that writing might transmit feeling, as it had long done with doctrine, information, and orders, was one that was now taken up with fervent enthusiasm. Spiritual conversation on paper was no longer rare and fragile, no longer limited to individuals of high learning and piety. It belonged to daily life and the common order.

Within a regime of feeling it was possible to create a new kind of relationship between rulers and ruled. The Catholic Church was reinvented in the time of Pius IX and charged with an unprecedented power. Worldwide order was transfigured. So was worldwide time, which was to be like railway time. The sense of a single globe, where the time in each place might be linked with the time everywhere else, even made it possible to feel each other's company in worship, however separate in space. '[Y]ou ask for the time at which on a sabbath our prayers might mingle together', James Wilson in Victoria remarked to his family in England, 'half past one o'clock at noon would answer the best'.[7]

The Europeans in Australia wanted to be tied to the large truths now abroad. They wanted membership of something worldwide. From this time, few people anywhere have been so inventive in cancelling isolation. To effect this cancellation feelings of a global kind were to be closely copied from more palpable sensations. The sense of unity with people at a distance was to be a reflection of feelings face to face, of talk and touch. The work began in a systematic way among the churches.

In the 1860s people in this country were much more willing to go to church than they had ever been before. The English novelist, Anthony Trollope, visiting Australia in 1871–72, was struck with the evidence of piety. Even more than in England, he said, 'religious teaching, and the exercise of religious worship, are held as being essential to civilization and well-being'.[8] He thought this keenness was a result of the Australian need for respectability. People here, on the whole, were better off than in England. They were more likely to educate their children and were likely to have been to school themselves. They were therefore more interested in appearances.

'Teaching produces prosperity; prosperity achieves decent garments; – and decent garments', he said, 'are highly conducive to church-going'.[9]

Certainly, churches already prosperous were also the most crowded. In New South Wales (according to the censuses) the number of people who called themselves Church of England grew by less than 50 per cent during the 1860s. But the number of Anglicans going to church more than doubled. It was the same with the Presbyterians, while Catholic congregations grew even more quickly.[10] Methodist churches had always been both numerous and full, and the men, women, and children who went to them were typically well off and well-dressed.

And yet piety in Australia was more than a matter of good clothes. It was part of the peculiar eagerness of the day. The worldwide ambitions of Christianity rested now on global commerce, including the distribution of books and newspapers (carrying many columns of foreign news), easier travel and speedier postage. During 1871 the quantity of new books imported from abroad by the two biggest colonies meant that every inhabitant might have bought two shillings-worth each – several small volumes.[11] Committee work, bookkeeping, letter-writing, and wide reading were all more common than hitherto. Lessons with universal currency, read in worldwide publications, were more easily tied to the events and the feelings of kitchen, street, and school.

In 1864 Pius IX issued his *Syllabus of Errors*, in which he condemned numerous new habits, including 'modern civilization' itself. In 1870 he secured from the First Vatican Council a statement of his own infallibility, when he issued formal edicts on faith and morals. Church hierarchy, reinforced in this way, was replicated in cities and provinces everywhere. By 1860 there were Catholic bishops in Sydney, Hobart, Adelaide, Melbourne, Perth, and Brisbane, and in New South Wales the process soon afterwards extended to Maitland, Bathurst, Goulburn, and Armidale. Most were Irish-born and they brought to Australia not only the growing power of the papacy but also the authoritarian habits of the Irish Church. Each bishop had his own pyramid of priestly officials and each was part of a network of ecclesiastical cooperation throughout Australia and the world. Each diocese made up a pattern of authority much more weighty for the faithful than even the secular state.

The processions of the Catholics, their bright vestments and high titles, their bell-ringing, their great building programs, altogether made a startling claim on the Australian landscape. Within Australian streets and across large expanses of bush they duplicated patterns of worship and reverence that had been laid down for the whole world and which were now enforceable, in detail, as never before. Few parts of the Church were more isolated than Western Australia, and yet the ritual and power of the new papacy were obvious even here. A tiny Catholic population (barely 2000 in 1854) possessed not only two bishops (one nominally attached to the settlement at Port Essington) but also communities of Spanish Benedictines

Mother Ursula Frayne of the Sisters of Mercy, portrait, undated, by an unknown artist. She helped in the administration of her Church in both Western Australia and Victoria. Her expression shows something of the new pleasures of nineteenth-century piety.

Reproduction courtesy of
Sisters of Mercy, Perth

and Irish Sisters of Mercy. The ceremonial life of these men and women and their accents of manner and voice must have shaped local piety in many small ways. The unusual variety – not only English, Irish, and Spanish but also Belgian, Italian, and French – was also proof of a regime which pervaded and subsumed the nations of the earth.

Convict transportation to Western Australia from 1850 and the assisted immigration of many young Irishwomen added to Catholic numbers. Tiny congregations were scattered through the western inland so that the priests were travellers, carrying with them for all occasions their vestments and the wherewithal for mass. In January 1859 Father Martin Griver, a Spaniard, was at Kojunup, near Albany:

> After breakfast I started for Mr Scott's, distant 28 or 30 miles in the bush. Mr Scott is a Protestant; last year I baptized two of his children with the father's consent, and even request. That night, Mrs Evans, who lives a mile away, came with her husband who is a Protestant to prayer and exhortation. Next day Mrs Scott and Mrs Evans came to confession and received holy Communion and I baptized another child of Mrs Scott. I stopt here all day because Mrs Evans wished to have Mass at her house the next day.[12]

Two devout women, Mrs Scott and Mrs Evans, here directed the steps of their priest. At the same time a cathedral was begun in Perth. Part of the cost of the high altar was borne by the King of Naples (soon to be deposed during the unification of Italy).[13] By such means Rome raised its colours in every section of this continent known to Europeans.

Other Christian denominations settled their structures of authority at the same time. They were states within the state (unlike Catholicism, with its sovereign head), but in their case, too, the fundamental purpose was at odds with democracy. Like the Catholics, the Anglicans had their lord bishops and in New South Wales there were enough to make up a provincial synod. The Presbyterians had long been divided into several sects but during 1859–65 most came to terms and joined forces. As in Scotland, Presbyterians had disagreed mainly about the doctrinal correctness of receiving subsidies from government. Now, with the increasing secularisation of the state, it was no longer the duty of government to fund spiritual life and such differences fell away. As in Italy, religion was officially marginalised. It had once owed a good deal to government support. Now it depended altogether on the hopes and feelings of the people.

There was no new doctrine. Indeed, doctrine partly made way for simpler priorities, for notions of universal value that were to be reproduced in a universal way. Inspiration came mainly from the United States, where religious life was in the throes of revival. From sect to sect throughout America a religion of logic and theology was now replaced by a religion of sentiment. Intellect, and the authority embedded in intellect, was replaced by feeling, the purpose of sermons shifted, and the intricacies of ancient faith gave way to the current concerns of home and family. Moral issues, especially drunkenness and temperance, filled the time of Christian ministers and the ministers themselves began to sound more like private men – husbands and fathers distinguished mainly by their superior feelings and eloquence. The American evangelist Henry Earl, for instance, came to Australia in 1864. Preaching here, he used a secular plainness, 'a style totally different', as a Melbourne reporter put it, 'to the received modes of pulpit oratory'.[14] Arguing against alcohol in Adelaide, another American, the Reverend William Taylor, brought the argument back to himself – as a mere man of flesh and feeling. It was a myth, he said, that alcohol was good for your health. 'He had stood the climates of almost every country in the world, with the exception of China, for the last 24 years, without the assistance of any intoxicating drink, and he would now run a race with any of them.' His physical form was an argument in itself. He was over 6 feet, one of his converts recalled, and well proportioned, 'with keen eyes, long flowing beard, and commanding voice'. Taylor spoke of Christ, too, in his mortal form, a non-drinking man as they all might be.[15]

Americans set the pace, but throughout the British Empire the direction was the same and success fed on success. Congregations multiplied. In this age of great cities it seemed good to be swept up in mass feeling, to be enclosed by the crush of crowds and to hear about other crowds equally moved – to read in the monthlies now published by all the more active sects about the great movements to which one belonged. In the schools new ideas about teaching stressed the usefulness of large classes and 'the sympathy of

numbers'.[16] Numbers – numbers of children, of factories, of national population – were proof of life's abundance. In religious worship a sense of
believers existing in unseen millions was combined with a sense of the eternal. We thus felt and heard about us, even beyond our own congregation, a
haunting and stately sweetness. As the Adelaide naturalist said of his honey-
scented bees (quoted above, at the opening of Part 3), Christians 'began to
set their wings in motion, and the buzzing of one soon excited others to follow its example'. There was a thrill in moving, as with any great body of
creatures, through such preordained cycles of emotion. Many times over, as
Thomas Carlyle remarked, in Christian ritual 'inmost ME is ... brought into
contact with inmost ME!'[17]

Shared excitement in any species depends on affinity, on like in step
with like. In this sense Trollope was right when he said that current piety
depended on 'decent garments'. It was easier to go to church when all felt
as one, properly dressed – when, like the bees, it was clear that all were of
one type. Also, these were mainly literate people. As Trollope said, they
had obviously been to school. Aware, in many cases, that they had done
better than their parents, they were self-consciously skilled and refined. I
say above (Chapter 1) that communities not much touched by literacy –
previously the case with many of the Europeans in Australia – were governed mainly by living speech. Such people understood humanity itself in
distinctive ways, keenly imagining, for instance, a reflection of themselves
in the voices and individual character of animals. Times had changed and
this was not true, generally, of the men and women Trollope saw. There
was now a closing of the ears in such matters. The imagined speech of animals – even the coarser voices of one's own kind – might be less interesting
now among the better read.

And not only less interesting. Such sounds and habits might seem posi-
tively repulsive. Charles Darwin's *Origin of Species* (1859) declared that
human beings were biologically connected with animals. Though few at
first grasped much of Darwin's ideas, these ideas, or rather this cast of
imagination, was common among younger men and women. Earlier generations had looked for hints of themselves in the animals they lived
among. Now the relationship was turned upside down. Men and women
saw hints of the animal – the wild, the dirty, the apparently aimless –
within humanity. It was a phenomenon they felt duty-bound to rise above.

In some churches ceremonies were more vivid than they had been in the
previous generation, with flowers set on the altar and surpliced choirs.
Colour and music became more central to church life. The singing of songs,
once mainly favoured by Methodists, became part of the Sunday liturgy of
other sects. Hymnbooks appeared in large numbers, with *Hymns Ancient
and Modern* (1861) an authorised work among Anglicans. The tones of
women and children thus entrenched everywhere on sacred time and space,
and the sound of one's own voice, carried up with so many more, became

a magnet for worshippers. Hymns and reshaped sermons meant a new idiom interwoven with psalms and scripture.[18]

In the previous generation 'New Testament Christianity' – a spirituality dwelling on the simple moral lessons taught by Jesus – had been preached by a leading few (Chapter 9). Something similar now touched the mass. It was manifest in ideas of ordinary kindness but also in exclamations of affection:

> How sweet the Name of Jesus
> sounds in a believer's ear!
> It soothes his sorrows, heals his wounds,
> and drives away his fear.
> It makes the wounded spirit whole,
> and calms the troubled breast;
> 'tis manna to the hungry soul,
> and to the weary, rest.[19]

God the avenger made his impact still, but less than hitherto. There was also less of that intellectual precision, that anxious theological inquiry, with which his Word had long been examined – and partly understood.

A new denomination, the Church (or Churches) of Christ, two or three generations old, offered a peculiarly neat answer to current hopes. Its origins were both British and American. Members simply called themselves 'Christians' and among themselves their message seemed so obviously true that they were sure the millions of other believers divided into sects throughout the world would quickly join them. They placed their faith in the New Testament, which they read as a message with one meaning for all, but they had their own publications, including the monthly *British Millennial Harbinger*. 'The desired unity can be found nowhere but in Christ and His simple word.' That word was to be interpreted by the moral sense of clear-thinking humanity, by the feelings of closeness, which came not only from two or three being gathered together but also from steam power and reliable postage. Precise theology, going beyond scripture, they saw as a source of argument – and 'Division among Christians', they said, 'is antichristian'. They had no trained ministry to start with, no one with doctrinal authority, and members depended on each other. Their gatherings therefore differed somewhat, because of their varied origins. The first in Adelaide, in the late 1840s, had been Scotch Baptists. The first in Sydney had been Wesleyan Methodists.[20] Such distinctions were considered immaterial.

In Victoria during the 1860s the Church of Christ was one of the ten leading sects (counting Sunday worshippers). It was also one of the few with more women than men. In South Australia the numbers were apparently even larger.[21] Though a worldwide communion, each fragment was self-governing. 'The One Body', its leaders said, 'manifests its life in numerous separate congregations'. Worshippers might meet in family groups, or less. In Victoria, according to the 1871 census, there were five individuals (boys or men) worshipping in a place or places near Winchelsea, there were two males and two females (perhaps a family) near Mount Greenock, and two females near Port Fairy. From gathering to gathering there were varied voices – singing their hymns together sometimes with no instruments beyond a tuning fork or pitch pipe.[22]

This was a rational age but it was also an age of apocalyptic hope. Who might set a boundary to divine emotion? The answer was vague – being anchored in feeling – but also strangely certain:

> Jesus shall reign where e'er the sun
> doth his successive journeys run;
> his kingdom stretch from shore to shore,
> till moons shall wax and wane no more.[23]

Singers of this generation told each other of a new day dawning, a new completeness. In time – out of time – the world, they were sure, would feel as 'One Body'.

II

The prophet of the Christian Israelites, John Wroe, had told his people in 1843 that when Christ's kingdom was established, when God gathered up his people, then, 'as a man's body is convulsed by fits, so this planet will be convulsed in the same way, till all the islands of the sea become one, and Jerusalem be in the centre of it' (Chapter 9).[24] The Europeans in Australia now began to experience some of this gathering to one point, in time and space. The Christian Israelites themselves continued to meet, although their numbers did not grow as those of other sects did. Melbourne in particular had begun to matter in their scheme of things. Wroe visited several times, he died at Fitzroy in 1863, and his headquarters in Yorkshire, Melbourne House, had been built with local gifts. In this and other ways Melbourne was a place where spiritual eagerness was marvellously present.[25]

Now from Melbourne emerged a Messiah. James Fisher had been a goldminer and he owned 140 acres at Nunawading, at the edge of the suburbs. 'His appearance is prepossessing', said an otherwise sceptical observer, 'for he has a fine well-knit figure'. His eyes were haggard and eager and his face showed much intelligence, 'but bearing the stamp of thought not culture'. Though the son of an English magistrate Fisher was largely illiterate. However, it was not learning that mattered now in gathering souls. He had been a Christian Israelite and he saw himself as John Wroe's successor, but also as the long-awaited offspring of the English seer, Joanna Southcott. He was heir as well to his own mother-in-law, Emma

Kefford, founder of the New Church of the Firstborn at Nunawading – a preacher herself frequently possessed by divine power. For several years Mrs Kefford's disciples had carried her message in preaching circuits beyond her home. With her encouragement James Fisher proclaimed himself the reincarnated Christ, demanding that believers obey him before all earthly powers.[26]

Fisher remembered hanging on the Cross, so he said, 'just as well as he remembered eating his supper last night'. But his authority on such points might have depended partly on the word of Emma Kefford. For instance, Fisher told one of his followers, Hyem Rintel, that he wanted Rintel's wife in addition to his own. The two were sisters. Rintel was stunned. He consulted Mrs Kefford, mother to both women, pointing out to her that Fisher's claim was forbidden by scripture itself. It was also, of course, contrary to the law of the state. The old woman was unmoved. 'She, to my surprise', said Rintel, 'declared that Fisher must be obeyed. ... "Oh", said she, "the Lord can do as he pleases"'.[27]

James Fisher and Pope Pius IX were very different. But both asked for a loyalty that transcended the tangible and secular. The stories they told their own faithful – millions in one case, less than fifty in the other – were vast indeed. During the 1860s Australia was visited by a number of men who represented, in various ways, similarly large and impalpable things. They gave the people glimpses beyond themselves and beyond colonial boundaries and they were met with enormous enthusiasm. The American evangelists already mentioned prefigured a time, near at hand, when Australia would be part of an international market in lecture tours. The Duke of Edinburgh – Prince Alfred – visited all the colonies during 1867–68 and was welcomed by cheering thousands as 'the representative of our ancient monarchy and our beloved Queen'. Trollope the novelist came partly to see his son, a squatter, and he was under commission to write a book about Australia. He travelled widely, writing as he went, but to the intense disappointment of the large numbers who read his stories, he gave only two public talks, in Hobart and in Melbourne.[28]

In Melbourne 3000 people heard Trollope speak on 'English Prose Fiction as a Rational Amusement'. Novels, the great man said, were part of daily life and good novels told truths of the most important kind. 'The novelist deals with the false and the forward as well as with the good and the gracious – with lust as well as love.' And, he said, 'did not Scripture teaching do the same?' The 'holiest of human ties' (as a party of Australian women put it) were the intimate ties of marriage and of blood.[29] Thus Trollope was right. Stories about home and family, with perfect assurance, made their way like hymns into our spiritual life.

Lust and love, romance and affection, were the most interesting issues of the day. Possessed of their own mystery and rationale, how might the state be used to affirm these new priorities of feeling? In 1857 the British parliament established a divorce court for English couples, replacing a system in which divorce had been more or less impossible. Now men and women in England might free themselves from spouses who had committed adultery, although women had to prove that their husbands had also beaten or deserted them, were bigamous, or guilty of some abominable sexual crime. Throughout the empire many insisted still that marriage was a sacred institution, an act of God, which no human agency could undo. But the tone and purposes of matrimony were changing. As with George and Margaret Stevenson (Chapter 7), husband and wife were more often seen as friends, even as equals, as rational beings who had freely agreed to share each other's lives and who, in extreme cases, might part and marry elsewhere. Men and women were to be guided by feeling, and feeling was subject to change.

In daily life there was less ceremony now between the sexes. The current generation, said Wilkie Collins in his highly popular story, *The Woman in White* (1859), lacked 'the formal grace and refinement of the old school of politeness'.[30] But as a result good marriage was all the more pleasant. In the words of John Stuart Mill (referring to the well read):

> The association of men with women in daily life is much closer and more complete than it ever was before. Men's life is more domestic. Formerly, their pleasures and chosen occupations were among men, and in men's company; their wives had but a fragment of their lives.

Men spent less time now, he said, among 'rough amusements and convivial excesses'. Their interests were less coarse and women, in turn, were likely to share them. The apparently happy mockery of men by women (Chapter 12) summed up the uncertain – often superficial – equality now common in the middle and upper ranks of life.[31]

In marriage, according to St Paul, a man and a woman became 'one flesh', a unity sacred and fixed. The divorce law cut across the doctrine built on such sayings – nothing was to be fixed anymore in this way – but it was not wholly radical. Certainly, it gave men and women unequal rights and it made everything depend on adultery. 'One flesh' might cease to be 'one flesh', especially, so it seemed, by the adultery of the wife. And yet in the debates on divorce even adultery was newly understood. Adultery still corrupted the sanctity of marriage but it was just as important in proving the vicissitudes of feeling. Instructed by numerous novels, men and women now laid down laws about the way marriage worked. Fiction, even bad fiction, trained their imagination and refined their sense of right. Trollope, for instance, said little about adultery, but his intricate stories about power and moral sensibility within married life made readers see a larger patterning in their own. Clearly, feeling was both long- and short-term. A man or woman might be 'unfeeling' for a while (cold and selfish) without losing the genuine feeling of a husband or wife. Divorce laws had to register that fact.

But they must also – this was the prevailing opinion – register a difference between the sexes. In the New South Wales parliament, when members came to discuss the subject, one of them explained that a man in his travels might be tempted into adultery and yet still love his wife. '[B]ut it was not so with woman', he said (and few disagreed), 'for she never fell until she ceased to love her husband'.[32]

Ministers at Whitehall wanted similar marriage laws to prevail throughout the empire. The marital status of each individual should be the same everywhere and therefore, since such a reform could not be forced on self-governing colonies, all were invited to copy it. This was a cogent appeal to reason, and yet life had its higher loyalties. For every Catholic and for many Anglicans divorce was anathema. Women might be asked to believe that divorce would free them from bad husbands. Marriage, they were told, was not a holy condition, a deep transformation of one's physical self, but a contract. And yet surely, some replied, a wife was God's permanent, perhaps his best, creation. She was not a business partner. If only we could vote, so a married woman told the Sydney *Herald*, we would demonstrate this truth. Our feelings, she said, were certainly beyond those of the men who would force a divorce law on us. 'If, Sir, we are labouring under a delusion as to the binding and sacred nature of the contract – as some men term it – that we have entered into ... do they imagine we should be thankful to have it so rudely dissipated by such coarse and unskillful hands?'[33] Resistance of this kind held up divorce reform in several colonies, as late as 1873 in New South Wales, but all eventually succumbed.

For many of the Europeans in Australia the future of civilisation depended on the education of feeling, on the abolition of coarseness, including drunkenness and violence. The refinement of the poor seemed most urgent, especially their family lives. In the 1820s and '30s savings banks had been established in most of the Australian colonies, making it possible for labouring men and women to plan for the future, to form for their own households habits of prudence and foresight (Chapter 11). Success in this regard came very slowly and yet, at the same time, some among the well read became more ambitious. One of the great projects of the 1850s was the better management of the children of the poor. Many parents seemed to lack the ability or will to plan not only for themselves but also for their offspring and just as their savings had sometimes been taken from them (forcibly in the case of convicts) and put away for their benefit, now it seemed useful to think of the removal, in certain cases, of their children. In England in 1851 Mary Carpenter, who had long experience in the teaching of slum children, published a book entitled *Reformatory Schools for the Children of the Perishing and Dangerous Classes and for Juvenile Offenders*. She followed this in 1853 with *Juvenile Delinquents, their Condition and Treatment*. Her arguments helped to shape a body of laws throughout the empire.[34]

As with the reformers of lunatic asylums, Mary Carpenter's writing was persuasive because her purpose was profound. In all children, she said, however difficult, there was 'an indestructible germ of a divine nature'. She also worked from a few basic principles, with terminology to match. She argued for two types of institution, reformatory schools and industrial schools, the first for children convicted of crime and the second for those judged to be neglected or destitute. Just as lunatic asylums were now 'hospitals for the insane' and promised cures, in these schools children would be drawn towards virtue. Their feelings would be softened and refined. '[A]s a general rule', she said, 'all children, however apparently vicious and degraded, are capable of being made useful members of society, and beings acting on a religious principle'.[35]

These ideas were quickly taken up in Australia. From colony to colony during the 1860s children were defined as 'criminal', 'vagrant', 'destitute', or 'neglected' and buildings were set aside as reformatories and industrial schools. For the first time governments gave themselves the power to come between children and their parents, not because any had been criminally convicted but because the children were, as it seemed, wrongly brought up. As with divorce, the state might now disassemble families, though families had long been thought of as the peculiar work of Providence. It was a type of power easily adopted in Australia because governments, especially in the convict colonies, had always been dictatorial. Besides children here were notoriously unruly, compared with children in Europe. Even in prosperous families, as a gentleman told his readers at Home, each 'runs wild in the most extraordinary, and often to his elders, unpleasant freaks'. Many labouring families seemed to abandon discipline altogether. 'Were they left to the care of only their parents', said a member of the Queensland parliament, 'knowing as we do, the little care children often receive in this country from their parents, it is probable they would grow up to be encumbrances to society'.[36]

Only in New South Wales and Victoria were there enough criminal children to justify reformatories. In South Australia, for instance, there was one building for all, the bulk of its inmates having been found (as the local Act put it) begging, wandering homeless, living in a brothel, or otherwise in an unprotected or uncontrollable state.[37] The first permanent home formed under the Act was an old hotel on the beach at Brighton 7 or 8 miles from Adelaide, a thirteen-room building with a detached cottage and stables and holding to begin with ninety-six children. They were visited during the first months by several medical men, who were afterwards questioned by a parliamentary committee in Adelaide. Medical insight alone could reveal the 'chemistry of life' among such a problematic body. 'Moral tone' – 'that subtle and indescribable feeling' to be found in any community and which was similar to the moral character of an individual – was to be read, with requisite skill, in the skin and bearing of its members. The children at Brighton by these criteria were unattractive. At least to start with, they were 'smothered in vermin', the eyes of most were infected with ophthalmia, and nearly all suffered from 'the itch'. Their skin, in general, was dingy, dry, and inflamed.[38]

Skin mattered. Europeans in these days, as the German philosopher Friedrich Nietzsche remarked, took an 'epidermal' interest in the world. What mattered to them, said Nietzsche, were those indications of life – 'warmth, movement, "storm", and undulations' – to be found on the material surface of things.[39] Physical cleanliness was proof of good feeling in every other sense. Moral self-respect depended on physical self-respect, on keeping clean, on acknowledging 'the power of soap and water'. Trollope had spoken of decent garments among church-going Australians. He might had added the evidence of regular washing – washing all over – and sufficient air and food. The native-born poet Charles Tompson (Chapter 1), now clerk of petty sessions at Camden, near Sydney, urged his poorer neighbours to take 'cold plunges and frequent ablutions' if they wanted to remain healthy. A few perhaps, eager to improve themselves, took his advice, and certainly this new sense of a patently cleaner self was not restricted to the well read. In elementary schools everywhere the lesson was the same and the new abundance of ironware, including baths and washstands, made it cheaper and easier to comply. Nevertheless, many among the poor seemed to belong to another age, surrounding themselves still (Chapter 13) with their own filth and the filth of beasts. Medical men often tested their feelings – professional concern as against physical disgust – in dealing with the dirty.[40]

The children at Brighton were tightly crowded and, in a sense, bound even more closely together by shared disease. Their fleas moved among them and their ophthalmia was carried by flies. The itch flourished on warm bodies, packed many abed. The doctors disagreed, however, on the ultimate causes of the itch. So much turned, both morally and physically, on propinquity of skin and it was not always easy to read the symptoms of closeness. (According to Trollope, the slightest pressure in shaking hands might lift, or bewilder, the hopes of lovers. Types of touch were dense with etiquette.) 'Looking over the children', said Dr J.P. Hall, speaking of the itch, 'there was scarcely one of them but what had got some sore – a sore head, sore legs, sore all over … just as if it was some sort of family complaint'. It was impetigo, he said, a well-known ailment but with local peculiarities as a result of food and climate. Dr Thomas Corbin, who had apparently read something of germ theory, spoke of 'itch insects' burrowing in the skin. Dr Robert Moore blamed 'a scrofulous taint in the constitution', caused partly by dirt. The offspring of the poor, he said, grow up dirty and 'children of this stamp will come in with itch'. He handled them carefully. He had been taken aback to see Hall, his colleague, touch a pustule – 'I should be sorry to do it myself'.[41]

Mary Carpenter had argued that institutions for children ought to be like family households, meaning 'decent' families, rich or poor. And yet, among masses of children this was very difficult. The parliamentarians in Adelaide were shocked to learn that for several days the washing arrangements among the reformatory children had involved two baths, for boys and for girls, placed in the same room. Only in time had canvas sheeting been hung between them. So far it had proved impossible not only to prevent overcrowding but also to keep the sexes apart and to prevent those 'attempts at familiarity' that were evidence of coarseness. At Brighton there were separate yards for the girls and boys to play in, but as the matron put it, 'the coals and all these sorts of things are in the girls' yard and the boys are employed to fill the coal scuttles, so that they must go into the girls' yard'.[42] Inevitably, there would be many similar problems until they had a home purpose-built.

The judgment of refined women was vital in such matters. Such women were the best regulators of feeling, of moral delicacy, domestic order, and physical health. Nuns, for instance, working as teachers, were highly important for the authority of the Catholic Church. Their headquarters were typically as close as possible to each cathedral but the women went far afield. Sisters of Mercy and Sisters of Charity were active in numerous dioceses. In Hobart the bishop brought in the Presentation nuns, with his own sister as mother superior. The Bishop of Maitland imported Dominicans. Two new orders were formed in Australia, the Sisters of the Good Samaritan in Sydney and the Sisters of St Joseph in Adelaide, the latter by Mary McKillop (Mary of the Cross) – generations afterwards a candidate for sainthood. St Joseph nuns worked especially among the children of the poor and they spread to Perth, Bathurst, and Newcastle, founding many small schools in the bush and setting before the children high examples of womanly feeling.[43]

The dictates of feeling might well seem to answer the need, so urgent now, for certitude and peace. But like feeling itself, the lessons were changeable from time to time and from soul to soul. The sight of destitute children might move someone like Mary McKillop to an almost sensual compassion. It seems to have moved Dr Moore to disgust. Ada Cambridge, a novelist and poet living in rural Victoria, wrestled with this issue, probably from the time she arrived with her husband, a Church of England clergyman, in 1870. In England she had written two books, *Hymns on the Litany* and *Hymns on the Holy Communion*. Now she began to have momentary doubts about the authority of conscience, although that authority pressed hard on every aspect of her life. The problem, she thought, was most vivid in the sexual dealings of husband and wife. Established doctrine said that a woman, whatever her inclination, must submit to her husband. Therefore so did the conscience of a good wife. But now that men and women were on such informal terms, might not conscience of this older kind give way to 'the conscience of the body'? 'Moral conscience', after all – as we understood it – was often a trap. Perverted by custom, so she said in verse, 'To what immoral deeds it sets its seal!' One such immoral deed, though she did not say so, was the murder of babies by their unmarried mothers (Chapter 6) – instinctive feeling cancelled by fear and shame.

We must listen no longer, surely, to 'our Heaven-sent light and guide'. We must turn instead to feeling and the palpable self. Trust 'the physical conscience', she said. 'Untamed and true, [it] … speaks in voice and face.' It shapes the touch of wife and husband. It shows itself in disgust – 'In cold lips stiffened to the loveless kiss, / In shamed limbs shrinking from unloved embrace.' Or, better, it appears in 'love-born passion', perfectly independent of any law. It was the here and now, said Ada Cambridge, which should prevail.

Were husband and wife really 'one flesh'? '[F]lesh', she said, 'is *us*' – all of us, but also each of us alone, wholly alone, dealing with the other.[44]

III

The well read in Melbourne were disturbed by the emergence of James Fisher, the Nunawading Messiah – a phenomenon quite at odds with democracy, science, reason, and feeling. 'We are very fond', said the *Argus*, 'of pluming ourselves on the intelligence of the age in which we live, and setting forth our vast superiority to the benighted generations that have gone before us'. Fisher's claims proved our presumption. '[T]he mere fact of endowing men with the franchise, and making them free', whatever we might think, does not make them 'intelligent creatures'.[45] The establishment of reformatories and industrial schools was inspired by the same harsh realisation. There was a great deal yet to be done. A decade after the coming of democracy another kind of order, unfeeling and irrational, still lay startlingly close at hand.

There was a similar gap in sensibility and culture between the cities – centres of civilisation – and what was now called 'the Bush'. 'The Bush', in Australian conversation, was no longer merely a type of vegetation, let alone, as in England, just a shrub. Trollope discovered that 'nearly every place beyond the influences of the big towns is called "bush", – even though there should not be a tree to be seen around'. Ada Cambridge, newly married and about to leave England for this country, had imagined when she heard about the Bush, 'a vast shrubbery, with occasional spears hurtling through it'.[46] In fact, 'the Bush' was a term that now encompassed both place and people.

Especially in New South Wales, the Bush was almost a separate dominion. Its geographical limits were vague, embracing everything, as Trollope said, beyond the influence of the big towns. By 1870 even the more remote parts, 100 miles or more from Sydney and beyond the old Limits of

Location, included 120,000 people – a quarter of the colony's population. This was a great arc of country, a varied space stretching from the blue, high-boned mountains of New England to the brittle red land that had shocked John Oxley (Chapter 5). The population equalled Queensland's and yet it lacked even Queensland's centres of order. The 1871 census listed seventy-seven towns and villages in these districts, but only twenty had more than 500 people and only one (Grafton, a river port in the north) had more than 2000. Some of the inland goldfields were more thickly populated than the towns and gold was indeed one of the magnets that had drawn so many so far. Near Armidale, two or three days' ride from the railhead and even further from the city, there were 658 people on the diggings at Rocky River. At Araluen, far to the south-west, there were 4239. Villages and goldfields made a network of settlement. The villages, especially, for all their smallness, were places of buying and selling, comfort and variety. Women lived in them while their men worked or looked for work elsewhere and in some the female population outnumbered the male. The interlinking rivers and creeks had once made up the imagined geography of inland Australia. Now one thought first of the placing of settlements and the pattern of tracks.

There was a real Bush and an imaginary Bush. For some the inland was a palpable place embellished with familiar journeys. For others it was a vacancy, interrupted by the merest scatter of civilised points. Fresh from England, Trollope was riding in a scrubby part with friends. 'There arose at last a feeling', he recalled, 'that go where one might … one was never going anywhere'. No one in the Bush, to city minds, was going anywhere, and for the Sydney government the many thousands of men, women, and children were a powerful challenge to law and order. To some extent these individuals were beyond the democratic settlement. They might even seem to be rebels against it. Even with manhood suffrage, many of the men were not listed as voters and of those who were listed less than half might vote.[47] The progress of civilisation demanded that the inland be better attached to the city, that a fabric of places be created that could all be understood as points within a universal scheme – understood in the same way by the man in the city and by the man in the Bush.

Being apparently empty, the land itself offered a way forward. In theory it might be settled, filled in, by the common man, by the decision-making individual, by the good husband and father – by that epitome of moral strength and feeling on whom the future of nations seemed to depend. Throughout Australia the vacant inland might be used for the reordering of society, for the formation of new peoples – a project, indeed, with a worldwide echo. In Britain the Chartists had argued for years that the independent ownership of small farms, each big enough for a man and his family, was essential to democracy. In Ireland land reform, designed to adjust the old ties of landlord and tenant, seemed to offer an answer to ancient suffering. In Russia in 1861, as a great act of emancipation, the serfs of the empire were freed, in part, from feudal obligations. At the same time they were given rights in the soil. In the United States the Homestead Act of 1862 allowed citizens to possess 160 acres each in the newly settled territories. In this last case the aim was to keep the American west safe from large speculators and plantation labour. In such schemes there was always some old enemy, a backward-looking aristocracy for the most part, to be dislodged or circumvented.

Hopes were equally large in Australia. Most of the land near the centres of government had long been granted in freehold tenure, fixing on the spot a hierarchy of gentlemen and smallholders (Chapter 5). By the 1840s, with the growth of the main towns, the large capitalists had begun to subdivide and the small ones multiplied, many working the soil as tenants. There had always been a charm in the image of the farmer wedded with his family to their patch of earth and sending grain, hay, vegetables, milk, and butter to urban markets. In New South Wales tenant farmers included many who had come as young assisted immigrants, not long married, in the 1830s. They were especially numerous around Sydney and in the coastal valleys to its north and south, where steamships picked up their produce for the capital. The Macarthurs had 160 families on Camden Park, with farms of varying sizes, furnishing a telling example to less wealthy landlords.[48] Settlement at Port Phillip added to the demand for farm produce in the south. The Archdeacon of Launceston, Robert Davies, invited new immigrants to settle as cottagers on his land at Norfolk Plains and James Cox placed families on 20 acres each at Clarendon, with huts and rations.[49]

Many of the children of these families were grown up by mid-century and the promises of democracy matched the hopes of the young men among them, youths working with their parents' cattle and crops. Reaching their twenties, looking forward to marriage, anxious to 'get a start', manhood suffrage gave them the right to vote, and they might vote indeed for farms of their own. In Sydney the principal reformer of land tenure was the minister for lands, John Robertson:

> Come all of you Cornstalks the victory's won,
> John Robertson's triumphed, the lean days are gone.

Such young men were less common in Victoria and here the call for farms came mainly from miners tired of digging. They included men convinced by Chartist logic that as citizens they had a right to the moral and financial independence embedded in freehold title. Such men led the demand to 'Unlock the Land'.[50]

In all the colonies democracy seemed to offer acreage for the masses and an end to any semblance of a 'feudal' elite. But reform had to make its way against the inclinations of the rich, and especially the squatters, who had monopolised much of the settled inland since the 1830s, relying on annual licences or leases from the Crown. 'The squatters want to frighten the people', said Caroline Chisholm to her Sydney audience (Chapter 12), 'but of this she was certain, when once men felt the desire to get their own land, when their wives entered into the project, – she had a good deal to do with women, and knew them well, – there would be no stopping them.'[51]

And yet even when the laws were passed success was contingent on space and distance – on the size of each colony, the availability of good Crown land, and the ease with which future farmers might reach their city market. Only Tasmania and Victoria were small enough to match those European states that were the best examples of agricultural and industrial efficiency, and Victoria alone possessed the necessary wealth and vigour. Farmers living beyond a day's journey from the city depended for their profits on rail transport. There was a railway across Victoria, from Melbourne to Echuca, on the Murray River, by 1864 so that even at the northern boundary small farmers might make a living. At the same time the steamship trade along the Murray came quickly into the hands of city merchants, so that enterprise throughout the colony was caught up in a tightening web of traffic. South Australia was much bigger and it became bigger still in 1863, when the entire region to the north, previously part of New South Wales, was transferred to the Adelaide government as its Northern Territory. Nevertheless, the area apparently good for farming was well defined – an outer line was drawn by the surveyor-general, George Goyder, in 1865 – and all was within 150 miles of the capital. Steam power, by sea or land, easily reached so far.[52]

In New South Wales, on the other hand, the number and the wide distribution of inland people sometimes made the task of settling the country correctly seem insuperable. Land reform offered 'free selection', which meant, in principle, that in most of those parts now occupied by squatters anyone might choose up to 320 acres of Crown land. Conditional on residence, improvement, and purchase (a set sum over a long period), the selector became the owner. But most of the land on offer was a long way from Sydney and trains did not run nearly so far. Even by the early 1870s the railway westward was a little short of Bathurst. To the south-west it was no further than Goulburn and in the north it only ran between Newcastle and the Hunter's upper limit. Besides, as in some other colonies, squatters managed to use the legislation to secure better title for themselves so that small farmers were squeezed out. In 1860, just before the first land acts, wheat acreage in New South Wales had been equal to Victoria's. By 1872, while its area had grown by a third, Victoria's had tripled.[53]

Indeed the Sydney government sometimes seemed non-existent in parts of the Bush. Briefly, at least, a few districts were overwhelmed with lawlessness. Convictions for bushranging increased from five in 1860 to fifty-nine in 1865, and for each man convicted many more robbed with impunity.

'The mails on the southern roads beyond Goulburn', said the Sydney *Empire*, 'have been stopped and plundered day after day'. The neighbour-hood of Mudgee and Bathurst was almost as dangerous. '[E]verywhere the police seem to be quite helpless, either to prevent crime or to detect the offenders.' Almost from the arrival of the Europeans in Australia, in 1788, there had been individuals and communities living beyond the reach of imperial and colonial government. In many parts of Van Diemen's Land, for instance – both its mainland and the coasts and islands of Bass Strait – there had been settlements following their own, more piecemeal laws (Chapter 5). Here, apparently, was the same thing again. The *Empire*, referring in 1864 to the previous two years, summarised in dramatic terms: '[I]t is no exag-geration to say that a large portion of the South-western and Western dis-tricts of the interior of this colony has been under the control of robbers rather than the Government.'[54]

Bushrangers might possess an extraordinary freedom. In places they could stop the clockwork of the state whenever they liked. In October 1863 Ben Hall's gang spent one Saturday evening in Bathurst itself, the provincial capital of the west, buying oranges, inspecting a gun shop, and in complete control of one of the public houses. Hall then joined forces with John Gilbert and held up Canowindra, 55 miles west of Bathurst, for three days. They brought money to town with them, stole little, and offered

Bushrangers attack a mail coach in New South Wales, a chromolithograph by Samuel Thomas Gill and dated 1864, when bushranging was at its worst.

Reproduction courtesy of National Library of Australia

open-handed hospitality at Robinson's hotel. 'Every dray and team that passed [through] was stopped', said the *Bathurst Times*, 'and the men belonging to them were lodged, fed, and supplied with drink, free of expense'. Townspeople wanting to move about were given signed passes.[55] Other bushrangers were less benign. Near Braidwood a gang led by the brothers Thomas and John Clarke killed four special constables in a single attack. The Clarkes had a remarkable hold over the local magistrates. One gentleman frequently failed to do his duty, 'in consequence', as he explained, 'of his having extensive properties, which he thought would be at the mercy of these fellows if he took any part in adjudicating any case in which they were concerned'.[56]

Perhaps the only answer, said the *Herald*, was a treaty, as if with alien powers. Travellers in the Bush would have to purchase their safety from the bushrangers under some general agreement. It might seem disgraceful to suggest such a thing for a British territory, but '[s]uch', said the editor, ' ... is the condition to which a considerable and important section of the country has been reduced'.[57]

The bushrangers flourished partly because they had so many allies in their own districts. It was hard to track and capture them, and it was hard to convict them when they came to court, because few people were prepared to testify against them. Many were boys and young men born in the inland and living within a network of kin. In other words, they were a new edition of the rural native-born (Chapter 1). Their loyalties, their narrow horizons, their skills, and their sensibility had been part of rural life since the 1820s. On the other hand they were not like the bushrangers of earlier days, most of whom had been escaped convicts. These ones, said the *Herald*, 'have their mothers, their sisters, their youthful companions – even their ministers of religion!' At Braidwood the police blamed their own continuous failure on 'the close family ties which bind together the greater proportion of the inhabitants' for 50 miles around.[58] The loyalty of the women was particularly telling. Where in the dark stretches of the Bush was to be found the delicate judgment of good womanhood? Surely the only excuse available for such females was the romantic character of the criminals – a quality 'always so seductive to the feminine imagination'. Society in those parts was, to all appearances, brutal in its feelings and 'corrupt in its domestic circles'.[59]

'[A] vast amount of ignorance and misconception prevails in town with respect to the behaviour and character of the labouring classes in the bush.' So remarked a *Herald* reader.[60] Within this confusion there was disagreement on one vital point. How indeed did feeling operate among these peculiar people? The bushrangers certainly demonstrated 'an innate love of wickedness', but that seemed to be part of a larger problem – 'an entire absence of moral sense' among the families from which they came. Nor was this surprising, perhaps, when schools were so few. With careless parents and no accredited teachers the children were 'brought up', as a school inspector from the Bathurst district said, 'in a state of unrestrained license, with no thought but self, [and] no aspiration beyond that of a mere animal nature'.[61]

Indeed, these people had a peculiar affinity with animals. Men and women embedded in speech, following the priorities that an oral culture set out for them, unreflecting, ignorant even of the 'conscience of the body', their way of life had always been typical of the mass of rural native-born. They lacked the refined self-consciousness that was now a matter for pride among the well read. Even the free selectors, people with a little property of their own, were to be found, as the *Herald* put it, 'herding ... in hovels little better than pigstyes'. Such men and women might be very clever in their own fashion, especially on horseback. They might be able to find their way through 'the intricacies of the wilderness' with an almost animal instinct.[62] But such skills were not likely to be admired among the well read. They 'rode like centaurs', said the *Sydney Morning Herald*, 'and ran like Kangaroos', but these were not the abilities of a globally minded and railway-making people. The lower ranks in the Bush were apparently like beasts themselves. They hardly belonged among us – 'reared if not born on horseback, illiterate as the animals they ride, and destitute of all moral training or sense of social responsibility'.[63]

The Catholic and Anglican churches made a startling effort among these people when they sent bishops to the Bush, to Grafton, Armidale, Bathurst, and Goulburn, all gilded with hierarchy and civilised virtue. Secular government placed its hopes on police, good postage, and schools. Police seemed particularly urgent during the worst years of bushranging, but in the end, as an Albury newspaper remarked, one schoolmaster was 'worth a dozen policemen'.[64] Postage had always been given high priority by government, as a medium of order and civilisation. Balranald, for instance, was 450 miles from Sydney, 250 from Melbourne and 300 from Adelaide but for all its isolation it exchanged mail twice a week with Deniliquin and once each with Wentworth, Hay, and Swan Hill, all by horseback. The men who did this work were called 'mailmen', not 'postmen', said Trollope. They served most places of significance, 'conveying letters, telegrams, and messages with wondrous accuracy'.[65]

Their mailbags, perhaps, were not well filled. The inhabitants of the Bush, said the *Empire*, were 'semi-barbarians'. Among them, imagination was governed by tales of 'daring adventure and brute courage'. They were not creatures of the written word:

> The ministers of refinement to them have been chiefly strolling players, dancing-masters, and tavern songsters. And their reading, such as it is, has been almost wholly confined to ballads and tales, the burden of which too frequently has been the feats of highwaymen and outlaws.[66]

Only a city writer could have imagined strolling players and dancing masters in the depths of the Bush. But something like tavern songsters certainly made their mark. Ballads of a kind later common among Australians were in many cases products of the 1860s and were sung first by bushmen:

> I sing of a commodity, it's one that will not fail yer,
> I mean that common oddity, the mainstay of Australia;
> Gold it is a precious thing, for commerce it increases,
> But stringy-bark and green-hide, can beat it all to pieces.

Ballads about bushranging had a similar currency.[67]

Throughout Australia governments tried hard with schools. One by one teachers brought together classes in the most difficult places. In South Australia, for instance, Andrew Heron, once a shepherd, worked in the remote Flinders Ranges as an 'itinerating teacher', riding backwards and forwards between the main homestead at Coonatto, a sheep run, and its outpost 10 miles away at Yanyarrie. He was then succeeded by his wife Elizabeth, who stayed at headquarters. The copper mines at Blinman, also in the ranges, and the little settlement far away at Palmerston (now Darwin), in the Northern Territory, likewise had women teachers. Twenty years previously it had seemed wrong for women to teach classes including big boys. Now they were prized for their qualities of feeling – for their 'patience and tact'. Where the people were backward and scattered, so it was thought, 'a competent energetic mistress is really the more suitable teacher'.[68]

Even in New South Wales, with the decline of bushranging during the late 1860s, there were glimmers of hope in this respect. It seemed after all that people in the remote Bush were not wholly lost to good feeling. In 1860 there had been only one government elementary school between Wagga Wagga and the Murray, an area stretching 400 miles downriver and 60 miles across. Ten years later there were nineteen. In May 1870 the ever-travelling school inspector visited Balranald and found twelve children in class. 'The attendance', he reported, 'has fallen off considerably, owing to the unpopularity of the teacher; the pupils present were slovenly attired and very lethargic'.[69] And yet, dull-eyed and unwelcoming, there they sat. Attendance, after all, was not yet compulsory.

Thoroughgoing success depended still on the shifting attitudes of parents, who might resent a heavy-handed discipline, who expected schools to be in easy reach and who kept their children at home whenever they were wanted for more urgent work. But taking his district as whole this inspector was optimistic. 'There is every reason', he said, 'to believe that a *desire* for education is steadily increasing'.[70] From the right kind of desire, felt in unison, all good things might come.

Chapter 15

Our Outer Edge

I

For a long time the roads that crossed the border between South Australia and Victoria were mainly bush tracks, with a capacity to confuse the inexperienced traveller. An Englishman, John Chapple, who used one of them in 1855 on his way to the Victorian goldfields, found that he was following in the footsteps of a number of Chinese with the same destination. He remarked in his diary, 'we know we are on the right road from the number of Chinese characters written about every two miles on the trees, the bark nicely shaven of about 12 inches x 18 inches and then six lines of writing neatly executed – I suppose, information for those poor fellows who cannot push on'. Some Chinese had failed altogether. There were fresh graves by the roadside and one man, presumably left to travel and to die alone, lay there unburied. Chapple buried him.[1]

The Chinese who came for Australian gold were from the region around Guangzhou, or Canton. Old trading links existed between that region and British ports, including ports in Australia, and there were British settlements there and nearby on Hong Kong. The miners, who were assembled in parties by Chinese merchants, were men of peasant background, used to working hard for a meagre return. Whatever money they made on the goldfields went partly to their families and partly to the merchants, who paid their passage. They were highly organised and interdependent, committed to each other and to those they left behind.[2] They were not like the loose atoms of humanity otherwise common on the diggings.

A few Chinese, from other parts, had come to Australia in the 1830s and '40s and worked as shepherds. The first miners reached Melbourne in 1852, and for the time being the majority came to this port. As many as 10,000 disembarked during 1854 and another 8000 during the first half of 1855, and at that point the Victorian parliament moved to slow the flood.

Every Chinese man arriving by sea was to be taxed £10 and no ship might carry more than one for every ten tons burthen, but even while the law was still under debate some began arriving at ports just outside Victoria's borders. The party followed by John Chapple, 400 of them (so he said), had landed at Guichen Bay, in South Australia. After only five years of immigration a fifth of the men on the Victorian goldfields (about 25,000) were Chinese and on some fields it was more than half.[3]

For many White diggers they were anathema. Their habits of work were different. When returns on one goldfield were slow Europeans were inclined to move on, but the Chinese persevered. They were therefore found on claims that the White diggers had kept, so they thought, in reserve in case their larger hopes failed. The Europeans usually dug on weekdays and spent Saturdays washing the piled-up dirt, but the Chinese dug and washed all at once. Since the Chinese were often on poorer claims much of their dirt yielded little and so they used more water and when water was scarce they were blamed for wasting it. In short, they upset many small efforts by the other diggers, many nicely patterned hopes and ideas of possession. '[T]hey are to the diggings', said a White man, 'what pigs, fowls, and dogs, are to the flower garden'.[4]

The Chinese, especially when they were gathered in large numbers, offended European sensibilities in other ways. The timbre of their voices, their strange manners and 'unmanly' appearance, multiplied a thousand-fold, were

Chinese goldminers washing for gold, 1870s, a chromolithograph by an unknown artist. Two use a cradle and three use pans, the most primitive means of washing. Their water comes from an elaborate reservoir but also direct from a stream.

Reproduction courtesy of National Library of Australia

unnerving, at least to some White men. It was not only the well read who were prouder now about the way they looked, about cleanliness, as they understood it, and dress (Chapter 14). Achievement differed, but many of all ranks at least pretended to new habits. These standards, shaped in a European way, could never, so it seemed, be reached by the Chinese. Besides, the Chinese worked hard and gold was obviously limited. In British colonies men of British descent, British voices, and British figures might be said to have the prior claim. '[S]hall we as men and as British subjects stand tamely by', they said, 'and allow the bread to be plucked from the mouths of ourselves, our wives, and children by these pig-tailed, moon-faced barbarians[?]'[5]

'Barbarians' was a telling term – a term easily taken up by a self-consciously civilised people. The bushrangers were called 'semi-barbarians' – unlike the Chinese, perhaps, there was hope for them. The Chinese were invaders, alien in every way.

In winter 1857 on the Buckland River diggings, south of Beechworth, the White miners, though greatly outnumbered, attacked the Chinese camps. The movement was well ordered to begin with, like the campaigns against the government and military on the Turon, Bendigo, and Ballarat (Chapter 11). The men met, appointed a chairman, proposed resolutions, and counted votes. They would avoid, they said, 'unnecessary violence or willful destruction of property'. But hatred – an ideological fervour – ran ahead of rhetoric and '[e]ye-witnesses [this is from a local paper] told of ruffianly behaviour, unmanly violence and unbounded rapacity'. Tents and stores were destroyed and an expensive joss house was burnt to the ground. When some Europeans tried to defend the Chinese they were beaten, and several fleeing Chinese died afterwards of exposure.[6] Such incidents made it appear that violence might be a necessary aspect of two such physically different peoples living side by side. The Chinese presented, to some European minds, the kind of deeply rooted danger that could be only met with blows.

American diggers took the lead on the Buckland. In New South Wales there were several riots at Lambing Flat (or Burrangong), west of Goulburn, between December 1860 and August 1861, and here the British and colonials were more obvious. A Miners Protection League was formed at Lambing Flat, partly with the aim of establishing a body of 'miners' police' to supplement the government force. The league also tried to stop tradesmen and townspeople carrying arms. Indeed, its aims went beyond local issues. Here was a working-man's campaign echoing the anti-transportation movement (Chapter 11), and similarly designed to keep out competition. Building on a common hatred for the Chinese the leadership aspired 'to organize and unite all the great labouring classes – the mining community – in fact, every member of the great working body – in one grand harmonious federation'. Their ultimate purpose was vague, but the miners, they said, were 'the working bees of the hive'. Bees laboured for a single purpose. They themselves must 'unite as one man'.[7]

Some on this occasion gave their best energies to talk, to explaining themselves, as at Eureka, rather than to action. At one meeting, for instance, a few men had speeches still undelivered when the majority began to shoulder their weapons. Their voices were overwhelmed with cries of 'no notice'. 'Groups collected, and all tried to speak at once, when the band, striking up, and moving slowly away, was the signal for the [end] ... of the meeting.' All advanced in a body on the Chinese tents, carrying a flag painted with the stars of the Southern Cross, once again like Eureka, but printed around the edge with 'Roll Up! Roll Up! No Chinese'.[8]

This time, too, Chinese miners were badly hurt. A *Herald* reporter saw: 'Men, or rather monsters, on horseback, armed with bludgeons and whips ... securing the unfortunate creatures by taking hold of their [pig]tails.' Their heads, he said, were pulled up and back across the saddle and their hair cut off in a kind of conquering fervour. A Chinese interpreter, Simon San Ling, complained of being chased into the bush with shouts of 'Cut off his tail'. He was robbed, he said, his tent was burnt and he lost about £100.[9] Such stories made a deep impact on Sydney readers. Uninvolved except as readers, they were forced to decide about events that cast a strange reflection on the new democracy. In spite of the apparent progress of civilisation – of democracy shaped by '*moral* force' – physical force still worked powerfully among them, a point proved not only by the riots at Lambing Flat but also by the bushranging that was to come to a head over the next few years. Perhaps the two were connected. '[T]he institution and the support of bushranging in this colony', said Chief Justice Stephen in Sydney, with no apparent doubt, 'are owing to the lawlessness, and spirit of self-will, which commenced with the Burrangong riots'.[10]

Whatever the exact link, if any, such dramatic action, such sudden mass feeling, seemed somehow momentous. For a generation schooled to believe that violence was an evil in itself – though often a necessary evil – any event like this raised large questions for the present and future. The Myall Creek massacre in 1838 and the hangings afterwards had seemed to signal a critical point in the local relationship of justice, in its widest sense, and public order. In South Australia there had been similar ambivalence about the killings near Lacepede Bay, in 1840, and the government response. In Victoria the deaths at Eureka had caused men and women to pause bewildered. Violence on that scale upset life's common round. It was always evidence, somehow, of 'self-will' – sheer impulse unrestrained. Might it still answer, on occasion, some deeper historic purpose? How was the regime of feeling, most obviously designed to govern issues of household and family, to manage such widely echoing questions? Physical revulsion was a feeling. So was racial pride. Both were powerfully expressed by the scattering of blood.

In other words, the current crisis touched on the very issue that worried Ada Cambridge (Chapter 14). Which was to be preferred? On the one hand we had the dictates of conscience, anchored in Christian doctrine, including the certainty that all human beings were equal before a just and all-seeing God. On the other hand we had feeling, the 'conscience of the body', embellished and strengthened by theories of race. The first implied peace. The second might justify fighting, among individuals and among great contesting bodies of men. The second left no room for any arbitrator, whether human or divine, possessed of the power to set feeling at rest. The intricacies of racial theory – classification, the hierarchy of types, the dangers of interbreeding – were increasingly part of scientific and wider debate. As with new forms of Christian worship (Chapter 14), they were most keenly worked out in the United States. Josiah Nott, an Alabama physician, was at present a leading authority and the book he helped to write, *Types of Mankind* (1854), which might well have been read in Australia before the goldfield troubles. 'Nations and races, like individuals,' said Nott, 'have each an especial destiny: some are born to rule, and others to be ruled. And such has ever been the history of mankind'.[11]

Destiny as large as this overshadowed even the teaching of the churches. It rendered irrelevant the simplicity of Andrew Eaton and his Aboriginal neighbours in north-western New South Wales (Chapter 8) – their shared ceremony, their mutual confidence. 'We were very friendly', said Eaton, 'They used frequently to sleep in the same hut with me ... They never attacked me at all'.[12]

The Europeans in Australia, in their first democratic days, had to make up their minds on a point more basic than democracy itself. Were they rulers in this way? Were the Chinese an altogether separate 'type' or 'species', as Nott and others would have them believe? If they followed such advice intermarriage, perhaps even close coexistence, was impossible. Any kind of intimacy, except the intimacy of violence, broke fundamental laws of human identity and human history. The older idealism was by no means dead, but at least in Sydney it was voiced mainly by those whose view of the world had been formed many years before, and especially by men who possessed a strong sense of living under the eye of the Almighty. John West, in former days a Congregationalist minister, editor of the *Launceston Examiner* and an opponent of convict transportation (Chapter 11), now edited the *Sydney Morning Herald*. His leaders were fierce on this question. So-called liberal democrats, he said, 'believe that certain races were born to be oppressed. ... They believe that men have different rights according to the colour of their skin, the twang of their language, or the latitude under which they were born' – so much, he said, for 'the doctrines of Christ [and] ... the principles of liberty'. Peter Faucett was a lawyer, originally an Irish Anglican and later a devout Catholic. 'What right had we', he asked from his seat in parliament, 'to talk of an inferior race? Did we dare in the sight of God who made them all to call any one inferior of race?'[13]

Those who read the new literature spoke of the 'hybrid' or 'Austral-Chinese race' that must result if nothing were done about these new invaders. A 'hybrid race' was itself inevitably 'an inferior caste'. Where it existed, they were now told, 'the progress of civilisation receded, and the principles of constitutional freedom retrograded'. So said a young man in Sydney, newly elected to parliament and keen to prove his learning. Such arguments were 'the greatest bosh ever uttered', retorted a churchman fifteen years his senior. What could experience find to condemn in the intermingling of blood? 'What race was so compound as the Anglo-Saxon race[?]' Legal wedlock was always 'moral and proper', said William Forster, another old colonist. Marriage between a Chinese man and a European woman, for instance, was certainly better than unblessed cohabitation. But no, said the innovators, a man and woman of the same race living in sin were far preferable to any couple who defied the laws of nature.[14]

William Windeyer had come as an infant from England in 1835. His father was Richard Windeyer, the lawyer who defended the Myall Creek murderers. Some time after those trials Windeyer senior had argued about race and justice before a gathering in Sydney (Chapter 9). He had spoken of anguished dealings with his own conscience. You are your brother's keeper, his conscience had told him, whoever that brother might be – 'and more than thy Brother's blood, his immortal spirit shall be required at thy hands'. William Windeyer was as ardent as his father (who died when he was twelve), but his mind was to move in the newer direction. At the King's School, Parramatta, he learned to love public recitation. 'I feel almost carried away when I am in a noble piece', he told his mother, 'out of myself'. Through public speaking he aimed 'to direct, to improve, to raise my country'. He was one of the first students at Sydney University. He was admitted to the bar, married (his wife was later a strong advocate of women's causes), and elected to parliament in 1860.[15]

At twenty-six years old William Windeyer was the opening speaker at a meeting called at the Mechanics School of Arts to discuss the Lambing Flat riots and Chinese immigration. It was, he told his audience, a question of profound importance. It 'affected our position as a nation [he meant New South Wales]', for surely we all aimed to see here 'a truly Anglo-Saxon community. (Great cheers.)' He would not argue, he said, about material riches or the threat posed by the Chinese to general prosperity. He was concerned with larger matters, with questions of morality and civilisation. 'He hoped to have here a people with the same physical and mental energies as their predecessors, with those glorious institutions which they had inherited from their fathers, and with that vigour that was required to maintain them.' The Chinese could have no part in such work. They were weak and degenerate, and therefore incompetent and vicious. Besides, no country inhabited by two such different races could ever be at peace. Civility and public order required that one must go.

Besides, there were deeper and broader questions of feeling – of the colour, the appearance, the massed numbers, the alien smell and touch of the Chinese in Australia. Only briefly did Ada Cambridge wonder whether the 'conscience of the body' should prevail in absolute terms over 'moral conscience'. Windeyer's father had spoken too of a 'whispering in the bottom of our hearts', of a voice from within and beyond that might conquer prejudice.[16] Now, however, among the more eager minds of the younger generation, Europeans were to be guided by the 'conscience of the body'. Living as one with the Chinese, said William Windeyer, should it ever happen, would mean dealing with them in the most intimate ways:

> Were they prepared to accept these people upon equal terms with themselves? not [only] to ride in the same coach with them – though that was very disagreeable as he knew by experience – (a laugh) – nor yet simply to buy and sell with them, or to eat at the same table with them; but to meet them as they were bound to do ... Were they prepared to intermingle with them in the way in which two people only could thoroughly intermingle – by giving them their daughters in marriage? (Loud cheers.) Were they prepared to do this? ('No! no!' and great cheering.)

It was the common man, he said, who must decide. It was the common man who, though ignorant of racial theory, best valued 'purity of race', because it was he whose daily life and labour forced him close to the new invaders. It was he who must leave his wife unprotected at home, he whose children were most at risk from 'their loathsome touch'.[17]

Windeyer was followed at the rostrum by Daniel Deniehy, who had made his name in 1853 with his speech against 'bunyip aristocracy' (Chapter 12). The Chinese for Deniehy were an antitype of masculine virtue even worse than hereditary peerage. 'We could only amalgamate with such races as had some features in common with our own', he said, ' ... some common feelings of civilisation and religion'. The Chinese were barbarians and '[i]t was perfectly impossible for any barbarian race to fuse with a race like the Europeans'. 'The best way', shouted a voice from the crowd, 'would be to drive them all down like a flock of sheep and send them back to their country'.[18] This was 'common feelings'. Such feelings shaped this democratic people – resounding in the shouts and cheers of the men gathered in the School of Arts and in the approving murmurs to be imagined elsewhere.

John West of the *Herald* resembled Horne Tooke and Hobbes Scott (Chapter 2). A precise scholar and writer, he was extremely careful about the rights of the people. But he also believed that the people might be wrong. Just as every man or woman must answer the demands of conscience, the mass had to be guided, he thought, by men of moral discrimination, like himself. 'It is part of the very pretty theory of democracy', he wrote at the height of this crisis, 'that it ensures the best men getting to the top of the tree'. And yet, he said, something had obviously gone wrong because the prejudices of the worst were already supreme, on the goldfields and in parliament, and the thoughts of individuals like himself were trampled under foot.[19]

In fact, in the end these were not matters of theory at all. They were matters of imagination. Theory, on either side, was only a tool. The issue was best set out not by John West or Josiah Nott but by writers who struggled at another level altogether with current drifts of thought – who had a better sense of the way imagination shaped ideas. Thirty years earlier, in Scotland, Thomas Carlyle had done something to this end in his book *Sartor Resartus* ('The Tailor Patched'). Our understanding of Creation depended, said Carlyle, on its outer coating. '*Man is a Spirit*, and bound by invisible bonds to *All Men*.' But it was physical appearance that kept up the connection. Each must be true to himself, but interlinking order was maintained by the appearance of himself and others, including clothes. Clothes were, besides, a metaphor for much else – Carlyle was a type of ethnographer. Think, in a courtroom, he said, of two men face to face, 'one dressed in fine Red, the other in coarse threadbare Blue'. Red, because he is Red, may condemn Blue to die and Blue – '(O wonder of wonders!)' – does so without question.[20] Since *Sartor Resartus*, Carlyle had moved his focus from garments to skin. His essay published in England in 1849, 'Occasional Discourse on the Nigger Question', was an early fanfare of uncomplicated racism.[21]

Humanity came parcelled for such writers, and perhaps for their entire generation, in a jumble of colour – as if seen through the stained glass now issuing from factories in its myriad sheets. In his glittering story of *Moby-Dick* (1851) Herman Melville made frequent play with tinctured skin, from the whiteness of the great whale itself to the 'red arm' that was the last visible sign of its hunters. Take the sailors on their first appearance in the story – one face 'a sun-toasted pear in hue', another 'satin wood', another 'slightly bleached', each marked by its own burden of sunshine. The flesh of Queequeg, the cannibal harpooner, was tattooed all over in large squares of black and purple-yellow, cut out in lozenges like a church window. The hero spent his last nights on shore with Queequeg, sleeping in the same bed, huddling away from his warm, unconscious weight. Melville copied a great deal from Carlyle, but colour for him was no universal predictor. 'A man can be honest in any sort of skin.' And again: 'Better sleep with a sober cannibal than a drunken Christian.'[22]

Like many in his time, Melville was taken with the physical beauty, the pale, bright skin of his own people. He also felt the existence of unplumbed savagery more surely than he did the existence of God. But he had an enthusiasm for justice – unrelenting justice – and he hated the regime of feeling. Men possessed of 'immaculate manliness', he thought, were led not by feeling but by a sometimes painful sense of right. A few among the Europeans in Australia, men and women, aimed to do as Melville did – 'To preach the Truth in the face of Falsehood.'[23] But most saw the matter like Carlyle.

II

During the northern summer, 1854, two families, the Thibous and the Icks, crossed the Atlantic from Antigua, in the West Indies, to Bristol, and from Bristol they sailed to Melbourne. They were shopkeepers, descended from White planters and Black slaves, and they were Wesleyan Methodists. Two of the Thibou children were named after Wesleyan luminaries – the namesake of one, the Reverend Adam Clarke, had written a six-volume commentary on scripture – and in Melbourne Edward Ick immediately joined the councils of his Church. To begin with Edward worked as a cook but he and his wife, Annie, later kept a boarding house in Caledonian Lane plus a restaurant in Swanston Street. Dark skin notwithstanding, both families did well. The Icks went on to manage the Wesleyan home for destitute immigrants in Carlton and they also bought a share in Enoch Thibou's importing business. One son enrolled at Melbourne University and graduated MA. He later went back for a medical degree.[24]

In Antigua such families were called 'free coloureds'. They had once been a separate class in law, superior to Black slaves but inferior to Whites. Their civil disabilities were abolished when the slaves were emancipated, in 1834, but they were disliked by both Black and White, which may be why this party left. In the West Indies, where men and women had been enslaved since the seventeenth century, race and law were now being hesitantly disentangled and evangelical Christians, including Wesleyans, were an important part of the movement for equality. Now, however, as a result of scientific racism, logic in such matters was partly turned upside down. Racial differences had been smoothed away in some places and in some minds, but elsewhere they were sharpened.

For many, Christianity was a marginal issue, eclipsed by the rule of science. No other membership, sacred or profane, mattered more now than membership of race. Old understanding still worked in Australia for families like the Icks and Thibous, helped by the fact that they were scattered in barely noticeable numbers among the majority. But it was less effective for the Chinese.

Race was another of those aspects of life in which patterns of sublime importance, so it seemed, were now being progressively uncovered by the best minds of the day. This new knowledge, whenever it should be enforced by law, seemed to promise an all-pervading regime of truth and order. Scientific racism pointed to a new kind of justice. This generation was the first among the Europeans in Australia, and among the Europeans in Europe, capable of making a wholesale attack on ancient ideas of right and wrong. The United States, wonderfully democratic and rich, seemed to be a source of answers for our brave new world, but it was science, in its multiplying forms, that made those answers applicable everywhere. The great question, as ever (Chapter 13), lay in understanding 'the delicate poise of

... body and mind', the relationship between automaton and eternal in human nature. But answers to that question varied.

Briefly, spiritualism – another mainly American invention – seemed to offer the most vivid solution. The great aim of spiritualism was to create a system of belief that would replace the 'decaying theologies' of church life with something equally profound but more up to date and certain. Certainty was to depend on scientific method. Among spiritualists God remained crucial as the source of life – and of all life equally. They were not racist. As a leading Australian spiritualist, Walter Lindesay Richardson, explained, their creed stood for 'the brotherhood of the human race and the absolute and unconditional freedom of each immortal soul'.[25] '[A]ll religious revelations are loopholes of light emanating from superior spheres', said another local advocate. It followed that 'no section of God's children can claim a monopoly of salvation'. The teachings of Confucius, for instance, were pressed on believers here as a sample of truth.[26]

The first spiritualist group in this country met in 1869 at the home of Dr James Motherwell, in Melbourne, and the Victorian Association of Progressive Spiritualists was founded, together with a monthly journal, the *Harbinger of Light*, in the following year. Twelve months later the association had a membership of over 300 and up to 1500 came to meetings. It apparently made little impact in other mainland capitals, but a few spiritualists met in Hobart and Launceston and there was keen activity in some Victorian goldfield towns. At Castlemaine, in particular, so said a sceptic: 'Spirits and mediums were as common ... as sparrows, and miracles were every-day occurrences.' Fisher, the Nunawading Messiah, partly used the language of spiritualism and churchmen spoke of him as a fanatic example of the new faith. But spiritualists said he represented 'old-time superstition'. They themselves were creatures of the future.[27]

Motherwell was a leading Melbourne physician and so was Richardson. For many men of scientific training spiritualism made perfect sense.[28] The British chemist, William Crookes, a Fellow of the Royal Society, tested its validity to his own satisfaction and published the results in the *Quarterly Journal of Science*. Magnetism and electricity were sources of energy currently offering enormous promise for the progress of humanity. So was 'psychic force', as Crookes called it. Each of these three forces, spiritualists said, might be understood in conjunction with the others. In particular, under certain precise conditions 'psychic force' gave human beings the power to communicate across distance. Even more wonderful, the spirits of the dead might speak to the living. The link was made by men or women (mediums) with high spiritual gifts – women especially distinguished themselves. And just as scientists were now intrigued by the air as the great interconnecting element of life, spiritualists spoke of 'aether', an even more fundamental substance that filled all space and was fraught with energy – with psychic, magnetic, and electric power, with feeling, sound, and light.[29]

Harmony of feeling was the essence of spiritualism. All depended on the 'motive power' of the heart. When groups gathered in 'seances', hoping to talk with the dead, 'low spirituality' (coarseness of feeling) and emotional jarring was bound to prevent success.[30] This was, or aimed to be, a precise science. The notes taken to document meetings were sometimes set out just as a meteorologist might record his experiments. For example: 'Two gentlemen and three ladies; room rather cold, ther[mometer] 56 deg.; cloudy night, damp atmosphere, no wind; invocation, music.' The party in this instance sat around a big heavy table for forty minutes and heard nothing from the dead except whimperings, as if from the table's surface. But then:

> Two more ladies joined the circle, and within fifteen minutes we had louder noises and movements. The table ... moved repeatedly west and south-west, towards Mr R. and Mrs B. Several questions were put, and the following among others: – 'Are you happier than when we last met?' No answer. 'Are you glad to meet us again?' 'Yes.' 'Can you suggest any improvement in the arrangement of those sitting?' No answer, &c.[31]

Some meetings were dramatically more successful. In many, however feeble, the 'chemistry of life' was manifest in spiritual form.

Spirit was clothed in flesh. Flesh embodied spirit. Seances were held in darkened rooms, but spiritualists loved light. They imagined 'magnetic light', halos and radiant forms like clouds, dense with electric energy. They believed that human bodies might be seen shining of their own accord. Photography – its light-filled miracles manufactured in darkness – was another science that overlapped with spiritualism and Melbourne photographers made a point of advertising in the *Harbinger of Light*.[32] Colour among spiritualists was an embodiment of feeling. Red was 'significant of sensuous experience', blue of 'intellectual and mental energies', yellow of 'light and spirituality'.[33] Leading minds debated the characteristics of a good marriage because feeling depended, in spiritualist theory, on the fine merging of spirit and flesh. Marriage without the right combination of feeling in both parties was fatal, they thought, to spiritual health. Indeed, for women it was 'prostitution'. Ada Cambridge used the same term and it may be that she took it from the spiritualists.[34]

Spiritualism seemed to make sense partly because it reflected all the energy of the communications revolution. Australians were prepared for it because they already knew about the telegraph, which for most of them was equally inexplicable. When telegraphy was first tried in Melbourne in 1853 the *Argus* called it 'the most perfect of human inventions ... anything more perfect than this is scarcely conceivable'.[35] Spiritualists were to look for another kind of perfection, something more obviously moral and humane. But while the telegraph never promised, all at once, a finer type of humanity as spiritualism did, it was vastly more efficient and more universally credible.

Spiritualism depended on the disembodied spirit guiding the hand of a medium who wrote down its communications on a piece of paper. With the telegraph each message was tapped out in Morse code in one place, carried by the 'the electric fluid' down the wire, and transcribed at the other end, again in code, by a stylus moving over a strip of paper. By 1861 such messages were being transmitted to neighbouring towns from all of the colonial capitals except Perth, the first line from Brisbane being deliberately built for the sake of connecting with Sydney.[36] Lines had very quickly stretched across the landscape and almost as quickly large numbers among the Europeans in Australia began to think of the telegraph as part of their lives. In Victoria the annual number of messages tripled in 1854–55, increased more than four times during 1856–57 and doubled again during 1857–58. Hobart and Launceston were linked in 1857 and then, in an extraordinary feat of engineering, a cable was laid across Bass Strait, running between Cape Otway, King Island, Circular Head, and Low Head, at the entrance to Port Dalrymple.

South Australians made best use of the system. Theirs was a compact population and Adelaide businessmen, like those in Hobart and Launceston, felt an urgent need to deal by wire with Melbourne, Australia's commercial heart. They also had a keen and ingenious superintendent of telegraphs, Charles Todd. By the early 1870s usage in South Australia amounted to nearly two messages per adult per annum.[37]

Todd worked closely with his counterpart in Melbourne – Samuel McGowan. His assistant, Edward Cracknell, took up the same post in Sydney and Cracknell's brother William was superintendent in Brisbane. In no other field did the mainland governments manage together so well and the telegraph quickly became part of government everywhere (once again, except the west). In South Australia there was a line linking the industrial school at Brighton with Adelaide, and it was used among other things to report deaths among the children. In Queensland the lunatic asylum at Woogaroo also had its own receiver, carrying orders for admission and news of escape.[38] By the beginning of the 1870s one in every eight messages sent in Victoria went on Her Majesty's service. In Queensland it was one in four. The telegraph held out enormous promise for policing. 'The wires', said the Sydney *Herald*, 'make us acquainted with every outrage committed on the great lines of communication almost as soon as it has happened'. Descriptions of stolen livestock could be communicated at once to all the main markets so as to stop their sale.[39] Railway systems, including the synchronising of clocks, depended absolutely on telegraph messages and telegraph poles, mainly ironbark, marched beside the tracks.[40]

The telegraph was a miracle for common imagination. Within a decade of its arrival in Australia the term 'bush telegraph' had been invented for the hurry of news among inland inhabitants – an old phenomenon newly named.[41] The presence of such marvellous technology, like the use of steam in previous years, not only led imagination towards even greater wonders, such as spiritualism, but also increased the hunger for news from distant parts. The telegraph became vital to newspaper work. Connection with the rest of the world took time, but the submarine network was steadily expanding (the Atlantic had been crossed in 1858) and it was obvious that the gap between this continent and all the others – and in particular the mother country – must soon disappear. Meanwhile attention was focused on the interlinking of the colonies and of the towns within each. Country newspapers featured staccato messages that had been passed along the line from the capital, news of all kinds being broadcast in this way – prices current and weather reports as well as brief leading items (the latter to be filled out in due course by more conventional means). These, with a mass of private messages, strengthened that sense of synchronised unity which now seemed to be the essence of progress – even that exhilarating harmony that spiritualists longed for.

In 1868 the French neurophysiologist, Emil du Bois-Reymond, explained to an audience in London how nerves worked in human bodies. He used as a model the Prussian telegraph system, then the best in Europe. Nerves, after all, were believed to transmit 'animal electricity', which made them very like wires:

> Just as the central station of the electric telegraph [he said] ... is in communication with the outermost borders of the monarchy through its gigantic web of copper wire, just so the soul in its office, the brain, endlessly receives dispatches from the outermost limits of its empire through its telegraph wires, the nerves, and sends out its orders in all directions to its civil servants, the muscles.

The same combination of imagery was more often used in reverse. The impact of the telegraph was so new and so dazzling that it was best explained in physiological terms, as if the people really were a single body, one palpable mass. Like spiritualism, this was a technology to be justified by the way it elevated and reflected our physical selves. Samuel Morse himself, one of its inventors, spoke of the electric network as 'those *nerves* which are to diffuse, with the speed of thought, a knowledge of all that is occurring throughout the land'.[42]

The image worked well in Australia. We were already prepared to take our main lessons from material things. Besides, the limits of the country, whether salt-water or desert, were as sharply tangible as flesh. A group of Sydney merchants argued, for instance, that the cost of sending telegraphic messages ought to be cut to the perfect minimum. They cited Rowland Hill and his postal reforms. As with the penny post, they said, if messages were very cheap the number sent would in fact increase the profits of all concerned. But their imagery went deeper. They spoke of the telegraph as a corporeal network. A capital city thus endowed became, they said, a 'centre of motive sensation'. There proceeded from it hour by hour 'vibration', 'pulsation', 'circulation and enlargement of cheap thought'. A flood of blessings 'continuously beats and reciprocates' through subordinate centres and, thinking thus 'in unison' every good thing about us was enlivened – 'business, trade, science, literature, philanthropy, social affection, and all the plans of public utility'.[43]

During winter 1867 it was announced that Prince Alfred, the Queen's second son, was to visit Australia and New Zealand. Alfred was a naval lieutenant in command of his own vessel and as he made his way from port to port his progress was tracked by telegraph and followed with excitement throughout the settled parts of this country. The *Armidale Express*, which appeared each Saturday on the high New England plateau in northern New South Wales, announced his approach on 5 October with a message sent from Sydney the previous afternoon: 'News has reached Adelaide that Prince Alfred was at the Cape of Good Hope.' And on 12 October: 'Prince Alfred declines visiting the Mauritius.' These messages had been carried part of the way by older means, but by the end of October the young man was telegraphically within reach. On Saturday, 2 November, the *Express* carried news from Adelaide of his 'magnificent' reception on Australian soil only the day before.

On Thursday, 12 March, however, the prince, standing on the grass overlooking one of the bright coves of Sydney Harbour – that 'mild and luminous floor of waters' – received a bullet in the back. Fired by Henry O'Farrell, a partly mad advocate of Irish independence, it entered 2 inches from the spine, travelled around the right side of the ribcage and halted just beneath the skin. Alfred fell forward, thinking his back was broken. The bullet, in fact, was easily cut out, but its impact echoed by telegraph across the country. Just as quickly the wires carried back reports of the stinging shock felt among the people. From Uralla – 'A great indignation meeting [to be held] in horror of the attempted murder.' From Albury – 'Great excitement.' From Braidwood – 'utmost horror.' These meetings were pure expressions of feeling. Hurt in a momentous way we thought and felt in unison. We were 'One Body'.[44]

There was no telegraph in Western Australia until 1869, and not until 1877 did a line link west with east, around the landward edge of the Great Australian Bight.[45] Far more urgent for most of the Europeans in Australia was the connection overseas and the chance of receiving instant news from the rest of the world – of 'continuously beating' in time with all kindred humanity. This vast undertaking was hindered by the fact that the coasts nearest to Europe were also far away from the main centres of Australian population. Many thousands of vacant square miles – vacant for European minds – lay between the great towns and the various points in the north at which a European submarine cable might be brought to the surface.

Success depended on better knowledge. From the mid-1850s Queensland had been busily explored, partly with the hope that the north might magnificently enrich squatters and businessmen. Halfway between

Brisbane and Cape York the Burdekin River, winding for many green miles parallel with the coast, was traced by the brothers Augustus and Francis Gregory in 1856. Later expeditions outlined a network of watercourses and Bowen, Cardwell, and Townsville were formed as centres of a pastoral province – the beginning, some thought, of a new colony.[46] In 1864 Francis and Alexander Jardine travelled overland to the tip of Cape York.

The question of the control of the north revived competition among colonial governments. All were drawn by its apparent fertility, by its closeness to East Indian traffic, and by the chance of linking up with the European cable. In earlier times (Chapter 5) Bass Strait, in the south, had been the continent's principal waterway. Our geographical balance had now tipped a little, our geographical boundaries expanded. We saw the country from a new angle. Now it seemed likely that the northern waters and islands, the archipelago that made a bridge with Asia, might have a similar role in Australian affairs. The continent was first crossed, from Melbourne to the Gulf, in 1861 by Robert O'Hara Burke and William John Wills. Richly funded, their purpose was to give Victorian enterprise a place in the north, but both leaders died of starvation on their way back. From Adelaide, John McDouall Stuart had made several similar attempts, reaching the centre of the continent, near today's Alice Springs, in 1860. Finally, starting again, in winter 1862 Stuart stooped on the beach at Chambers Bay and washed in its warm salt water.

Adelaide had been planned in the 1830s as a continental hub, as 'the London of Australia', partly because it commanded the western entrance to Bass Strait. The hopes of South Australians were renewed, from 1863, by possession of the Northern Territory, through which might run the overseas connection. This was the great ambition of Charles Todd, and William Cracknell in Queensland was his only – but an urgent – competitor. The line northward from Brisbane reached Cardwell in 1869 and Cracknell had long looked forward to an extension westward from there to the Gulf.[47] But with Stuart's success, planning immediately began in Adelaide for a line following in his tracks. The project was set back by commercial and technical problems, and in the end by Queensland's rival claims. But at length Todd's diplomatic cunning sealed negotiations with the owners of the submarine cable.[48] In winter 1870 work began.

Engineering achievements prove the power of an independent people. They demonstrate its ownership of water, air, and soil. The Zig-Zag railway, a series of tunnels and viaducts built in 1867–69 backwards and forwards up the eastern side of the Blue Mountains, near Sydney, was the first of its kind anywhere in the world. The cable under Bass Strait was innovative too.[49] Todd's Overland Telegraph was a labour of endurance. It was also a vast and intricate administrative effort – the line extending nearly 1700 miles, from Port Augusta, at the head of Spencer Gulf, to Port Darwin. The work went on simultaneously in three sections, often in extreme temperatures and in country that, over many miles, had never been seen before by Europeans except for Stuart and his men, with drays carrying water, provisions, tons of coiled wire, insulators, and batteries to the depots built for the purpose, and so to each point of labour. Hundreds were employed and five died. There were 36,000 timber poles and occasional iron ones, all set within a cleared corridor 30 feet wide or else as a fragile line within a landscape already void of trees.[50]

So was imposed on both blue-green forest and purple-tawny desert 'the magical dominion of the human mind' (Chapter 2). On 22 August 1872 all was complete. The man who pulled the two ends together, at Frew Ponds in the north, also by accident closed the electrical circuit. His yelp was the opening note for immediate conversation with the world.[51]

III

Self-government was a great triumph for the Europeans in Australia. It led to engineering marvels, manhood suffrage, and a larger effort to gather knowledge about land and people. It was combined with a nicer sense of the way each colony sat within the land mass as a whole and within its encircling waters. And it seemed to entail a duty to the original inhabitants. 'I only ask honorable members', said a member of Queensland's upper house in 1864, 'to consider the responsibility which the possession of this land entails upon us'. We have been 'manifestly unjust', he said, to the Aboriginal people. We must find ways of doing better.[52]

The same point was made in each colonial capital. But once again, ideas of duty were shaped by vagaries of imagination and at mid-century imagination was straitened in distinctive ways. Men and women increasingly thought of themselves as fixed types. They communicated with freedom and openness and across great distances, but they communicated mainly with people who looked liked themselves. The charm of reaching out lay in the discovery of similar thought, similar taste, similar feeling – in finding reflections of self both near at hand and a long way away. Each 'ME ', in Carlyle's terms, was part of a far-flung, timeless normality. And that normality had its outer edge. According to Josiah Nott, the 'form' of every species of mankind was fixed, whatever its circumstances. Established in the beginning, he said, it *remained unchanged … for ages*.[53] This was theory erected on the imaginative habits of the day, on shared inclination. That inclination was formed by reading – by diverse and numerous communication, including newspapers, monthlies, and books. Europeans everywhere struggled to know what they themselves were like, and what they were unlike. They wanted a certain permanent feeling of self.

In Australia this concern with like and unlike meant discussions about 'the native character', including the Aborigines as physical beings – 'the

peculiar character of their constitutions'.[54] One might be perfectly ignorant of racial theory and still sense, within this large, interconnected
world, an everlasting difference in mind and body, a boundary between
Black and White.

A few of the Europeans in Australia aspired to understand the difference by something like scientific method.[55] Most thought with less refinement. Several generations of settlement had established a body of common
knowledge both about the land and about its people. This was especially
true among bushmen and in Queensland, from the moment of separation,
government itself was dominated by the language, knowledge, and priorities of the Bush. The inland parts of the new colony had been taken up
partly by capitalists from Europe but also by some who had come here –
themselves or their forebears – much earlier, who had become people of the
Bush. There were several old Hawkesbury families among the Queensland
squatters, of the type mentioned in Chapter 1. Joseph Fleming, whose
brother had led the massacre at Myall Creek in 1838, was at Talavera, on
the Maranoa. His cousins, the Halls, were next door. Augustus Gregory,
the surveyor-general, had grown up in Western Australia. He was an explorer in both colonies. George Clark, born in Tasmania (where his mother
had managed the island's best school for young ladies), was a breeder of
sheep at Talgai, also on the Maranoa.[56]

In no other Australian parliament were bush terms used with such ease
– 'brigalow scrub', for instance (though the clerks differed about its
spelling). *Acacia harpophylla*, thin hard black stems set close, silver leaves,
and yellow-balled blossom, was one of the main obstacles to movement
through the Bush. It gave a hard, dense complexion to the land and squatters knew it well. These gentlemen and their stockmen agreed and disagreed about the 'native character'. Everywhere among them Aboriginal
matters were 'a sort of standing gossip'.[57] It was generally understood that
the Queensland Blacks were cannibals. Did they eat White men? 'They
don't like whites.' What about 'unnatural vices'? They were 'very particular' – 'They are so particular that they won't allow the daughter to sleep at
the same fire with the son, when they have arrived at the age of puberty.'
How do troubles start with settlers? 'I believe the young men are incited to
commit depredations by the old men and women.' Would you take their
word? 'I would not trust them as far as I could throw a bullock by the
tail.'[58] These were remarks from various mouths.

It was also understood that the Aborigines differed from one part of
the continent to another. Europeans were now aware in a detailed fashion
how the indigenous population stretched from shore to shore. Those living
around the Murray and Darling Rivers, it was said in Queensland, were
'more skilful in warfare, and are a finer race of men' than ours. In Western
Australia, '[t]he blacks are far more treacherous [than those in Queensland]'.
Also, they 'never act in large bodies'.[59]

In earlier days high policy on the Aborigines had come from England – from Whitehall and the churches. Now the colonials thought for themselves. In doing so they used their own day-to-day knowledge. In government eyes the most urgent point was the protection of landholders and their livestock, especially on the frontier. In South Australia, for instance, violence between Black and White was managed in the criminal courts, although many more Aborigines were hanged for killing Europeans than the other way around. Since Aboriginal attacks were supposed to be a result of the need to eat, the Adelaide government set up numerous ration depots throughout the settled territory, and because rations depended on good behaviour the Blacks were thus brought within the power of local officials.[60]

From colony to colony methods varied, but also from one European to another. 'Among the settlers', said Maurice O'Connell, president of the legislative council in Brisbane, 'there are some who treat the blacks more skilfully than others'.[61] Power of imagination varied. Some argued with precision, striving to put justice even before feelings of loyalty to their own people – Herman Melville's prescription. The editor of the Melbourne *Argus*, Edward Wilson, believed in the high destiny of the settlers. '[T]he Anglo-Saxon', he said, 'was ... justified in taking possession of this fine country, and developing its magnificent resources, as the original occupant never would have done'. Such, he believed, was 'the onward march of the white man'. But this happy destiny was no excuse for the cruelty and fraud that had been used in the process. 'We have shot them down like dogs', he said. We have poisoned large numbers. 'In the guise of friendship we have issued corrosive sublimate in their damper and consigned whole tribes to the agonies of an excruciating death.' Indeed we have used science and Christian ideas to justify murder. We have blamed the disappearance of our victims on 'natural law' and 'the hand of Providence'.[62] The just hopes of our own race had become, in short, a crutch for the feeble conscience of each member.

The *Argus* was still Melbourne's leading newspaper. There was a peculiar spiritual energy in Melbourne (Chapter 14) and also a keen interest in moral debate. Here government policy was shaped partly by cynicism, partly by openness. It spoke sometimes of coercion, sometimes of willing attention to Aboriginal wishes. But, as usual throughout the continent, it was always overshadowed by a sense of difference. In 1860, following a parliamentary inquiry, a Central Board for Aborigines was formed. Its members were inclined to think that the only hope for the Blacks, including the hope that they might look after themselves, lay in their being isolated. Reserves were set aside under the care of White men. '[M]y method of managing the blacks', said John Green, at Coranderrk on the upper Yarra, 'is to allow them to rule themselves as much as possible'. And yet his discipline was very rigid. Just as reformatories brought some White children under the concentrated power of the state, at Coranderrk Black children were kept as far as possible from their parents, so as to be fully imbued with European feeling.[63]

The difference between 'native character' and the character of Europeans seemed to be worth underlining on the land itself. In the 1830s in Van Diemen's Land the few remaining Aborigines had been removed to Flinders Island (Chapter 9). In Western Australia, Rottnest Island, 12 miles off the coast at Fremantle, was used for the special confinement of Black men who had been convicted of crimes. In Queensland, too, there were suggestions that an island or islands somewhere might help in preserving the lives of some of the Blacks. '[T]he only way I can see', said a squatter, 'is to kidnap them and take them entirely away to some islands, and make them work'.[64]

But this was, as yet, a distant possibility. The Aborigines in Queensland were very numerous and they fought more fiercely perhaps than any elsewhere. On some stations they were regularly fed, they worked a little, and squatters ignored their occasional killing of stock. In other places they were driven off or murdered. In 1848 a body of Native Police had been formed by the Sydney government, with Aboriginal troopers and White officers. They were employed in the north of the colony, the men being brought from the far south. This force was taken over by the new government in Brisbane in 1859 as a fundamental means of order, although its activities were already

Six men from the Queensland Native Police, a picture taken by an unknown photographer in the 1860s. They took off their uniforms in the heat of battle so as to move quickly through the bush.

Reproduction courtesy of Capricornia Collection, University of Central Queensland

controversial there. Then and afterwards the press drew frequent attention to violent clashes and to the apparent decimation of the Queensland tribes.

The Native Police possessed bush skills as well as horses and firearms, but the local people could strike back with devastating effect. In October 1857 nine members of the Fraser household, including a mother and four daughters, were murdered by Jiman men at Hornet Bank, on the Dawson River west of Bundaberg. Three years later, further inland in newly settled country on the Nogoa, at Cullinlaringoe, nineteen men, women, and children were killed by the Gayiri. In both cases large numbers of Blacks were hunted down in retaliation.[65]

The Native Police were the authorised agents of the Queensland government. The government itself was therefore guilty of systematic and lawless violence. The arguments of Brisbane papers on this point were echoed by British ministers and in winter 1861 a parliamentary inquiry, chaired by the squatter and colonial treasurer Robert Ramsay Mackenzie, took up the matter. Attention was focused on two things: the activities of the force and, more broadly, the future control of the Blacks.

But underneath was a larger problem. It is a problem that bears on the chapter, and on all the previous chapters in this volume. During the long series of questions and answers – twenty-nine witnesses and 3791 exchanges, bullying, bluff, fumbling, authoritative – some members of the inquiry clearly wondered about the character of their own people, the Europeans in Australia, tested now by trials of the severest kind.

Most gentlemen on both sides of the table – including many who were concerned for the Aborigines – agreed that the inland's safety depended on the Native Police. The methods of the force were described by Lieutenant Frederick Wheeler, whose detachment patrolled the south-west. In attacking Aborigines he acted, so Wheeler said, as a result of letters from squatters. When they told him that Blacks were killing their livestock he went straight away and 'dispersed' the culprits. 'What do you mean by dispersing?', Mackenzie asked him. 'Firing at them', Wheeler replied. He strictly forbade the shooting of women who might be camped with the offenders. 'It is only sometimes, when it is dark', he said, 'that a gin is mistaken for a blackfellow, or might be wounded inadvertently'. Mackenzie referred to one case as 'indiscriminate slaughter'. 'I don't think there was any indiscriminate slaughter', Wheeler said, 'there were only two blacks shot'.[66] The numbers were often larger. Eighteen were said to have been killed in a battle on the Maranoa (though the officer in charge put it at three or four).[67]

It was widely agreed that fatalities could not be helped. After all, the old inhabitants fought hard and dense scrub made it impossible for White men to work as the police did in South Australia – arresting Blacks and bringing them in for trial. Witnesses remembered 'the old system', before the arrival of the Native Police. There had been 'massacres' then on both sides, said an officer. Many more had died. 'The settlers were all driven away by force from their stations', said Jacob Lowe, speaking of the Macintyre River district, in the south. But they had retaliated – 'of course, we went out, and shot them, and killed a good number'. Now, the Native Police made that unnecessary. Certainly, said Lowe, '[t]here would be more bloodshed, if the whites were allowed to have their own way in punishing the blacks'. Around Brisbane and Ipswich, said Captain John Coley, 250 White men had been killed by Blacks in those days. At Kilcoy, he added (speaking apparently from rumour), Evan Mackenzie and his stockmen had responded to two deaths by administering bullets and poison to the enemy – 'they destroyed hundreds of them'. The force, he was sure, 'has been a great saving of life to whites and blacks'.[68]

By the late 1860s the Native Police had a reputation for extreme brutality. '[T]he longer the force existed', according to a Theophilus Pugh, of the *Moreton Bay Courier*, 'the worse it became'. It now had more damaging firearms, but also its White officers were increasingly inured to blood. This was only to be expected, remarked George Clark of Talgai. Habitual killing had its effect. 'It has been said that, in the course of time, a butcher came to like the smell of blood, and delighted in the killing of a beast.' The habits of these officers, he said, was proof of the same thing.[69] They were addicted now to easy murder.

But still it seemed better not to leave policing to settlers and White troopers. Europeans, whether organised or not, according to Gregory, were always 'more cruel' and 'more uncontrolable' than Black troopers. The Native Police were 'decidedly not more cruel than the settlers', said John Ker Wilson, a Maranoa squatter. Our own people, in other words, were the fundamental problem. Some settlers, said Wilson, showed a lack of 'brains and common sense' in dealing with the Aborigines, lurching between gentleness and blood.[70] Without a force of some kind, George Clark agreed, 'the whites would just shoot them down as they used to do'. William Archer, near Rockhampton, welcomed Blacks on his run. But he, too, thought that without the Native Police the White settlers 'would very soon exterminate the blacks'. If the force were disbanded he would leave, he said, rather than face 'a war of extermination'.[71]

What did this mean from the point of view of intellect and imagination? The squatter St George Gore said of the violence now enveloping them: 'It is a question as to which is the stronger race.'[72] Readers of Josiah Nott, detached and visionary, could have had no doubt on such an issue. But bushmen were not readers. They might know the language of racism, and they might like it, but they were not men of doctrine. Their minds were not shaped to take in large stories of racial destiny. Wrapped in narrow horizons, it must have been an open question to many 'as to which was the stronger race'.

This narrowness of vision, this intimate sense of difference, appeared even in dealings between Europeans and Chinese. Gold was found to the west of Rockhampton in 1861 and at Gympie in 1867. The Chinese shifted direction accordingly and a later series of rushes further north, to the Cape, Gilbert, and Palmer Rivers – within reach of the Gulf – brought thousands overland. There was fighting at Gympie and on the Gilbert. On the Cape River a Chinese killed a European in a pub brawl. But nowhere on the Queensland goldfields were the Chinese attacked in the wholesale, ideological fashion of Buckland River and Lambing Flat.[73]

Fears of a 'hybrid race' had no effect on Queensland capitalists who wanted to bring in Melanesians to work as indentured labourers, bound for periods of six months to two years at a very low, set wage. During 1863–71 more than 3000 arrived – nearly all from the New Hebrides and Loyalty Islands, a thousand miles away. Some worked on the new sugar plantations around Mackay and Maryborough.[74] Queenslanders were also keen to engage with both the wealth and the peoples of Asia – for years the main purpose of exploring the north and opening up the Gulf. Government and parliament were enraptured with the chance of 'enormous trade' with Chinese, Malays, and island people.[75] Theirs was just the kind of profiteering, at the risk of our racial character, which distressed idealists in the south, men like Deniehy and Windeyer.

All this made no difference to the fact that in its management of frontier violence the Queensland government systematically broke the law. The problem made little impact on Robert Herbert, the premier, who spoke scornfully of those who wanted justice for the Aborigines – 'those who prefer the dark-skinned cannibal to their own fellow Christian'. In justifying themselves to Whitehall he and his colleagues pretended that the Blacks, unlike ourselves, were a merciless people. They punished every trespass, Black or White, with death. Even among themselves the strong claimed a right to dispossess the weak. The current troubles 'can never terminate', Herbert said, 'except with the gradual disappearance of [this] ... unimprovable race'.[76] Our overwhelming needs, so he implied, and even more the fundamental difference between Black and White, created purposes beyond the law.

The Aborigines were human beings and, according to long-established principle, British subjects, but no official record was kept of their deaths at the hands of the Native Police. There were few inquests. Officers did not report even the numbers killed.[77] No attempt was made as in earlier days, by Saxe Bannister in New South Wales and George Arthur in Van Diemen's Land (Chapter 8), to declare martial law, so as to give what settlers themselves said were hundreds of deaths some kind of legality. A police force was not a military body and it was not entitled to act as this one did. 'You would have to pass a law', a squatter remarked, 'to render killing no murder'.[78] Maurice O'Connell, once a squatter himself, had no doubt that the force must be given up. The killings that would result from its absence, he said, might be dealt with by a combination of civil and martial law. At least the government would then cease to be party to 'a wholesale system of extermination'.[79]

O'Connell felt especially the impact of these deeds on civilised opinion. Whatever the legal position, 'the horror of all right-thinking people', he said, 'is very greatly excited by the knowledge that cruelty and injustice have been committed under the guise of law'. There is after all, he said, 'an instinctive feeling against taking human life'.[80] The government did in fact make adjustments to the law but nothing effective was done to curtail the Native Police.

The legal problems were the more easily overlooked partly because the Aborigines seemed to be, like animals, creatures without moral motives. They behaved for mysterious reasons of their own, which put them, in a sense, outside the law. Like a horse with its rider, for instance, 'by a certain instinct' they could sense the purposes of a White man.[81] This was 'animal' instinct, not moral instinct, or conscience – the 'instinctive feeling' mentioned by O'Connell. The indiscriminate sense of kin, the tug of duty, the glimpse of God in one's neighbour – moral imagining 'dark with excessive brightness' – was apparently beyond the Blacks. John Leopold Zillman, once a missionary, argued otherwise before the committee:

> [W]ith the blackfellows it is just the same as with us: they have a natural conscience, as we find in the Epistles of Saint Paul, we have a natural conscience which distinguishes between the good and bad. They have the same conscience, and the fear of doing wrong, and they feel a gladness when they are doing right.[82]

His listeners thought differently.

The idea that Black and White might have been equally present in the mind of St Paul – or rather, in the mind of the Almighty – had once been fundamental to every elaborate scheme for higher civilisation in Australia. In a single generation all had changed.

In 1860 Emma McPherson, an Englishwoman who had lived with her husband on Keera Station, near Bingera in north-west New South Wales, published in London a book entitled *My Experiences in Australia*. Two chapters she spent on the Aborigines. 'I was naturally', she said, 'very anxious to learn all I could about this strange race'. She felt in many small ways for the people who lived on Keera. During one visit with her husband to their camp she carried her box of watercolours, to their intense interest. Among the paint and dye brought from Europe to Australia red especially intrigued the Blacks – a sacramental colour used in their own painting, and the colour of blood. King Sandy, the leading man, according to Mrs McPherson, was 'especially happy' when her husband put his finger in the paint and covered his black cheeks with 'remarkable hieroglyphics'. 'I soon made him desist, however', she said, 'for there was something melancholy in seeing the childish eagerness with which this really fine looking old savage submitted or rather petitioned to be thus bedaubed'.[83]

Keera, said Emma McPherson, was the '*tourai*' of these people. It was 'the little domain which belonged to them and they to it'. She was sure, all the same, like most of her own kind, that the Aborigines were 'almost the lowest' of human types. The overrunning of their country, its bedaubing with pain, was therefore sad but just. '[T]o call the conflicts which occasionally take place with the aborigines by the name of *murder*', she said, 'is simply absurd'.[84] Keera was barely 20 miles from Myall Creek. It was also less than twenty years between the murders on that place, murders then punished with the full force of the law, and her own gentle inquiries.

Afterword

I

It is hard to say exactly how the Europeans in Australia, in the first years of democracy, thought about the country itself. For the time being the appearance of the land was not an important topic among them. It was still easy to appreciate examples of vivid beauty, especially manifest in a mass of colour. The newly immigrant author, Henry Kingsley, in his novel, *The Recollections of Geoffrey Hamlyn* (1859), wrote about a laughing party of horsemen in the bush:

> startling the brilliant thick-clustered lories (richest coloured of all the par-
> rots in the world), as they hung chattering on some silver-leafed acacia,
> bending with their weight the fragile boughs down towards the clear still
> water, lighting up the dark pool with strange, bright reflections of crimson
> and blue.[1]

This was typical. Here certainly was beauty – but none of that independent mystery, that unknown, even ghostly presence that had been evident to many even twenty years earlier. This seemed now to be a place that came to life, as it did for Kingsley, during the passage of newcomers. It was not a place where life – larger and more mysterious – might pause until such wanderers had gone.

Leading explorers had once been men of trained imagination, used to grappling with the deeper impressions made on them by landscape. Many were writers who were proud of being able to set out on paper interwoven layers of experience. Now explorers were likely to think about what they saw mainly in terms of commercial usefulness and material form. During 1861 there was talk of founding a new colony in the northern parts of Western Australia where cotton might be grown, and Francis Gregory led an expedition to investigate. Leaving Fremantle in April the party reached Nickol Bay, nearly a thousand miles to the north, in October. They made their way back by sea. There was to be no new colony in fact, but graziers soon followed in the explorers' tracks, settling especially between the De Grey and Fortescue Rivers. Gregory's journal, which was published, was

334

characteristic of its time. There were touches of whimsy. At the mouth of
the De Grey, at the beginning of high tide, for instance, he was struck with
way the blue-green ocean mass was met by smaller creatures. 'Swarms of
beautiful bright-crimson crabs', he said, 'about two inches diameter, were
to be seen issuing from their holes to welcome the coming flood'.[2] There
was uncharacteristic whimsy in that word 'welcome'.

And with the people too:

> [W]e came suddenly on a party of natives, digging roots. One woman, with
> a child of about five years of age, hid close to our line of march, and did
> not move until she was afraid of being run over by the pack-horses, when
> she ran away, leaving the child gazing upon the monster intruders with a
> look of passive wonder. It was a poor, ill-conditioned looking object, suf-
> fering from a cutaneous disorder. On giving it a piece of damper, it quickly
> began to devour it, tearing it to fragments with its sharp and attenuated fin-
> gers, with all the keenness of a hawk.

But the drama of landscape Gregory rendered in more straightforward terms:

> In one place the river [the Fortescue] had cut through a ridge of altered rocks,
> and exhibited a very singular contortion of the strata, the laminae being crip-
> pled up into an arch of 100 feet high, showing a dip on each flank of 45
> degrees, forming a cave beneath running for some distance into the hill.[3]

Gregory had grown up in Australia. He found the land inexhaustibly interesting but he took its appearance for granted more than a new immigrant
might have done. More important, he saw no need to dwell on its mani-
festations of power and in this he was a man of his time.

Even among old settlers and the native-born, according to Anthony
Trollope: 'It is taken for granted that Australia is ugly.'[4] Difference from
the rest of the world proved ugliness. The Europeans in Australia might
delight in feeling for or with others like themselves, here and elsewhere, but
for the moment they felt little for the land and little, too, for its first inhabitants. Edward Wilson, of the Melbourne *Argus*, summed up their prag-
matic indifference. The invading 'Anglo-Saxon', he said:

> takes possession of the land as a matter of course. He alters water-courses,
> drives off game, fences, clears, and cultivates, tears open the very bowels of
> the earth and walks away with uncounted wealth, while the original occu-
> pant of the soil, not only looks helplessly on, but sinks, contaminated by
> new vices, and wasted by imported diseases, into premature extermination.[5]

The culprit here was the man in the Bush. The man in town did and
thought nothing one way or the other.

The idealism of the 1850s and '60s came wholly from abroad – shining
parcels of thought introduced together with 'new vices' and 'imported diseases'. Democracy itself was valued to start with as a regimen of distant

manufacture and reformers carefully stressed its British credentials. (There was no manhood suffrage in Britain until 1918, but it had been talked about there sixty years earlier.)[6] Democracy, in its ideal form, was in no way tied to the Australian soil and it was, so far, sharply at odds with life in the Bush. The cities and the south-eastern goldfields, places open to the wide world, were its best home. The great hope of reformers in this period – of all high-minded men and women, especially the young – was to impose on the country something unlike its old self. Agendas varied and at least in principle ambitions might contradict each other. But an emphatic foreign-ness was their common theme. There was to be a moral and self-respecting workforce to replace the convicts. There was to be temperance instead of drunkenness. There was to be settled family life instead of the old pre-dominance of single men. There was to be free enterprise, with government giving up any idea of shaping the economy as it had done in convict days. There was to be egalitarianism and democracy instead of hierarchy and the property vote. There was to be self-conscious and deliberate racial purity, democracy itself being a special creation of the Anglo-Saxon race. Self-gov-ernment alone contradicted this interlinking with the remainder of the world. But it was self-government which allowed the people go about their own refashioning.

Convictism summed up memories of the old regime very neatly. Convict labour and convict degradation did most to make the Australian past seem contemptible. The movement against slavery in the United States – care-fully watched elsewhere, from the publication of *Uncle Tom's Cabin* in 1852 until the end of the Civil War in 1865 – forced comparisons between Australia and America. 'Convicts were slaves', wrote John West in the *Sydney Morning Herald*, looking back. They were treated like slaves – '[T]here have been convict quarters in the Australian bush not very much above the quality of those devoted to niggers.'[7]

The importance of distinguishing, as day from night, the democratic present from the corrupt and selfish past was to survive, even throughout the twentieth century. But the moment of real urgency was brief. By the end of the period dealt with in this volume Australian attitudes were already mellowing. In writing, and probably in speech, the Europeans in Australia wondered again about their understanding of the land. In his poems from the early 1870s Adam Lindsay Gordon laughed like Kingsley's riders at the impact of horsemen among wildlife. But the sadder lines of Henry Kendall glanced at something larger: 'The ruins of Time', as he put it, 'in revisited places'. All at once, for instance, Kendall told of 'the ruthless Australasian wastes' and of 'the wild old times', as if Australia's sometimes frightening landscape was a mirror for the dreadful, half-forgotten past.[8] Marcus Clarke's famous convict story, at first entitled *His Natural Life* (1870–72), also made a single package of these two samples of terror – a dimly fearful time in a dimly fearful place.

This was also, by 1870, the age of weekly newspapers, managed in the cities but meant mainly for country readers – the *Australasian*, the *Town and Country Journal*, the *Queenslander*. These dwelt on more manageable peculiarities – the skills of rural life, rural ambition, and rural adventure. Whether or not Australia was frightening, such printed detail, including serialised stories of the Bush – some of them from expert hands – made it gradually harder to think that the land was ugly and dull.[9]

In town and country from the 1870s the Europeans in Australia became more assured in their local patriotism. They continued to scatter further afield. They populated new coastal towns in the far north, including Broome in Western Australia and, in Queensland, Cooktown, Cairns, and Townsville. In and beyond these towns there was also a thickening population of Chinese, Melanesians, and Malays, complicating even more Australian ideas about race. A hardening of racial ideals in the last decades of the nineteenth century meant that the north became a problem for the future – at least from the point of view of other parts of Australia – instead of the source of hope it had once been.[10]

Partly inspired by the threat of foreign labour, working men began to organise in a settled, long-term fashion. Trade unionism was well established during the 1870s and soon labouring men sat in parliament. Miners and shearers, men of mobile habits, were essential in this long campaign.[11] For this reason, too, the Bush was now in closer conversation with the town and a collective sense of self became more tightly tied to the Australian soil.

In the 1840s and 1850s, in every colony, children had gone to school in unprecedented numbers (Chapter 7). And so Trollope was to find in 1871–72, when some of those children were approaching middle age: 'The labourer born in the colonies is better educated than the man who has come from the old country.' Habits of literacy fed ideas of equality and yet 'the education of youths', as Trollope also remarked, was 'quick, perfunctory, and perhaps superficial'. This was a land of 'rough plenty', of a certain prosperity widely dispersed, but 'literary luxury', as he called it, was another matter.[12] The possession of good clothes – another aspect of 'rough plenty' – was the reason, so the great man guessed, why so many people went to church. The reason was really more complicated (Chapter 14). And indeed, with good clothes still, from the 1870s numbers of churchgoing dwindled again.[13] Never again were the Europeans in Australia so apparently devout as they were when Trollope saw them. So another age took shape.

II

In June 1833, at work on his farm at Swan River, George Fletcher Moore had noticed a small hill. On it, as he wrote in his diary that night, 'stood a sort of pillar of clay'. It was about 5 feet high and had once filled up the centre of a hollow tree. The wood had fallen away and left the clay exposed:

> This pillar [said Moore] was the work of white ants. As it interfered with the working of the plough, I commenced breaking and digging it down; not without some small curiosity. Numbers of centipedes were found about the outside, where pieces of the wood still remained. The clay, which was surprisingly stiff, hard, and dry, broke off in large fragments. At length, near the level of the surface of the ground, a rounded crust was uncovered, looking like the crown of a dome. On breaking through this, the whole city of the ants was laid bare – a wonderful mass of cells, pillars, chambers, and passages. The spade sunk perhaps two feet among the crisp and cracking ruins, which seemed formed either of the excavated remnants of the tree, or a thin shell-like cement of clay. The arrangement of the interior was singular: the central part had the appearance of innumerable small branching pillars, like the minutest stalactital formations, or like some of the smaller coralline productions. Towards the outer part, the materials assumed the appearance of thin laminae, about half the substance of a wafer, but most ingeniously disposed in the shape of a series of low elliptic arches, so placed that the centre of the arch below formed the resting-place for the abutment of the arch above. These abutments again formed sloping platforms for ascent to the higher apartments. In other places, I thought I could discern spiral ascents, not unlike geometrical staircases.

He was mightily impressed. It was like the remnant of an ancient civilisation – 'an ingenious specimen of complicated architecture, and such an endless labyrinth of intricate passages, as could bid defiance alike to art and to Ariadne's clue'.

Moore wrote like an historian of cities and empires – like an Edward Gibbon (Ancient Rome) or a George Grote (Ancient Greece). Like any good historian, he knew that, even among these desiccated ruins, he confronted something neither static nor wholly dead. '[E]ven the affairs of the ants', he said, 'are subject to mutation'. The story uncovered by his spade was only one episode in a longer tale. 'This great city was deserted – a few loiterers alone remained, to tell to what race it had formerly belonged.' The ants, by living within the tree had apparently killed it and made it useless even to themselves. 'Their great store-houses had been exhausted – even the roots had been laid under contribution.' At last, so Moore imagined, 'its myriads of inhabitants had migrated *en masse*, to commence anew their operations in some other soil'.[14]

The two ant-nests, old and new, might be taken to stand for the two generations that are described in this volume – the generation that coloured life around about the 1830s and that of the goldrush years and after. The notion of an intricate way of life given over and replaced by something new certainly matches what I say here. At length, with the coming of democracy, the habits of earlier days seemed to be, in the minds of the young, as dried up and use-less as Moore's 'great city'. The Europeans in Australia made for themselves another mental habitation, like the ants. Like the ants, moreover, they were gatherers from the world beyond, living by traffic and communication. In rehousing themselves they drew their main materials, all that coloured glass, all those entrancing ideas, from Britain and the United States.

But ants are not much given, apparently, to the impulse of delight. In this respect the Europeans in Australia were more like those small crimson creatures at the mouth of the De Grey, who hurried from their houses to feel the weight of the incoming tide.

Notes

Foreword

1 Geoffrey Blainey, *The Tyranny of Distance: How Distance Shaped Australia's History* (Melbourne 1966).

2 Harold Bloom, *The Western Canon: The Books and School of the Ages* (London 1995), pp. 48–9.

3 Elizabeth Gaskell, *Mary Barton: A Tale of Manchester Life* (London 1970; first pub. 1848), p. 38.

4 Charles Dickens, *The Old Curiosity Shop* (London 1953; first pub. 1841), pp. 370–1; Virginia Woolf, *To the Lighthouse* (London 1977; first pub. 1927), p. 39.

5 Barron Field, *First Fruits of Australian Poetry* (Canberra 1990; first pub. 1819).

6 Alan Atkinson and Marian Aveling (eds), *Australians 1838* (Sydney 1987).

7 Rob Pascoe, *The Manufacture of Australian History* (Melbourne 1979), pp. 42–69; Stephen Garton, 'What Have We Done? Labour History, Social History, Cultural History', in Terry Irving (ed.), *Challenges to Labour History* (Sydney 1994).

8 The sources for the latter are already numerous. See especially Keith Windschuttle, 'The Myths of Frontier Massacres in Australian History', in three parts, *Quadrant*, October, November, and December 2000; Bain Attwood and Stephen Foster (eds), *Frontier Conflict: The Australian Experience* (Canberra 2003); Keith Windschuttle, *The Fabrication of Aboriginal History*, vol. 1 (Sydney 2003); Stuart Macintyre and Anna Clark, *The History Wars* (Melbourne 2003); Robert Manne (ed.), *Whitewash: On Keith Windschuttle's Fabrication of Aboriginal History* (Melbourne 2003); Discussion in *History Australia: Journal of the Australian Historical Association*, vol. 1, no. 1 (December 2003).

9 Alan Atkinson, 'Honey and Wax' (review of Windschuttle, *The Fabrication of Aboriginal History*, vol. 1), *Journal of Australian Colonial History*, vol. 4 (2002) (appeared January 2004).

10 Keith Windschuttle, quoted in 'History Made Implausible', 27 September 2003, *Australian* web page, www.theaustralian.news.com.au/common/story (seen 18 October 2003).

11 Edward Gibbon, *The History of the Decline and Fall of the Roman Empire* (ed. David Womersley) (London 1994; first pub. 1776–88), vol. 2, p. 147 (originally vol. 3, chapter 30, fn. 82).

12 Alan Atkinson, *The Commonwealth of Speech: An Argument about Australia's Past, Present and Future* (Melbourne 2002).

13 Ken Macnab and Russel Ward, 'The Nature and Nurture of the First Generation of Native-Born Australians', *Historical Studies*, no. 39 (November

1962); Ward, *The Australian Legend* (Melbourne 1966); Portia Robinson, *The Hatch and Brood of Time: A Study of the First Generation of Native-Born White Australians 1788–1828* (Melbourne 1985); John Molony, *The Native-Born: The First White Australians* (Melbourne 2000).

14 Michael Roe, *Quest for Authority in Eastern Australia 1835–1851* (Melbourne 1965); John Gascoigne, *The Enlightenment and the Origins of European Australia* (Cambridge 2002).

15 C.M.H. Clark, *A History of Australia*, vol. 2 (*New South Wales and Van Diemen's Land 1822-1838*) (Melbourne 1968), pp. 41–60. See also Michael Persse's account of Wentworth, *Australian Dictionary of Biography*, vol. 2, pp. 582–9.

16 His face appears in a collective portrait of the Anti-Slavery Convention, 1840, by Benjamin Robert Haydon (National Portrait Gallery, London), but it is too much obscured and too small to show what he looked like. I am grateful to Jennifer Mamujee of the National Portrait Gallery for help with this picture.

17 Peter Hammond, 'Murder, Manslaughter and Workplace Relations in Convict New South Wales 1824–1838', BA thesis, University of New England 2003.

18 See, for instance, Alan Atkinson, 'Four Patterns of Convict Protest', *Labour History*, no. 37 (November 1979); J.B. Hirst, *Convict Society and Its Enemies: A History of Early New South Wales* (Sydney 1983); Alan Atkinson and Marian Aveling (eds), *Australian 1838* (Sydney 1987); Hamish Maxwell-Stewart, 'The Bushrangers and the Convict System of Van Diemen's Land, 1803–1846', PhD thesis, University of Edinburgh 1990; Kirsty M. Reid, 'Work, Sexuality and Resistance: The Convict Women of Van Diemen's Land, 1820–1839', PhD thesis, University of Edinburgh 1995; Ian Duffield and James Bradley (eds), *Representing Convicts: New Perspectives on Convict Forced Labour Migration* (London 1997); Joy Damousi, *Depraved and Disorderly: Female Convicts, Sexuality and Gender in Colonial Australia* (Cambridge 1997); Kay Daniels, *Convict Women: Rough Culture and Reformation* (Sydney 1998); Cassandra Pybus and Hamish Maxwell-Stewart, *American Citizens, British Slaves: Yankee Political Prisoners in an Australian Penal Colony 1839–1850* (Melbourne 2002).

19 Brian Plomley and Kristen Anne Henley, 'The Sealers of Bass Strait and the Cape Barren Island Community', *Tasmanian Historical Research Association Papers and Proceedings*, vol. 37 (1990); Iain Stuart, 'Sea Rats, Bandits and Roistering Buccaneers: What Were the Bass Strait Sealers Really Like?', *Journal of the Royal Australian Historical Society*, vol. 83 (1997); Rebe Taylor, 'Savages or Saviours? The Australian Sealers and Tasmanian Aboriginal Culture', *Journal of Australian Studies*, no. 66 (2000).

20 Lionel Frost, *Australian Cities in Comparative View* (Melbourne 1990).

21 Pike, Douglas, *Paradise of Dissent: South Australia 1829–1857* (Melbourne 1967); Stuart Macintyre, *Colonial Liberalism: The Lost World of Three Victorian Visionaries* (Melbourne 1991).

22 Miriam Dixson, *The Real Matilda: Woman and Identity in Australia 1788 to the Present* (Melbourne 1994); Atkinson and Aveling, op. cit.; Patricia Grimshaw and others, *Creating a Nation 1788–1990* (Melbourne 1994); Marilyn

Lake, 'The Constitution of Political Subjectivity and the Writing of Labour History', in Irving op. cit.; Miriam Dixson, *The Imaginary Australian: Anglo-Celts and Identity – 1788 to the Present* (Sydney 1999); Marilyn Lake, *Getting Equal: The History of Australian Feminism* (Sydney 1999); Annemieke van Drenth and Francisca de Haan, *The Rise of Caring Power: Elizabeth Fry and Josephine Butler in Britain and the Netherlands* (Amsterdam 1999); Iris Marion Young, 'The Logic of Masculinist Protection: Reflections on the Current Security State', *Journal of Women in Culture and Society*, vol. 29 (2003), pp. 3–6.

23   Henry Reynolds, *The Other Side of the Frontier: An Interpretation of the Aboriginal Response to the Invasion and Settlement of Australia* (Townsville 1981) (and see Bibliography, below); Lyndall Ryan, *The Aboriginal Tasmanians* (St Lucia 1981).

24   Atkinson, 'Honey and Wax'.

25   Geoffrey Serle, *The Golden Age: A History of the Colony of Victoria 1851–1861* (Melbourne 1963); Weston Bate, *Lucky City: The First Generation at Ballarat 1851–1901* (Melbourne 1978).

26   F.G. Clarke, *The Land of Contrarieties: British Attitudes to the Australian Colonies 1828–1855* (Melbourne 1977), pp. 102–5; Anne Coote, 'Imagining a Colonial Nation: The Development of Popular Concepts of Sovereignty and Nation in New South Wales with Particular Reference to the Period between 1856 and 1860', *Journal of Australian Colonial History*, vol. 1 (1999); Anne Coote, 'The Development of Colonial Nationhood in New South Wales, c. 1825–1865', PhD thesis, University of New England, forthcoming.

27   P. Loveday and A.W. Martin, *Parliament, Factions and Parties: The First Thirty Years of Responsible Government in New South Wales, 1856–1889* (Melbourne 1966); A.W. Martin, *Henry Parkes: A Biography* (Melbourne 1980).

28   J.B. Hirst, *The Strange Birth of Colonial Democracy: New South Wales 1848–1884* (Sydney 1988); Mark McKenna, *The Captive Republic: A History of Republicanism in Australia 1788–1996* (Cambridge 1996).

29   Richard Sennett, *The Fall of Public Man* (Cambridge 1977); Ann Douglas, *The Feminization of American Culture* (London 1996); Susan West, 'Bushranging, the Policing of Rural Banditry and Working Class Identity in New South Wales, 1860–1880', PhD thesis, University of Newcastle 2003.

30   Henry Reynolds, *North of Capricorn: The Untold Story of Australia's North* (Sydney 2003).

31   Raymond Evans, Kay Saunders and Kathryn Cronin, *Exclusion, Exploitation and Extermination: Race Relations in Colonial Queensland* (Sydney 1975); Raymond Evans, *Fighting Words: Writing about Race* (St Lucia 1999); Raymond Evans and Bill Thorpe, 'Indigenocide and the Massacre of Aboriginal History', *Overland*, no. 163 (Winter 2001).

32   Thomas L. Haskell, 'Capitalism and the Origins of the Humanitarian Sensibility' (in two parts), *American Historical Review*, vol. 90 (1985).

33   W.K. Hancock, *Australia* (London 1930), pp. 74–75, 84. See also the work of Eleanor Dark, Marjorie Barnard, and Florence Eldershaw.

34   Richard Windeyer, 'On the Rights of the Aborigines of Australia', June 1844, ML MSS 1400, p. 43; Henry Reynolds, *This Whispering in Our Hearts* (Melbourne 1998).

35   Tom Roberts, 1897, quoted in Bob Birrell, *Federation: The Secret Story* (Sydney 2001), pp. 125–6.

36   Alan Atkinson, 'Irony and Bluster: An Historian Responds to His Critics', *Australian Historical Association Bulletin*, no. 88 (June 1999).

Part 1

1   *South Australian Register*, 27 March 1841 (paragraphing added).

Chapter 1: Bound by Birth

1   John Hunter, *An Historical Journal of the Transactions at Port Jackson and Norfolk Island* (London 1793), p. 70.

2   James Tucker, *Ralph Rashleigh* (Sydney 1962), p. 173.

3   Hunter, op. cit., p. 70; Mrs Charles Meredith, *Notes and Sketches of New South Wales* (London 1844), pp. 69–70, 149. I am grateful to Elizabeth Davidson for advice on ants.

4   Meredith, op. cit., p. 149.

5   A.G.L. Shaw, *Convicts and the Colonies: A Study of Penal Transportation from Great Britain and Ireland to Australia and Other Parts of the British Empire* (London 1966), pp. 84, 363–5; Wray Vamplew (ed.), *Australians: Historical Statistics* (Sydney 1987), pp. 104, 106.

6   G.P. Harris to his mother, 6 November 1803, in Barbara Hamilton-Arnold (ed.), *Letters and Papers of G.P. Harris 1803–1812* (Melbourne 1994), p. 44.

7   Irene Schaffer (ed.), *Land Musters, Stock Returns and Lists, Van Diemen's Land 1803–1822* (Hobart 1991), pp. 8–14, 23.

8   W.H. Leigh, *Reconnoitering Voyages, Travels and Adventures in the New Colonies of South Australia* (London 1839), p. 103; James Ross, *Dr Ross's Recollections of a Short Excursion to Lake Echo in Van Diemen's Land 1823* (Hobart 1992), p. 41; Keith Thomas, *Man and the Natural World: Changing Attitudes in England 1500–1800* (London 1983), p. 138.

9   G.T.W.B. Boyes to his wife, 12 April 1824, in Peter Chapman (ed.), *The Diaries and Letters of G.T.W.B. Boyes*, vol. 1 (Melbourne 1985), p. 183.

10 Amasa Delano, *A Narrative of Voyages and Travels* (Boston, Mass., 1817), pp. 441, 458–9; Ross, op. cit., pp. 49, 55–6; David Burn, *A Picture of Van Diemen's Land* (Hobart 1973; first pub. 1840–41), pp. 125–6.

11 Ibid., pp. 92–3.

12 *Sydney Gazette*, 28 July, 4, 11 August 1810; Alan Atkinson, *The Europeans in Australia: A History*, vol. 1 (Melbourne 1997), p. 331.

13 Sidney J. Baker, *The Australian Language: The Meanings, Origins and Usage from Convict Days to the Present* (Sydney 1978), p. 312; Philip Conolly to Bishop Poynter, 13 November 1819, quoted in W.T. Southerwood, 'New Light on the Foundation of Australian Catholicism', *Australasian Catholic Record*, vol. 61 (1984), p. 165.

14 Trial of Edward Powell and others, 14–18 October 1799, *HRA*, series 1, vol. 2, pp. 403–22.

15 *Sydney Gazette*, 2 June 1805.

16 *Hobart Town Gazette*, 13, 20 March 1819; Lyndall Ryan, *The Aboriginal Tasmanians* (St Lucia 1981), pp. 75–8; Marie Fels, 'Culture Contact in the County of Buckinghamshire, Van Diemens Land 1803–11', *Tasmanian Historical Research Association Papers and Proceedings*, vol. 29 (1982), pp. 47–68; Brian Plomley and Kristen Anne Henley, 'The Sealers of Bass Strait and the Cape Barren Island Community', *Tasmanian Historical Research Association: Papers and Proceedings*, vol. 37 (1990), pp. 61–2; Keith Windschuttle, *The Fabrication of Aboriginal History*, vol. 1 (Sydney 2003), pp. 48–56.

17 T.H. Scott to R. J. Wilmot Horton, 4 September 1823, CO 201/147, f. 348.

18 J.O. Balfour, *A Sketch of New South Wales* (London 1845), p. 69; Roger Therry, *Reminiscences of Thirty Years' Residence in New South Wales and Victoria* (London 1863), pp. 121–2; Richard Cartwright, evidence before Commissioner Bigge, 26 November 1819, in John Ritchie (ed.), *The Evidence to the Bigge Reports* (Melbourne 1971), vol. 1, p. 157; Michael J. Belcher, 'The Child in New South Wales Society: 1820 to 1837', PhD thesis, University of New England 1982, pp. 111–12; Michael Sturma, *Vice in a Vicious Society: Crime and Convicts in Mid-Nineteenth Century New South Wales* (St Lucia 1983), p. 78. For ages see AOT CSO 918.

19 J.T. Bigge, *Report of the Commissioner of Inquiry, on the State of Agriculture and Trade in the Colony of New South Wales* (London 1823), p. 76. The literacy figures come from an analysis of signatories in the Anglican marriage registers, combined for New South Wales with the 1828 census (work done by Trin Truscett), and for Van Diemen's Land (Hobart registers only) with evidence of local birth or arrival as children. For school attendance, see AOT CSO 1/918; *Statistics of Tasmania 1804–54*, no. 25; T.H. Scott to George Arthur, 13 February 1826, *HRA*, series 3, vol. 5, pp. 154–9; Scott to Ralph Darling, 1 May 1826, *HRA*, series 1, vol. 12, pp. 309–18; Scott to Arthur, 25 March 1828, *HRA*, series 3, vol. 7, pp. 139–50.

20 Henry Home, Lord Kames, *Sketches of the History of Man* (Edinburgh 1778), vol. 2, p. 172; Ross, op. cit., p. 46.

21 Bigge, *Report ... on the State of Agriculture and Trade ...* , p. 82; T.H. Scott to R. Wilmot Horton, 4 September 1823, CO 201/147, f. 348.

22 Bigge, *Report ... on the State of Agriculture and Trade ...* , pp. 75; Tucker, op. cit., p. 103.

23 Peter Cunningham, *Two Years in New South Wales* (Sydney 1966; first pub. 1827), p. 207.

24 Elizabeth Gaskell, quoted by Clement Shorter in his introduction to Gaskell, *The Life of Charlotte Brontë* (Oxford 1919), p. xi.

25 *Sydney Gazette*, 9, 30 October 1823. West's authorship is clearly implied in later correspondence: *Sydney Gazette*, 13 January, 10, 17, 24 February, 31 March, 14 April 1825.

26 *Sydney Gazette*, 30 October 1823; Cunningham, op. cit., p. 209; Nolan, op. cit., pp. 311–13.

27 James Backhouse, *A Narrative of a Visit to the Australian Colonies* (London 1843), p. 21; William Macarthur, 'A few Memoranda respecting the aboriginal Natives' [1835?], ML A2935; Sir William Macarthur's reminiscences, as recorded by Elizabeth Onslow, March 1870, ML A2935, pp. 239–42.

28 John McGarvie to T.H. Scott, 19 June 1828, AONSW 4/330, ff. 245–7; Petition of Edward Ready, 9 July 1829, AONSW 4/331, p. 61.

29 Charles Tompson jnr, 'Retrospect; or, A Review of my Scholastic Days', in his *Wild Notes from the Lyre of a Native Minstrel* (Sydney 1826), p. 15; Sir William Macarthur's reminiscences, p. 239.

30 W.C. Wentworth, *Australasia* (London 1823); Reminiscences of Jane Maria Cox, 1873, National Library MS 1559/25, p. 8. It is not certain that William Wentworth was D'Arcy's son. John Ritchie's chronology, in *The Wentworths: Father and Son* (Melbourne 1997), pp. 23–4, 52–3, making William's birth 'at least five weeks premature', might not have convinced D'Arcy himself.

31 *Sydney Gazette*, 21 August 1803; Leigh, op. cit., p. 93; Meredith, op. cit., p. 150; George Fletcher Moore, *Diary of Ten Years Eventful Life of an Early Settler in Western Australia* (London 1884), p. 52; Edward West Marriott (ed.), *The Memoirs of Obed West: A Portrait of Early Sydney* (Bowral 1988), p. 36.

32 Leigh, op. cit., p. 101; George Augustus Robinson, journal, 26 December 1835, in N.J.B. Plomley (ed.), *Weep in Silence: A History of the Flinders Island Aboriginal Settlement* (Hobart 1987), p. 330.

33 *Launceston Advertiser*, 21 September 1829; Alexander Harris, *The Emigrant Family; or, the Story of an Australian Settler* (Canberra 1967; first pub. 1849), p. 74; Charles Rowcroft, *Tales of the Colonies; or the Adventures of an Emigrant* (London 1858), p 12; Longford (Norfolk Plains) petty sessions, 8 September 1830, 20 June 1836, LC 362/3. See also Alexander Harris, *Settlers and Convicts; or, Recollections of Sixteen Years' Labour in the Australian Backwoods* (Melbourne 1953; first pub. 1847), p. 62.

34 *Sydney Gazette*, 7 August 1803, 3 June 1804, 2 June, 22 December 1805, 18 June 1809.

35 Charles Harpur, 'Midsummer Noon in the Australian Forest', in Adrian Mitchell (ed.), *Charles Harpur* (Melbourne 1973), pp. 25–6.

36 Tompson, 'Retrospect; or, A Review of my Scholastic Days', pp. 1–18.

37 'Betsey Bandicoot' to the editor, *Sydney Gazette*, 30 October 1823.

38 Bigge, *Report … on the State of Agriculture and Trade …* , pp. 81–2; *Monitor*, 5 July 1827; *Australian*, 28 January 1831; Edith Wharton, *Ethan Frome* (London 1938), p. 5; Stephen Nicholas and Richard H. Steckel, 'Heights and Living Standards of English Workers During the Early Years of Industrialization, 1770–1815', *Journal of Economic History*, vol. 51 (1991), pp. 938–41.

39 Ralph Darling to William Huskisson, 10 April 1828, *HRA*, series 1, vol. 15, p. 131; Cunningham, op. cit., p. 207; Meredith, op. cit., p. 50; Belcher, op. cit., p. 63.

40 Bigge, *Report … on the State of Agriculture and Trade …* , pp. 81–2; Balfour, op. cit., pp. 5–6.

41 Bigge, *Report … on the State of Agriculture and Trade …* , pp. 12–13; Edward Curr, *An Account of the Colony of Van Diemen's Land* (London 1824), pp. 14–17.

42 Ibid., pp. 35–8; Backhouse, op cit., pp. 132–3.

43 G.T.W.B. Boyes to his wife, 6 May 1824, in Chapman op. cit., p. 192; Diary of Christiana Brooks, March 1826, ML MSS 4661, p. 47; Cunningham, op. cit., pp. 207–8, 211; *Monitor*, 24 August 1834 (I owe this reference to Erin

Ihde); Glen McLaren, *Beyond Leichhardt: Bushcraft and the Exploration of Australia* (Fremantle 1996), p. 160.

44   Tucker, op. cit., pp. 102–3, 194 (original emphasis).

45   'An Australian Journalist', *The Emigrant in Australia, or Gleanings from the Gold-Fields* (London 1852) p. 10; Baker, op. cit., p. 29.

46   Population return, 10 September–26 October 1821, and Lachlan Macquarie to Lord Bathurst, 27 June 1822, *HRA*, series 1, vol. 10, pp. 575, 675; James Atkinson, *An Account of the State of Agriculture and Grazing in New South Wales* (London 1826), p. 62; Malcolm R. Sainty and Keith A. Johnson (eds), *Census of New South Wales, November 1828* (Sydney 1980); Carol J. Baxter (ed.), *Musters of New South Wales and Norfolk Island 1805–1806* (Sydney 1989), pp. xvi, 122–42; McLaren, op. cit., pp. 30–1.

47   Returns of population and livestock in Van Diemen's Land, October 1819, March 1820, *HRA*, series 3, vol. 4, pp. 638–9; Backhouse, op. cit., p. 29; Schaffer, op. cit., pp. 131–52; Sharon Morgan, *Land Settlement in Early Tasmania: Creating an Antipodean England* (Cambridge 1992), p. 72.

48   Cunningham, op. cit., p. 298.

49   W.C. Wentworth to Lord Fitzwilliam, 13 January 1817, ML A756; W.C. Wentworth to Lord Bathurst, 22 April 1817, CO 201/88, f. 692; W.C. Wentworth, *Statistical, Historical, and Political Description of the Colony of New South Wales, and Its Dependent Settlements in Van Diemen's Land* (London 1819), p. vi; Ritchie, *The Wentworths*, pp. 165–6.

50   W.C. Wentworth to D'Arcy Wentworth, 10 April 1817, 25 May 1818, ML A756; Mark Hutchinson, 'W.C. Wentworth and the Sources of Australian Historiography', *Journal of the Royal Australian Historical Society*, vol. 77 (1992), pp. 63–4.

51   W.C. Wentworth to D'Arcy Wentworth, 10 November 1818, 13 April 1819, ML A756, pp. 108–9, 142. The old supposition that the marriage was forbidden by Elizabeth's father (as in Ritchie, *The Wentworths*, pp. 167, 175) jars with the immediate evidence, with his character and with hers.

52   Wentworth, *Statistical, Historical, and Political Description*, pp. 241, 249. The same sense of present and future empire appears in Wentworth's poem, 'Australasia' (see note 30).

53   *Edinburgh Review*, vol. 32, (July–October 1819), pp. 28–48; Minute, n.d., on W.C. Wentworth to Henry Goulburn, 20 May 1820, CO 201/102, p. 821; *Quarterly Review*, vol. 24 (October 1820), p. 56.

54   *Rob Roy* appeared on 31 December 1817, but the publication date is usually given as 1818.

55   Sir Walter Scott, *Rob Roy* (London 1831), p. 202; Lord Byron, 'Childe Harold's Pilgrimage', in *The Complete Poetical Works* (ed. Jerome J. McGann), vol. 2 (Oxford 1980), p. 103.

56   Scott, *Rob Roy*, pp. 126–30; Wentworth, *Statistical, Historical, and Political Description …* , pp. 236–42.

57   Ibid., pp. 245–6.

58   Address to Governor Darling (probably composed by Hall), n.d., enclosed with Darling to Lord Bathurst, 1 February 1826, *HRA*, series 1, vol. 12, p. 145 (compare Haman's words, in the Book of Esther, 3:8); Wentworth, *Australasia*; *Monitor*, 19 June 1827.

59 Charles Harpur, 'On Tennyson', in Mitchell, op. cit., p. 126.

60 Richard Cartwright, evidence before Commissioner Bigge, 26 November 1819, in Ritchie, *The Evidence to the Bigge Reports*, vol. 1, p. 155; *Monitor*, 23 March 1827; E.S. Hall to Sir George Murray, 17 November 1828, *HRA*, series 1, vol. 14, p. 580; James Macarthur, *New South Wales; its Present State and Future Prospects* (London 1837), pp. 36–7; Ken Macnab and Russel Ward, 'The Nature and Nurture of the First Generation of Native-Born Australians', *Historical Studies*, no. 39 (November 1962), pp. 299–303.

61 Philip Burnard, evidence in Thomas Wood *vs.* Henry Kable jr and Charles Kable, Supreme Court, 15 July 1822, AONSW SZ 798, p. 382; William Cox and others to John Wylde, 18 September 1822, AONSW SZ 799, ff. 350–2, *Sydney Gazette*, 1, 8 July 1824.

62 G.W. Evans, *A Geographical, Historical, and Topographical Description of Van Diemen's Land* (London 1822), pp. 64–5; John Pascoe Fawkner, Reminiscences (version beginning 'Yes, tis England'), SLV La Trobe MS 8695, pp. 16, 26. Harry Hugh Thrupp was born 12 September.

63 *Hobart Town Gazette*, 30 September 1820, 27 January, 28 April 1821; Indictment of Robert Hunter, Joseph Potaski, James Flin and Edward Brady, 6 January 1821, NSWSA SZ 804; *Sydney Gazette*, 3 March 1821; Marjorie Tipping, *Convicts Unbound: The Story of the* Calcutta *Convicts and their Settlement in Australia* (Melbourne 1988), p. 301. I am very grateful to Marjorie Tipping for help with the Potaski story. The rape docs not appear in any contemporary public record, presumably out of regard for Mrs Thrupp.

64 Papers relating to the inquest on Patrick McCooey, 20 February 1827, and trial of William Puckeridge and Edward Holmes, 16 March 1827, AONSW SC T24A; *Australian*, 20 March 1827.

65 *Sydney Gazette*, 17, 20 March 1827; *Australian*, 20 March 1827; Minutes of the Executive Council, 18, 19 March 1827, AONSW 4/1515, pp. 134–42.

66 Samuel Sneyd, evidence before select committee on the Native Police Force, 23 May 1861, p. 48, Queensland legislative assembly *Votes and Proceedings*, 1861; Norma Townsend, 'Masters and Men and the Myall Creek Massacre', *Push from the Push*, no. 20 (April 1985), pp. 7, 10–11.

Chapter 2: The Well Read

1 James I, 1607, quoted in William Taylor, 'The King's Mails, 1603–1625', *Scottish Historical Review*, vol. 42 (1963), p. 143.

2 John Stuart Mill, 1852, quoted in David Vincent, *The Culture of Secrecy: Britain, 1832–1998* (Oxford 1998), p. 30.

3 Harriet Beecher Stowe, *Uncle Tom's Cabin; or, Life among the Lowly* (London 1981; first pub. 1852), p. 193.

4 *Sydney Gazette*, 4 February 1815; Macquarie to Bathurst, 24 February 1820, 27 July 1822, *HRA*, series 1, vol. 10, pp. 263, 677–8; Michael Smithson, 'A Misunderstood Gift: The Annual Issue of Blankets to Aborigines in New South Wales, 1826–48', *Push: A Journal of Early Australian Social History*, no. 30 (1992), pp. 74–5.

5 R.H.W. Reece, *Aborigines and Colonists: Aborigines and Colonial Society in New South Wales in the 1830s and 1840s* (Sydney 1974), pp. 63–4, 108–9;

Alan Atkinson, *The Europeans in Australia: A History*, vol. 1 (Melbourne 1997), pp. 331–3.

6   Proclamation, 4 May 1816, *HRA*, series 1, vol. 9, pp. 142–3.

7   Atkinson, *The Europeans in Australia*, vol. 1, pp. 70, 338–40.

8   *Monitor* (Sydney), 15 June 1827.

9   Ellis Bent to Lord Bathurst, 14 October 1814, CO 201/75, f. 200; Bent to Bathurst, 1 July 1815, CO 201/79, f. 11.

10   Robert Townson to Joseph Corbett, 19 March 1816, enclosed with William Wilberforce to Henry Goulburn, 19 April 1817, CO 201/88, f. 689: Brian H. Fletcher, *The Grand Parade: A History of the Royal Agricultural Society of New South Wales* (Sydney 1988), pp. 15–16.

11   *Sydney Gazette*, 7, 14 May, 4 (original emphasis), 18 June, 9 July 1814.

12   Alan Atkinson, *Camden: Farm and Village Life in Early New South Wales* (Melbourne 1988), p. 7.

13   Lachlan Macquarie to Lord Bathurst, 7 May 1814, *HRA*, series 1, vol. 8, pp. 250–1; *Sydney Gazette*, 9, 30 March, 11 May 1816; Proclamations, 4 May, 20 July 1816, *HRA*, series 1, vol. 9, pp. 142–3, 362–4; Carol Liston, 'The Dharawal and Gandangara in Colonial Campbelltown, New South Wales, 1788–1830', *Aboriginal History*, vol. 12 (1988), pp. 51–4.

14   William Lawson jr to Nelson Lawson, 14 June 1824, ML FM3/210 (original in London Guildhall); *Sydney Gazette*, 12 August 1824; Sir Thomas Brisbane to Lord Bathurst, 3 November 1824, *HRA*, series 1, vol. 11, pp. 409–11; David Roberts, 'Bells Falls Massacre and Bathurst's History of Violence: Local Tradition and Australian Historiography', *Australian Historical Studies*, no. 105 (October 1995), pp. 618–24.

15   A.G.L. Shaw, *Convicts and the Colonies: A Study of Penal Transportation from Great Britain and Ireland to Australia and other parts of the British Empire* (London 1966), pp. 364–5.

16   Ibid., pp. 81, 97.

17   Return of population in Van Diemen's Land, 30 October 1815, *HRA*, series 3, vol. 2, p. 137; Shaw, op. cit., pp. 186, 364–5.

18   William Sorrell to Macquarie, 8 December 1817, and Macquarie to Sorrell, *HRA*, series 3, vol. 2, pp. 290, 292; Shaw, op. cit., pp. 186–8; Kay Daniels, *Convict Women: Rough Culture and Reformation* (Sydney 1998), p. 109.

19   William Wilberforce to Henry Goulburn, 19 April 1817, enclosing Robert Townson to Joseph Corbett, 19 March 1816, CO 201/88, ff. 683–9.

20   Robert Torrens to Lord Bathurst, [January–April 1816], CO 201/81. f. 3 (and minute thereon); Torrens' memorial, [July–August 1816], CO 201/82, ff. 228–9; *Edinburgh Review*, vol. 32 (July–October 1819), pp. 38–9.

21   Ellis Bent to Lord Bathurst, 14 October 1814, CO 201/75, ff. 203–4; Bent to Bathurst, 1 July 1815, CO 201/79, ff. 3–5; J.H. Bent to Macquarie, 21 May 1816 (with attached depositions by William Henshall, Daniel Read, and William Blake), enclosed with J.H. Bent to Bathurst, 12 June 1816, CO 201/82, ff. 150–6.

22   John Ritchie, *Punishment and Profit: The Reports of Commissioner John Bigge on the Colonies of New South Wales and Van Diemen's Land, 1822–1823; Their Origins, Nature and Significance* (Melbourne 1970), pp. 16–30, 67–82.

23   *Monitor*, 26 May 1826.
24   Charles Tompson, 'Retrospect; or, A Review of my Scholastic Days', in his *Wild Notes, from the Lyre of a Native Minstrel* (Sydney 1826), p. 17; Henry Savery, *The Hermit in Van Diemen's Land* (ed. Cecil Hadgraft) (St Lucia 1964; first pub. in book form 1829–30) p. 140.
25   W.C. Wentworth, *Statistical, Historical, and Political Description of the Colony of New South Wales, and Its Dependent Settlements in Van Diemen's Land* (London 1819), p. 49; W.C.Wentworth, *Australasia* (London 1823).
26   John Clare, 1826, quoted in A.S. Byatt, *Unruly Times: Wordsworth and Coleridge in their Time* (London 1997), pp. 261–9 (Clare quoted pp. 268–9).
27   James Ross, *Dr Ross's Recollections of a Short Excursion to Lake Echo in Van Diemen's Land 1823* (Hobart 1992), pp. 25, 42–3.
28   Wentworth, *Australasia*; Chris Cunningham, *The Blue Mountains Rediscovered: Beyond the Myths of Early Australian Exploration* (Sydney 1996), pp. 74–84, 127–39.
29   *Sydney Gazette*, 6 July 1816; Atkinson, *The Europeans in Australia*, vol. 1, pp. 57, 188.
30   *Sydney Gazette*, 12 February 1814, 10 June 1815.
31   Macquarie to Lord Bathurst, 28 June 1813, *HRA*, series 1, vol. 7, p. 780; Atkinson, *The Europeans in Australia*, vol. 1, pp. 306, 338.
32   William Balmain, 'Government of New South Wales', 1802, ML A78–3, pp. 61–4; Atkinson, *The Europeans in Australia*, vol. 1, pp. 233–4, 238.
33   Carol J. Baxter (ed.), *General Muster and Land and Stock Muster of New South Wales, 1822* (Sydney 1988), pp. 536–86; Irene Schaffer (ed.), *Land Musters, Stock Returns and Lists, Van Diemen's Land 1803–1822* (Hobart 1991), pp. 130–52.
34   Macquarie to Lord Bathurst, 1 December 1817, and, *HRA*, series 1, vol. 9, pp. 495–501; Macquarie to Bathurst, 22 March 1819, *HRA*, series 1, vol. 10, pp. 52–65; *Monitor*, 26 June 1827; John Ritchie, *The Wentworths: Father and Son* (Melbourne 1997), p. 163.
35   *Hobart Town Gazette*, 6 October, 15 December 1821, 5 January, 20 April 1822, 13 (letter from 'Settler'), 20 August 1824; Edward Curr, *An Account of the Colony of Van Diemen's Land* (London 1824), pp. 89–90; R.M. Hartwell, *The Economic Development of Van Diemen's Land 1820–1850* (Melbourne 1954), pp. 167–8.
36   Baxter, op. cit.
37   *Sydney Gazette*, 28 June 1822; Barron Field, *Geographical Memoirs on New South Wales* (London 1825), p. v.
38   John Gascoigne, *The Enlightenment and the Origins of European Australia* (Cambridge 2002), pp. 77–80.
39   *Hobart Town Courier*, 3 May 1828; Fletcher, op. cit., pp. 24–30.
40   Sir John Jamison to Lord Bathurst, 2 September 1822, CO 201/107, ff. 365–7; *Sydney Gazette*, 26 July 1822, 27 February, 6 March, 8, 15 May, 24 July 1823; S.J. Butlin, *Foundations of the Australian Monetary System 1788–1851* (Sydney 1953), pp. 146–50.
41   *Hobart Town Gazette*, 25 October 1823, 9, 30 April 1824; Edward Lord and others to Lord Bathurst, 2 August 1823, *HRA*, series 3, vol. 4, pp. 475–7; *Australian Dictionary of Biography*, vol. 2, p. 128.

42   Lord and others to Bathurst, 2 August 1823, *HRA*, series 3, vol. 4, pp. 475–7.

43   *Hobart Town Gazette*, 8 March, 9 August 1823, 23, 30 April 1824.

44   George Arthur to R. J. Wilmot Horton, 28 July 1823, 28 October 1824, *HRA*, series 3, vol. 4, pp. 78–81, 225–7.

45   *Hobart Town Courier*, 17 May 1828. The terms 'Australia' and 'Australasia' were used by the *Hobart Town Gazette* (19 January 1822, 8 March 1823) to refer to the mainland.

46   T.H. Scott to G.W. Norman, 10 June 1832, Norman MSS C200, Kent Archives Office; Alexander Stephens, *Memoirs of John Horne Tooke* (London 1813), vol. 2, pp. 325–6, 464, 479, 483; T.H. Scott to James Macarthur, 11 April 1831, ML A2955; Kelvin Grose, 'Thomas Hobbes Scott's Background, 1783–1823', *Journal of the Royal Australian Historical Society*, vol. 68 (1982), pp. 49–53.

47   John Horne Tooke, *The Diversions of Purley*, vol. 2 (London 1805), pp. 2–14; Stephens, op. cit., p. 323.

48   Tooke, op. cit., vol. 1 (London 1798), pp. 75, 317; Olivia Smith, *The Politics of Language 1791–1819* (Oxford 1984), pp. 118, 123–53.

49   James Macarthur to John Macarthur jr, 6–11 June 1827, ML A2931 (original emphasis); Grose, op. cit., pp. 53–7; Phillip McCann and Francis A. Young, *Samuel Winderspin and the Infant School Movement* (London 1982), pp. 67–8; Hans Aarsleff, *The Study of Language in England 1780–1860* (Minneapolis 1983), p. 73, 88–96.

50   Scott to R.J. Wilmot Horton, 4 September 1823, CO 201/147, pp. 343–50.

51   Scott to James Macarthur, 11 April 1831, ML A2955.

52   *Hobart Town Courier*, 3 May 1828; Scott to G.W. Norman, 25 February 1832, Norman MSS C200, Kent Archives Office (original emphasis); Scott to James Macarthur, 10 March 1837, ML A2955; Stephens, op. cit., p. 477.

53   Vicesimus Knox, *Essays, Moral and Literary* (London 1821), vol. 2, pp. 70–1; Vicesimus Knox, 'Remarks on the Tendency of Certain Clauses in A Bill now Pending in Parliament to Degrade Grammar Schools' (1821), in *The Works of Vicesimus Knox, D.D.* (London 1824), vol. 4, pp. 277–383; *Dictionary of National Biography*, vol. 1, pp. 1062–3.

54   Knox, *Essays, Moral and Literary* , vol. 2, pp. 70–1; Knox, 'Remarks on the Tendency ... ' , p. 334.

55   *Monitor*, 1 September 1826.

56   T.L. Mitchell, *Three Expeditions into the Interior of Eastern Australia* (London 1839), vol. 1, pp. 5–6; James Macarthur's speech, 30 August 1853, in E.K. Silvester (ed.), *The Speeches, in the Legislative Council of New South Wales, on the Second Reading of the Bill for Framing a New Constitution for the Colony* (Sydney 1853), p. 141; Alan Atkinson, 'The Position of John Macarthur and His Family in New South Wales before 1843', MA thesis, University of Sydney 1971, pp. 303–10.

57   John Macarthur to John Macarthur jnr, 17 April 1824, ML A2899, p. 114; Atkinson, 'The Political Life of James Macarthur', pp. 28–35; Atkinson, 'The Position of John Macarthur ... ', pp. 303–14.

58   *Sydney Gazette*, 16, 23 December 1820; Christine Bramble, 'Relations between Aborigines and White Settlers in Newcastle and the Hunter District', BLitt thesis, University of New England 1981, pp. 41–3.

59   'Philadelphus' [Saxe Bannister], *Remarks on the Indians of North America, in a Letter to an Edinburgh Reviewer* (London 1822), p. 31; Saxe Bannister, *Humane Policy; or, Justice to the Aborigines of New Settlements Essential to a Due Expenditure of British Money, and to the Best Interests of the Settlers* (London 1830), pp. 2–3, 7, 40–1, 81, 87, 162.

60   'Philadelphus', op. cit., p. 3.

61   Threlkeld to G. Burder and W.A. Hankey, 20 January 1826, in Neil Gunson (ed.), *Australian Reminiscences and Papers of L.E. Threlkeld, Missionary to the Aborigines 1824–1859* (Canberra 1974), vol. 2, p. 196; Scott to George Arthur, 21 April 1826, *HRA*, series 3, vol. 5, p. 15; Scott to Ralph Darling, 1 August 1827, enclosing Scott to Richard Sadleir, 29 July 1826, *HRA*, series 1, vol. 12, pp. 55–64; R.J. Burne, 'Archdeacon Scott and the Church and School Corporation', in C. Turney (ed.), *Pioneers of Australian Education* (Sydney 1969), pp. 21–2.

62   Bannister, *Humane Policy*, pp. 149, 234–5.

63   Threlkeld to Bannister, 25 July 1826, in Gunson, op. cit., vol. 1, p. 92; *Sydney Gazette*, 21 May 1827.

64   'Philadelphus', op. cit., p. 3; Lancelot Threlkeld, 'Second Half Yearly Report of the Aboriginal Mission', 21 June 1826, in Gunson, op. cit., vol. 2, p. 209.

65   Ibid., p. 210.

66   Bannister to Threlkeld, 22 October 1825 (extract), ML BT 53, p. 1540; Bannister, *Humane Policy*, p. 234; Saxe Bannister, evidence before select committee on Aborigines (British Settlements), 31 August 1835, *Parliamentary Papers*, 1836 (538) VII, pp. 175–6.

67   Speech by J.H. Plunkett, *Sydney Morning Herald*, 29 June 1849.

68   Saxe Bannister, evidence, 31 August 1835, pp. 175–6.

69   Ralph Darling to William Huskisson, 27 March 1828, enclosing Scott to Darling, 1 August 1827, *HRA*, series 1, vol. 12, pp. 54–64; James Macarthur, *New South Wales; Its Present State and Future Prospects* (London 1837), p. 215.

70   Jack Davis, in Adam Shoemaker, 'An Interview with Jack Davis', *Westerly*, December 1982, p. 114.

71   *Dictionary of National Biography*, vol. 1, p. 1062. The best efforts of the Baillieu Library at Melbourne University and the National Library of Scotland have failed to locate a copy of this book.

72   *Sydney Gazette*, 29 September, 31 October, 1 December 1825; *Australian*, 3 November , 8 December 1825.

73   Atkinson, 'The Position of John Macarthur ... ', pp. 314–17; Atkinson, *The Europeans in Australia*, vol. 1, pp. 163, 167.

Chapter 3: Making a Name

1   Cecil Hadgraft, introduction to Henry Savery, *The Bitter Bread of Banishment* (that is, *Quintus Servinton*) (Sydney 1984; first pub. Hobart 1830–31), pp. vii–xiv.

2   Henry Savery, *The Hermit in Van Diemen's Land* (ed. Cecil Hadgraft) (St Lucia 1964; first pub. in book form 1829–30), pp. 153, 154. The spelling of this surname varies, and Savery probably used this version to suggest kinship with William Stukeley (d. 1765), a scholar who wrote about Stonehenge

(note the awkward detail on Stonehenge in *Quintus Servinton*, op. cit., pp. 175–6). *The Hermit in London; or, Sketches of English Manners*, apparently by Felix McDonogh, appeared in London in 1819.

3   Bruce Bennett, 'Ego, Sight and Insight in Convict Fiction by Henry Savery and John Boyle O'Reilly', *Journal of Australian Colonial History*, vol. 2 (2000), pp. 29–30, 39.

4   From Andrew Marvell, 'A Dialogue between the Body and Soul'. And see James H. Smith, 'Njama's Supper: The Consumption and Use of Literary Potency by Mau Mau Insurgents in Colonial Kenya', *Comparative Studies in Society and History*, vol. 40 (1998), pp. 524–48.

5   Patricia Miles, 'In Search of Alexander Harris', *Push: A Journal of Early Australian History*, no. 30 (1992), pp. 59–60; Lorraine Neate, 'Alexander Harris – A Mystery No More', *Journal of the Royal Australian Historical Society*, vol. 86 (2000), p. 199. The pocket-book is mentioned in Alexander Harris, *Settlers and Convicts: Recollections of Sixteen Years' Labour in the Australian Backwoods* (Melbourne 1953; first pub. 1847), p. 21.

6   Ibid., pp. 44, 45, 99.

7   *Sydney Gazette*, 16 December 1824.

8   *Sydney Gazette*, 17 March 1821; *Hobart Town Gazette*, 17 May 1823, 14, 21, 28 May 1824; *Australian Dictionary of Biography*, vol. 2, p. 515.

9   Return of population, New South Wales, 27 September–12 November 1819, *HRA*, series 1, vol. 10, p. 286; Return of population, co. Buckinghamshire, VDL, 1 March 1820, *HRA*, series 3, vol. 4, p. 638; Charles Rowcroft, *Tales of the Colonies; or, The Adventures of an Emigrant* (London 1858), pp. 8, 13.

10 Return of population, New South Wales, 10 September–26 October 1821, *HRA*, series 1, vol. 10, p. 575.

11 *Sydney Gazette*, 7 January 1828.

12 Launceston petty sessions, 15, 30 November 1824, AOT LC 347/1.

13 Peter Gay, *The Bourgeois Experience: Victoria to Freud*, vol. 3 *(The Cultivation of Hatred)*, (London 1994), pp. 306–12.

14 Lord Byron, 'Don Juan', Canto II, stanza 4.

15 *Australian*, 13 January 1825. See also *Australian*, 18 November, 30 December 1824, 29 September 1825 (women fighting), 5 April 1826; Miriam Dixson, *The Real Matilda: Woman and Identity in Australia 1788 to the Present* (Melbourne 1994), pp. 93–4.

16 Edward Gibbon, *The History of the Decline and Fall of the Roman Empire* (ed. David Womersley), (London 1994; first pub. 1776–88), vol. 1, p. 405; *Australian*, 23 December 1824; *Sydney Gazette*, 13 January, 10 February 1825.

17 *Sydney Gazette*, 13 November 1823, 4 March 1824; *Hobart Town Gazette*, 10 December 1824; *Australian*, 8 September 1825; Michael Roe, 'Mary Leman Grimstone (1800–1850?): For Woman's Rights and Tasmanian Patriotism', *Tasmanian Historical Research Association: Papers and Proceedings*, vol. 38 (1989), pp. 9–32.

18 Diary of Christiana Brooks, 1 April 1826, ML MSS 4661, p. 47.

19 *Monitor*, 29 December 1826.

20 *Monitor*, 2 June, 9, 16 June, 1 September 1826, 20 January, 9 March, 12 July 1827.

21 *Monitor*, 16 June, 8 September 1826, 23, 30 March, 26, 28 June 1827. But see also Leonore Davidoff and Catherine Hall, *Family Fortunes: Men and*

Women of the English Middle Class 1780–1850 (London 1987), pp. 160–1. 'Corinna' has not been identified, but she seems to have lived in the Upper Hunter Valley with a brother with initials 'W.L.C.'.

22   *Monitor*, 21 July, 11 August, 17 February 1827.

23   *Monitor*, 2 June, 15 December 1826.

24   Alan Atkinson, *The Europeans in Australia: A History*, vol. 1 (Melbourne 1997), pp. 222–4, 231.

25   *Australian*, 25 November 1824; Eric Irvin, *The Theatre Comes to Australia* (St Lucia 1971), pp. 6–10; Robert Jordan, *The Convict Theatres of Early Australia 1788–1840* (Sydney 2002), pp. 150–78.

26   Irvin, op. cit., pp. 7–49; Davidoff and Hall, op. cit., pp. 436–8.

27   Barron Field (ed. and author), *Geographical Memoirs on New South Wales* (London 1825), p. 435.

28   *Monitor*, 9, 23 June, 21 July, 11, 25 August 1826 (original emphases); *Australian*, 10, 21, 24 June, 22 July, 26 August 1826; *Hobart Town Gazette*, 24 February 1827; Henry Widowson, *Present State of Van Diemen's Land* (London 1829), p. 31; Davidoff and Hall, op. cit., pp. 438–42.

29   Publisher's note, quoting *Penny Magazine*, 28 April 1832, in James Ross, *Dr Ross's Recollections of a Short Excursion to Lake Echo in Van Diemen's Land 1823* (Hobart 1992), p. 9.

30   Savery, *The Hermit in Van Diemen's Land*, p. 125.

31   *Sydney Gazette*, 3 February 1825, 5 March 1828; W.C. Wentworth to William Carter, 8 June 1825, ML A1440; J.O. Balfour, *A Sketch of New South Wales* (London 1845), pp. 69–70.

32   Papers in the case of R. *v.* Nathaniel Lowe, May 1827, AONSW SC T24A.27/56; *Australian*, 26 June 1826; *Sydney Gazette*, 21 May 1827.

33   Wentworth to Sir Thomas Brisbane, 26 February 1825, and Wentworth to John Ovens, 19 March 1825, ML A1440; J.B. M[artin], *Reminiscences* (Camden, NSW, 1884), p. 33.

34   *Sydney Gazette*, 17 October 1827.

35   C.H. Chambers to Rev. George Middleton, 9 March 1825, and Wentworth to William Carter, 8 June 1825, ML A1440.

36   T.H. Scott to George Arthur, 21 April 1826, *HRA*, series 3, vol. 5, p. 166.

37   Edmund Burke, *Reflections on the Revolution in France* (London, n.d. [The Scott Library]), p. 74 (original emphasis).

38   Thomas Chittenden to Eliza Chittenden, December 1824, in Stephen Jones's statement, [December 1824], papers in case R. *v.* Martin Benson and others, January 1825, AONSW CP T128.10.

39   Henry Dumaresq to his mother, 25 November 1825, ML A2571; T.H. Scott to George Arthur, 5 April 1826, ML A2172 (original emphasis).

40   *Australian*, 5 May 1825.

41   *Sydney Gazette*, 2, 16 June 1825; Wentworth to Frederick Goulburn, 3 June 1825, ML A1440.

42   *Sydney Gazette*, 1, 4 February 1826; *Australian*, 2 February 1826.

43   John Macarthur sr to John Macarthur jr, 16 May 1827, ML A2899.

44   *Sydney Gazette*, 7 June 1826, 17, 29 March 1827; James Macarthur to John Macarthur jr, 17 May 1827, ML A2931.

45   *Australian*, 18 October 1826, 31 March 1827; *Sydney Gazette*, 31 March 1827.

46   Peter Cunningham, *Two Years in New South Wales* (Sydney 1966; first pub. 1827), vol. 1, p. 45; Widowson, op. cit., p. 22; Mrs Augustus Prinsep, *The Journal of a Voyage from Calcutta to Van Diemen's Land* (London 1833), pp. 51, 56; Balfour, op. cit., pp. 37–8.

47   *Australian*, 5 May 1825; Cunningham, op. cit., vol. 2, p. 70.

48   Edward Curr, *An Account of the Colony of Van Diemen's Land* (London 1824), p. 19; *Hobart Town Courier*, 5 July 1828.

49   J.S. Mill, 'The Spirit of the Age, 1', 9 January 1831, in John M. Robson (gen. ed.), *Collected Works of John Stuart Mill*, vol. 22 (Toronto 1986), p. 228.

50   *Hobart Town Gazette*, 5 May 1821, 21 December 1822; *Sydney Gazette*, 11 November 1824, 14 July, 11 August 1825; *Australian*, 29 September, 17 November 1825; *Monitor*, 24 November 1826. The Hobart historians were 'J.H.' and Evan Henry Thomas.

51   *Monitor*, 29 December 1826.

52   *Australian*, 11 November 1824; *Sydney Gazette*, 18 November 1824; *Hobart Town Gazette*, 3 December 1824; Charles Tompson, 'On the Death of Maj. Gen. Macquarie, the Late Much Lamented Governor of Australia', in his *Wild Notes, From the Lyre of a Native Minstrel* (Sydney 1826), p. 41; Atkinson, *The Europeans in Australia*, vol. 1, p. 226.

53   *Australian*, 5 May 1825.

54   Mark Hutchinson, 'W.C. Wentworth and the Sources of Australian Historiography', *Journal of the Royal Australian Historical Society*, vol. 77 (1992), p. 78.

55   James Macarthur to John Macarthur jr, 27 May 1827, ML A2931.

56   Hutchinson, op. cit., pp. 65–70.

57   Marilyn Butler, *Romantics, Rebels and Revolutionaries* (Oxford 1981), p. 119; J.C.L. Simonde de Sismondi, *Histoire des Républiques Italiennes du Moyen Age* (Paris 1840), vol. 1, pp. 5–6.

58   W.C. Wentworth, *Statistical, Historical, and Political Description of The Colony of New South Wales, and Its Dependent Settlements in Van Diemen's Land* (London 1819), pp. 345–6.

59   George Arthur to R.W. Hay, 12 March 1827, *HRA*, series 3, vol. 5, pp. 584–5; *Hobart Town Gazette*, 17 March 1827.

60   William Gellibrand to John Burnett, 20 March 1827, and William Gellibrand and others to Lord Bathurst, 21 March 1827, *HRA*, series 1, vol. 5, pp. 656–7, 658; *Tasmanian*, 29 March, 12 April 1827; *Hobart Town Gazette*, 31 March 1827.

61   *Australian*, 27 October 1825.

62   Sir Walter Scott, *Ivanhoe* (Edinburgh 1998), p. 17.

63   Wentworth, op. cit., pp. 346–51; John Macarthur's annotation in the copy now at Camden Park, p. 348; Hutchinson, op. cit., pp. 68–9.

64   *Sydney Gazette*, 21 November 1825.

Chapter 4: Convict Opinion

1   Alan Atkinson, 'The Free-Born Englishman Transported: Convicts Rights as a Measure of Eighteenth-Century Empire', *Past and Present*, no. 144 (August 1994); Alan Atkinson, *The Europeans in Australia: A History*, vol. 1 (Melbourne 1997), p. 5.

2   Charles Dickens, *Great Expectations* (Ware, Herts., 1992), p. 184.

3   Returns of population, New South Wales and Van Diemen's Land, 27 September–12 November 1819, 10 September–26 October 1821, *HRA*, series 1, vol. 10, pp. 286, 575, 578. J.T. Bigge, *Report of the Commissioner of Inquiry on the State of Agriculture and Trade in the Colony of New South Wales* (London 1823), pp. 79–80. The 1821 muster, unlike that of 1819, has no category for 'convict' children. It also makes separate provision for convicts with pardons and tickets of leave, probably counted as 'free' in 1819.

4   The term 'servants of the Crown' was in use when Sorrell arrived in 1817 (*Hobart Town Gazette*, 1816–17), but deeds from David Collins' time show it was not used by him.

5   Sorrell to Macquarie, 26 March 1818, *HRA*, series 3, vol. 2, p. 310.

6   *Sydney Gazette*, 7 December 1816; *Hobart Town Gazette*, 28 March, 26 December 1818; W.C. Wentworth, *Statistical, Historical, and Political Description of the Colony of New South Wales, and Its Dependent Settlements in Van Diemen's Land* (London 1819), p. 155.

7   William Sorrell to George Arthur, 22 May 1824, *HRA*, series 3, vol. 4, p. 144; Edward Curr, *An Account of the Colony of Van Diemen's Land* (London 1824), pp. 8–9. The acquisition of land in Hobart at this time was usually undocumented, title depending on convention.

8   Atkinson, 'The Free-Born Englishman Transported', p. 103; Atkinson, *The Europeans in Australia*, vol. 1, pp. 261–2.

9   Joy Damousi, *Depraved and Disorderly: Female Convicts, Sexuality and Gender in Colonial Australia* (Cambridge 1997), pp. 18–19.

10   Sir Thomas Brisbane to Lord Bathurst, 28 April 1823, and enclosure in Brisbane to Bathurst, 14 May 1825, *HRA*, series 1, vol. 11, pp. 75, 573; Bathurst to Ralph Darling, 12 March 1826, and Darling to Bathurst, 26 October 1826, *HRA*, series 1, vol. 12, pp. 218–19, 659–60; *Monitor*, 17 November 1826; *Hobart Town Gazette*, 14 June 1828.

11   *Sydney Gazette*, 28 July 1821; James Lawrence's story of his life, n.d. [1842?], ML Dixson MS Q168, item 1, p. 56; 'The McGreavys: A Family Saga', *Push*, no. 28 (1990), pp. 99–106.

12   John Hunter to Duke of Portland, 20 June 1797, *HRA*, series 1, vol. 2, p. 23 (the original in italics); Atkinson, *The Europeans in Australia*, vol. 1, pp. 171–2.

13   James Ross, *Dr Ross's Recollections of a Short Excursion to Lake Echo in Van Diemen's Land 1823* (Hobart 1992), pp. 36–9.

14   J.E. Calder, 'Early Troubles of the Colonists', (published in Hobart *Mercury*, 17, 27 November 1873), collected in ML as 'Scraps of Tasmanian History', vol. 1, p. 202.

15   Thomas Miller, evidence, 20 April 1815, enclosed with Thomas Davey to Lachlan Macquarie, 30 April 1815, *HRA*, series 3, vol. 2, p. 103.

16   William Lucas, evidence, 28 October 1814, ibid., pp. 83–4; David Burn, *A Picture of Van Diemen's Land* (Hobart 1973; first pub. 1840–41), p. 95; Calder, op. cit., p. 177.

17   Evidence of William Merry, 22 August 1814, of William Holsgrove, 26 October 1814, and of John Peachey, 9 September 1816, and Robert Knopwood and others to Davey, 30 August 1814, *HRA*, series 3, vol. 2, pp. 77, 79, 82, 591; Calder, op. cit., pp. 155–7, 164, 173, 185, 198, 199, 200;

John West, *The History of Tasmania* (ed. A.G.L. Shaw) (Sydney 1971; first pub. 1852), p. 360; T.E. Wells, *Michael Howe, the Last and Worst of the Bushrangers of Van Diemen's Land* (ed. George Mackaness) (Dubbo 1979; first pub. 1818), pp. 31, 36–7.

18   W.H. Craig, evidence, 22 August 1814, *HRA*, series 3, vol. 2, p. 78.

19   Thomas Seals, evidence, 10 July 1816, and Michael Howe and others to Davey, [November 1816], *HRA*, series 3, vol. 2, pp. 162–3, 643–4.

20   Seals, evidence, 10 July 1816, p. 163; Calder, pp. 153–4, 156.

21   Wells, op. cit., pp. 6, 27, 38, 40. Sir John Ferguson (*Bibliography of Australia*, vol. 1 [Sydney 1941], p. 282) calls it an 'unofficial' publication, but this seems misleading.

22   Bethia Penglase, 'An Enquiry into Literacy in Early Nineteenth Century New South Wales', *Push from the Bush*, no. 16 (October 1983), pp. 42–5, 51–3; Deborah Oxley, 'Female Convicts', in Stephen Nicholas (ed.), *Convict Workers: Reinterpreting Australia's Past* (Cambridge 1988), pp. 93–4, and see final tables, pp. 212–13.

23   Sir George Gipps to Lord Stanley, 1 April 1843, *HRA*, series 1, vol. 22, p. 616.

24   Numerous examples can be found, for instance, in quotations in Deborah Bird Rose, *Dingo Makes Us Human: Life and Land in an Aboriginal Australian Culture* (Cambridge 2000).

25   *Australian*, 28 February 1834.

26   Henry Tingley to Thomas Tingley, 15 June 1835, in C.M.H. Clark (ed.), *Select Documents in Australian History 1788–1850* (Sydney 1950), p. 131; Alexander Harris, *Settlers and Convicts: Recollections of Sixteen Years' Labour in the Australian Backwoods* (Melbourne 1953; first pub. 1847), pp. 184–5.

27   Longford (Norfolk Plains) petty sessions, 28 July 1830, AOT LC 362/2.

28   Ibid., 3 October 1836, AOT LC 362/3, p. 332.

29   Ibid., 17 or 18 May 1830, 27, 29 October 1836, AOT LC 362/3.

30   Ibid., 22 April, 5 May 1829, AOT LC 362/1.

31   Penglase, op. cit., pp. 51–3; Shergold, op. cit., pp. 212–13. Compare Scott's reports on NSW and on VDL, in letter to George Arthur, 13 February 1826, *HRA*, series 3, vol. 5, pp. 154–9; Scott to Ralph Darling, 1 May 1826, *HRA*, series 1, vol. 12, pp. 309–18; Scott to Arthur, 25 March 1828, *HRA*, series 3, vol. 7, pp. 139–50.

32   Arthur to Lord Bathurst, 21 April 1826, 23 March 1827, *HRA*, series 3, vol. 5, pp. 153, 623.

33   Grace Heinbury, evidence, 21 March 1842, Report of the committee appointed to inquire into the present state of female convict discipline, [1841], AOT CSO 22/50, p. 266; Elizabeth Fenton, *The Journal of Mrs Fenton: A Narrative of Her Life in India, the Isle of France (Mauritius), and Tasmania During the Years 1826–1830* (London 1901), p. 365.

34   Michael Bogle, *Convicts* (Sydney 1999), pp. 41–8.

35   Jane Franklin to Elizabeth Fry, 3 August 1841, University of Tasmania, RS 16/1(2); Deborah Oxley, 'Representing Convict Women', in Ian Duffield and James Bradley (eds), *Representing Convicts: New Perspectives on Convict Forced Labour Migration* (London 1997), p. 95.

36   Mary Hughs to Rev. John Espy Keane, 5 June 1832, AONSW 4/2152.2;
     Mary Haigh, evidence, 23 March 1842, report of the committee appointed to
     inquire into the present state of female convict discipline, pp. 313–14; Alan
     Atkinson, 'Convicts and Courtship', in Patricia Grimshaw and others (eds),
     Families in Colonial Australia (Sydney 1985), p. 21; Kirsty M. Reid, 'Work,
     Sexuality and Resistance: The Convict Women of Van Diemen's Land,
     1820–1839', PhD thesis, University of Edinburgh 1995, p. 114. Compare
     Melanie Tebbutt, *Women's Talk?: A Social History of 'Gossip' in Working-
     Class Neighbourhoods, 1880–1960* (Aldershot, Hants., 1997), pp. 74–6 (I
     owe this reference to Kirsty Reid).

37   H. Mayhew and J. Binny, *The Criminal Prisons of London and Scenes of
     Prison Life* (London 1862), p. 272; Leonore Davidoff and Catherine Hall,
     Family Fortunes: Men and Women of the English Middle Class 1780–1850
     (London 1987), p. 401.

38   Walter J. Ong, 'African Talking Drums and Oral Noetics', in his *Interfaces of
     the Word: Studies in the Evolution of Consciousness and Culture* (Ithaca,
     N.Y., 1977), p. 104.

39   Babette Smith, *A Cargo of Women: Susannah Watson and the Convicts of the
     Princess Royal* (Sydney 1988), p. 94. See also Laura Gowing, *Domestic
     Dangers: Women, Words, and Sex in Early Modern London* (Oxford 1996),
     pp. 131–3 (I owe this reference to Kirsty Reid).

40   Reid, op. cit., p. 242. Compare Paula J. Byrne, *Criminal Law and Colonial
     Subject: New South Wales, 1810–1830* (Cambridge 1993), p. 45.

41   Reid, op. cit., p. 106; Charles Wilkes, *Narrative of the U.S. Exploring Expedition,
     During the years 1838, 1839, 1840, 1841, 1842* (London 1845), p. 127.

42   R.C. Snelling and T.J. Barron, 'The Colonial Office and Its Permanent
     Officials', in Gillian Sutherland (ed.), *Studies in the Growth of Nineteenth-
     Century Government* (London 1972), pp. 141, 143; David Vincent, *The
     Culture of Secrecy: Britain, 1832–1998* (Oxford 1998), pp. 30–2.

43   James Stephen to Arthur, 4 January 1824, ML A2164; Stephen to his wife,
     27 October 1841, quoted in Vincent, op. cit., p. 44; Peter Murdoch, evidence
     before select committee on transportation, 22 March 1838, *Parliamentary
     Papers*, 1837–8 (669) XXII, p. 115; Raymond Williams, *Keywords: A
     Vocabulary of Culture and Society* (London 1983), p. 49.

44   Cassandra Pybus and Hamish Maxwell-Stewart, *American Citizens, British
     Slaves: Yankee Political Prisoners in an Australian Penal Colony 1839–1850*
     (Melbourne 2002), p. 20.

45   Arthur to Bathurst, 26 March 1827, *HRA*, series 3, vol. 5, p. 716; Arthur to
     Stephen, 20 April 1827, ML A2164. Dispatches are listed at the back of each
     volume of *HRA*, series 1 and series 3.

46   Scott to Arthur, 9 October 1825, ML A2172 (original emphasis); Stephen to
     Arthur, 9 October [1826?], and Arthur to Stephen, 20 April 1827, ML
     A2164; West, op. cit., p. 205.

47   Richard P. Davis, *The Tasmanian Gallows: A Study of Capital Punishment*
     (Hobart 1974), pp. 12–13; Pybus and Maxwell-Stewart, op. cit., pp. 21–4. I
     am grateful to Hamish Maxwell-Stewart for advice here.

48   Arthur to Bathurst, 24 March 1827, *HRA*, series 3, vol. 5, p. 693; Arthur to
     William Wilberforce, 9 October 1828, ML A2165.

49   Arthur to Bathurst, 16 March 1827, *HRA*, series 3, vol. 5, pp. 608–9.

50   Peter Murdoch, evidence before select committee on transportation, 22 March 1838, *Parliamentary Papers*, 1837–8 (669) XXII, op. cit., p. 116.

51   Scott to Arthur, 29 April 1825, ML A2164; Arthur to Robert Hay, 15 November 1826, *HRA*, series 3, vol. 5, pp. 434–5; A.G.L. Shaw, *Sir George Arthur, Bart, 1784–1854: Superintendent of British Honduras, Lieutenant-Governor of Van Diemen's Land and of Upper Canada, Governor of the Bombay Presidency* (Melbourne 1980), pp. 143, 148.

52   Arthur to William Wilberforce, 9 October 1828, ML A2165.

53   Marie Fels, 'Culture Contact in the County of Buckinghamshire, Van Diemen's Land, 1803–11', *Tasmanian Historical Research Association Papers and Proceedings*, no. 29 (1982), pp. 61–3; Hamish Maxwell-Stewart, 'The Bushrangers and the Convict System of Van Diemen's Land, 1803–1846', PhD thesis, University of Edinburgh 1990, pp. 154–6 (Hamish Maxwell-Stewart kindly gave me access to his thesis); Alan Atkinson, 'Writing About Convicts: Our Escape from the One Big Gaol', *Tasmanian Historical Studies*, vol. 6, no. 2 (1999), pp. 18–20.

54   Edward Curr, *An Account of the Colony of Van Diemen's Land* (London 1824), pp. 71–2.

55   *Hobart Town Gazette*, 20 January 1827; Henry Melville, *History of the Island of Van Diemen's Land from the Year 1824 to 1835 Inclusive* (London 1835), p. 2; J. Syme, *Nine Years in Van Diemen's Land* (Dundee 1848), p. 16; Atkinson, 'Writing About Convicts', pp. 18–20.

56   Bigge, op. cit., p. 81; Charles Sturt, *Two Expeditions into the Interior of Southern Australia* (London 1833), vol. 1, pp. lvi–lvii; Henry Savery, *The Hermit in Van Diemen's Land* (ed. Cecil Hadgraft) (St Lucia 1964; first pub. in book form 1829–30), p. 134.

57   *Monitor*, 22 December 1826.

58   John Macarthur, evidence, n.d., in John Ritchie (ed.), *The Evidence of the Bigge Reports* (Melbourne 1971), vol. 2, p. 79.

59   Nicholas Bayly to Sir Henry Bunbury, 13 March 1816, CO 201/88, f. 95.

60   *Hobart Town Courier*, 3 May 1828.

61   [John Montagu?], 'Remarks on the Correspondence ... ', [March 1827], *HRA*, series 3, vol. 5, p. 672; J. Dunmore Lang, evidence before select committee on transportation, 30 May 1837, *Parliamentary Papers*, 1837 (518) XIX, pp. 255, 260; W. Ullathorne, *The Catholic Mission in Australasia* (Liverpool 1837), pp. 19–20.

62   Maria Turner to Steven Bumstead, 15 [no month] 1841, and Eliza Churchill, evidence, March 1842, both in report of the committee appointed to inquire into the present state of female convict discipline, [1843], AOT CSO 22/50, pp. 286–9, 294.

63   Arthur, Appendix to enclosure 2, 20 December 1826, in Arthur to Robert Hay, 23 March 1827, *HRA*, series 3, vol. 5, p. 683; George Arthur, evidence before select committee on transportation, 27 June 1837, *Parliamentary Papers*, 1837 (518) XIX, pp. 287–92.

64   Lang, op. cit., 30 May 1837, pp. 240–1, 245–6.

65   *Monitor*, 12 June 1827; *Launceston Advertiser*, 3 August 1829.

66   Sandra Blair, 'The "Convict Press": William Watt and the *Sydney Gazette* in the 1830s', *Push from the Bush*, no. 5 (December 1979), pp. 98–119; Sandra

Blair, 'Patronage and Prejudice: Educated Convicts in the New South Wales Press', *Push from the Bush*, no. 8 (December 1980), p. 82.

67   *Sydney Gazette*, 1 March 1834 (the words quoted are in italics).

68   *Monitor*, 12, 22 June 1827; Thomas Chatfield to his wife, 12 September 1832, in Report from His Majesty's Commissioners for Inquiring into the Administration and Practical Operation of the Poor Laws, appendix C, p. 159, *Parliamentary Papers*, 1834, XXXVII, 44.

69   William Ullathorne, evidence before select committee on transportation, 8 February 1838, *Parliamentary Papers*, 1837–8 (669) XXII, p. 21. For women, see Joy Damousi, *Depraved and Disorderly: Female Convicts, Sexuality and Gender in Colonial Australia* (Cambridge 1997); Kay Daniels, *Convict Women: Rough Culture and Reformation* (Sydney 1998).

70   Port Macquarie petty sessions, 2 April 1832, AONSW 4/5637; Muswellbrook petty sessions, 31 July 1832, AONSW 4/5599; Alan Atkinson, 'Four Patterns of Convict Protest', *Labour History*, no. 37 (November 1979), pp. 33–6.

71   Alan Atkinson and Marian Aveling (eds), *Australians 1838* (Sydney 1987), p. 147.

72   Savery, op. cit., p. 159.

73   Arthur, evidence before select committee on transportation, 30 June 1837, op. cit., p. 304; A.G.L. Shaw, *Convict and the Colonies: A Study of Penal Transportation from Great Britain and Ireland to Australia and Other Parts of the British Empire* (London 1966), pp. 212–16; J.B. Hirst, *Convict Society and Its Enemies* (Sydney 1983), pp. 62–5; Maxwell-Stewart, op. cit., pp. 107–10.

74   Arthur, evidence before select committee on transportation, 30 June 1837, op. cit., pp. 304–5.

75   Return of floggings in New South Wales, 1830–37, 22 October 1838, *HRA*, series 1, vol. 19, p. 654; Shaw, *Convicts and the Colonies*, pp. 200–2; Shaw, *Sir George Arthur*, p. 87; Raymond Evans and William Thorpe, 'Power, Punishment and Penal Labour: *Convict Workers* and Moreton Bay', *Australian Historical Studies*, vol. 25 (1992), pp. 97–8,103.

76   James Tucker, *Ralph Rashleigh* (Sydney 1962), p. 59.

77   W.H. Suttor, *Australian Stories Retold*, quoted in H.M. Suttor, *Australian Milestones and Stories of the Past, 1770–1914* (Sydney 1925), vol. 1, pp. 251–3; Rob Meppem, 'Convict Runaways, Rebels and Protesters, 1824 to 1830', BA thesis, University of New England 1991, p. 6.

78   Charles Darwin, 1839, quoted in F.W. and J.M. Nicholas, *Charles Darwin in Australia* (Cambridge 1989), p. 73.

79   *Sydney Herald*, 11 February 1836.

80   Sandra J. Blair, 'The Revolt at Castle Forbes: A Catalyst to Emancipist Emigrant Confrontation', *Journal of the Royal Australian Historical Society*, vol. 64 (1978), pp. 89–107; Hamish Maxwell-Stewart and Bruce Hindmarsh, ' "This is the Bird that Never Flew": William Stewart, Major Donald Macleod and the *Launceston Advertiser*', *Journal of Australian Colonial History*, vol. 2 (2000), pp. 1–28; Peter Hammond, 'Murder, Manslaughter and Workplace Relations in Convict New South Wales 1824–1838', BA thesis, University of New England 2003.

81   Ralph Darling to Sir George Murray, 7 October 1830, *HRA*, series 1, vol. 15, pp. 769–70; Meppem, op. cit., pp. 4–16.

82   George Suttor to E.B. Suttor, in *Sydney Gazette*, 21 October 1830.
83   *Australian*, 22 October 1830.

Chapter 5: 'A Most Extensive Scale'

1   John Oxley, *Journal of Two Expeditions into the Interior of New South Wales* (London 1820), pp. 39–40, 41, 58, 108, 113, 184.
2   T.L. Mitchell, *Three Expeditions into the Interior of Eastern Australia* (London 1839), vol. 1, pp. 25, 164, 194, 217, 247; Anne Coote, 'The Development of Colonial Nationhood in New South Wales, c. 1825–1865', PhD thesis, University of New England, forthcoming.
3   Rowland Hill, *Post Office Reform; Its Importance and Practicability* (London 1837), p. 77; Brian Austen, 'The Impact of the Mail Coach on Public Coach Services in England and Wales, 1784–1840', *Journal of Transport History*, series 3, vol. 2 (1981), pp. 32–4; Leonore Davidoff and Catherine Hall, *Family Fortunes: Men and Women of the English Middle Class 1780–1850* (London 1987), pp. 403–5.
4   J.B. Harley, 'Maps, Knowledge, and Power', in D. Cosgrove and S. Daniels (eds), *The Iconography of Landscape: Essays on the Symbolic Representation, Design and Use of Past Environments* (Cambridge 1988), pp. 280–3; Avril M.C. Maddrell, 'Discourses of Race and Gender and the Comparative Method in Geography School Texts 1830–1918', *Environment and Planning D: Society and Space*, vol. 16 (1998), pp. 84–7.
5   Charles Sturt, *Two Expeditions into the Interior of Southern Australia* (London 1833), vol. 1, p. 114; 'An Intending Colonist of South Australia', 14 July 1835, in Brian Dickey and Peter Howell (eds), *South Australia's Foundation: Select Documents* (Adelaide 1986), p. 60.
6   W.H. Dutton, evidence before committee on police and gaols, 9 June 1835, NSW Legislative Council *Votes and Proceedings*, 1824–37, p. 335; William Hobbs, evidence during the first inquiry into the Myall Creek massacre, 30 July 1838, AONSW 4/5601.
7   Patrick Byrne, evidence before Commissioner Bigge, 12 October 1820, in John Ritchie (ed.), *The Evidence to the Bigge Reports*, vol. 1 (Melbourne 1971), p. 183 (emphasis added); David Roberts, ' "Binjang" or the "Second Vale of Tempe": The Frontier at Wellington Valley, New South Wales, 1817–1851', PhD thesis, University of Newcastle 2000, p. 49.
8   T.B. Atkinson, shipboard diary, 2 June 1857, SLV La Trobe MS 12599.
9   Roberts, op. cit., pp. 62–6, 69.
10   W.C. Wentworth, *Statistical, Historical, and Political Description of the Colony of New South Wales, and Its Dependent Settlements in Van Diemen's Land* (London 1819), p. 89; 'Epsilon', 'Star of Australia', in *Australian Magazine*, January 1838, p. 71.
11   Rebe Taylor, 'Savages or Saviours? The Australian Sealers and Tasmanian Aboriginal Culture', *Journal of Australian Studies*, no. 66 (2000), p. 74.
12   J.S. Cumpston, *Kangaroo Island 1800–1836* (Canberra 1970), pp. 51 (quoting George Sutherland, 1831), 105 (quoting George Bates, 1886); John Hart, 1854, T.F. Bride (ed.), *Letters from Victorian Pioneers* (Melbourne 1893), p. 302; D.R. Hainsworth, *The Sydney Traders: Simeon Lord and his Contemporaries 1788–1821* (Melbourne 1972), pp. 137–47.

13   W.H. Leigh, *Reconnoitering Voyages, Travels and Adventures in the New Colonies of South Australia* (London 1839), pp. 124–6; Cumpston, op. cit., p. 53; J.W. Bull, *Early Experiences of Life in South Australia* (Adelaide 1884), pp. 5–6; Lyndall Ryan, *The Aboriginal Tasmanians* (St Lucia 1981), p. 70.

14   Charles Throsby to Lachlan Macquarie, 4 September 1820, quoted in T.M. Perry, *Australia's First Frontier: The Spread of Settlement in New South Wales 1788–1829* (Melbourne 1963), p. 99.

15   Roger Milliss, *Waterloo Creek: The Australia Day Massacre of 1838, George Gipps and the British Conquest of New South Wales* (Sydney 1992), pp. 81–96.

16   'Itinerary of Roads throughout New South Wales', *The New South Wales Calendar and General Post Office Directory, 1832* (Sydney 1832), pp. 46–154.

17   Perry, op. cit., pp. 138, 139; Sharon Morgan, *Land Settlement in Early Tasmania: Creating an Antipodean England* (Cambridge 1992), pp. 166–9.

18   Wentworth, op. cit., p. 415 (original emphasis).

19   Mrs Charles Meredith, *Notes and Sketches of New South Wales* (London 1844), p. 80; Davidoff and Hall, op. cit., pp. 202–5; Rob Linn, *Power, Progress and Profit: A History of the Australian Accounting Profession* (Melbourne 1996), pp. 18–27.

20   Edward Curr, *An Account of the Colony of Van Diemen's Land* (London 1824), p. 78; George Fletcher Moore, *Diary of Ten Years Eventful Life of an Early Settler in Western Australia* (London 1884), p. 200; John Perkins and Jack Thompson, 'Cattle Theft, Primitive Capital Accumulation and Pastoral Expansion in Early New South Wales, 1800–1850', *Australian Historical Studies*, no. 111 (October 1998), p. 296.

21   Moore, op. cit., p. 55.

22   James Macarthur, *New South Wales; Its Present State and Future Prospects* (London 1837), pp. 186, 188. For Macarthur's authorship, see Alan Atkinson, 'James Macarthur as Author', *Journal of the Royal Australian Historical Society*, vol. 67 (1981).

23   *Sydney Gazette*, 28 April 1835; Iain Stuart, 'Sea Rats, Bandits and Roistering Buccaneers: What Were the Bass Strait Sealers Really Like?', *Journal of the Royal Australian Historical Society*, vol. 83 (1997), p. 54.

24   W.H. Dutton, evidence before committee on police and gaols, 9 June 1835, p. 335.

25   Sir John Jamison, evidence before committee on police and gaols, 10 June 1835, ibid., p. 338.

26   John West, *The History of Tasmania* (ed. A.G.L. Shaw) (Sydney 1971; first pub. 1852), p. 105.

27   P.A. Pemberton, *Pure Merinos and Others: The 'Shipping Lists' of the Australian Agricultural Company* (Canberra 1986), pp. 46–50; Mark Hannah, 'Aboriginal Workers in the Australian Agricultural Company, 1824 to 1857', BA thesis, University of New England 2000, pp. 66–7.

28   Stephen H. Roberts, *History of Australian Land Settlement 1788–1920* (Melbourne 1968), p. 68 (quoting E.M. Curr, 7 March 1832); Jennifer Duxbury, 'Conflict and Discipline: The Van Diemen's Land Company', *Push from the Bush*, no. 25 (October 1987), pp. 37–45.

29   Governor Darling's instructions, 17 July 1825, *HRA*, series 1, vol. 12, p. 123.

30   Alexandra Hasluck, *Thomas Peel of Swan River* (Melbourne 965), p. 11.

31 Lord Bathurst to Ralph Darling, 1 (two letters), 11 March 1826, and Darling to Bathurst, 10 October, 24 November, 4 December 1826, *HRA*, series 1, vol. 12, pp. 192–4, 218, 640–1, 700, 730; William Huskisson to Darling, 28, 30 January 1828, *HRA*, series 1, vol. 13, pp. 739–40, 741–2.

32 Sir George Murray to Darling, 12 January 1829, *HRA*, series 1, vol. 14, p. 610.

33 The naming of county Plantagenet suggests a connection with the Duke of Beaufort. Beaufort's eldest son married two of Wellington's nieces, his brother had been Governor of the Cape (married a Poulett, as in Stirling's Lake Poulett) and his brother-in-law under-secretary in the Colonial Office.

34 J.M.R. Cameron, *Ambition's Fire: The Agricultural Colonization of Pre-Convict Western Australia* (Nedlands 1981), pp. 63–5.

35 Elizabeth Fenton, *The Journal of Mrs Fenton: A Narrative of Her Life in India, the Isle of France (Mauritius), and Tasmania During the Years 1826–1830* (London 1901), p. 352.

36 'Regulations for the guidance … of Settlers', 3 February 1829, *HRA*, series 3, vol. 6, pp. 606–8.

37 'List of Persons who have claimed Land', 17 February 1830, *HRA*, series 3, vol. 6, p. 639; Marnie Bassett, *The Hentys: An Australian Colonial Tapestry* (London 1954), pp. 39–40, 53; F.K. Crowley, 'Master and Servant in Western Australia 1829–1851', *Western Australian Historical Society Journal and Proceedings*, vol. 4, pt 5 (1953), pp. 95–7.

38 James Stirling to Sir George Murray, 30 January 1830, *HRA*, series 3, vol. 6, p. 621.

39 Moore, op. cit., pp. 35, 40.

40 Ibid., p. 159; Ian Berryman (ed.), *A Colony Detailed: The First Census of Western Australia 1832* (Perth 1979). The list is not quite complete in describing occupations.

41 Hasluck, *Thomas Peel of Swan River*, p. 112; George Stokes to James Stirling [1836], in Marian Aveling (ed.), *Westralian Voices: Documents in Western Australian Social History* (Nedlands 1979), p. 10; P.C. Statham, 'Peter Augustus Lautour', *Journal of the Royal Australian Historical Society*, vol. 72 (1986), pp. 229–30.

42 Thomas Bannister to Lord Egremont, West Sussex Record Office MF72 PHA136; Crowley, op. cit., p. 103; T.W. Mazzarol, 'Tradition, Environment and the Indentured Labourer in Early Western Australia', *Studies in Western Australian History*, vol. 3 (November 1978), pp. 30–7.

43 *Sydney Gazette*, 1 January 1831 (original emphasis); Berryman, op. cit., p. 18.

44 Pamela Statham, 'Swan River Colony 1829–1850', in C.T. Stannage (ed.), *A New History of Western Australia* (Nedlands 1981), pp. 190–2; Cameron, op. cit., pp. 130–5.

45 'Resolutions proposed and carried at a meeting', York, 12 May 1838, and J. R. Phillips to colonial secretary, 12 September 1838, WAA CSO 62, ff. 29, 302; *South Australian Register*, 22 February 1840; Donald S. Garden, *Albany: A Panorama of the Sound* (Melbourne 1977), p. 95.

46 J.S. Marais, *The Colonisation of New Zealand* (London 1927), p. 73; R.B. Madgwick, *Immigration into Eastern Australia 1788–1851* (Sydney 1969), p. 223; Douglas Pike, *Paradise of Dissent: South Australia 1829–1857* (Melbourne 1967), p. 517.

47 *South Australian Gazette*, 3 November 1838.

48   Alexander Baring, speech in the House of Commons, 29 July 1834, in Dickey and Howell, *South Australia's Foundation: Select Documents* (Adelaide 1986), p. 34; Anonymous paper beginning 'Probable causes of the difficulties', September 1835, MLSA PRG 174/13, p. 216.

49   [E.G. Wakefield], *Sketch of a Proposal for Colonizing Australasia*, n.d., pp. 8–9, 34–6, enclosed with Robert Gouger to R.W. Hay, 25 June 1829, CO 201/206, f. 468; Erik Olssen, 'Mr Wakefield and New Zealand as an Experiment in Post-Enlightenment Experimental Practice', *New Zealand Journal of History*, vol. 31 (1997), p. 201.

50   E.G. Wakefield, *A Letter from Sydney*, in his *A Letter from Sydney and other Writings on Colonization* (London 1929), pp. 44–5, 47; Peter Dillon to R.W. Hay, 7 October 1832, CO 323/168. Dillon says that Dixon met Robert Gouger, Wakefield's friend, in King's Bench prison. But Dixon was in England only during the first half of 1829, when *A Letter from Sydney* was being written and before Gouger was incarcerated: *Sydney Gazette*, 2 June 1828, 24 December 1829. There is no record of Dixon's imprisonment. See also Pike, op. cit., p. 53.

51   Pike, op. cit., p. 55 (quotation not attributed).

52   Wakefield, *A Letter from Sydney*, p. 58.

53   Ibid., p. 47.

54   Samuel Stephens to G.F. Angas, 3, 21 August, 27 October 1835, MLSA PRG 174/1; Angas to Thomas Bannister, 8 December 1836, MLSA PRG 174/10; Unattributed quotation in Eric Richards, 'The Peopling of South Australia, 1836–1986', in Eric Richards (ed.), *The Flinders History of South Australia: Social History* (Adelaide 1986), p. 117.

55   'New Colony of South Australia', 1835, in Dickey and Howell, op. cit., p. 65 (original emphasis).

56   Wakefield, *A Letter from Sydney*, pp. 68–9.

57   William Tooke to Anthony Bacon, 27 October 1831, CO 13/1, f. 68; E.G. Wakefield, *England and America*, in his *A Letter from Sydney and Other Writings on Colonization*, p. 156.

58   Alan Atkinson, *Camden: Farm and Village Life in Early New South Wales* (Melbourne 1988), pp. 38–41, 123–4, 213–21.

59   Wakefield, *England and America*, p. 113; Macarthur, op. cit., pp. 54, 159, 163.

60   Wakefield, *England and America*, p. 181; Hill, op. cit., pp. 35, 75–80; M.J. Daunton, *Royal Mail: The Post Office Since 1840* (London 1985), p. 23.

61   George Arthur, evidence before select committee on transportation, 27 June 1837, *Parliamentary Papers*, 1837 (518) XIX, pp. 287–92.

62   Rowland Hill to G.F. Angas, 8 June 1835, John Hull to Angas, 6 June 1835, Samuel Stephens to Angas, 27 October 1835 (original emphasis), and George Stevenson to Angas, 24 May 1836, MLSA PRG 174/1; 'A Return of all the Expenses attendant upon the execution of the Commission for the Colonization of South Australia ... until the 31st of December last', 30 January 1837, CO 13/8, f. 33; Pike, op. cit., pp. 138–9.

63   Wakefield, *A Letter from Sydney*, pp. 55–7.

64   Margaret and Alistair Macfarlane, *John Watts: Australia's Forgotten Architect and South Australia's Postmaster General 1841–1861* (Bonnells Bay, N.S.W., 1992), p. 69.

65   James Gardner to Mrs Thomas Gardner, 4 July 1841, belonging to Mr D. Barber, England, and copy kindly supplied by Bill Gammage.

66   Moore, op. cit., pp. 174–5, 196–7, 211–12.
67   Louisa Clifton, diary, 23 May 1841, in Lucy Frost (ed.), *No Place for a Nervous Lady* (Melbourne 1984), pp. 60–1.
68   Mary Arlett to Charles Fahey, 27 March 1833, AONSW 4/2443.5; Richard Corbett to his sister, 22 May 1853, La Trobe MS 6748.

Chapter 6: Conscience

1   John Blackman, 'The Experiences of a King's School "Bolter"', *The King's School Magazine*, March 1907, p. 281; Biographical information kindly supplied by Peter Yeend, of The King's School.
2   Blackman, op. cit., p. 284.
3   [Charlotte Barton], *A Mother's Offering to Her Children* (Sydney 1841), pp. 100, 155, 177, 197; Patricia Clarke, *Pioneer Writer: The Life of Louisa Atkinson: Novelist, Journalist, Naturalist* (Sydney 1990), pp. 54–9. For authorship, see Marcie Muir, *Charlotte Barton: Australia's First Children's Author* (Sydney 1980), pp. 9–19.
4   T.L. Mitchell, *Three Expeditions into the Interior of Eastern Australia* (London 1839), vol. 1, p. 192.
5   George Fletcher Moore, *Diary of Ten Years Eventful Life of an Early Settler in Western Australia* (London 1884), p. 53.
6   [Barton], op. cit., pp. 85–100.
7   Trial of Thomas Holden, 10 December 1835, Yass bench book, AONSW 4/5709; Brian Harrison, 'Animals and the State in Nineteenth-Century England', *English Historical Review*, vol. 88 (1973), pp. 786–9; John E. Archer, *By a Flash and a Scare: Incendiarism, Animal Maiming, and Poaching in East Anglia 1815–1870* (Oxford 1990), pp. 198–218; Dave Grossman, *On Killing* (Boston 1996), pp. 6–15 (I owe this reference to Iain Spence); Hamish Maxwell-Stewart and Bruce Hindmarsh, ' "This is the Bird that Never Flew": William Stewart, Major Donald MacLeod and the *Launceston Advertiser*', *Journal of Australian Colonial History*, vol. 2 (2000), p. 4.
8   William Shakespeare, *Richard III*, act V, sc. iii.
9   L.F. Fitzhardinge (ed.), *Sydney's First Four Years* (that is, Watkin Tench, *A Narrative of the Expedition to Botany Bay* and *A Complete Account of the Settlement at Port Jackson*) (Sydney 1979), p. 208.
10 Moore, op. cit., p. 206; Alexandra Hasluck, 'Yagan the Patriot', *Early Days: Journal and Proceedings of the Western Australian Historical Society*, vol. 5, pt 7 (1961), pp. 46–7.
11 *Perth Gazette*, 23 March 1833; P.E.C. de Mouncey, 'The Historic Duel at Fremantle between George French Johnson, a Merchant, and William Nairne Clark, a Solicitor, in the Year, 1832', *Early Days: The Western Australian Historical Society Journal and Proceedings*, vol. 1, pt 5 (1929), pp. 1–15. For the other fatal duels, both in Sydney, see *Sydney Gazette*, 5 May 1828, and *Australian*, 7 May 1828.
12 *Monitor*, 7 September 1838; 'Garryowen' [Edmund Finn], *The Chronicles of Early Melbourne 1835 to 1852* (Melbourne 1888), p. 775; Paul de Serville, *Port Phillip Gentlemen and Good Society in Melbourne before the Gold Rushes* (Melbourne 1980), pp. 106–11, 214–16.

13   James Backhouse, *A Narrative of a Visit to the Australian Colonies* (London 1843), p. 156; W.G. Broughton, evidence before committee on education, 15 July 1844, Report, p. 82, NSW legislative council *Votes and Proceedings*, 1844, vol. 2.

14   Alexander Tolmer, 'Journal of an Expedition to Kangaroo Island', 4 September 1844, SRSA GRG 5/4/34; John Stuart Mill, *The Early Draft of John Stuart Mill's Autobiography* (ed. Jack Stillinger) (Urbana, Ill,. 1961), pp. 172, 173; Alexander Harris, *Settlers and Convicts: Recollections of Sixteen Years' Labour in the Australian Backwoods* (Melbourne 1953; first pub. 1847), p. 231 (the original is in italics throughout).

15   Statement of Jeremiah Leary, 15 February 1834, in Margaret Hazzard, *Punishment Short of Death: A History of the Penal Settlement at Norfolk Island* (Melbourne 1984), p. 135.

16   *Sydney Gazette*, 27 January 1825 (the first passage originally in italics); Deposition of Eliza Campbell, 15 November 1824, AONSW SC 720.25/10; Papers for R. *v.* Martin Benson and others, January 1825, AONSW CP T128/10.

17   Reports of Supreme Courts trials, *Sydney Morning Herald*, 1849; Appendices in 'Supreme Court [NSW] Criminal Jurisdiction', unpublished guide, AONSW; Indictments, SA Supreme Court, 1837–50, SRSA GRG 36/1; Indictment register, WA Supreme Court, 1830–87, SROWA CONS 3422/1. I am grateful for Andrew Messner and Peter Hammond for help with this material.

18   *Monitor*, 1 August 1838.

19   *Sydney Gazette*, 24 March 1828, 5 May 1832, 22 February 1838.

20   Indictments, S.A. Supreme Court, 1837–50, SRSA GRG 36/1; R.H.W. Reece, *Aborigines and Colonists: Aborigines and Colonial Society in New South Wales in the 1830s and 1840s* (Sydney 1974), pp. 30, 48–9, 55.

21   Census of South Australia, 1840, MLSA PRG 174/13, p. 878; D.W. Meinig, *On the Margins of the Good Earth: The South Australian Wheat Frontier, 1869–1884* (Adelaide 1970), pp. 19–20; Douglas Pike, *Paradise of Dissent: South Australia 1829–1857* (Melbourne 1967), pp. 300–1.

22   *South Australian Register*, 25 January 1840.

23   Portia Robinson, *The Hatch and Brood of Time: A Study of the First Generation of Native-Born White Australians 1788–1828* (Melbourne 1985), pp. 36–7. Byrne lists only six cases tried in Sydney before 1830 and none of the mothers were convicts: Paula J. Byrne, *Criminal Law and Colonial Subject: New South Wales 1810–1830* (Cambridge 1993), pp. 250–7.

24   Criminal indictments, SA Supreme Court, 1837–50, SRSA GRG 36/1 (Rau, May 1840; Hydress, September 1844; Lygoe, March 1845); *South Australian Register*, 18, 21 September 1844.

25   *Sydney Herald*, 12 August 1840.

26   J.N. Dickinson, in *Sydney Morning Herald*, 12 September 1846; Judith A. Allen, *Sex and Secrets: Crimes Involving Australian Women since 1880* (Melbourne 1990), p. 33; Shurlee Swain and Renate Howe, *Single Mothers and their Children: Disposal, Punishment and Survival in Australia* (Melbourne 1995), pp. 95–6.

27   W.H. Leigh, *Reconnoitering Voyages, Travels and Adventures in the New Colonies of South Australia* (London 1839), p. 131 (original emphasis).

28   Mrs Charles Meredith, *Notes and Sketches of New South Wales* (London 1844), p. 68.

29   John Cashen, 'Master and Servant in South Australia', *Push from the Bush*, no. 6 (May 1980), pp. 23–33 (quoting *South Australian Gazette*).

30   E.J.P. Joske, 'Health and Hospital: A Study of Community Welfare in Western Australia, 1829–1855', MA thesis, University of Western Australia 1973, pp. 147–53, 242–4, 250–3; Alan Atkinson and Marian Aveling (eds), *Australian 1838* (Sydney 1987), pp. 351–2; Pamela Statham (comp.), *Dictionary of Western Australians 1829–1914*, vol. 1 (Nedlands 1979), p. 85.

31   Ian L.D. Forbes, 'Aspects of Health Care', in Eric Richards (ed.), *The Flinders History of South Australia: Social History* (Adelaide 1986), p. 261.

32   Report of the Board appointed by His Excellency the Acting Governor to enquire into the management and condition of the Infirmary, 17 September 1838, SRSA GRG 24/90/369.

33   *Southern Australian*, 2 June 1838; Atkinson and Aveling, op. cit., p. 353–4.

34   Brian Dickey, *Rations, Residence, Resources: A History of Social Welfare in South Australia since 1836* (Adelaide 1986), pp. 3–5; Robert Dare, 'Paupers' Rights: Governor Grey and the Poor Law in South Australia', *Australian Historical Studies*, vol. 25 (1992), pp. 231–41.

35   Michael Smithson, 'A Misunderstood Gift; The Annual Issue of Blankets to Aborigines in New South Wales 1826–48', *Push: A Journal of Early Australian Social History*, no. 30 (1992), pp. 86, 96–104.

36   *Sydney Herald*, 24 May 1838; Launceston petty sessions, 27 February 1839, AOT LC 347/25.

37   W.C. Wentworth, evidence of before select committee on police and gaols, 19 July 1839, NSW legislative council *Votes and Proceedings*, 1839, vol. 2, p. 317.

38   Alan Atkinson, 'The Parliament in the Jerusalem Warehouse', *Push from the Bush*, no. 12 (1982), pp. 86–7.

39   *Sydney Herald*, 31 January 1833; Alan Atkinson, 'The Political Life of James Macarthur', PhD thesis, Australian National University 1976, pp. 133–9.

40   *Sydney Gazette*, 29 January 1833; *Report of the Proceedings of the General Meeting of the Supporters of the Petitions to His Majesty and the House of Commons, Held at the Committee Rooms, May 30, 1836* (Sydney 1836), pp. 12–13; Atkinson, 'The Political Life of James Macarthur', pp. 139–42.

41   *Sydney Gazette*, 29 January 1833.

42   *Australian*, 2 June 1835; Atkinson, 'The Parliament in the Jerusalem Warehouse', pp. 82–4; Atkinson and Aveling, op. cit., pp. 333–6.

43   *Murray's Review*, 26 June 1835; West, John, *The History of Tasmania* (ed. A.G.L. Shaw) (Sydney 1971; first pub. 1852), p. 136; Atkinson and Aveling, op. cit., pp. 333–4.

44   Ibid.

45   *South Australian Register*, 12 February 1842 (original emphasis); Pike, op. cit., p. 393.

46   *Sydney Gazette*, 4 February 1840; *Australian*, 11 June 1840; *Commercial Journal*, 24 June, 8, 15 July 1840; *New Moral World*, 4 January, 1 February 1840; John F.C. Harrison, *Quest for a New Moral World: Robert Owen and the Owenites in Britain and America* (New York 1969), pp. 47–87; D.W.L.

Webster, 'Radicalism and the Sydney Press c. 1838–1846', MA thesis, University of Melbourne 1978, p. 56. Alan Mayne kindly helped with these references.

47   A.W. Martin, *Henry Parkes: A Biography* (Melbourne 1980), p. 23.

48   Clarinda Parkes to Sarah Parkes, 10 March 1839, in A.T. Parkes, *An Emigrant's Home Letters* (Sydney 1896), pp. 66–8 (the original does not survive).

49   James Macarthur, evidence before select committee on transportation, 5 February 1838, *Parliamentary Papers*, 1837–8 (669) XXII, pp. 6–7; Henry Parkes to his sister, 10 February 1839, ML A1044.

50   Macarthur, evidence before select committee on transportation, 19 May 1837, *Parliamentary Papers*, 1837 (518) XIX, p. 164.

51   Alan Atkinson, *The Europeans in Australia: A History*, vol. 1 (Melbourne 1997), pp. 136–8, 142–4, 267–72.

52   G.T.W.B. Boyes to his wife, 5 November 1824, in Peter Chapman (ed.), *The Diaries and Letters of G.T.W.B. Boyes*, vol. 1 (Melbourne 1985), p. 208; *Sydney Gazette*, 22 March, 31 May 1826; *Monitor*, 19 May, 2 June 1826; G. Burder to W.A. Hankey, 13 October 1825, 4 September 1826, and Lancelot Threlkeld, 'Explanation', 13 February 1827, in Neil Gunson (ed.), *Australian Reminiscences and Papers of L.E. Threlkeld, Missionary to the Aborigines 1824–1859* (Canberra 1974), vol. 2, pp. 187–8, 213, 224 ; Meredith, op. cit., p. 49. See also Leonore Davidoff and Catherine Hall, *Family Fortunes: Men and Women of the English Middle Class 1780–1850* (London 1987), pp. 429–36; Annemieke van Drenth and Francisca de Haan, *The Rise of Caring Power: Elizabeth Fry and Josephine Butler in Britain and the Netherlands* (Amsterdam 1999), p. 44.

53   Brian Fletcher, 'Elizabeth Darling: Colonial Benefactress and Governor's Lady', *Journal of the Royal Australian Historical Society*, vol. 67 (1982), pp. 309–10, 312–13.

54   Frances Macleay to William Macleay, 21 April 1826, ML A4300, p. 164.

55   Elizabeth Windschuttle, ' "Feeding the Poor and Sapping their Strength": The Public Role of Ruling-Class Women in Eastern Australia, 1788–1850', in Elizabeth Windschuttle (ed.), *Women, Class and History: Feminist Perspectives on Australia 1788–1978* (Sydney 1980), p. 58; Fletcher, op. cit., p. 311.

56   Penny Russell, ' "Her Excellency": Lady Franklin, Female Convicts and the Problem of Authority in Van Diemen's Land', *Journal of Australian Studies*, no. 53 (1997), pp. 40–50 (quoting Jane Franklin, 19 January 1843).

57   Derek Phillips, 'The State and the Provision of Education in Tasmania, 1839 to 1913', PhD thesis, University of Tasmania 1988, p. 120.

58   The number of letters to the Colonial Secretary from the country benches (not counting Port Phillip) was 927 in 1835 and 912 in 1845 and except in 1836 and 1841 it was never more than 1000 (figures collected by Dr Patricia Curthoys). See also Michael J. Belcher, 'The Child in New South Wales Society, 1820 to 1837', PhD thesis, University of New England 1982, pp. 157, 183.

59   William Macarthur to John Macarthur jr, 5 June 1832, ML A2935; Mitchell, op. cit., vol. 1, pp. 156–8.

60   George Arthur, evidence before select committee on transportation, 27 June 1837, *Parliamentary Papers*, 1837 (518) XIX, p. 291; Backhouse, op. cit.

61   *Hobart Town Gazette*, 17 March 1827; Thomas Carlyle, 'Signs of the Times', 1829, in Thomas Carlyle, *Critical and Miscellaneous Essays* (London 1899), vol. 2, p. 77; *Australian*, 18 December 1838 (original emphasis); Ivon Asquith, '1780–1855', in George Boyce, James Curren, and Pauline Wingate (eds), *Newspaper History from the Seventeenth Century to the Present Day* (London 1978), p. 100.

62   *Sydney Morning Herald*, 10 June 1847; William Ullathorne, *From Cabin-Boy to Archbishop: The Autobiography of Archbishop Ullathorne* (London 1941), p. 159; Alan Atkinson, 'A Slice of the Sydney Press', *Push from the Bush*, no. 1 (May 1978), pp. 87–91.

63   *South Australian Gazette*, 3 November 1838; James Macarthur in *Sydney Morning Herald*, 1 May 1844.

64   Convict indents (printed), for Sarah McGregor, no. 44, *Kains*, arrived 11 March 1831, and Mary Maloney, no. 36, *Palambam*, arrived 31 July 1831, NSWAO 4/4016; Charlotte Anley, *The Prisoners of Australia: A Narrative* (London 1841), pp. 24–5.

65   *Sydney Gazette*, 25 February 1834; 'Waldron (Charles)', in L.M. Mowle (ed.), *A Genealogical History of Pioneer Families of Australia* (Adelaide 1978), p. 370.

66   *Sydney Gazette*, 25 February 1834.

67   Ibid.

68   *Sydney Gazette*, 25 (original emphasis), 27 February 1834.

69   *Sydney Gazette*, 27 February 1834; *Australian*, 28 February 1834 (original emphasis).

70   *Sydney Herald*, 24 February 1834; *Sydney Gazette*, 25, 27 February 1834; Anley, op. cit., p. 25.

Part 2

1   *South Australian Register*, 12 December 1840 (paragraphing added). Thanks to Mary Notestine for entomological advice.

Chapter 7: Men and Women

1   Leonore Davidoff and Catherine Hall, *Family Fortunes: Men and Women of the English Middle Class 1780–1850* (London 1987), p. 385.

2   James Tucker, *Ralph Rashleigh* (Sydney 1962), pp. 105–6. See also James Backhouse, *A Narrative of a Visit to the Australian Colonies* (London 1843), p. 29.

3   Launceston petty sessions, 28 August 1824, AOT LC 347/1; William Wilson Dobie, *Recollections of a Visit to Port-Phillip Australia, in 1852–55* (Edinburgh 1856), pp. 72–3.

4   Sophia Dumaresq to Mrs Winn, 20 February 1830, ML ZA 2571.

5   Annie Baxter, 16 June 1848, quoted in Paul de Serville, *Rolph Boldrewood: A Life* (Melbourne 2000), p. 81.

6   Hamish Maxwell-Stewart, Paul Donnelly and Timothy Millett, 'Dr Martin and the Forty Thieves', in Lucy Frost and Hamish Maxwell-Stewart (eds), *Chain Letters: Narrating Convict Lives* (Melbourne 2001), p. 183.

7   Monitor, 1 September 1826; George Arthur to John Burnett, 23 February 1832, and Burnett to Arthur, 24 February 1832, ML A2165; Alan Atkinson, 'Convicts and Courtship', in Patricia Grimshaw and others (eds), *Families in Colonial Australia* (Sydney 1985), pp. 19–31.

8   *Aberdeen Journal*, 18 April 1827 (extract kindly supplied by Central Library, Aberdeen); Convict indents for Robert Simpson, Prince Regent, arrived 27 September 1827, NSWAO 4/4011, and for Ann Durrant, Louisa, arrived 3 December 1827, NSWAO 4/4013; Ann Durrant, ticket of leave, 8 April 1838, AONSW 4/4118, no. 318/45.

9   List of persons applying for the publication of banns at Parramatta, 12 April 1839, with remarks by Rev. Cunninghame Atchison, NSWAO 4/2436.8; Report of principal superintendent of convicts an applications to marry, 17 April 1839, AONSW 4/4510, f. 118; Malcolm R. Sainty and Keith A. Johnson (eds), *Census of New South Wales, November 1828* (Sydney 1980), pp. 133, 339; N.G. Butlin, C.W. Cromwell and K.L. Suthern (eds), *General Return of Convicts in New South Wales, 1837* (Sydney 1987), pp. 554, 555.

10   George and Margaret Stevenson, journal, 16 November 1836, 21 January 1837, MLSA PRG 174/1.

11   Ibid., 8 January 1837.

12   T.B. Atkinson, shipboard diary, 28 June 1857, SLV La Trobe MS 12599.

13   Ibid., 28 May 1857.

14   Penny Russell, 'Introduction', in Penny Russell (ed.), *For Richer, For Poorer: Early Colonial Marriages* (Melbourne 1994), pp. 3–4.

15   G.A. Robinson, journal, 15, 25 October 1830, in N.J.B. Plomley (ed.), *Friendly Mission: The Tasmanian Journals and Papers of George Augustus Robinson, 1824–1834* (Hobart 1966), pp. 249, 256–7; Miriam Dixson, *The Real Matilda: Woman and Identity in Australia 1788 to 1975* (Melbourne 1994), p. 60.

16   James Stirling to Sir George Murray, 20 January 1830 (extract), *Parliamentary Papers*, 1830, XXI, 675, p. 5; *Perth Gazette*, 5 January 1833; Backhouse, op. cit., p. 536.

17   Elizabeth Dent, deposition, 17 December 1832, SROWA 3472/11, no. 55; *Perth Gazette*, 5 January 1833; Alan Atkinson, 'Women Publicans in 1838', *Push from the Bush*, no. 8 (December 1980), pp. 88–106; Davidoff and Hall, op. cit., pp. 299–301.

18   Indictment register, W.A. Supreme Court, 1830–87, SROWA CONS 3422/1; E.J.P. Joske, 'Health and Hospital: A Study of Community Welfare in Western Australia 1829–1855', MA thesis, University of Western Australia 1973, p. 251 (quotation from surgeon's report, 24 June 1836). The husband may be the 'John Dent' who died a lunatic in Fremantle gaol in 1848 (ibid., p. 305).

19   Walter Ong, 'System, Space, and Intellect in Renaissance Symbolism', in his *The Barbarian Within, and Other Fugitive Essays and Studies* (New York 1962), pp. 81–2.

20   James Ross, 'An Essay on Prison Discipline', quoted in John Gascoigne, *The Enlightenment and the Origins of European Australia* (Cambridge 2002), p. 135.

21   Michael Roberts, 'Sickles and Scythes: Women's Work and Men's Work at Harvest Time', *History Workshop*, issue 7 (Spring 1979), pp. 3–28; K.D.M. Snell, *Annals of the Labouring Poor: Social Change and Agrarian England 1660–1900* (Cambridge 1987), pp. 15–66; Davidoff and Hall, op. cit., pp. 274–5.

22   Longford (Norfolk Plains), petty sessions, 3 September 1830, AOT LC 362/2.

23   *Monitor*, 1 August 1838.

24   *Sydney Gazette*, 31 October 1827, 30 September 1830; *Australian*, 31 October 1827; John Piper jr to John Piper sr, [February 1831?], ML CY A256, p. 753; *Monitor*, 5 February 1831; Marsden to Alexander Macleay, 12 Oct 1832, 1 March 1833, AONSW 4/2191.3; David Kent, 'Customary Behaviour Transported: A Note on the Parramatta Female Factory Riot of 1827', *Journal of Australian Studies*, no. 40 (March 1994), pp. 75–9; Kay Daniels, *Convict Women: Rough Culture and Reformation* (Sydney 1998), pp. 145–56.

25   Kent, op. cit., pp. 75–9.

26   Jesse Pullen, statement, 9 February 1829, and Josiah Spode to John Burnett, 5 April 1832, in Eustace Fitzsymonds (ed.), *A Looking-Glass for Tasmania* (Hobart 1980), pp. 165–6, 214; *Monitor*, 5 February 1831 (original emphasis).

27   *Sydney Herald*, 10 March 1834; Jane Franklin to Elizabeth Fry, 3 August 1841, University of Tasmania, RS 16/1(2) (original emphasis); Daniels, op. cit., p. 150.

28   Elizabeth Fry, *Observations on the Visiting, Superintendence, and Government of Female Prisoners* (London 1827), pp. 44–7 (original emphasis).

29   John Ruskin, *Sesame and Lilies* (London 1960), p. 107; Annemieke van Drenth and Francisca de Haan, *The Rise of Caring Power: Elizabeth Fry and Josephine Butler in Britain and the Netherlands* (Amsterdam 1999), p. 70.

30   Fry, op. cit., p. 22; [Charlotte Anley], 'Extracts from a letter written by a Lady residing in New South Wales, for the information of the Committee of the Ladies Society for the reformation of Female Prisoners', July 1836, CO 201/266, ff. 533–6; Charlotte Anley to Samuel Marsden, 13 September [1837], ML A1677-4, pp. 1064–5; Charlotte Anley, *The Prisoners of Australia: A Narrative* (London 1841), pp. 24–7 (original emphasis); Information kindly supplied by Mr Paul Anley.

31   Thomas James Lempriere, *The Penal Settlements of Early Van Diemen's Land* (Launceston 1954), p. 45; Frances O'Donoghue, 'Winding Down the Convict Machine: Brisbane in 1838', *Push from the Bush*, no. 13 (November 1982), p. 14.

32   'An Unpaid Magistrate', *Observations on the 'Hole and Corner Petition' in a Letter to the Rt Hon. Edward G. Stanley, Principal Secretary of State for the Colonial Department* (Sydney 1834), pp. 31–2 (original emphases); Tucker, op. cit., pp. 121–2.

33   [Anley], 'Extracts from a letter ... ', July 1836, CO 201/266, ff. 535; Jane Franklin to Elizabeth Fry, 3 August 1841, University of Tasmania, RS 16/1(2).

34   Thomas Cook, *The Exile's Lamentations* (Sydney 1978), p. 79; John Clay, *Maconochie's Experiment* (London 2001), pp. 150–5, 163.

35   Sir Richard Bourke to Thomas Spring Rice, 15 January 1835, *HRA*, series 1, vol. 17, pp. 638–9; Bourke to Lord Glenelg, 4 November 1837, *HRA*, series 1, vol. 19, p. 154; Van Diemen's Land Census, 1842, *Hobart Town Gazette*, 20 May 1842.

36   Anon., 'Excursion to Port Arthur', in *Elliston's Hobart Town Almanack*, 1837 (Hobart 1837), pp. 97–8; Dora Heard (ed.), *The Journal of Charles*

O'Hara Booth, Commandant of the Port Arthur Penal Settlement (Hobart 1981), p. 26.

37 Anon., 'Excursion to Port Arthur', p. 96; Heard, op. cit., pp. 24–5 (quoting Booth, 28 October 1833, and Jane Franklin, March 1837).

38 Ruskin, op. cit., p. 107; Margaret Hazzard, *Punishment Short of Death: A History of the Penal Settlement at Norfolk Island* (Melbourne 1984), p. 140; Raymond Nobbs (ed.), *Norfolk Island and Its Second Settlement, 1825–1855* (Sydney 1991), p. 19.

39 George Arthur, evidence before select committee on transportation, 30 June 1837, *Parliamentary Papers*, 1837 (518) XIX, p. 309; Lempriere, op. cit., pp. 66–8, 79, 85–7, 95; A.G.L. Shaw, *Convict and the Colonies: A Study of Penal Transportation from Great Britain and Ireland to Australia and Other Parts of the British Empire* (London 1966), pp. 211–13; Maggie Weidenhofer, *Port Arthur: A Place of Misery* (Melbourne 1981), pp. 29–41.

40 Arthur, evidence, 30 June 1837, pp. 308–10; Matthew Forster, 7 March 1840, quoted in Ian Brand, *Penal Peninsula: Port Arthur and Its Outstations 1827–1898* (Launceston 1989), p. 52; John Burnet, 1833, quoted in Shaw, op. cit., p. 212.

41 F.J. Cockburn, *Letters from the Southern Hemisphere* (Calcutta 1856), p. 67.

42 G.C. Mundy, *Our Antipodes* (London 1852), vol. 3, p. 206; Weidenhofer, op. cit., pp. 36–9.

43 Tucker, op. cit., pp. 121–2.

44 *Launceston Advertiser*, 14 December 1829; Shayne Breen, 'Justice, Humanity and the Common Good: John Pascoe Fawkner's Ideology of Utilitarian Justice, 1829–30', *Tasmanian Historical Studies*, vol. 4 (1994), pp. 31–41.

45 Handbill headed 'Volunteer Association', 29 September 1830, and Edward Abbott to John Burnett, 1 October 1830, in Fitzsymonds, op. cit., pp. 185–6; John Reynolds, *Launceston: History of an Australian City* (Melbourne 1969), pp. 54–6.

46 John Batman to George Arthur, 25 June 1835, *Historical Records of Victoria*, vol. 1, p. 5; John Pascoe Fawkner, 'Constitution and Form of Government', n.d. (c. 1835), SLV La Trobe MS 13273.

47 *Launceston Advertiser*, 1 June 1829; Fawkner, 'Constitution and Form of Government'.

48 *Launceston Advertiser*, 1 February 1830.

49 William Ullathorne, evidence before the select committee on transportation, 8 February 1838, *Parliamentary Papers*, 1837–8 (669) XXII, p. 27; Cook, op. cit. p. 44; Daniels, op. cit., pp. 112–16.

50 New South Wales census, 1841, NSW legislative council *Votes and Proceedings*, 1841, no pagination (counting males and females fourteen years and over).

51 G.A. Robinson, journal, 27 December 1836, 3 January 1837, in N.J.B. Plomley (ed.), *Weep in Silence: A History of the Flinders Island Aboriginal Settlement* (Hobart 1987), pp. 407, 413.

52 Batman to Arthur, 25 June 1835, *Historical Records of Victoria*, vol. 1, pp. 6–10; C.P. Billot (ed.), *Melbourne's Missing Chronicle, Being the Journal of Preparations for Departure to and Proceedings at Port Phillip by John Pascoe Fawkner* (Melbourne 1982), pp. 68–9 (3 May 1836); C.P. Billot, *The Life and Times of John Pascoe Fawkner* (Melbourne), pp. 140–6.

53   Anne Colman, 'New Worlds: Attitudes to Immigrants and Immigration in Port Phillip, New York and Rio de Janeiro, 1835–1850', PhD thesis, University of Melbourne 1999, pp. 47–8.

54   *Port Phillip Patriot*, 20 January 1840; Colman, op. cit., pp. 11, 57, 132–6, 166–7, 175, 180, 215.

55   George Arden, *Latest Information with Regard to Australia Felix* (Melbourne 1840, pp. 85–7; John Dunmore Lang, *Emigration to Port Phillip* (London 1848), p. 2; Colman, op. cit., p. 150.

56   Cook, op. cit., p. 69.

57   Ibid., pp. 46, 50, 66–7, 70, 97.

58   Answers (n.d.) from Thomas Arkell, Francis N. Rossi, Watson Augustus Steel, Cyrus M. Doyle, John Grono, Thomas Hyndes, to questionnaire from committee on immigration, NSW legislative council *Votes and Proceedings*, 1838, pp. 191, 194, 206, 207, 212; Penelope Selby to her mother, 15 December 1848, in Lucy Frost (ed.), *No Place for a Nervous Lady* (Melbourne 1984), p. 177.

59   Caroline Chisholm, evidence before select committee on immigration, 4 September 1845, NSW legislative council *Votes and Proceedings*, 1845, pp. 639–40.

60   Penelope Selby to her sisters, 6 November 1844, in Frost, op. cit., p. 168; William Wilson Dobie, *Recollections of a Visit to Port-Phillip, Australia, in 1852–55* (Edinburgh 1856), p. 73.

61   Rica Erickson, *The Drummonds of Hawthornden* (Nedlands 1975), pp. 39–40, 105–6, 124–5.

62   Eliza Brown to William Bussey, 30 December 1851, in Peter Cowan (ed.), *A Faithful Picture: The Letters of Eliza and Thomas Brown at York in the Swan River Colony 1841–1852* (Fremantle 1977), p. 134; *The Catholic Almanac*, 1854, extract in Patrick O'Farrell (ed.), *Documents in Australian Catholic History* (London 1969), vol. 1, pp. 317–18.

63   Mary Anne Kettle, evidence in Kettle *v.* McVitie, 1 July 1852, *Bell's Life in Sydney*, 3 July 1852.

64   Anthony Trollope, *The Small House at Allington* (London 1909), p. 191.

65   Derek Phillips, 'The State and the Provision of Education in Tasmania, 1839 to 1913', PhD thesis, University of Tasmania 1988, pp. 464–6; Alan Atkinson, ' "He Filled us Full of Laughter": Contact and Community in Australian Experience' in Richard White and Hsu-Ming Teo (eds), *Cultural History in Australia* (Sydney 2003), pp. 44–7.

66   'School Establishments of New South Wales', 1838, in W.W. Burton, *The State of Religion and Education in New South Wales* (London 1840), between pp. lxv–lxvi; 'State of Education in New South Wales', 1843, and W.G. Broughton, evidence before committee on education, 15 July 1844, Report, pp. 55, 82, NSW legislative council *Votes and Proceedings*, 1844, vol. 2.

67   D.F. Bourke, *The History of the Catholic Church in Western Australia* (Perth 1979), pp. 24–25; David Mossman, *State Education in Western Australia 1829–1960* (Nedlands 1972), p. 9; Sister Ursula to Reverend Mother Cecilia, 19 December–1 January 1849, and same to same, 5 August 1849, in Geraldine Byrne (ed.), *Valiant Women: Letters from the Foundation Sisters of Mercy in Western Australia, 1845–1849* (Melbourne 1981), pp. 119, 139.

68   *Census of New South Wales*, 1861 (Sydney 1862); Atkinson, ' "He Filled Us Full of Laughter" ', p. 45.

69   John Dunmore Lang, in *Sydney Morning Herald*, 23 February 1844; Kathleen Tillotson, *Novels of the Eighteen-Forties* (Oxford 1954), p. 4; James D. Hart, *The Popular Book: A History of America's Literary Taste* (Berkeley 1961), pp. 90–1; Catherine Helen Spence, *Clara Morison* (Adelaide 1971; first pub. 1854), pp. 75, 78.

70   Deborah Brandt, *Literacy as Involvement: The Acts of Writers, Readers, and Texts* (Carbonvale, Ill. 1990), p. 6.

71   *Hobart Town Courier*, 15 February 1845, 13 February 1847; Van Diemen's Land Census, 1848; *Hobart Town Gazette*, 28 March 1848; Mrs McWhirter, 'Opening the Valentines', *Sydney Morning Herald*, 15 February 1850.

72   *Sydney Morning Herald*, 1, 2, 5 October 1858; Alan Atkinson, 'Classified Cupid', *Push from the Bush*, no. 22 (April 1986), pp. 30–8.

73   *Sydney Morning Herald*, 4 March 1850.

Chapter 8: Black and White

1   Somed Ali, deposition, 26 December 1832, SROWA 3472/11, no. 52; *Perth Gazette*, 5 January 1833.

2   James Purkis, David Patterson, and John Wittenoom jr, depositions, 26 December 1832, SROWA 3472/11, no. 52.

3   Lyndall Ryan, *The Aboriginal Tasmanians* (St Lucia 1981), p. 14; Henry Reynolds, *Fate of a Free People: A Radical Re-Examination of the Tasmanian Wars* (Melbourne 1995), pp. 142–3.

4   Convict indent for Andrew Eaton, *Surrey*, arrived 17 May 1836, AONSW X639; Albert Eugene Casey (ed.), *O'Kief, Coshe Mang, Slieve Lougher and Upper Blackwater in Ireland* (Birmingham, Alabama, 1964), vol. 5, p. 246; Andrew Eaton, evidence taken by Edward Denny Day following the massacre at Myall Creek, 30 August 1838, AONSW 4/5601.

5   Charles Sturt, *Narrative of an Expedition into Central Australia* (Adelaide 2001; first pub. 1849), pp. 93–4.

6   Charles Sturt, *Two Expeditions into the Interior of Southern Australia* (London 1833), vol. 1, p. 64; E.J. Stormon (trans. and ed.), *The Salvado Memoirs: Historical Memoirs of Australia and Particularly of the Benedictine Mission of New Norcia and of the Habits and Customs of the Australian Natives by Dom Rosendo Salvado, O.S.B.* (Nedlands 1977), p. 122.

7   T.L. Mitchell, *Three Expeditions into the Interior of Eastern Australia* (London 1839), vol. 1, p. 207; Elizabeth Macarthur to Eliza Kingdon, 8 March 1817, in Sibella Macarthur Onslow (ed.), *Some Early Records of the Macarthurs of Camden* (Sydney 1914), pp. 311–12; T.L. Mitchell to George Fife Angas, 12 December 1837, MLSA PRG 174/1.

8   James Backhouse, journal, 7 January 1834, in N.J.B. Plomley (ed.), *Weep in Silence: A History of the Flinders Island Aboriginal Settlement* (Hobart 1987), p. 267; Mitchell, op. cit., pp. 303–4.

9   Sir Thomas Brisbane to Earl Bathurst, 2 November 1824, and enclosed proclamation, 14 August 1824, *HRA*, series 1, vol. 11, pp. 409–11, 898; Saxe Bannister to Ralph Darling, 5 September 1826, *HRA*, series 1, vol. 12,

pp. 577–8; John Ferry, 'An Examination of the Various Aboriginal Evidence Bills of New South Wales, South Australia and Western Australia in the Period 1839–1849, As Well As an Analysis of the Racial Attitudes Which Were Espoused During the Controversies', BA thesis, University of New England 1980, pp. 9–11.

10   Darling to Bathurst, 6 October 1826, *HRA*, series 1, vol. 12, p. 609.

11   G.A. Robinson, journal, 16, 24 June 1830, in N.J.B. Plomley (ed.), *Friendly Mission: The Tasmanian Journals and Papers of George Augustus Robinson 1829–1834* (Hobart 1966), pp. 175–6, 183; A.G.L. Shaw, *Sir George Arthur, Bart, 1784–1854: Superintendent of British Honduras, Lieutenant-Governor of Van Diemen's Land and of Upper Canada, Governor of the Bombay Presidency* (Melbourne 1980), pp. 126–9; Reynolds, *Fate of a Free People*, pp. 111–14; Geoff Lennox, 'The Van Diemen's Land Company and the Tasmanian Aborigines: A Reappraisal', *Tasmanian Historical Research Association: Papers and Proceedings*, vol. 37 (1990), pp. 170–4; Keith Windschuttle, *The Fabrication of Aboriginal History*, vol. 1 (Sydney 2003), pp. 249–69.

12   George Arthur to Sir George Murray, 4 November 1828, and enclosed executive council minutes, 30, 31 October 1828, proclamation and instructions to police magistrates, both 1 November 1828, and instructions to military officers, 3 November 1828, *HRA*, series 3, vol. 7, pp. 625–35; Reynolds, *Fate of a Free People*, pp. 30–52, 72–3.

13   Brisbane's proclamation, 14 August 1824, op. cit., p. 410–11; Arthur's proclamation, 1 November 1828, op. cit., p. 631 (emphasis added); Ryan, op. cit., pp. 101–10; Lennox, op. cit., pp. 189–90. Compare Reynolds, *Fate of a Free People*, pp. 107–11.

14   Robinson, journal, 15 January 1831, in Plomley, *Friendly Mission*, p. 315; Ryan, op. cit., pp. 10–12; Reynolds, *Fate of a Free People*, pp. 114–19; Shaw, op. cit., pp. 129–31; John Connor, *The Australian Frontier Wars 1788–1838* (Sydney 2002), pp. 93–101.

15   The 1907 edition of *Webster's International Dictionary* gives 'to drive out' as a meaning still extant.

16   William Shakespeare, *Macbeth*, act IV, sc. i; *Sydney Gazette*, 21 May 1827; *Australian*, 8 December 1838; John Ruskin, *Sesame and Lilies* (London 1960), pp. 22–3; Henry Reynolds, *An Indelible Stain?: The Question of Genocide in Australia's History* (Melbourne 2001), pp. 52–66; Alan Atkinson, 'Historians and Moral Disgust', in Bain Atwood and Stephen Foster (eds), *Frontier Conflict: The Australian Experience* (Canberra 2003), pp. 117–18.

17   George Fletcher Moore, *Diary of Ten Years Eventful Life of an Early Settler in Western Australia* (London 1884), p. 183.

18   Neville Green, 'Aborigines and White Settlers', in C.T. Stannage (ed.), *A New History of Western Australia* (Nedlands 1981), p. 84.

19   Bill Gammage, 'The Wiradjuri War', *Push from the Bush*, no. 16 (November 1983), pp. 3–17 (quoting J.C. Crawford, 13 February 1839); Connor, op. cit., pp. 55–61.

20   Norma Townsend, 'Masters and Men and the Myall Creek Massacre', *Push from the Bush*, no. 20 (April 1985), p. 9; Connor, op. cit., pp. 55–61.

21   Andrew Burrowes, evidence taken by Edward Denny Day about the massacre at Myall Creek, 30 July 1838, and from others, 28 July–27 August 1838,

AONSW 4/5601; R.H.W. Reece, *'Aborigines and Colonists: Aborigines and Colonial Society in New South Wales in the 1830s and 1840s'* (Sydney 1974), pp. 334–45; Townsend, op. cit., pp. 17–20.

22 William Hobbs and George Anderson, evidence in Myall Creek trial, 15 November 1838, *Sydney Gazette*, 20 November 1838.

23 Alastair H. Campbell, *John Batman and the Aborigines* (Melbourne [1987?]), pp. 99–102.

24 George Arthur to Sir Richard Bourke, 25 March 1835, *Historical Records of Victoria*, vol. 1, p. 23.

25 Saxe Bannister, *Humane Policy; or, Justice to the Aborigines of New Settlements Essential to a Due Expenditure of British Money, and to the Best Interests of the Settlers* (London 1830), p. 81; Thomas Bannister, Memoranda, 1835, and Thomas Bannister to Sir Charles Burrell, 22 June–3 July 1835, SLV Bannister Papers, pp. 45–51 (original emphasis); J.T. Gellibrand to Joseph Ball, 19 February 1836, quoted Campbell, op. cit., p. 152.

26 Campbell, op. cit., pp. 99–106.

27 Ibid., pp. 149–50.

28 Bannister, *Humane Policy*, pp. 232–3; Campbell, op. cit., pp. 121–3, 135–6 (quoting 'Memorandum for Mr Batman', 23 October 1835), 149–50; J.H. Wedge to James Simpson, 9–11 August 1835, SLV M1436; J.H. Wedge to Lord John Russell, 10 January 1840, Papers Relative to the Aborigines, Australian Colonies, *Parliamentary Papers*, 1844 (627) XXXIV, pp. 119–21.

29 Campbell, op. cit., pp. 183–4, 196.

30 Thomas Bannister to George Arthur, 8 December 1835, and Arthur to Sir Richard Bourke, 13 January 1836, *HRV*, vol. 1, pp. 21–2; Wedge to Russell, 10 January 1840, p. 120.

31 W.W. Burton to Sir Richard Bourke, 22 November 1835, *HRV*, vol. 2A, pp. 154–6.

32 Burton to Bourke, 22 November 1835, *HRV*, vol. 2A, pp. 154–6; Burton to Sir George Gipps, 12 June 1838, and enclosures, AONSW SC 5/1161; S.G. Foster, ' "The Purposes, Duties and Arts of Life": Judge Burton's Plan for Black Villages', *Push from the Bush*, no. 9 (July 1981), pp. 47–54.

33 Thomas Babington Macaulay, 'Minute on Education', 2 February 1835, in W. Theodore de Bary (ed.), *Sources of Indian Tradition* (New York 1958), vol. 2, pp. 44–6; C.A. Bayly, *Empire and Information: Intelligence Gathering and Social Communication in India, 1780–1870* (Cambridge 1999), pp. 255–83.

34 Alexander Maconochie, 'Observations on the Treatment of the Aborigines in New South Wales', 1838, in Plomley, *Weep in Silence*, p. 1007; Robert Lyon, 'A Glance at the Manner and Language of the Aboriginal Inhabitants of Western Australia; With a Short Vocabulary', 1833, in Neville Green (ed.), *Nyungar – The People: Aboriginal Customs in the Southwest of Australia* (Perth 1979), p. 156; L.E. Threlkeld, 'Reminiscences', in Neil Gunson (ed.), *Australian Reminiscences and Papers of L.E. Threlkeld, Missionary to the Aborigines 1824–1859* (Canberra 1974), vol. 1, p. 42.

35 L.E. Threlkeld to George Burder and W.A. Hankey, 2 February 1825, in Gunson, op. cit., vol. 2, p. 178; G.M. Langhorne to Sir Richard Bourke, 26 November 1836, and Alexander Macleay, draft memorandum, 9 December 1836, *HRV*, vol. 2A, pp. 157–60, 161–7.

36   W.W. Burton, *The State of Religion and Education in New South Wales* (London 1840), p. 242 (quoting Bishop Broughton, 16 July 1838); Campbell, op. cit., pp. 197–8, 205–8, 210.

37   Letters patent for the foundation of South Australia, 19 February 1835, in Brian Dickey and Peter Howell (eds), *South Australia's Foundation: Select Documents* (Adelaide 1986), p. 75.

38   Henry Reynolds, *The Law of the Land* (Melbourne 1992), pp. 103–15.

39   J.T. Bigge, *Report of the Commissioner of Inquiry on the State of Agriculture and Trade in the Colony of New South Wales* (London 1823), p. 83; *Sydney Gazette*, 8 January 1824; James Backhouse, *A Narrative of a Visit to the Australian Colonies* (London 1843), p. 447; Alan Atkinson, *Camden: Farm and Village Life in Early New South Wales* (Melbourne 1988), pp. 228–9, 231.

40   John Dunmore Lang, 'Colonial Nomenclature', in his *Poems: Sacred and Secular* (Sydney 1873), pp. 153–6; *Van Diemen's Land Monthly*, October 1835, p. 94; Journal of G.A. Robinson, 22 May 1838, in Plomley, *Weep in Silence*, p. 563; Campbell, op. cit., p. 158.

41   Moore, op. cit., pp. 88, 233.

42   Threlkeld, 'Reminiscences', p. 70; Atkinson, *Camden*, p. 231.

43   Neville Green, 'Aboriginal and Settler Conflict in Western Australia, 1826–1852', *Push from the Bush*, no. 3 (May 1979), p. 91.

44   *Sydney Gazette*, 16, 23 December 1820; Plomley, *Friendly Mission*, pp. 28, 43 (quotation not attributed); Christine Bramble, 'Relations between Aborigines and White Settlers in Newcastle and the Hunter District', BLitt thesis, University of New England 1981, pp. 41–3.

45   *Sydney Gazette*, 23 September, 14 October 1826; *Australian*, 6 March 1827; R. v. Ridgway, Chip, Colthurst, and Stanley, report in 'Decisions of the Superior Courts of New South Wales, 1788–1899', www.law.mq.edu.au/scnsw/html (accessed November 2002).

46   James Stirling, proclamation, 18 June 1829, quoted in Enid Russell, *A History of the Law in Western Australia and Its Development from 1829 to 1979* (Nedlands 1980), p. 313; John Summers, 'Colonial Race Relations', in Eric Richards (ed.), *The Flinders History of South Australia: Social History* (Adelaide 1986), pp. 284–5.

47   F.C. Irwin to James Stirling, 18 May 1830, in Report from the Select Committee on Aborigines (British Settlements), *Parliamentary Papers*, 1837 (425) VII, evidence, pp. 127–8; *Perth Gazette*, 30 May, 7 June, 11 July 1835; Moore, op. cit., p. 271; Green, 'Aboriginal and Settler Conflict in Western Australia, 1826–1852', pp. 72–3, 89.

48   Moore, op. cit., p. 188.

49   Henry Reynolds, *The Other Side of the Frontier: An Interpretation of the Aboriginal Response to the Invasion and Settlement of Australia* (Townsville 1981), pp. 26–32; Tony Swain, *A Place for Strangers: Towards a History of Australian Aboriginal Being* (Cambridge 1993), pp. 122–4; Connor, op. cit., pp. 71–3.

50   James Dawson, *Australian Aborigines: The Languages and Customs of Several Tribes of Aborigines in the Western District of Victoria, Australia* (Melbourne 1881), pp. 110–11.

51   Francis Armstrong, 'Manners and Habits of the Aborigines of Western Australia', 1836, in Green, *Nyungar – The People*, p. 187.

52 Lyon, op. cit., p. 177; Threlkeld, 'Reminiscences' and 'Memoranda of Events at Lake Macquarie', 8 October 1828, in Gunson, op. cit., vol. 1, pp. 56, 97.

53 *Perth Gazette*, 20 July 1833.

54 Isaac Scott Nind, 'Description of the Natives of King George's Sound (Swan River Colony) and Adjoining Country', 1831, in Green, *Nyungar – The People*, pp. 50–1; Threlkeld, 'Reminiscences', vol. 1, p. 46.

55 Green, *Nyungar – The People*, pp. 143–4; Penelope Hetherington, 'Child Labour in Swan River Colony, 1829–1850', *Australian Historical Studies*, no. 98 (April 1992), pp. 45–6.

56 *Perth Gazette*, 20 July 1833.

57 Green, *Nyungar – The People*, pp. 97–8.

58 C.G. Teichelmann and C.W. Schurmann, *Outlines of a Grammar, Vocabulary, and Phraseology, of the Aboriginal Language of South Australia* (Adelaide 1840); Matthew Moorhouse, *A Vocabulary, and Outline of the Grammatical Structure of the Murray River Language* (Adelaide 1846).

59 Moore, op. cit., p. 233; John Ramsden Wollaston, *Wollaston's Picton Journal (1841–1844)* (ed. A. Burton and Percy W. Henn) (Nedlands 1975), pp. 8–9; Reynolds, *The Other Side of the Frontier*, pp. 10–11.

60 Note quoted in Eliza Brown to William Bussey, 2 October 1843, in Peter Cowan (ed.), *A Faithful Picture: The Letters of Eliza and Thomas Brown at York in the Swan River Colony 1841–1852* (Fremantle 1977), p. 42; Moore, op. cit., p. 227; Stormon, op. cit., p. 74.

61 *Sydney Gazette*, 20 November 1838; 'Papers Relative to the Massacre of Australian Aborigines', enclosed with Sir George Gipps to Lord Glenelg, 19 December 1838, CO 201/277, ff. 208–79; Reece, op. cit., pp. 148–9.

62 *Sydney Gazette*, 29 November 1838; *Australian*, 1, 6 December 1838; W.W. Burton to Gipps, 13 December 1838, in 'Papers Relative to the Massacre of Australian Aborigines', ff. 214–16; Reece, op. cit., pp. 149–56.

63 *Sydney Gazette*, 29 November 1838; Samuel Sneyd, evidence before select committee on the Native Police Force, 23 May 1861, p. 48, Queensland legislative assembly *Votes and Proceedings*, 1861; *Sydney Morning Herald*, 21 June 1844, 6 May 1872.

64 Thomas O'Halloran, report, 1840, in J.W. Bull, *Early Experiences of Life in South Australia* (Adelaide 1884), pp. 119–26; Kathleen Hassell, *The Relations Between the Settlers and Aborigines in South Australia, 1836–1860* (Adelaide 1966), pp. 52–62; Robert Foster, Rick Hosking and Amanda Nettelbeck, *Fatal Collisions: The South Australian Frontier and the Violence of Memory* (Adelaide 2001), pp. 13–19.

65 Charles Cooper's address to grand jury, *South Australian Register*, 7 November 1840.

66 *Western Australian Journal*, 8 April 1837; James Macarthur, in *Sydney Morning Herald*, 19 August 1842, and in *Australian*, 22 August 1842.

67 John Coley, evidence before select committee on the Native Police Force, 14 May 1861, pp. 19, 20, Queensland legislative assembly *Votes and Proceedings*, 1861; Reece, op. cit., pp. 48–9.

68 Thomas Carlyle, 'Occasional Discourse on the Nigger Question', 1849, in his *Critical and Miscellaneous Essays*, (London 1899), vol. 4, p. 350; Reginald Horsman, 'Origins of Racial Anglo-Saxonism in Great Britain before 1850', *Journal of the History of Ideas*, vol. 37 (1976), pp. 399–410.

69   Letter to the editor, *South Australian Register*, 25 November 1846; James Tucker, *Ralph Rashleigh* (Sydney 1962), p. 68 (and for the date of writing, see Colin Roderick's introduction, pp. ix–x).

70   Benjamin Disraeli, *Tancred; or, The New Crusade* (London 1927; first pub. 1847), p. 201;

Chapter 9: God and Humanity

1   *Sydney Gazette*, 9 August 1836. See also E.J. Stormon (trans. and ed.), *The Salvado Memoirs: Historical Memoirs of Australia and Particularly of the Benedictine Mission of New Norcia and of the Habits and Customs of the Australian Natives by Dom Rosendo Salvado, O.S.B.* (Nedlands 1977), pp. 128–9.

2   Lady Mary Fox, *Account of an Expedition to the Interior of New Holland* (London 1837); G.C. Bolton, 'A Whig Utopia in Northern Australia', *Push from the Bush*, no. 5 (December 1979), pp. 120–8.

3   Fox, op. cit., pp. 10–23, 27–8, 186–93.

4   Bolton, op. cit., p. 126.

5   Evidence of George Arthur before select committee on transportation, 27 June 1837, *Parliamentary Papers*, 1837 (518) XIX, p. 285.

6   Mary Haigh's story, 23 March 1842, AOT CSO 22/50, pp. 304–5; Michael Sturma, 'Death and Ritual on the Gallows: Public Executions in the Australian Penal Colonies', *Omega*, vol. 17 (1986–87), pp. 92–6; Alan Atkinson, *The Europeans in Australia: A History*, vol. 1 (Melbourne 1997), pp. 220–1.

7   Colin Arrott Browning, *The Convict Ship* (London 1844), pp. 93–101, 254–5.

8   John and Elizabeth Claborne to Mary Griffiths, 23 August 1830, AONSW 4/2444.8.

9   Maria Gawler, 1 November 1838, in David Hilliard and Arnold D. Hunt, 'Religion', in Eric Richards (ed.), *The Flinders History of South Australia: Social History* (Adelaide 1986), p. 199.

10   Isaac Dole to editor, *Monitor*, 1 October 1836.

11   Stephen Doust, 15 May 1857, in Alan Atkinson, *Camden: Farm and Village Life in Early New South Wales* (Melbourne 1988), p. 174; E.G. Clancy, 'The Commencement of the Primitive Methodist Mission in New South Wales', *Push from the Bush*, no. 27 (1989), pp. 23–4.

12   Anon., *South Australia, in 1842, by One Who lived There Nearly Four Years* (London 1843), pp. 20–1; Arnold D. Hunt, 'The Bible Christians in South Australia', *Journal of the Historical Society of South Australia*, no. 10 (1982), pp. 14–18.

13   David Hilliard, 'Emanuel Swedenborg and the New Church in South Australia', *Journal of the Historical Society of South Australia*, no. 16 (1988), pp. 70–3 (quoting William Holden, 1890).

14   Andrew Anderson to Reuben Hancock (extract), n.d., *Times and Seasons*, 1 August 1845, pp. 989–90; Marjorie B. Newton, 'The Gathering of the Australian Saints', *Push from the Bush*, no. 27 (1989), pp. 1–16.

15   J.F.C. Harrison, *The Second Coming: Popular Millenarianism 1780–1850* (London 1979), pp. 109–11; Barbara Taylor, *Eve and the New Jerusalem: Socialism and Feminism in the Nineteenth Century* (London 1983), pp. 162–6 (quotation from Joanna Southcott, 1802, p. 163).

16 Harrison, op. cit., pp. 107–8; *Private Communications given by J. Wroe from the Beginning of 1843, to the End of 1852*, 1853, in Alan Atkinson, 'Our First Chance of Kingdom Come', *Push from the Bush*, no. 19 (April 1985), pp. 69, 74–5, 80.

17 Ibid., p. 79.

18 Ibid., p. 61.

19 Ibid., pp. 70–2, 81–2. Compare Harrison, op. cit., pp. 150–2.

20 Report of the select committee on the lunatic asylum, Tarban Creek, NSW legislative council *Votes and Proceedings*, 1846 (second session), p. 343.

21 *Private Communications*, in Atkinson, 'Our First Chance of Kingdom Come', pp. 65–7.

22 William Godwin, 'On Frankness and Reserve', in his *Thoughts on Man; His Nature, Productions and Discoveries* (London 1831), p. 304; Angela Esterhammer, 'Godwin's Suspicion of Speech Acts', *Studies in Romanticism*, vol. 39 (2000), pp. 553–78.

23 Godwin, op. cit., p. 303.

24 Ibid., p. 300.

25 Sir Thomas Brisbane to Lord Bathurst, 31 December 1824, *HRA*, series 1, vol. 11, pp. 430–2; Connor, op. cit., p. 61.

26 *Perth Gazette*, 28 March, 6 June 1835; Neville Green, 'Aborigines and White Setters' in C.T. Stannage (ed.), *A New History of Western Australia* (Nedlands 1981), p. 85–6.

27 *South Australian Register*, 30 May 1840.

28 Richard Windeyer, 'On the Rights of the Aborigines of Australia', June 1844, ML MSS 1400, p. 43.

29 *Australian*, 13 December 1838 (original emphasis); *South Australian Register*, 30 May 1840.

30 John Jarvis, *Archbold's Summary of the Law Relative to Pleading and Evidence in Criminal Cases* (1838), in John Ferry, 'An Examination of the Various Aboriginal Evidence Bills of New South Wales, South Australia and Western Australia in the Period 1839–1849, As Well As an Analysis of the Racial Attitudes Which Were Espoused During the Controversies', BA thesis, University of New England 1980, p. 94.

31 Saxe Bannister to R.J. Wilmot Horton, 16 August 1824, *HRA*, series 4, vol. 1, pp. 554–5; Ferry, op. cit., pp. 97–105.

32 *Sydney Morning Herald*, 21 June 1844; *South Australian Register*, 17 July 1844; Enid Russell, *A History of the Law in Western Australia and Its Development from 1829 to 1979* (Nedlands 1980), pp. 319–20.

33 It is true that the saying 'man is a bundle of habits' can be traced to the clergyman-philosopher William Paley. See Athena Vrettos, 'Defining Habits: Dickens and the Psychology of Repetition', *Victorian Studies*, vol. 42 (1999–2000), p. 399.

34 Bishop J.B. Polding, evidence before select committee on Aborigines, 10 September 1845, NSW legislative council *Votes and Proceedings*, 1845, p. 952.

35 Rev. Francis Cameron, evidence before select committee on the Aborigines, 13 April 1846, NSW legislative council *Votes and Proceedings*, 1846 (second session), p. 571.

36 Moses (Tjalkabota), 1948, quoted in Barry Hill, *Broken Song: T.G.H. Strehlow and Aboriginal Possession* (Sydney 2002), p. 423.

37   Henry Reynolds, *Fate of a Free People: A Radical Re-Examination of the Tasmanian Wars* (Melbourne 1995), pp. 134–47.
38   Ibid., pp. 7–9 (quoting petition of Walter George Arthur and others to Queen Victoria, February 1846).
39   Stormon, op. cit., pp. 39, 40.
40   Polding to Central Council of the Society for the Propagation of the Faith, p. 304; Patrick O'Farrell, *The Catholic Church and Community in Australia: A History* (Melbourne 1977), p. 34.
41   Fr Luigi Pesciaroli to Cardinal Bishop of Viterbo, 29 January 1844, in P.F. Moran, *History of the Catholic Church in Australasia* (Sydney 1891), vol. 1, p. 414; Jean Woolmington, 'Missionary Attitudes to the Baptism of Australian Aborigines before 1850', *Journal of Religious History*, vol. 13 (1984–85), pp. 283–93.
42   Stormon, op. cit., p. 122.
43   Polding to Fr Francis Murphy, 2 July 1843, in Moran, op. cit., vol. 1, pp. 409–10 (emphasis added).
44   Fr Raymond Vaccari to Polding, 19 December 1843, in Moran, op. cit., vol. 1, p. 412.
45   Stormon, op. cit., p. 67.
46   G.A. Robinson, journal, 7 December 1835, 19, 20 January, 19 August 1837, in N.J.B. Plomley (ed.), *Weep in Silence: A History of the Flinders Island Aboriginal Settlement* (Hobart 1987), pp. 315, 417, 473.
47   James Backhouse, journal, 6 January 1834, ibid., p. 267.
48   Robert Clark to G.A. Robinson, 2 September 1837 (extract), ibid., p. 707; N.J.B. Plomley, *A Word-List of the Tasmanian Aboriginal Languages* (Hobart 1976), p. 39, and for meanings, ibid., pp. 238, 240, 247 ('coethee' may be the same as 'go.zee'), 366, 416.
49   Robinson, journal, 12, 14 October 1832, in Plomley, *Weep in Silence*, pp. 228, 234.
50   Ibid., 14 October 1835, p. 300.
51   Ibid., 15 January, 8 February 1836, 3, 22 June 1837, pp. 336–7, 344, 447, 455. For a similar, richer characterisation of Robinson, see Cassandra Pybus, *Community of Thieves* (Melbourne 1991).
52   Laurence Frayne, memoir, c. 1845, ML MS 681/1, p. 59. But see Plomley, *A Word-List of the Tasmanian Aboriginal Languages*, pp. 242–3.
53   Elizabeth Chittenden to Thomas Chittenden, December 1824, in papers relating to R. *v.* Martin Benson and others, January 1825, AONSW CP T128/10; *Australian*, 27 January 1825.
54   Thomas James Lempriere, *The Penal Settlements of Early Van Diemen's Land* (Launceston 1954), p. 31.
55   'Memorial Addressed to His Majesty's Government by the Society for Promoting Christian Knowledge', n.d., enclosed with Lord Glenelg to Sir Richard Bourke, 30 November 1835, *HRA*, series 1, vol. 18, p. 212.
56   Minutes of the Congregational Church, Hobart, 1832–62, AOT NS 477/1, 4 March, 2 November 1836; Francis and Harriet Edgar to members of their Church, 5 January 1835, AOT NS 663/13.
57   James Backhouse, *A Narrative of a Visit to the Australian Colonies* (London 1843), pp. 193, 309.

58   *Monitor*, 31 August 1836; Sir Eardley Wilmot's annotations, n.d., on the evidence of Mrs Slea, 27 December 1841, AOT CSO 22/50, p. 230.

59   Colin Arrott Browning, *The Convict Ship, and England's Exiles* (London 1847), pp. vii–viii (original emphasis).

60   Memoir of Laurence Frayne, c. 1845, pp. 46–7.

61   Lachlan Macquarie to Lord Bathurst, 18 May 1818, *HRA*, series 1, vol. 9, p. 801.

62   Maurice Lepailleur, journal, 2 August 1840, in F. Murray Greenwood (ed. and trans.), *Land of a Thousand Sorrows: The Australian Prison Journal, 1840–1842, of the Exiled Canadien Patriote, François-Maurice Lepailleur* (Melbourne 1980), p. 34.

63   Polding to Fr Thomas Brown, 14 June 1837, J418, Downside Abbey manuscripts (AJCP mfm M996, p. 308).

64   Michael J. Belcher, 'The Child in New South Wales Society: 1820 to 1837', PhD thesis, University of New England 1982, pp. 157–8.

65   Ralph Darling to Lord Bathurst, 6 September 1826, *HRA*, series 1, vol. 12, pp. 543–4; O'Farrell, op. cit., pp. 21–9.

66   Ullathorne, n.d., quoted in O'Farrell, op. cit., p. 34.

67   William Ullathorne, *From Cabin-Boy to Archbishop: The Autobiography of Archbishop Ullathorne* (London 1941), pp. 32, 35, 38.

68   Ibid., pp. 19, 30.

69   W. Ullathorne, *A Reply to Judge Burton, of the Supreme Court of New South Wales, on 'The State of Religion' in the Colony* (Sydney 1840), p. 80.

70   Darling to Bathurst, 6 September 1826, *HRA*, series 1, vol. 12, p. 544; Alexander Maconochie, *Australiana: Thoughts on Convict Management, and Other Subjects Connected with the Australian Penal Colonies* (London 1839), p. 125.

71   Ullathorne, *From Cabin-Boy to Archbishop*, pp. 81, 86. In telling this story, and in quoting Mrs Anderson, Ullathorne gives Stiles' name incorrectly as 'Short'. Stiles' interest in Catholic method blossomed as Tractarianism (*Australian Dictionary of Biography*, vol. 2, pp. 483–4).

72   William Ullathorne, *The Catholic Mission in Australasia* (Liverpool 1837), p. 33; William Ullathorne, evidence before select committee on transportation, 8 February 1838, *Parliamentary Papers*, 1837–8 (669) XXII, pp. 20, 27; Bishop J.B. Polding to Central Council of the Society for the Propagation of the Faith, in Moran, op. cit., vol. 1, p. 305 (Moran dates this letter as 10 January 1870, but it was clearly written 1839); W.W. Burton, *The State of Religion and Education in New South Wales* (London 1840), p. civ; Ullathorne, *From Cabin-Boy to Archbishop*, pp. 81–2.

73   Burton, op. cit., p. 311 (original emphasis).

74   Ibid., pp. 304–5; Bishop J.B. Polding to Cardinal Prefect of Propaganda, 12 March 1842, in Moran, op. cit., vol. 1, p. 237; 4 December 1843, Sisters of Charity Archives, Sydney; Ullathorne, *From Cabin-Boy to Archbishop*, pp. 147–8; W.B. Ullathorne, *The Autobiography of Archbishop Ullathorne with Selections from His Letters* (London 1891), p. 153.

75   John Pascoe Fawkner, 'Constitution and Form of Government', n.d. (c. 1835), SLV La Trobe MS 13273; Bishop R.W. Willson, evidence before select committee on lunatic asylums, 13 August 1863, NSW legislative assembly *Votes and Proceedings*, 1863–4, vol. 4, p. 885.

76   Reverend James Clow to Reverend J.D. Lang, 31 December 1837, SLV La Trobe MS 9570/74.

77   'Report for the Select Committee Appointed to Consider the Propriety of Bringing in a General Educational Measure', 9 December 1851, *Votes and Proceedings of the Legislative Council of South Australia*, 1851; A.G.L. Shaw, *Sir George Arthur, Bart, 1784–1854: Superintendent of British Honduras, Lieutenant-Governor of Van Diemen's Land and of Upper Canada, Governor of the Bombay Presidency* (Melbourne 1980), pp. 203, 205; John Gascoigne, *The Enlightenment and the Origins of European Australia* (Cambridge 2002), pp. 26–34.

78   Matthew, 7:12; James Macarthur (two speeches), in *Australian*, 16 January 1843, and *Sydney Morning Herald*, 20 April 1855.

79   Bishop W.G. Broughton, evidence before select committee on education, 15 July 1844, NSW legislative council *Votes and Proceedings*, 1844, pp. 85, 90.

80   Mark, 15:32; Fox, op. cit., pp. 206–7.

Part 3

1   *South Australian Register*, 5 March 1842.

Chapter 10: Feeding on Stories

1   Laurence Frayne, memoir, c. 1845, ML MS 681/1, p. 4. Frayne here transcribes from Ross's essay, pp. 4–5, originally published in *The Van Diemen's Land Annual and Hobart-Town Almanack* (Hobart 1833).

2   Frayne, memoir, pp. 5, 60, 68.

3   Thomas Cook, *The Exile's Lamentations* (Sydney 1978), pp. 44–5; Frayne, memoir, pp. 16, 23.

4   Ibid., pp. 5, 19.

5   James Porter, autobiography, 1840s, typescript copy, p. 89, Dixson Library MS Q168; Frayne, memoir, p. 8.

6   Ibid., pp. 11, 21, 57.

7   Saxe Bannister, *Humane Policy; or, Justice to the Aborigines of New Settlements Essential to a Due Expenditure of British Money, and to the Best Interests of the Settlers* (London 1830), p. 233; Frayne, memoir, p. 4.

8   Ibid., pp. 23, 65–6, 68.

9   Report of the committee appointed to inquire into the present state of female convict discipline, [1843], AOT CSO 22/50, pp. 259–73, 290–322; Lucy Frost, 'Eliza Churchill Tells ... ', in Lucy Frost and Hamish Maxwell-Stewart (eds.), *Chain Letters: Narrating Convict Lives* (Melbourne 2001), pp. 79–82.

10   *South Australian Register*, 11, 18 September 1841; Kathleen Hassell, *The Relations Between the Settlers and Aborigines in South Australia, 1836–1860* (Adelaide 1966), pp. 66–71; Robert Clyne, 'At War with the Natives: From the Coorong to the Rufus, 1841', *Journal of the Historical Society of South Australia*, no. 9 (1981), pp. 99–108; Robert Foster, Rick Hosking, and Amanda Nettelbeck, *Fatal Collisions: The South Australian Frontier and the Violence of Memory* (Adelaide 2001), pp. 31–4.

11   Oliver MacDonagh, *Early Victorian Government 1830–1870* (London 1977), pp. 6, 24–5.

12   John Ruskin, *Sesame and Lilies* (London 1960), p. 22; David Vincent, *The Culture of Secrecy: Britain, 1832–1998* (Oxford 1998), pp. 46–9 (quotation from John Bowring to Lord John Russell, 1833).

13   [Charles Dickens and W.H. Wills], 'A Visit to the Registrar-General', *Household Words*, 30 November 1850, vol. 2, pp. 235–40.

14   MacDonagh, op. cit., p. 1.

15   [Charles Dickens and W.H. Wills], 'Valentine's Day at the Post-Office', *Household Words*, 30 March 1850, vol. 1, pp. 7–8; James Raymond to Board of Inquiry on the General Post Office, 26 February 1851, NSW legislative council *Votes and Proceedings*, 1851, session 2, p. 487.

16   Cook, op. cit., pp. 36–7. The relevant legislation was 5 Gul. IV (1835).

17   Records of the *William Metcalfe*, arrived 13 March 1844, NSWAO 4/4894, pp. 8, 9, 77; Baptismal register, Catholic church, Campbelltown; *Douglas Jerrold's Weekly Newspaper*, 6 November 1847; Margaret Kiddle, *Caroline Chisholm* (Melbourne 1969), pp. 54–9, 85.

18   Caroline Chisholm, *Emigration and Transportation Relatively Considered* (London 1847), pp. 23–4, 33.

19   Elizabeth Studham, 1842, quoted in Frost, op. cit., p. 87. In taking down this statement the clerk added his own inverted commas (omitted here) to the second 'Churchill', as if the usage sounded strange to him.

20   N.J.B. Plomley (ed.), *Weep in Silence: A History of the Flinders Island Aboriginal Settlement* (Hobart 1987), pp. 791–836.

21   Saxe Bannister, evidence before select committee on Aborigines (British settlements), 14 March 1837, *Parliamentary Papers*, 1837 (425) VIII, pp.14–20.

22   Charles Griffiths, *The Present State and Prospects of the Port Phillip District of New South Wales* (Dublin 1845), pp. 187–90; M.F. Christie, *Aborigines in Colonial Victoria 1835–86* (Sydney 1979), pp. 92–135.

23   Alexander Harris, *The Emigrant Family: or, The Story of an Australian Settler* (Canberra 1967; first pub. 1849).

24   Roger Therry, *Reminiscences of Thirty Years' Residence in New South Wales and Victoria* (London 1863), pp. 213–16.

25   William Shakespeare, *Julius Caesar*, act II, sc. i; Grace Karskens, 'Revisiting the Worldview: The Archaeology of Convict Households in Sydney's Rocks Neighborhood', *Historical Archaeology*, vol. 37 (2003), pp. 45–7.

26   T.L. Mitchell, *Three Expeditions into the Interior of Eastern Australia* (London 1839), vol. 1, p.157; Ludwig Leichhardt to his mother, 27 August 1843, in Marcel Aurousseau (ed.), *The Letters of F.W. Ludwig Leichhardt* (Cambridge 1968), vol. 2, p. 672.

27   James Gardner to Mrs Thomas Gardner, 4 July 1841, letter belonging to Mr D. Barber, England (copy supplied by Bill Gammage).

28   Karskens, op. cit., pp. 45–7.

29   George Fletcher Moore, *Diary of Ten Years Eventful Life of an Early Settler in Western Australia* (London 1884), p. 124.

30   Harris, *The Emigrant Family*, pp. 10, 20.

31   James Atkinson, *An Account of the State of Agriculture and Grazing in New South Wales* (London 1826), p. 31; Mitchell, op. cit., vol. 1, pp. 41, 71; John

Pickard, 'Trespass, Common Law, Government Regulations, and Fences in Colonial New South Wales, 1788–1828', *Journal of the Royal Australian Historical Society*, vol. 84 (1998), pp. 132–4.

32   Mrs Charles Meredith, *Notes and Sketches of New South Wales* (London 1844), p. 57; James Backhouse, *A Narrative of a Visit to the Australian Colonies* (London 1843), pp. 28–9; J. Syme, *Nine Years in Van Diemen's Land* (Dundee 1848), p. 132.

33   W.G. Broughton to W.B. Boydell, 23 May 1845, letter kindly shown me by Boydell's descendants, Tamworth; Pickard, op. cit., p. 138.

34   Longford (Norfolk Plains) petty sessions, 19 April 1836, AOT LC362/3.

35   James Atkinson, op. cit., pp. 92–3; Meredith, op. cit., pp. 130–1; Alexander Harris, *Settlers and Convicts: Recollections of Sixteen Years' Labour in the Australian Backwoods* (Melbourne 1953; first pub. 1847), pp. 72–3.

36   William Shakespeare, *The Tempest*, act I, sc. ii; Moore, op. cit., pp. 137–8.

37   Census of South Australia, 1840, SLSA PRG 174/13, p. 878; Harris, *Settlers and Convicts*, p. 152; A.J. Boyd, *Old Colonials* (Sydney 1882), pp. 19–26.

38   See, for instance, Harris, *The Emigrant Family*, p. 76.

39   Ibid., p. 15.

40   Moore, op. cit., pp. 37, 50.

41   Ibid., p. 133 (original emphasis).

42   J.R. Booth to Edward Deas Thomson, 25 May 1838, AONSW 4/2439-1.

43   Glen McLaren, *Beyond Leichhardt: Bushcraft and the Exploration of Australia* (Fremantle 1996), pp. 144–5. I have relied a great deal on McLaren at this point.

44   Ludwig Leichhardt to his mother, 27 August 1843, to William Nicholson, 6 February 1844, and to Sir Thomas Mitchell, 24 July 1844, in Aurousseau, op. cit., vol. 2, pp. 673, 721, 780; McLaren, op. cit., pp. 222–3.

45   Ludwig Leichhardt, *Journal of an Overland Expedition in Australia* (London 1847), pp. 400–1, 407; McLaren, op. cit., p. 164.

46   Aurousseau, op. cit., vol. 3, p. 982.

47   Leichhardt, *Journal*, pp. 182–3.

48   Ibid., p. 118; McLaren, op. cit., pp. 171–2.

49   Penelope Selby to her sisters, 21 November 1842, in Lucy Frost (ed.), *No Place for a Nervous Lady* (Melbourne 1984), p. 164; T.B. Atkinson, ship's journal, 14 July 1857, SLV La Trobe MS 12599.

50   William Wilson Dobie, *Recollections of a Visit to Port-Phillip, Australia, in 1852–55* (Edinburgh 1856), pp. 56–7.

51   Edgar Allan Poe, 'The Murders in the Rue Morgue', in *The Complete Tales and Poems of Edgar Allan Poe* (London 1982), pp. 141, 146–7 (original emphasis).

52   W. Ullathorne, *A Reply to Judge Burton, of the Supreme Court of New South Wales, on 'The State of Religion' in the Colony* (Sydney 1840), p. 80; John Gascoigne, *The Enlightenment and the Origins of European Australia* (Cambridge 2002), pp.141–2.

53   Nathaniel Hawthorne, *The Scarlet Letter: A Romance* (London 1965; first pub. 1850), pp. 115, 230; Richard Sennett, *The Fall of Public Man* (Cambridge 1977), pp. 146, 169–74.

54   Charles Dickens, *The Old Curiosity Shop* (London 1941), p. 306.

55 Mitchell, op. cit., vol. 1, pp. 180–200.
56 William Westgarth, *Australia Felix; or, A Historical and Descriptive Account of the Settlement of Port Phillip, New South Wales* (Edinburgh 1848), pp. 283–4.
57 *South Australian Register*, 24 October 1840.
58 T.L. Work, 'The Early Printers of Melbourne', *Australasian Typographical Journal*, August 1897, p. 2, and July 1898, p. 1; Elizabeth Morrison, 'The Contribution of the Country Press to the Making of Victoria, 1840–1890', PhD thesis, Monash University, 1991, vol. 2, p. 54; Anne Colman, 'New Worlds: Attitudes to Immigrants and Immigration in Port Phillip, New York and Rio de Janeiro, 1835–1850', PhD thesis, University of Melbourne 1999, pp. 74.
59 John Badcock, evidence before select committee on Crown lands, 5 July 1849, NSW legislative council *Votes and Proceedings*, 1849, pp. 567, 569; 'Garryowen' [Edmund Finn], *The Chronicles of Early Melbourne 1835 to 1852* (Melbourne 1888), p. 852.
60 George Eliot, *Middlemarch* (London 1967; first pub. 1872), p. 396.
61 Alexis de Tocqueville, *Democracy in America* (trans. George Lawrence; ed. J.P. Mayer and Max Lerner) (New York 1966), vol. 1, pp. 309–13; John Stuart Mill, *The Early Draft of John Stuart Mill's Autobiography* (ed. Jack Stillinger) (Urbana, Ill., 1961), p. 172.
62 William Ullathorne, evidence before select committee on transportation, 8 February 1838, *Parliamentary Papers*, 1837–8, XXII, 669, pp. 14, 27–8.
63 Ralph Waldo Emerson, 'The Over-Soul', in his *Essays and Lectures* (New York 1983), p. 390; Raymond Williams, *Keywords: A Vocabulary of Culture and Society* (London 1983), p. 294.
64 *Sydney Morning Herald*, 22 September 1854.
65 *South Australian Register*, 18 September 1841.
66 Charles Dickens, *Nicholas Nickleby* (London 1907; first pub. 1838–39), p. 814; Charles Dickens, *Dombey and Son* (London 1970; first pub. 1848), p. 738.
67 Harris, *Settlers and Convicts*, p. 230.
68 'Abstracts from the Returns of the Commissioners of Crown Lands', 1 July 1839 to 31 December 1843, NSW legislative council *Votes and Proceedings*, 1843, p. 474; Returns from the 1846 census, NSW *Government Gazette*, 4 November 1846.
69 Michael Sturma, *Vice in a Vicious Society: Crime and Convicts in Mid-Nineteenth Century New South Wales* (St Lucia 1983), pp. 102–5 (quotation from Charles Lockhart, 1851).
70 *South Australian Register*, 24 April 1841; Charles Symmons, Fourth Annual Report of the Protector of the Natives (Western Australia), 31 December 1843, Papers Relative to the Aborigines, Australian Colonies, *Parliamentary Papers*, 1844 (627); XXXIV, p. 434; *People's Advocate*, 17 February 1849 (I owe this reference to Anne Coote); Therry, op. cit., pp. 213–16.
71 *Geelong Advertiser*, 28 June, 2 July 1845.
72 W.H. Hovell to editor, *Sydney Morning Herald*, 9 February 1847; *Melbourne Argus*, 18 July 1848; 'Bunyips', *Push: A Journal of Early Australian Social History*, no. 27 (1989), pp. 37–48; Robert Holden, *Bunyips: Australia's Folklore of Fear* (Canberra 2001), pp. 2–4, 88–99, 175–6.

Chapter 11: Digging Deep

1   G. Wotherspoon, 'Savings Banks and Social Policy in New South Wales 1832–71', *Australian Economic History Review*, vol. 18 (1978), pp. 141–51, 161–3; Patricia Curthoys, ' "A Provision for Themselves and Their Families?": Women Depositors of the Savings Bank of New South Wales, 1846–1871', *Journal of the Royal Australian Historical Society*, vol. 84 (1998), pp. 155–9. For the Hobart bank, see AOT CON 73/1; 'Return of Cash received on account of Convicts and deposited in the savings Bank during 1842', AOT CO 280/153, ff. 450–6.

2   Henry Capper, *South Australia: Containing Hints to Emigrants; Proceedings of the South Australian Company* (London 1838), p. 106; Douglas Pike, *Paradise of Dissent; South Australia 1829–1857* (Melbourne 1967), p. 183.

3   Alan Atkinson, *Camden: Farm and Village Life in Early New South Wales* (Melbourne 1988), p. 51; Curthoys, op. cit., pp. 159–60.

4   C. Rudston Read, *What I Heard, Saw, and Did at the Australian Gold Fields* (London 1853), p. 48 (original emphasis).

5   Benjamin Boyce to his family, 22 July 1842, 1 February 1844, NLA MS 1247; Eric Richards, 'A Voice from Below: Benjamin Boyce in South Australia, 1839–46', *Labour History*, no. 27 (November 1974), pp. 65–75.

6   Jeremiah Howgego, diary 1832–34, quoted in Leonore Davidoff and Catherine Hall, *Family Fortunes: Men and Women of the English Middle Class 1780–1850* (London 1987), pp. 446–7.

7   'A Melbourne Merchant', *The Gold Era of Victoria* (London 1855), p. 129.

8   Caroline Chisholm, evidence before select committee on the petition from distressed mechanics and labourers, 14 November 1843, NSW legislative council *Votes and Proceedings*, 1843, p. 741.

9   Ludwig Leichhardt to unknown correspondent, c. 2 March 1844, in Marcel Aurousseau (ed.), *The Letters of F.W. Ludwig Leichhardt* (Cambridge 1968), vol. 2, p. 739; Samuel Bailey Dowsett, evidence before select committee on the city corporation, 4 June 1849, NSW legislative council *Votes and Proceedings*, 1849, vol. 2, p. 153.

10   *Sydney Gazette*, 16 July 1831; Alan Atkinson and Marian Aveling (eds), *Australians 1838* (Sydney 1987), pp. 133–6.

11   Ibid.

12   Andrew Messner, 'Chartist Political Culture in Britain and Colonial Australia, c. 1835–1860', PhD thesis, University of New England 2000, pp. 3–6, 242–373.

13   R.B. Walker, *The Newspaper Press in New South Wales, 1803–1920* (Sydney 1976), p. 40; Benjamin Sutherland, evidence before select committee on the petition from distressed mechanics and labourers, 13 November 1843, NSW legislative council *Votes and Proceedings*, 1843, p. 728.

14   *New Moral World*, 4 January 1840, and Robert Cochrane and others to G.A. Fleming, 25 August 1839, ibid., 1 February 1840. I owe these references to Andrew Messner.

15   Michael Sturma, *Vice in a Vicious Society: Crime and Convicts in Mid-Nineteenth Century New South Wales* (St Lucia 1983), pp. 45–7, 57–9.

16   'Mr Nash', speech in *Launceston Examiner*, 21 April 1847.

17   C.E. Stanley (private secretary) to the magistrates, March 1847, and Sir William Denison to Earl Grey, 4 December 1847, Further Correspondence on the Subject of Convict Discipline and Transportation, *Parliamentary Papers*, 1849 (217) XLVIII, pp. 70, 92–3; *Launceston Examiner*, 31 March 1847, 27 June 1849.

18   Dan Huon, 'By Moral Means Only: The Origins of the Launceston Anti-Transportation Leagues 1847–1849', *Tasmanian Historical Research Association Papers and Proceedings*, vol. 44 (1997), pp. 97–9.

19   *Launceston Examiner*, March 1844, quoted in West, op. cit., p. 210; Sturma, op. cit., pp. 52–6.

20   *Launceston Examiner*, 12 May 1847; Robert Pitcairn and others to Earl Grey, 22 October 1847, and 'Tabular Analysis of Opinions on the Subject of Transportation to Van Diemen's Land', n.d., enclosed with Sir William Denison to Earl Grey, 4 December 1847, Further Correspondence, pp. 81–2, 101.

21   Huon, op. cit., p. 102.

22   Messner, op. cit., pp. 265–74.

23   *Launceston Examiner*, 20 June 1850.

24   John West, *The History of Tasmania* (ed. A.G.L. Shaw) (Sydney 1971; first pub. 1852), p. 533.

25   C.T. Stannage, *The People of Perth: A Social History of Western Australia's Capital City* (Perth 1979), pp. 77–83.

26   [Charlotte Barton], *A Mother's Offering to Her Children* (Sydney 1841), pp. 1–7; Robert Dundas Murray, *A Summer at Port Phillip* (Edinburgh 1843), pp. 195–6; Ralph Waldo Emerson, 'History', in Ralph Waldo Emerson, *Essays and Lectures* (New York 1983), pp. 244–5 (original emphasis).

27   Charles Sturt, *Two Expeditions into the Interior of Southern Australia* (London 1833), vol. 1, pp. xxxiv–xl, 197–200.

28   *South Australian Register*, 14 August 1841.

29   Ludwig Leichhardt, *Journal of an Overland Expedition in Australia* (London 1847), p. 220. See also David Matthew Watson to his mother, 26 March 1853, SLV La Trobe MS 8297; Peter Ackroyd, *Dickens* (London 1990), p. 663.

30   [Barton], *A Mother's Offering to Her Children*, pp. 1–7.

31   Anon., 'A Visit to the Northern Mines of South Australia', *South Australian Register*, 28 November 1846; Geoffrey Blainey, *The Rush that Never Ended: A History of Australian Mining* (Melbourne 1969), pp. 106–11.

32   Thomas Paten to A.W. Blane, 23 January 1852, Noel Butlin Archives Centre 78/1/20 (Pennie Pemberton helped with this material); R.B. Dockray, 'Camden Station', *Institution of Civil Engineers Minutes of Proceedings*, vol. 8 (1849), pp. 171–2 (copy supplied by Miss C. Arrowsmith, of the Institution of Civil Engineers); family papers in my possession (Paten was my great-great-uncle); John Gascoigne, *The Enlightenment and the Origins of European Australia* (Cambridge 2002), p. 97.

33   J. Syme, *Nine Years in Van Diemen's Land* (Dundee 1848), p. 36; Blainey, op. cit., pp. 9–11.

34   James Ward, *A History of Gold as a Commodity and as a Measure of Value* (London n.d. [1852]), pp. 121–2; P. Just, *Australia; or, Notes taken During a Residence in the Colonies from the Gold Discovery in 1851 till 1857* (Dundee 1859), p. 58.

35   G.B. Earp, *What We Did in Australia* (London 1853), pp. 114–15.

36   Ward, op. cit., p. 9.

37   Ibid., pp. 13–15.

38   R.S. Anderson, diary, 1 June, 1 October 1852, SLV La Trobe MS 8492; 'A Melbourne Merchant', op. cit., p. 122.

39   James Bonwick, *Notes of a Gold Digger, and Gold Digger's Guide* (Melbourne 1852), p. 25.

40   Anderson, diary, 1 October 1852.

41   *Banner*, 30 August, 6 September 1853.

42   Henry Mundy, memoirs, 1909, SLV La Trobe MS 10416, p. 271.

43   Olcher Fedden to his father, 31 December 1852, 16 May 1853, SLV La Trobe MS 8379; Richard Connebee's advertisement, attached to Bonwick, op. cit.; Read, op. cit., pp. 16–17; William Westgarth, *Victoria: Late Australia Felix, or Port Phillip District of New South Wales* (Edinburgh 1853), p. 258; Elizabeth Morrison, 'The Contribution of the Country Press to the Making of Victoria, 1840–1890', PhD thesis, Monash University 1991, p. 83; Neville A. Ritchie, ' "In-Sites", Historical Archaeology in Australasia: Some Comparisons with the American Colonial Experience', *Historical Archaeology*, vol. 37 (2003), p. 12.

44   Anderson, diary, 13 January 1852; Seth Rudolphus Clark, diary, 17 June 1853, SLV La Trobe MS 10436.

45   Just, op. cit., p. 113.

46   George Baker, diary, 1852–53, notes at end, SLV La Trobe MS 11374; George Henry Wathen, *The Golden Colony: or Victoria in 1854* (London 1855), pp. 76–8.

47   Anderson, diary, 31 December 1851, 13 January 1852; Alexander Dick, memoirs, c. 1907, SLV La Trobe MS 11241, pp. 189–90; Mundy, memoirs, pp. 671–2.

48   Thomas Livingstone Mitchell, diary, 19 June 1851, ML ZC71; A.G. Mannon to his parents, 3 June 1853, ML A3030; Antoine Fauchery, *Letters from a Miner in Australia* (Melbourne 1965), pp. 64–5.

49   W.J. Wills to his father, 12 February 1853, SLV La Trobe MS 9504; Fauchery, op. cit., pp. 65–8.

50   A.G. Mannon to his parents, 3 June 1853, ML A3030; Wathen, op. cit., p. 56.

51   Read, op. cit., pp. 2–3.

52   'A Melbourne Merchant', op. cit., pp. 41–2; Just, op. cit., p. 85; Peter Stoneley, 'Rewriting the Gold Rush: Twain, Harte and Homosociality', *Journal of American Studies*, vol. 30 (1996), pp. 189–90.

53   Olcher Fedden to his father, 16 May 1853, SLV La Trobe MS 837; Thomas McCombie, *The History of the Colony of Victoria* (Melbourne 1858), pp. 240–1.

54   *Argus*, 2 January 1852, 3 August 1853; Dick, memoirs, p. 139.

55   *Gold-Diggers Advocate*, 20 May, 26 August, 2, 9 September 1854; Messner, op. cit., pp. 318–21.

56   William Rayment, diary, May 1853, SLV La Trobe MS 4471.

57   Ward, op. cit., p. 123.

58   James Daniel to his mother, 2 November 1852, SLV La Trobe MS 10222.

59   Mundy, memoirs, p. 228.

60 Bonwick, op. cit., p. 27; David Mackenzie, *The Gold Digger: A Visit to the Gold Fields of Australia in February 1852* (London [1853?]), p. 49; Read, op. cit., p. 43 (original emphasis).

61 Baker, diary, 29 December 1852, 9 January 1853; Mundy, memoirs, p. 228.

62 Ward, op. cit., pp. 15–16.

63 Baker, diary, 14 December 1852.

64 W.C. Newton, diary, 1 March 1853, SLV La Trobe MS 10251.

65 Mundy, memoirs, pp. 619–20.

66 James Muir, diary, 5 November 1852, SLV La Trobe MS 10056; William Tomlinson, diary, 5 November 1852, SLV La Trobe MS 12183.

67 [E. Ramsay-Laye], *Social Life and Manners in Australia* (London 1861), p. 37.

68 Mundy, memoirs, p. 228.

69 Henry Brown, *Victoria, As I Found It, During Five Years of Adventure* (London 1862), p. 140.

70 Petitions presented 13 October 1853, Victorian legislative council *Votes and Proceedings*, 1853–4, vol. 1, pp. 107, 111, 116, and vol. 3, pp. 1051–3. For Isabella (not 'Lizzy') Singleton, see *Australian Dictionary of Biography*, vol. 6, pp. 129–30.

71 'Laughing no Crime, or Twenty Pounds No Comedy', by 'A Gold Digger' (preface dated Canadian Gully, 21 October 1853), in James Oddie (ed.), *From Tent to Parliament, The Life of Peter Lalor; History of the Eureka Stockade* (Melbourne 1954), p. 10.

72 Earp, op. cit., p. 133.

73 Olcher Fedden to his father, 31 December 1852, SLV La Trobe MS 8379; Diary of William Rayment, May 1853, SLV La Trobe MS 4471; *American Journal of Medical Sciences*, 1855, quoted in David Goodman, *Gold Seeking: Victoria and California in the 1850s* (Sydney 1994), p. 179; Read, op. cit., pp. 190–1; Dick, memoirs, p. 17.

74 Tomlinson, diary, 29 December 1852; Earp, op. cit., pp. 26–7; 'A Melbourne Merchant', op. cit., p. 42.

75 Earp, op. cit., p. 124 ; Dick, memoirs, p. 204.

76 Ibid., p. 197; Weston Bate, *Lucky City: The First Generation at Ballarat 1851–1901* (Melbourne 1978), pp. 33–6.

77 Dick, memoirs, pp. 197–8; Baker, diary, 11 January 1853; Just, op. cit., p. 39. The Bathurst paper pre-dated the goldrush.

78 J.D. Owens, evidence before select committee on the goldfields, 8 September 1853, p. 9, Victorian legislative council *Votes and Proceedings*, 1853–54, vol. 3.

79 Charles H. Parrott, evidence ibid., 19 September 1853, p. 71; Westgarth, op. cit., p. 259.

80 J.B. Hirst, *The Strange Birth of Colonial Democracy: New South Wales 1848–1884* (Sydney 1988), pp. 200–1.

81 Geoffrey Serle, *The Golden Age; A History of the Colony of Victoria 1851–1861* (Melbourne 1963), p. 110; Matthew Higgins, 'Near-Rebellion on the Turon Goldfields in 1853', *Journal of the Royal Australian Historical Society*, vol. 68 (1983), pp. 304–6.

82 Messner, op. cit., pp. 287–323.

83 Sir Charles Hotham to Duke of Newcastle, 18 November 1854, quoted in Serle, op. cit., pp. 163–8.

84   Samuel Lazarus, diary, 29 November, 1 December 1854, SLV MS 11484.

85   Dick, memoirs, pp. 22–3; W.B. Withers, *The History of Ballarat, from the First Pastoral Settlement to the Present Time* (Ballarat 1870), p. 99. For other precedents for the flag's design, see Len Fox, *The Eureka Flag* (Sydney 1992), p. 33.

86   J.C. Byrne, evidence before commission on the condition of the goldfields, 26 December 1854, p. 102, Victorian legislative council *Votes and Proceedings*, 1854–55, vol. 2.

87   Ann Diamond, evidence ibid., 26 December 1854, p. 111.

88   *Argus*, 10 April 1855; Serle, op. cit., p. 168.

89   Lazarus, diary, 3 December 1854; Dick, memoirs, p. 30.

90   Raffaello Carboni, *The Eureka Stockade* (Melbourne 1855), pp. 75, 93; Alan Atkinson, *The Commonwealth of Speech: An Argument about Australia's Past, Present and Future* (Melbourne 2002), pp. 68–73.

Chapter 12: Ink and Affection

1   Family papers in my possession; John Feather, *The Provincial Book Trade in Eighteenth-Century England* (Cambridge 1985), pp. 87–8.

2   Henry Spencer, *Men That Are Gone from the Households of Darlington* (Darlington, co. Durham, 1864[?]), pp. 72, 76; C.J. Hunt, *The Book Trade in Northumberland and Durham to 1860* (Newcastle-upon-Tyne 1975), p. 5; Family papers in my possession.

3   *Australian Typographical Circular*, July 1859, p. 151.

4   *Weekly Times* (Creswick), 22 March 1855.

5   *Port Phillip Gazette*, 1 February 1830; C.P. Billot, *The Life and Times of John Pascoe Fawkner* (Melbourne 1985), pp. 216–17.

6   *Port Phillip Patriot*, 30 January 1840.

7   'Garryowen' [Edmund Finn], *The Chronicles of Early Melbourne 1835 to 1851* (Melbourne 1888), p. 840.

8   *Port Phillip Gazette*, 29 January 1840.

9   Anne Colman, 'New Worlds: Attitudes to Immigrants and Immigration in Port Phillip, New York and Rio de Janeiro, 1835–1850', PhD thesis, University of Melbourne 1999, pp. 13–14.

10   *Argus*, 9 March 1849.

11   'Garryowen', op. cit., pp. 916–17; T.L. Work, 'The Early Printers of Melbourne', *Australasian Typographical Journal*, August 1898, pp. 1–2.

12   These notices began on 22 October 1852 and continued for several months.

13   *Port Phillip Gazette*, 29 January 1840.

14   James Backhouse, *A Narrative of a Visit to the Australian Colonies* (London 1843), p. 384.

15   *Express*, n.d., quoted in *Gold-Diggers Advocate*, 9 September 1854; William Westgarth, *Victoria; Late Australia Felix, or Port Phillip District of New South Wales* (Edinburgh 1853), pp. 363, 369–73; 'A Melbourne Merchant', *The Gold Era of Victoria* (London 1855), p. 45.

16   *Banner*, 8 November 1853.

17   'A Melbourne Merchant', op. cit., p. 56.

18   T.B. Atkinson to W.G. Atkinson, 3, 9 September 1858, SLV La Trobe MS 12599; Family papers in my possession.

19 *Banner*, 19 August 1853; R.M. Abbott, diary, 5 January 1854, Royal Historical Society of Victoria MS 4626; *Bendigo Advertiser*, 4 April 1885; *Australian Dictionary of Biography*, vol. 2, pp. 131–2.

20 *Banner*, 4, 28 October 1853; Abbott, diary, 24 January 1854.

21 *Banner*, 23 August, 11 November 1853, 25 August 1854.

22 David Watson to his family, 18 October 1853, SLV La Trobe MS 8297; Abbott, diary, 11 January, 21 March, 10 May 1854; Thomas A. Darragh, *Printer and Newspaper Registration in Victoria 1838–1924* (Wellington, NZ, 1997), pp. 1, 2, 90, 91.

23 David Goodman, *Gold Seeking: Victoria and California in the 1850s* (Sydney 1994), p. xxiv.

24 *Banner*, 13 September 1853.

25 Charles James Atkinson, death certificate (died 10 May 1857); T.B. Atkinson to W.G. Atkinson, 3, 9 September 1858, SLV La Trobe MS 12599; *Australian Typographical Circular*, January 1859, p. 104, February 1859, p. 110, and August 1860, p. 5.

26 T.L. Work, 'The Early Printers of Melbourne', *Australasian Typographical Journal*, March 1898, p. 1.

27 David Watson to his family, 25 October 1855, SLV La Trobe MS 8297; City of Melbourne rate books, 1854–56.

28 Thomas Stubbs *v.* Jeremiah Harnett and William Shaw (tried in Supreme Court, 6 March 1858), VPRS 267/159; *Argus*, 8 March 1858; *Avoca Mail*, 5 July 1898; T.L. Work, 'The Early Printers of Melbourne', *Australasian Typographical Journal*, December 1898, pp. 1–2.

29 Silas Andrews, 'A True Story of Early Victorian days, from a Diary' (entry in this copy dated 14 June 1852, but Andrews arrived June 1853), SLV La Trobe MS 10943; Melbourne *Herald*, 12 January 1854.

30 James Wilson to his family, 12 July 1853, SLV La Trobe MS 12416.

31 *The Times*, 19 December 1851; James Daniel to Austin Daniel, 1 August 1852, 14 March 1853, SLV La Trobe MS 10222; mother to son, both unnamed, 31 December 1857, SLV La Trobe MS 10943.

32 W.W. Burton, *The State of Religion and Education in New South Wales* (London 1840), p. 306.

33 James Macarthur, *New South Wales; Its Present State and Future Prospects* (London 1837), pp. 281–2.

34 *Port Phillip Gazette*, 29 January 1840.

35 John M. Ward, *Earl Grey and the Australian Colonies 1846–1857: A Study of Self-Government and Self-Interest* (Melbourne 1958), pp. 230–5.

36 Ward, op. cit., pp. 228–30, 245–65.

37 Correspondence on intercolonial postage, August–October 1852, NSW legislative council *Votes and Proceedings*, 1853, vol. 2, pp. 663–7; Ward, op. cit., pp. 288–97.

38 *Sydney Morning Herald*, 4 January 1851, 10 March 1852; *Letter of Instructions issued by … the Australasian League*, Sydney 1851 Appendix C; Ward, op. cit., pp. 196–226.

39 James Bonwick, *Notes of a Gold Digger, and Gold Digger's Guide* (Melbourne 1852), p. 23; C. Rudston Read, *What I Heard, Saw, and Did at the Australian Gold Fields* (London 1853), pp. 29–30, 97; P. Just, *Australia;*

or Notes taken During a Residence in the Colonies from the Gold Discovery in 1851 till 1857 (Dundee 1859), p. 71; Alexander Dick, memoirs, c. 1907, SLV La Trobe MS 11241, p. 140.

40   *South Australian Register*, 21 October 1852.

41   C.N. Connolly, 'Politics, Ideology and the New South Wales Legislative Council, 1856–72', PhD thesis, Australian National University 1974, pp. 27–44, 307–11; Alan Atkinson, 'The Political Life of James Macarthur', PhD thesis, Australian National University 1976, pp. 380–2; Ged Martin, *Bunyip Aristocracy: The New South Wales Constitution Debate of 1853 and Hereditary Institutions in the British Colonies* (Sydney 1986), pp. 92–4.

42   *South Australian Register*, 16 October 1851. The South Australian censuses for 1851 and 1855 give no figures for literacy and I rely here on the census of 1861.

43   *South Australian Register*, 16 October 1851.

44   *South Australian Register*, 7, 14 October 1852.

45   *South Australian Register*, 7, 14, 21 October 1852; Mel Davies, 'Cornish Miners and Class Relations in Early Colonial South Australia: The Burra Burra Strikes of 1848–49', *Australian Historical Studies*, vol. 26 (1995), pp. 576–94.

46   *South Australian Register*, 7, 14 October 1852; Census of South Australia 1855, *South Australian Government Gazette*, 2 August 1855, p. 565.

47   *South Australian Register*, 7, 14 October 1852.

48   *South Australian Register*, 21, 22 February 1856; Mark McKenna, 'The Story of the "Australian Ballot"', in Marian Sawer (ed.), *Elections Full, Free and Fair* (Sydney 2001), pp. 49–54.

49   Electoral Act, 1856 (19 Vic. no. 24), *Hobart Town Gazette*, 1856, vol. 1, between pp. 160–1 (i.e. 19 and 26 February 1856); Terry Newman, 'Tasmania and the Secret Ballot', *Australian Journal of Politics and History*, vol. 49 (2003), pp. 93–101.

50   T.L. Work, 'The Early Printers of Melbourne', *Australasian Typographical Journal*, October 1897, p. 2.

51   *Port Phillip Gazette*, 4 January 1940.

52   Raffaello Carboni, *The Eureka Stockade* (Melbourne 1855), pp. 25, 126.

53   Ibid., pp. 83–4, 86.

54   Herman Melville, *Moby-Dick, or The Whale* (New York 1962; first pub. 1851), p. 1; Carboni, op. cit., p. 13.

55   Ibid., pp. 46, 90, 107.

56   Ibid., p. 20. See also John Ruskin, *Sesame and Lilies* (London 1960), pp. 22–3.

57   William Westgarth, *Victoria: Late Australia Felix*, p. 361.

58   *Sydney Morning Herald*, 16 August 1853.

59   Ibid.

60   Thomas Carlyle, *Sartor Resartus* (ed. J.A.S. Barrett) (London 1897; first pub. 1833–34), p. 76.

61   Read, op. cit., p. 13 (original emphasis); Matthew Higgins, 'Near-Rebellion on the Turon Goldfields in 1853', *Journal of the Royal Australian Historical Society*, vol. 68 (1983), p. 305.

62   *Argus*, 3 August 1855.

63   *Banner*, 12 September 1854.

64   William Westgarth, *Victoria and the Australian Gold Mines in 1857* (London 1857), p. 271; Henry Mundy, memoirs, 1909, SLV La Trobe MS 10416, p. 245.

65   William Howitt, *Life in Victoria: or, Victoria in 1853, and Victoria in 1858* (Kilmore, Vic., 1977), pp. 252–3. Andrew Messner helped me with Chartist forms of address.

66   'A Young Woman' to the editor, *Empire*, 16 July 1860.

67   *Banner*, 25 August 1854.

68   Matthew Arnold, 'To My Friends' (1849).

69   *Mount Alexander Mail*, 10 November 1854; Caroline Chisholm, *Emigration and Transportation Relatively Considered* (London 1847), pp. 5, 9, 13, 18.

70   *Argus*, 11 November 1854.

71   Caroline Chisholm to Robert Lowe, n.d., quoted in Patricia Grimshaw, 'The Moral Reformer and the Imperial Major: Caroline and Archibald Chisholm', in Penny Russell (ed.), *For Richer, for Poorer: Early Colonial Marriages* (Melbourne 1994), p. 113.

72   *Empire*, 11 December 1860; Eneas Mackenzie, *Memoirs of Mrs Caroline Chisholm with an Account of Her Philanthropic Labours in India, Australia and England* (London 1852), pp. 5, 23; Patricia Grimshaw and others, *Creating a Nation 1788–1990* (Melbourne 1994), pp. 88–9, 102–5.

73   *Empire*, 11 December 1860.

74   *Sydney Morning Herald*, 13 August 1857.

75   *Empire*, 11 December 1860.

Chapter 13: Railway Dreaming

1   NSW Statistical Register, 1846–55, pp. 13, 14, in NSW legislative assembly *Votes and Proceedings*, 1856–57, vol. 2; G.J.R. Linge, *Industrial Awakening: A Geography of Australian Manufacturing 1788 to 1890* (Canberra 1979), pp. 407–10.

2   *Sydney Morning Herald*, 27 September 1855.

3   'Fair Play' to editor, *Sydney Morning Herald*, 11 November 1858; Alan Atkinson, *Camden: Farm and Village Life in Early New South Wales* (Melbourne 1988), pp. 51, 58–9.

4   Frederick Calf, evidence before select committee on railway management, 27 October 1858, and William Hanson, ibid., 3 November 1858, pp. 86, 116, *Proceedings of the Parliament of South Australia*, 1858, vol. 2.

5   Oliver MacDonagh, 'Government, Industry and Science in Nineteenth Century Britain: A Particular Study', *Historical Studies*, no. 65 (October 1975), pp. 506–10; Wray Vamplew (ed.), *Australians: Historical Statistics* (Sydney 1987), p. 88.

6   Estimates for 1860, pp. 26–7, 75–6, Additional estimates for 1860, pp. 8–9, and Further additional estimates for 1860, p. 5, Victorian legislative assembly *Votes and Proceedings*, 1859–60, vol. 1; Geoffrey Serle, *The Golden Age: A History of the Colony of Victoria 1851–1861* (Melbourne 1963), pp. 365–6.

7   M.E. Hoare, 'Learned Societies in Australia: The Foundation Years in Victoria, 1850–1860', *Records of the Australian Academy of Science*, vol. 1, no. 1 (December 1966), pp. 17–19 (W.H. Archer, assistant registrar-general,

paper delivered to the Institute for the Advancement of Science, Melbourne, quoted ibid., pp. 12–13).

8   Charles Harpur, 'To Myself June 1855', in Adrian Mitchell (ed.), *Charles Harpur* (Melbourne 1973), p. 97.

9   J.H. Clark, evidence before select committee on railway management, 8 October 1858, and William Hanson, ibid., 3 November 1858, pp. 48, 95, *Proceedings of the Parliament of South Australia*, 1858, vol. 2.

10 Samuel Tuke, *Description of the Retreat, an Institution near York for Insane Persons of the Society of Friends* (York 1813), pp. 175–6; Andrew T. Scull, *Museums of Madness: The Social Organization of Insanity in Nineteenth-Century England* (London 1979), p. 102.

11 Tuke, op. cit., p. 132.

12 George Eliot, *Middlemarch* (London 1967; first pub. 1872), p. 618.

13 Robert Bowie, Return of patients, Yarra Bend asylum, 6 February 1857, pp. 4–8, Victorian legislative assembly *Votes and Proceedings*, 1856–7, vol. 2; R.T. Tracy, 'Inaugural lecture of the Course on Obstetrics and Diseases of Women and Children', *Australian Medical Journal*, April 1865, p. 120; Janet McCalman, *Sex and Suffering: Women's Health and a Women's Hospital – The Royal Women's Hospital, Melbourne 1856–1996* (Melbourne 1998), pp. 29, 37.

14 William Westgarth, *Victoria: Late Australia Felix, or Port Phillip District of New South Wales* (Edinburgh 1853), p. 29; P. Just, *Australia; or, Notes taken During a Residence in the Colonies from the Gold Discovery in 1851 till 1857* (Dundee 1859), p. 114.

15 Richard Eades, evidence before select committee on night soil, Melbourne, 25 April 1866, p. 5, and William Gregory, ibid., 1 May 1866, p. 22, and appendices, p. 40, Victorian legislative assembly *Votes and Proceedings*, 1866 (second session), vol. 1.

16 Herman Melville, *Moby-Dick, or, The Whale* (New York 1962; first pub. 1851), p. 5; *Sydney Morning Herald*, 1 February–29 March 1851 (quotations 22 March). The author was possibly Charles St Julian, for whom see Marion Diamond, *Creative Meddler: The Life and Fantasies of Charles St Julian* (Melbourne 1990).

17 Thomas Carlyle, *Sartor Resartus* (ed. J.A.S. Barrett) (London 1897; first pub. 1833–34), p. 113.

18 Georg Neumayer, report on 'magnetical, nautical, and meteorological observations' for 1858–9, June 1860, pp. 2, 259, Victorian legislative assembly *Votes and Proceedings*, 1859–60, vol. 4.

19 Neumayer, preface to his report, June 1860, p. v (quotation from Humboldt's *Cosmos: Sketch of a Physical Description of the Universe*, vol. 2).

20 William McCrea to James McCulloch, 25 February 1859, Victorian legislative assembly *Votes and Proceedings*, 1869, vol. 1, p. 477.

21 W.M. Turnbull, evidence before select committee on water from the Yan Yean reservoir, and F.T.W. Ford, ibid., both 2 November 1858, pp. 7, 13–14, 17, Victorian legislative assembly *Votes and Proceedings*, 1858–9, vol. 1; Richard Youl, evidence before select committee on the Yan Yean purification, 1 May 1860, Victorian legislative assembly *Votes and Proceedings*, 1859–60, vol. 2, p. 1; *Argus*, 23 January 1869.

22   W.M. Turnbull, evidence before select committee on the Yan Yean purification, 4 May 1860, p. 9, Victorian legislative assembly *Votes and Proceedings*, 1859–60, vol. 2.

23   D.E. Wilkie, evidence before select committee on water for the Yan Yean reservoir, 4 November 1858, p. 27, and J. Smith, ibid., 12 January 1859, pp. 82–3, Victorian legislative assembly *Votes and Proceedings*, 1858–9, vol. 1.

24   'Inhabitants and Houses', p. 56, and 'Land and Livestock', p. 17, Victorian census, 1871, Victorian legislative assembly *Votes and Proceedings*, 1872, vol. 2; Bernard Barrett, *The Inner Suburbs: The Evolution of an Industrial Area* (Melbourne 1971), pp. 123–4.

25   William McCrea, chief medical officer, report on small pox, 6 April 1869, Victorian legislative assembly *Votes and Proceedings*, 1869, vol. 1, pp. 501–3.

26   W.H. Christie, postmaster-general, report for 1855, p. 18, NSW legislative assembly *Votes and Proceedings*, 1856–7, vol. 2.

27   John Vader and Brian Murray, *Antique Bottle Collecting in Australia* (Sydney 1975), p. 29; James Boow, *Early Australian Commercial Glass: Manufacturing Processes* (Sydney 1991), pp. 25–6, 41–4, 102–4, 108.

28   [Louisa Anne Meredith], 'Shadows of the Golden Image', *Household Words*, 4 April 1857, pp. 317–18 (for the author, see Anne Lohrli, *Household Words, A Weekly Journal 1850–1859, Conducted by Charles Dickens* (Toronto 1973), p. 165); Grace Karskens, 'Revisiting the Worldview: The Archaeology of Convict Households in Sydney's Rocks Neighborhood', *Historical Archaeology*, vol. 37 (2003), p. 50.

29   Vader and Murray, op. cit., p. 51.

30   Ibid., p. 14; Tim Murray and Alan Mayne, '(Re)Constructing a Lost Community: "Little Lon", Melbourne, Australia', *Historical Archaeology*, vol. 37 (2003), pp. 92, 93, 96–7.

31   George Stephenson, evidence before select committee on railways, 29 March 1841, *Parliamentary Papers*, 1841 (354) VIII, pp. 125–6; D.N. Hagarty, 'The Selection, Design and Delivery of the First Locomotives and Rolling Stock', part 1, *Australian Railway History Society Bulletin*, vol. 48, no. 719 (September 1997), p. 318.

32   [Charles Dickens], 'Railway Dreaming', *Household Words*, 10 May 1856, pp. 386–8; Wolfgang Schivelbusch, *The Railway Journey: Trains and Travel in the 19th Century* (trans. Anselm Hollo) (Oxford 1979), pp. 58–66.

33   [Charles Dickens], 'Railway Nightmares', *Household Words*, 13 November 1858, p. 451.

34   *Banner*, 7 October 1853, 7 April 1854; Sir Henry Young to Duke of Newcastle, 25 March 1854, NSW legislative council *Votes and Proceedings*, 1854, vol. 1, pp. 1158–60.

35   *Sydney Morning Herald*, 20 August 1855.

36   *Argus*, 12 September 1854.

37   George Stephenson, evidence before select committee on railways, 29 March 1841, *Parliamentary Papers*, 1841 (354) VIII, p. 125

38   *Argus*, 12 September 1854.

39   William Morgan, evidence before select committee on the railway accident, 28 July 1858, p. 59, NSW legislative assembly *Votes and Proceedings*, 1858, vol. 3.

40   John Fishlock, evidence before coronial inquiry, 10 July 1858, papers relative to the railway accident, p. 11, Fishlock, evidence before commission of inquiry, 5 August 1858, p. 7, and George Carter, evidence before select committee on the railway accident, 21 July 1858, p. 42, NSW legislative assembly *Votes and Proceedings*, 1858, vol. 3; *Sydney Morning Herald*, 12 July 1858.

41   Report from the select committee on railways, 6 June 1848, NSW legislative council *Votes and Proceedings*, 1848, p. 462; Frances de Courcy, evidence before select committee on the petition of Mrs de Courcy, 21 December 1859, and B.H. Martindale, ibid., 18 February 1860, NSW legislative assembly *Votes and Proceedings*, 1859–60, vol. 3, pp. 389–392, 396; Death certificate of Frances de Courcy (died 9 August 1860).

42   Robert Stephenson, evidence before select committee on railways, 2 July 1839, and Edward Bury, ibid., 9 July 1839, *Parliamentary Papers*, 1839 (517) X, pp. 213, 236; Rowland Hill, evidence before select committee on railways, 22 April 1844, *Parliamentary Papers*, 1844 (318) XI, pp. 503–11.

43   Charles Cowper to P.W. Flower, 4 March 1853, NSWAO 15087/1/1, pp. 541, 546; *Sydney Morning Herald*, 27 September 1855; Andrew Clarke, report upon railways, 15 November 1856, p. xxxviii, Victorian legislative assembly *Votes and Proceedings*, 1856–57, vol. 4; B.H. Martindale to John Robertson, 17 April 1858, p. 6, NSW legislative assembly *Votes and Proceedings*, 1858, vol. 3; D.N. Hagarty, 'The Selection, Design and Delivery of the First Locomotives and Rolling Stock', part 2, *Australian Railway History Society Bulletin*, vol. 48, no. 720 (October 1997), pp. 369–74. Neil Marshall and Andrew Grant helped with this detail.

44   Charles Nealds to B.H. Martindale, 12 July 1858, p. 6, NSW legislative assembly *Votes and Proceedings*, 1858, vol. 3; correspondence respecting the claim of Mrs Want, July 1858–December 1859, NSW legislative assembly *Votes and Proceedings*, 1859–60, vol. 3, pp. 369–77.

45   *Sydney Morning Herald*, 27 September 1855; George C. Darbyshire, 'Specification of the Rolling Stock Proposed to be Manufactured in Victoria', 29 October 1856, in Andrew Clarke, report on railways, Victorian legislative assembly *Votes and Proceedings*, 1856–7, vol. 4; plans for stations at Campbelltown, 1858, and Parramatta, 1859, Permanent way plans and drawings of railway infrastructure, NSWAO R301.1, roll 303, plan D198, and R301.1, roll 256, plan 3576; Schivelbusch, op. cit., pp. 88–92. John Ferry gave me good advice here.

46   Schivelbusch, op. cit., pp. 35–7.

47   Ibid., pp. 35, 41–50; Graeme Davison, *The Unforgiving Minute: How Australia Learned to Tell the Time* (Melbourne 1993), pp. 40, 47, 52–5, 60–5.

48   Ann Kershaw, 20 August 1863, quoted in Susan West, 'Bushranging, the Policing of Rural Banditry and Working Class Identity in New South Wales, 1860–1880', PhD thesis, University of Newcastle 2003, p. 147.

49   John Ruskin, *The Seven Lamps of Architecture*, in *The Complete Works of John Ruskin* (ed. E.T. Cook and Alexander Wedderburn) (London 1903), vol. 8, p. 159.

50   Scull, *Museums of Madness*, pp. 247–8; John Walton, 'The Treatment of Pauper Lunatics in Victorian England: The Case of Lancaster Asylum, 1816–1870', in Andrew Scull (ed.), *Madhouses, Mad-Doctors, and Madmen: The Social History Psychiatry in the Victorian Era* (London 1981), p. 168.

51   F.J. Cockburn, *Letters from the Southern Hemisphere* (Calcutta 1856), p. 52
     (original emphasis). No one identifiable as a Frenchmen appears in the men's
     casebooks for the asylum, 1849–55 (search by Caroline Evans).

52   *Argus*, 26 September 1859; Speeches in legislative assembly, 13 May 1869,
     Queensland Parliamentary Debates, vol. 9, pp. 155–65.

53   Report of select committee on administration of justice in country districts —
     petitions of Joseph Wilkes and others, 18 February 1857, and minutes of evi-
     dence, NSW legislative assembly *Votes and Proceedings*, 1856–7, vol. 1, pp.
     987–1025 (quotation p. 1013). The numbering of questions and names of
     questioners have been left out here.

54   Robert Bowie, 'The Yarra Bend Lunatic Asylum', *The Statistical Register of
     Victoria* (Melbourne 1854), p. 191.

55   Bishop R.W. Willson, evidence before select committee on lunatic asylums, 13
     August 1863, NSW legislative assembly *Votes and Proceedings*, 1863–4, vol.
     4, p. 888.

56   *The Statistical Register of Victoria*, pp. 255–6; Willson, evidence before select
     committee on lunatic asylums, 13 August 1863, p. 888; Henry Challinor, evi-
     dence before select committee on the Woogaroo Lunatic Asylum, 22 June
     1869, Queensland legislative assembly *Votes and Proceedings*, 1869, vol. 1,
     pp. 965–6; Cathy Coleborne, ' "She Does Up Her Hair Fantastically": The
     Production of Feminity in Patient Case-Books of the Lunatic Asylum in 1860s
     Victoria', in Jane Long, Jan Gothard, and Helen Brash (eds), *Forging
     Identities: Bodies, Gender and Feminist History* (Nedlands 1997), p.55, 60.

57   G.W. Vivian, 'Report on the Proposed New Lunatic Asylum', 6 August 1856,
     p. 7, Victorian legislative assembly *Votes and Proceedings*, 1856–7, vol. 4.

58   Edward Paley, annual report on hospitals for the insane, February 1870, p. 5,
     Victorian legislative assembly *Votes and Proceedings*, 1870 (first session),
     vol. 2.

59   D.I. McDonald, 'Frederick Norton Manning (1839–1903)', *Journal of the
     Royal Australian Historical Society*, vol. 58 (1972).

60   Sir George Bowen to Earl of Carnarvon, 12 November 1966, CO 234/16, f.
     277; Howard le Couteur, 'Gramschi's Concept of Hegemony and Social
     Formation in Early Colonial Queensland, *Limina*, vol. 6 (2000), pp. 32–3.

61   J. Lort Stokes, *Discoveries in Australia* (London 1846), vol. 2, p. 319.

62   John Dunmore Lang, *Freedom and Independence for the Golden Lands of
     Australia: The Right of the Colonies, and the Interest of Britain and of the
     World* (London 1852), p. 28–32; *Argus*, 1 August 1862.

63   Charles Tiffin's correspondence with other members of government, 1861–7,
     in report of select committee on the Woogaroo Lunatic Asylum, Queensland
     legislative assembly *Votes and Proceedings*, 1869, vol. 1, pp. 934–8; Kearsey
     Cannan, evidence before commission of inquiry on lunatic asylum, Woo-
     garoo, 29 May 1867, Queensland legislative assembly *Votes and Proceedings*,
     1867, vol. 2, p. 1067; Raymond L. Evans, 'Charitable Institutions of the
     Queensland Government to 1919', MA thesis, University of Queensland
     1969, pp. 24–40.

64   K.I. O'Docherty to colonial secretary, 18 February 1869, in report of select
     committee on the Woogaroo Lunatic Asylum, Queensland legislative assem-
     bly *Votes and Proceedings*, 1869, vol. 1, p. 994.

65   Case of Richard Pritchard, 1861–62, casebook quoted in Evans, op. cit., p. 35; K.I. O'Docherty to Charles Lilley, 18 February 1869, and Henry Challinor, evidence before select committee on the Woogaroo Lunatic Asylum, 22 June 1869, Queensland legislative assembly *Votes and Proceedings*, 1869, vol. 1, pp. 960, 994.

66   John Brosnan, evidence before inquiry into the lunatic asylum, Woogaroo, 25 February 1869, Edward Kennedy, ibid., 4 March 1869, and John Gee to commissioners, 31 March 1869, Queensland legislative assembly *Votes and Proceedings*, 1868–69, pp. 695, 706, 758.

67   Evelyn Shlomowitz, ' "How Much More Generally Applicable are Remedial Words than Medicines": Care of the Mentally Ill in South Australia, 1858–1884', *Journal of Australian Colonial History*, vol. 4 (2002), pp. 81–2, 93–7; Coleborne, op. cit., pp 63–4.

68   F.N. Manning, evidence before select committee on the Woogaroo Lunatic Asylum, 6 July 1869, Queensland legislative assembly *Votes and Proceedings*, 1869, vol. 1, p. 972.

69   Ibid., Anthony Trollope, *The Last Chronicle of Barset* (London 1909), vol. 1, pp. 168–9. See also Marian Quartly, 'South Australian Lunatics and their Custodians, 1836–1846', *Australian Journal of Social Issues*, no. 2 (1966), p. 19.

70   Anon., 'The Hospital for the Insane', *Australian Medical Journal*, vol. 4 (October 1859), pp. 281–2.

Chapter 14: To Feel as One

1   Matthew Arnold, 'On Dover Beach' (1851?).

2   *Sydney Morning Herald*, 5 May 1862.

3   Frank M. Murtaugh, *Cavour and the Economic Modernization of the Kingdom of Sardinia* (New York 1991), pp. 65–8, 71–2, 85–95.

4   Matthew Arnold, 'Empedocles on Etna' (1852) (the voice of Empedocles but the opinion of Arnold); Matthew Arnold, *Culture and Anarchy* (first pub. 1869).

5   Edward Payne (Mudgee) to his family, [1858?], in Gerry Tomlinson, *'Bring Plenty of Pickles': Letters from an Emigrant Family* (Waddesdon, Bucks, 1986), p. 54.

6   Anne Brontë, *The Tenant of Wildfell Hall* (London 1979; first pub. 1848), pp. 408–9.

7   James Wilson to his family, 28 January 1853, La Trobe MS 12416.

8   Anthony Trollope, *Australia and New Zealand* (Melbourne 1876; first pub. 1873), p. 146.

9   Ibid., p. 146.

10   *Census of New South Wales*, 1861 and 1871; *New South Wales Statistical Register*, 1861, pp. 118–30, and 1871, pp. 16–17; Hans Mol, *The Faith of Australians* (Sydney 1985), p. 54. Mol understates the change. To the single heading for 1861, 'Churches and Chapels', is added in 1871 a heading for other buildings used for worship. Mol sets aside the latter, failing to notice that the 1861 figures include these too.

11   NSW *Statistical Register*, 1871, p. 69; 'Interchange', p. 13, *Statistical Register of Victoria*, 1871, Victorian legislative assembly *Votes and Proceedings*,

1872, vol. 2; F.B. Smith, 'Religion and Freethought in Melbourne, 1870 to 1890', MA thesis, University of Melbourne 1960, pp. 2–4, 116, 330–1.

12   Martin Griver, diary 14 February, 1859, in D.F. Bourke, *The History of the Catholic Church in Western Australia* (Perth 1979), p. 68.

13   Bourke, op. cit., p. 73.

14   *Argus*, 8 August 1864.

15   *South Australian Advertiser*, 28 August 1865; Joseph Nicholson, quoted in C. Irving Benson, *A Century of Victorian Methodism* (Melbourne 1935), pp. 132–3; Ann Douglas, *The Feminization of American Culture* (London 1996), passim.

16   Derek Phillips, 'The State and the Provision of Education in Tasmania, 1839 to 1913', PhD thesis, University of Tasmania 1988, pp. 321–6.

17   Thomas Carlyle, *Sartor Resartus* (ed. J.A.S. Barrett) (London 1897; first pub. 1833–34), p. 155.

18   David Hilliard, *Godliness and Good Order: A History of the Anglican Church in South Australia* (Adelaide 1986), p. 60; Owen Chadwick, *The Spirit of the Oxford Movement: Tractarian Essays* (Cambridge 1990), pp. 234–5; Stephen Judd and Kenneth Cable, *Sydney Anglicans: A History of the Diocese* (Sydney 2000), pp. 116–17.

19   John Newton, 'How Sweet the Name of Jesus Sounds' (1779).

20   G. Chapman, *One Lord, One Faith, One Baptism: A History of Churches of Christ in Australia* (Melbourne 1989), pp. 49–50, 55–6; R.J. Leach, 'Churches of Christ in Australia 1846–1905: An Inter-Colonial Comparison', MLitt thesis, University of New England 1997, pp. 6–9, 19, 78–80 (quotation from Thomas Campbell, *Declaration and Address* [1809]).

21   'Religions of the People', p. 7, Victorian census, 1871, Victorian legislative assembly *Votes and Proceedings*, 1872, vol. 2; 'Religious, Moral, and Intellectual Progress', p. 5, Statistical Register of Victoria, 1871, Victorian legislative assembly *Votes and Proceedings*, 1873, vol. 2.

22   'Religions of the People', pp. 135, 164, 168, Victorian census, 1871, op. cit.; Leach, op. cit., pp. 30, 31–2.

23   Isaac Watts, 'Jesus Shall Reign' (1719) (from *Hymns Ancient and Modern*).

24   *Private Communications given by J. Wroe from the Beginning of 1843, to the End of 1852*, 1853, in Alan Atkinson, 'Our First Chance of Kingdom Come', *Push from the Bush*, no. 19 (April 1985), p. 61.

25   Guy Featherstone, 'The Nunawading Messiah: James Fisher and Popular Millenarianism in Nineteenth-Century Melbourne', *Journal of Religious History*, vol. 26 (2002), pp. 46–8.

26   *Argus*, 10 July 1871; *Age*, 12 July 1871.

27   *Age*, 12 July 1871.

28   *Sydney Morning Herald*, 13 March 1868; Marcie Muir, *Anthony Trollope in Australia* (Adelaide 1949), pp. 41–3.

29   Petition from 'Mothers and Daughters' of Narellan, 15 September 1870, NSW legislative assembly *Votes and Proceedings*, 1870–1, vol. 4, p. 29; *Argus*, 19 December 1871.

30   Wilkie Collins, *The Woman in White* (London 1906), p. 98.

31   John Stuart Mill, *The Subjection of Women* (ed. Susan Moller Okin) (Indianapolis 1988; first pub. 1869), p. 102.

32   M.C. Stephen, in *Sydney Morning Herald*, 10 September 1870.

33   *Sydney Morning Herald*, 23 September 1870.

34   Susan Magarey, 'The Invention of Juvenile Delinquency in Early Nineteenth-Century England', *Labour History*, no. 34 (May 1978), pp. 13–19; Brian Dickey, *Rations, Residence, Resources: A History of Social Welfare in South Australia since 1836* (Adelaide 1986), pp. 53–62; Robert van Krieken, 'Towards "Good and Useful Men and Women": The State and Childhood in Sydney, 1840–1890', *Australian Historical Studies*, no. 93 (October 1989), pp. 411–17.

35   Mary Carpenter, *Reformatory Schools for the Children of the Perishing and Dangerous Classes and for Juvenile Offenders* (London 1851), pp. 69, 347–8.

36   Western Wood, speech in legislative council, 1 June 1865, *Queensland Parliamentary Debates*, 1865, p. 361; R.E.N. Twopeny, *Town Life in Australia* (London 1883), p. 83.

37   Dickey, op. cit., pp. 57–60. The legislation was the Destitute Persons Relief Act, 1867.

38   William Wilkins, 1858, quoted in M.J. Ely, 'The Management of Schools is New South Wales 1848–1880: Local Initiative Suppressed', *Journal of Educational Administration*, vol 9 (1971), p. 83.

39   Friedrich Nietzsche, *The Will to Power* (trans. Anthony M. Ludovici), vol. 1 (New York 1964), pp. 63–4.

40   F.B. Smith, *The People's Health, 1830–1910* (Canberra 1979), pp. 217–19 (quotation, p. 218, from British pamphlet); Alan Atkinson, *Camden: Farm and Village Life in Early New South Wales* (Melbourne 1988), pp. 109–201 (Charles Tompson, 1850, quoted p. 200); Janet McCalman, *Sex and Suffering: Women's Health and a Women's Hospital – The Royal Women's Hospital, Melbourne 1856–1996* (Melbourne 1998), p. 18.

41   R.W. Moore to Henry Ayers, 22 July 1867, and J.P. Hall, R.W. Moore, and T.W. Corbin, evidence before select committee on management of destitute poor, 19, 23 and 30 August 1867, pp. ii, 17–18, 30–1, 44–5, *Proceedings of the Parliament of South Australia*, 1867, vol. 3.

42   Sarah Ann Phillips, evidence before select committee on management of destitute poor, 19 August 1867, and T.W. Corbin, ibid., 30 August 1867, pp. 13–14, 43, *Proceedings of the Parliament of South Australia*, 1867, vol. 3.

43   Paul Gardiner, *An Extraordinary Australian: Mary MacKillop* (Sydney 1993), pp. 57–74, 79–84.

44   Ada Cambridge, 'The Shadow', and 'The Physical Conscience', in *Unspoken Thoughts* (Canberra 1988; first pub. 1887), pp. 8 (original emphasis), 65. See also, Ada Cambridge, 'The Lonely Seas', *Atlantic Monthly*, vol. 108 (1911), pp. 96–7.

45   *Argus*, 11 July 1871.

46   Trollope, op. cit., p. 193; Ada Cambridge, *Thirty Years in Australia* (Sydney 1989; first pub. 1901–02), p. 2.

47   G.L. Buxton, *The Riverina, 1861–1891: An Australian Regional Study* (Melbourne 1967), p. 123; Susan West, 'Bushranging, the Policing of Rural Banditry and Working Class Identity in New South Wales, 1860–1880', PhD thesis, University of Newcastle 2003, pp. 116, 281.

48   Atkinson, *Camden,* pp. 68–72.

49 W. Henty, *On Improvements in Cottage Husbandry* (Launceston [1851]), p. 22; *Australian Dictionary of Biography*, vol. 1, p. 292. See also Alan Atkinson and Marian Aveling (eds), *Australians 1838* (Sydney 1987), p. 127.

50 Anon., 'The Free Selector's Song – 1861', in Russel Ward (ed.), *The Penguin Book of Australian Ballads* (London 1964), p. 87; Alan Atkinson, 'Towards Independence: Recipes for Self-Government in Colonial New South Wales', in Penny Russell and Richard White (eds), *Pastiche I: Reflections on 19th Century Australia* (Sydney 1994), pp. 88–9; Andrew Messner, 'Chartist Political Culture in Britain and Colonial Australia, c. 1835–1860', PhD thesis, University of New England 2000, pp. 324–37.

51 *Empire*, 11 December 1860; Anne Coote, 'The Development of Colonial Nationhood in New South Wales, c. 1825–1865', PhD thesis, University of New England, forthcoming.

52 D.W. Meinig, *On the Margins of the Good Earth: The South Australian Wheat Frontier, 1869–1884* (Adelaide 1970), pp. 45–50; G.J.R. Linge, *Industrial Awakening: A Geography of Australian Manufacturing, 1788 to 1890* (Canberra 1979), p. 179.

53 Wray Vamplew (ed.), *Australians: Historical Statistics* (Sydney 1987), p. 76.

54 *Empire*, 21 November 1864; West, op. cit., p. 24 and appendix 1.

55 *Bathurst Times*, in *Empire*, 20 October 1863; D.J. Shiel, *Ben Hall, Bushranger* (St Lucia 1983), pp. 140–9.

56 Report of the commission appointed to inquire into state of crime in the Braidwood district, 9 February 1867, NSW legislative assembly *Votes and Proceedings*, 1867–8, vol. 2, pp. 121–3.

57 *Sydney Morning Herald*, 6 January 1865; West, op. cit., pp. 134–5.

58 John Carroll to Henry Parkes, 31 December 1866, NSW legislative assembly *Votes and Proceedings*, 1867–8, vol. 2, p. 276.

59 *Empire*, 17 June 1867; *Sydney Morning Herald*, 28 February, 29 October 1863.

60 *Sydney Morning Herald*, 27 July 1864.

61 Sir Alfred Stephen, in *Sydney Morning Herald*, 27 April 1865; W. Dwyer, inspector's annual report, 20 December 1865, NSW legislative assembly *Votes and Proceedings*, 1866, vol. 2, p. 564; *Empire*, 17 June 1867.

62 *Sydney Morning Herald*, 18 August 1864; *Empire*, 17 June 1867.

63 *Sydney Morning Herald*, 28 August 1863; West, op. cit., p. 85 (wrongly attributed quotation).

64 Buxton, op. cit., p. 86 (country newspaper quoted, but wrongly attributed).

65 Joseph Docker, postmaster-general's annual report, 26 April 1872, NSW legislative assembly *Votes and Proceedings*, 1872, vol. 1, pp. 1185, 1205; Trollope, op. cit., p. 194.

66 *Empire*, 17 June 1867.

67 Anon., 'Stringy-bark and Green-hide', in Ward, *The Penguin Book of Australian Ballads*, p. 71; Russel Ward, *The Australian Legend* (Melbourne 1966), pp. 160–9.

68 Report of the Central Board of Education 1869, p. 8, *Proceedings of the Parliament of South Australia*, 1870–1, vol. 2; Ibid., 1870, p. 2, *Proceedings of the Parliament of South Australia*, 1871, vol. 2; Ibid., 1872, p. 2, *Proceedings of the Parliament of South Australia*, 1873, vol. 2; Ibid., 1873,

p. 22, *Proceedings of the Parliament of South Australia*, 1874, p. 22; 1874, p. 37, *Proceedings of the Parliament of South Australia*, 1875, vol. 2; William Jessop (1862), quoted in Hans Mincham, *The Story of the Flinders Ranges* (Adelaide 1965), p. 100; Jill Statton (ed.), *Biographical Index of South Australians 1836–1885*, vol. 2 (Adelaide 1986), p. 726.

69   Edward H. Flannery, inspector's annual report, 28 January 1871, NSW legislative assembly *Votes and Proceedings*, 1870–1, vol. 4, pp. 199–208 (quotation p. 205); Buxton, op. cit., pp. 86–9.

70   Flannery, annual report 19 February 1872, NSW legislative assembly *Votes and Proceedings*, 1872, vol. 2, pp. 481 (original emphasis), 483.

Chapter 15: Our Outer Edge

1   John Chapple, diary, 17, 19 April 1855, SLV MS 11792.

2   Charles Price, *The Great White Walls are Built: Restrictive Immigration to North America and Australia 1836–1888* (Canberra 1974), pp. 53–60.

3   Geoffrey Serle, *The Golden Age: A History of the Colony of Victoria 1851–1861* (Melbourne 1963), pp. 388–9.

4   *Argus*, 14 July 1857; C.N. Connolly, 'Miners' Rights', in Ann Curthoys and Andrew Markus (eds), *Who are Our Enemies?: Racism and the Working Class in Australia* (Sydney 1978), pp. 36–9.

5   John Stewart (Lambing Flat), *Sydney Morning Herald*, 7 February 1861.

6   *Argus*, 14 July 1857; Serle, op. cit., pp. 325–6 (quoting *Ovens and Murray Advertiser*).

7   *Sydney Morning Herald*, 7 February 1861; P.A. Selth, 'The Burrangong (Lambing Flat) Riots, 1860–1861', *Journal of the Royal Australian Historical Society*, vol. 60 (1974), pp. 53–4 (Miners Protection League prospectus and John Stewart quoted p. 53).

8   *Sydney Morning Herald*, 7 February 1861; D.L. Carrington, 'Riots at Lambing Flat, 1860–1861', *Journal of the Royal Australian Historical Society*, vol. 46 (1960); R.B. Walker, 'Another Look at the Lambing Flat Riots 1860–61', *Journal of the Royal Australian Historical Society*, vol. 56 (1970).

9   *Sydney Morning Herald*, 9 July, 4 September 1861.

10   *Sydney Morning Herald*, 27 April 1865.

11   Reginald Horsman, *Josiah Nott of Mobile: Southerner, Physician, and Racial Theorist* (Baton Rouge 1987), pp. 181–200 (quotation pp. 192–3); Andrew Markus, *Australian Race Relations 1788–1993* (Sydney 1994), pp. 11–14.

12   Andrew Eaton, evidence taken by Edward Denny Day following the massacre at Myall Creek, 30 August 1838, AONSW 4/5601.

13   *Sydney Morning Herald*, 15 June 1860, 13 March, 13 September 1861; 'Peter Faucett'. *Australian Dictionary of Biography*, vol. 4, pp. 157–8.

14   Daniel Deniehy, Charles Kemp and William Forster, speeches in legislative assembly, *Sydney Morning Herald*, 15 June 1860.

15   William Windeyer to Maria Windeyer, 12 March 1851, in Alan Atkinson, 'Some Documents and Data from the King's School, Parramatta', *Push from the Bush*, no. 4 (September 1979), p. 79; *Australian Dictionary of Biography*, vol. 6, pp. 420–2.

16   Richard Windeyer, 'On the Rights of the Aborigines of Australia', June 1844, ML MSS 1400, p. 43.

17   William Windeyer, in *Sydney Morning Herald*, 1 August 1861; Audrey Tate, *Ada Cambridge: Her Life and Work 1844–1926* (Melbourne 1991), pp.115–16.

18   Daniel Deniehy, in *Sydney Morning Herald*, 1 August 1861.

19   *Sydney Morning Herald*, 22 July 1861.

20   Thomas Carlyle, *Sartor Resartus* (ed. J.A.S. Barrett) (London 1897; first pub. 1833–34), pp. 102–3.

21   Thomas Carlyle, 'Occasional Discourse on the Nigger Question', 1849, in his *Critical and Miscellaneous Essays*, (London 1899), vol. 4.

22   Herman Melville, *Moby-Dick; or, The Whale* (ed. Luther S. Mansfield and Howard P. Vincent) (New York 1962; first pub. 1851), pp. 21, 23–4, 29, 189, 566, and explanatory notes, passim.

23   Ibid., p. 47, 114; Ann Douglas, *The Feminization of American Culture* (London 1996), pp. 289–326. And see Herman Melville, *Billy Budd* (1924).

24   Family papers in my possession (the Icks were my wife's forebears).

25   Caleb S. Weeks, 'Spiritualism the All-Embracing Religious Faith', *Harbinger of Light*, November 1870, p. 33 (original emphasis); W.L. Richardson, quoted in Alfred J. Gabay, *Messages from Beyond: Spiritualism and Spiritualists in Melbourne's Golden Age 1870–1890* (Melbourne 2001), p. 69.

26   'Excelsior' to editor, *Argus*, 22 July 1871; *Harbinger of Light*, December 1873, p. 548.

27   *Australasian Sketcher*, 17 May 1873; F.B. Smith, 'Religion and Freethought in Melbourne, 1870 to 1890', MA thesis, University of Melbourne 1960, pp. 31 (quoting E.W. Cole), 33–5, 67–74.

28   A.J. Gabay, 'The Séance in the Melbourne of the 1870s: Experience and Meanings', *Journal of Religious History*, vol. 13 (1984).

29   Editorial, *Harbinger of Light*, November 1873, p. 520; William Crookes, 'Notes of an Enquiry into the Phenomena Called Spiritual, During the Years 1870–73', ibid., June 1874, pp. 639–42; Smith, op. cit., pp. 88–94; Gabay, *Messages from Beyond*, pp. 101–3, 184–9.

30   Smith, op. cit., p. 34; Gabay, op. cit., p. 212.

31   *Harbinger of Light*, July 1871, p. 130.

32   'The Editor of the British Journal of Photography, on Dark Circles & Spirit Photographs', *Harbinger of Light*, April 1871, p. 159; 'Spirit Photography', ibid., August 1872, pp. 288–9.

33   Smith, op. cit., pp. 49, 144–6.

34   'What Constitutes True Marriage', *Harbinger of Light*, December 1871, p. 264; Enoch Aster to editor, ibid., March 1873, p. 394.

35   Ann Moyal, *Clear across Australia: A History of Telecommunications* (Melbourne 1984), p. 17 (wrongly attributed quotation?); Smith, op. cit., p. 139.

36   Moyal, op. cit., pp. 23–4.

37   Statistical register of South Australia, 1871, p. 84, in *Proceedings of the Parliament of South Australia*, 1867, vol. 3. W. Turner, deputy postmaster-general, annual report, 31 March 1872, p. 43, Victorian legislative assembly *Votes and Proceedings*, 1872, vol. 2; Moyal, op. cit., pp. 19–21.

38   Sarah Dring, evidence before select committee on management of destitute poor, 26 August 1867, p. 38, *Proceedings of the Parliament of South*

Australia, 1867, vol. 3; Henry Challinor, evidence before select committee on the Woogaroo Lunatic Asylum, 22 June 1869, Queensland legislative assembly *Votes and Proceedings*, 1869, vol. 1, p. 37; K.T. Livingston, *The Wired Nation Continent: The Communication Revolution and Federating Australia* (Melbourne 1996), pp. 46–7, 50.

39   Samuel W. McGowan, general superintendent of electric telegraph, half-yearly report, 31 December 1857, p. 6, Victorian legislative assembly *Votes and Proceedings*, 1859–60, vol. 2; *Sydney Morning Herald*, 16 May 1862.

40   Turner, op. cit., p. 43; W.J. Cracknell, superintendent of electric telegraphs, annual report, 8 April 1872, Queensland legislative assembly *Votes and Proceedings*, 1872, p. 1409.

41   Susan West, 'Bushranging, the Policing of Rural Banditry and Working Class Identity in New South Wales, 1860–1880', PhD thesis, University of Newcastle 2003, pp. 128–9.

42   Laura Otis, 'The Metaphoric Circuit: Organic and Technological Communication in the Nineteenth Century', *Journal of the History of Ideas*, vol. 63 (2002), pp. 105–28 (du Bois-Reymond quoted p. 114 and Morse pp. 118–19; emphasis in Otis).

43   Petition from 'Bankers, Merchants and Others', n.d. (ordered to be printed 16 July 1872), NSW legislative assembly *Votes and Proceedings*, 1872, vol. 1, pp. 1231–2 (partly quoting Joshua Leavett).

44   Matthew Arnold, 'Empedocles on Etna' (1852); *Sydney Morning Herald*, 13, 16 March 1868; *Armidale Express*, 14, 21 March 1868.

45   Moyal, op. cit., pp. 28–30, 56–9.

46   Bolton, op. cit., pp. 14–32.

47   W.J. Cracknell, annual report, 19 June 1865, Queensland legislative assembly *Votes and Proceedings*, 1865, p. 1245.

48   Peter Taylor, *The End to Silence: The Building of the Overland Telegraph from Adelaide to Darwin* (Sydney 1980), pp. 35–41.

49   Moyal, op. cit., pp. 26–7; Robert Lee, *Colonial Engineer: John Whitton 1819–1898 and the Building of Australia's Railways* (Sydney 2000), pp. 163–7.

50   Taylor, op. cit., pp. 30, 49–50, 76–7, 84, 158.

51   Ibid., pp. 153–4.

52   Western Wood, speech in legislative council, 11 May 1864, *Queensland Parliamentary Debates*, vol. 1, pp. 31–2.

53   Josiah Nott, *Types of Mankind*, 1854, quoted Horsman, op. cit., p. 195 (original emphasis).

54   A.C. Gregory, evidence before select committee on the Native Police Force, 22 May 1861, p. 41, Queensland legislative assembly *Votes and Proceedings*, 1861.

55   Tom Griffith, *Hunters and Collectors: The Antiquarian Imagination in Australia* (Melbourne 1996), pp. 28–40.

56   Mary McManus, *Reminiscences of the Early Settlement in the Maranoa District* (Brisbane 1913), pp. 4–5; *Australian Dictionary of Biography*, vol. 3, pp. 403–4.

57   Alfred Brown, evidence before select committee on murders by the Aborigines on the Dawson River, 23 June 1858, 15 July 1858, p. 33, NSW legislative assembly *Votes and Proceedings*, 1858, vol. 2; Lt Carr, evidence before select committee on the Native Police Force, 27 June 1861, p. 135, and

Carden Collins, ibid., 13 June 1861, p. 65, Queensland legislative assembly *Votes and Proceedings*, 1861.

58   C.M. Frazer, ibid., 3 May 1861, p. 2; Jacob Lowe, ibid., 8 May 1861, p. 9; James Davies, ibid., 12 June 1861, pp. 57, 58; John Hardie, ibid., 20 June 1861, p. 100.

59   W.B. Tooth, evidence before select committee on murders by the Aborigines on the Dawson River, 23 June 1858, p. 26, NSW legislative assembly *Votes and Proceedings*, 1858, vol. 2; A.C. Gregory, evidence before select committee on the Native Police Force, 22 May 1861, p. 40, Queensland legislative assembly *Votes and Proceedings*, 1861.

60   John Summers, 'Colonial Race Relations', in Eric Richards (ed.), *The Flinders History of South Australia: Social History* (Adelaide 1986), pp. 301, 303.

61   M.C. O'Connell, evidence before select committee on the Native Police Force, 19 June 1861, p. 84, Queensland legislative assembly *Votes and Proceedings*, 1861.

62   *Argus*, 17 March 1856; M.F. Christie, *Aborigines in Colonial Victoria 1835–86* (Sydney 1979), pp. 150–3.

63   Ibid., pp. 157–77 (John Green, 1863, quoted p. 167).

64   James Davies, evidence before select committee on the Native Police Force, 12 June 1861, p. 56, and Carden Collins, ibid., 13 June 1861, p. 65, Queensland legislative assembly *Votes and Proceedings*, 1861; John Bramston, speech in legislative council, 11 May 1864, *Queensland Parliamentary Debates*, vol. 1, p. 32.

65   Arthur Laurie, 'Hornet Bank Massacre, October 27, 1857', *Journal of the Royal Historical Society of Queensland*, vol. 5, no. 5 (1957); Gordon Reid, *A Nest of Hornets: The Massacre of the Fraser Family at Hornet Bank Station, Central Queensland, 1857, and Related Events* (Melbourne 1982), pp. ix, 75–100; Henry Reynolds, *An Indelible Stain?: The Question of Genocide in Australia's History* (Melbourne 2001), pp. 124–6.

66   Frederick Wheeler, evidence before select committee on the Native Police Force, 9, 16 May 1861, pp. 17, 29, Queensland legislative assembly *Votes and Proceedings*, 1861.

67   John Ker Wilson, ibid., 18 June 1861, p. 73; Lt Carr, ibid., 27 June 1861, p. 129.

68   Jacob Lowe, ibid., 8 May 1861, pp. 6–7, 9, 10; John Coley, ibid., 14 May 1861, pp. 19, 21; John Ker Wilson, ibid., 18 June 1861, p. 71; John O'Connell Bligh, ibid., 8 July 1861, p. 155. For Kilcoy, see Raymond Evans, Kay Saunders and Kathryn Cronin, *Exclusion, Exploitation and Extermination: Race Relations in Colonial Queensland* (Sydney 1975), p. 49.

69   William Miles, T.P. Pugh and George Clark, speeches in legislative assembly, 4 October 1867, *Queensland Parliamentary Debates*, third series, vol. 5, pp. 338, 340, 341.

70   A.C. Gregory, evidence before select committee on the Native Police Force, 22 May 1861, p. 43, Queensland legislative assembly *Votes and Proceedings*, 1861; James Davies, ibid., 12 June 1861, p. 55; John Ker Wilson, ibid., 18 June 1861, pp. 72, 74; J.L. Zillman, 18 June 1861, p. 78; C.R. Haley, ibid., 19 June 1861, p. 81; Lt Carr, ibid., 27 June 1861, p. 134.

71   William Archer, evidence before select committee on murders by the Aborigines on the Dawson River, 22 June 1858, p. 19, NSW legislative

assembly *Votes and Proceedings*, 1858, vol. 2; Archibald Archer and William Miles, speeches in legislative assembly, 4 October 1867, *Queensland Parliamentary Debates*, vol. 4, pp. 337, 338.

72   St George Gore, one of the select committee on the Native Police Force, 8 July 1861, p. 156, Queensland legislative assembly *Votes and Proceedings*, 1861.

73   G.C. Bolton, *A Thousand Miles Away: A History of North Queensland to 1920* (Brisbane 1963), pp. 54-5; C. May, 'Chinese in Queensland', in James Jupp (ed.), *The Australian People* (Sydney 1988), pp. 311-12.

74   Evans, Saunders and Cronin, op. cit., pp. 149-51, 157-9; K. Saunders, 'Pacific Islander Recruitment', in Jupp, op. cit., pp. 722-5.

75   W.H. Walsh, speech in legislative assembly, 28 June 1866, *Queensland Parliamentary Debates*, vol. 3, p. 445; Henry Reynolds, *North of Capricorn: The Untold Story of Australia's North* (Sydney 2003), p. ix.

76   Executive council minute, 4 July 1865, CO 234/12, ff. 355-6; R.G.W. Herbert, memorandum, 20 June 1866, CO 234/16, f. 300.

77   D.T. Seymour, commissioner of police, to H.D. Pitt, 15 June 1866, and monthly reports from officers of the native police, February–March 1866, CO 234/16, ff. 306, 311-16.

78   John Ker Wilson, evidence before select committee on the Native Police Force, 18 June 1861, p. 72, Queensland legislative assembly *Votes and Proceedings*, 1861.

79   M.C. O'Connell, ibid., 19 June 1861, pp. 82-5.

80   Ibid., p. 83.

81   Frederick Wheeler, ibid., 16 May 1851, p. 31; James Davies, ibid., 12 June 1861, p. 58; C.R. Haly, ibid., 19 June 1861, p. 80.

82   J.L. Zillman, ibid., 18 June 1861, p. 78.

83   'A Lady' [Emma McPherson], *My Experiences in Australia: Being Recollections of a Visit to the Australian Colonies in 1856-7* (London 1860), p. 219 (I am grateful to Meg Vivers for help with this material); Howard Morphy, *Ancestral Connections: Art and an Aboriginal System of Knowledge* (Chicago 1991), p. 148.

84   'A Lady', op. cit., pp. 202, 238-9; Margaret Vivers, 'Evidence of European Women in Early Contact History, with Particular Reference to Northern New South Wales and Queensland', BA thesis, Universtiy of New England 2003, pp. 28-9.

Afterword

1   Henry Kingsley, *The Recollections of Geoffrey Hamlyn* (Melbourne 1970; first pub. 1859), p. 225.

2   F.T. Gregory, 'Journal of the North-west Australian Exploring Expedition', 10, 17 June, 26 September 1861, in Augustus Charles Gregory and Francis Thomas Gregory, *Journals of Australian Explorations* (Brisbane 1884), p. 86.

3   Ibid., pp. 63, 65.

4   Anthony Trollope, *Australia and New Zealand* (Melbourne 1876; first pub. 1873), p. 204.

5   *Argus*, 17 March 1856.

6   J.B. Hirst, *The Strange Birth of Colonial Democracy: New South Wales 1848–1884* (Sydney 1988), pp. 48–57.

7   *Sydney Morning Herald*, 18 August 1864.

8   Henry Kendall, 'The Glen of Arrawatta' and 'Narrara Creek', in *Poems of Henry Clarence Kendall* (Melbourne 1903), pp. 43, 174.

9   H.M. Green, *A History of Australian Literature, Pure and Applied* (Sydney 1961), vol. 1, pp. 339–40.

10 L. Manderson, 'Malays', in James Jupp (ed.), *The Australian People* (Sydney 1988), pp. 691–3; Henry Reynolds, *North of Capricorn: The Untold Story of Australia's North* (Sydney 2003), pp. x–xi, xiv–xv.

11 D.J. Murphy, 'Introduction: The Labor Parties in Australia', in D.J. Murphy (ed.), *Labor in Politics: The State Labor Parties in Australia 1880–1920* (St Lucia 1975), p. 9.

12 Trollope, op. cit., pp. 307, 311–12, 318, 321.

13 Hans Mol, *The Faith of Australians* (Sydney 1985), pp. 53–5.

14 George Fletcher Moore, *Diary of Ten Years Eventful Life of an Early Settler in Western Australia* (London 1884), pp. 201–2.

Bibliography

1. Works from the Period and Published Documents

Anley, Charlotte, *The Prisoners of Australia: A Narrative* (London 1841).

Anon. (ed.), *A Bloodthirsty Banditti of Wretches: Informations on Oath Relating to Michael Howe and Others between 1814 and 1818* (Hobart 1985).

Anon., *South Australia, in 1842, by One Who Lived There Nearly Four Years* (London 1843).

Arden, George, *Latest Information with Regard to Australia Felix* (Melbourne 1840).

Aspinall, Clara, *Three Years in Melbourne* (London 1862).

Atkinson, Alan, 'Some Documents and Data from the King's School, Parramatta', *Push from the Bush*, no. 4 (September 1979).

[Atkinson, Alan], 'Bunyips', *Push: A Journal of Early Australian Social History*, no. 27 (1989).

[Atkinson, Alan], 'The McGreavys: A Family Saga', *Push: A Journal of Early Australian Social History*, no. 28 (1990).

Atkinson, James, *An Account of the State of Agriculture and Grazing in New South Wales* (London 1826).

Aurousseau, Marcel (ed.), *The Letters of F.W. Ludwig Leichhardt* (three volumes; Cambridge 1968).

'Australian Journalist, An', *The Emigrant in Australia, or, Gleanings from the Gold-Fields* (London 1852).

Aveling, Marian (ed.), *Westralian Voices: Documents in Western Australian Social History* (Nedlands 1979).

Backhouse, James, *A Narrative of a Visit to the Australian Colonies* (London 1843).

Balfour, J.O., *A Sketch of New South Wales* (London 1845).

Bannister, Saxe, *Humane Policy; or, Justice to the Aborigines of New Settlements Essential to a Due Expenditure of British Money, and to the Best Interests of the Settlers* (London 1830).

Baxter, Carol J. (ed.), *General Muster and Land and Stock Muster of New South Wales, 1822* (Sydney 1988).

Baxter, Carol J. (ed.), *Musters of New South Wales and Norfolk Island 1805–1806* (Sydney 1989).

Beale, Edgar (ed.), *The Earth between Them: Joseph Beale's Letters Home to Ireland from Victoria, 1852–53* (Sydney 1975).

Berryman, Ian (ed.), *A Colony Detailed: The First Census of Western Australia 1832* (Perth 1979).

Bigge, J.T., *Report of the Commissioner of Inquiry into the State of the Colony of New South Wales* (London 1822).

Bigge, J.T., *Report of the Commissioner of Inquiry on the State of Agriculture and Trade in the Colony of New South Wales* (London 1823).

Bigge, J.T., *Report of the Commissioner of Inquiry on the Judicial Establishments of New South Wales and Van Diemen's Land* (London 1823).

Billot, C.P. (ed.), *Melbourne's Missing Chronicle, Being the Journal of Preparations for Departure to and Proceedings at Port Phillip by John Pascoe Fawkner* (Melbourne 1982).

Bonwick, James, *Notes of a Gold Digger, and Gold Digger's Guide* (Melbourne 1852).

Boyd, A.J., *Old Colonials* (Sydney 1882).

Bride, T.F. (ed.), *Letters from Victorian Pioneers* (Melbourne 1893).

Brontë, Anne, *The Tenant of Wildfell Hall* (London 1979; first pub. 1848).

Brown, Henry, *Victoria, As I Found It, During Five Years of Adventure* (London 1862).

Browning, Colin Arrott, *The Convict Ship* (London 1844).

Browning, Colin Arrott, *The Convict Ship, and England's Exiles* (London 1847).

Bull, J.W., *Early Experiences of Life in South Australia* (Adelaide 1884).

Burn, David, *A Picture of Van Diemen's Land* (Hobart 1973; first pub. 1840–41).

Burton, W.W., *The State of Religion and Education in New South Wales* (London 1840).

Butlin, N.G., C.W. Cromwell, and K.L. Suthern (eds), *General Return of Convicts in New South Wales, 1837* (Sydney 1987).

Byrne, Geraldine (ed.), *Valiant Women: Letters from the Foundation Sisters of Mercy in Western Australia, 1845–1849* (Melbourne 1981).

Cambridge, Ada, *Thirty Years in Australia* (Sydney 1989; first pub. 1901–02).

Cambridge, Ada, *Unspoken Thoughts* (Canberra 1988; first pub. 1887).

Capper, Henry, *South Australia: Containing Hints to Emigrants; Proceedings of the South Australian Company* (London 1838).

Carboni, Raffaello, *The Eureka Stockade* (Melbourne 1855).

Carlyle, Thomas, *Critical and Miscellaneous Essays* (London 1899).

Carlyle, Thomas, *Sartor Resartus* (ed. J.A.S. Barrett) (London 1897; first pub. 1833–34).

Carpenter, Mary, *Reformatory Schools for the Children of the Perishing and Dangerous Classes and for Juvenile Offenders* (London 1851).

Casey, Albert Eugene (ed.), *O'Kief, Coshe Mang, Slieve Lougher and Upper Blackwater in Ireland* (seventeen volumes; Birmingham, Alabama, 1952–79).

Chapman, Peter (ed.), *The Diaries and Letters of G.T.W.B. Boyes*, vol. 1 (Melbourne 1985).

Chisholm, Caroline, *Emigration and Transportation Relatively Considered* (London 1847).

Clark, C.M.H. (ed.), *Select Documents in Australian History 1788–1850* (Sydney 1950).

Clarke, Alfred, *Raw Gold and Sovereigns, Free Trade in Money, and No Export Duty on Gold* (Geelong 1855).

Cockburn, F.J., *Letters from the Southern Hemisphere* (Calcutta 1856).

Collins, Wilkie, *The Woman in White* (London 1906).

Cook, Thomas, *The Exile's Lamentations* (Sydney 1978).

Cowan, Peter (ed.), *A Faithful Picture: The Letters of Eliza and Thomas Brown at York in the Swan River Colony 1841–1852* (Fremantle 1977).

Cunningham, Peter, *Two Years in New South Wales* (Sydney 1966; first pub. 1827).

Curr, Edward, *An Account of the Colony of Van Diemen's Land* (London 1824).

Dawson, James, *Australian Aborigines: The Languages and Customs of Several Tribes of Aborigines in the Western District of Victoria, Australia* (Melbourne 1881).

de Bary, W. Theodore (ed.), *Sources of Indian Tradition* (New York 1958).

de Tocqueville, Alexis, *Democracy in America* (trans. George Lawrence; ed. J.P. Mayer and Max Lerner) (New York 1966).

Delano, Amasa, *A Narrative of Voyages and Travels* (Boston, Mass., 1817).

Dickens, Charles, *Nicholas Nickleby* (London 1907; first pub. 1838–39).

Dickens, Charles, *The Old Curiosity Shop* (London 1953; first pub. 1841).

Dickens, Charles, *Dombey and Son* (London 1970; first pub. 1848).

Dickens, Charles, *Great Expectations* (Ware, Herts., 1992; first pub. 1860–61).

Dickey, Brian, and Peter Howell (eds), *South Australia's Foundation: Select Documents* (Adelaide 1986).

Disraeli, Benjamin, *Tancred; or, The New Crusade* (London 1927; first pub. 1847).

Dobie, William Wilson, *Recollections of a Visit to Port-Phillip, Australia, in 1852–55* (Edinburgh 1856).

Earp, G.B., *What We Did in Australia* (London 1853).

Eliot, George, *Middlemarch* (London 1967; first pub. 1872).

Emerson, Ralph Waldo, *Essays and Lectures* (New York 1983).

Evans, G.W., *A Geographical, Historical, and Topographical Description of Van Diemen's Land* (London 1822).

Fauchery, Antoine, *Letters from a Miner in Australia* (Melbourne 1965).

Fenton, Elizabeth, *The Journal of Mrs Fenton: A Narrative of Her Life in India, the Isle of France (Mauritius), and Tasmania During the Years 1826–1830* (London 1901).

Field, Barron, *First Fruits of Australian Poetry* (Canberra 1990; first pub. 1819).

Field, Barron, *Geographical Memoirs on New South Wales* (London 1825).

Fitzsymonds, Eustace (ed.), *A Looking-Glass for Tasmania* (Hobart 1980).

Foster, John Fitzgerald Leslie, *The New Colony of Victoria, Formerly Port Phillip* (London 1851).

Fox, Lady Mary, *Account of an Expedition to the Interior of New Holland* (London 1837).

Frost, Lucy (ed.), *No Place for a Nervous Lady* (Melbourne 1984).

Frost, Lucy, *A Face in the Glass: The Journal and Life of Annie Baxter Dawbin* (Melbourne 1992).

Fry, Elizabeth, *Observations on the Visiting, Superintendence, and Government of Female Prisoners* (London 1827).

'Garryowen' [Edmund Finn], *The Chronicles of Early Melbourne 1835 to 1852* (Melbourne 1888).

Gaskell, Elizabeth, *Mary Barton: A Tale of Manchester Life* (London 1970; first pub. 1848).

Gaskell, Elizabeth, *The Life of Charlotte Brontë* (Oxford 1919; first pub. 1857).

Godwin, William, *Thoughts on Man; His Nature, Productions and Discoveries* (London 1831).

Green, Neville (ed.), *Nyungar – The People: Aboriginal Customs in the Southwest of Australia* (Perth 1979).

Greenwood, F. Murray (ed. and trans.), *Land of a Thousand Sorrows: The Australian Prison Journal, 1840–1842, of the Exiled Canadien Patriote, François-Maurice Lepailleur* (Melbourne 1980).

Griffiths, Charles, *The Present State and Prospects of the Port Phillip District of New South Wales* (Dublin 1845).

Gunson, Neil (ed.), *Australian Reminiscences and Papers of L.E. Threlkeld, Missionary to the Aborigines 1824–1859* (Canberra 1974).

Hall, William H., *Practical Experience at the Diggings of the Gold Fields of Victoria* (London 1852).

Halloran, Laurence, *Proposals for the Foundation and Support of a Public Free Grammar School, in the Town of Sydney, New South Wales* (Sydney 1825).

Hamilton-Arnold, Barbara (ed.), *Letters and Papers of G.P. Harris 1803–1812* (Melbourne 1994).

Hargraves, E.H., *Australia and its Gold Fields* (London 1855).

Harris, Alexander, *Settlers and Convicts: Recollections of Sixteen Years' Labour in the Australian Backwoods* (Melbourne 1953; first pub. 1847).

Harris, Alexander, *The Emigrant Family: or, The Story of an Australian Settler* (Canberra 1967; first pub. 1849).

Hawthorne, Nathaniel, *The Scarlet Letter: A Romance* (London 1965; first pub. 1850).

Heard, Dora (ed.), *The Journal of Charles O'Hara Booth, Commandant of the Port Arthur Penal Settlement* (Hobart 1981).

Henty, W., *On Improvements in Cottage Husbandry* (Launceston [1851]).

Hill, Rowland, *Post Office Reform; Its Importance and Practicability* (London 1837).

Home, Henry, Lord Kames, *Sketches of the History of Man* (Edinburgh 1778).

Howitt, William, *Life in Victoria: or, Victoria in 1853, and Victoria in 1858* (Kilmore, Vic., 1977).

Hunter, John, *An Historical Journal of the Transactions at Port Jackson and Norfolk Island* (London 1793).

Jones, H. Berkeley, *Adventures in Australia, in 1852 and 1853* (London 1853).

Just, P., *Australia; or, Notes taken During a Residence in the Colonies from the Gold Discovery in 1851 till 1857* (Dundee 1859).

Knox, Vicesimus, *Essays, Moral and Literary* (two volumes; London 1821).

Knox, Vicesimus, *The Works of Vicesimus Knox, D.D.* (seven volumes; London 1824).

'Lady Long Resident in New South Wales, A', [Charlotte Barton], *A Mother's Offering to Her Children* (Sydney 1841).

'Lady, A' [Emma McPherson], *My Experiences in Australia: Being Recollections of a Visit to the Australian Colonies in 1856–7* (London 1860).

Lang, John Dunmore, *Emigration to Port Phillip* (London 1848).

Lang, John Dunmore, *Freedom and Independence for the Golden Lands of Australia: The Right of the Colonies, and the Interest of Britain and of the World* (London 1852).

Lang, John Dunmore, *Poems: Sacred and Secular* (Sydney 1873).

Leichhardt, Ludwig, *Journal of an Overland Expedition in Australia* (London 1847).

Leigh, W.H., *Reconnoitering Voyages, Travels and Adventures in the New Colonies of South Australia* (London 1839).

Lempriere, Thomas James, *The Penal Settlements of Early Van Diemen's Land* (Launceston 1954).

M[artin], J.B., *Reminiscences* (Camden, NSW, 1884).

Macarthur Onslow, Sibella (ed.), *Some Early Records of the Macarthurs of Camden* (Sydney 1914).

Macarthur, James, *New South Wales; Its Present State and Future Prospects* (London 1837).

Mackenzie, David, *The Gold Digger: A Visit to the Gold Fields of Australia in February 1852* (London [1853?]).

Mackenzie, Eneas, *Memoirs of Mrs Caroline Chisholm with an Account of Her Philanthropic Labours in India, Australia and England* (London 1852).

McCombie, Thomas, *The History of the Colony of Victoria* (Melbourne 1858).

McManus, Mary, *Reminiscences of the Early Settlement in the Maranoa District* (Brisbane 1913).

Maconochie, Alexander, *Australiana: Thoughts on Convict Management, and Other Subjects Connected with the Australian Penal Colonies* (London 1839).

Marriott, Edward West (ed.), *The Memoirs of Obed West: A Portrait of Early Sydney* (Bowral 1988).

Mayhew, H., and J. Binny, *The Criminal Prisons of London and Scenes of Prison Life* (London 1862).

'Melbourne Merchant, A', *The Gold Era of Victoria* (London 1855).

Melville, Herman, *Moby-Dick; or, The Whale* (ed. Luther S. Mansfield and Howard P. Vincent) (New York 1962; first pub. 1851).

Meredith, Mrs Charles, *Notes and Sketches of New South Wales* (London 1844).

Mill, John Stuart, *The Early Draft of John Stuart Mill's Autobiography* (ed. Jack Stillinger) (Urbana, Ill,. 1961).

Mill, John Stuart, *The Subjection of Women* (ed. Susan Moller Okin) (Indianapolis 1988; first pub. 1869).

Mitchell, Adrian (ed.), *Charles Harpur* (Melbourne 1973).

Mitchell, T.L., *Three Expeditions into the Interior of Eastern Australia* (two volumes; London 1839).

Moore, George Fletcher, *Diary of Ten Years Eventful Life of an Early Settler in Western Australia* (London 1884).

Moorhouse, Matthew, *A Vocabulary, and Outline of the Grammatical Structure of the Murray River Language* (Adelaide 1846).

Moran, P.F., *History of the Catholic Church in Australasia* (two volumes; Sydney 1891).

Mossman, Samuel, *Emigrants' Letters from Australia* (London 1853).

Mundy, G.C., *Our Antipodes* (three volumes; London 1852).

Murray, Robert Dundas, *A Summer at Port Phillip* (Edinburgh 1843).

Nichols, Mary (ed.), *The Diary of the Reverend Robert Knopwood, 1803–1838, First Chaplain of Van Diemen's Land* (Hobart 1977).

Nietzsche, Friedrich, *The Will to Power* (trans. Anthony M. Ludovici) (two volumes; New York 1964).

O'Farrell, Patrick (ed.), *Documents in Australian Catholic History* (London 1969), vol. 1.

Oxley, John, *Journal of Two Expeditions into the Interior of New South Wales* (London 1820).

Parkes, A.T., *An Emigrant's Home Letters* (Sydney 1896).

Perry, Sarah Susannah, *'Durable Riches'; or, A Voice from the Golden Land* (ed. Alfred J. Perry) (London 1857).

'Philadelphus' [Saxe Bannister], *Remarks on the Indians of North America, in a Letter to an Edinburgh Reviewer* (London 1822).

Plomley, N.J.B. (ed.), *Friendly Mission: The Tasmanian Journals and Papers of George Augustus Robinson, 1824–1834* (Hobart 1966).

Plomley, N.J.B., *A Word-List of the Tasmanian Aboriginal Languages* (Hobart 1976).

Plomley, N.J.B. (ed.), *Weep in Silence: A History of the Flinders Island Aboriginal Settlement* (Hobart 1987).

Poe, Edgar Allan, *The Complete Tales and Poems of Edgar Allan Poe* (London 1982).

Prinsep, Mrs Augustus, *The Journal of a Voyage from Calcutta to Van Diemen's Land* (London 1833).

Read, C. Rudston, *What I Heard, Saw, and Did at the Australian Gold Fields* (London 1853).

Report of the Proceedings of the General Meeting of the Supporters of the Petitions to His Majesty and the House of Commons, Held at the Committee Rooms, May 30, 1836 (Sydney 1836).

'Resident, A' [E. Ramsay-Laye], *Social Life and Manners in Australia* (London 1861).

Ritchie, John (ed.), *The Evidence of the Bigge Reports* (Melbourne 1971).

Robson, John M. (gen. ed.), *Collected Works of John Stuart Mill* (33 volumes; Toronto 1986).

Ross, James, *Dr Ross's Recollections of a Short Excursion to Lake Echo in Van Diemen's Land 1823* (Hobart 1992).

Rowcroft, Charles, *Tales of the Colonies; or, The Adventures of an Emigrant* (London 1858).

Ruskin, John, *Sesame and Lilies* (London 1960).

Ruskin, John, *The Complete Works of John Ruskin* (ed. E.T. Cook and Alexander Wedderburn) (39 volumes; London 1903–12).

Sainty, Malcolm R., and Keith A. Johnson (eds), *Census of New South Wales, November 1828* (Sydney 1980).

Savery, Henry, *The Bitter Bread of Banishment* (that is, *Quintus Servinton*) (Sydney 1984; first pub. 1830–31).

Savery, Henry, *The Hermit in Van Diemen's Land* (ed. Cecil Hadgraft) (St Lucia 1964; first pub. 1829–30).

Schaffer, Irene (ed.), *Land Musters, Stock Returns and Lists, Van Diemen's Land 1803–1822* (Hobart 1991).

Scott, Sir Walter, *Ivanhoe* (Edinburgh 1998; first pub. 1819).

Scott, Sir Walter, *Rob Roy* (London 1831; first pub. 1818).

Sidney, Samuel, *The Three Colonies of Australia: New South Wales, Victoria, South Australia; Their Pastures, Copper Mines, and Gold Fields* (London 1853).

Silvester, E.K. (ed.), *The Speeches, in the Legislative Council of New South Wales, on the Second Reading of the Bill for Framing a New Constitution for the Colony* (Sydney 1853).

Simonde de Sismondi, J.C.L., *Histoire des Républiques Italiennes du Moyen Age* (Paris 1840).

Spence, Catherine Helen, *Clara Morison* (Adelaide 1971; first pub. 1854).

Spence, Catherine Helen, *Tender and True: A Colonial Tale* (London 1862),

Spencer, Henry, *Men That Are Gone from the Households of Darlington* (Darlington, co. Durham, 1862).

Stephens, Alexander, *Memoirs of John Horne Tooke* (two volumes; London 1813).

Stokes, J. Lort, *Discoveries in Australia* (two volumes; London 1846).

Stoney, H. Butler, *Victoria: A Description of Its Principal Cities, Melbourne and Geelong: and Remarks on the Present State of the Colony* (London 1856).

Stormon, E.J. (trans. and ed.), *The Salvado Memoirs: Historical Memoirs of Australia and Particularly of the Benedictine Mission of New Norcia and of the Habits and Customs of the Australian Natives by Dom Rosendo Salvado, O.S.B.* (Nedlands 1977).

Stowe, Harriet Beecher, *Uncle Tom's Cabin; or, Life among the Lowly* (London 1981; first pub. 1852).

Sturt, Charles, *Narrative of an Expedition into Central Australia* (Adelaide 2001; first pub. 1849).

Sturt, Charles, *Two Expeditions into the Interior of Southern Australia* (two volumes; London 1833).

Suttor, H.M., *Australian Milestones and Stories of the Past, 1770–1914* (Sydney 1925).

Syme, J., *Nine Years in Van Diemen's Land* (Dundee 1848).

Teichelmann, C.G., and C.W. Schurmann, *Outlines of a Grammar, Vocabulary, and Phraseology, of the Aboriginal Language of South Australia* (Adelaide 1840).

Therry, Roger, *Reminiscences of Thirty Years' Residence in New South Wales and Victoria* (London 1863).

Thomas, Evan Kyffin (ed.), *The Diary and Letters of Mary Thomas (1836–1866)* (Adelaide 1925).

Tomlinson, Gerry, *'Bring Plenty of Pickles': Letters from an Emigrant Family* (Waddesdon, Bucks., 1986).

Tompson, Charles, *Wild Notes, from the Lyre of a Native Minstrel* (Sydney 1826).

Tooke, John Horne, *The Diversions of Purley* (two volumes; London 1786, 1805).

Trollope, Anthony, *Doctor Thorne* (London 1924; first pub. 1858).

Trollope, Anthony, *The Small House at Allington* (London 1909; first pub. 1864).

Trollope, Anthony, *The Last Chronicle of Barset* (London 1909; first pub. 1867).

Trollope, Anthony, *Australia and New Zealand* (Melbourne 1876; first pub. 1873).

Tucker, James, *Ralph Rashleigh* (Sydney 1962).

Tuke, Samuel, *Description of the Retreat, an Institution near York for Insane Persons of the Society of Friends* (York 1813).

Ullathorne, W., *A Reply to Judge Burton, of the Supreme Court of New South Wales, on 'The State of Religion' in the Colony* (Sydney 1840).

Ullathorne, William, *The Catholic Mission in Australasia* (Liverpool 1837).

Ullathorne, William, *From Cabin-Boy to Archbishop: The Autobiography of Archbishop Ullathorne* (London 1941).

Wakefield, E.G., *A Letter from Sydney and other Writings on Colonization* (London 1929).

Ward, James, *A History of Gold as a Commodity and as a Measure of Value* (London [1852]).

Ward, Russel (ed.), *The Penguin Book of Australian Ballads* (London 1964).

Wathen, George Henry, *The Golden Colony: or, Victoria in 1854* (London 1855).

Wells, T.E., *Michael Howe, the Last and Worst of the Bushrangers of Van Diemen's Land* (ed. George Mackaness) (Dubbo 1979; first pub. 1818).

Wentworth, W.C., *Australasia* (London 1823).

Wentworth, W.C., *Statistical, Historical, and Political Description of the Colony of New South Wales, and Its Dependent Settlements in Van Diemen's Land* (London 1819).

West, John, *The History of Tasmania* (ed. A.G.L. Shaw) (Sydney 1971; first pub. 1852).

Westgarth, W., *Personal Recollections of Early Melbourne and Victoria* (Melbourne 1888).

Westgarth, William, *Australia Felix; or, A Historical and Descriptive Account of the Settlement of Port Phillip, New South Wales* (Edinburgh 1848).

Westgarth, William, *Victoria: Late Australia Felix, or Port Phillip District of New South Wales* (Edinburgh 1853).

Westgarth, William, *Victoria and the Australian Gold Mines in 1857* (London 1857).

Widowson, Henry, *Present State of Van Diemen's Land* (London 1829).

Wilkes, Charles, *Narrative of the U.S. Exploring Expedition, During the Years 1838, 1839, 1840, 1841, 1842* (London 1845).

Wilson, William Dobie, *Recollections of a Visit to Port-Phillip, Australia, in 1852–55* (Edinburgh 1856).

Withers, W.B., *The History of Ballarat, from the First Pastoral Settlement to the Present Time* (Ballarat 1870).

Wollaston, John Ramsden, *Wollaston's Picton Journal (1841–1844)* (ed. A. Burton and Percy W. Henn) (Nedlands 1975).

2. Books by Modern Scholars

Aarsleff, Hans, *The Study of Language in England 1780–1860* (Minneapolis 1983).

Allen, Judith A., *Sex and Secrets: Crimes Involving Australian Women since 1880* (Melbourne 1990).

Amos, Keith, *The Fenians in Australia 1865–1880* (Sydney 1988).

Anderson, R.D., *Education and the Scottish People 1750–1918* (Oxford 1995).

Archer, John E., *By a Flash and a Scare: Incendiarism, Animal Maiming, and Poaching in East Anglia 1815–1870* (Oxford 1990).

Atkinson, Alan, and Marian Aveling (eds), *Australian 1838* (Sydney 1987).

Atkinson, Alan, *Camden: Farm and Village Life in Early New South Wales* (Melbourne 1988).

Atkinson, Alan, *The Europeans in Australia: A History*, vol. 1 (*The Beginning*) (Melbourne 1997).

Atkinson, Alan, *The Commonwealth of Speech: An Argument about Australia's Past, Present and Future* (Melbourne 2002).

Attwood, Bain, and Stephen Foster (eds), *Frontier Conflict: The Australian Experience* (Canberra 2003).

Austin, A.G., *Australian Education 1788–1900* (Melbourne 1972).

Baker, Sidney J., *The Australian Language: The Meanings, Origins and Usage; From Convict Days to the Present* (Sydney 1978).

Barcan, Alan, *Two Centuries of Education in New South Wales* (Sydney 1988).

Barrett, Bernard, *The Inner Suburbs: The Evolution of an Industrial Area* (Melbourne 1971).

Barrett, John, *That Better Country: The Religious Aspect of Life in Eastern Australia 1835–1850* (Melbourne 1966).

Bassett, Marnie, *The Hentys: An Australian Colonial Tapestry* (London 1954).

Bate, Weston, *Lucky City: The First Generation at Ballarat 1851–1901* (Melbourne 1978).

Bate, Weston, *Victorian Gold Rushes* (Melbourne 1988).

Bayly, C.A., *Empire and Information: Intelligence Gathering and Social Communication in India, 1780–1870* (Cambridge 1999).

Benson, C. Irving, *A Century of Victorian Methodism* (Melbourne 1935).

Billot, C.P., *The Life and Times of John Pascoe Fawkner* (Melbourne).

Birman, Wendy, *Gregory of Rainworth, a Man in His Time* (Nedlands 1979).

Blainey, Geoffrey, *The Tyranny of Distance: How Distance Shaped Australia's History* (Melbourne 1966).

Blainey, Geoffrey, *The Rush that Never Ended: A History of Australian Mining* (Melbourne 1969).

Bloom, Harold, *The Western Canon: The Books and School of the Ages* (London 1995).

Bogle, Michael, *Convicts* (Sydney 1999).

Bolger, Peter, *Hobart Town* (Canberra 1973).

Bolt, Christine, *Victorian Attitudes to Race* (London 1971).

Bolton, G.C., *A Thousand Miles Away: A History of North Queensland to 1920* (Brisbane 1963).

Boow, James, *Early Australian Commercial Glass: Manufacturing Processes* (Sydney 1991).

Bourke, D.F., *The History of the Catholic Church in Western Australia* (Perth 1979).

Boyce, George, James Curren, and Pauline Wingate (eds), *Newspaper History from the Seventeenth Century to the Present Day* (London 1978).

Brandt, Deborah, *Literacy as Involvement: The Acts of Writers, Readers, and Texts* (Carbonvale, Ill. 1990).

Bridge, Carl, *A Trunk Full of Books: History of the State Library of South Australia and Its Forerunners* (Adelaide 1986).

Broeze, Frank, *Mr Brooks and the Australian Trade: Imperial Business in the Nineteenth Century* (Melbourne 1993).

Broome, Richard, *Aboriginal Australians: Black Response to White Dominance 1788–1980* (Sydney 1982).

Brown-May, Andrew, *Melbourne Street Life: The Itinerary of Our Days* (Melbourne 1988).

Burgmann, Verity, and Jenny Lee (eds), *A Most Valuable Acquisition: A People's History of Australia since 1788* (Melbourne 1988).

Burroughs, Peter, *Britain and Australia 1831–1855: A Study in Imperial Relations and Crown Lands Administration* (Oxford 1967).

Butler, Marilyn, *Romantics, Rebels and Revolutionaries* (Oxford 1981).

Butlin, S.J., *Foundations of the Australian Monetary System 1788–1851* (Sydney 1953).

Buxton, G.L., *The Riverina, 1861–1891: An Australian Regional Study* (Melbourne 1967).

Byatt, A.S., *Unruly Times: Wordsworth and Coleridge in their Time* (London 1997).

Byrne, Paula J., *Criminal Law and Colonial Subject: New South Wales 1810–1830* (Cambridge 1993).

Cameron, J.M.R., *Ambition's Fire: The Agricultural Colonization of Pre-Convict Western Australia* (Nedlands 1981).

Campbell, Alastair H., *John Batman and the Aborigines* (Melbourne [1987?]).

Cannon, Michael, *Australia in the Victorian Age* (three volumes; Melbourne 1971).

Castles, Alex C., *An Australian Legal History* (Sydney 1982).

Castles, Alex C., and Michael C. Harris, *Lawmakers and Wayward Whigs: Government and Law in South Australia 1836–1986* (Adelaide 1987).

Chadwick, Owen, *The Spirit of the Oxford Movement: Tractarian Essays* (Cambridge 1990).

Chapman, G., *One Lord, One Faith, One Baptism: A History of Churches of Christ in Australia* (Melbourne 1989).

Charlwood, *The Long Farewell: The Perilous Voyages of Settlers under Sail in the Great Migrations to Australia* (Melbourne 1981).

Christie, M.F., *Aborigines in Colonial Victoria 1835–86* (Sydney 1979).

Clark, C.M.H., *A History of Australia* (six volumes; Melbourne1962–87).

Clarke, F.G., *The Land of Contrarieties: British Attitudes to the Australian Colonies 1828–1855* (Melbourne 1977).

Clarke, Patricia, *Pioneer Writer: The Life of Louisa Atkinson: Novelist, Journalist, Naturalist* (Sydney 1990).

Clay, John, *Maconochie's Experiment* (London 2001).

Collins, Patrick, *Goodbye Bussamarai: The Mandandanji Land War, Southern Queensland 1842–1852* (St Lucia 2002).

Connell, R.W., and T.H. Irving, *Class Structure in Australian History: Documents, Narrative and Argument* (Melbourne 1980).

Connor, John, *The Australian Frontier Wars 1788–1838* (Sydney 2002).

Cosgrove, D., and S. Daniels (eds), *The Iconography of Landscape: Essays on the Symbolic Representation, Design and Use of Past Environments* (Cambridge 1988).

Critchett, Jan, A *'Distant Field of Murder'*: Western District Frontiers, 1834–1848 (Melbourne 1990).

Crowley, F.K., *Australia's Western Third: A History of Western Australia from the First Settlements to Modern Times* (London 1960).

Cumes, J.W.C., *Their Chastity Was Not Too Rigid: Leisure Times in Early Australia* (Melbourne 1979).

Cumpston, J.H.L., *Augustus Gregory and the Inland Sea* (Canberra 1972).

Cumpston, J.S., *Kangaroo Island 1800–1836* (Canberra 1970).

Cunningham, Chris, *The Blue Mountains Rediscovered: Beyond the Myths of Early Australian Exploration* (Sydney 1996).

Currey, C.H., *Sir Francis Forbes, First Chief Justice of the Supreme Court of New South Wales* (Sydney 1968).

Curthoys, Ann, and Andrew Markus (eds), *Who are Our Enemies?: Racism and the Working Class in Australia* (Sydney 1978).

Damousi, Joy, *Depraved and Disorderly: Female Convicts, Sexuality and Gender in Colonial Australia* (Cambridge 1997).

Daniels, Kay, *Convict Women: Rough Culture and Reformation* (Sydney 1998).

Darragh, Thomas A., *Printer and Newspaper Registration in Victoria 1838–1924* (Wellington, NZ, 1997).

Daunton, M.J., *Royal Mail: The Post Office Since 1840* (London 1985).

Davidoff, Leonore, and Catherine Hall, *Family Fortunes: Men and Women of the English Middle Class 1780–1850* (London 1987).

Davidoff, Leonore, *Worlds Between: Historical Perspectives on Gender and Class* (Cambridge 1995).

Davis, Richard P., *The Tasmanian Gallows: A Study of Capital Punishment* (Hobart 1974).

Davison, Graeme, *The Rise and Fall of Marvellous Melbourne* (Melbourne 1978).

Davison, Graeme, *The Unforgiving Minute: How Australia Learned to Tell the Time* (Melbourne 1993).

Davison, Graeme, *The Use and Abuse of Australian History* (Sydney 2000).

Denholm, David, *The Colonial Australians* (London 1979).

de Serville, Paul, *Port Phillip Gentlemen and Good Society in Melbourne before the Gold Rushes* (Melbourne 1980).

de Serville, Paul, *Rolph Boldrewood: A Life* (Melbourne 2000).

Diamond, Marion, *The Seahorse and the Wanderer: Ben Boyd in Australia* (Melbourne 1988).

Diamond, Marion, *Creative Meddler: The Life and Fantasies of Charles St Julian* (Melbourne 1990).

Dickey, Brian, *Rations, Residence, Resources: A History of Social Welfare in South Australia since 1836* (Adelaide 1986).

Dixson, Miriam, *The Real Matilda: Woman and Identity in Australia 1788 to the Present* (Melbourne 1994).

Dixson, Miriam, *The Imaginary Australian: Anglo-Celts and Identity – 1788 to the Present* (Sydney 1999).

Donovan, P.F., *A Land Full of Possibilities: A History of South Australia's Northern Territory* (St Lucia 1981).

Douglas, Ann, *The Feminization of American Culture* (London 1996).

Duffield, Ian, and James Bradley (eds), *Representing Convicts: New Perspectives on Convict Forced Labour Migration* (London 1997).

Dunstan, David, *Governing the Metropolis – Politics, Technology and Social Change in a Victorian City: Melbourne, 1850–1891* (Melbourne 1984).

Dyster, Barrie, *Servant and Master: Building and Running the Grand Houses of Sydney 1788–1850* (Sydney 1989).

Eaden, P.R., and F.H. Mares (eds), *Mapped But Not Known: The Australian Landscape of the Imagination* (Adelaide 1986).

Erickson, Rica, *The Drummonds of Hawthornden* (Nedlands 1975).

Erickson, Rica, *The Brand on His Coat: Biographies of Some Western Australian Convicts* (Nedlands 1983).

Evans, Raymond, *Fighting Words: Writing about Race* (St Lucia 1999).

Evans, Raymond, Kay Saunders, and Kathryn Cronin, *Exclusion, Exploitation and Extermination: Race Relations in Colonial Queensland* (Sydney 1975).

Feather, John, *The Provincial Book Trade in Eighteenth-Century England* (Cambridge 1985).

Fels, Marie, *Good Men and True: The Aboriginal Police of the Port Phillip District 1837–1853* (Melbourne 1988).

Ferry, John, *Colonial Armidale* (St Lucia 1999).

Finnane, Mark (ed.), *Policing in Australia: Historical Perspectives* (Sydney 1987).

Finnane, Mark, *Punishment in Australian Society* (Melbourne 1997).

Fitzgerald, Shirley, *Rising Damp: Sydney 1870–90* (Melbourne 1987).

Fletcher, Brian H., *The Grand Parade: A History of the Royal Agricultural Society of New South Wales* (Sydney 1988).

Foster, Robert, Rick Hosking, and Amanda Nettelbeck, *Fatal Collisions: The South Australian Frontier and the Violence of Memory* (Adelaide 2001).

Fox, Len, *The Eureka Flag* (Sydney 1992).

Frost, Lionel, *Australian Cities in Comparative View* (Melbourne 1990).

Frost, Lucy, and Hamish Maxwell-Stewart (eds), *Chain Letters: Narrating Convict Lives* (Melbourne 2001).

Gabay, Alfred J., *Messages from Beyond: Spiritualism and Spiritualists in Melbourne's Golden Age 1870–1890* (Melbourne 2001).

Galison, Peter, and Emily Thompson (eds), *The Architecture of Science* (Cambridge, Mass., 1999).

Garden, Donald S., *Albany: A Panorama of the Sound* (Melbourne 1977).

Garden, Donald S., *Northam: An Avon Valley History* (Melbourne 1979).

Gardiner, Paul, *An Extraordinary Australian: Mary MacKillop* (Sydney 1993).

Gascoigne, John, *The Enlightenment and the Origins of European Australia* (Cambridge 2002).

Gay, Peter, *The Bourgeois Experience: Victoria to Freud* (five volumes; London 1984–99).

Gilbert, Alan D., *Religion and Society in Industrial England: Church, Chapel and Social Change, 1740–1914* (London 1976).

Glynn, Sean, *Urbanisation in Australian History, 1788–1900* (Melbourne 1975).

Golder, Hilary, *Divorce in 19th Century New South Wales* (Sydney 1985).

Goodman, David, *Gold Seeking: Victoria and California in the 1850s* (Sydney 1994).

Gowing, Laura, *Domestic Dangers: Women, Words, and Sex in Early Modern London* (Oxford 1996).

Grabosky, Peter N., *Sydney in Ferment: Crime, Dissent and Official Reaction 1788 to 1973* (Canberra 1977).

Greenop, Frank S., *History of Magazine Publishing in Australia* (Sydney 1947).

Gregson, Jesse, *The Australian Agricultural Company 1824–1875* (Sydney 1907).

Griffith, Tom, *Hunters and Collectors: The Antiquarian Imagination in Australia* (Melbourne 1996).

Grimshaw, Patricia, and others (eds), *Families in Colonial Australia* (Sydney 1985).

Grimshaw, Patricia, and others, *Creating a Nation 1788–1990* (Melbourne 1994).

Grimshaw, Patricia, Susan Janson, and Marian Quartly (eds), *Freedom Bound I: Documents on Women in Colonial Australia* (Sydney 1995).

Grossman, Dave, *On Killing* (Boston 1996).

Hainsworth, D.R., *The Sydney Traders: Simeon Lord and his Contemporaries 1788–1821* (Melbourne 1972).

Hancock, W.K., *Australia* (London 1930).

Hannaford, Ivan, *Race: The History of an Idea in the West* (Washington 1996).

Harrison, John F.C., *Quest for a New Moral World: Robert Owen and the Owenites in Britain and America* (New York 1969).

Harrison, J.F.C., *The Second Coming: Popular Millenarianism 1780–1850* (London 1979).

Hart, James D., *The Popular Book: A History of America's Literary Taste* (Berkeley 1961).

Hartwell, R.M., *The Economic Development of Van Diemen's Land 1820–1850* (Melbourne 1954).

Hasluck, Alexandra, *Thomas Peel of Swan River* (Melbourne 1965).

Hasluck, Alexandra, *Portrait with Background: A Life of Georgiana Molloy* (Melbourne 1966).

Hassell, Kathleen, *The Relations Between the Settlers and Aborigines in South Australia, 1836–1860* (Adelaide 1966).

Hazzard, Margaret, *Punishment Short of Death: A History of the Penal Settlement at Norfolk Island* (Melbourne 1984).

Hetherington, Penelope, *Childhood and Society in Western Australia* (Nedlands 1988).

Hill, Barry, *Broken Song: T.G.H. Strehlow and Aboriginal Possession* (Sydney 2002).

Hilliard, David, *Godliness and Good Order: A History of the Anglican Church in South Australia* (Adelaide 1986).

Hirst, J.B., *Adelaide and the Country 1870–1917: Their Social and Political Relationship* (Melbourne 1973).

Hirst, J.B., *Convict Society and Its Enemies: A History of Early New South Wales* (Sydney 1983).

Hirst, J.B., *The Strange Birth of Colonial Democracy: New South Wales 1848–1884* (Sydney 1988).

Hodge, Brian, *Major Controversies of the Australian Goldrush: Contenders, Pretenders and Prevaricators* (Tambaroora, NSW, 2003).

Holden, Robert, *Bunyips: Australia's Folklore of Fear* (Canberra 2001).

Hollinsworth, David, *Race and Racism in Australia* (Katoomba, NSW 1998).

Holthouse, Hector, *River of Gold: The Story of the Palmer River Gold Rush* (Sydney 1967).

Horsman, Reginald, *Josiah Nott of Mobile: Southerner, Physician, and Racial Theorist* (Baton Rouge 1987).

Hughes, Robert, *The Fatal Shore: A History of the Transportation of Convicts to Australia 1787–1868* (London 1988).

Hunt, C.J., *The Book Trade in Northumberland and Durham to 1860* (Newcastle-upon-Tyne 1975).

Hutchinson, Mark, and Stuart Piggin (eds), *Reviving Australia: Essays on the History and Experience of Revival and Revivalism in Australian Christianity* (Sydney 1994).

Inglis, K.S., *The Australian Colonists: An Exploration of Social History, 1788–1870* (Melbourne 1974).

Irvin, Eric, *The Theatre Comes to Australia* (St Lucia 1971).

Irving, Terry (ed.), *Challenges to Labour History* (Sydney 1994).

Jaensch, Dean (ed.), *The Flinders History of South Australia: Political History* (Adelaide 1986).

Jalland, Pat, *Australian Ways of Death: A Social and Cultural History 1840–1918* (Melbourne 2002).

Jordan, Robert, *The Convict Theatres of Early Australia 1788–1840* (Sydney 2002).

Judd, Stephen, and Kenneth Cable, *Sydney Anglicans: A History of the Diocese* (Sydney 2000).

Jupp, James (ed.), *The Australian People: An Encyclopedia of the Nation, Its People and Their Origins* (Sydney 1988).

Karskens, Grace, *The Rocks: Life in Early Sydney* (Melbourne 1997).

Kercher, Bruce, *An Unruly Child: A History of Law in Australia* (Sydney 1995).

Kiddle, Margaret, *Men of Yesterday: A Social History of the Western District of Victoria, 1834–1890* (Melbourne 1961).

Kiddle, Margaret, *Caroline Chisholm* (Melbourne 1969).

King, Hazel, *Richard Bourke* (Melbourne 1971).

Kingston, Beverley, *The Oxford History of Australia*, vol. 3 (*1860–1900: Glad, Confident Morning*) (Melbourne 1988).

Kociumbas, Jan, *The Oxford History of Australia*, vol. 2 (*1770–1860: Possessions*) (Melbourne 1992).

Lee, Robert, *Colonial Engineer: John Whitton 1819–1898 and the Building of Australia's Railways* (Sydney 2000).

Lee, Robert, *The Greatest Public Work: The New South Wales Railways – 1848 to 1889* (Sydney 1988).

Levi, J.S., and G.F. Bergman, *Australian Genesis: Jewish Convicts and Settlers 1788–1850* (Adelaide 1974).

Linge, G.J.R., *Industrial Awakening: A Geography of Australian Manufacturing 1788 to 1890* (Canberra 1979).

Linn, Rob, *Power, Progress and Profit: A History of the Australian Accounting Profession* (Melbourne 1996).

Liston, Carol, *Sarah Wentworth, Mistress of Vaucluse* (Sydney 1988).

Livingston, K.T., *The Wired Nation Continent: The Communication Revolution and Federating Australia* (Melbourne 1996).

Lohrli, Anne, *Household Words, A Weekly Journal 1850–1859, Conducted by Charles Dickens* (Toronto 1973).

Long, Jane, Jan Gothard, and Helen Brash (eds), *Forging Identities: Bodies, Gender and Feminist History* (Nedlands 1997).

Loveday, P., and A.W. Martin, *Parliament, Factions and Parties: The First Thirty Years of Responsible Government in New South Wales, 1856–1889* (Melbourne 1966).

Madgwick, R.B., *Immigration into Eastern Australia 1788–1851* (Sydney 1969).

Manne, Robert (ed.), *Whitewash: On Keith Windschuttle's Fabrication of Aboriginal History* (Melbourne 2003).

Marais, J.S., *The Colonisation of New Zealand* (London 1927).

Markus, Andrew, *Fear and Hatred: Purifying Australia and California, 1850–1901* (Sydney 1979).

Markus, Andrew, *Australian Race Relations 1788–1993* (Sydney 1994).

Martin, A.W., *Henry Parkes: A Biography* (Melbourne 1980).

Martin, Ged, *Bunyip Aristocracy: The New South Wales Constitution Debate of 1853 and Hereditary Institutions in the British Colonies* (Sydney 1986).

Martin, Henri-Jean, *The History and Power of Writing* (trans. Lydia G. Cochrane) (Chicago 1994).

McCalman, Iain, Alexander Cook, and Andrew Reeves (eds), *Gold: Forgotten Histories and Lost Objects of Australia* (Cambridge 2001).

McCalman, Janet, *Sex and Suffering: Women's Health and a Women's Hospital – The Royal Women's Hospital, Melbourne 1856–1996* (Melbourne 1998).

McCann, Phillip, and Francis A. Young, *Samuel Wilderspin and the Infant School Movement* (London 1982).

MacDonagh, Oliver, *Early Victorian Government 1830–1870* (London 1977).

MacDonald, Peter F., *Marriage in Australia: Age at First Marriage and Proportions Marrying, 1860–1971* (Canberra 1975).

Macfarlane, Margaret and Alistair, *John Watts: Australia's Forgotten Architect and South Australia's Postmaster General 1841–1861* (Bonnells Bay, NSW, 1992).

Macintyre, Stuart, *Colonial Liberalism: The Lost World of Three Victorian Visionaries* (Melbourne 1991).

Macintyre, Stuart, *A Concise History of Australia* (Cambridge 1999).

McKenna, Mark, *The Captive Republic: A History of Republicanism in Australia 1788–1996* (Cambridge 1996).

McLaren, Glen, *Beyond Leichhardt: Bushcraft and the Exploration of Australia* (Fremantle 1996).

McQueen, Humphrey, *A New Britannia: An Argument Concerning the Social Origins of Australian Radicalism and Nationalism* (London 1970).

Meinig, D.W., *On the Margins of the Good Earth: The South Australian Wheat Frontier, 1869–1884* (Adelaide 1970).

Milliss, Roger, *Waterloo Creek: The Australia Day Massacre of 1838, George Gipps and the British Conquest of New South Wales* (Sydney 1992).

Mills, R.C., *The Colonization of Australia 1829–42* (London 1911).

Mincham, Hans, *The Story of the Flinders Ranges* (Adelaide 1965).

Modystack, William, *Mary MacKillop, a Woman before Her Time* (Adelaide 1982).

Mol, Hans, *The Faith of Australians* (Sydney 1985).

Molony, John, *An Architect of Freedom: John Hubert Plunkett in New South Wales 1832–1869* (Canberra 1973).

Molony, John, *The Native-Born: The First White Australians* (Melbourne 2000).

Morgan, Sharon, *Land Settlement in Early Tasmania: Creating an Antipodean England* (Cambridge 1992).

Morphy, Howard, *Ancestral Connections: Art and an Aboriginal System of Knowledge* (Chicago 1991).

Morrison, Ian, *The Publishing Industry in Colonial Australia* (Melbourne 1996).

Mossenson, David, *State Education in Western Australia 1829–1960* (Nedlands 1972).

Moyal, Ann, *Clear across Australia: A History of Telecommunications* (Melbourne 1984).

Muir, Marcie, *Anthony Trollope in Australia* (Adelaide 1949).

Muir, Marcie, *Charlotte Barton: Australia's First Children's Author* (Sydney 1980).

Mullins, Steve, *Torres Strait: A History of Colonial Occupation and Culture Contact 1864–1897* (Rockhampton 1995).

Nadel, George, *Australia's Colonial Culture: Ideas, Men and Institutions in Mid-Nineteenth Century Eastern Australia* (Cambridge, Mass., 1957).

Neal, David, *The Rule of Law in a Penal Colony: Law and Power in Early New South Wales* (Cambridge 1991).

Nicholas, F.W. and J.M., *Charles Darwin in Australia* (Cambridge 1989).

Nicholas, Stephen (ed.), *Convict Workers: Reinterpreting Australia's Past* (Cambridge 1988).

Nobbs, Raymond (ed.), *Norfolk Island and Its Second Settlement, 1825–1855* (Sydney 1991).

Nolan, Sidney J., *The Australian Language: The Meanings, Origins and Usage from Convict Days to the Present* (Sydney 1978).

Oddie, James (ed.), *From Tent to Parliament, The Life of Peter Lalor; History of the Eureka Stockade* (Melbourne 1954).

O'Donoghue, Frances, *The Bishop of Botany Bay: The Life of John Bede Polding, Australia's First Catholic Archbishop* (Sydney 1982).

O'Farrell, Patrick, *The Catholic Church and Community in Australia: A History* (Melbourne 1977).

O'Farrell, Patrick, *The Irish in Australia* (Sydney 1986).

Ong, Walter J., *Interfaces of the Word: Studies in the Evolution of Consciousness and Culture* (Ithaca, N.Y., 1977).

Ong, Walter, *The Barbarian Within, and Other Fugitive Essays and Studies* (New York 1962).

Oxley, Deborah, *Convict Maids: The Forced Migration of Women to Australia* (Cambridge 1996).

Pearl, Cyril, *Brilliant Dan Deniehy, a Forgotten Genius* (Melbourne 1972).

Pemberton, P.A., *Pure Merinos and Others: The 'Shipping Lists' of the Australian Agricultural Company* (Canberra 1986).

Perrott, Monica, *A Tolerable Good Success: Economic Opportunities for Women in New South Wales 1788–1830* ((Sydney 1983).

Perry, T.M., *Australia's First Frontier: The Spread of Settlement in New South Wales 1788–1829* (Melbourne 1963).

Philipp, June, *A Great View of Things: Edward Gibbon Wakefield* (Melbourne 1971).

Piggin, Stuart, *Evangelical Christianity if Australia: Spirit, Word and World* (Melbourne 1996).

Pike, Douglas, *Paradise of Dissent: South Australia 1829–1857* (Melbourne 1967).

Poirier, Richard (ed.), *Raritan Reading* (New Brunswick 1990).

Powell, Alan, *Far Country: A Short History of the Northern Territory* (Melbourne 1982).

Price, Charles, *The Great White Walls are Built: Restrictive Immigration to North America and Australia 1836–1888* (Canberra 1974).

Purcell, Marie, *By Degrees: A Story of the Potaskie/McDonald Family 1802–1987* (Melbourne 1987).

Pybus, Cassandra, *Community of Thieves* (Melbourne 1991).

Pybus, Cassandra, and Hamish Maxwell-Stewart, *American Citizens, British Slaves: Yankee Political Prisoners in an Australian Penal Colony 1839–1850* (Melbourne 2002).

Rankin, D.H., *The History of the Development of Education in Victoria 1836–1936: The First Centenary of Educational Effort* (Melbourne 1939).

Read, Peter, *A Hundred Years War: The Wiradjuri People and the State* (Sydney 1988).

Reece, R.H.W., *Aborigines and Colonists: Aborigines and Colonial Society in New South Wales in the 1830s and 1840s* (Sydney 1974).

Reid, Gordon, *A Nest of Hornets: The Massacre of the Fraser Family at Hornet Bank Station, Central Queensland, 1857, and Related Events* (Melbourne 1982).

Reynolds, Henry, *The Other Side of the Frontier: An Interpretation of the Aboriginal Response to the Invasion and Settlement of Australia* (Townsville 1981)

Reynolds, Henry, *With the White People: The Crucial Role of Aborigines in the Exploration and Development of Australia* (Melbourne 1990).

Reynolds, Henry, *The Law of the Land* (Melbourne 1992).

Reynolds, Henry, *Fate of a Free People: A Radical Re-Examination of the Tasmanian Wars* (Melbourne 1995).

Reynolds, Henry, *This Whispering in Our Hearts* (Melbourne 1998).

Reynolds, Henry, *An Indelible Stain?: The Question of Genocide in Australia's History* (Melbourne 2001).

Reynolds, Henry, *North of Capricorn: The Untold Story of Australia's North* (Sydney 2003).

Reynolds, John, *Launceston: History of an Australian City* (Melbourne 1969).

Richards, Eric (ed.), *The Flinders History of South Australia: Social History* (Adelaide 1986).

Ritchie, John, *Punishment and Profit: The Reports of Commissioner John Bigge on the Colonies of New South Wales and Van Diemen's Land, 1822–1823; Their Origins, Nature and Significance* (Melbourne 1970).

Ritchie, John, *The Wentworths: Father and Son* (Melbourne 1997).

Roberts, Stephen H., *The Squatting Age in Australia 1835–1847* (Melbourne 1935).

Roberts, Stephen H., *History of Australian Land Settlement 1788–1920* (Melbourne 1968).

Robin, A. de Q., *Charles Perry, Bishop of Melbourne* (Nedlands 1967).

Robinson, Portia, *The Hatch and Brood of Time: A Study of the First Generation of Native-Born White Australians 1788–1828* (Melbourne 1985).

Robson, L.L., *The Convict Settlers of Australia* (Melbourne 1965).

Roe, Michael, *Quest for Authority in Eastern Australia 1835–1851* (Melbourne 1965).

Russell, Enid, *A History of the Law in Western Australia and Its Development from 1829 to 1979* (Nedlands 1980).

Russell, Penny (ed.), *For Richer, For Poorer: Early Colonial Marriages* (Melbourne 1994).

Russell, Penny, and Richard White (eds), *Pastiche I: Reflections on 19th Century Australia* (Sydney 1994).

Ryan, Lyndall, *The Aboriginal Tasmanians* (St Lucia 1981).

Sawer, Marian (ed.), *Elections Full, Free and Fair* (Sydney 2001).

Schedvin, C.B., and J.W. McCarty (eds), *Urbanization in Australia: The Nineteenth Century* (Sydney 1974).

Schivelbusch, Wolfgang, *The Railway Journey: Trains and Travel in the 19th Century* (trans. Anselm Hollo) (Oxford 1979).

Schivelbusch, Wolfgang, *Disenchanted Night: The Industrialisation of Light in the Nineteenth Century* (trans. Angela Davies) (Oxford 1988).

Scull, Andrew T., *Museums of Madness: The Social Organization of Insanity in Nineteenth-Century England* (London 1979).

Scull, Andrew (ed.), *Madhouses, Mad-Doctors, and Madman: The Social History Psychiatry in the Victorian Era* (London 1981).

Sennett, Richard, *The Fall of Public Man* (Cambridge 1977).

Serle, Geoffrey, *The Golden Age: A History of the Colony of Victoria 1851–1861* (Melbourne 1963).

Shaw, A.G.L., *A History of the Port Phillip District: Victoria before Separation* (Melbourne 1996).

Shaw, A.G.L., *Convict and the Colonies: A Study of Penal Transportation from Great Britain and Ireland to Australia and Other Parts of the British Empire* (London 1966).

Shaw, A.G.L., *Sir George Arthur, Bart, 1784–1854: Superintendent of British Honduras, Lieutenant-Governor of Van Diemen's Land and of Upper Canada, Governor of the Bombay Presidency* (Melbourne 1980).

Shaw, G.P., *Patriarch and Patriot: William Grant Broughton 1788–1853* (Melbourne 1978).

Shiel, D.J., *Ben Hall, Bushranger* (St Lucia 1983).

Smith, Babette, *A Cargo of Women: Susannah Watson and the Convicts of the Princess Royal* (Sydney 1988).

Smith, F.B., *The People's Health, 1830–1910* (Canberra 1979).

Smith, Olivia, *The Politics of Language 1791–1819* (Oxford 1984).

Snell, K.D.M., *Annals of the Labouring Poor: Social Change and Agrarian England 1660–1900* (Cambridge 1987).

Solomon, R.J., *Urbanisation: The Evolution of an Australian Capital* (Sydney 1976).

Souter, Gavin, *Company of Heralds: A Century and a Half of Australian Publishing* (Melbourne 1981).

Stannage, C.T. (ed.), *A New History of Western Australia* (Nedlands 1981).

Stannage, C.T., *The People of Perth: A Social History of Western Australia's Capital City* (Perth 1979).

Sturma, Michael, *Vice in a Vicious Society: Crime and Convicts in Mid-Nineteenth Century New South Wales* (St Lucia 1983).

Sullivan, Martin, *Men and Women of Port Phillip* (Sydney 1985).

Sutherland, Gillian (ed.), *Studies in the Growth of Nineteenth-Century Government* (London 1972).

Swain, Shurlee, and Renate Howe, *Single Mothers and their Children: Disposal, Punishment and Survival in Australia* (Melbourne 1995).

Swain, Tony, *A Place for Strangers: Towards a History of Australian Aboriginal Being* (Cambridge 1993).

Tate, Audrey, *Ada Cambridge: Her Life and Work 1844–1926* (Melbourne 1991).

Taylor, Barbara, *Eve and the New Jerusalem: Socialism and Feminism in the Nineteenth Century* (London 1983).

Taylor, Peter, *The End to Silence: The Building of the Overland Telegraph from Adelaide to Darwin* (Sydney 1980).

Tebbutt, Melanie, *Women's Talk?: A Social History of 'Gossip' in Working-Class Neighbourhoods, 1880–1960* (Aldershot, Hants., 1997).

Thomas, Keith, *Man and the Natural World: Changing Attitudes in England 1500–1800* (London 1983).

Tillotson, Kathleen, *Novels of the Eighteen-Forties* (Oxford 1954).

Tipping, Marjorie, *Convicts Unbound: The Story of the Calcutta Convicts and their Settlement in Australia* (Melbourne 1988).

Townsend, Norma, *Valley of the Crooked River: European Settlement on the Nambucca* (Sydney 1993).

Travers, Robert, *The Phantom Fenians of New South Wales* (Sydney 1986).
Turner, Naomi, *Catholics in Australia: A Social History* (two volumes; Melbourne 1992).
Turney, C. (ed.), *Pioneers of Australian Education* (Sydney 1969).
Vader, John, and Brian Murray, *Antique Bottle Collecting in Australia* (Sydney 1975).
Vamplew, Wray (ed.), *Australians: Historical Statistics* (Sydney 1987).
van Drenth, Annemieke, and Francisca de Haan, *The Rise of Caring Power: Elizabeth Fry and Josephine Butler in Britain and the Netherlands* (Amsterdam 1999).
Vincent, David, *The Culture of Secrecy: Britain, 1832–1998* (Oxford 1998).
Waldersee, James, *Catholic Society in New South Wales 1788–1860* (Sydney 1974).
Walker, R.B., *The Newspaper Press in New South Wales, 1803–1920* (Sydney 1976).
Ward, John M., *Earl Grey and the Australian Colonies 1846–1857: A Study of Self-Government and Self-Interest* (Melbourne 1958).
Ward, Rowland S., *The Bush Still Burns: The Presbyterian and Reformed Faith in Australia 1788–1988* (Melbourne 1989).
Ward, Russel, *The Australian Legend* (Melbourne 1966).
Waterson, D.B., *Squatter, Selector, and Storekeeper: A History of the Darling Downs, 1859–93* (Sydney 1968).
Weidenhofer, Maggie, *Port Arthur: A Place of Misery* (Melbourne 1981).
White, John, and Barbara J. Hancock (eds), *The Postal History of New South Wales 1788–1901* (Sydney 1988).
White, Richard, *Inventing Australia* (Sydney 1981).
White, Richard, and Hsu-Ming Teo (eds), *Cultural History in Australia* (Sydney 2003).
Williams, Raymond, *Keywords: A Vocabulary of Culture and Society* (London 1983).
Windschuttle, Elizabeth (ed.), *Women, Class and History: Feminist Perspectives on Australia 1788–1978* (Sydney 1980).
Windschuttle, Keith, *The Fabrication of Aboriginal History*, vol. 1 (Sydney 2003).

3. Articles in Learned Journals

Adams, David, ' "Superior" Boys Schools in a Pioneering Community: The Swan River Settlement, 1829 to 1855', *Early Days: Journal of the Royal Western Australian Historical Society*, vol. 8, pt 5 (1981).
Archer, John E., 'The Nineteenth-Century Allotment: Half an Acre and a Row', *Economic History Review*, vol. 50 (1997).
Armstrong, Nancy, and Leonard Tennenhouse, 'The Interior Difference: A Brief Genealogy of Dreams, 1650–1717', *Eighteenth-Century Studies*, vol. 23 (1989–90).
Atkinson, Alan, 'A Slice of the Sydney Press', *Push from the Bush*, no. 1 (May 1978).
Atkinson, Alan, 'Four Patterns of Convict Protest', *Labour History*, no. 37 (November 1979).
Atkinson, Alan, 'Women Publicans in 1838', *Push from the Bush*, no. 8 (December 1980).
Atkinson, Alan, 'James Macarthur as Author', *Journal of the Royal Australian Historical Society*, vol. 67 (1981).
Atkinson, Alan, 'The Parliament in the Jerusalem Warehouse', *Push from the Bush*, no. 12 (1982).
Atkinson, Alan, 'Our First Chance of Kingdom Come', *Push from the Bush*, no. 19 (April 1985).
Atkinson, Alan, 'Classified Cupid', *Push from the Bush*, no. 22 (April 1986).
Atkinson, Alan, 'The Free-Born Englishman Transported: Convicts Rights as a Measure of Eighteenth-Century Empire', *Past and Present*, no. 144 (August 1994).
Atkinson, Alan, 'Irony and Bluster: An Historian Responds to His Critics', *Australian Historical Association Bulletin*, no. 88 (June 1999).
Atkinson, Alan, 'Writing About Convicts: Our Escape from the One Big Gaol', *Tasmanian Historical Studies*, vol. 6, no. 2 (1999).

Austen, Brian, 'The Impact of the Mail Coach on Public Coach Services in England and Wales, 1784–1840', *Journal of Transport History*, series 3, vol. 2 (1981).

Bavin, Louise, 'Punishment, Prisons and Reform: Incarceration in Western Australia in the Nineteenth Century', *Studies in Western Australian History*, no. 14 (*Historical Refractions*, ed. Charlie Fox) (1993).

Bennett, Bruce, 'Ego, Sight and Insight in Convict Fiction by Henry Savery and John Boyle O'Reilly', *Journal of Australian Colonial History*, vol. 2 (2000).

Blair, Sandra J., 'The Revolt at Castle Forbes: A Catalyst to Emancipist Emigrant Confrontation', *Journal of the Royal Australian Historical Society*, vol. 64 (1978).

Blair, Sandra, 'The "Convict Press": William Watt and the Sydney Gazette in the 1830s', *Push from the Bush*, no. 5 (December 1979).

Blair, Sandra, 'Patronage and Prejudice: Educated Convicts in the New South Wales Press', *Push from the Bush*, no. 8 (December 1980).

Bolton, G.C., 'A Whig Utopia in Northern Australia', *Push from the Bush*, no. 5 (December 1979).

Boyce, James, 'Journeying Home: A New Look at the British Invasion of Van Diemen's Land: 1803–1823', *Island*, no. 66 (Autumn 1996).

Breen, Shayne, 'Justice, Humanity and the Common Good: John Pascoe Fawkner's Ideology of Utilitarian Justice, 1829–30', *Tasmanian Historical Studies*, vol. 4 (1994).

Broeze, F.J.A., 'Western Australia Until 1869: The Maritime Perspective', *Early Days: Journal of the Royal Western Australian Historical Society*, vol. 8, pt 6 (1982).

Brown, Wendy, 'Finding the Man in the State', *Feminist Studies*, vol. 18 (1992).

Buck, A.R., ' "The Poor Man": Rhetoric and Political Culture in Mid-Nineteenth Century New South Wales', *Australian Journal of Politics and History*, vol. 42 (1996).

Byrne, Paula J., 'A Colonial Female Economy: Sydney, Australia', *Social History*, vol. 24 (1999).

Carrington, D.L., 'Riots at Lambing Flat, 1860–1861', *Journal of the Royal Australian Historical Society*, vol. 46 (1960).

Cashen, John, 'Master and Servant in South Australia', *Push from the Bush*, no. 6 (May 1980).

Castles, Alex C., 'The Vandemonian Spirit and the Law', *Tasmanian Historical Research Association Papers and Proceedings*, vol. 38 (1991).

Clancy, E.G., 'The Commencement of the Primitive Methodist Mission in New South Wales', *Push from the Bush*, no. 27 (1989).

Clyne, Robert, 'At War with the Natives: From the Coorong to the Rufus, 1841', *Journal of the Historical Society of South Australia*, no. 9 (1981).

Cohen, Esther, 'Law, Folklore and Animal Love', *Past and Present*, no. 110 (February 1986).

Connor, John, 'British Frontier Warfare Logistics and the "Black Line", Van Diemen's Land (Tasmania), 1830', *War in History*, vol. 9 (2002).

Cooper, Robert Alan, 'Jeremy Bentham, Elizabeth Fry, and English Prison Reform', *Journal of the History of Ideas*, vol. 42 (1981).

Coote, Anne, 'Imagining a Colonial Nation: The Development of Popular Concepts of Sovereignty and Nation in New South Wales with Particular Reference to the Period between 1856 and 1860', *Journal of Australian Colonial History*, vol. 1 (1999).

Cowburn, Philip M., 'The Attempted Assassination of the Duke of Edinburgh, 1868', *Journal of the Royal Australian Historical Society*, vol. 55 (1969).

Craig, Cairns, 'Scott's Staging of the Nation', *Studies in Romanticism*, vol. 40 (2001).

Crowley, F.K., 'Master and Servant in Western Australia 1829–1851', *Western Australian Historical Society Journal and Proceedings*, vol. 4, pt 5 (1953).

Cunningham, Hugh, 'The Language of Patriotism, 1750–1914', *History Workshop: A Journal of Socialist Historians*, issue 12 (Autumn 1981).

Currey, C.H., 'The Foundation of the Benevolent Society of New South Wales, on May 6, 1818', *Journal of the Royal Australian Historical Society*, vol. 48 (1962).

Curthoys, Patricia, ' "A Provision for Themselves and Their Families?": Women Depositors of the Savings Bank of New South Wales, 1846–1871', *Journal of the Royal Australian Historical Society*, vol. 84 (1998).

Dare, Robert, 'Paupers' Rights: Governor Grey and the Poor Law in South Australia', *Australian Historical Studies*, vol. 25 (1992).

Davies, Mel, 'Cornish Miners and Class Relations in Early Colonial South Australia: The Burra Burra Strikes of 1848–49', *Australian Historical Studies*, vol. 26 (1995).

Davies, Susanne, 'Aborigines, Murder and the Criminal Law in Early Port Phillip, 1841–1851', *Historical Studies*, vol. 22 (1987).

de Mouncey, P.E.C., 'The Historic Duel at Fremantle between George French Johnson, a Merchant, and William Nairne Clark, a Solicitor, in the Year, 1832', *Early Days: The Western Australian Historical Society Journal and Proceedings*, vol. 1, pt 5 (1929).

Dockray, R.B., 'Camden Station', *Institution of Civil Engineers Minutes of Proceedings*, vol. 8 (1849).

Dowd, B.T., and Averil Fink, 'James Mudie, Harlequin of the Hunter' (two parts), *Journal of the Royal Australian Historical Society*, vols 54 (1968) and 55 (1969).

Duxbury, Jennifer, 'Conflict and Discipline: The Van Diemen's Land Company', *Push from the Bush*, no. 25 (October 1987).

Dwight, Alan, 'South Sea Islanders to New South Wales', *Journal of the Royal Australian Historical Society*, vol. 68 (1983).

Ely, M.J., 'The Management of Schools is New South Wales 1848–1880: Local Initiative Suppressed', *Journal of Educational Administration*, vol. 9 (1971).

Esterhammer, Angela, 'Godwin's Suspicion of Speech Acts', *Studies in Romanticism*, vol. 39 (2000).

Evans, Raymond, and Bill Thorpe, 'Indigenocide and the Massacre of Aboriginal History', *Overland*, no. 163 (Winter 2001).

Evans, Raymond, and William Thorpe, 'Power, Punishment and Penal Labour: *Convict Workers* and Moreton Bay', *Australian Historical Studies*, vol. 25 (1992).

Featherstone, Guy, 'The Nunawading Messiah: James Fisher and Popular Millenarianism in Nineteenth-Century Melbourne', *Journal of Religious History*, vol. 26 (2002).

Fels, Marie, 'Culture Contact in the County of Buckinghamshire, Van Diemens Land 1803–11', *Tasmanian Historical Research Association Papers and Proceedings*, vol. 29 (1982).

Ferguson, J.A., 'Edward Smith Hall and the "Monitor"', *Journal of the Royal Australian Historical Society*, vol. 17 (1931).

Fletcher, Brian, 'Elizabeth Darling: Colonial Benefactress and Governor's Lady', *Journal of the Royal Australian Historical Society*, vol. 67 (1982).

Foster, S.G., ' "The Purposes, Duties and Arts of Life": Judge Burton's Plan for Black Villages', *Push from the Bush*, no. 9 (July 1981).

Foster, Robert, 'Feasts of the Full-Moon: The Distribution of Rations to Aborigines in South Australia, 1836–1861', *Australian Aboriginal Studies*, vol. 13 (1989).

Gabay, A.J., 'The Séance in the Melbourne of the 1870s: Experience and Meanings', *Journal of Religious History*, vol. 13 (1984).

Gaffney, Carmel, 'Towards an Australian Pastoral in the Poetry of Charles Harpur', *Meridian*, vol. 16 (1997).

Gammage, Bill, 'The Wiradjuri War', *Push from the Bush*, no. 16 (November 1983).

Goodin, Vernon W.E., 'Public Education in New South Wales before 1848' (two parts), *Journal of the Royal Australian Historical Society*, vol. 36 (1950).

Goodman, David, 'Reading Gold-Rush Travellers' Narratives', *Australian Cultural History*, no. 10 (1991).

Green, Neville, 'Aboriginal and Settler Conflict in Western Australia, 1826–1852', *Push from the Bush*, no. 3 (May 1979).

Hagarty, D.N., 'The Selection, Design and Delivery of the First Locomotives and Rolling Stock' (two parts), *Australian Railway History Society Bulletin*, vol. 48 (1997).

Hallam, Silvia, 'Aboriginal Women as Providers: The 1830s on the Swan', *Australian Aboriginal Studies*, vol. 15 (1991).

Hallam, Silvia, 'Some Little-Known Aborigines of the 1830s in the Perth Area', *Early Days: Journal of the Royal Western Australian Historical Society*, vol. 10, pt 3 (1991).

Harrison, Brian, 'Animals and the State in Nineteenth-Century England', *English Historical Review*, vol. 88 (1973).

Hasluck, Alexandra, 'Yagan the Patriot', *Early Days: Journal and Proceedings of the Western Australian Historical Society*, vol. 5, pt 7 (1961).

Henningham, J.P., 'Two Hundred Years of Australian Journalism: A History Waiting to be Written', *Australian Cultural Studies*, no. 7 (1988).

Hetherington, Penelope, 'Child Labour in Swan River Colony, 1829–1850', *Australian Historical Studies*, no. 98 (April 1992).

Hetherington, Penelope, 'Aboriginal Children as a Potential Labour Force in Swan River Colony, 1829–1850', *Journal of Australian Studies*, no. 33 (June 1992).

Higgins, Matthew, 'Near-Rebellion on the Turon Goldfields in 1853', *Journal of the Royal Australian Historical Society*, vol. 68 (1983).

Hilliard, David, 'Emanuel Swedenborg and the New Church in South Australia', *Journal of the Historical Society of South Australia*, no. 16 (1988).

Hoare, M.E., 'Learned Societies in Australia: The Foundation Years in Victoria, 1850–1860', *Records of the Australian Academy of Science*, vol. 1, no. 1 (December 1966).

Horsman, Reginald, 'Origins of Racial Anglo-Saxonism in Great Britain before 1850', *Journal of the History of Ideas*, vol. 37 (1976).

Hudson, Paul, 'English Emigration to New Zealand, 1839–1850: Information Diffusion and Marketing a New World', *Economic History Review*, vol. 54 (2001).

Hunt, Arnold D., 'The Bible Christians in South Australia', *Journal of the Historical Society of South Australia*, no. 10 (1982).

Huon, Dan, 'By Moral Means Only: The Origins of the Launceston Anti-Transportation Leagues 1847–1849', *Tasmanian Historical Research Association Papers and Proceedings*, vol. 44 (1997).

Hutchinson, Mark, 'W.C. Wentworth and the Sources of Australian Historiography', *Journal of the Royal Australian Historical Society*, vol. 77 (1992).

Hyams, B.K., 'The Teacher in South Australia in the Second Half of the Nineteenth Century', *Australian Journal of Education*, vol. 15 (1971).

Ihde, Erin, ' "A Smart Volley of Dough-Boy Shot": A Military Food Riot in Colonial Sydney', *Journal of Australian Colonial History*, vol. 3 (2001).

Iliffe, Narelle, 'First Fruits: Baptists in New South Wales, c. 1830–1856', *Journal of Australian Colonial History*, vol. 1 (1999).

Janda, Mary Ann, 'Public Punishment and Private Pleasure: Literacy from Without and Within', *a/b: Auto/Biography Studies*, vol. 16 (2001).

Karskens, Grace, 'Revisiting the Worldview: The Archaeology of Convict Households in Sydney's Rocks Neighborhood', *Historical Archaeology*, vol. 37 (2003).

Kent, David, and Norma Townsend, 'Deborah Oxley's "Female Convicts": An Accurate View of Working-Class Women?', *Labour History*, no. 65 (November 1993).

Kent, David, 'Customary Behaviour Transported: A Note on the Parramatta Female Factory Riot of 1827', *Journal of Australian Studies*, no. 40 (March 1994).

Knox, Bruce, ' "Care is More Important than Haste": Imperial Policy and the Creation of Queensland, 1856–9', *Historical Studies*, vol. 17 (1976).

Kociumbas, Jan, 'Science as Cultural Ideology: Museums and Mechanics Institutes in Early New South Wales and Van Diemen's Land', *Labour History*, no. 64 (May 1993).

Kristeva, Julia, 'Women's Time' (trans. Alice Jardine and Harry Blake), *Signs: Journal of Women in Culture and Society*, vol. 7 (1981).

Laugero, Greg, 'Infrastructures of Enlightenment: Road-Making, the Public Sphere, and the Emergence of Literature', *Eighteenth-Century Studies*, vol. 29 (1995).

Laurie, Arthur, 'Hornet Bank Massacre, October 27, 1857', *Journal of the Royal Historical Society of Queensland*, vol. 5, no. 5 (1957).

Leary, Rachel, 'Rewriting the Hobart Rivulet', *Island*, no. 75 (Winter 1998).

le Couteur, Howard, 'Gramschi's Concept of Hegemony and Social Formation in Early Colonial Queensland', *Limina*, vol. 6 (2000).

Lennox, Geoff, 'The Van Diemen's Land Company and the Tasmanian Aborigines: A Reappraisal', *Tasmanian Historical Research Association Papers and Proceedings*, vol. 37 (1990).

Lindsay, Elaine, 'Figuring the Sacred: Geography, Spirituality and Literature', *Kunapipi*, vol. 17 (1995).

Liston, Carol, 'The Dharawal and Gandangara in Colonial Campbelltown, New South Wales, 1788–1830', *Aboriginal History*, vol. 12 (1988).

Lyons, Martyn, 'Texts, Books, and Readers: Which Kind of History?', *Australian Cultural History*, no. 11 (1992).

McCabe, Kris, 'Discipline and Punishment: Female Convicts on the Hunter', *Journal of Australian Colonial History*, vol. 1 (1999).

MacDonagh, Oliver, 'Government, Industry and Science in Nineteenth Century Britain: A Particular Study', *Historical Studies*, no. 65 (October 1975).

McDonald, Barry, 'Evidence of Four New England Corroboree Songs Indicating Aboriginal Responses to European Invasion', *Australian Aboriginal Studies*, vol. 20 (1996).

McDonald, D.I., 'Frederick Norton Manning (1839–1903)', *Journal of the Royal Australian Historical Society*, vol. 58 (1972).

McLaren, Angus, 'Phrenology, Medium and Message', *Journal of Modern History*, vol. 46 (1974).

Macnab, Ken, and Russel Ward, 'The Nature and Nurture of the First Generation of Native-Born Australians', *Historical Studies*, no. 39 (November 1962).

Macnab, Ken, and Russel Ward, 'The Nature and Nurture of the First Generation of Native-Born Australians', *Historical Studies*, no. 39 (November 1962).

Maddrell, Avril M.C., 'Discourses of Race and Gender and the Comparative Method in Geography School Texts 1830–1918', *Environment and Planning D: Society and Space*, vol. 16 (1998).

Magarey, Susan, 'The Invention of Juvenile Delinquency in Early Nineteenth-Century England', *Labour History*, no. 34 (May 1978).

Manuel, Deane, 'Roads Not Taken: Some Minor Concerns of Adelaide's Newspapers at the Mid-Nineteenth Century', *Journal of the Historical Society of South Australia*, no. 8 (1980).

Marks, Lynne, 'Railing, Tattling, and General Rumour: Gossip, Gender, and Church Regulation in Upper Canada', *Canadian Historical Review*, vol. 81 (2000).

Markus, Andrew, 'Explaining the Treatment of Non-European Immigrants in Nineteenth Century Australia', *Labour History*, no. 48 (May 1985).

Maxwell-Stewart, Hamish, ' "I Could Not Blame the Rangers ... ": Tasmanian Bushranging, Convicts and Convict Management', *Tasmanian Historical Research Association Papers and Proceedings*, no. 42 (1995).

Maxwell-Stewart, Hamish, and Ian Duffield, 'Beyond Hell's Gates; Religion at Macquarie Harbour Penal Station', *Tasmanian Historical Studies*, vol. 5 (1997).

Maxwell-Stewart, Hamish, and Bruce Hindmarsh, ' "This is the Bird that Never Flew": William Stewart, Major Donald MacLeod and the *Launceston Advertiser*', *Journal of Australian Colonial History*, vol. 2 (2000).

Mayne, A.J.C., ' "The Question of the Poor" in the Nineteenth-Century City', *Historical Studies*, no. 81 (October 1983).

Mazzarol, T.W., 'Tradition, Environment and the Indentured Labourer in Early Western Australia', *Studies in Western Australian History*, vol. 3 (November 1978).

Messner, Andrew, 'Contesting Chartism from Afar: Edward Hawkesley and the *People's Advocate*', *Journal of Australian Colonial History*, vol. 1 (1999).

Messner, Andrew, 'Land, Leadership, Culture, and Emigration: Some Problems in Chartist Historiography', *Historical Journal*, vol. 42 (1999).

Messner, Andrew, 'Popular Constitutionalism and Chinese Protest on the Victorian Goldfields', *Journal of Australian Colonial History*, vol. 2 (2000).

Miles, Patricia, 'In Search of Alexander Harris', *Push: A Journal of Early Australian History*, no. 30 (1992).

Morrison, Elizabeth, 'Reading Victoria's Newspapers 1838–1901', *Australian Cultural History*, no. 11 (1992).

Murray, Tim, and Alan Mayne, '(Re)Constructing a Lost Community: "Little Lon", Melbourne, Australia', *Historical Archaeology*, vol. 37 (2003).

Neate, Lorraine, 'Alexander Harris – A Mystery No More', *Journal of the Royal Australian Historical Society*, vol. 86 (2000).

Newman, Terry, 'Tasmania and the Secret Ballot', *Australian Journal of Politics and History*, vol. 49 (2003).

Newton, Marjorie B., 'The Gathering of the Australian Saints', *Push from the Bush*, no. 27 (1989).

Nicholas, Stephen, and Richard H. Steckel, 'Heights and Living Standards of English Workers During the Early Years of Industrialization, 1770–1815', *Journal of Economic History*, vol. 51 (1991).

O'Donoghue, Frances, 'Winding Down the Convict Machine: Brisbane in 1838', *Push from the Bush*, no. 13 (November 1982).

O'Grady, Desmond, 'Carboni Redivivus', *Overland*, no. 160 (Spring 2000).

Olssen, Erik, 'Mr Wakefield and New Zealand as an Experiment in Post-Enlightenment Experimental Practice', *New Zealand Journal of History*, vol. 31 (1997).

Otis, Laura, 'The Metaphoric Circuit: Organic and Technological Communication in the Nineteenth Century', *Journal of the History of Ideas*, vol. 63 (2002).

Palmer, Sarah, ' "The Most Indefatigable Activity": The General Steam Navigation Company, 1824–50', *Journal of Transport History*, series 3, vol. 3 (1982).

Penglase, Bethia, 'An Enquiry into Literary in Early Nineteenth Century New South Wales', *Push from the Bush*, no. 16 (October 1983).

Perkins, John, and Jack Thompson, 'Cattle Theft, Primitive Capital Accumulation and Pastoral Expansion in Early New South Wales, 1800–1850', *Australian Historical Studies*, no. 111 (October 1998).

Pickard, John, 'Trespass, Common Law, Government Regulations, and Fences in Colonial New South Wales, 1788–1828', *Journal of the Royal Australian Historical Society*, vol. 84 (1998).

Picker, Greg, ' "A Nation is Governed By All That Has Tongue in the Nation": Newspapers and Political Expression in Colonial Sydney, 1825–1850', *Journal of Australian Studies*, no. 62 (September 1999).

Pickering, Paul A., ' "The Oak of English Liberty": Popular Constitutionalism in New South Wales, 1848–1856', *Journal of Australian Colonial History*, vol. 3 (2001).

Pickering, Paul A., ' "And Your Petitioners &c": Chartist Petitioning in Popular Politics', *English Historical Review*, vol. 116 (2001).

Plomley, Brian, and Kristen Anne Henley, 'The Sealers of Bass Strait and the Cape Barren Island Community', *Tasmanian Historical Research Association Papers and Proceedings*, vol. 37 (1990).

Quartly, Marian, 'South Australian Lunatics and their Custodians, 1836–1846', *Australian Journal of Social Issues*, no. 2 (1966).

Ramson, W.S., 'For the Term of a Natural Life: Lexical Evidence of the Convict Experience', *Australian Cultural History*, no. 6 (1987).

Richards, Eric, 'A Voice from Below: Benjamin Boyce in South Australia, 1839–46', *Labour History*, no. 27 (November 1974).

Ritchie, Neville A., ' "InSites", Historical Archaeology in Australasia: Some Comparisons with the American Colonial Experience', *Historical Archaeology*, vol. 37 (2003).

Roberts, David, 'Bells Falls Massacre and Bathurst's History of Violence: Local Tradition and Australian Historiography', *Australian Historical Studies*, no. 105 (October 1995).

Roberts, David Andrew, ' "A Sort of Inland Norfolk Island"? Isolation, Coercion and Resistance on the Wellington Valley Convict Station, 1823–26', *Journal of Australian Colonial History*, vol. 2 (2000).

Roberts, Michael, 'Sickles and Scythes: Women's Work and Men's Work at Harvest Time', *History Workshop*, issue 7 (Spring 1979).

Roe, Michael, 'Mary Leman Grimstone (1800–1850?): For Woman's Rights and Tasmanian Patriotism', *Tasmanian Historical Research Association Papers and Proceedings*, vol. 38 (1989).

Russell, Penny, ' "Her Excellency": Lady Franklin, Female Convicts and the Problem of Authority in Van Diemen's Land', *Journal of Australian Studies*, no. 53 (1997).

Seaman, Keith, 'The Press and the Aborigines: South Australia's First Thirty Years', *Journal of the Historical Society of South Australia*, no. 18 (1990).

Selth, P.A., 'The Burrangong (Lambing Flat) Riots, 1860–1861', *Journal of the Royal Australian Historical Society*, vol. 60 (1974).

Serjeantson, R.W., 'The Passions and Animal Language, 1540–1700', *Journal of the History of Ideas*, vol. 62 (2001).

Shaw, G.P., ' "Filched from Us": The Loss of Universal Manhood Suffrage in Queensland 1859–1863', *Australian Journal of Politics and History*, vol. 26 (1980).

Shlomowitz, Evelyn, ' "How Much More Generally Applicable are Remedial Words than Medicines": Care of the Mentally Ill in South Australia, 1858–1884', *Journal of Australian Colonial History*, vol. 4 (2002).

Shoemaker, Adam, 'An Interview with Jack Davis', *Westerly*, December 1982.

Smith, James H., 'Njama's Supper: The Consumption and Use of Literary Potency by Mau Mau Insurgents in Colonial Kenya', *Comparative Studies in Society and History*, vol. 40 (1998).

Smithson, Michael, 'A Misunderstood Gift; The Annual Issue of Blankets to Aborigines in New South Wales 1826–48', *Push: A Journal of Early Australian Social History*, no. 30 (1992).

Southerwood, W.T., 'New Light on the Foundation of Australian Catholicism', *Australasian Catholic Record*, vol. 61 (1984).

Statham, P.C., 'Peter Augustus Lautour', *Journal of the Royal Australian Historical Society*, vol. 72 (1986).

Stoneley, Peter, 'Rewriting the Gold Rush: Twain, Harte and Homosociality', *Journal of American Studies*, vol. 30 (1996).

Stuart, Iain, 'Sea Rats, Bandits and Roistering Buccaneers: What Were the Bass Strait Sealers Really Like?', *Journal of the Royal Australian Historical Society*, vol. 83 (1997).

Sturma, Michael, 'Myall Creek and the Psychology of Mass Murder', *Journal of Australian Studies*, no. 16 (May 1985).

Sturma, Michael, 'Death and Ritual on the Gallows: Public Executions in the Australian Penal Colonies', *Omega*, vol. 17 (1986–87).

Summers, Anne, ' "In a Few Years We Shall None of Us That Now Take Care of Them Be Here": Philanthropy and the State of Thinking of Elizabeth Fry', *Historical Research*, vol. 67 (1994).

Taylor, Antony, 'Shakespeare and Radicalism: The Uses and Abuses of Shakespeare in Nineteenth-Century Popular Politics', *Historical Journal*, vol. 45 (2002).

Taylor, Rebe, 'Savages or Saviours? The Australian Sealers and Tasmanian Aboriginal Culture', *Journal of Australian Studies*, no. 66 (2000).

Taylor, William, 'The King's Mails, 1603–1625', *Scottish Historical Review*, vol. 42 (1963).

Thorpe, William, 'Archibald Meston and Aboriginal Legislation in Colonial Queensland', *Historical Studies*, vol. 21 (1984).

Tipping, Marjorie, 'The Pre-Arthurian Legend, or Convict Families in Van Diemen's Land from 1803 to 1824', *Bulletin of the Centre for Tasmanian Historical Studies*, vol. 3, no. 1 (1990–91).

Townsend, Norma, 'Masters and Men and the Myall Creek Massacre', *Push from the Push*, no. 20 (April 1985).

van Krieken, Robert, 'Towards "Good and Useful Men and Women": The State and Childhood in Sydney, 1840–1890', *Australian Historical Studies*, no. 93 (October 1989).

Vrettos, Athena, 'Defining Habits: Dickens and the Psychology of Repetition', *Victorian Studies*, vol. 42 (1999–2000).

Walker, R.B., 'Another Look at the Lambing Flat Riots 1860–61', *Journal of the Royal Australian Historical Society*, vol. 56 (1970).

Walker, R.B., 'German-Language Press and People in South Australia, 1848–1900', *Journal of the Royal Australian Historical Society*, vol. 58 (1972).

Woolmington, Jean, 'Missionary Attitudes to the Baptism of Australian Aborigines before 1850', *Journal of Religious History*, vol. 13 (1984–85).

Wotherspoon, G., 'Savings Banks and Social Policy in New South Wales 1832–71', *Australian Economic History Review*, vol. 18 (1978).

4. Unpublished Research

Alexander, Alison, 'The Public Role of Women in Tasmania, 1803–1914', PhD thesis, University of Tasmania 1989.

Alexander, Dan, 'The Press and Race Relations in Van Diemen's Land: The Influence of Newspaper Reporting on Lieutenant-Governor Arthur's Aboriginal Policies' 1824–1831', BA thesis, University of Tasmania 1997.

Atchison, J.F., 'Port Stephens and Goonoo Goonoo: A Review of the Early Period of the Australian Agricultural Company', PhD thesis, Australian National University 1973.

Atkinson, Alan, 'The Position of John Macarthur and His Family in New South Wales before 1843', MA thesis, University of Sydney 1971.

Atkinson, Alan, 'The Political Life of James Macarthur', PhD thesis, Australian National University 1976.

Barnes, Karen, 'Dr James Ross, "The Colonial Janus": Scholar, Pressman, Educator and Disseminator of Culture in Van Diemen's Land 1822–1838', BA thesis, University of Tasmania 1998.

Belcher, Michael J., 'The Child in New South Wales Society, 1820 to 1837', PhD thesis, University of New England 1982.

Bills, N. George, 'Governor George Arthur and Colonial Liberties in Van Diemen's Land, 1824–36', BEd thesis, University of Tasmania 1979.

Bramble, Christine, 'Relations between Aborigines and White Settlers in Newcastle and the Hunter District', BLitt thesis, University of New England 1981.

Breen, Shayne, 'Place, Power and Social Law: A History of Tasmania's Central North 1810–1900' PhD thesis, University of Tasmania 1997.

Brown, Joan C., 'The Development of Social Services in Tasmania 1803–1900', MA thesis, University of Tasmania 1969.

Brown-May, A.J., ' "The Itinerary of Our Days": The Historical Experience of the Street in Melbourne, 1837–1923', PhD thesis, University of Melbourne 1993.

Colman, Anne, 'New Worlds: Attitudes to Immigrants and Immigration in Port Phillip, New York and Rio de Janeiro, 1835–1850', PhD thesis, University of Melbourne 1999.

Connolly, C.N., 'Politics, Ideology and the New South Wales Legislative Council, 1856–72', PhD thesis, Australian National University 1974.

Coote, Anne, 'The Development of Colonial Nationhood in New South Wales, c. 1825–1865', PhD thesis, University of New England, forthcoming.

Crowe, K.J., 'Missionary Reformer: The Social Work and Ideas of Robert Willson, First Catholic Bishop of Hobart', BA thesis, University of Tasmania 1968.

Dunstan, 'Governing the Metropolis: Politics, Technology and Social Change in a Victorian City, Melbourne 1850–1891', PhD thesis, University of Melbourne 1983.

Ferry, John, 'An Examination of the Various Aboriginal Evidence Bills of New South Wales, South Australia and Western Australia in the Period 1839–1849, As Well As an Analysis of the Racial Attitudes Which Were Espoused During the Controversies', BA thesis, University of New England 1980.

Green, Anne, 'Against the League: Fighting the "Hated Stain"', BA thesis, University of Tasmania 1994.

Hammond, Peter, 'Murder, Manslaughter and Workplace Relations in Convict New South Wales 1824–1838', BA thesis, University of New England 2003.

Hannah, Mark, 'Aboriginal Workers in the Australian Agricultural Company, 1824 to 1857', BA thesis, University of New England 2000.

Jaques, W.R.C., 'The Impact of the Gold Rushes on South Australia 1852–54', BA thesis, University of Adelaide 1963.

Joske, E.J.P., 'Health and Hospital: A Study of Community Welfare in Western Australia, 1829–1855', MA thesis, University of Western Australia 1973.

Leach, R.J., 'Churches of Christ in Australia 1846–1905: An Inter-Colonial Comparison', MLitt thesis, University of New England 1997.

Lendrum, S.D., 'Special Legal Problems Relating to the Aborigines in the First Fifteen Years after Settlement', LLB thesis, University of Adelaide 1976.

McCormick, John, 'Religious Pluralism: State Aid to Religion in Tasmania, 1837–1869', BA thesis, University of Tasmania 1974.

Maxwell-Stewart, Hamish, 'The Bushrangers and the Convict System of Van Diemen's Land, 1803–1846', PhD thesis, University of Edinburgh 1990.

Meppem, Rob, 'Convict Runaways, Rebels and Protesters, 1824 to 1830', BA thesis, University of New England 1991.

Messner, Andrew, 'Chartist Political Culture in Britain and Colonial Australia, c. 1835–1860', PhD thesis, University of New England 2000.

Moneypenny, Maria, ' "Going Out and Coming In": Co-operation and Collaboration between Aborigines and Europeans in Early Tasmania', BA thesis, University of Tasmania 1994.

Morrison, Elizabeth, 'The Contribution of the Country Press to the Making of Victoria, 1840–1890', PhD thesis, Monash University, 1991.

Oats, W.N., 'Quakers in Australia in the Nineteenth Century', PhD thesis, University of Tasmania 1982.

Parrott, Jennifer, ' "Wise as a Serpent and Gentle as a Lamb": Elizabeth Fry and the Extension of Her Prison Reform Work to the Australian Colonies', BA thesis, University of Tasmania 1990.

Phillips, Derek, 'The State and the Provision of Education in Tasmania, 1839 to 1913', PhD thesis, University of Tasmania 1988.

Reid, Kirsty M., 'Work, Sexuality and Resistance: The Convict Women of Van Diemen's Land, 1820–1839', PhD thesis, University of Edinburgh 1995.

Roberts, David, ' "Binjang" or the "Second Vale of Tempe": The Frontier at Wellington Valley, New South Wales, 1817–1851', PhD thesis, University of Newcastle 2000.

Ross, Lynette, 'Death and Burial at Port Arthur 1830–1877', BA thesis, University of Tasmania 1995.

Smith, F.B., 'Religion and Freethought in Melbourne, 1870 to 1890', MA thesis, University of Melbourne 1960.

Trevena, Bill, 'Country Newspaper People: A Select Biographical Dictionary of Country Newspaper Men and Women, Working in Victoria between 1840 and 1980', MA thesis, University of Melbourne 1985.

Vivers, Margaret, 'Evidence of European Women in Early Contact History, with Particular Reference to Northern New South Wales and Queensland', BA thesis, University of New England 2003.

Webster, D.W.L., 'Radicalism and the Sydney Press c. 1838–1846', MA thesis, University of Melbourne 1978.

West, Susan, 'Bushranging, the Policing of Rural Banditry and Working Class Identity in New South Wales, 1860–1880', PhD thesis, University of Newcastle 2003.

Index